Jews and the American Soul

JEWS
and the
AMERICAN SOUL

Human Nature in the Twentieth Century

Andrew R. Heinze

PRINCETON UNIVERSITY PRESS

PRINCETON AND OXFORD

Library of Congress Cataloging-in-Publication Data
Heinze, Andrew R.
Jews and the American soul : human nature in
the twentieth century / Andrew R. Heinze.
p. cm.
Includes bibliographical references and index.

ISBN: 0-691-11755-1 (alk. paper)

1. Jews—United States—Intellectual life—20th century. 2. Psychological
literature—United States—History. 3. United States—Civilization—Jewish
influences. 4. Psychology and religion—United States—History. 5. Psychology—Popular
works—History—20th century. 6. Self-actualization (Psychology)—Religious
aspects—Judaism—History—20th century. I. Title.

E184.36.I58H45 2004
150'.89'924073—dc22   2004043404

British Library Cataloging-in-Publication Data is available
This book has been composed in ITC New Baskerville

Printed on acid-free paper. ∞

www.pupress.princeton.edu

Printed in the United States of America

1 3 5 7 9 10 8 6 4 2

*This book is dedicated to the memory of
Abraham Lincoln, who argued for America,
and to the tradition of Abraham of Ur,
who argued for humanity*

Rabbi Yohanan ben Zakkai had five primary disciples . . . and he said to them: "Go out and discern which is the good path to which a man should cling." One replied: "A good eye." Another said: "A good friend." The third said: "A good neighbor." The fourth said: "One who sees the consequences of a deed." Rabbi Elazar said: "A good heart." Rabbi Yohanan ben Zakkai said to them: "I prefer the words of Rabbi Elazar because all of your words are included in his words."

—The Talmud

The philosopher Kant once declared that nothing proved to him the greatness of God more convincingly than the starry heavens and the moral conscience within us. The stars are unquestionably superb, but where conscience is concerned God has been guilty of an uneven and careless piece of work, for a great many men have only a limited share of it or scarcely enough to be worth mentioning. This does not mean, however, that we are overlooking the fragment of psychological truth which is contained in the assertion that conscience is of divine origin! but the assertion needs interpretation.

—Sigmund Freud

Psychological explanation—To trace something unknown back to something known is alleviating, soothing, gratifying and gives moreover a feeling of power.

—Friedrich Nietzsche

Contents

Illustrations

Acknowledgments

WRITING HISTORY IS HARD and often grueling work, but one of its rewards is the joy of learning from what other scholars have written. The first debt I want to acknowledge is to the scores of historians from whom I have learned in the course of writing *Jews and the American Soul*. My endnotes contain many of their names. To those whose names are missing as a result of my having to trim and edit the manuscript: please accept my acknowledgment here.

Without the following sources of funding, this book would have taken much longer to complete: a sabbatical and research support from the Dean of Arts and Sciences and the Faculty Development Fund at the University of San Francisco; a seed grant and a supplemental grant from the Lucius N. Littauer Foundation; a Loewenstein-Wiener fellowship from the American Jewish Archives in Cincinnati; and a senior fellowship from the Center for Religion and American Life at Yale, which enabled me to complete the book during the 2002–03 academic year. For those commitments to my scholarship, I am deeply appreciative.

I depended on the courteous help of archivists and staff at the following institutions: the Manuscript Division, Rare Books and Special Collections Division, Prints and Photographs Division, Motion Picture, Broadcasting and Recorded Sound Division, the Serial and Government Publications Division, and the Main Reading Room of the Humanities and Social Sciences Division at the Library of Congress in Washington, D.C.; the Rare Books and Manuscripts Division of the Boston Public Library; the Francis A. Countway Library of Medicine in Boston; the Manuscript Department of the Houghton Library at Harvard University; the Rare Book, Manuscript and Special Collections Library at Duke University; the History of American Psychology Archives at the University of Akron; the Department of Special Collections at the Mugar Memorial Library of Boston University; the American Jewish Archives at the Hebrew Union College, Cincinnati; Erich Fromm Archiv in Tübingen, Germany; the Film and Television Archive at the University of California, Los Angeles; the Museum of Television and Radio in Los Angeles; the NRLF Division of the Doe Library, University of California, Berkeley; and the Richard A. Gleeson Library, University of San Francisco.

One of the pleasures that came with *Jews and the American Soul* was making the acquaintance of David Hollinger. In 1998, when I asked David to read some of the material that went into the book, I was a babe wandering in the woods of intellectual history. Most of my previous scholarship dealt with immigration and popular culture, and I had no training in the history of ideas. I didn't know if David would give me the time of day, but he did. With the eye of the superlative scholar, he read that first essay and everything else I gave him afterward. For his steady encouragement, I am grateful.

I met Deborah Dash Moore without knowing it when I was preparing my first book for publication. She was the anonymous reviewer whose wisdom guided my revisions. Since then, Deborah has been a rock of support. Everyone who knows her admires her intellectual rigor and her deep understanding of Jewish life in America. Early on, when I needed inspiration more than I needed to analyze it, Deborah told me that I had hit on something important. I believed her then and thank her now, by her real name.

Months after I had drafted the two preceding paragraphs, I discovered that David Hollinger and Deborah Dash Moore were the scholars Princeton University Press had chosen to review my manuscript, a coincidence that allows me to add one more line here, thanking both for their kind and careful comments on the entire text.

As I worked out the ideas for this book, I was fortunate to receive extensive feedback from the editors and anonymous reviewers of the journals that published my essays: Joanne Meyerowitz and the *Journal of American History*; Tom Davis and *Religion and American Culture*; Lucy Maddox and the *American Quarterly*; Marc Lee Raphael and *American Jewish History*; Murray Baumgarten and *Judaism*. I thank these journals for permission to use material from my previously published articles: "*Schizophrenia Americana*: Aliens, Alienists and the 'Personality Shift' of Twentieth-Century Culture," *American Quarterly* 55 (June 2003), 227–56, part of which appears in Chapter 1; "Jews and American Popular Psychology: Reconsidering the Protestant Paradigm of Popular Thought," *Journal of American History* 88 (December 2001), 950–78, parts of which appear in Chapters 1, 7, and 8; "*Peace of Mind* (1946): Judaism and the Therapeutic Polemics of Postwar America," *Religion and American Culture* 12 (Winter 2002), 31–58, parts of which appear in Chapters 9 and 10; "Clare Boothe Luce and the Jews: A Chapter from the Catholic-Jewish Disputation of Postwar America," *American Jewish History* 88 (September 2000), 361–76, part of which appears in Chapter 11; and "The Americanization of *Mussar*: Abraham Twerski's Twelve Steps," *Judaism* 48 (Fall 1999), 450–69, part of which appears in Chapter 14.

I have enjoyed the help and encouragement of a good number of colleagues. Paula Fass and Mitchell Ash each read a chapter of the manuscript and gave me wise advice. Patrick Allitt, Arnold Eisen, Tony Fels, Ellen Herman, Regina Morantz-Sanchez, Ira Robinson, Joan Shelley Rubin, Michael Sokal, Richard Weiss, and Leila Zenderland offered valuable comments on parts of the work that appeared as journal articles.

Along with David Hollinger and Deborah Dash Moore, Robert Orsi and Moses Rischin graciously agreed to write on my behalf as I applied for research support. As directors of the Center for Religion and American Life at Yale, Jon Butler and Harry Stout expressed their faith in the potential of this book by selecting me for a coveted senior fellowship. David Myers gave me good feedback on a paper about Martin Buber and Erich Fromm, and Robert Middlekauff, Michael Meyer, and Nicole Barenbaum kindly answered specific questions about Puritans, German and Reform Jews, and Jewish psychotherapists, respectively. I assume sole responsibility for any factual errors in this book.

I want to express my appreciation for the opportunities I was given to present ideas for this book before warm and generous audiences at the following places: the Biennial Scholars' Conference in American Jewish History, which convened at the Jewish Theological Seminary in 1996; a conference of the Immigration and Ethnic History Society on immigrants and World War II, which met at New York University in 1997; the annual conference of the American Historical Association in 1998; the Oxford Centre for Hebrew and Jewish Studies, for the conference "Jews in the Social and Biological Sciences" in 1998; the University of Denver, where I was honored to give the John C. Livingston Memorial Lecture in 1999; Yale University, where I was honored to speak at the Institute for the Advanced Study of Religion in 2000; Arizona State University, for the conference "Key Texts in American Jewish Culture" in 2000; the annual conference of the Association for Jewish Studies in 2001; the University of Arizona, where I was honored to give the Shaol Pozes Memorial Lecture in 2001; the annual conference of the Western Jewish Studies Association in 2002; and San Diego State University, where I was honored to give the Maurice Friedman Lecture in 2002.

Finally, though they may not realize it, some of my colleagues helped simply by expressing enthusiasm for my work: Jeanne Abrams, Joyce Antler, Laurence Baron, Andrew Bush, Hasia Diner, Leonard Dinnerstein, Samuel Haber, Mitchell Hart, Paula Hyman, William Issel, Pamela Nadell, Elliot Neaman, Abraham Peck, Riv-Ellen Prell, Kevin Proffitt, Jonathan Sarna, Shalendra Sharma, Daniel Soyer, and Beth Wenger.

My agent, Carol Mann, guided *Jews and the American Soul* to the right publisher and spoke words of praise when I was weary and needed to hear them. My primary editor at Princeton, Fred Appel, shared my enthusiasm for the book, guided it diligently through production, and made it better with many wise suggestions for revising the manuscript. I also benefited from the advice and enthusiasm of collaborating editor Brigitta van Rheinberg, the fine assistance of production editor Gail Schmitt, and the careful copyediting of Eric Schramm.

Though indirectly, Rabbi Zelig Pliskin, formerly of Baltimore and now Jerusalem, has a place in these acknowledgments because it was through his writings that I learned about the vital and dynamic moral tradition of *musar*, which reshaped my understanding of Jewish values.

I thank the members of my family who have taken an interest in my writing over the years, and want to conclude with a few words for three people who have been at my side in an unusual way and taken special pleasure in my work on this book.

I have been blessed with extraordinarily devoted parents who enabled me, as a child, to feel at home in the world.

I thank my mother: your gentle disposition, sensitivity to human qualities that others overlook, vivacious imagination, love of art, and whimsical sense of humor make you an inspiration and a friend.

I thank my father, a man of few words and deep feelings: your great loyalty, heartfelt devotion, and frequent praise helped me set my sights high and pick myself up when fallen low.

To Mary J. Heinze from Texas, witty mistress and subtle mind, chef, laundress, and gardener, angst-wrestler and *mensch extraordinaire*. You called to me in the depths, and I remembered who I was. You showed me what *musar* really means. What greater gift is there?

Jews and the American Soul

Introduction

Jews and the American Soul

WHEN THOMAS JEFFERSON drafted the Declaration of Independence, he took "life, liberty, and property"—the standard trio of rights assumed by British citizens—and, for reasons unknown, replaced "property" with an elusive psychological ideal: the pursuit of happiness. In doing so, he anticipated what would become a national passion for achieving peace of mind.

Though often described as the most religious of modern societies, America is certainly the most "psychological," for it has been a tireless host to new ideas about the psyche. Since the late 1800s, when psychology began to vie with religion for the right to determine how we understand ourselves, Americans have developed an extraordinarily large and dynamic market for psychological, as well as religious, advice. However, if we are curious about the history of American ideas of human nature in the twentieth century, we quickly encounter a problem.

That problem might be called the myth of Protestant origins, if we understand myth to mean not a false story but one that, for all its richness, remains radically incomplete and therefore misleading. According to this myth, modern American views of human nature are aftereffects, mutations, or extenuations of Protestant modes of thought, starting with the Puritans and moving up in time through such seminal thinkers as John Dewey and William James, who were raised as Protestants and ended up as great post-Protestant thinkers of the twentieth century.[1]

If American history had stopped at 1900, this account would be sound enough. But standing on the other side of 2000, we must dismiss it as outmoded. Where are the Catholics, who became a more and more significant presence in the United States after 1900? And perhaps even more urgently, we must ask, where are the Jews, whose numbers include some of the most eminent commentators on human nature to be embraced by Americans in the twentieth century? (By the opening of the twenty-first century, we should note, a new wave of non-Christian newcomers from Asia and the Islamic world had formed a foundation for further additions to American thought about the human condition.)

Because thinkers of Jewish origin were so important in this domain of American life, they pose an especially blunt challenge to the old Protestant story. It is well known that Jews authored many of the terms Americans use to describe their pursuit of happiness—the search for *identity*, the desire for *self-actualization,* the wish to avoid an *inferiority complex* and to stop *compensating* for inner weaknesses, *rationalizing* powerful drives and *projecting* them on to others, and the quest for an *I-Thou relationship*— to name a few. Nevertheless, historians have been content to treat Jewish thinkers as isolated individuals inexplicably dotting a post-Protestant landscape. About a thinker like Freud, whose impact on America was simply too conspicuous to be ignored, we are told that his ideas lost whatever Jewish aspect they may have possessed once Americans adapted them to meet the needs of a Protestant public.

This book explores a new hypothesis: that modern American ideas about human nature have Jewish as well as Christian origins. Only by looking at the interaction between Jews and Christians (both Protestants and Catholics) will we arrive at a more complete picture of popular thought in the twentieth century.[2]

The story to be told here uncovers ethnic and religious elements of American thought that have lingered in the shadows of history. We will bring together parts of the national past that are usually studied in isolation: the history of immigration, ethnic identity and race, popular psychology and religious inspiration, and the moral traditions of both Jews and Christians. Because the United States is an ethnically and religiously complex society with a buoyant consumer demand for psychological and spiritual advice, we will see how new ideas about the mind and soul have ricocheted back and forth between natives and newcomers, Christians and Jews, intellectuals and the mass media.[3]

Jews and the American Soul focuses on psychological and religious thinkers whose ideas attracted a mass audience. The book highlights a variety of psychologists and psychiatrists, rabbis, philosophers, intellectuals, journalists, and creative writers. My goal is straightforward: to uncover and track the flow of Jewish values, attitudes, and arguments into the mainstream of American thought.

A word should be said here about the term "Jewish values." Since Jews first arrived in North America, they have lived not in a segregated world of their own but alongside other Americans in a society of ever-shifting values and complicated involvements between people of various faiths and backgrounds. And even in other times and places, "Jewish values" have never existed in a vacuum, subsisting unchanged from generation to generation, immune to the winds of history. Instead, the ways in which Jewish people have chosen to live constantly changed, for the simple reason that the conditions and surroundings in which Jews found themselves constantly changed. The very definition of "Jewish" has been unstable since ancient times. And yet, Jewish values exist as a real, identifiable, and consequential force in the history of Western civilization and, as we shall see in the pages that follow, in the history of modern American culture.

Over the years our histories of colonial New England have produced profound observations about the transformation of a Puritan mentality into a distinctive American culture. From them we have learned that certain cultural tendencies and myths—about the wilderness, about an American sacred destiny, about the possibility of a morally self-regenerating society—grew in the ideologically rich soil of New England Puritanism.

The story to be told in these pages runs parallel in some respects to the Protestant narrative of spiritual pilgrimage, dissarray, and quest for redemption. The extensive Jewish engagement with modern psychologies happened not by accident but as a result of the religious and moral transformation of Jewish life in the nineteenth and twentieth centuries. Jews in the Western world embarked on an errand not in the wilderness, like that of the American Puritans, but into modern culture. Their errand was not to create a City on a Hill, a moral place from which to regenerate the world; it was to create a moral space within European and American culture, from which to secure themselves as citizens and to purge the evils they associated with Christian civilization.

Before we begin, I want to explain the meaning of my title, *Jews and the American Soul.* "Jews" does not refer to all or even most Jews but to a select group whose ideas entered into the mainstream of American thought. The Jewish background of the people I discuss was significant; it made a tangible difference in their values. In what follows, I avoid the parochial assumption that the mere fact of being a Jew automatically makes one's ideas or values Jewish. That might have been true for *shtetl* Jews living a fairly cloistered life in communities that operated on the basis of Jewish law, but it is certainly not true of Jewish men and women living in modern societies. Imagine an American of Jewish parentage who has had no contact with Judaism or Jewish culture and whose social life does not differ from that of other Americans. Unless we indulge in a kind of genetic mysticism, we would have no reason to describe that person's ideas or values as Jewish.[4]

By the same token, neither should we be so cautious as to assume that a Jewish perspective will be found only among those who are immersed in Judaism or *Yiddishkeyt* ("Jewishness," Jewish culture). Half a century ago Albert Einstein gave a vivid, though not definitive, answer to the question of what makes a person a Jew. In an attempt to explain the apparent paradox of people, like him, who had abandoned Judaism but still considered themselves thoroughly Jewish, he rejected as insufficient the definition, "A Jew is a person professing the Jewish faith":

> The superficial character of this answer is easily recognized by means of a simple parallel. Let us ask the question: What is a snail? An answer similar in kind to the one given above might be: A snail is an animal inhabiting a

snail shell. This answer is not altogether incorrect; nor, to be sure, is it exhaustive; for the snail shell happens to be but one of the material products of the snail. Similarly, the Jewish faith is but one of the characteristic products of the Jewish community. It is, furthermore, known that a snail can shed its shell without thereby ceasing to be a snail. The Jew who abandons his faith (in the formal sense of the word) is in a similar position. He remains a Jew.[5]

In short, the integrity of our story depends not on quick assumptions about whether someone is capable of speaking from a Jewish point of view, but on solid evidence and plausible suggestions that a particular statement, attitude, or idea comes out of a clearly identifiable Jewish context. In order to say that a point of view is Jewish we must make the case that it either derives from Judaism or Jewish culture or reflects a state of mind shared by Jews in response to bigotry or social ostracism.[6]

The other phrase in my title, "The American Soul," must be understood figuratively. I do not mean to imply that a nation has a soul, or that the people of the United States are so fundamentally similar as to have one common mentality that we refer to as a soul. I use the phrase "American Soul" as a metaphor for public ideas about the psyche and human nature ("psyche" being Greek for "soul").

This leads to the question, *which* public? Americans have always encompassed a variety of "publics" based on racial, religious, ethnic, gender, regional, and socioeconomic differences among others. There are also "taste" publics: groups of people who share a passion for a certain kind of music, art, recreation, or hobby. The public with which this book is most concerned cannot be profiled precisely, but it includes that great multitude of Americans who have taken an interest in mass-marketed inspirational literature and have been eager to know (via books, newspapers, magazines, radio, and television) what psychologists and psychiatrists, as well as spiritual leaders, think about human nature. Those who make up this public have often belonged to religious communities but, rather than restricting themselves to religious doctrine, have remained open to the mass market of ideas.

Our story opens with the era of the great mass immigration that brought two million Jews from Europe. That era, from the 1880s to the 1920s, also witnessed the rise of modern psychology as a force in American society. New ideas about the divisibility of the psyche appeared simultaneously with new ideas about the ethnic divisibility of the nation, and Jews played an important symbolic and intellectual role in that transformation of popular attitudes.

In order to fully understand why psychological ideas became so important so quickly in America, and why Jewish psychological thinkers were disproportionately involved in the dissemination of those ideas, we will travel back in time to examine the rise of new concepts of the psyche, especially in the nineteenth century, to see how closely interwoven they were with varieties of Christian thought and to identify some of the Jewish religious innovations that made Judaism more attentive to the psychic condition of the individual.

As a point of departure, we will look at an unusual, and quite early, interaction of American and Jewish values of individual development—the adaptation of Benjamin Franklin's famous self-improvement plan into the Hebrew ethical literature of eastern Europe, a genre known as *musar*—in the early 1800s. The intellectual and moral restlessness that led Jews to adapt new techniques of self-improvement also led to the psychoanalytic moralism of Sigmund Freud and Alfred Adler, the first major approach to the psyche to emerge out of a Jewish moral environment.

Once we have viewed the trajectory of Western and Jewish conceptions of the psyche, we will return to America and examine the reasons why popular psychology became a booming cultural industry, outstripping theology and philosophy as a guide for a literate mass audience seeking advice about how to live. We then turn to Jewish thinkers in the field of psychological advice between the 1890s and 1940s. Through them, Jewish concerns and values first entered into American popular thought.

As popularizers of psychology, a number of men conveyed a Jewish moral perspective into American conversations about the nature of intelligence, personality, race, the subconscious mind, mass behavior, and evil. Jewish interpreters of the psyche, no less than Protestants, hoped to move public values in a direction that would produce the kind of society they wanted to inhabit. Sensitive to both overt and implicit Christian biases in popular thought, they campaigned against them and counterpoised Jewish moral reference points, which had previously been rare in public forums. For them psychology was a potent instrument with which to combat pernicious stereotypes about ethnic minorities in general and Jews in particular. It also gave them a means of reaffirming a rationalist code of emotional restraint that, in America, had become outmoded by more spectacular views of the psyche as a source of divine power or a machine that could be programmed for perfection.

As they went about the business of issuing prescriptions for the psychological and moral improvement of America, they encouraged greater public appreciation for the sensitive and intellectually intense individual and greater vigilance about the evil people produced when they formed a mob. According to their moral critique of society, the proverbial neurotic Jew, whose credentials for assimilation had been challenged by nativists, possessed certain characteristics that were ideally suited to a fast-paced urban America. By the same standards, the bigot was redefined as a psychopath and as the primary obstacle blocking the road to a more democratic future.

After World War II, Jewish interpreters of the psyche increased in both numbers and variety. The most popular inspirational book to appear since 1900, *Peace of Mind* (1946), was written by a rabbi, Joshua Loth Liebman, who became not only the first rabbi with an interfaith audience of national dimensions but also the clergyman most closely associated with the problem of psychic pain, mental readjustment, and the Freudian vogue after the war. Liebman was the first American clergyman of national stature to have undergone psychoanalysis, and his *Peace of Mind* heralded a postwar romance with the psychological and therapeutic values that had been growing steadily since the 1890s. Religion *needed* the insights of depth psychology, Liebman argued; without them it could not guide Americans toward spiritual maturity.

Liebman's career marked a turning point in American culture. Jewish psychological thinkers had written popular books before, but his was the first best-seller by a religious Jew. For the first time Judaism, and an explicit Jewish theology, had to be taken seriously in the arena of public opinion about the human condition. *Peace of Mind* contained a strong polemic beneath its appealing message about the healing of American psychic pain. Liebman defined Judaism as a religion of love, not the legalistic faith Christianity had traditionally deemed it, and unflinchingly asserted Judaism's unique ability to lead Americans toward the ideal of loving the neighbor as oneself. He called for a new democratic "God-idea for America" rooted in Jewish values.

Peace of Mind elicited sharp criticism from both Jewish intellectuals and traditionalist Christians. The most interesting controversy over Liebman's Freudian religious vision, however, involved Fulton Sheen and Clare Boothe Luce, the two most charismatic leaders of American Catholicism in the 1940s and 1950s. Psychology provided a perfect focal point for a culture clash between Jews and Catholics as they moved from the periphery toward the center of a society traditionally dominated by Protestants. For many Jews, psychology and Freud represented a path toward a more sophisticated, cosmopolitan America; for many Catholics, Freud signified a heretical departure from fundamental religious values. This postwar culture clash expressed itself with particular poignance in the life and career of Clare Luce, a convert to Catholicism whose stirring public confession of faith and renunciation of Freudianism led her to be accused, wrongly, of antisemitism. Our story takes up the circumstances of that allegation and reveals the intriguing personal relationships with Jewish men that lay hidden beneath Luce's public role in the Catholic-Jewish clash over Freud.

Although many Jewish thinkers took up the cudgels of psychology in the second half of the twentieth century, a few played a formative role in the development of humanism, the most powerful psycho-spiritual movement in America after the 1950s. We remain surprisingly unaware, or forgetful, of the strong Protestant and Jewish sources of postwar humanism. Our story compares two triads of thinkers—one Protestant, the other Jewish—whose ideas established the foundation of a distinctly American humanist philosophy: Paul Tillich–Rollo May–Carl Rogers, and Martin Buber–Erich Fromm–Abraham Maslow. We will see how Buber, Fromm, and Maslow stressed Jewish values of "relatedness" while Tillich, May, and Rogers focused on a Protestant concern for "acceptance." We will also examine the immigrant and Jewish context of Erik Erikson's pioneering theory of identity and see how a rising generation of writers, including Saul Bellow, Philip Roth, and Allen Ginsberg, added a Jewish dimension to the postwar "crisis of conformity" out of which humanism arose.

We then explore a phenomenon closely related to humanism, the conspicuous presence of Jewish women in public discussions of human potential. Jewish women took up psychology, either formally or informally, in greatly disproportionate numbers and created a niche for themselves as moralists in the mass market of advice and self-help. In the 1950s, by a seemingly odd coincidence, Betty Friedan, Ayn Rand, Ann Landers, Abigail Van Buren, and Joyce Brothers all became, or were on the verge of becoming, public advisers of wide influence, especially in relation to American women, and Gertrude Berg, who had emerged as the archetypal Jewish mother in the age of radio, consummated that career by moving to television and incorporating psychology into the didactic repertoire of her popular sitcom, *The Goldbergs*. Our story will focus especially on Joyce Brothers, for she became the most influential popular psychologist in America between the 1950s and the 1990s. Though entirely overlooked by historians of postwar America, Brothers was a figure of real significance who imparted a practical feminism to a multitude of American housewives in the suburban age. Her stream of advice over the course of a generation reveals many of the philosophical and ethical complexities inherent in the Jewish and American embrace of psychological values, which promised human liberation while struggling to produce a coherent substitute for traditional religion. Her complexities were, in many respects, the complexities of an entire generation of American women whose worlds were shaken and permanently altered by the feminist revolt of the 1960s.

Our story moves to a close by turning to the ways in which Judaism figured into American meditations on evil, suffering, and redemption in the final decades of the century. The key figure of that chapter of our history is Rabbi Harold Kushner, whose book of consolation, *When Bad Things Happen to Good People*, exalted him as a popular authority on the enduring question of theodicy—why does an omnipotent and benevolent God allow the innocent to suffer? To interpret Kushner's theodicy, we must first consider the surprising prominence of the Holocaust and Hasidism in American popular thought, because they established the background for Kushner's conception of suffering and redemption.

The Holocaust filtered into public awareness through a variety of Jewish interpreters, the two most significant being Viktor Frankl and Elie Wiesel. Wiesel, in particular, had a powerful effect on American thinking, for he came to personify the ultimate suffering of the Holocaust victim and the prospect of spiritual rejuvenation, or redemption, through the Hasidic traditions in which he was raised. Wiesel's popular neo-Hasidic lore formed part of a larger emergence of Hasidism into American culture, including the inspirational writings of Abraham Twerski, a Hasidic psychiatrist who created a unique blend of *musar* and the Twelve Step program of recovery from addiction. Twerski was one of the more prolific rabbis to follow Joshua Liebman's lead into the mass market, but Kushner was by far the most important and *When Bad Things Happen to Good People* probably the most consequential work of theodicy written for an American mass audience since the nineteenth century. Kushner proposed a controversial idea of God that became a touchstone for subsequent American meditations on evil, and he created a coherent theory of suffering and redemption that tapped popular interest in the Holocaust and Hasidism.

Between the Hebrew version of Benjamin Franklin in the early 1800s and American versions of the Baal Shem Tov, the founder of Hasidism, in the late 1900s, our story contains many new twists and turns in the history of ideas about the mind and soul. We will see that American understandings of human nature in the twentieth century evolved out of an intriguing and, until now, unexamined exchange between Jews and Christians.

One Nation under Stress, Divisible:
Jewish Immigrants
and the National Psyche

Chapter 1

Jews and the Psychodynamics of American Life

IN OCTOBER 1912 *McClure's Magazine* gave Sigmund Freud his first mass audience. Hundreds of thousands of American readers learned of the Viennese doctor who analyzed dreams in order to cure the psychic ills of his patients. Nothing like this had been imagined before—that the everyday dreams of ordinary people might be coherent, comprehensible, and therapeutic.

Freud himself had visited America in 1909 to lecture at Clark University in Worcester, Massachusetts, and his theory of dreams found its way to the average American the following year when the nation's major newspapers reviewed *Abnormal Psychology*, a book by a Jewish psychiatrist from Boston, Isador Coriat. "It is not too much to expect that we shall begin to know ourselves eventually, or at least much better than now," the *Philadelphia Inquirer* said of Coriat's presentation of Freud, which was "written in such popular style that it ought to appeal to a large circle of readers."

When the mass-circulation *McClure's* took note of Freud, it forecast the unique popularity the Viennese doctor was destined to enjoy in America. That success left him ambivalent—he realized that his ideas would be simplified and altered as they made their way through the world's largest market of readers. But something much larger than Freudianism was appearing in *McClure's* America. Within a six-month period of Freud's debut, the popular magazine published a medley of reports on Jews, on the psyche, and on Jews, like Isador Coriat, who had become important psychological experts in America. *McClure's* marked a turning point in the history of American thought and culture. From then on, new interpretations of the human psyche, and Jewish newcomers who specialized in interpreting the psyche, gained greater and greater importance in American life.[1]

Founded in the 1890s by Sam McClure, an Irish immigrant, *McClure's* became a sharp gauge of American society at the turn of the century. The magazine's writers included Ida Tarbell, Lincoln Steffens, and Ray Stannard Baker, the stars of American journalism, and such gifted novelists as Jack London, Stephen Crane, and Willa Cather. The first muckraking journal of the Progressive era, *McClure's* kept American readers informed about organized crime, big business, and Progressive politics and boldly dramatized the need for workmen's compensation, child labor laws, and other reforms. It was one of the first magazines to present anthropologist Franz Boas's pioneering theories about race and to introduce Americans to the latest findings in psychology.[2]

In its very first year of publication, 1893, *McClure's* reported on the new Harvard psychology laboratory run by Hugo Münsterberg, a German Jew of prodigious ability and escalating reputation. Hoping to make Harvard a leader in the new discipline, William James, the school's most eminent philosopher and psychologist, wooed Münsterberg away from the University of Freiburg. *McClure's* described the young German as a "man of original inspiration." "In his genius," the story concluded, "the hopes and destiny of experimental psychology at Harvard are now centred." Münsterberg proved the writer correct. He became the best-known professional psychologist in America over the next twenty years, to the point of alienating colleagues with his success as an evangelist of the psychological word. "Professor Münsterberg is a wizard at telling us why we do things," *Cosmopolitan* declared in 1915, twelve months before the six-foot, two-hundred-pound professor collapsed and died of a cerebral hemorrhage while teaching elementary psychology to a class of Radcliffe women.[3]

Soon after its feature on Münsterberg, *McClure's* carried a short story by Israel Zangwill, the British Jewish writer whose 1908 play *The Melting Pot* became an American legend. Zangwill's little melodrama for *McClure's* was called " 'Incurable.' A Ghetto Tragedy." The tragedy is that of Sarah Kretznow, a thirty-five-year-old Polish immigrant who lives as a bedridden invalid in an East End hospital. Knowing that she will never leave her sickbed and that her husband has taken an interest in another woman, Sarah decides to give him a divorce. But her passions remain alive. Foreshadowing his theme, Zangwill opens Sarah's story with a description of the tiny hospital, which contains "a miniature synagogue" in which the women's section is "religiously railed off from the men's, as if these grotesque ruins of sex might still distract each other's devotions." "Yet," Zangwill concludes, knowing that one of the "incurable" retains her ardor, "the rabbis knew human nature."[4]

These unrelated stories, an account of a psychology laboratory and a melodrama about London Jews, had a thread in common. They both involved a new Jewish presence in American life. Passages about rabbis knowing human nature were still unusual, and seemingly contrary to common knowledge, which associated rabbis with Jewish legalism rather than intuitive understanding of the soul. Stories about a new breed of men called psychologists who commanded esoteric knowledge of the mind were also uncommon. Americans in 1893 continued to look to religion, Protestantism for the vast majority, for information about their psychological states. But as the tide of public opinion began shifting toward this new source of knowledge and inspiration, Jewish thinkers found themselves with a kind of authority in the moral domain that had not been possible before. As long as religion dictated what people knew about human nature, Christian followed Christian and Jew followed Jew. In the universe of psychology, however, that axiom did not hold. Christian and Jew alike became sufferers of mental and emotional problems that were addressed equally well by Christian or Jewish experts.

Before taking a closer look at what *McClure's* was saying about the psyche and about Jews around 1912, we should survey what Americans already knew. The vast majority understood both—the psyche and Jews—primarily in religious terms.

Popular ideas about the psyche followed a gradual arc from the eighteenth century through the twentieth. The word itself derives from the Greek term for soul or spirit. The first edition of the *Encyclopaedia Britannica* (1771) did not contain the term *psyche* but had an entry for *soul*, defined as "a spiritual substance, which animates the bodies of living creatures." The soul's "primary operations of willing and thinking" had "no connection with the known properties of [the] body." Two centuries later, in the 1990s, *psyche* appeared in a standard American dictionary with two meanings, one resembling that of the 1771 *Britannica* and the other not. The first definition corresponded to *soul*, a metaphysical entity that coexisted with the body. The second reflected the Freudian revolution: "the totality of the id, ego, and superego including both conscious and unconscious components."[5]

In 1912 most Americans accepted the explanation of the psyche that was given in the After School Library, a guide to proper living whose editorial board included such prominent leaders as former president Theodore Roosevelt; James Cardinal Gibbons, archbishop of Baltimore; and Nicholas Murray Butler, the president of Columbia University. The After School Library treated the psyche in the language of the day, as "the will," and concentrated on the problem of "moral growth," rather than *spirituality*, the term that came into favor several generations later. There was one great and simple conflict: temptation versus willpower. If willpower is to win, if we want to avoid wild temptation, we must train ourselves in advance when we have time to think about what tempts us. In that way we can strengthen the "moral fiber," forming "a habit of feeling and action which would by and by help us to do right unhesitatingly and spontaneously. . . . We wish to have a will so firm that it can never yield to wrong, but so firm that it yields instantly to right—a perfectly disciplined will. It is the untrained horse that balks or that shies; but the thoroughbred horse stands still the moment his master speaks, and he turns to the right or left at the lightest touch of the bridle."[6]

There was another popular way of interpreting the psyche, which also stressed self-control but emphasized thinking more than willing. The willpower school derived from America's old-fashioned Protestantism, whereas the mindpower school came out of a newer, transcendentalist Christianity. The person who determined to master his or her thoughts, "who does not shrink from self-crucifixion," will "never fail to accomplish the object upon which his heart is set." Not merely bad habits, but bad habits of thought, were the culprits in every case of human failure. If only we decided upon a worthy goal and concentrated all our thoughts upon it, we would attain self-mastery in accordance with the underlying laws of the mind: "Yes, humanity surges with uncontrolled passion, is tumultuous with ungoverned grief, is blown about by anxiety and doubt. Only the wise man, only he whose thoughts are controlled and purified, makes the winds and the storms of the soul obey him. . . . Keep your hand firmly upon the helm of thought. In the bark of your soul reclines the commanding Master; He does not sleep: awake Him. Self-control is strength; Right Thought is mastery; Calmness is power."[7]

The metaphors of the wild horse and the rushing waters were often invoked, as they were by these authors, to describe the unknown, unpredictable, innermost nature of the human psyche. To imagine the soul as an atmosphere—"the winds and the storms of the soul"—also comforted people in their search for a description of elusive inner states. That image is ancient and deeply rooted in Western culture. In Indo-European and Semitic languages the words for soul and for breath or wind have the same root. The same may be said about images of the will being "firm" lest it "yield" to wrong, and of moral "fiber" that may be weak or strong. Americans in 1912, like the ancients (and like Americans today), perceived the psyche in terms of natural forces and substances: winds capable of blowing hot and cold, fibers that may be weakened or strengthened, horses that may be wild or tamed, waters that overwhelm if they are not navigated.

The psyche has always invited metaphors because it cannot be completely defined by science. So to say that Americans in 1912 were just beginning to know something about the psyche is not to say that they were ignorant about human nature whereas we are not. The statement is historical, meaning that a new vocabulary of the psyche associated with the new discipline of psychology was emerging in the early decades of the century. That vocabulary would change the way people defined themselves. Some of the new psychological concepts amounted to old wine in new bottles, repeating with different words, such as "behavior modification," something that people already understood, perhaps better, in simpler terms—"changing habits." Other ideas, like those about the complexity of unconscious drives, increased the public's awareness of subtleties in human behavior.

Whatever advances the sciences of human behavior produced, the rise of the psyche as a focus of public attention constituted one of the major cultural events of the twentieth century. Most Americans came to believe that they desperately needed new information about themselves and new techniques for healing their psychic pains, and many believed that religion had exhausted its resources in that area. Americans in 1912 sensed that cultural change without knowing what they detected.

As for Jews, they commanded very little of America's public attention before the 1880s. This was primarily a demographic fact. At the time of the nation's founding there were a few thousand American Jews in a population of several million; they constituted less than one-tenth of one percent of the total. Between 1830 and 1880, however, the Jewish population increased from roughly 6,000 to 250,000 as a result of immigration from Germany. German Jews in America prospered almost immediately. Some rose to become leaders in finance, retailing, and mining, forming America's first real Jewish elite: the Guggenheims, Schiffs, Sutros, Kuhns, Loebs, Lehmanns, and others. Still, an 1856 catalog of *Religion in America* noted that "the fewness of the Jews, until of late years," had caused them "to be overlooked" by Protestant missionaries. An encyclopedia published that same year reminds us that the eastern European Jew remained an exotic in American eyes. Despite a title that sounds harsh to modern ears, "The Polish Jew Boy" was a complimentary description of the boldness and tenacity of Jewish boys who left home to start out on careers as traveling merchants in Europe. *The Pictorial Family Encyclopedia* detailed the religious customs of "those interesting people" who "were persecuted throughout every part of Europe" yet found protection under "the noble sympathising Pole." That picturesque rendering joined others such as "The Cossacks and Circassians," "Confucius and the Chinese," "The Mississippi and its Tributaries," and "Adventures among the Indian Gauchos."[8]

Unfortunately, the popular image of the Jew did not begin and end with exoticism. Negative stereotypes crossed the Atlantic before many Jews did. American antisemitism did not attain the depth of its European source, but hoary Christian notions framed the typical view of Jews. At bottom stood the belief that Jews subscribed to a hollow legalistic creed wholly lacking the redemptive spiritual power of Christianity. That ancient thesis flowered into many derogatory opinions and superstitions, including bizarre conceptions of the Jew as the satanic archenemy and saboteur of Christianity. Without detouring into the history of anti-Jewish myth and practice, we may say that under the best circumstances in the nineteenth century—and America offered Jews the best circumstances available in the Christian world—Jews were constantly on the defensive. For example, Isaac Leeser, the religious leader of Philadelphia's Jewish community and the leading spokesman for American Judaism, wrote an essay entitled "The Jews and their Religion" in an encyclopedia of American religious groups published in 1844, in which he observed:

> The Jews, and their predecessors the Israelites, have been always regarded with suspicion, and not rarely with aversion, by those who hold opinions different from them. . . . One would suppose that the Judaeophobia must be owing to some monstrous doctrines which the Jewish religion contains, which would render its professors dangerous to the state as unsafe citizens or rebellious subjects, by teaching them to imbrue their hands in blood, or to plunder the unwary of their possessions. Perhaps calumny has asserted these things; perhaps ignorance may have imagined that this could be so. But how stands the case?

Leeser followed that question with fifteen eloquent pages on the grandeur and depth of Jewish belief and practice.[9]

The basic pattern of Christian suspicion and Jewish defensiveness continued into the next century. In 1900 *McClure's* published a piece on Jesus, "The Life of the Master," that typified the pattern. Explaining that Jesus was "of pure Jewish blood" and "filled with the noblest spirit of Jewish religion," the article emphasized the difference between Christ and the Pharisees as conveyors of that spirit. "Two different views of God and man" separated Christ from the Pharisees. "According to the fancy of the Pharisees in all ages," the author explained, using a phrase that suggested the unbroken chain leading from ancient to modern Jewry, "the Divine purpose is to select from the bloom on the human tree a few buds and bring them to perfection, while the rest is left to perish." Whereas Jesus cared for the outcast and the afflicted, the Pharisees despised them. "The Pharisees made their great mistake," the essay concluded, "because they did not know God." That was a standard interpretation. Here, at least, it did not come encased in the vulgar antisemitism that was common in European journalism. The Jews were not a cancerous growth or a parasite on the body politic; they simply lacked the spirituality and healing temper of Christians.[10]

Yet the winds of popular theology were about to shift. Before 1912 it was the rare American, such as the pioneering sociologist Lester Ward, who compared a Pharisee favorably with Jesus by pointing out that "the 'golden rule' of Christ was laid down independently by Hillel." In that year, however, the publishing houses of Williams & Norgate of Covent Garden, London, and G. P. Putnam's Sons of New York came out with a remarkable book by the British Christian scholar R. Travers Herford. In *Pharisaism*, Herford deliberately broke with virtually every preceding

Christian interpreter of Judaism, by attempting to "make clear the Pharisaic conception of religion," and "as far as may be possible for one who is not a Jew, to present their case from their own standpoint, and not, as is so often done, as a mere foil to the Christian religion." His lucid treatment of the theology of the Pharisees was aimed at a popular rather than an academic audience. "I am not without hope that a small book may be read where a large one would be passed by," Herford wrote in his preface, "and that the ends of justice—in this case justice to the Pharisees—may thereby be the better attained." Like the thunderstorm that punctures a long-gathering humidity, this Unitarian minister from Manchester shattered the "erroneous associations" that Christians had built up around the concept of "Torah," which had been pejoratively construed as "Law" in the narrowest sense, and he cleared away the stale charges of hypocrisy, pride, and selfishness that had long been leveled at the sages of Torah: "Why should not the Christian be glad to own that the Jew, even the Pharisee, knew more of the deep things of God than he had supposed, and after a way which was not the Christian way, yet loved the Lord his God with heart and soul and strength and mind,—yes, and his neighbor as himself?"[11]

Herford's *Pharisaism* appeared within months of Freud's debut in *McClure's*. Just as the Pharisaic Jew faced a promotion into the ranks of the spiritually sound, the Jew as psychotherapeutic healer began to appear in the popular press. In November 1912 *McClure's* followed up its report on Freudian dream interpretation with another story containing several American cases from the files of Abraham Brill and Boris Sidis.

"THE DREAM OF THE WILD HORSE"

Mrs. L. was thirty-eight, in good physical health, and the mother of four healthy children, but she suffered from nervousness, depression, anxiety, and insomnia. In the autumn of 1908 she walked into the Vanderbilt psychiatric clinic in Manhattan, one of the first and few clinics of its type in the United States. For six years Mrs. L. had endured these problems, which erupted some time before she immigrated to New York City from Austria. The clinic's receiving doctor diagnosed her as a case of manic-depressive insanity.

Mrs. L. came under the care of Dr. Abraham A. Brill. A Jewish immigrant from Austro-Hungarian Galicia, Brill was the foremost Freudian in America and the first translator of Freud for the American market. After getting to know Mrs. L., Brill decided that she had been misdiagnosed. He noted that her first attack came two years after her husband left for America and that, even before he left, the couple had been practicing *coitus interruptus* to prevent another pregnancy after the birth of their fourth child. Brill was both a devoted Freudian and a sensible man who knew about the forced separations and sexual frustration of immigrants, so he sought the sexual etiology of Mrs. L.'s illness.

She told him that the attacks usually came in the early autumn, coinciding with the Jewish High Holy Days, but there was not much more she could think of to help the doctor solve her problem. He turned to her dreams for insight. Mrs. L. recalled having had a vivid dream before her first attacks. In the dream a horse came upon her and bit her. She had grown up around horses and, after being persuaded by Brill to speak freely, she explained that her first exposure to sex came from watching horses mate. Brill inquired further about events after her husband's departure. After overcoming her initial discomfort, Mrs. L. told him that she had experienced persistent sexual thoughts prompted by a salesman who came to her house several times to negotiate for the feather beds she was selling before her departure for the United States. The salesman behaved suggestively toward the lonely housewife. While remaining faithful to her husband, Mrs. L. felt distressed by her erotic desires and, adding to her guilt feelings, she began to recall earlier experiences of masturbation with thoughts of what she had witnessed of the horses' mating.

Once Mrs. L. talked candidly about the past, Brill unraveled the sexual frustration and guilt she was feeling. His knowledge of Judaism enabled him to explain the timing of her anxiety attacks. "The incidents enumerated above took place before the Jewish Day of Atonement," Brill reported, "and it was on this day, which is the most solemn day for the orthodox Jew, that her actions appeared to her in the most lurid colors." "It is a day of fasting and confession," he added, "and she certainly had a lot to confess." Several weeks after encountering the salesman, Mrs. L. emigrated, and every year "with the approach of this solemn day, the depression returned." She, however, had forgotten the original cause of her distress. A journalist interested in the case emphasized that the patient saw no connection between her previous experience and the mood attacks. But, he reported, "Dr. Brill said gently . . . without knowing it, you have taken it too much to heart, and allowed yourself to brood over it. . . . But, now that we know what is wrong, we can easily make things right." Soon after, Mrs. L.'s symptoms disappeared.

"The Young Man Who Was Afraid of a Closed Door"

Around the same time that Mrs. L. sought help for her troubles, a young man came to Boris Sidis, a Jewish immigrant from Kiev who had become one of America's most renowned psychiatrists. Sidis practiced in New

York City and in Brookline, Massachusetts, before setting up his own sanatorium, the Sidis Psychotherapeutic Institute, in Portsmouth, New Hampshire.

Mr. M. feared being alone in a closed place. His anxiety included such physical symptoms as severe headaches and convulsive shivering. Before his case was presented to Sidis, doctors assumed that Mr. M.'s malady was physical and they drugged him. "But to Dr. Sidis' trained eye," a journalist reported, "the clinical picture presented was not of physical so much as mental trouble." M. could not be hypnotized, so Sidis used a procedure of his own devising, *hypnoidization*, in which he induced a state of mind halfway between sleep and consciousness. By means of this method, Sidis brought the most active ideas of the subconscious into the patient's field of awareness.

In a hypnoidal state, Mr. M. reported having violent dreams, which he never consciously recalled, in which "brutal, terrible-looking men" attacked his mother and father. On learning of these dreams, Sidis asked the young man if they reminded him of anything that had ever happened to him. M. said yes. "Then, welling up from the remote depths of his mind, came a sad and ugly story," *McClure's* recounted. "Years before, when he was not more than six or seven, his home had been invaded, in the dead of a winter night, by a party of drunken soldiers, who knocked down his mother, beat his father unmercifully, and killed an older brother." The boy fled to a deserted barn, where neighbors found him the next morning crouched in a corner shivering with cold. The corner of the barn was the small space that prompted his fear and anxiety. "Even as he told the story he passed into one of his attacks, shivering violently, limbs trembling, teeth chattering, face deathly pale." Having freed Mr. M. enough to recall that horrifying episode, Dr. Sidis helped him to integrate the suppressed memory into his conscious memories, thereby relegating them to the emotional past.

McClure's did not mention the Jewish identity of the patients or the doctors, but simply presented these accounts as vivid illustrations of the psychological revolution that had just begun to unfold in Europe and America. We know that Mrs. L. was a Jew because Brill gave the full account of her case, including sexual details that *McClure's* omitted, in a book he published on Freudianism in 1913. (The magazine article did not mention that her attacks coincided with Yom Kippur.) We do not know that Mr. M. was a Jew, but he probably was. The story of the drunken soldiers breaking into the family home places his childhood in Europe, probably eastern Europe, and resembles Jewish accounts from tsarist Russia. Elsewhere Sidis reported on eastern European Jewish immigrants who came to him for help, knowing that he spoke Yiddish and knew what life had been like in Mother Russia. Regardless of Mr. M.'s background, it was significant that psychiatric cases of immigrants appeared right along with those of native-born Americans in this literature of psychopathology and recovery. Because immigrants and their children constituted roughly one-third of the American population, the psychological dimension of their lives was an important part of the psychology of American life in general. *McClure's* also understood that the story of a woman like Mrs. L. was universal; her torment came not from being a Jew but from being a conscientious woman with normal sexual drives.[12]

In its coverage of new psychological inquiries, *McClure's* ended up showcasing the new role of Jews as psychological authorities. Just as Brill and Sidis were the focus of the report on dream interpretation, the only two American experts cited in an article on "Stammering and Its Cure" were Brill and Isador Coriat. Readers learned that the surgical "cure" of cutting off part of the stammerer's tongue was barbaric because Brill and Coriat discovered that stammerers were often reacting to a very upsetting experience in their past—"stammering was not so much a disease in itself as a psycho-neurotic symptom." In a 1912 article on child geniuses, *McClure's* also introduced Americans to Boris Sidis's theory that the proper upbringing will make a genius of any child. The story featured his son, William James Sidis, perhaps the most famous American child prodigy of the early twentieth century. And in that same year, the magazine reported on Hugo Münsterberg's pathbreaking use of word-association tests as lie detectors in criminal prosecutions, "a method which, in theory at least, is capable of extracting any piece of information from any man's mind, against either his will or his conscious knowledge."[13]

The flurry of reports on the new psychotherapies and their Jewish proponents coincided with equally extensive stories on the Jewish immigration to America. Between 1881 (when the assassination of Tsar Alexander II started an era of antisemitic persecution) and 1924 (when Congress radically reduced immigration from eastern Europe), more than two million Jews from Russia, Poland, Austria-Hungary, and Rumania entered the United States. Nearly all of them came to stay, in contrast to most other immigrants, many of whom repatriated. As a result eastern European Jews formed one of America's largest foreign populations. In March 1913 one of *McClure's* lead writers, Burton J. Hendrick, devoted an extraordinary number of pages to the saga of Jewish immigrants in business and the professions. Illustrated with pictures of such eminent figures as Rabbi Solomon Schechter, president of the Jewish Theological Seminary, and Abraham Cahan, author and editor of the *Jewish Daily Forward (Forverts)*, and with sympathetic portraits of youngsters such as "Ethel Zbarsch, a little orphan whose parents were massacred in Kieff, Russia," Hendrick's article suggested that the future of America would have a lot to do with the future of its Jews. Commenting on "what are perhaps the two keenest business intellects in the world—the Yankee and the Jew," Hendrick marveled at what Jewish immigrants had accomplished in the span of a generation, once they were "unhindered by the restrictions that interfere with their success in eastern Europe." In succeeding issues, Hendrick concluded, "A well known writer, himself a distinguished Jew, Mr. Abraham Cahan . . . will show, by concrete example, the minute workings of that wonderful machine, the Jewish brain."[14]

The "concrete example" came from Cahan's novel *The Rise of David Levinsky,* which *McClure's* serialized in the spring and summer of 1913 (and presented as virtually a true story). An immigrant from Lithuania, Cahan achieved the unusual feat of becoming a respected American novelist, as well as a journalist in charge of the country's most dynamic foreign-language newspaper. His protagonist, David Levinsky, is a Talmud scholar from Lithuania who immigrates to New York City, switches occupations, and turns himself into a wealthy but unhappy garment manufacturer. *The Rise of David Levinsky* fit perfectly into *McClure's* concern with recent developments in psychology because it was the first psychological novel about the assimilation of immigrants in America. Continuing a motif he had used in his novella *Yekl: A Tale of the New York Ghetto* (1896), Cahan explored the psychic and psychosexual conflicts of the immigrant self-made man. Levinsky served a double psychological purpose, for, according to *McClure's,* he was also supposed to provide a case study of "the Jewish brain." At the dawn of the age of psychology, the mind that accounted for extraordinary economic success in America became a compelling model of psychic unrest.[15]

THE JEWISH PATIENT AND AMERICAN DEMOCRACY

One of the qualities that made Ray Stannard Baker one of the great journalists of the Progressive era was his ability to detect the key crises and changes of his time. Baker sensed the importance of the psychotherapeutic trend in America and linked it to Jews in an interesting way. Best known for his classic study of racial segregation and tension in the South, *Following the Color Line* (1908), Baker also turned his curiosity to the Jewish immigrants of New York City. In *The Spiritual Unrest* (1910) he poignantly depicted the religious disorientation of newcomers on the Lower East Side. Jews made a different and unexpected appearance in another of Baker's books, *New Ideals in Healing* (1908), which illustrated how sophisticated psychological theories were changing the American medical and religious scene. "Both clergyman and physician," Baker observed of the traditional minister and the traditional doctor, were "sensible to the fact that they have lost in some degree the authority which they formerly exercised over the lives of men." "Men everywhere are questioning the validity of old beliefs," he continued, "demanding of old professions and institutions new proofs of their right to continued existence and approval."[16]

Baker's study focused on two new movements in Boston, the Emmanuel movement, which combined pastoral care with the latest psychiatric knowledge, and the "Social Service" movement that began at the Massachusetts General Hospital. In those manifestations of the New England conscience, Baker saw a powerful means of personal and national regeneration. Through the merger of religion and psychology, Americans who felt overburdened by their hectic urban civilization would find their way to a new optimistic faith in themselves. "The basis of the whole system is a vital belief based partly on religion, partly on the applications of new psychological knowledge that a man is, indeed, largely the master of his fate. . . . If he says, 'I do,' 'I will,' instead of saying weakly and hopelessly, 'I cannot,' 'I do not,' his life will become a new thing. This is the phenomenon of the 'new birth,' the 'transformed life.' In short, it is a living faith in the free will of men, as against the old fatalism."[17]

By "the old fatalism," Baker referred to the nation's Calvinist heritage, which he saw being replaced by the therapeutic faith of a medical innovator like Richard Cabot, chief of medicine at Massachusetts General Hospital. Cabot introduced the idea of treating "the whole man," which meant that healing a patient depended on being concerned about the psychological and social conditions of his or her life. Baker perceived Cabot's interest in "the broader needs of men" as representing the highest principles of democracy. "Though a member of no church," Cabot "had grown up in the atmosphere of that humanitarianism which has so long marked the best thought of New England," and "his view of life is profoundly religious." His father was Ralph Waldo Emerson's biographer, and Cabot infused an Emersonian spirit into his medical service. "When you reach the core of any man, you reach, it seems to me, the divine spark in him," Cabot stated. The individual "must be treated not merely as an individual and unrelated sick man, but as a component and essential part of our close-knit social life, where one man who is sick endangers the whole city in which he lives."[18]

Cabot's conception of treating "the whole man" came out of his encounters with Jewish nervous patients. Jewish immigrants were conspicuous in the psychiatric clinics of America's big cities for two reasons: immigrants in general often ended up in psychiatric care simply because doctors could not understand them, and Jews suffered disproportionately from nervous disorders. In an admirable display of self-criticism, Cabot reflected on his initial failure to view Jewish patients as individuals. Referring to "the vague misty composite photograph of all the hundreds of Jews who in the past ten years have shuffled up" in the wards of the Massachusetts General Hospital, Cabot observed that he perceived "*not* Abraham Cohen, but *a Jew*," not "the sharp, clear outlines of this unique sufferer" but "a nervous, complaining whimpering Jew." To reduce his foreign patients to a caricature like that, Cabot realized, was to betray the democratic and Emersonian principles in which he had been raised. Ray Stannard Baker perceived Cabot's therapeutic philosophy of treating "the whole man" as a vital means of regenerating American democracy in an urban age.[19]

To Elwood Worcester, reverend of Boston's Emmanuel Church and creator of the popular Emmanuel healing movement, the ambitious Jewish immigrant personified the dilemma of the modern American businessman. "The Jew, however humble may be the beginning of his business career, is too intelligent not to perceive the great opportunities for the acquisition of wealth which this country affords him." He "bends his whole energy to lifting himself out of his humble circumstances into affluence," leaving himself "in a state of constant fatigue." Jews exemplified the psychic predicament of American businessmen who "confined themselves exclusively to business and who had never learned to play." Believing that American conditions produced nervousness, Worcester considered immigrant Jews even more vulnerable to that affliction than their Yankee counterparts. A therapeutic that worked for them would work for everyone.[20]

To show how the mental as well as the physical hygiene of the individual affected the welfare of the larger society, Baker told the "Story of an Ambitious Russian Jew." During one of his visits to Massachusetts General, Baker saw a "bright, healthy-looking Jewish boy" of about fifteen chatting with the resident social worker (itself a new vocation) about his recovery from a terrible physical state six months earlier. "He belonged to a Russian Jewish family," Baker learned. "His father was a peddler, and he had eight brothers and sisters. The family was very poor. But the boy was alert-minded and ambitious, eager to get ahead in America. Though he had been in this country only eight months he spoke English pretty well. He was working in a grocery store thirteen hours a day at $2.50 a week, and going to night school afterward. Think of it, for a growing boy! He said he never played on the street because his uncle would think him a 'bum.' " The overstressed boy came to the hospital exhausted and suffering from headaches. The staff there fixed his headaches by ordering an eye exam and getting him glasses, had his adenoids removed to clear his breathing, convinced his family to let him spend more time outdoors, arranged a job mowing lawns, and then sent him for three weeks of vacation in the country. "The result," Baker wrote, "was that he came back well and strong and happy and grateful: a citizen saved."[21]

As the parable of the "Ambitious Russian Jew" suggested, Jews were coming to play an interesting role in the popular imagination as a kind of psychotherapeutic test case for the future of America.

THE SPLIT PERSONALITY AND THE DIVIDED NATION

Stories like Baker's came out of a historical coincidence: the era between the 1880s and the 1920s was one of intense immigration and also of rising concern about psychological matters. In those decades, new ideas about the fragility and divisibility of the psyche developed alongside a new anxiety about the ethnic fragility and divisibility of the nation. Because Jews were so conspicuous in urban America and so involved in the new psychology, they appeared prominently in public conversation as Americans coped with the fact that both the individual and society were more internally complex than had previously been thought.

The link that Baker perceived between the mental health of the Jewish immigrant and the social health of urban America had a tantalizing linguistic dimension, summed up in the relation between the words *alien* and *alienist*. That twist of the English language established a connection between the psychological concept of mental disturbance and the political concept of a noncitizen. An individual could be alienated from a polity or from the mind itself. In politics, the alien represented a disruptive and discordant element of the whole, an invasive and potentially contaminating force. Unlike an external enemy, an alien resided in the body that it might infect. In psychology, too, health and wholeness—or sanity—depended on the absence of alien notions in the mind. To restore a sound mental constitution was the task of the alienist, just as the civic leader ensured the security of the national constitution.

After the 1880s both the psyche and the nation came to be seen as fragile and divisible. French studies of hysteria, especially the investigations of psychologist Pierre Janet, alerted European and American doctors and psychologists to the phenomenon of split and even multiple personalities and to the general problem of psychological "dissociation." Under the influence of hypnosis, patients displayed completely distinct traits from those that normally identified them. What an earlier age perceived as spirit possession, the late nineteenth century understood as a psychological break. A new lexicon of phrases described the fragmented self: double consciousness, dual consciousness, alternate consciousness, secondary self, subconscious self, subliminal self, co-consciousness, mental dissociation. Although the psychological revolution of those years started with pathological cases of hysteria, its concepts very quickly became definitive for interpreting the "normal" or "healthy" mind. Everyone, it seemed, had a fragile, divisible psyche. Hysterics simply showed the extremities of a universal condition. In his *Principles of Psychology* (1890), William James introduced Americans to the new understanding of personality as an entity capable of dissociation or fragmentation. "Any man becomes, as we say, *inconsistent* with himself if he forgets his engagements, pledges, knowledges, and habits," James wrote, "and it is merely a question of degree at what point we shall say that his personality is changed."[22]

Well-publicized cases of split personality dramatized the frightening proportions of a disunified soul. Although William James and others had been talking about the subject for a number of years, the reading public received a massive exposure in 1905 when Boris Sidis and another of the nation's most eminent psychiatrists, Morton Prince, published books about multiple personalities. The young, well-educated Bostonian whom Prince made famous, "Sally Beauchamp" (Clara Norton Fowler), contained uncomfortably within herself what psychiatrists were calling three fully developed and distinct personalities. Prince "cured" Sally by hypnotic suggestions that eliminated the most unruly of the woman's inner selves and reintegrated the whole personality around an acceptable type of behavior. Sidis described a case not of multiple personality but of a rare total amnesia, which left a young Connecticut minister, Thomas Hanna, apparently without any memories of who he was and without any of the abilities he had learned since infancy. Sidis suspected that somewhere in Hanna's subconscious there lay memories of his identity prior to the accident that incapacitated him (he fell from a carriage). Hanna's therapy involved being reeducated to speak, read, and write, skills he learned so quickly that Sidis hypothesized the presence of residual memory. Sidis also put Hanna into a hypnoid state during which he began to dredge up images from the past. The doctor gradually revived and reintegrated the forgotten Thomas Hanna into the full consciousness of his patient. Of Hanna, whose dreams harbored memories of the original self, Sidis observed, "To the patient himself it appeared as if another being took possession of his tongue."[23]

In 1906 the case of Susan Norris, "The Woman Who Lost Herself," riveted public attention on the close link between personal and cultural identity. A forty-five-year-old spinster from Lowell, Massachusetts, Norris turned up at the Lowell Alms House oblivious of her original identity. She had taken on the additional personalities of "Sarah Wilson" and "Margaret Kelly," the names by which she was known to local authorities. A well-educated teacher, Norris remembered nothing of her life up to the day she told her family she was going to North Adams, a trip from which she never returned. In the interim she traveled to California and back. Norris "seems to be an astonishingly clear case of multiple person-

ality," the *Boston Herald* reported, "one of the most remarkable psychological phenomena admitted by present-day psychologists." Interviewers discovered that Norris had forgotten everything she had ever read,
including the Bible, and recalled nothing about religion. " 'I guess I
haven't any religion,' she said. 'But if you some day wished to attend
such exercises, what denomination would you prefer?' 'I don't know. I
would have to go to them all and then judge.' 'Do you know the difference between Protestantism and Catholicism?' 'I seem to have heard the
words somewhere, but they do not mean anything to me.' " That line of
questioning suggested the degree of cultural discomfort her case provoked. What did it mean that a mentally sound person could forget her
identity so completely as to be unaware of her religion, the foundation
of her social and moral universe?[24]

In these and other such cases, a person was either internally divided
into disparate personalities or driven by amnesia into a second life and
personality that remained beyond the recognition of the original self. The
disturbed individual faced one of two very bleak horizons: possibly irrepa-
rable inner conflict or complete loss of memory of one's original nature.

The disturbing possibilities for the individual personality mapped perfectly onto those for the American nation. Behind the immigration restriction movement, the reemergence of the Ku Klux Klan, the institu-
tionalization of Jim Crow, the rise of scientific racism, and even the
Progressive movement itself was a fear that America faced one of two
bleak horizons: permanent internal conflict along ethnic and racial
lines, or a transformation of national personality so complete as to eradi-
cate memory of the original Republic.

At precisely the time that a newer understanding of the human personality called into question the traditional idea of a cohesive, unified self,
Americans were starting to reevaluate the coherence and unity of their
nation, which seemed threatened by ethnic division. The 1880s marked
the rise of modern psychology and also the beginning of American immigration restriction. The shift in federal policy about immigrants began
with the passage of the Chinese Exclusion Act of 1882 and the planning
of a new reception center at Ellis Island where aliens would be screened
more carefully than before. Previously, those Americans whose votes mattered most had not been particularly concerned about ethnic differences
in the population. They relied on discriminatory laws and customs to
regulate their internal diversity and did not interpret that diversity as a
fundamental social problem. Between the 1880s and the 1920s, however,
when mass immigration changed the social landscape, the most established Americans spotted trouble in their "divided heritage" and "dualis-
tic national identity." Suddenly, assimilation became a major problem

and not, as it had been before, a process that occurred in the case of some groups but perhaps not others. Paralleling the alarm about immigrants in the North and West, white southerners reacted to the social and economic advances of blacks by erecting (with national support) the legal apparatus of racial segregation. Fully in place by 1914, those laws rigidified a dual racial system among Americans. A leading historian of the era has observed, "The acute consciousness of assimilation as a problem marked a great crisis in ethnic relations."[25]

The crisis took the form of an abrupt awareness that the personality of the nation, like that of the individual, could be pathologically split or maladjusted. The fear of a monstrous Jekyll-and-Hyde bifurcation of the national personality did not infect only those rabid nativists who considered the mass of Jewish, Slavic, and Mediterranean immigrants to be like a parasitic growth on an Anglo-Saxon civilization. Others shared the opinion of Theodore Roosevelt, who generally approved of immigration and displayed clear sympathies for Jews, but who insisted that new Americans abandon their emotional ties to their native culture in favor of an uncomplicated loyalty to the United States. Roosevelt loved Israel Zangwill's play "The Melting Pot" (1908), which dissolved the religious and ethnic differences of Americans in a messianic vision of national unity. For the same reasons he decried "hyphenated Americanism," which by 1915 was widely viewed as the country's most pressing problem. The American of German or Irish origin, Roosevelt intoned, was politically acceptable, but the German American and the Irish American were not. "I set my face like flint against all hyphenated Americanism and all hyphenated Americans," Roosevelt wrote to Hugo Münsterberg after ethnic tension in Austria-Hungary erupted into world war. "It would be a dreadful thing to reduce us to the condition of the Balkan peninsula. . . . I believe in treating all our citizens, of whatever national origin, on an exact equality, but . . . I tolerate no divided allegiance in our citizenship. . . . If a man is in good faith a good American, I care not a rap for his creed, his birthplace or his ancestry."[26]

By the early 1920s, not long after Roosevelt's death, an uglier temper dominated the public mind, a mood that went well beyond complaints about dual loyalty and led straight to the most potent restriction of immigration in the history of the United States. The Johnson-Reed or National Origins Act of 1924 prohibited further immigration from Asia and authorized a quota that radically reduced the number of immigrants from eastern and southern Europe. On the road to that legislation, a congressional report titled "Analysis of the Metal and the Dross in America's Modern Melting Pot" used the metaphor of mental illness to describe the effects of immigration on the American character. The report claimed that "social inadequacy" and "racial degeneracy" were turning America into "a custodial asylum for degenerates."[27]

That line of argument came not only from populist hysteria but also from the published papers of influential psychiatrists. A cutting-edge textbook of 1913, *The Modern Treatment of Nervous and Mental Disorders*, which included some of the most sophisticated findings of modern psychology, also contained a chapter on "Immigration and the Mixture of Races in Relation to the Mental Health of the Nation." That chapter quoted generously from the world's most notorious racialist authors and concluded, "Mental defectiveness is likely to increase in this country as the result of the changes in the character and sources of immigration." The textbook emphasized the close connection between individual psychology and national mental health: "for if racial characteristics profoundly affect political, social, and religious ideals we must look for a similar influence upon the individual make-up which so largely determines trends in mental disease." It then catalogued a variety of "racial" defects, starting with the tendency of the Japanese in California toward suicide: "This is in accordance with the general attitude of the Japanese toward self-destruction. The strong tendency to delusionary trends of a persecutory nature in West Indian negroes, the frequency with which we find hidden sexual complexes among Hebrews and the remarkable prevalence of mutism among Poles . . . are familiar examples of the influence of racial traits upon mental diseases."[28]

The fear that America was split into healthy and unhealthy ethnic elements received strong corroboration from Edward A. Ross's *The Old World in the New* (1914), a superb example of florid pseudoscience from the pen of a respected sociologist at the University of Wisconsin. With stunning nonchalance, Ross assembled unattributed quotations, bald stereotypes, and popular science jargon to slander the intelligence, appearance, and character of the new immigrants. Benefiting from an innovative brand of statistical analysis, he wrote, "I scanned 368 persons as they passed me in Union Square, New York, at a time when the garment-workers of the Fifth Avenue lofts were returning to their homes. Only thirty-eight of these passers-by had the type of face one would find at a county fair in the West or South." "To the practised eye," he went on, "the physiognomy of certain groups unmistakably proclaims inferiority of type." In addition to the physical ugliness Ross found in these newcomers, he detected moral turpitude. Whereas northern Europeans were "truth-tellers . . . even when they were dirty, ferocious barbarians," immigration officials "report vast trouble in extracting the truth from certain brunet nationalities." The inferior morality of the new immigrants was "as certain as any social fact." As to intelligence, Ross expostulated, "the fewer brains they have to contribute, the lower the place immigrants take

among us, and the lower the place they take, the faster they multiply."
Ross was capable of greater subtlety on the subject of assimilation, but
here he espoused the idea of two Americas, one from the Old World
dwelling like a sick secondary personality within the brave new world
created by the rugged American pioneers who were Ross's heroes.[29]

Social psychologists more dispassionate than Ross also viewed immigrants as test cases but of a different theory, that of adjustment. Adjustment signified a proper fit between the individual and his or her social
roles. A maladjusted personality had to be reorganized so as to find a
productive place in society. According to adjustment psychology, hostility
came from the frustrations of maladjusted people; social conflict would
disappear when the rupture between person and social role was healed.[30]

Immigrants were the perfect test case of the importance of adjustment,
and the first great study of American immigration, *The Polish Peasant in
Europe and America* (1918–21), interpreted them in those terms. The
book's chief author, William Isaac Thomas, was a social psychologist from
the University of Chicago, the school that produced pathbreaking studies of urban sociology and immigrant life. Thomas argued that immigrants experienced profound disorientation and maladjustment. They
occupied a peculiar middle ground, a place of tension between Old
World and New World values. The shock of immigration was such that
Polish Americans suffered basic problems of social abnormality in which
"individual disorganization" acquired "an unusual extension" to the
community at large.[31]

Ideas about the splitting of personality and the maladjustment of the
individual appeared on both sides of the Atlantic, but, like Freudianism,
they found more fertile soil in America than in Europe. In America, talk
about personality disturbances mingled with talk about ethnic disrup-
tions. The new interpretation of personality as something internally divided or out of adjustment gave Americans a meaningful vocabulary for
describing society in a period of massive immigration and racial recon-
figuration. And with so many Americans or their parents having moved
from one culture to another, the notion of a divisible or internally
strained personality made sense.[32]

JEWISH INTERPRETATIONS OF THE ETHNICALLY SPLIT PERSONALITY

In the opening years of the twentieth century, a number of gifted writers
from immigrant or African American backgrounds constructed a vivid
image of the ethnically split personality: the American who felt internally
divided by distinct ethnic loyalties. In European and American literature,
the motif of a divided personality had been popular for some time, the

most famous being the protagonist of Robert Louis Stevenson's *The Strange Case of Dr. Jekyll and Mr. Hyde* (1886). The rising ethnic nationalism of the era added a new dimension to the image. The movements for Irish, Jewish, and Polish self-determination, for example, accentuated a feeling of dual identity among Irish, Jews, and Poles living in the United States. Even those who came from sovereign nations like Germany expressed the same feeling. George Sylvester Viereck, one of the most influential German American writers of the period, spoke of Germany and America as projections of his own "twofold racial consciousness." African American and Jewish writers produced the most memorable, early explorations of the ethnically split American personality. Of all the groups within the American mosaic, those two had the most profound consciousness of estrangement coexisting with an equally profound yearning for membership in the larger society. In *The Souls of Black Folk* (1903) W.E.B. Du Bois penned the century's most eloquent depiction of "the problem of ever feeling one's "twoness,—an American, a Negro; two souls." Du Bois yearned for an integration of his ethnically split personality, a merger of his "double self into a better and truer self" in which "neither of the older selves [would] be lost."[33]

Jews, like blacks, were especially prone to ponder the problem of a split ethnic American identity. Although they were beneficiaries of the American color line, Jews possessed a high degree of ethnic self-awareness, they remained apprehensive about antisemitism in the United States, and they felt their marginality within Christian civilization. Alongside Du Bois, three Jewish writers, Abraham Cahan, Mary Antin, and Horace Kallen, contributed landmark commentaries on the problem of the ethnically split personality.

In his two best-known characters, Yekl/Jake Podkovnik and David Levinsky, Abraham Cahan drew on his own (triply) fragmented Russian-Yiddish-American identity to examine the divided personality of the American immigrant. Both Podkovnik and Levinsky exchange a more or less traditional eastern European Jewish personality for a secular Americanized self. The drama at the heart of these stories comes from the deep internal discord occasioned by that exchange. On the opening page of *The Rise of David Levinsky*, Cahan presents the subjective experience of split identity for the Russian Jew by having Levinsky distinguish between "my inner self" and the personality of the wealthy American businessman he had become. That wording appeared in the novel's 1913 serialization in *McClure's*. Four years later, when the book was published by Harper and Brothers, Levinsky referred instead to "my inner identity." Because *McClure's* presented Levinsky's story as if it were nonfiction, with the banner heading "The Autobiography of an American Jew" and the prefatory remark "Levinsky is, in fact, an actual type," the split-identity phenomenon was highlighted as a new fact of American life.[34]

Mary Antin's classic autobiography, *The Promised Land*, also focused public attention on the divided identity of the immigrant, though with an ostensibly happier resolution. The top nonfiction best-seller of 1912, *The Promised Land* juxtaposes an Old World and a New World personality. Like Du Bois, Antin refers to a double consciousness, but unlike him, she manages to integrate them. She has built a new "I," a "second self," upon the foundations of the old self inherited from her parents and ancestors. Antin presents her self-analysis as completely typical of the immigrant, especially the immigrant Jew. That was her rationale for writing the autobiography of an unknown person. "It is because I understand my history . . . to be typical of many," she writes, "that I consider it worth recording." What was the essence of that typical experience? The awareness that "it is painful to be consciously of two worlds." And where did that awareness come from? From the fact that "all the processes of uprooting, transportation, replanting, acclimatization, and development took place in my own soul." Antin connected the social and psychological dimensions of assimilation. *The Promised Land* was intended as a refutation of those nativists who denied that immigrants like Antin could successfully assimilate in America. Its author displayed a rare gift for addressing the problem of split identity on the personal and national levels simultaneously. According to her story, psychic rifts in the individual and cultural rifts in society would heal once the immigrant integrated into the American way of life.[35]

The social philosopher Horace Kallen, a favorite pupil of William James, considered the split-identity problem more intractable. Kallen's momentous 1915 essay "Democracy Versus the Melting-Pot" was the cornerstone of American cultural pluralism, the idea that the country's ethnic groups need not and would not "melt away" their ethnic differences as they became Americans. The essay was a critique of Ross's *The Old World in the New*, which had riveted public attention on the problem of an ethnic split in the American nationality, a nationality that, in the view of Ross and many others, had previously been unified and cohesive. But Kallen also criticized the new school of immigrant autobiographers, of which Mary Antin was the greatest, for whitewashing the inner tension and struggle of the ethnic American. Antin and the others "protest too much. . . . Their 'Americanization' appears too much like an achievement, a *tour de force*, too little like a growth." The newcomer "cannot change his grandfather," Kallen wrote. He doubted Mary Antin's claim that she finessed a smooth merger of her "first self"—her Jewish ancestry—into her ultimate "second self": "One senses, underneath the excellent writing, a dualism and the strain to overcome it. The same dualism

is apparent in different form among the Americans, and the strain to
overcome it seems even stronger." Kallen objected even more vehe-
mently to those Anglo-Saxonists who accepted Edward Ross's idea of
competing personalities in the American bosom, one truly "inner" and
the other an alien import. Kallen believed that it was neither possible
nor desirable to revive an older America in the more cosmopolitan world
of 1915. Americans must accept the new pluralism of their society rather
than bury their heads in nativist nostalgia for "the old American life."[36]

JEWISH ALIENISTS: DIAGNOSES AND PRESCRIPTIONS
FOR A DIVIDED AMERICA

As psychological authorities, Jews added a new element to American
thinking about the divided psyche and the divided nation: the image of
the immigrant Jew struggling for both mental and social security. If, as
Ray Stannard Baker and others were claiming, the Jewish alien represented a test case for the mental and civic health of the nation, then
Jewish alienists would have something distinctive to say about it.

As social outsiders and often immigrants themselves, those doctors
had a special capability to analyze the Jewish patients who flowed into
psychiatric clinics out of proportion to their admittedly large numbers
in the nation's big cities. The ability to understand Yiddish, for example,
made it possible for Boris Sidis to treat patients like the man who scrib-
bled a message in that language when asked, in a hypnoid state, to revert
mentally to his life at age seven. "Papa, I want you to come to me. Chaim
wants to lick [hit] me," the childlike penmanship read. That episode
occurred during an experiment in "personality-metamorphosis," about
which Sidis reported: "My friends present at the experiment and myself
were surprised to see the hand changing its direction, and instead of
writing from left to right, started from right to left . . . in the modern
rabbinical script used by the Eastern Jews." "The subject," Sidis explained, "knew no other alphabet when he was of that age."[37]

In a 1910 symposium on psychotherapy in which Boris Sidis was the
only Jewish doctor, he was also the only one to note the ethnicity of
the patients in the cases he discussed. Where his colleagues omitted any
references to national origin, apparently assuming that this was not relevant to the psychodynamics of a case, Sidis identified each patient as
"American," "Irish," or "Russian," the last generally designating Russian
Jews. He did not explicitly discuss possible effects of ethnicity on psychology, but he implied that ethnicity was a relevant fact of a patient's identity. Rather than create a fictitious homogeneity among patients, which
his colleagues did by deleting references to nationality, Sidis showed an

awareness of contrasts between natives and newcomers, insiders and out-siders in the American social order.[38]

Joseph Jastrow, the single most prolific popularizer of psychology in the United States between the 1890s and the 1940s, advised his readers to do as the immigrant family did and boldly relocate for better opportu-nities even if it meant temporary "maladjustment." That was the advice the Polish-born psychologist gave to a twenty-four-year-old secretary who felt out of her element in a blue-collar milltown and sought guidance through Jastrow's syndicated newspaper column, asking him if she should pick up stakes and move to more propitious surroundings. Her query was perfectly suited to the guiding metaphor of the book in which it was included, Jastrow's popular 1930 volume *Piloting Your Life*. The individual seeking happiness and proper adjustment was like a ship at sea, Jastrow suggested, with "the psychologist as helmsman." Encourag-ing his reader to take the risk of improving her situation though it "costs something in the way of maladjustment, temporarily," he explained that "emigration from the less promising environments and immigration to the more promising ones . . . getting away, being thrown on one's own responsibilities to shape or choose one's environment, is indispensable to a rich independence of character."[39]

The most obvious effect of Jews as popular psychological writers was their introduction of the Jew and the immigrant as positive figures into a literature that would otherwise have done without them. To see the difference we can compare two contemporaneous books that both pre-sented numerous case histories, Brill's *Psychanalysis* (1913) and Morton Prince's *The Unconscious* (1914). Both psychiatrists worked with many patients in New York and Boston, respectively, some of whom were Jews, and Prince had close working relationships with Jewish colleagues. None-theless, Prince's book typified the genre in making virtually no reference to Jews. The exception was one case study of a Protestant woman who had a dream featuring a "poor Jewess" who, in Prince's analysis, symbol-ized the city's poor slum dwellers. Concerned primarily with understand-ing the stricken "New England conscience," Prince dispensed with others such as Jews by treating them as symbols within that framework.[40]

But Brill's book features Jews and Jewish themes throughout. To illus-trate a psychologically loaded cryptogram, he mentions the Yvel Jewelry Company, which is really the Levy company, but "looks better and is perhaps more profitable than would be the Levy Jewelry Company." Not only the phenomenon of name-changing as a factor in assimilation but also the social psychology of Jewish humor attracted Brill's pen. Drawing on Freud's *Wit and Its Relation to the Unconscious*, Brill explained how Jewish jokes provide a safe outlet for retaliatory aggression, while "Jewish jokes not produced by Jews never rise above the level of the comical strain or the brutal mockery." A lengthy description from Brill's clinical work in Zurich told the story of a Swiss bank official whose agnosticism and collegial affiliations with Jews during his twenties and early thirties had alienated his religious and antisemitic father. Desperate to reestablish rapport with his father, the man ultimately reverted to the familial antisemitism, refusing anymore to work with Jews, and he subsequently experienced a cathartic vision in which he, as Christ, was reunited with his father, who appeared as God.[41]

Jewish authorities presented cases of individual personality dissociation or dysfunction that reminded readers of ethnic divisions in the age of immigration. Isador Coriat devoted a third of his *The Meaning of Dreams* (1915), one of the first popular expositions of Freudian dream theory, to a dream containing ethnically specific hidden wishes. The dreamer was a "Jewish friend" of the author whose inner fears were riveted on the question of his social acceptance among his American colleagues. In the dream, Coriat's friend, who had gone to medical school with Dr. X, was with Dr. and Mrs. X in the dining room of their home when the doorbell rang, at which point Mrs. X said, "That is a rabbi; we don't want any more rabbis in here," and she dived under the table as if to hide and motioned to the subject to hide in the closet. When it turned out there was a package and not a rabbi at the door, relaxed conversation resumed between the three. In this demonstration of dream as wish-fulfillment, Coriat explained, "The subject himself was Hebrew and had often felt, because of his religious belief, that perhaps he was only tolerated by the doctor and his wife." Freudians spoke of personality splits more subtle than the famous cases of multiple personality. In their eyes, everyone suffered internal division from the conflict between urgent desires and the need to repress them. The desires of the Jewish subject in Coriat's dream analysis were basically social: the healing of his psychic rift depended on his integration as a Jew into the larger society.[42]

In a detailed case history recorded in *Psychanalysis*, Abraham Brill also showed that dreams revealed the human personality as a site of profound conflicts that were bound up with social divisions in American society. The story of "a bright, thoroughly Americanized young man of Russian-Jewish extraction" suggested that beneath the surface of adjustment lay deep ambivalences about the Jew's situation, ancestry, and future in Christian America. That case referred to a twenty-three-year-old driver, born in New York of immigrant parents, who entered a Manhattan clinic in 1909 in a state of inner turmoil, believing that Christians were about to kill all the Jews. Brill subjected the patient to rigorous dream analysis over a period of several months. Once the young man gave up his resistance and began to enjoy the voyage back into his childhood, he and Brill traversed (and Brill reported in full detail) a history of polymorphous sexuality, including sodomy and exhibitionism, with strong homosexual tendencies. At sixteen the "hypersexual" young man began peddling in rural New York, where he took "a strange feeling of pleasure" in exposing himself to women, and where, after a while, he fell in love with a farmer's daughter. His desire to marry the Christian girl, however, met his father's strong objections. The powerful father-son conflict, Brill deduced in proper Freudian style, lay at the source of his obsession with an imminent Christian massacre of Jews. While in this state of "wavering between his father and his beloved," he read a newspaper account of a massacre of Jews in Russia. "As his father was a Russian Jew a thought something like the following suddenly flashed through his mind: 'If my father were only there!' which may be completed, 'he would be killed and I could marry a Christian'; but this conscious perception was naturally at once suppressed. A few days later he began to compare notes about Jews and Christians which finally developed into the obsession 'All Jews will be killed by Christians.' "

Brill explained further that the young man's ambivalence was "intensified by the fact that his father was an orthodox Jew and he wanted to be an American." He was ashamed to be seen with his father because gentile boys made derogatory remarks about him, calling him Jew and Sheeny. "He himself often applied the same epithets to him, which was naturally followed by a reproach and an outburst of affection." In the story of the Jewish driver, Brill located a number of inner conflicts. Two of these, the conflict between homosexual and heterosexual desires and the love-hate relationship with the father, were Freudian universals. A third, though, represented a specifically American ethnic layer of the psychic unrest: the conflict between Americanizing child and immigrant parent, couched in the larger context of Jewish-Christian conflict.

This young man's analysis with Brill lasted four months. He saw Brill at first three hours each week, then two, then one, after which "there was still much to be done" because "his homosexual component had to be dealt with." A few months later Brill discharged him as cured. "Since then he has become more ambitious," Brill concluded, in what appears to have been an understatement, given that the young man "gave up his position as driver and is now the owner of a well paying business." Thanks to Freud, another Jew became an American success story. A young man who had walked into a Manhattan psychiatric clinic an obsessive compulsive, bisexual wage-earner walked out several months later a normal, heterosexual businessman.[43]

The new literature of psychological healing was full of cures, from Ray Stannard Baker's "Ambitious Russian Jew" to Abraham Brill's "bright, thoroughly Americanized young man of Russian-Jewish extraction." Though we must take such claims lightly as evidence of psychotherapeutic success (we do not know what happened to the patient the day after), they were loaded with cultural meaning. Baker's immigrant lad symbolized the value of a new therapeutic ethos, one that treated the alien not as a generic "Jew" but as an individual. By relieving the boy of what were considered Jewish tendencies toward mental overwork, the "new ideals in healing" had achieved a powerful democratic goal, "a citizen saved," as Baker put it.

Brill also documented the salvation of a citizen, even though his ostensible purpose was to expose the American public to Freudian theory. His patient was a prototype of the divided soul, a man driven by inner conflicts to an obsessive fear of Jewish annihilation. What more dramatic way could have been conceived to demonstrate the redemptive power of psychology than to cure that patient and turn him into a well-adjusted, prosperous American? The rifts between the Jew and the Christian and between the Orthodox immigrant father and the secular son were healed through the psychoanalysis.

As both aliens and alienists, Jews figured into public speculation about the idea that the human psyche and the American nation were divisible rather than solid, pluralistic rather than unified. Alongside the older archetype of the tormented New England soul struggling to make sense of a post-Calvinist universe, there now appeared another very different kind of character: the tormented Jewish soul navigating roughly between Old World and New and struggling for acceptance in a Christian world.

The rise of psychological thinking in America, and of Jews as psychological thinkers, leads us to two important questions. Why did Americans provide such a rich audience for psychological knowledge? And why were Jewish thinkers so keen to participate in public conversations about human nature? We have gotten a glimpse of the answers to those questions, but a fuller understanding will require us to turn back in time and explore two areas of history: (1) the cataclysm of Jewish intellectual and moral life after the Enlightenment, and (2) the rise of an enormous American market for books on how to live a more meaningful life. Those two trends first came together in a strange and fascinating way in the early 1800s when Benjamin Franklin, the godfather of American advice, appeared in Hebrew.

Part II

The Moral Universe of the Jews

Chapter 2

Benjamin Franklin in Hebrew:
The *Musar* Sage of Philadelphia

JEWISH AND AMERICAN IDEAS about the psyche did not deeply intermingle until the twentieth century, but we have evidence of an unlikely meeting of the two in the early 1800s. The moral revolution that led Jewish thinkers to create bold new theories of human nature was prefaced by the sudden appearance of Benjamin Franklin's moral philosophy in the Jewish ethical literature of eastern Europe. Judaism had always adapted ideas from other civilizations; this had been a key to its survival in times of crisis. And so it was when Jews imported Franklin's unique plan of moral self-improvement. That exchange signified a deep intellectual and moral restlessness in the Jewish world. It also foreshadowed the merger of Jewish and American values that would occur many years later when a wide array of Jews took up the business of moral instruction in America.

FRANKLIN'S CHART OF VIRTUES

Benjamin Franklin (1706–90) was not a church-going man. Raised a Presbyterian in the early 1700s, he came to doubt many of the cardinal points of faith, everything except those "Essentials of every Religion" that Presbyterianism shared with the other religions of the American colonies. These essentials were the existence of a Deity who "made the World, and govern'd it by his Providence," who prized "the doing Good to Man," and who punished Crime and rewarded Virtue "either here or hereafter." Franklin supported religion in general and contributed to Philadelphia's Jewish community as well as to Christian denominations because he believed those Bible-based organizations promoted the general welfare. Described by one historian as a "printer and friend of the human race," he was too much a rationalist to endure enthusiastic Christianity and too nimble a thinker to put up with dull expositions of Scripture. So Franklin devised his own private liturgy. He also created a personal spiritual tool, a unique plan of moral improvement, so sensible, so logical, and so captivating as to enthrall readers across the world for generations after his death in 1790.[1]

Published in his renowned *Autobiography*, Franklin's "bold and arduous Project of arriving at moral Perfection" focused on a simple chart. Set up as a grid, the chart had seven columns for each day of the week, and thirteen rows for each of the moral qualities Franklin hoped to improve: Temperance, Silence, Order, Resolution, Frugality, Industry, Sincerity, Justice, Moderation, Cleanliness, Tranquility, Chastity, and Humility. At the end of each day, Franklin went over each of the thirteen boxes for the day and placed dots in the boxes for those qualities he failed to cultivate properly, one dot for each transgression. If he overate twice on a Tuesday, for example, he would make two marks for Temperance that day. Every week he would concentrate on one of the thirteen characteristics, with the goal of attaining a clear set of boxes for that virtue. In thirteen weeks, he would complete a full cycle and begin again, so that by the end of one year he would have gone through the entire list of qualities four times. Franklin believed that this regimen would virtually guarantee a high moral character in an individual if it were pursued over a lifetime. He himself worked at it for a few years, until his busy schedule overtook him. He reported being "surpriz'd to find myself so much fuller of Faults than I had imagined," and he never got much of a grip on Order. In retrospect, Franklin concluded, "tho' I never arrived at the Perfection I had been so ambitious of obtaining, but fell far short of it, yet I was by the Endeavour a better and a happier Man than I otherwise should have been, if I had not attempted it."[2]

Franklin published a description of his self-examination plan because he considered it an excellent device for the moral instruction of young men, one that he hoped would spread far and wide. "Tho' my Scheme was not wholly without Religion," he wrote, "there was in it no Mark of any of the distinguishing Tenets of any particular Sect." "I had purposely avoided them," Franklin explained, because he wanted his method to be "serviceable to People in all Religions." "I would not have any thing in it that should prejudice any one of any Sect against it."[3]

Franklin's autobiography traveled quickly through the United States and then succeeded as well in Great Britain and continental Europe, where French, German, Dutch, Italian, and Spanish translations found many avid readers. Perhaps more surprising was the fact that part of the book, Franklin's distinctive chart for self-improvement, appeared far beyond the cosmopolitan universe of western Europe—in an 1808 Hebrew treatise for the ethical education of Polish yeshiva boys.

ACCOUNTING OF THE SOUL: FRANKLIN MEETS MUSAR

The treatise, *Accounting of the Soul (Ḥeshbon ha-Nefesh)*, was written by Menachem Mendel Lefin (1749–1826), a *maskil* (Enlightenment thinker) from Podolia, a region of southeastern Poland. A disciple of Moses Men-

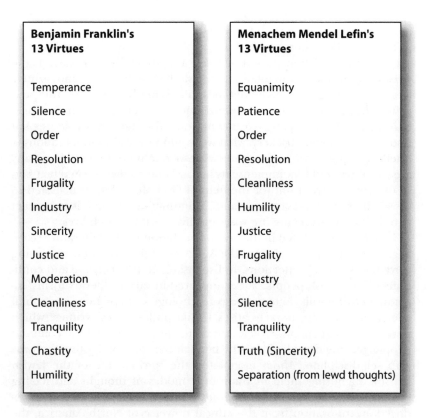

Benjamin Franklin's 13 Virtues	Menachem Mendel Lefin's 13 Virtues
Temperance	Equanimity
Silence	Patience
Order	Order
Resolution	Resolution
Frugality	Cleanliness
Industry	Humility
Sincerity	Justice
Justice	Frugality
Moderation	Industry
Cleanliness	Silence
Tranquility	Tranquility
Chastity	Truth (Sincerity)
Humility	Separation (from lewd thoughts)

The lists of virtues from the self-improvement plans of Benjamin Franklin and Menachem Mendel Lefin.

delssohn, Lefin wanted to preserve traditional Judaism while introducing Jewish readers to modern scientific and general literature. Toward that end he published a variety of religious and secular works and translations, one of which was his adaptation of Franklin's moral regimen.[4]

Lefin's book became a classic in the Jewish genre known as *musar*, a word derived from the Biblical Hebrew root meaning "chastise," "chasten," "try." Although *musar* is normally translated as "ethics" or "morality"—perhaps the best English approximations—the word actually has a different sense. Ethics and morality derive from the Greek concept of custom and customary, meaning conformity to certain mores or customs. *Musar*, however, suggests rigorous discipline; Bible translators often render it as "instruction." In the book of Proverbs, where the word appears most frequently, the sense of *musar* can be understood from the admonition: "Take fast hold of instruction [*musar*]; let it not go; keep it; for it is your life" (Proverbs 4:13). *Musar* thus suggests a deeply internal activity, an absorbing of proper habits through serious discipline.

The nemesis against which this discipline works is the *yetzer hara,* the evil inclination. Often personified as a mighty and clever warrior, the *yetzer hara* represents the totality of selfish desires, from lust and laziness to avarice and aggression. Sometimes called simply "the *yetzer,*" this powerful inner force (Judaism recognizes no external agent akin to Christianity's Devil) leads people astray not only through unruly desires but also through mental trickery, what we would now call rationalizations— intellectual justifications for doing what we ought not to do. "How many are its names, and how immense its havoc," one medieval *musar* text said of the *yetzer,* "were it not for the help of God Most High vouchsafed to those who seek to be saved from it." The function of *musar* is to instruct people how to overcome the *yetzer* and live spiritually rich lives.[5]

Though firmly rooted in the Torah and Talmud, *musar* literature really began to take shape in the Middle Ages, and it flowered into a stunning garden of spiritual reflections. Indispensable to the daily life and continuity of the Jewish people, *musar* appeared in various literary forms, including ethical wills, letters, poetry, anthologies of epigrams and moral tales, and systematic moral treatises. Unlike philosophical writings, which were directed at an elite of learned men, *musar* addressed the common people, placing new ideas into the familiar narrative of fighting the *yetzer* with self-discipline. *Musar* modulated the spiritual life of the Jewish masses, anchoring them in traditional modes of thought and feeling while allowing for timely innovations. When *Accounting of the Soul* introduced an innovation from the ethical universe of North America, the Jews of eastern Europe were ready to receive it. By 1900 the book had become a standard text in the great yeshivas of Lithuania.[6]

Accounting of the Soul is an extraordinary example of American Protestant and European Jewish moral traditions intersecting with each other. Commercial metaphors flourished in both, which is not surprising given that both Yankees and Jews were famous for their mercantile skills. The idea of keeping a spiritual ledger and making sure one's ethical books were in order appealed to New England Protestants and European Jews, whose survival in their respective wildernesses depended on solvency. *Accounting of the Soul* begins with a parable of two merchants, one fortunate and the other not. To survive, the second merchant has no choice but to make a careful accounting of his business, appraising the conditions of the market and calculating "to a hair" his income and expenses. Only then can he change his mercantile habits sufficiently to find prosperity in the long run. Such a parable would have been perfectly intelligible to Americans. Like Benjamin Franklin, Emerson and Thoreau relied on commercial metaphors to convey moral values. The lists of income and expenses in the first chapter of *Walden*, for example, had satirical value but also depicted Thoreau's spiritual quest "in terms his contemporaries could readily understand—the accountant's ledger." The same logic led Americans at the end of the nineteenth century to delight in philosopher William James's reference to the "cash value" of an idea.[7]

Franklin's ledger of virtues, which had no clear Protestant source, paralleled Jewish ethical writing in fascinating ways. A likely Puritan model for Franklin was Cotton Mather's *Bonifacius: An Essay upon the Good* (1710), which he said had "an Influence on my conduct thro' life" because of its great practical morality. In *Bonifacius*, Mather calls for a disciplined self-examination but he does not detail one. The treatise contains neither a plan for daily self-scrutiny nor a list of moral qualities to be cultivated. It does, however, allude to a Jewish ethical treatise that presented a novel plan of daily introspection. In his discussion of the moral obligations of physicians, Mather makes the following detour: "One *Jacob Tzaphalon*, a famous Jew in the former century, published at *Venice*, a book entitled *Precious Stones*. There are several *prayers* in the book; and among them a pretty long one, *for physicians when they go to visit their patients*. When the Psalmist says, 'Thou hast made me wiser than my enemies'; it may be read, 'Thou hast made me wise from my Enemies.' We should learn *wisdom* from them. . .—O *Christianity*, certainly thou wilt outdo *Judaism* in thy devotions!" Jacob Tzahalon's *Precious Stones* was a creative abridgment of *The Duties of the Heart*, an eleventh-century *musar* classic composed by the Spanish pietist Baḥya ibn Paquda. *The Duties of the Heart* constructs a series of spiritual "gateways," each representing a specific quality, through which the morally earnest Jew must pass to achieve love of God. In *Precious Stones* Tzahalon condensed *The Duties of the Heart* and divided it into thirty parts so that the reader could read one part each day and complete the cycle every month.[8]

In Jewish ethical writing, the technique of creating a series of moral attributes was conventional. The Talmud often lists moral qualities as a homiletic device, for which the Torah itself provided a precedent in the Ten Commandments and various lists of divine attributes held up for human imitation. The classic works of *musar* guided readers on tours of an intricate moral realm. By the sixteenth century the ethical traits and precepts from a medieval *musar* book, *The Paths of Life*, had been systematized according to a daily and weekly plan, as a means of heightening the ability of students to understand and practice them. In Franklin's own time, in fact almost exactly when he was devising his moral regimen, an Italian kabbalist, Moses Chaim Luzzatto, produced one of the most important of all *musar* volumes, *The Path of the Upright*. Luzzatto outlined eight qualities that, like Franklin's list of traits, were to be treated in

ascending order of development: watchfulness, zeal, cleanliness, abstinence, purity, saintliness, humility, and holiness.[9]

The ideal of striving for a temperamental mean between opposite
traits—for example, between stinginess and prodigality—passed into
both Jewish and Protestant ethics from the Greeks. Like other colonial
readers, Franklin was familiar with Greek literature. Historians have suggested Xenophon's *Memorabilia* and Aristotle's *Ethics* as likely sources of
his philosophy of self-improvement. The Aristotelian emphasis on a life
of moderation formed a perfect foundation for Franklin's ethical
thought. The Greek connection may explain the natural affinity between
Franklin and the Jewish ethical tradition, because Judaism permanently
incorporated Aristotle's *Ethics* through the twelfth-century writings of
Moses Maimonides. Maimonides produced a Jewish version of the
Golden Mean that affected Jewish culture as deeply as any single concept
could. "The moral man will remain always aware of his dispositions and
will evaluate his actions, and will inquire every day into the traits of his
soul," Maimonides prescribed, "and whenever he perceives his soul tending toward one of the extremes, he will hurry to remedy it and not allow
the evil trait to strengthen itself through the repetition of bad actions."[10]

JEWISH AND PROTESTANT RATIONALIST MORALITY

By comparing the motives behind the moral routines of Menachem Mendel Lefin and Benjamin Franklin, we can shed light on this first instance
of the Americanization of *musar.* Franklin's moral system reflected a lifelong effort to replace the Puritan dogma of his childhood with a fully
rational philosophy of life, freed from the supernaturalism and mystery
he associated with the religion of his ancestors. Cotton Mather, like any
good Puritan, insisted that there was a real difference between one's
actions and one's spiritual condition. Puritanism relied so heavily on the
concept of salvation by God's grace alone that it had to guard against
crediting a person's works too much. Good deeds might be a sign of
God's grace, meaning that the doer of the deeds had been predestined
for salvation, but they could never stand on their own as spiritually significant. Summing up this element of Puritan theology, Mather declared,
"No *good works* can be done by any man until he be *justified.*" In other
words, all of the unsaved man's works were "*dead works.*"[11]

Franklin disagreed. He believed that the opposite was true: good works
were easily available to all civic-minded souls. The Puritans believed in
self-examination as part of the storm and stress of being, but Franklin
saw it as a way of making a happy and orderly universe still happier and
more orderly. Furthermore, he wryly defined moral transgressions not

as sins but as errata, mistakes, on the pages of one's life. His morality was completely practical; it involved no inner dramas and nothing remotely mystical. He saw few mysteries in life and shunned any sort of appeal to a hidden source of wisdom.[12]

In all these ways, Franklin echoed John Locke, the most influential philosopher in the Anglo-American world. Even Franklin's concept of errata reflected the Lockean metaphor of the human mind as a blank sheet of paper on which impressions are collected. Locke's magisterial *Essay Concerning Human Understanding* (1690) lucidly expounded the superiority of reason to revelation. Locke insisted on the value of empirically tested ideas (those proved by experience) and cautioned against "enthusiasm," or emotionally driven beliefs (which he considered prejudices). We have scant knowledge of the true nature of things in the world, Locke explained, so our suppositions about the "real essences" of things were "useless." Therefore we should pursue only useful knowledge: the ideas we form from our sensations and observations. Like his famous brief for religious toleration (which paved the way for British acceptance of Jews as citizens), Locke's emphasis on useful knowledge and his distrust of unverifiable personal revelations formed a mainstream of American thought. Both Franklin and later generations of Jewish psychological thinkers in America waded comfortably in those waters.[13]

Franklin's Lockean moral plan matched the concerns of Lefin, who wanted to combat the mysticism that he saw infiltrating the Jewish world through Hasidism. An energetic *maskil*, Lefin hoped to modernize the thinking of the *shtetl*, the better to argue for the naturalization of Polish Jewry. He considered Hasidism the primary obstacle blocking his plan and intended *Accounting of the Soul* as a weapon against Hasidic enthusiasm. Camouflaged in what appears to be a pure discussion of ethics, Lefin conveyed a pointed message: Trust not in wonder-working *tzaddikim* (Hasidic rabbis), trust not in fiery emotional devotions as a moral purgative; rather, follow the well-trodden path of steady, rational commitment to self-rectification.[14]

Even though Lefin wanted only to reinforce rabbinic Judaism by importing a modern technique of character formation, it was difficult to embrace Franklin without embracing his defiance of ancestral authority. Franklin replaced the religious authority of his Puritan ancestors with the authority of practical experience. As Lefin assimilated Franklin, he approached the border of heretical disrespect of the Sages, the chain of rabbinic authority linking the Talmud to the present. While praising "our blessed Sages . . . whose rebuke we cannot answer," Lefin complained that the masters of *musar* "addressed only the intellectual spirit," the rational mind. "From where," he publicly wondered, "are we to draw counsel in our attempts to subdue the animal spirit so that it is subject to our will?" Just as Franklin discounted "the mere Exhortation to be good, that does not instruct and indicate the Means," so Lefin noted that the Sages, despite their profundity in many areas, had little to teach about psychological conditioning; they relied for the most part on the old technique of rewards and punishments. An answer came not from the vast chain of tradition but from the vast North American continent. "A few years ago a new strategy was developed," one that Lefin called "a wonderful innovation in this work" of spiritual accounting. Instead of older methods that required long hours stolen from sleep to pore over one's traits, "this method actually leaves the entire day open and orderly, with the mind clear for the Divine service. It clears the path so that a person can make his spiritual accounting, tempers the fires of *musar* and facilitates character development."[15]

From this point to the end of the century, Benjamin Franklin became a minor icon in the literature of *musar.* Jewish literati started to speak of "the English *ḥakham*" (sage) and "the *musar* Sage in Philadelphia" and to praise "the wonderful device that the sage Benjamin Franklin of the city of Philadelphia in North America invented." "It was a *goy* that lit the candle that serves as the light of Israel," a Hebrew periodical of Vienna reported in 1833. Though not unheard of, it was unusual for a gentile to receive such accolades. Franklin had entered the great chain of tradition. Where Judaism's sages left a gap, an American provided the missing link.[16]

MAJOR AND MINOR KEYS: AMERICAN OPTIMISM
MEETS THE ROD OF *MUSAR*

Not only did Lefin insert Franklin into the Jewish ethical tradition, but he also injected a dose of Franklin's American optimism. Franklin's ethical plan assumes a virtually unlimited faith in the power of the individual to change. Such a faith could come only by erasing all the deep and idiosyncratic perversities of character that traditionalist Christians and Jews took for granted. Franklin piously believed in the perfectionist possibility: if only he had applied himself unceasingly to his plan of self-improvement, he would have eradicated every moral flaw on his list.

Lefin's *Accounting of the Soul*, too, sounded a note of optimistic individualism that clashed with the minor key of *musar. Musar* tended toward a dim view of human nature. It emphasized the potency of the *yetzer hara*, the mighty efforts required to defeat it, and, in some of the darker works, the hellish punishments that would meet the morally lazy soul. Of course, *musar* writers held out the possibility of repentance for sin and urged their readers to take the "straight path." Nonetheless, *musar* liked to dwell on the "obstinacy of the human heart" and on the commensurate need for "the rod of terror and dread" to discipline one's unruly inclinations.[17]

Lefin continues in the traditional mode of describing the *yetzer hara* as a mighty and indefatigable foe, but he unmistakably endorses Franklin's optimism about human nature.

> At the end of the year, carefully review the charts of summation. With God's help, what you see will make you quite happy, for you will find that the violations have diminished year by year, season by season and week by week. You will thus know that God has desired your actions and has led you on the path of truth. As our Sages said: *In the path that man wishes to follow, he is led.* When you follow this path securely for a few more seasons, you will find that all traces of the violation of a particular trait have disappeared from your notebook. You can then eliminate that trait from the book and substitute another trait of yours which needs correction. Slowly but surely you will be able to replace all of the original traits with new ones, until you reach the point where your notebook will be entirely devoid of markings of any violations—testimony to the purity of your heart and the triumph of your intellectual spirit over the animal spirit. The entire purpose of your creation was to achieve this.

Lefin concludes this passage traditionally, saying that success at self-improvement enables the individual to serve God "in joy for as long as you live, until you return to the dust and your spirit returns to . . . the radiance of the Divine Presence." Yet the message of Divine service now mixes freely with the motif of individual happiness, and Judaism's optimism about the Hereafter now finds a direct parallel in earthly optimism about self-mastery.[18]

When Lefin announced to his readers that he was presenting a "marvelous innovation," he intended only to enrich Jewish moral scrutiny with a simple and sensible new device. In order to resist the *yetzer*'s many devices or tricks (*taḥbulot*), the individual needed a superior set of ethical devices or tricks. Benjamin Franklin's chart was such a device, one so new, Lefin implies, that the *yetzer*, like a warrior faced with an unknown weapon, will be helpless before it. "His heart should be confident," Lefin said of the man who applied the new technique diligently, "that within but a few years he will merit that his spiritual illnesses will be cured, that he will be blessed and that his end will be good." Whether or not the "*musar* sage of Philadelphia" really provided a match for the *yetzer hara*, his scheme of moral improvement tipped the scales of Jewish ethical thought toward a new optimistic individualism, just as it had done to Puritan ethics.[19]

JUDAISM AND THE SCIENCE OF THE PSYCHE

Lefin's use of Franklin also signaled a new sensitivity to philosophical and psychological ideas that might be blended with *musar.* Franklin's preoccupation with habit and its effect on character came straight from Locke. So did his dictum that "vicious Actions are not hurtful because they are forbidden, but forbidden because they are hurtful." Given Locke's empiricist belief in human experience as the source of all knowledge, it followed that the character of a person could be known by his or her effects upon the world. Because character depended on habits, the sure way to improve character was to change one's habits. Locke's successors added scientific information about the nervous system to his psychology of habit, producing a more complicated system of character formation, which Lefin adopted in *Accounting of the Soul.*[20]

Lefin combined new knowledge about nerves with *musar*'s emphasis on the will and habits. He explained that the repetition of an action (i.e., habit) conditioned the nervous system. By repeating morally troubling experiences, one deepened the sensory "traces" of those experiences in the memory, and the build-up of such negative traces compromised whatever chance willpower might have to subdue the *yetzer.* By the same token, the will could be strengthened and the *yetzer* weakened if the individual developed new habits, producing new experiences and sensations that built up positive traces in the memory. Eventually this kind of reeducation would give the individual a greater conviction of his ability to overcome bad habits. Willpower would be reinforced by changes in the messages that the nervous system conveyed to the brain.[21]

The linkage of nerves and psychological states in *Accounting of the Soul* revealed an intense effort to deepen the understanding of the soul by tapping scientific theories. Shifting the focus of *musar* onto the subtle mechanisms of the psyche, Lefin imported into Jewish ethical thought a more explicit concern with the subconscious dimension of human behavior. "The ideas that are hidden in the heart of man," he wrote, "accompany him in every place and time and act upon him both consciously and unconsciously [*poalim b'nafsho me-daato u'shelo me-daato*] according to their strength in his mind." *Accounting of the Soul* presents Franklin's plan as having both a behavioral and an introspective component. Not only should one strive for better habits, but through the method of self-examination the sensitive person will "discover that there are subtleties and novel specifics pertaining to the trait under inspection." From the weekly charting of virtues "there will flower . . . a precious collection" of insights into the psyche.[22]

Accounting of the Soul was the first sign of a collective need among European Jews to find more dynamic approaches to the inner life of the individual. The last sign appeared at the end of the century, when Jews alienated from the synagogue began to congregate in the temple of Freud. To follow the path between those signposts, we must turn to those events in Western intellectual life that transformed the moral universe of the Jews.

Chapter 3

Jews and the Crisis of the Psyche

SINCE THE LATE 1600s European and American thinkers had been inquiring into the workings of the psyche and developing new conceptions of human psychology. By the nineteenth century, those conceptions were forcing Christian civilization into an intellectual crisis, as psychological theorists of various types wrenched the psyche from the hands of theologians. Yet the most influential new interpretations of the mind remained wedded to various forms of Christian and metaphysical experience, which were either implicitly dismissive or overtly hostile to Judaism. Those Christian undertones put Jewish thinkers under pressure to renovate Judaism in the hope of making it more responsive to the individual psyche. The principal renovations—Reform Judaism, Ethical Culture, Modern Orthodoxy, the *Musar* movement, and *Ḥabad* Hasidism—were all systems of moral reform with a strong psychological emphasis. The result of these initiatives was a new emphasis on Jewish morality as the solution for the psychic problems of the individual. Only within this context of a revolution in the moral universe of the Jews can we begin to understand the bold new psychologies that Jewish thinkers would construct for the twentieth century.

THE CREATION OF THE MODERN SELF

In the sixteenth and seventeenth centuries, a whole range of social and intellectual changes set the stage for a new conception of the "self" and of a personal psyche. The individualism that has long been associated with the Renaissance, an individualism marked by such cultural forms as portrait painting, took on a sharp outline after 1500. Not only did the art of individual portraiture soar to great heights, but the mass-marketing of mirrors and the popularity of writing personal letters, keeping diaries, and reading self-improvement books all gave new meaning to "self-reflection." Some of Europe's greatest literature opened up new pathways for interpreting the individual as a self-defining subject. Between 1595 and 1610, Shakespeare changed the entire course of Western literature by creating self-reflective characters who changed themselves "on the basis of self-overhearing," establishing what we consider the modern sensibility of "talking to ourselves endlessly, overhearing what we say, then pondering and acting upon what we have learned." Shortly before and soon after Shakespeare, Michel de Montaigne created a new mode of literary introspection in the *Essays* (1580), René Descartes claimed that the subjective mind was the ultimate judge of reality in his *Discourse on Method* (1637), and John Locke linked personal identity with one's own consciousness, rather than with God and Church, in the *Essay Concerning Human Understanding* (1690). By 1700 "something recognizably like the modern self" had appeared among the elite of northwestern Europe and America.[1]

Without abandoning Christianity, Descartes and Locke placed a new emphasis on the power of the rational mind. For them and their followers, the mind came equipped not with ideas from God but with the capacity to comprehend the laws of the physical world. By isolating the rational mind from the senses, they moved away from earlier approaches to human nature that closely linked psychological states and physical substances. (Such terms as *sanguine, phlegmatic,* and *good-humoured* reflect that older view, as does *melancholy,* which comes from the word meaning "black bile.") There was more disagreement than agreement among philosophers about the specifics of how the soul, mind, and body related to each other, but the Enlightened tended to reject superstitious beliefs that spirits inhabited bodies or that mental illness came from demons. Instead, they replaced supernatural explanations of disease with medical experimentation and treatment.[2]

One problem with the Enlightenment emphasis on human rationality, however, was that it flattened the psyche into a one-dimensional sheet of Reason. By the late 1700s the model of the rational, morally self-disciplined person began to give way to other images and theories of human nature, which emphasized the reality of inner forces capable of overcoming the rational mind. In the new genre of sentimental novels, writers explored the emotional recesses of the individual and delighted in a new kind of heroine who was "driven by forces beyond her control." The exquisite psychodramas of Sigmund Freud a century later culminated a long intellectual and cultural trend in which students of human nature, and their growing audience of middle-class readers, abandoned the abstract human nature of Descartes and Locke and focused more intently on the stormy convolutions of the individual mind.[3]

Until Freud, new understandings of the psyche were intertwined with varieties of Christian experience and post-Christian mysticism. Three trends dominated the nineteenth century, each with its own religious manifestation. A naturalist psychology—which formed the basis of the academic discipline "Psychology"—merged with liberal Protestantism (and in France with Catholicism). Mesmerism encouraged Christian mind-cure movements, spiritualism, theosophy, and occultism. And

German philosophies of self blended with romantic Protestantism. All three of those approaches presented Jews with distinct problems and challenges.

NATURALIST PSYCHOLOGY

For men and women in the early nineteenth century, scientific discoveries about electricity and the chemistry of the brain stirred a deep curiosity about the electrical and chemical basis of feelings, thoughts, and life itself. Until the 1830s, a general ignorance of physical properties made it easy for people to speculate about the power of natural forces over thoughts, feelings, and behavior. It was commonly thought that the activity of the soul, or psyche, depended on the play of electricity, magnetism, heat, and gravity. Inspired in part by Luigi Galvani's discovery of the link between electricity and the nerve impulses of frogs, Mary Shelley wrote the prototypical monster story, *Frankenstein* (1818), in which a scientist successfully animates dead matter, creating a man with the intelligence and sensitivity of the most human soul. The idea of galvanic natural forces animating human life—possibly without the participation of God—came out of the most radical branch of late Enlightenment philosophy.

The philosophical radicals of the late 1700s and early 1800s theorized that human emotions, usually considered part of the soul, actually derived from nature. Emotions resulted from the repeated, adaptive responses of the human organism to its environment over the generations. This line of thought had strong materialist implications, tending as it did to dismiss the soul as a convenient fiction and to define the mind in purely physical terms. Potentially, it challenged long-established religious teachings that prized the soul as the source of the human will and moral choice.[4]

By the 1870s, a naturalist approach to the psyche—one that viewed the mind in organic terms as part of nature—provided the basis for a new academic discipline of psychology. Because of its potential to reduce all human life to physiology, the new psychology had to be reconciled with religious belief, at least in the universities where most psychologists did their work. Psychologists performed the appropriate acts of reconciliation, insisting that their investigations of the mind did not defy religion. Relying on the fundamental distinction between mind and body that Descartes had made two centuries earlier, they claimed that science concerned itself only with the body. They experimented on the brain but left the mind (the soul) undisturbed, free for the continuing speculations of religious philosophers. When the English philosopher Herbert Spencer was attacked for the alleged atheism of his *Principles of Psychology* (1855), he responded with some pain that, on the contrary, his science lacked the wherewithal to prove or disprove the existence of God.

As long as theologians ceased their search for scientific proof of religious truths, psychologists would meet them halfway by respecting the boundaries of theology. The new science of mind "succeeded in becoming a science," explains an eminent historian of psychology, "in large part because of its defense of a theological conception of human nature typically associated with liberal Protestant theology" (and, in French universities, with Catholicism). The merger of science and Christianity was announced with impeccable clarity by G. Stanley Hall, a founder of academic psychology in the United States. Hired by the Johns Hopkins University in 1884 to fill the nation's first endowed position in psychology, Hall soothed the audience of his inaugural lecture by observing, "The new psychology . . . is I believe Christian to its root and centre."[5]

MESMERISM

Mesmerism generated another kind of inquiry into covert forces animating the psyche. Originating in the 1770s with Austrian physician Franz Anton Mesmer (1734–1815), mesmerism was a method of healing that built on the medically popular idea of magnetic forces within the body. Mesmer introduced the principle of *animal magnetism*, a kind of psychic fluid that a gifted healer could influence, thus curing the kinds of illnesses and disturbances often associated with demonic possession. Mesmerism worked on the theory that this fluid filled the entire universe and served as a mysterious medium of connection between people, like a liquid ground of being. In the nineteenth century, especially in France, where Mesmer spent most of his adult life performing sensational healings, mesmerism evolved along more psychological lines, ultimately producing the concept of *rapport* between healer and patient and the idea of sleep or sleeplike states as a therapeutic vehicle. In the 1880s that evolution yielded pioneering French studies of psychiatric hypnosis.[6]

Along the way, however, mesmerism stimulated spiritualism and a number of Christian and post-Christian mystical beliefs. In America a Maine clockmaker, Phineas Quimby, gave up clocks for humans in the 1830s, becoming a famed mesmerist and developing a special theory about disease—that it consisted of an error in the mind. His doctrine, which he called "Christian science" and the "science of health," stressed that people were spiritual beings who shared in God's wisdom and whose souls stood in a direct relation to the Divine Mind. "Mind-cure" became a powerful American movement, culminating in Mary Baker Eddy's Christian Science and coinciding with a massive outbreak of spiritualism

between 1850 and 1900. Mind-cure advocates were the first Christians
to expound on the unconscious as a key source of spiritual healing. They
drew heavily on Swedenborgianism, the mystical belief system based on
Swedish philosopher Emanuel Swedenborg's accounts of communication with dead souls and his doctrine of spiritual spheres surrounding
the earth. Two popular and representative books by Warren Evans, a
Methodist Episcopal minister turned Swedenborgian, *The Mental Cure*
(1869) and *Mental Medicine* (1871), claimed that the healing powers of
the unconscious were a psychological form of Christianity. Christ had
worked saving grace through the impressionable unconscious, Evans believed, and now men and women might again achieve immediate communication with God.[7]

In Europe, occultism was as popular as spiritualism and mind cure
were in America, but, unlike those American phenomena, it often included antisemitism. Modern occultism, which emerged in the late nineteenth century, differed from mysticism by focusing on the self and the
attainment of inner insight, rather than on mysticism's classical aim of
union with God. Not unlike Swedenborgianism, with its conception of
higher spiritual spheres and direct psychic communications through appointed souls, the Theosophical movement of Madame Blavatsky,
founded in New York City in 1875, proliferated throughout Europe in
its effort to tap humanity's latent psychic powers. Blavatsky's eclectic system had an interesting racial cosmology, according to which Jews and
certain other "archaic root races" were destined to die out, while the
Aryans, the root race of the nineteenth century, passed into a final, spiritualized human consciousness that was already on the horizon. Theoso-
phists who were more piously antisemitic than Blavatsky herself built on
this idea. French adherents helped produce and transfer to Russia the
infamous *Protocols of the Elders of Zion* in the 1890s. After World War I,
Alfred Rosenberg, a Baltic German and (like Adolf Hitler and Heinrich
Himmler) an occultist, introduced the *Protocols* into the Nazi movement,
which feasted on the idea of a Judeo-Masonic conspiracy behind the Bolshevik Revolution.[8]

Long haunted by the image of a demonic and sinister Jewry, European
Christian culture could hardly avoid incorporating it into mystical cos-
mologies that highlighted the play of mysterious psychic forces. In Russia, all sorts of occult and mystic beliefs abounded for the same reason
spiritualism and mind cure did in America. They constituted a potent
reaction against the scientific despiritualization of the psyche. The great
drift toward theosophy and mysticism merged with a resurgent popular
interest in Slavic folk mythology, especially the peasant tendency to combine beliefs in supernatural beings with Christianity. Ancient superstitions about Jews found deep nourishment in this atmosphere of gothic

irrationalism. One prominent Russian occultist presented a confused notion of Kabbala to support an accusation of the blood libel, which was enjoying new life under the Tsars at the turn of the century. This was a bizarre inversion of the mesmeric idea: instead of healing Christian folk, hidden forces now drained their life substance.[9]

THE GERMAN PSYCHOLOGY OF SELF

Along with naturalism and mesmerism, a German philosophy of self encouraged psychological inquiry in the nineteenth century. In the wake of the Enlightenment, a younger generation of Germans took up a romantic philosophy of the "I" (*ich*), which focused on the deep inner relationship of oneself with others and with the universe. German romanticism aimed to restore a sense of harmony and unity to a human psyche that had been understood as terribly divided by the conflict between reason and passion. Romanticism also produced a powerful intellectual quest for an underlying force of existence, in which all individual personalities merged. One of the most memorable and influential of these unifying forces was the Will to Life (or Will to Live) of Arthur Schopenhauer (1788–1860). Schopenhauer believed that "a way from *within* stands open to us," a mysterious force connecting human beings "to that real inner nature of things." The inner essence of all human beings is the will-to-life, a primordial life force that exists in powerful tension with the rational mind. Schopenhauer's meditations on the qualities of the inner force laid a foundation for Freud's theories about the power of unconscious sexual drives.[10]

Just as naturalist psychology allied with liberal Protestantism and mesmerism blended with Christian spiritualism and occultism, the new German psychologies of self melded with romantic Protestantism. They represented an impassioned search for the authentic inner life of the individual and for the secret relationship that united the individual with the spiritual order of the universe. According to Friedrich Schleiermacher (1768–1834), the theologian who reformulated Protestantism in the spirit of German romanticism, religion was not the product of reason but of emotion and intuition. It had to address the reality expressed so concisely by Goethe's young Werther (1774): "Ah, what I know, everyone can know—my heart is mine alone." Religion's concern was the ineffable motion of the individual soul toward the Infinite. Challenging both the rationalism of the Enlightenment and the dogmatics of Christianity, Schleiermacher postulated a God that spoke anew to every generation in the mysterious language of one's innermost consciousness. As if to demonstrate how thoroughly the dichotomy of Christianity versus

Judaism permeated the European mind, Schleiermacher explained himself by referring to those allegedly polar opposites. Judaism, he believed, represented dead religion, the kind of worn-out doctrine that could not serve the modern quest for spiritual fulfillment. Judaism's one redeeming value, the concept of Messiah, was conveyed to modern men and women through the still-living faith of Christianity.[11]

Romantic Christianity threw German Jews into a predicament that was well illustrated by the religious conversions of Henriette Herz and Rahel Varnhagen. In the lives of these extraordinary hostesses of Berlin's brightest salons, we can see both the power of contemporary German philosophy over Jewish intellectuals and the unique challenge that a somewhat mystical Christianity presented to the highly rationalist mentality of emancipated Jews. Children of the German Jewish bourgeoisie of the late eighteenth century, Herz (née de Lemos) and Varnhagen (née Levin) gravitated toward the cultural high life of Berlin, befriended (and romanced) leading Romantic thinkers, and learned to hold Judaism in contempt as a meaningless, defunct religion. Herz and Varnhagen delighted, sometimes agonizingly, in the inward search that the German Romantics prescribed. The effort to get into sublime touch with one's soul struck each of them as a basically Christian experience. The only Judaism they knew was riddled with outer forms of worship they did not understand and supported by rationalist arguments they did not respect. In their sincere conversions to Christianity, Herz and Varnhagen showed that the primary threat to Jewish existence in the modern world was a transcendentalist "religion of the heart" that promised intuitive union with Christ.[12]

JEWS AND THE CRISIS OF THE PSYCHE

Because each of the major streams of psychological inquiry—naturalist, mesmerist, and German romantic—was clearly connected to a type of Christian experience, and sometimes spilled over into antisemitism, the Jewish engagement with them was ambivalent. That ambivalence would underlay much of the Jewish psychological impact on the culture of the twentieth century, for Jewish thinkers introduced their ideas in tension with Christian society. In the nineteenth century, however, Jews, like Christians, adapted new psychological concepts into their religious universe, producing a variety of innovative moral systems that recognized the importance of the individual psyche. There were five major innovations: Reform Judaism, the Ethical Culture movement, and Modern Orthodox Judaism in Germany and America, and, in eastern Europe, the *Musar* movement and *Ḥabad* Hasidism. Together those initiatives amounted to a Jewish moral revolution offering different answers to the same question: How does Judaism satisfy the psychic needs of the individual?

REFORM AND ETHICAL CULTURE

Two of the most direct responses to this question in nineteenth-century Western culture were Reform and its derivative, Ethical Culture. Based on the widespread German search for religious forms that accurately reflected the inner spirit of men and women, the Reform movement in Judaism aimed to reconstruct the religion so as to bring law and spirit into a pure connection with each other. The Reformers agreed with Christian critics that most of the 613 commandments of rabbinic Judaism were antiquated ceremonials. They honed the body of law down to those rules governing the ethics of interpersonal behavior. For Jews living in modern societies rather than segregated Jewish communities, communal standards of diet and dress seemed irrelevant, whereas standards governing the individual moral conduct of a citizen became all-important.

Rabbi Abraham Geiger (1810–74), the chief formulator of the philosophy of Reform Judaism, believed that rabbinic Judaism had lost touch with its essence and stagnated, falling behind the moral development of mankind. A native of Frankfurt, Geiger held pulpits in Wiesbaden, Breslau, Frankfurt, and Berlin, and he managed to be both a prolific scholar and a militant reformer. Hoping to restore the essence and moral vigor of Judaism, Geiger called for a complete religious overhaul. He believed in retaining whatever rituals were personally meaningful to people. Whereas the chain of rabbinic tradition formerly guided the spiritual life of the Jewish people, now, according to Reform, the personal needs of modern people determined which elements of tradition were essential and which were dispensable. In keeping with the times, Geiger found his inspiration in a psychological crisis of faith. Having desanctified Judaism's basic texts as human rather than divine creations, he still experienced real longing for an unbounded connection to those scriptures. A self-described "stormy soul," he wrote passionately of Scripture and certain rabbinic commentaries as constituting "a part of my personality."[13]

At its apex the Reform ideal of a renewed Judaism attuned to the individual psyche produced a powerful doctrine of Jewish moral superiority. When Geiger was a philology student at the University of Heidelberg, he envied the success of Germans at modernizing Christianity, but by the end of his life he believed that Judaism defined the moral future of humanity. He centered the Reform movement on the moral grandeur of the Hebrew Bible, especially the revelation of Moses at Sinai and the

injunctions of the Prophets. Geiger came to the conclusion that the people of Israel had a genius for religion and held the keys to universal
spiritual growth. As the Greeks had been gifted with the arts, so were
the Hebrews with morality. The acute moral sense that God imparted to
ancient Israel continued to belong to Israel's descendants, as God's spirit
expressed itself unendingly through the moral workings of the Jewish
people. Reform envisioned itself as the modern incarnation of the
Prophets, and the religion of humanity.[14]

Reform spun off yet another moral innovation in the nineteenth century, the Ethical Culture movement of Felix Adler (1851–1933), which
took Jewish rationalist moralism all the way into a nontheistic universal
faith of pure morality. An immigrant from Germany, Adler was educated
at Columbia University and, like his father, became a Reform rabbi, hold-
ing the pulpit of New York City's prestigious Temple Emanu-El. Too
much of a rationalist to continue as a rabbi, he decided to create a new
movement that retained the ethics of Judaism without the theology. In
1876 Adler founded the Society for Ethical Culture, which advocated a
vigorous moral philosophy for agnostic or atheist Jews and Christians. In
some respects Ethical Culture paralleled the Social Gospel movement
that emerged out of Christianity to deal with the new problems that came
with life in urban, industrial America. Both tried to revivify a sense of
moral commitment in society, but the Social Gospelers focused on the
disparities between rich and poor, whereas Ethical Culture concerned
itself more with psychological matters.[15]

Felix Adler attempted to apply a coherent moral system to what he
considered the basic psychological problem of modern people, the de-
basement of the self as a result of science's reevaluation of the world. "A
reconstructed ethical ideal," he wrote, "must relieve mankind of the
pain, the depression, due to profound self-depreciation and self-con-
tempt." Adler culled the great ethical insights of East and West, but his
background allowed him to dwell on Jewish sources, both biblical and
talmudic, which he considered an excellent vehicle of moral instruction.
He believed that Bible stories about ethical dilemmas possessed a rare
"interweaving of moral causes and effects." They were "true moral pictures" ideally suited "to train the power of observation." Adler thought
it extraordinary that ancient Judaism resisted speculating about the un-
knowable spirit of God and instead labored over an ethical conception
of the human soul. The fruit of that labor was the belief that people
would best honor the unknown holiness of God through respectful conduct toward each other. He lauded Judaism's "awe-inspired respect for
the personality of others."[16]

SAMSON RAPHAEL HIRSCH AND MODERN ORTHODOXY

In the founding of Modern Orthodoxy, we encounter yet another creative effort to establish Jewish morality as perfectly suited to the modern psyche. Like Felix Adler and the leaders of Reform, Samson Raphael Hirsch (1808–88), the formulator of Modern Orthodox Judaism, emphasized the supreme importance of Judaism's interpersonal ethics. Born and educated in Hamburg, Hirsch studied with Rabbi Isaac Bernays (the grandfather of Sigmund Freud's wife, Martha Bernays), who was known for combining secular knowledge with traditional Judaism. Although Hirsch had once been a close friend of his contemporary Abraham Geiger, the two ended up as founders of opposite movements within Judaism. Unlike Geiger, whose moral passion led him to Reform, Hirsch fashioned a new kind of Orthodoxy, one that allowed Jews to observe the commandments while following a modern way of life. To reconcile tradition and modernity, he strove to demonstrate that Jewish practice nourished the psyche.

Hirsch believed that *halakhah,* Jewish law, contained eternal truths given to all humanity at the beginning of history. Those truths might have been forgotten over time had not God created a covenant with Israel based on commandments that preserved them. By diligently keeping the entirety of the law, Jews became conveyors of universal moral principles and fulfilled a spiritual mission to humanity.[17]

Breaking from the insularity of a ghettoized Judaism, Hirsch's new type of Orthodoxy concerned itself fully with the scriptural challenge to "love thy neighbor as thyself." He called that commandment "the summarizing final maxim for the whole of our social behavior, in feelings, word and deed." Interpreting Leviticus 19:18, in which the commandment appears, Hirsch interpreted the Hebrew word for love (*ahavah*) to mean "equally giving oneself up for others and bringing others most intimately near to oneself." Blending Jewish and German ideas about *duty*—one's ethical obligations to others—Hirsch spoke about love in a way that he hoped would appeal to modernized Jews who were familiar with German romantic writings about the self and the inner connection of the self with others and with the cosmos: "His own self-love, too, is only a consciousness of duty. He sees in himself only a creation of God, entrusted to himself to attain that bodily, mental and moral perfection for which God has designed him and placed him in his earthly existence, and for which He had given him directions in His Torah. In exactly the same way, and from the same consciousness of duty, he directs his love to the well-being of his neighbor, [and] loves him as being equally a creation of God."[18]

Hirsch focused on the psychology of the modern Jew, claiming that only the Torah-observant person would find peace of mind. The Jew who abandoned the law in search of a modern identity, rather than achieving a balance between tradition and modernity, was doomed to psychological malaise. That was the meaning he saw in Leviticus 26:16, in which God warns the Israelites what will happen to them if they abandon the commandments: "I will decree consternation over you, which brings lassitude, and fever which destroys the eyesight with weakness and fills the mind with woe." Hirsch approached that passage with the observation, "It is the mind that governs the body, and psychical unrest has physical results." The word "consternation," he suggested, referred to "the dismay and enervation which arises out of the feeling of helplessness . . . out of the loss of self-confidence." And he interpreted "eyesight" in a figurative, psychological sense: it is "the mental outlook" that is destroyed. The psychic disorder of those who abandon the Torah will finally lead to paranoia—"ye shall flee when none pursueth you." The lesson of Hirsch's biblical psychoanalysis was plain: the Jewish psyche without the law is a sick psyche.[19]

In the most economically advanced and philosophically modern areas of Europe and America, Reform Judaism, Ethical Culture, and Modern Orthodoxy emerged to create new moral systems that addressed the psychic needs of the individual. Each movement claimed that its moral psychology was a proper and healthy adaptation to modern conditions. Each declared itself the truest path of Western moral development and presented the Jewish people or the Jewish ethical tradition, or both, as vital to the moral welfare of humanity.

Jews in the Tsar's domains of Poland, Russia, and Lithuania, in Rumania, and in the Austro-Hungarian territories of Galicia, Moravia, and Bohemia also produced bold moral innovations, but they did not develop them in the context of Christian-Jewish tension and polemic. They responded to modernization itself, aiming to strengthen traditional Jewry against secular knowledge and values filtering in from the West. In eastern Europe, where Jews continued to live in conditions of severe economic and political stress, a psyche-centered moral revolution emerged in two forms: the *Musar* movement of Rabbi Israel Salanter and the Ḥabad Hasidism of Rabbi Shneur Zalman of Lyady.

ISRAEL SALANTER AND THE *MUSAR* MOVEMENT

Aiming to incite a revolution in the souls of young men and ultimately in every Jew, Rabbi Israel Salanter took the *musar* tradition and turned it into a highly focused, powerful movement within eastern European Jewry. Salanter (1810–83) was born Israel Lipkin in Zagory, Lithuania. A child prodigy, he was sent to study in the town of Salant, where he trained under Rabbi Joseph Zundel, a man of great scholarly and ethical qualities. By the 1840s Israel Lipkin had become Israel Salanter, following a custom of identifying sages by a locale in which they studied or taught. In an effort to reinvigorate Judaism, Salanter shifted his attention from Talmud, the usual pursuit of Jewish scholars, to *musar*, and then he went a step further, turning *musar* into a full-blown movement. He started separate schools of young men who devoted themselves to techniques of ethical improvement and inner awakening instead of the conventional study of *halakhic* questions. By 1900 the *Musar* movement had spread throughout the prestigious yeshivas of Lithuania.[20]

Drawing some of his inspiration from Lefin's *Accounting of the Soul*, Salanter created a psychological theory about the evil inclination and built an entire moral system around it. Salanter brooded over the gap between knowing and doing, between awareness of what is right and inability to act on that awareness. He concluded that the primary reason for the discrepancy lay in the nature of subconscious drives, which he associated with the *yetzer hara*. He likened the unconscious to a torrential stream "in which the intellect drowns, if we do not place it aboard a ship." Convinced that the spirit of Judaism would collapse without the firm foundation of *musar*, he insisted on the necessity of painstaking self-evaluation. Without an awareness of the unconscious forces at work within the soul, the individual was doomed to lack self-control. *Musar* would redeem morality by turning the attention of the individual inward to the psyche.[21]

The psychological drama of the potentially unmoored Jew reflected real changes in eastern Europe. After 1840, when the reign of Nicholas I commenced, the tsarist government initiated a long campaign to modernize the sizable Jewish population under its power. A decisive step in this process was the abolition of Jewish communal authority, by which the rabbinic courts regulated daily life and handled internal conflicts. As the official government intervened more and more in Jewish affairs, as the communal control of the rabbis eroded, and as the newer ideas of religious modernizers penetrated the school system and literature of the Jewish communities, religious innovators like Salanter wanted to give individual Jews the wherewithal to survive with their faith and traditions intact. He saw his intensive, emotionally compelling techniques of inner transformation as a powerful weapon in the hands of the individual Jew. As the superstructure of rabbinic authority crumbled, Salanter constructed a moral infrastructure in its place.[22]

SHNEUR ZALMAN AND *ḤABAD* HASIDISM

The *Musar* movement competed with Hasidism for the souls of eastern European Jews, many of whom were attracted by Hasidism's own unique focus on the individual psyche as a site of moral transformation. Unlike most other forms of mysticism in the nineteenth century, Hasidism had a strong ethical orientation, and, unlike earlier theosophical and esoteric trends in Judaism, it took mysticism down from the heavens and disseminated it in the fields of everyday life. This was especially true of *Ḥabad* Hasidism, the most buoyant of the various Hasidic sects. (*Ḥabad* is an acronym for three Hebrew words meaning wisdom, understanding, and knowledge.) Centered on the Belorussian town of Lubavitch—thus known as Lubavitcher Hasidism—*Ḥabad* combined mystical enthusiasm for God with an "intense preoccupation with the human mind and its impulses."[23]

To some degree, this new emphasis on individual psychology characterized all of Hasidism. Hasidic thought retained some of the older kabbalistic theosophical motifs, with their complicated articulations and descriptions of the cosmos, but its central concern was the individual person. Described by Gershom Scholem as "practical mysticism at its highest," Hasidism transformed kabbalism into an ethico-spiritual path for all men and women to follow. Instead of monopolizing their spiritual secrets, the great holy men of Hasidism, the *tzaddikim*, aimed to teach their adherents as much as was within their grasp. The *Tzaddik* became, in the banal sociological language of the late-twentieth century, a "role model" of the most absolute kind. By learning from the *Tzaddik*, the average Jew strove to fulfill the heavy burden of the *mitzvot* (commandments). In the hands of the *Tzaddik*, the *mitzvot* were themselves transformed into divine chariots, on which the Jew could fly to God. Every ethical act—there were no *mitzvot* that were not understood as ethical acts—suddenly radiated with the potential splendor of Unification with the Holy Name.[24]

Rabbi Shneur Zalman (1745–1813), the founder of *Ḥabad* Hasidism, came out of the eighteenth-century world in which Hasidism originated, but his innovations in Hasidic thought were established and disseminated in the nineteenth century. Shneur Zalman deviated from most other Hasidic leaders by developing a sophisticated, rationalist method of individual striving. Simple faith in God or in the *Tzaddik*, he believed, cannot overcome the inner forces of the *yetzer*. Only through laborious study and meditation could the individual achieve his desire for proper obedience to God's will. Shneur Zalman saw meditation as a necessary part of every commanded action, and as a commanded activity itself. One of the focal points of contemplation should be the fundamental idea that God's goodness pervades every corner of the universe, including the pockets of evil that were spread everywhere at the time of Creation.[25]

Shneur Zalman understood the psychological oscillation between melancholy and ecstasy as fundamental to human existence and to the structure of the universe. Those emotions gave people an arena in which to display a kind of spiritual heroism; the individual did brave and constant battle against all his inherent tendencies to worldly affirmation. His mood swings were markers of an intense spiritual pilgrimage. The constant struggle with the *yetzer* thus became a cause of rejoicing, for the Jew carried on an uplifting, cathartic struggle. By confronting moodiness with intense self-examination, the individual scored a victory over the power of evil and caused God to rejoice.[26]

The *Musar* movement and *Ḥabad* Hasidism both taught the spiritual necessity of dynamic introspection, and both emphasized the individual's ability to transform himself by turning crude elements of personality into morally redemptive traits. Despite the differences between them, they testified to the intense psycho-moral atmosphere of eastern European Jewry.

Reform Judaism, Ethical Culture, Modern Orthodoxy, the *Musar* movement, and *Ḥabad* were all passionate attempts to create moral and spiritual systems that addressed the psychic needs of the individual in a new way. At the dawn of the twentieth century, an even bolder moral psychology came out of the secular Jewish world of Vienna.

Chapter 4

Freud and Adler:
The Rise of Jewish
Psychoanalytic Moralism

These *Greeks* have a lot on their conscience—
falsification was their true trade; the whole of European
psychology is sick with Greek *superficiality*; and without
that little bit of Judaism.
—Friedrich Nietzsche (1887)[1]

A Galician Jew who was riding in a train had made
himself very comfortable; he had unbuttoned his coat,
and had put his feet on the seat, when a fashionably
dressed gentleman came in. The Jew immediately put
on his best behavior and assumed a modest position.
The stranger turned over the pages of a book, did
some calculation, and pondered a moment and
suddenly addressed the Jew. "I beg your pardon, how
soon will we have Yom Kippur?" "Aha!" said the Jew, and
put his feet back on the seat before he answered.
—Sigmund Freud (1905)[2]

As WE HAVE SEEN, the three primary approaches to the psyche in the
nineteenth century were intertwined with Christian thought, but a
fourth arose in the 1890s out of the Jewish moral universe. The psychological systems of Sigmund Freud and Alfred Adler, both of which became strongly influential in America, culminated the Jewish search for
a rationalist moral psychology. The thinking of Freud and Adler was
rooted in the complex social and intellectual environment of German-
ized Austrian Jews. Intensely self-conscious about their Jewishness, as
were all of Germany's and Austria's eminent Jewish intellectuals, Freud
and Adler could not avoid layering their theories with values that were
either Jewish in origin or reflections of the tense Christian-Jewish dialectic within German culture. The fourth wave of nineteenth-century European psychology reflected its Jewish origins in several ways. Like the
rabbinic innovations that preceded them, Freudian and Adlerian psy-

chology were overwhelmingly moral in their focus, rather than cognitive or metaphysical. They also displayed an acute awareness of the stigma of Jewish "particularism" (clannishness) and, like the rabbinic responses, they exalted themselves as universal solutions for the moral reconstruction of modern society. Unlike any of the psychologies that preceded them, they emphasized the emotional content of family life, a theme that reflected the intense inwardness that social ostracism had produced in European Jewry.

Freud's Jokes and Nietzsche's Guts

Freud loved the irony of Jewish jokes, which he found so dexterous that he cited them frequently in *Wit and Its Relation to the Unconscious.* The joke about the men on the train struck Freud as evocative of the blunt intimacy between Jews, which betrayed the formality and hierarchy of life in "society." He called this trait, somewhat stiffly, "the democratic mode of thought of the Jew who recognizes no difference between master and servant."[3]

Freud was engrossed with the power of jokes to express the deep emotional interdependencies among Jews. He highlighted this function in his analysis of jokes about the *shnorrer,* a beggar so devoid of a sense of hierarchy that his begging was never begging.

> The *shnorrer,* who was a regular Sunday dinner guest at a certain house, appeared one day accompanied by a young stranger, who prepared to seat himself at the table. "Who is that?" demanded the host. "He became my son-in-law last week," was the reply, "and I have agreed to supply his board for the first year."

> The *shnorrer* supplicates the baron for money to visit the bathing resort Ostend, as the physician has ordered him to take sea-baths for his ailment. The baron remarks that Ostend is an especially expensive resort, and that a less fashionable place would do just as well. But the *shnorrer* rejects that proposition by saying, "Herr Baron, nothing is too expensive for my health."

Freud commented, "One is forced to laugh at the insolence of the demand," and he went on to clarify the religious and cultural context of the joke: "The truth is that the *shnorrer* who mentally treats the rich man's money as his own, really possesses almost the right to this mistake, according to the sacred codes of the Jews." He based this claim on the commandment of *tzedakah,* which obligates Jews to give to the needy; any opportunity to give is seen as spiritually benefiting the giver. The rich man in the joke "is obligated by the mandate to give alms, and strictly speaking must be thankful that the *shnorrer* gives him an opportunity to be charitable." Though noting the superiority of *tzedakah* to the "ordinary, bourgeois conception of alms," Freud elucidated that the tight web of interdependence among Jews created tensions and frustrations that were exorcised through humor. "Naturally the resistance which is responsible for this joke is directed against the law which even the pious find very oppressing."[4]

Although Freud's older contemporary Friedrich Nietzsche would not have looked so fondly at the *shnorrer* and his democratic demeanor, Nietzsche admired the life-affirming vigor of the Jewish religion as it appeared in the Hebrew Bible. When he said that European psychology needed a little bit of Judaism, he most likely meant that the Greek philosophical emphasis on the mind, as distinct from the flesh, had bequeathed to Christian culture a false rendering of human behavior. It produced theories of an unreal human nature that lacked blood and guts, or what Freud called *libido*. Freud shared Nietzsche's disillusionment with contemporary values, dissatisfaction with the direction of psychology, and belief that a close study of language would light the path to a new moral order. That language, for Freud, was the symbolic language that masked vital and even violent emotional connections between people, that "little bit of Judaism" to which Nietzsche referred.[5]

FREUD VERSUS ADLER

Not only because of his unparalleled genius and literary output, but also because of his manifest interest in things Jewish, Freud has commanded much more attention from scholars than Adler. In a recent history of Western culture, Jacques Barzun observes that Adler "has been unjustly overshadowed" by Freud and Jung, both of whom became darlings of the academic avant-garde after World War II. The impact of Freud on American thought has merited an excellent two-volume history, whereas Adler's American influence is usually mentioned in passing. Historians of European Jewish thought and culture, too, routinely highlight Freud and leave Adler in the shadows. In Jewish history, Adler invited his own obscurity by converting (nominally) to Christianity, failing to establish a large coterie of Jewish adherents, as Freud did, and saying relatively little about Jewish affairs. Yet as a socialist, Adler, like many socialists, could not have been expected to emphasize either his Jewish background or the destiny of Jews as a group, when his ideology defined these things as irrelevant. Here I will allow Adler to share the spotlight with Freud and will treat both men as part of a single trend in Jewish culture.[6]

Fourteen years Freud's junior, Adler joined the master's circle, the Vienna Psychoanalytic Society, in 1902, and spent nine years among the Freudians. Then, during a special meeting in the autumn of 1911 at the Café Arkadan, Freud moved to expel Adler and his associates. The motion passed by a vote of eleven to five, with five abstentions. Six of Adler's comrades promptly resigned, bid their colleagues a courteous farewell, and joined Adler at the Café Central, where the group celebrated their newly given independence. Freud forced a final reckoning because Adler had developed a psychoanalytic theory that challenged his own in a way that was too fundamental to be ignored and too divergent to be accommodated.[7]

In shorthand and stilted English, one of Adler's notebooks records his view of those irreconcilable differences. "This leads to the question: what is the main conception of Freud? <u>Self interest</u>. So he finds the strength of wish fulfillments the main problem of life. The whole body and mind is loaded with cravings for lust which can be moderated only because of the sorry narrowness of our common life which does not allow <u>to get</u> everything out of it what is desired." The underlinings express <u>some</u> of the emotional distaste Adler had developed for a Freudian psychology that seemed self-indulgently preoccupied with desire and oblivious to obligation.

> It is easy now to understand why Freud still gives so much importance to the "Oedipus Complex." The boy in the simplest form is possessive. He wants to have his mother for himself. Freud of course pictures this craving as a sexual one and all his strivings are explained as originated out of the sexual drive. That he wants it of this type of a pampered style, a getting type expecting everything from others, a burden, socially not adjusted, not a help, everything done by others believing his right to lay his hands on everything he wants is thoroughly overlooked. It is now clear enough that Freud has the misconception of a pampered child.

A pampered child. Adler could not have produced a more scathing commentary than those three words. As a socialist, Adler wanted to create more socially committed and less self-concerned individuals; Freudianism had started to appear to him as almost retrograde in its absorption with personal sexuality. Never completely satisfied with Freud's focus on sex as the overriding human motive, he believed that people had a more fundamental striving to power or dominance, and that a proper therapy would work against excessive displays of ego. And yet, Adler did not lose sight of the essential contribution Freud had made to an understanding of the hidden factors of human behavior: "I do not deny the [singular?] merits of Freud. His attacks against a damaging Puritanism, and against the stalemate Psychiatry, his intense efforts to trace neurotic symptoms to psychological sources, his interest in facts which rule the attitudes of an individual without ones knowledge and understanding should give him a first rank among the contemporary thinkers."[8]

Adler continued to share Freud's assumption that unconscious motives rooted in childhood shaped the adult personality, but Adlerian and Freudian psychology ended up with very different focal points. Freud believed that neurotic and hysterical behavior derived from suppressed sexual drives. Those drives were fundamental to all human beings, and they conflicted with the standards of moral behavior that ruled Western society. Therefore, modern people all suffered a terrible conflict between the urgings of the libido and the restraints society imposed on those urges. The difference between psychologically sick and psychologically healthy people lay in their ability to handle the conflict between primal desire and social convention. The libido expressed itself very early in childhood, focusing on parents and other family members and establishing basic patterns of emotional life that determined how one related to other people in adulthood. By cutting through the resistance of the adult patient, who refuses to acknowledge the presence of forbidden drives within himself or herself, the psychoanalyst brings those covert elements into the daylight of consciousness. Only then can the patient achieve a mature self-understanding and self-acceptance. Freud's psychoanalytic process operated on the principle that by talking freely about one's innermost thoughts to the quietly observing therapist, the patient will inevitably focus on the source of inner conflict, usually through symbols in dreams. Hence, psychoanalysis was known as the "talking cure." "The task of a psycho-analytic treatment," Freud explained, "is to make conscious everything that is pathogenically unconscious."[9]

Adler diverged from Freud by insisting that a different force motivated all human behavior. Weakened by rickets when he was young, Adler was as fascinated by the problem of organic defects as Freud was by infantile sensual attractions. In the first book he published after the break with Freud, *The Neurotic Constitution*, Adler argued that, in childhood, every person is afflicted with a feeling of inferiority that derives from either an actual or an imagined defect. In an effort to overcome the sense of inferiority, the individual develops a strategy or life plan that will produce a feeling of strength or mastery. These strategies include both overt activities, such as professional accomplishment, and oblique actions, such as emotional manipulation of others. Freud's neurotic was driven by unconscious libidinal impulses; Adler's acted out of unconscious drives toward dominance. Partly as a result of his socialist sympathies, Adler's psychotherapeutic solution differed markedly from Freud's. After World War I, Adler turned his attention increasingly to the problem of juvenile delinquency and criminality, focusing on psychological maladjustment in children and adolescents and advocating educational reform to make schools more responsive to the psychic needs of the young. Concerned about the proper adjustment of individuals within society, Adler defined three fundamental "life-problems," those involving community, work, and love (*Gemeinschaft, Arbeit, Liebe*). The gist of his psychotherapeutic philosophy was to guide the individual away from a "pampered" style of self-concern and into a socially responsible, mature interest in the welfare of one's intimates, one's colleagues, and one's fellow citizens.[10]

FREUD AND ADLER: THE MORAL GROUNDING OF SECULAR THINKERS

To locate Freud and Adler within the larger context of Jewish thought and culture, we must begin with the fact that both men were thoroughly secular. Like other Jewish thinkers, they had assimilated ideas and values from European society. This, however, did not mean that they magically erased the fundamental values of their upbringing. The moral education of secular Jews originated in lessons they learned from parents and teachers in a fairly segregated Jewish environment. In his sweeping history of *The Austrian Mind*, William Johnston observes that even the most secular of Austria's thinkers "imbibed during childhood Jewish or Christian attitudes that could not easily be shed." The term "secular Jew" fails to express the complexity and nuance of Jewish intellectual life, which amounted to more than a mere rejection of traditional Judaism. "Throughout the nineteenth century," historian Yosef Hayim Yerushalmi explains, "Jews who lost faith in the God of their fathers sought and found a spectrum of novel secular Jewish surrogates," such as Zionism, socialism, Yiddishism, and Hebraism. In the same vein, Freud and Adler expressed a Jewish sensibility through the invention of psychoanalytic moralism.[11]

Though Freud was born in 1856 and Adler in 1870, both participated in the same startling phenomenon of Jewish intellectual and artistic achievement in fin-de-siècle Vienna. One of numerous ethnic minorities in Austria-Hungary, Jews composed approximately 10 percent of the population of Vienna at the turn of the century. Their cultural impact, though, was out of all proportion to their numbers; no other ethnic group "produced so many thinkers of transcendent originality." In addition to Freud and Adler, Karl Kraus, Arthur Schnitzler, Gustav Mahler, Edmund Husserl, and Ludwig Wittgenstein (Jewish on his father's side) were some of the many Jewish intellectuals and artists who honeycombed Vienna. Theodor Herzl, the founder of Zionism, and Viktor Adler, the founder of the Austrian Social Democratic Party, also belonged to this illustrious coterie. Jewish entrepreneurs started Vienna's most illustrious newspapers, for a largely Jewish readership. "Without this audience for witticism and novelty," William Johnston concludes, "Austrian literature might have been as impoverished after 1850 as it has become since 1938." Catholics brought forth such intellectual giants as Franz Brentano, Ernst Mach, and Carl Menger, but this does not demand an explanation in the largely Catholic territories of Austria and Hungary. The huge disproportion of Jewish innovators does.[12]

In a 1919 essay, "The Intellectual Pre-Eminence of the Jews in Modern Europe," American social theorist Thorstein Veblen suggested that emancipated Jews—emancipated both into modern society and out of traditional Judaism—composed a unique group of marginal intellectuals. Not fully accepted into European society, even when they completely assimilated its customs, they existed always at the margins and developed a uniquely skeptical point of view. Intensely in modern society but not completely of it, Jews were perfectly positioned to create novel critiques of the status quo. Another way to understand the idea of Jewish marginality appeared in a recent *New Yorker* assessment of its legendary artist, Saul Steinberg. Steinberg's Romania "sat on the edge of three civilizations—Gallic, Germanic, and Russian Orthodox—which meant that for a young Jew like Steinberg nothing seemed quite 'natural.' Everything looked tentative. The usual split between what's real and what's artificial didn't mean much to him." The idea of a unique vantage point, based on the estrangement of European Jews, may provide a partial explanation for the explosion of mental and artistic talent in Vienna and other capitals of Western culture.[13]

But Viennese Jews were only one of many minorities—Czechs, Germans, Poles, Galicians, Ruthenes, Slovaks, Magyars, Romanians, Croats, Serbs—struggling for acceptance. And, like modernizing Jews, Catholic and Protestant intellectuals also experienced a crisis of estrangement from their religious traditions. So the reasons for the Jews' unparalleled creativity must be found elsewhere. Like Austrian Germans, Jews were cosmopolitan, especially compared to the provincial ethnic groups of eastern Europe. What separated their experience from that of all other minorities, however, was their history as a ghettoized population. They were urban to the core. They had "lost touch with mysticism and the soil" in a period of rising nationalism that romanticized the national sod. In that sanctified ground, only the *volk* (a category that never included Jews) claimed roots. Long uprooted from a homeland and scattered among the nations, Jews had developed the mental equivalent of a national home through their veneration of religious texts. The *Beit Midrash* (house of study) was the center of the Jewish world and beckoned to every Jewish male beyond the age of four. In this homeland of the mind, the scholar triumphed over every other type of hero. Jews cultivated disdain for physical strength and indifference to the robust physicality that landed peoples valued and infused into their icons.[14]

The ideal of scholarship persisted in new forms after modernized Jews entered the German and Austrian bourgeoisie. An urban and commercial people, Jews quickly succeeded at business across Europe. Almost without exception, the fathers of the Freuds and the Adlers were merchants and manufacturers a generation or two removed from the ghetto. These men and their wives abandoned traditional Judaism and reared their sons in the Germanic ethos of *Bildung* (education, cultivation). They wanted to see the younger generation distinguish itself through careers in medicine, law, science, and letters. In this way, the old stigmatic association of Jews and business could be muted and the old Jewish ideal of literacy could be expressed through prestigious professions.

Sigmund Freud and Alfred Adler matched this generational profile. When they were youngsters, their families migrated to Vienna from the eastern reaches of Austria-Hungary, their fathers were middling merchants, their mothers were lively *balebostes* (Jewish homemakers), and both boys attended the same *gymnasium* (high school) before moving on to medical studies at the University of Vienna. Characteristic of Jewish families in that milieu, Freud's and Adler's fathers developed strong affectionate bonds with them, and their mothers, despite modest budgets, raised them in a cultured environment with music lessons and other such advantages. To the degree we can generalize about family life in any cultural group, we may say that Jewish families were intensely and affectionately inward, perhaps as a response to the hostility they perceived in the outer world. Children were at the center of a strong centripetal force, and boys especially were doted on in a way that was countercultural. It was not a coincidence, then, that both Freud and Adler, despite great differences in their childhoods, recalled fathers and mothers who focused their energies and affections on them. Adler grew up on the fringes of Jewish Vienna in close proximity to Christians. Although he had many Christian friends and recalled nostalgically his enjoyment of their many playful activities, Adler never lost sight of the gulf between their homes and his. His home was more affluent and cultured than theirs (he and his brothers and sisters were all trained in music). He attributed this superior atmosphere to the competence of his mother and to the fact that his father was uncommonly solicitous of his feelings and attentive to his interests as he grew up. In their turn, Freud and Adler were solicitous fathers.[15]

Both men considered their fathers to be essential moral guides, and from them they learned to think of the family as an arena of important moral commitments. "The part of Jakob Freud's legacy that lived on most vitally within his son was comprised in the values he had conveyed to the young boy as his first teacher," writes one of Freud's more sophisticated biographers. Adler believed his father possessed a keen ability to focus on people's actions rather than their words. From him, the future psychologist "realized that I must in the future judge mankind *not by their spoken words and sentiments, but by their actions.*"[16]

Outside the family, young Jews, like young Catholics, received a basic moral education from their religious school teachers. In Freud's case, we know some of the details of that schooling. The Jewish religious school in which young Sigmund was educated followed an explicit program of ethical instruction through biblical stories. Freud's beloved teacher Samuel Hammerschlag believed that the Torah, "a source of instruction at the disposal of our youth from ancient times," was an unparalleled medium for molding the spirit and imagination of young Jews. Not through dry "systematic instruction," but through presentations of vivid biblical stories such as that of Joseph in Genesis, the Religion School of the Jewish community of Vienna aimed to shape the moral and intellectual character of its students. The formative education of Freud, and of virtually all Austrian and German Jews, consisted of equal parts Kantian philosophy, with its emphasis on the morally free individual, and Jewish exegesis, with its Hebraic constellation of moral heroes. Students were reared in a supremely rationalist monotheism with morality rather than theology at its core. In this way, secular Jews shared fully in the moral though not the dogmatic universe of German Judaism.[17]

Peter Gay, a devotee and biographer of Freud, has long insisted that Freud's Jewishness had little to do with his thinking as a psychiatrist. Partly to refute those who search too eagerly for links between Judaism and psychoanalysis, Gay argues that Freud's Jewishness was a strictly private matter. While he is probably right to say that Judaism played no role in the formation of psychoanalysis, Gay misses the presence of Jewish moral values in the mind of this secular thinker. When he notes the potent influence of Samuel Hammerschlag on Freud's mental development, it is to emphasize that Hammerschlag failed to undo the secularism of the Freud household, because he "was far more interested in ethics than in theology." But that is exactly the point on which Freud's Jewishness turned. Those ethics were not an abstraction, nor were they Greek or German, although there were elements of Greek and German thought mixed in with them. Those ethics derived from Judaism.[18]

MORAL VALUES AND THE JEWISH-CHRISTIAN DIVIDE

In addition to a Jewish ethical education, another strong factor shaped the psyches of Jewish youth: an ever-present tension with the Christian world. An interesting parallel in the childhood experiences of Freud and

Adler, involving conflicts between Jewish parents and Christian caretakers, illustrated the well-defined Jewish atmosphere that pervaded even the homes of non-observant families. Austrian Catholics and Jews inhabited totally distinct worlds, yet there were many intersections between them, one of which was the practice of employing gentile nurses and nannies for Jewish children. When Sigmund Freud was a child, his Catholic nursemaid took him to church and taught him about Christian doctrines of heaven and hell. His parents eventually dismissed her, and Freud's mother remembered the woman many years later as an especially baneful influence on her beloved "Siggy." Adler, as a boy, had been put in the care of a governess for a short time, during which she apparently exposed him to some earthy adult songs at a nearby cabaret. As in Freud's case, the Jewish parents were taken aback at this culture clash with the gentile world and fired the governess. These examples of parental protectiveness reflected feelings of an essential cultural difference between Jews and Christians. Indeed, the familial intensity of Jewish life, with its distinctive focus on what later generations would call "child development," went hand in hand with suspicion of the contaminating effects that certain gentile habits might have on the young.[19]

The tension of the Jewish-Christian relationship deeply affected the moral sensibility of Austrian and German Jews in the late nineteenth century. "In the youth of every German Jew comes a moment which is remembered for one's entire life," reminisced Walter Rathenau, the eminent statesman and writer who was assassinated in 1922, "when for the first time it is fully understood that one has entered the world as a second-class citizen, and that no virtue and no service can free him from this condition." Jews in Central Europe were no more able than American blacks to elude the racial identity they had been assigned. For an eminent example, we may turn to the case of one of Germany's greatest composers, Felix Mendelssohn. This grandson of philosopher Moses Mendelssohn grew up as a Christian, married the daughter of a minister, and did his share to embellish Protestant liturgical music. Those facts of Mendelssohn's life, however, did not inhibit Richard Wagner and Franz Liszt from stereotyping him as a producer of "Jewish" music, which was code for imitative rather than creative accomplishments.[20]

As bad as it had been, antisemitism actually worsened and became starkly racial after the 1870s, the decade in which a German enthusiast coined the term itself, by forming a League of Anti-Semites (*Antisemiten-Liga*). That decade also witnessed the publication of one of the most notorious antisemitic tracts of the modern era, *The Talmud Jew.* The offspring of August Rohling, a fanatical Rhineland priest who was a professor of Semitic languages at the University of Prague, *The Talmud Jew* rejuvenated old charges that the Talmud compelled Jews to attack Christians at every opportunity. In 1882, a Viennese journalist used *The Tal-*

mud Jew to incite a crowd of hundreds. His acquittal on charges of religious incitement seemed to recommend the book as authoritative on its subject.[21]

By 1900 a multitude of disappointed people believed that the Jews, and the materialist Jewish spirit, had caused the collapse of traditional Austrian and German values. The more that Jews ascended in business, the professions, journalism, and the arts, the more their success seemed to justify any theory about a Jewish intention to control and distort Christian civilization. A new "Germanic ideology" combined reactionary mysticism about a Teutonic past with virulent condemnations of modern liberalism and of Jews as "the very incarnation of modernity." "This *ressentiment* of Jews had a certain seductive force for Germans," historian Fritz Stern has explained:

> and it may have also brought them some advantage, permitting them a sense of moral superiority while categorizing certain specific traits—ruthless ambition, dogged self-assertion, a desire for power and money—as typically Jewish. That prejudice . . . masked a double anxiety: fear of possible contamination by those very traits that one maligned or might already be infected with; anxiety that Jews, by these very same qualities, might effectively challenge the position and intellectual patrimony of their Christian colleagues.[22]

In that milieu, secular Jews became preoccupied with the nagging question of Jewish traits that allegedly separated them from society. The drive to eliminate those traits and make Jews into "universal" men and women was the most powerful spiritual motive of secular intellectuals and artists. Stefan Zweig observed that his academic success might have reflected "a secret longing to resolve the merely Jewish—through flight into the intellectual—into humanity at large." He believed this to be the prototypical psychological experience of his generation of secular Jews: "A 'good' family . . . means a Jewry that has freed itself of all defects and limitations and pettiness which the ghetto has forced upon it, by means of adaptation to a different culture and even possibly a universal culture."[23]

Secular intellectuals shared the belief in a ghettoized Jewish personality that clashed with modern civilization. The consciousness of a set of Jewish traits to be overcome was so sharp as to lead the gifted, vitriolic Viennese writer Karl Kraus to deny that he, as a cultivated individual, could have any Jewish characteristics (*jüdische Eigenschaften*), and to insist that such characteristics could have no place in the world of *Geist* (mind/spirit), which contained the universal values of freedom and culture. Even the Jewish nationalism of another Viennese writer, Theodor Herzl, did not waver from this path of Jewish *self-overcoming*. Herzl's Zionism proposed not to universalize Jewish traits but, rather, to enact a universal culture within the safety of a sovereign territory.[24]

Both Freudian and Adlerian psychology partook of this generational drive for the universal. In spite of the antisemitic rejection he suffered as a student at the University of Vienna (and which he took very much to heart), Freud tenaciously believed that "an active fellow-worker could not fail to find some nook or cranny in the framework of humanity." Although psychoanalysis was a general method of therapy and not at all dependent upon Jewish culture, it did develop within the social world of Vienna Jewry. Nearly all of Freud's students were Jewish, as were many of the patients whose cases led to his seminal theories. Freud spoke candidly about the special intimacy he felt with his Jewish colleagues. He liked to refer to the "consanguineous Jewish traits" that attracted Jews to one another and distinguished them emotionally from gentiles. Precisely because of his awareness of the Jewish dimensions of psychoanalysis, he wanted to evangelize the new science through Christian followers such as Carl Jung and Oscar Pfister. To his disciple Karl Abraham, who felt Freud had elevated Jung over him in order to spread psychoanalysis to the Swiss, Freud wrote: "I think that we as Jews, if we wish to join in, must develop a bit of masochism, be ready to suffer some wrong. Otherwise there is no hitting it off. Rest assured that, if my name were Oberhuber, in spite of everything my innovations would have met with far less resistance."

Burdened by a common stereotype of Jews as incapable of true scientific objectivity (as they were also presumably incapable of true artistic creativity), Freud knew that he faced an epic challenge of Jewish self-overcoming. Only by relentlessly and even tyrannically promoting his theories of the unconscious to a wider public would he be able to turn an enterprise of imaginative Jews into a universally applicable method of psychological investigation.[25]

Sensitivity to the accusation of Jewish self-interestedness and insularity seemed almost to form a foundation for Adler's psychological system. Unlike Freud, who relished his Jewish associations and considered conversion a cowardly act of social conformity, Adler followed the well-trodden path of baptism in order to remake himself into the truly universal man, the man of deep commitments to others in society. Describing Adler as "a moralist without a dogmatic belief in any religion," his close friend and first biographer, Phyllis Bottome, also noted that he "respected and prized his race and its many contributions to mankind, but he generally distrusted the orthodox Jews' attitude toward their God. It seemed to him to be a form of refined selfishness to keep God for one tribe or for one set of human beings, rather than to share a universal Deity with the common family of mankind." Adler invoked a moral imperative of social *interdependence*. His psychological theory emphasized the importance of the individual developing social feeling (*Gemein-schaftsgefühl*), which meant contributing to one's neighbors and to the larger society. Strongly affected by the Bible stories he learned early in life, Adler especially gravitated toward the injunction to love one's neighbor as oneself and to the story of Cain and Abel ("Am I my brother's keeper?"). Adlerian psychology universalized those precepts.[26]

Though secular Jews felt pressure to free themselves from stigmatic Jewish traits, there was one that they not only accepted but cherished: the ethical sense they believed to be their special inheritance. In this respect, they shared entirely in the Jewish moralist movement of the nineteenth century. Although most Jewish intellectuals were unable to maintain the religious practices of their ancestors and often received little religious instruction from their parents, they nevertheless grew up in a Jewish, not a Christian, ethical world. A key element of that world was the belief that Jews were as naturally prone to civility as gentiles were to violence. Writing of "the splendid urge which prompts us to settle our problems with our fellow man in a moral way," Arnold Zweig asked Freud, "Is this impulse not inborn within us? Have not we, the Jews, produced this impulse in many more individuals than has any other modern race?" Albert Einstein described the belief in Jewish moral superiority this way: "Judaism seems to me to be concerned almost exclusively with the moral attitude in life and to life. I look upon it as the essence of an attitude to life which is incarnate in the Jewish people rather than the essence of the laws laid down in the Torah and interpreted in the Talmud."[27]

Freud shared with Einstein the Lamarckian view of Jews as having acquired an ethical gene. Named after Jean-Baptiste de Monet de Lamarck (1744–1829), Lamarckism holds that temporary human adaptations can turn into genetic traits. In other words, by developing a culture that enforced certain ethical norms, Jews eventually developed a genetic disposition toward ethical behavior. Perceiving Jews as more emotionally disciplined and more rational than Christians, Freud believed that Jewish moral superiority lay in a capacity to sublimate the sensual into the spiritual. Jews retained the "inclination toward spiritual interests" that had been granted them in the time when they accepted the de-materialized God of Moses. After the destruction of the Temple, they inaugurated a grand tradition of Torah study that sustained spiritual discipline. Out of this tradition, Freud thought, Jews collectively incorporated or, in Einstein's words, *incarnated* superior ethical traits. Those characteristics no longer required formal religion, as they were naturally conveyed through the Jewish people. Adler, as a lifelong socialist, did not share Freud's ethnocentrism. Yet he shared the view that the "most valuable, ethical ideals" of Judaism should "be expressed through social and political action."[28]

Several factors, then, shaped the intellectual world of Sigmund Freud and Alfred Adler: a Jewish family setting with close emotional bonds to morally self-conscious fathers, a rising and increasingly racialist anti-semitism, an intense self-consciousness of one's Jewishness, a corresponding desire to eliminate putatively Jewish traits for the sake of integrating into modern culture, and, finally, an underlying belief in a Jewish ethical inclination that came from and transcended Jewish religion. The biographies of Freud and Adler contrasted in many respects, but both showed the influence of these environmental factors.

JEWISH RATIONALIST MORALISM AND THE DRAMA OF FAMILY LIFE

Freud and Adler were deeply rooted in the rationalism that characterized modern European Jews. The Viennese feuilletonist Peter Altenberg commented obliquely on that mentality in one of his sketches: "When Gentiles see the thick green woven cord around my neck, at the end of which there hangs a good-sized police whistle, they never tactlessly ask me what it's for; they just quietly conclude that I am an out-and-out lunatic, and that's all there is to it. The Jews always do ask, because they can't help hoping that there might be a rational explanation for it, after all." Altenberg was referring to a quality he perceived in Jews generally, but his observation certainly applied to the temper of secular European Jews. Long after German artists and intellectuals turned to romanticism, mysticism, and *volkish* nationalism, Jews held on doggedly to the rationalist ideals of the German Enlightenment.[29]

We can get a quick sense of that characteristic by comparing Freud and Adler to Carl Jung, the third member of the trio of psychoanalytic pioneers. A minister's son, Jung felt the inadequacies of formal Christianity as keenly as Freud and Adler did those of Judaism. All three men were in a state of rebellion against dogma and religious formalism, but where Freud and Adler had no affection for the religious life, Jung yearned for the "inner light" he found lacking in his father's churched Protestantism. He described himself as an unconventional Christian who was "wholly rooted in Christian conceptions," especially that deep stratum of consciousness which esoteric spirituality sought to uncover. Jung possessed a lifelong interest in esoterica and mysticism.[30]

Freud could not have been more different. When he was a student at the University of Vienna in the 1870s, Freud revered his teacher Franz Brentano, the former Dominican priest who became one of Austria's preeminent philosophers. Brentano's arguments for the existence of

God challenged Freud's youthful view of himself as a confirmed materialist. Yet as much as he felt drawn to his Catholic professor's blend of
religious faith and scientific spirit, Freud would not follow the road to
belief, because he considered it loaded with land mines of superstition
and mysticism that would destroy the scientific ideal. "It is unfortunately
a slippery slope which one treads in admitting the concept of God," he
wrote a friend, confiding, "I am afraid of being captured by . . . spiritualism, homeopathy, Louise Lateau, and so forth." (Miss Lateau was famous
for her displays of stigmata—issues of blood from the hands, feet, fore-
head, and abdomen—that occurred during trances in which she witnessed Christ's passion.) As he matured, Freud came to believe that Jews
enjoyed a kind of immunity from supernaturalism, as a result of their
upbringing. Discussing the break with Carl Jung, he wrote his colleague
Sandor Ferenzci: "It has seldom been so clear to me as now what a psychological advantage it signifies to be born a Jew and to have been spared
in one's childhood all the atavistic nonsense."[31]

Adler matched Freud as an arch-rationalist. "He had very strong objections to any unprovable theories," a close friend and biographer recalled,
"but especially when they might disturb our personal control of our own
destinies. . . . Spiritualism, theosophy, astrology, even telepathy, he
greatly distrusted." Adler referred to "that large group of people that
interests itself in spiritualism, psychic research, telepathy and similar
movements" as misguided by a vain anxiety "to grow beyond the boundaries of mere humanity." He believed those metaphysical practitioners to
be "desirous of possessing powers which human beings do not possess."[32]

The achievement of Freud and Adler was to adapt the rationalist moralism of German Jewry to the discipline of psychology, and to do so with
a pioneering focus on family dynamics. In the language of psychology,
these two psychoanalysts replicated the sophistication of Jewish domestic
life, which evolved through centuries of rabbinic commentary on the
proper behavior of spouses, parents, and children. Since ancient times,
the Jewish home had been a quasi-sacred precinct in which vital ceremonies were enacted and in which carefully calibrated norms of behavior
were followed. For centuries Jews had cordoned off the home and made
it the center of emotional life, in stark contrast to the public domain
where they had to remain emotionally guarded. The popular midrashic
method of Bible interpretation reinforced the interior world of familial
relationships. Midrash took the vivid scriptural stories about the relationships of siblings, spouses, parents, and children and turned them into
examples, illustrations and lessons for Jewish families in all times and
places. The parental anguish of Abraham and Sarah, the sibling rivalries
of Jacob and Esau and Rachel and Leah, the courtship of Jacob and

Rachel—these and many other interpersonal struggles were read as exciting moral melodrama by Jews living thousands of years later.[33]

Freud and Adler read the Bible as youngsters, acquired a simple midrashic understanding from religious school, and developed a psychological concept of the family "complex" that echoed a familiar narrative within Jewish culture. "My early familiarity with the Bible story (at a time almost before I had learnt the art of reading)," Freud recalled in his autobiography, "had, as I recognized much later, an enduring effect upon the direction of my interest." Freud and Adler were equally impressed by such biblical accounts of sibling conflict as that of Joseph and his brothers and that of Cain and Abel. The biblical theme of a younger brother usurping or surpassing the position of the first-born son struck them as especially informative about the role of family dynamics in shaping the individual's emotional and psychic destiny. To illustrate "that delicate and fine way in which personalities were described" in the Hebrew Bible, Adler selected the case of Jacob: "He did not like to be a second child and did not like the elder. He wanted always to overcome the elder. He fell in love with a second child and wanted to remove the elder girl. And when Joseph brought to him his two children he crossed his hands and gave the greater blessing with the right hand to the second boy. Of course you can believe that this is coincidence but I believe it is that people have understood each other better than we do."[34]

An emphasis on family dynamics distinguished Freudian and Adlerian psychology—and thus the Jewish psychoanalytic movement—from other approaches to the psyche. For Freud the essential drive was libido, and for Adler it was the striving for dominance, but in both cases what shaped the individual's character was the way in which these drives played out in relation to other family members. In the context of what Freud called "the family complex" and what Adler called "the family constellation," the birth order of siblings and the respective relationship of children to mother and father, and to mother and father substitutes, became all-important factors of human psychology. Most important, these factors were understood by Freud and Adler to be dynamic, not static. No simple arithmetic governed the personalities of first child, second child, male child, and female child. Instead, the development of personality depended on the intricate and intimate interactions that took place within the family.[35]

Uniquely focused on family dynamics, the psychoanalytic moralism of Freud and Adler shattered the molds of European psychology. Freud rejected the conventional psychiatric view of sickness as an alien force intruding on the body and argued instead that mental disturbances were embedded in the character of patients. By insisting that doctors treat the moral character of the person, Freud "restored an ethical, and therefore a social, conception of human sickness." The same can be said of Adler, who labored mightily to explain and correct such destructive traits as avarice, envy, suspiciousness, cruelty, and self-deprecation. The psycho-analysts departed not only from mainstream psychiatry but also from academic psychology. Unlike experimental psychologists, Freud and Adler were not interested in the characteristics humans shared with ani-mals, because animals had impulses without beliefs and therefore lacked moral agency. They also differed from academic psychology by ignoring the science of perception. Experiments to determine how humans per-ceived and responded to physical stimuli were the bread-and-butter of modern psychological investigation, but those did not interest the psy-choanalysts, who wanted to know how people perceived and responded to other people in an intimate sphere.[36]

By freeing the psyche from the determinism of family relationships, Freud and Adler brought Jewish rationalist moralism to a peak. Both Freudian and Adlerian psychotherapy aimed to liberate the individual from fixed patterns of behavior by bringing unconscious motives into the daylight. Not unlike the *Musar* movement of Israel Salanter, psycho-analytic moralism held that one's character depended on the desire and the ability to see beneath the surface of habit. No matter how convention-ally upright one's behavior may seem, it cannot be truly moral unless freely chosen out of self-awareness. As Freud put it, "The property of being conscious or not is in the last resort our one beacon-light in the darkness of depth-psychology." Adler also invoked the terminology of light and darkness in describing the supreme value of rational awareness. "The law of psychic development," he wrote, "is the most important indi-cator to any human being who wishes to build up his destiny consciously and openly, rather than to allow himself to be the victim of dark and mysterious tendencies."[37]

Freud and Adler were heir to decades of German and French specula-tion about the unconscious, but they focused uniquely on the family as the critical context for understanding the moral dimension of uncon-scious drives. Convinced that they had discovered universal laws of psy-chological conduct, these two analysts followed the path of rabbinic mor-alists—Abraham Geiger, Felix Adler, Samson Raphael Hirsch, Israel Salanter, Shneur Zalman—and propounded an ultimate moral solution for the crisis of the modern psyche.

The psychoanalytic moralism of Freud and Adler stood apart from previous psychologies that were bound up with varieties of Christian ex-perience. This was so not only because psychoanalysis grew up in the world of Viennese Jews, but also because it deviated from the values of Christian liberalism, spiritualism, and romanticism that accompanied the earlier trends of psychological inquiry. The liberal Protestantism that accompanied naturalist psychology failed to comprehend the dark irrationalism of human behavior. The spiritualism and occultism that accompanied mesmeric psychology was abhorrent to Jews who worshiped the rules of reason. The romanticism that accompanied Germanic self psychology was too tightly interwoven with Christian triumphalism and *volkish* nationalism to be acceptable to Jews.

During the lifetimes of these men, Europe proved that psychologies do not exist outside of culture. By 1900 German culture allowed a dangerous discussion of the differences between the Germanic and the Jewish soul: one was lofty, capable of merging with the divine; the other was crude, incompatible even with civilization, not to mention the godly. Both Freud and Adler died in exile, refugees from what Freud once called "the atavistic nonsense" of the gentile world. But their ideas found a home in the United States, as did the ideas of many others who conveyed Jewish moral concerns into an American market far larger than the one Benjamin Franklin had once so richly served.

Sigmund Freud at Clark University, 1909. Seated from left: Sigmund Freud,
G. Stanley Hall, Carl Jung. Standing from left: A. A. Brill, Ernest Jones, Sandor
Ferenczi. (Courtesy of Clark University Archives.)

Alfred Adler, 1933. Adler's ideas found an extremely receptive audience in the United States, to which he immigrated in the late 1920s. (Courtesy of the Library of Congress.)

By Pach - Apr. 1892

William James in 1892. One of America's greatest thinkers, James was also one of the most cosmopolitan, encouraging the involvement of Jews in academia. Photo by Pach. (Reproduced by permission of the Houghton Library, Harvard University. Shelf mark pfMS1092.)

Part III

Jewish Morality and the Psychological Shift of American Culture, 1890–1945

Chapter 5

Popular Psychology:
The Great American Synthesis
of Religion and Science

WRITING FROM EXILE in Palestine in the winter of 1937, Arnold Zweig remarked to Sigmund Freud on the extraordinary American mass market for books. "We manage not only to balance our budget but also to make up for past losses," the frequently cash-strapped novelist told his friend, "but this has been achieved only through American miracles, the Book of the Month, for example." Thoughts of the success of their writings among Americans provided a cheerful intermission in a correspondence that primarily brooded over the future of the Jews and of civilization under Hitler.[1]

In the twentieth century Americans turned the Western interest in the psyche into a veritable cult, one that rivaled traditional religions and forced them, sooner or later, to accept psychological conceptions of human nature. The foundation for that shift in values was laid in the half-century between the 1890s and 1940s. By the 1950s social commentators were speaking of America as a "therapeutic" culture inhabited by a new kind of human being, "psychological man." A Jewish moral sensibility first entered into American popular thought through the mass market of popular psychology. Let us then turn to that mass market and examine its nature and scope.

For a public anxious about urban life and accustomed to reading for inspiration and moral advice, popular psychology combined elements of religion and science in appealing ways. American psychologists basked in the popular demand for advice because, unlike their European peers, they stressed the practical side of their science and saw themselves as social reformers and moral guides. In the early decades of the twentieth century, popular ideas about the psyche fell into a spectrum defined by two poles. One, associated with William James, was transcendentalist—it depicted human consciousness as a source of hidden spiritual power. The other, associated with John B. Watson, was behaviorist—it depicted the mind as totally conditioned by environmental forces. Both drew on powerful currents in the American Protestant tradition and both promised grand transformations of human nature.

THE AMERICAN AUDIENCE FOR ADVICE

The American public that had begun to welcome Freud and his disciples
in the 1910s and 1920s was a public used to reading for advice about
living. By the mid-1700s the literacy rate of white colonial America exceeded Britain's. Compared to the large population of illiterate peasants
in Europe whose lives were only indirectly affected by the ideas contained
in books and newspapers, the farmers and traders of New England "lived
easily in the world of print." Their Puritanism required them to seek
religious nourishment through their own personal reading of the Bible
and secondarily through the religious commentaries published by their
ministers. To be illiterate was to be spiritually crippled. Where Protestants were unfree, as in the South after the mass conversions of African
and African American slaves in the 1700s, they were largely prevented
from reading—a sure sign of their masters' belief in the logic that the
man or woman who could read the Bible would gain inner freedom. "A
free people were a people of the Word," one historian has written of
New England Protestants, "with the Bible as their token of identity." Not
surprisingly, after Emancipation ex-slaves rushed to learn how to read;
by 1913, the Year of Jubilee marking the fiftieth anniversary of the Emancipation Proclamation, the literacy rate of black Americans was roughly
70 percent, compared to less than 10 percent in 1865.[2]

After the American Revolution, the ability to read anchored a national
principle of self-determination. The leaders of the Revolutionary generation, guided by an Enlightenment belief in the necessity of individual
reasoning, formed an ideal that asked men and women to educate themselves, thereby making themselves over into true democratic citizens.
Thomas Jefferson expressed the basic premise of that ideal when he
claimed, in his great statement on religious liberty, "God has created the
mind free." His meaning was simple: as long as no institution or force
prevented people from exercising their intellectual freedom, they alone
were accountable for the quality of their thoughts and actions. It was the
novelty of Freud, a century later, to argue that the individual's freedom
of conscious thought was shackled not by an external force but by unconscious forces within the mind itself.[3]

Although religious literature dominated the market of the 1700s, a
reading public for extra-religious instruction still emerged—witness the
success of Benjamin Franklin's *Poor Richard's Almanack*. A blend of meteo-
rology and morals, the *Almanack* appeared annually for a quarter-century
between 1733 and 1758. The book was the country's first secular best-
seller, secular not because Poor Richard was irreligious but because he
personified Franklin's desire to create a reading public that was not dom-

inated by the ministry and formal religion. Through the character of Richard Saunders, Franklin captivated Americans with such aphorisms as "He that lives carnally won't live eternally"; "The favour of the Great is no inheritance"; "Great Talkers, little Doers"; "An empty Bag cannot stand upright"; and "There are no Gains, without Pains." The distance between Franklin's worldview and Freud's was suggested by Poor Richard's saying, "A good Man is seldom uneasy, an ill one never easie." The *Almanack* prescribed maxims for success but more often emphasized the importance of a strong moral character and, when expedient, Franklin even cited scripture for proof: "But, after all, do not depend overmuch upon your own Industry, and Frugality, and Prudence, though excellent Things, for they may all be blasted without the Blessing of Heaven; and therefore ask that Blessing humbly; and be not uncharitable to those that at present seem to want it, but comfort and help them. Remember Job suffered, and was afterwards prosperous."[4]

Franklin proved the existence of a mass desire for advice that was moral but not formally religious, and an industry arose to reaffirm the fact in the middle and late nineteenth century. The extraordinary demographics of the United States, where population doubled nearly every generation, fueled the rise of a mass market between 1790 and 1910. In that period, framed by Franklin's *Autobiography* (1791) and the first American edition of Freud's *Interpretation of Dreams* (1913), the number of Americans rose spectacularly from 4 million to 91 million. The explosion of population came with huge bursts of economic activity, a transportation and information revolution, and the rise of mass-production and mass-marketing. After the 1830s success books poured off American presses, encouraging young men to apply Franklinesque methods of self-discipline and perseverance as a "way to wealth" and good citizenship. Horatio Alger, Jr., the Massachusetts minister who became the greatest success writer after the Civil War, wrote about boys like Harry Walton, the hero of *Bound to Rise* (1873). By the end of that novel Harry has just begun to earn decent wages en route to his goal of becoming a printer. But by studiously following "In Franklin's Footsteps" (the title of a chapter), he redeemed his family from a debt that had once seemed hopeless.[5]

The saga of self-reliant success also permeated newspapers and magazines once biographical sketches of successful people became a distinct type of feature story. These portraits repeated endlessly the same basic formula: the boy's boy becomes the man's man. In small-town papers, that man might be a storekeeper, artisan, or salesman, while in the metropolitan press he was a business magnate; in either case he was self-sufficient and beneficent. By the 1880s, when William Dean Howells wrote *The Rise of Silas Lapham*, the first great novel to depict the American gospel of success, it was a boilerplate item of the protagonist's biography that his poor but pious parents "taught their children the simple virtues of the Old Testament and Poor Richard's Almanac."[6]

A second type of self-help literature also appeared in the nineteenth century. Though sharing the Protestant values of the success stories, the genre of "self-culture" de-emphasized career and concentrated on the inner person. Self-culture emphasized the development of a well-balanced character based on liberal education and a rational, humanistic outlook on life. An American and more democratic version of the German concept of *Bildung*, self-culture encouraged the individual to develop inner potential and to shun everything vulgar and artificial. It was a secular rendition of the old Puritan emphasis on the inner light, the state of grace that differentiated the saintly person from the one who trusted in the externals of respectable behavior. Emerson's essays and Thoreau's *Walden* stood at the summit of American self-culture, calling for individual self-awareness of a high order that transcended the conventional idea of personal success.[7]

One of the greatest nineteenth-century self-culture writers, Unitarian minister Edward Everett Hale was still publishing in the early years of the new century a classic message about "how to live." Hale emphasized the importance of not wasting time, of reading, speaking, writing, and listening with concentration and focus, and of being a well-prepared person, able to meet events as they come. In a parable about two friends—Ferguson, who is punctual and well organized, and Horace, who is not—Hale eschewed the old moralism when he denied that these traits meant Ferguson would succeed and Horace would not. Yet he maintained the Franklinesque emphasis on personal efficiency: Ferguson's self-discipline would make for a more satisfying existence that allowed for maximal personal development, while Horace's disorderliness promised frustration, "blunders and annoyance."[8]

As self-culture evolved from the nineteenth into the twentieth century, it adapted bits and pieces of the new world of Freud but cleaved to the old ways of Franklin. Dorothea Brande showed the resilience of the old-fashioned path to individual betterment. A journalist and editor who wrote the artistic self-help classic *Becoming a Writer* (1934), Brande also wrote the second-best-selling nonfiction title of 1936, *Wake Up and Live!* In that book she tried to startle her readers into a meaningful life of self-restraint, graciousness, thoughtfulness, and efficiency. Brande was aware of Freudian theory, to which she occasionally referred, but she still recommended Franklin's system of self-examination. She devised a variant of his famous chart but with only six categories—Work, Courage, Decision, Speech, Meals, Sleep—which she deemed the most troublesome for most people.[9]

Urban Malaise and the Advent of Psychological Advice

To the older types of self-help advice, Americans added a new one, psychological advice for alleviating urban malaise. In 1881 New York City neurologist George Beard published an influential book, *American Nervousness*, which sounded the alarm for the new affliction. Beard diagnosed the proverbial American "drive" as a neurotic problem, one that left many of his patients with symptoms of exhaustion and anxiety. He attributed those problems to "modern civilization" with its noise, its schedules and timetables, its frantic stock markets, its rapid-fire news reportage, its technologies and its many mental demands. Americans suffered especially, he believed, because America had developed the most rapid, most total version of urban life.[10]

Urbanism did not come easily to rural and small-town people who developed a romantic attachment to the countryside as soon as they left it. Thomas Jefferson recorded the common wisdom when he observed that farms and farmers were the lifeblood of America's unique democracy. Cities, Jefferson thought, signified decay; they belonged to Europe, while open land enabled Americans to replenish the national vigor in every generation. "Those who labour in the earth," he wrote, "are the chosen people of God." An American pastoral ideal coursed through the literary veins of the country for generations after Jefferson, often in the form of naïve romanticism but sometimes in such refined works as *Walden* (1854). There, the town of Concord was sufficiently busy and commercial to elicit Thoreau's indictment of life-suffocating over-civilization: "Men have become the tools of their tools." A half-century after *Walden*, cities that had doubled, tripled, and quadrupled in size evoked a new term of apprehension: "the urban wilderness." Prompting the kind of anxiety that Americans had once associated with dangerous uncharted forests, the slums and factories of the American city invited sociologist Robert A. Woods to write an exposé of *The City Wilderness* (1898), Upton Sinclair to name his novel of Chicago *The Jungle* (1906), and Edward Alsworth Ross to open his influential sociological study, *Social Control* (1901), with the image of "crowded city thoroughfares," which symbolized social chaos.[11]

Diagnoses of an American urban pathology became popular in the early 1900s. A high school civics textbook of the 1920s warned the young about "the ever-increasing strains which greater wealth and greater complexity of life place upon them." The textbook's author, Edward A. Ross, taught that the city produced both material and psychological superficiality. Whereas the country fostered producer values such as frugality and thrift, the city favored consumer values of spending and extravagance;

while the country encouraged mental solidity, the city produced superficiality—"snapshot judgments and shallow thinking." According to this eminent social scientist, city life caused enough psychological disorientation to prompt concern that "America might lose her soul."[12]

Whether from the medical perspective of Dr. Beard or the sociological perspective of Dr. Ross, a new and critical American problem became the focus of public attention at the turn of the century. The recognition of urban malaise happened to coincide with a mighty development in American intellectual life, the rise of psychology as the charismatic science of humankind.

Between 1880 and 1920 the intensely rapid development of American psychology was one of the most notable events in the world of science. Parallel to the rise of the United States from third-rate to world-power status during those decades, American psychologists moved from a position of intellectual subservience to one of considerable authority. Those were the years in which the older Ivy League schools were transformed into modern universities, a status they shared with impressive state universities in California and the Midwest and with new research-oriented schools such as Johns Hopkins, Stanford, Chicago, and Clark. University laboratories, Ph.D.'s, and the publications of American professors of psychology multiplied rapidly, so much so that by the 1920s psychology was the only science in which America exceeded Europe. And on the popular level, enthusiasm was immense. Journalist Frederick Lewis Allen recalled of the Roaring Twenties that "the prestige of science was colossal," and of all the sciences, it was "the youngest and least scientific"—psychology—"which most captivated the general public." Psychology's prestige depended on the willingness of Americans to accept the idea that Hugo Münsterberg had expressed so concisely in 1909: "The misjudgment and the depression of the insane are only an exaggeration of that which may occur in any man."[13]

Perhaps the most sensational coincidence of the new psychology and the feeling of urban malaise came with the Leopold and Loeb kidnapping-murder case of 1924, in which psychiatric diagnoses of the young criminals blended with mass anxiety about the degenerative qualities of America's fast-paced, excitement-oriented and narcissistic urban life. Coming soon after the 1920 federal census revealed the unprecedented fact that more Americans (51 percent) lived in towns and cities than on farms, the case of Nathan Leopold's and Richard Loeb's psychosexual deviance connected in the public mind to the portfolio of city living: "joy rides, jazz parties, petting parties, freedom in sex relations and the mania for speed on every turn." More important in the long run than typical expressions of anti-urban anxiety, the prominence of psychiatrists in the trial established a new interpretive precedent: the boys' behavior was abnormal rather than simply criminal. Initially, a confused public wondered how two brilliant teenagers from wealthy and cultured Chicago homes could in cold blood arbitrarily select an acquaintance for murder. By the end of the trial, a defense led by Clarence Darrow had successfully shifted public focus from the idiosyncrasies of Leopold and Loeb to the ordinariness of abnormal male behavior in the wake of a vicious world war, where boys of the same age learned to kill without conscience. Psychological problems in the boys' childhood coupled with the bloodthirstiness of the times, the defense contended, made Leopold's and Loeb's crime one that might have been committed by any child from an apparently normal home. In this case, abnormality became an "unfortunate extension of normality." For those who questioned such an argument, the chief psychiatric witness for the defense, a prominent Freudian, explained that a sound psychiatric examination revealed the workings of the mind as clearly as an X-ray exposed the interior of the body.[14]

Between the 1880s and the 1920s, then, Americans began to develop a powerful new psychological mode of interpreting themselves. Their problems looked more and more like psychological problems, and their solutions increasingly took psychotherapeutic forms. Psychotherapeutic theories first appealed to the educated readers of literary magazines and books at the turn of the century and then began working their way into the vocabulary and thought of everyone else through public school textbooks, newspaper stories, and radio shows after World War I. In the 1920s, Freudianism and behaviorism threw the country into a psychological fit, and books that popularized psychology or combined it with folk wisdom and religious inspiration started to show up routinely on the list of American best-sellers, a trend that continued for the rest of the century. After World War II the psychological impact was so total as to leave no area of American society unaffected. Psychological experts came to preside over "a vast audience," one historian explains—they became "familiar figures in most communities, in the media, and in virtually every corner of popular culture." That phenomenon led the eminent sociologist Philip Rieff to speak in the 1950s of the "tyranny of psychology" and later to publish an influential analysis of American culture titled *The Triumph of the Therapeutic* (1966). Since then, it has been routine for scholars to define America as a "therapeutic culture."[15]

THE SPIRITUAL FUNCTION OF POPULAR PSYCHOLOGY

The phenomenal rise of a mass market for psychology meant that growing numbers of Americans were dissatisfied with exclusively religious answers to questions about human nature. Joseph Jastrow, the son of an

eminent rabbi, boldly defined the new ratio between religion and psychology. Many human problems that "in older periods of social management [were] referred to such institutions as the Church" had come to
be identified "as flesh and bone of our mental tissue," Jastrow explained
in *Keeping Mentally Fit*, a book that went through four editions between
1928 and 1930. In the suggestively titled *Piloting Your Life: The Psychologist
as Helmsman*, Jastrow declared: "We have arrived at a psychological
age. . . . Morals and good citizenship haven't retired, but they are viewed
as conditioned upon mental fitness. . . . Mental hygiene projects the program of right living with the psychologist at the helm."[16]

Jastrow's claims were not exaggerated. Popular psychology fulfilled a
quasi-religious function for an ever-widening public. It aimed to explain
human nature and improve the conduct of the individual, to suggest
ethical rules for social interaction, to offer inspiration and consolation to
the troubled, and to search for an ultimate *ground of being*, a fundamental
principle of human growth that promises happiness, contentment, or
some kind of this-worldly redemption.[17]

Popular psychology leaped into the breach of public thought that was
created by the simultaneous withdrawal of philosophy and theology between 1900 and 1945. Once a thriving industry of ideas for the educated
public, American philosophy retreated from that role after it became a
formal academic discipline. By the 1920s the nation's academic philosophers occupied themselves with abstruse or technical issues of logic and
epistemology and disdained the perennial questions of morality and
faith that most concerned the general public. Much of the ancient burden of philosophy—defining and explaining human nature and behavior—was taken up by psychology and medicine. By 1900 psychology had
entered the university auditorium and psychiatry was leaving its confinement in the asylum. From then on, doctors of the mind and body
were the ones who brooded over questions of human conduct, told the
public what was normal, ideal, and deviant, and envisioned great
schemes of personal and social improvement. Ministers presided over
declining congregations and faced increasing prejudices about the inca-
pacity of their "effeminate" religion to meet the challenges of George
Beard's nervous urban-industrial civilization.[18]

Popular psychology allowed Americans to combine the age-old desire
for miraculous healing with a belief in the importance of scientific credibility. The psychological experts of the turn of the century broke through
the somatic assumptions of their elders—the idea that most afflictions
had organic sources and could be cured, if at all, only by physical methods. Under that regime, people with all kinds of physical symptoms were
usually diagnosed as having lesions in the brain or weakness in the ner-

vous system, for which doctors recommended physical therapy (nutrition, rest, massage, electricity, nerve tonics) and old-fashioned willpower—the refusal to indulge in exhausting releases of emotional or sexual energy. In stark contrast to the old school, the new psychotherapies promised exciting revelations of inner conflicts and transformations. They had the drama of faith-healing, a simile that was not lost on the public. In a full-page feature on psychiatrist Isador Coriat's *The Meaning of Dreams* (1915), one newspaper headlined "Blind Girl's Dreams Restore Sight in Newest Science." After summarizing a dramatic case of hysterical blindness, in which Coriat deciphered an adolescent's dreams, uncovered the genitive trauma, and restored her eyesight, the reporter exhorted, "Ah, the reader may smile with superior wisdom, this is some tale of an Australian 'medicine man' or Hottentot 'witch doctor.' . . . On the contrary, it is a story of present-day fact, told by Dr. Isador H. Coriat."[19]

While conveying some of the drama associated with faith-healing and miraculous cures, the new psychology promised much more. It preserved an aura of mystery about the psyche but insisted that the mind operated according to comprehensible rules. The *New York Times* devoted a full page of its Sunday magazine to Coriat's dream book, highlighting both the theme of mysterious revelation and that of rationalist science. Dreams hold a key to "the riddle of life," for they "reveal our true selves, our inner motives and desires, often hidden both from the world and ourselves." They perform that spiritual function by virtue of the precision of the psyche, "for every dream is predetermined by our unconscious mental life." The *Boston Advertiser* emphasized the coincidence of spiritually expansive freedom with scientific necessity. "Dr. Coriat . . . makes it plain even to a lay reader that dreams follow definite laws," the paper explained while exulting in "the freedom which this method brings to the burdened mind." The *Globe* relied on quasi-religious imagery in its review, which headlined: "Visions of the Night Express our Repressed Wishes." That paper highlighted the mix of mystery and rationality with an interesting analogy to motion pictures, which, like psychoanalysis, were not yet two decades old in 1915. "The dream also is a highly visualized product, like the cinematograph, and like it, too, it is constantly in motion. Just as behind the limited area of the motion picture, as projected on the screen, there may be many feet of film of which the moving picture is the condensed product, so the dream picture is the condensed product of a long series of dream thoughts which lie behind it." Darkness and light framed the experiences of movie watching and psychological exploration. In each case there was a clear and logical delineation of images but also a formative unseen realm behind the visible reality.[20]

FUNCTIONALISM: THE AMERICAN WAY OF DOING PSYCHOLOGY

There was both a demand and a supply side to the extraordinary growth of popular psychology in America. We have seen the demand side, the large market of readers who were eager for advice about their personal development and who liked the blend of science and inspiration that popular psychology offered. On the supply side, there is one overriding reason why psychology spread so quickly into popular thought: the activist mentality of American psychologists, who saw themselves as agents of social and moral improvement.

America's distinctive way of doing psychology was known as *functionalism.* Just as American philosophy was known for pragmatism, which held that truth was discovered through solving real problems (rather than metaphysical paradoxes), so the founders of American psychology saw their discipline as practical rather than speculative. They wanted to examine how people behaved, how they functioned in society, rather than merely describe the thought process. Thinking of moral behavior in terms of *functions,* John Dewey wrote, "brings morals to earth."

> Honesty, chastity, malice, peevishness, courage, triviality, industry, irresponsibility are not private possessions of a person. They are working adaptations of personal capacities with environing forces. . . . They can be studied as objectively as physiological functions, and they can be modified by change of either personal or social elements.[21]

In John Dewey (1859–1952) functionalism had its most influential voice, one that called for the steady perfecting of America as the world's most democratic social order. Perhaps more than any philosopher of the twentieth century, Dewey focused his entire intellectual energy on the question of how people should live in society. His impassioned combination of moral and scientific ideals reflected two powerful influences of his early adulthood, Calvinism and Darwinism. Born into a devout Congregationalist family in Burlington, Vermont, Dewey came of age within the church, undergoing a conversion experience in his early twenties. In those years he also took up the study of philosophy and wrote a number of scholarly essays in which he aimed to reconcile religion and science. Adapting his ancestral religion to the realities of Darwin's universe, Dewey came to think "God embodied himself in matter, just as the body incarnated the individual soul."[22]

By the 1890s Dewey had left Protestantism behind and moved toward a purely scientific faith. He came to believe that to examine human behavior was to inquire into the true nature of the world. Dewey transformed American thought about the psyche when he challenged the simplifications by which psychologists obscured the complexity of human behavior. He rejected the idea that people responded mechanically to stimuli in their environment. He objected to arguments that mind controlled body or that body controlled mind. Instead, Dewey argued, human behavior was like an integrated circuit, a continuous flow in which sensations and emotions and thoughts constantly interacted. It was a complicated, organic *co-ordination* of functions toward one end: a satisfactory adjustment of the person to the environment. That happy adjustment he called *self-realization.* Dewey's concept of human nature invoked the idea of *process;* self-realization for the individual and for society was always unfolding and never static or accomplished. In 1932 the great historian Carl Becker suggested that the key words of his generation were "relativity, process, adjustment, function, complex." If we assign relativity to Einstein and complex to Freud and Adler, then process, adjustment, and function belong to Dewey.[23]

To understand why American functionalism was so distinctive, we can look at how Americans departed from the dominant German approach to psychology. The founding father of modern experimental psychology was Wilhelm Wundt, who set up the first psychological laboratory at the University of Leipzig in 1879. Wundt commanded the homage not only of Germany's first professional psychologists but also of America's. He maintained a clear sense of the limitations of psychologists' knowledge and therefore divided psychology into two branches, only one of which—experimental psychology—was viable. The other, *Völkerpsychologie*—which might translate as "cultural psychology"—consisted of the social attitudes, values, language, and institutions that determine how a person in society thinks and acts. That domain, Wundt believed, belonged more to the anthropologist than to the psychologist. *Völkerpsychologie* concerned an area of human behavior that followed specific cultural norms rather than universal psychological patterns. Wundt's American students, however, ignored his caution about the limits of psychological knowledge and authority. When they recrossed the Atlantic to establish the nation's leading psychology departments, they translated German psychology into American terms: they authorized themselves to use psychology as a tool for understanding every aspect of society. "For in the hands of the young, vigorous, practically minded Americans," one historian has written of this avant-garde, "psychology was not just to be a means of exploring traditional philosophical and scholarly problems: it was to be a means of getting the millennium on stage."[24]

The same spirit motivated the "new psychiatrist" who replaced the old-fashioned alienist. More bureaucrats than healers, alienists administered the insane asylums established in the middle decades of the nineteenth century. By the 1880s, out of touch with advances in psychology and neurology, they were sliding into a muggy backwater of American society. The new breed of physician, however, pumped a contagious idealism into the domain of mental illness and psychotherapy. Even more important for the social history of the twentieth century, the psychiatrist moved out of the asylum and into the mainstream of American society, becoming an authority on the everyday problems that stood between people and their peace of mind.

The "new psychiatrist" of the early 1900s saw himself as a missionary figure in the science of human nature. In his "dual capacity as psychologist and physician," the psychiatrist was uniquely qualified to lay the foundation for all the social sciences and to bring a whole new sophistication to the study of criminality, education, and "all forms of social maladjustment and even of unhappiness." Inspired by Clifford Beers's *A Mind That Found Itself* (1908), a true story about recovery from mental illness that did for public feeling about mental health what *Uncle Tom's Cabin* had done for abolitionism, a mental hygiene movement emerged with the goal of keeping the mind healthy so it would not descend into madness. The National Committee for Mental Hygiene, the organization Beers founded, expressed a millennial mission to "hasten the time when the minds of men will be capable of adjustments which will permit the spirit of humanity and charity to rule instead of envy and malice, vengeance to give way to justice, war to peace, despair to hope."[25]

THE PROTESTANT ORIGINS OF POPULAR PSYCHOLOGY

The evangelical spirit of American psychological thinkers came straight out of the Protestant heritage. It was not accidental that William James and John Watson, two of the towering figures in the history of American psychological thought, both evangelized the general public rather than confine themselves to academia. Those two men were raised in utterly different Christian environments—James in a highly literate, transcendentalist-spiritualist home and Watson in an unstable rural fundamentalist family—but they were both "evangelicals of the religion of science" aiming "to bring enlightenment by exposing everyone to the truth." G. Stanley Hall, who stood with James as the founding father of American psychology, was also an ardent popularizer whose religious upbringing deeply affected his understanding of human nature. His classic work, *Adolescence* (1904), was saturated in Christian references. Hall felt sure that the transition from self-centered childhood to other-centered adulthood proved the maxim, "All are thus born twice," and he warned the Church that if it failed to communicate the experience of rebirth, "psychology . . . will preach it."[26]

America's Calvinist tradition bequeathed to posterity a fascination and preoccupation with the inner states of the individual. The Puritans developed a dynamic religious psychology in which men and women were responsible for constant spiritual introspection and self-interpretation. Each person looked inward for signs of the divine spirit at work. Those signs appeared in states of severe psychic tension and distress, in bouts of despondency about the redemption of one's soul. Once such an experience registered, the churchgoer appeared before the community of believers and testified to it, giving a public spiritual account and autobiography. The American Puritan structure of spiritual narration conditioned an entire population to speak and write about private experiences, and it elicited from the most articulate religious leaders profound inquiries into the nature of the psyche. Long after the custom of the public testimonial died out, the New England elite continued to ponder the psychodynamics of religious experience, leaving eloquent volumes that aimed to decipher the mysterious interplay of thought and feeling, perception and sensation, will and desire. Among their legacies was a unique literature focused on the alienation and travail of the spiritually striving individual.[27]

William James was one of the most eloquent inheritors of that tradition to point it in a psychotherapeutic direction. James was the grandson of Irish immigrants, not the descendant of Puritans, and he grew up largely in New York City, not Boston, but he nevertheless had a deep familiarity with the New England style of self-discipline and containment. He believed that style had become self-defeating, for it left people in a state of enervation, too fatigued and overwrought to enjoy whatever success their work ethic had achieved. In two addresses, "The Energies of Men" and "The Gospel of Relaxation," which were widely circulated as a small book called *On Vital Reserves*, James responded to Dr. Beard's problem by proposing a theory of "reserve energy." "It is evident," he wrote, "that our organism has stored-up reserves of energy that are ordinarily not called upon, but that may be called upon." From this premise, James argued that men and women have the willpower to alter their habits in such a way as to open up those reserves of power. Known for his theory that acts dictated feelings, James urged his listeners and readers to change whichever habits seemed to produce fatigue or listlessness; by doing so, they would counteract the deadening effects of the New England conscience—a worried form of behavior that stunted creativity: "Why do we hear the complaint so often that social life in New England is either less rich and expressive or more fatiguing than it is in some other parts of the world? To what is the fact, if fact it be, due unless to the overactive conscience of the people, afraid of either saying something too trivial and obvious, or something insincere, or something unworthy of one's interlocutor, or something in some way or other not adequate to the occasion?"[28]

James ratified the popular desire to see the subconscious as a divining rod, a mysterious *sanctum sanctorum* where contact with divine energy is made, latent powers are released, and the self is transformed. In *The Varieties of Religious Experience,* he used the idiom of psychology to describe the possibility of divine workings within the human mind. "The *subconscious self* is nowadays a well-accredited psychological entity," James explained, as he suggested that "the subconscious continuation of our conscious life" could account for the apparently real power of religious experiences. If we leave aside the specifics of various religious practices and concentrate only on "what is common and generic," James wrote,

> we have in *the fact that the conscious person is continuous with a wider self through which saving experiences come,* a positive content of religious experience which, it seems to me, *is literally and objectively true as far as it goes.* . . . The further limits of our being plunge, it seems to me, into an altogether other dimension of existence from the sensible and merely "understandable" world. Name it the mystical region, or the supernatural region, whichever you choose. . . . Yet the unseen region in question is not merely ideal, for it produces effects in this world. When we commune with it, work is actually done upon our finite personality, for we are turned into new men, and consequences in the way of conduct follow in the natural world upon our regenerative change.[29]

James was only the most eminent spokesman of a massive therapeutic trend that emerged out of Protestant America as a cure for American nervousness. "We are just now witnessing a very copious unlocking of energies," he declared in a presidential address to the American Philosophical Association in 1906, "by . . . those converts to 'New Thought,' 'Christian Science,' 'Metaphysical Healing,' or other forms of spiritual philosophy, who are so numerous among us today." Christian Science alone claimed nearly 100,000 self-identified adherents by 1910, and hundreds of thousands of Americans read the mind-cure treatises of the New Thought movement, which peaked with Ralph Waldo Trine's *In Tune with the Infinite* (1897), a volume that eventually sold more than a million and a half copies. The mind-curists combined a whole range of Christian sensibilities, from the evangelical to the socialist, and their writings on the supreme importance of mind could easily be fit into the lives of Methodists and Episcopalians as well as those who had abandoned formal Protestant denominations.[30]

The advocates of New Thought rebelled against the dark pessimism of Calvinism but tried to salvage Calvinist ideas about the synchronicity of faith and works in the life of the saintly individual. By opening themselves to the influx of the divine spirit, their philosophy claimed, women and men enabled themselves to work more efficiently both at their careers and in service to others. Despite the mystical sound of their slogans, they insisted that they were pursuing the most rational of courses; after all, they centered their lives on the ideal of mental power in an orderly universe. That universe was so orderly that mind always governed matter. Even when it failed to cure bodily illness, as the Christian Scientists believed it always could, the human mind was the indispensable means of relieving those nervous problems that prevented otherwise capable people from living full lives.[31]

Another popular approach, equally rooted in the Calvinist heritage, denied the very existence of an autonomous mind and claimed that human transformation was a function of the environment. "We are not the creatures of reason we think we are," said the founder of behaviorism, John Broadus Watson (1878–1958). "The mistake the psychologists made—William James included—was to look upon emotions as 'mental states' and not *as ways of behavior which had to be learned like other sets of habits.*" Behaviorism countered the transcendentalist model of human nature with a mechanical model of stimulus-and-response, by which the human, like the white rat of the behaviorist's laboratory, was supposedly governed. As surely as food (and symbols of food) stimulated salivation, events in a person's environment stimulated emotional responses within the body. Every personality trait was a habitual emotional response created in childhood by a specific stimulus.[32]

Watson's behaviorism, which soared to popularity in the 1920s, tapped a well of optimistic environmentalism that ran deep in Protestant America. One of the most important treatises on child-rearing in the nineteenth century, Horace Bushnell's "Christian Nurture" (1847), preached the overwhelming importance of the home environment. Bushnell, minister of the North Congregational Church in Hartford, declared that both "the declaration of scripture, and the laws of physiology" showed that parents shaped their children's personalities early in life. The child remains for many years "within the matrix of the parental life." From the start "the child is held as a mere passive lump in the arms, and he opens into conscious life under the soul of the parent streaming into his eyes and ears, through the manners and tones of the nursery." If parental influence was so complete, good parenting could transform the nature of the growing person.[33]

On the surface, Watson's behaviorism had nothing in common with the evangelical Protestantism that conditioned his childhood in rural South Carolina. (Watson's devout mother named him after a well-known preacher, John Broadus, and expected the boy to become a minister.) The intellect and the will, those essentials of biblical religion, Watson considered fictions because in reality human behavior consisted entirely of conditioned responses. But his system, too, spoke to a public wanting both the idealism of religion and the certainty of science. Watson's view of the psyche offered a very attractive blend of democratic and Calvinist values: behaviorism insisted that all people were fundamentally the same and, if raised in the right environment, equally capable of becoming productive, emotionally self-controlled citizens. Watson brooded about the problem of volatility and unpredictability in human emotional life— "our adult emotional behavior is harumscarum, disorderly, and unpredictable"—and he believed he had found a solution as ultimate as the Infinite of the mind-cure folks. "Since the gut cannot be legislated out of existence," he offered a scheme of salvation as grand as any that Calvinist theologians had produced: "Why can't we train it or have it trained to behave in an orderly way, the way the rest of our body behaves?" By "unconditioning" people out of their bad behaviors and reconditioning them into good, behaviorism would one day be capable of freeing humanity of crippling fears and extravagant emotions, making real civilization possible for the first time in the history of the species.[34]

Both the transcendentalist and the behaviorist approach to human nature promised beatific transformations of the individual and society. They were the most embracing and enduring perspectives to emerge from the American Protestant tradition. Each identified hidden sources of great power that, if tapped, would transform the quality of human life by eliminating emotional and psychological obstacles. In the enormity of their promise, they replicated the drama of religious conversion and regeneration.

We have seen how America's Protestant heritage yielded a powerful American interest in personal development and a massive audience for popular psychology, but our picture is incomplete because Jews, too, became part of that story in the early years of the twentieth century. If popular psychology formed a bridge between Protestantism and modern science, what kind of bridge existed in the case of Jewish thinkers? How did they adapt Jewish values to American inquiries into human nature?

Chapter 6

Jewish Psychological Evangelism:
A Collective Biography
of the First Generation

"I HAVE YOUR VERY CORDIAL LETTER," Joseph Jastrow wrote Hugo Münsterberg in the fall of 1892, "and it gives me very great pleasure to learn of your willingness to assist the section of Psychology at the World's Fair." It may have been a coincidence that the nation's first public exhibition of psychology, which took place at the Chicago World's Fair of 1893, was produced by a pair of Jews—the only Jews in the nation's first cohort of prominent psychologists.

The University of Wisconsin's Jastrow and Harvard's Münsterberg were not close friends and lived far apart, but evidently they were more anxious than their peers to bring "the new psychology" to the general public. They were both twenty-nine years old when they began planning what they wanted to be "a strong collective exhibit," something that would make a real showing of psychology's presence, rather than an array of "relatively small exhibits from various colleges." They worked feverishly toward the big day; Jastrow set up the apparatus and Münsterberg wrote a pamphlet explaining in layman's terms what the various instruments measured. Among others there was the chronoscope, which measured reaction times to a thousandth of a second; the kymograph, which, with the help of the sphygmograph, recorded the pulse as it varied with emotional states; the ergograph, which scored muscular work according to attention and fatigue; and the galvanoscope, which registered the effect of emotions on the glands of the skin. For a nominal fee, visitors made use of the sizable testing laboratory to learn about their sensitivity to sights and sounds and other perceptual features of their minds.[1]

A little more than two decades later, when Jastrow and Münsterberg were at or near the top of their careers both as academics and as popularizers of psychology, they corresponded about the ups and downs of popularity. Having just finished another of the books that he published at an astonishing rate, Münsterberg wrote Jastrow in a moment of self-congratulation hastily dressed as modesty. Of his 1913 best-seller *Psychology and Industrial Efficiency,* a landmark of American applied psychology, Münsterberg mentioned that the book "went through six large editions in the first six months and has in the mean time been translated into seven languages." About the new volume (which may have been either *Psychology and Social Sanity* or *Psychology: General and Applied,* both of which appeared in 1914), he dissembled: "It seems that the new one will take a similar course, but I can assure you that this wide popularity of my books fills me only with the feeling of the Greek orator who asked what mistake he had made, because everybody applauded."[2]

Jews were among the founders of American popular psychology and, no less than their colleagues from Protestant backgrounds, they wanted to introduce their values into popular thought. We have already come across the names of some of the most influential Jewish popularizers at work in America—Jastrow, Münsterberg, Brill, Coriat, and Sidis—and to that list we must add Alfred Adler, who lived in the United States for a number of years, Adler's primary American disciple, Walter Béran Wolfe, and Boston neurologist Abraham Myerson. Together these men produced an abundance of books and articles for the mass market, hundreds of newspaper interviews and public lectures, and, in the case of Jastrow and Brill, many radio addresses as well. Their names were widely known, not only to people in the upper and middle classes, but also to the multitude of immigrants and wage-earners who showed up at clinics and hospitals in New York and Boston. (Myerson alone saw 25,000 patients in his career.) They had many differences between them and much in common with their Christian peers, but these thinkers shared a Jewish moral perspective, which they introduced into the vast American market of popular psychology.[3]

These were not the only Jewish thinkers whose writings affected American ideas of human nature in the half-century before World War II. Others will also appear in our story. But the men named above formed the core of the first generation of Jewish psychological evangelists, thinkers who were powerfully driven to reach a mass audience and whose writing and speaking contained a clearly Jewish point of view.[4]

Before moving ahead with the story of how they changed public conversation about human nature, we must briefly sketch their biographies, with an eye toward appreciating how Jewish origins affected their attitudes and values. For the sake of simplicity, we will group them according to their three areas of expertise: psychology, psychiatry, and psychoanalytic psychiatry (Freudian or Adlerian). Those professional differences would have placed these doctors in very different worlds had they not all wanted to publicize their ideas about the psyche. In becoming public moralists, they transcended their disciplinary boundaries.

THE PSYCHOLOGISTS: MÜNSTERBERG AND JASTROW

Hugo Münsterberg (1863–1916)

Fifty-three years old, six feet tall, and more than two hundred pounds, Hugo Münsterberg broke the desk on his lecture platform when he suddenly keeled over from a cerebral hemorrhage while teaching his Elementary Psychology class at Radcliffe in the winter of 1916. The sixty or so women in Room Five of the old Brown and Nichols building panicked at the sight of their stricken professor, who was dead within ten minutes.

Münsterberg's death made news all across the country. The *Passaic News* called Münsterberg "America's most noted international figure," while the *Chicago Post* declared that "Chicagoans today set aside personal prejudices" about the professor's controversial pro-Germanism "and became a unit in declaring him one of the leading thinkers of the time." Many obituaries referred to him as "Harvard's famous psychologist" and "noted savant." One of Münsterberg's last printed messages stated that the findings of psychology about human memory boded well for a lasting peace after the war that had made a living hell out of his own life as Germany's most vocal defender in the United States. His laboratory studies showed that specific memories faded quickly once their motives disappeared. "The subtle power of our mind to forget will become mankind's blessing," he wrote. "Unless all psychological signs deceive us, after this war ends peace will really be lasting."[5]

The venerable American stereotype of the excitable, balding German professor with the bushy black mustache probably gained some (if not most) of its substance from Münsterberg. One young man wrote to the *Louisville Courier-Journal*, describing the excitement of Herr Doktor's classes at Harvard. Hundreds of people attended those lectures, including many visitors, like himself, who were not Harvard students. To those packed halls, Münsterberg made unusual demonstrations of the practical uses of psychology and of people who had highly developed physical senses. Yet he cautioned his students not to applaud, reminding them, "This is not a vaudeville performance." "Ze study of ze mind," he would say in his heavily accented English, "is a very zerious zubject." A former student wrote to a New York paper: "He was a master of the human mind. . . . Professor Muensterberg had almost an absolute control of the thoughts of those who came within the zone of his personal influence." Another former student living in Hartford recalled Münsterberg's "prodigious and tenacious memory." "His mind was replete with ideas," wrote Gustave Feingold, Ph.D., "and his advice was sought by hundreds of people . . . lawyers and judges, physicians and financiers, manufacturers and railroad presidents, ship owners and army officers, not to mention plain, everyday mortals of the street . . . whether in matters of private life, of choosing a career, or guiding a business."[6]

Münsterberg's sensational campaign against spiritualism and his long friendship with William James reverberated in the press even after he was gone. A Boston psychic and "explorer in the field of spirit return" told the press that a medium channeled a message to her from the departed psychologist, who evidently no longer spoke with a German accent. From beyond the grave Münsterberg not only testified to the linguistic achievement of 100 percent Americanism but also discovered "absolute proof that excarnate beings can and do communicate with their earth-friends." "Spirit-return is a truth," the message concluded; "I am Hugo Munsterberg." The *Des Moines Register* reported on the differing views of Münsterberg and James about spiritualism and on the latter's alleged promise to communicate from the beyond within three years of his death. "The three years have passed and a couple more have gone by, but no one has heard a word from him. It is strange that Professor Muensterberg, disbeliever in spirits, should get into communication with the earth less than a week after his funeral. . . . Professor Muensterberg was so strongly given to imparting solid and detailed information about concrete matters, in terms understandable to the laiety [*sic*], that it is strange he said not a word about the world in which he now lives."[7]

Münsterberg entered the terrestrial world fifty-three years earlier in Danzig. He was the extraordinary son of parents who nearly typified the German Jewish bourgeois family of the late nineteenth century. His father, Moritz (1825–80), grew up in Breslau, where his family had lived for two generations, and set off as a very young man to establish himself in business in Danzig, where he married his first wife and became a partner in his father-in-law's lucrative lumber business. Located on the Black Sea, the firm bought lumber in Russia and sold it largely to merchants in England and Scotland. Well-traveled and cosmopolitan, Moritz nevertheless devoted a lot of attention to his children: two sons from his first marriage and two more from his second union with Anna Bernhardi, cousin to his prematurely deceased first wife. Hugo was Anna's first son, born on June 1, 1863. Anna, too, died young, before Hugo reached his thirteenth year. Stricken by the death of yet another wife, Moritz thereafter focused all his spare time and energy on the upbringing of his four sons. Like most middle-class German Jewish fathers, he reared the boys according to strict standards of *Bildung*—character formation based on self-discipline, academic attainment, and cultural education. For many Jewish boys, including the four Münsterberg sons, *Bildung* also entailed several years of moral education at the local synagogue culminating in confirmation, the German bourgeois equivalent of becoming a bar mitzvah.[8]

An intellectually precocious, obedient, and well-mannered child, Hugo was close to his parents and delighted in the praise and adoration of uncles, aunts, and cousins whom he visited during Jewish holidays and summer vacations. Moritz and Anna were artistically cultivated—Anna especially loved music and painting—and Hugo shared those passions as well, becoming an avid writer of poetry, a student of the cello, and a fan of the theater. By seventeen Hugo was parentless but he remained close with his brothers; all four made a ritual of a yearly reunion in Danzig even after Hugo lived in America, where Emil, Otto, and Oskar also visited him numerous times. The intimacy of family relations in Hugo's boyhood would be a recurring nostalgic theme for the frenetically busy and high-strung public man he was to become.[9]

Hugo had little use for Judaism once he left home. He tended to deny the glaring realities of antisemitism in the 1880s, despite (or because of) his brothers' expressions of anxiety about it, and he envisioned for himself an uncomplicated ascent in the German professional world. Yet the Jewish proprieties of his youth kept Hugo apart from the in-crowd; he crowed, for example, about the heavy drinking of his German schoolmates. According to one biographer, Münsterberg's "inability to call or count upon psychological support from either Germans or Jews had at least one important consequence. Sensing that he must play a lone hand in life, he ventured everything in a quest for personal achievement and influence."[10]

Münsterberg's coming to America was a story of intellectual alliance between two illustrious thinkers. Between 1890 and 1892 William James courted the young Prussian, intent on bringing him to Harvard to create and maintain a top-notch laboratory and program in experimental psychology. Temperamentally, the two men had little in common except for bouts of nervous exhaustion, the price they were willing to pay for their extraordinary productivity. James, nineteen years older than Münsterberg, gave a father figure's encouragement to the hypersensitive and egocentric young student who had already produced a German masterwork and who revolted against his teacher, Wilhelm Wundt, declaring James rather than Wundt to be the true leader of modern psychology. Münsterberg's pride and formality assumed comic proportions in his correspondence with James. It took Münsterberg two years of repeated requests from James to be addressed informally before he changed his greeting from *Verehrter Herr Professor* to *Verehrter Herr James,* which was like meeting a request for milk by switching from whipped cream to heavy cream. Soon after he arrived at Harvard, Münsterberg was mortified by a colleague's criticism of his English; he nursed his pride by telling James that he would thenceforth express himself only in German! But James was patient and nurturing, and Münsterberg excelled as expected. In supporting Münsterberg, James made concrete his desire that American universities integrate Jewish scholars and "grow to be the organizers of what is new and untried in moral and social lines . . . instead of being guardians of what is traditional and secure."[11]

Münsterberg pulled off a trick that would have been impossible if he had stayed in Germany. From afar in the United States, he could construct the kind of Germany that tempted the imagination of every idealistic German Jewish intellectual and artist—he portrayed the Fatherland as a society permeated with moral idealism. The qualities he associated with America—impulsiveness, extravagance, and hedonism—could be criticized from the vantage point of the expatriate German professor. Münsterberg was himself impulsive, extravagant, and far from ascetic in his tastes, and the kind of celebrity that he enjoyed was possible only in America, where an impulsive, extravagant, pleasure-loving public produced a mass market for psychological advice (instead of saving money and enduring the stringencies of the old-time religious instruction on proper behavior). At Harvard he immediately attained a revered position that would have eluded him as a Jew, though a baptized one, in Germany. He proclaimed his love for the Fatherland but, when offered the chair in philosophy at the University of Königsberg (the chair that Immanuel Kant once occupied), Münsterberg preferred to stay in Cambridge. Whether or not antisemitism was the reason for the academic rebuffs he suffered before leaving Germany, he believed it was, and, despite his retention of German citizenship, he envisioned that his wife and daughters would live out their lives in America, which they did. Loving American affluence while attacking it with German idealism, extolling German duty while refusing it with American individualism, Münsterberg ended up playing the stereotypical Jewish role of the self-consciously exiled intellectual.[12]

The psychic underside of Münsterberg's radical identification as a German appeared most vividly in a poem he wrote as a young man while daydreaming during his studies. The poem describes the youthful scholar working away in a garret. Suddenly, he starts to grow, and keeps growing to gigantic proportions. Bursting out of the confines of the house and towering over the city, the young giant smashes a church along with nearby houses, breaks off the church steeple, and uses it as a walking stick, with which he strides through forests and across the ocean. Confronting the final face of nature, outer space, the giant recognizes the limits of his power and aspiration, shrinks to his original state, and quietly resumes his studies. The young man's poem added a note of irony to the older man's claim that he did not dream and that Freud's unconscious realm was a total fiction. A young Jew rises to an awesome height in society; he crushes buildings—the statist and aristocratic institutions that forbade entry to Jews; he takes a church steeple—the symbol of Christian dominance above which no synagogue roof was allowed to rise; he strides with his stick through forested lands—the lumber trade that enabled a Jewish businessman like Moritz Münsterberg to project Hugo into German culture but that also differentiated Hugo from most German university students, whose fathers were in elite rather than mercantile vocations; he crosses the ocean—leaving behind the social confines of the Old World. In Münsterberg's dream, complete with a Freudian steeple and a Nietzschean superman, the young scholar expressed the rebellion of a prodigious intellect against the boundaries society had erected against him. In real life, Hugo tried to transcend those boundaries anticlimactically, by a mechanical conversion to Protestantism. (In Heinrich Heine's day, that act was at least somewhat novel, whereas Münsterberg's generation provided thousands of new Christians for the Fatherland, including two of his three brothers.)[13]

According to the most complete biography of Münsterberg, the psychologist's Jewish background was "well known in America, at least in the academic community," even though Münsterberg himself rarely mentioned it. There is evidence enough that Americans outside of academia also knew of his Jewish origins. The *Brooklyn Eagle* eulogized the psychologist with the headline, "Hugo Muensterberg was of Jewish Parentage," and commented, "He was one of many Jews whose devotion to an academic life unfortunately ended their connection with their religion." *The Churchman*, a New York City paper, noted tersely that "from the standpoint of religion Professor Münsterberg could not be pleasing to Christians" because he was "intellectually the kind of man who gives reason to fear materialistic tendencies in our large universities."[14]

A thousand miles westward in Peoria, a rabbi commemorated the psychologist's death with a mini-sermon in the local press. Acknowledging Münsterberg's professional attainments, Rabbi A. Cohen commented that there was "another side to the personality of Professor Hugo Munsterberg which I, as a Jew, am particularly interested in."

> Now, we cannot overlook the humorous situation of this gifted scholar. He wrote, taught and instructed the whole world on the subject of psychology, but he did not know the psychology of his own soul. He championed the cause of Germanism, although Germany refused to recognize him according to his merits. He preached the gospel of superiority of the Teuton, forgetting that he himself is the son of a noble, ancient Semitic race, that gave the world just as much as any other race can boast of. . . . The fact, however, remains, that the Jew seems to be willing to forget the slurs and insults of his enemies and takes up the work of repaying good for evil in the most practical manner.[15]

Here we find Münsterberg symbolizing not simply the secular thinker insufficiently proud of his "race" but something more: the secular Jew whose spiritual maturity enabled him to rise above the calumnies of Christian antagonists and contribute to the betterment of their common world.

Joseph Jastrow (1863–1944)

A diminutive man, balding and bespectacled, with gently playful brown eyes, Joseph Jastrow penned a description of himself at fifty-two. Preparing for an annual summer vacation in Maine, he made an index card by which he could be identified if lost en route: "JASTROW, the chief citizen of Scampville. May be shipped to Maine by parcel post insured and prepaid or smuggled into a trunk. Can lose himself and find himself without trouble. Will wear any kind of clothes and eat anything. Requires to be introduced to all captains of boat and train conductors. Is a good deal of a nuisance, but doesn't mind being told so. Very amusing to the fellow-passengers: hence a good travelling companion. A great collector of useless stuff. . . . No guarantee that he will be returned." The quirky little man was a noted scholar and the single most prolific disseminator of psychology to the American public between the 1890s and the 1940s.[16]

Born in Warsaw to Bertha (Wolfsohn) and Marcus M. Jastrow, Joseph Jastrow arrived with his family in the United States in 1866. He grew up in Philadelphia, where his father was a congregational rabbi, and graduated from the University of Pennsylvania. Two years later at age twenty-three, Jastrow received the first Ph.D. to be awarded by an American university with a psychology laboratory, at Johns Hopkins. (The 1886 class of doctorates at Johns Hopkins included Woodrow Wilson, seven years Jastrow's senior.) In 1888 Jastrow started a long career at the University of Wisconsin, where he built one of the nation's earliest and best psychology laboratories. Fascinated by animal behavior, which he felt was primary to and comparable with human activity, Jastrow helped establish the field of comparative psychology in the United States. He also pioneered in the psychology of delusion, which constituted a lifelong interest and a major theme of his writings for the general public. His magazine and newspaper articles and books on superstition, magical thinking, credulity, and parapsychology were so abundant as to suggest that a primary motive behind Jastrow's popularization of psychology was the desire to rid the American public of phantasms. From 1927 to 1932 he wrote a syndicated advice column, "Keeping Mentally Fit," which served as the basis for several popular books: *Keeping Mentally Fit* (1928), *Piloting Your Life* (1930), and *Effective Thinking* (1931). One of the first radio psychologists, he spoke to the public on NBC from 1935 to 1938. From the lectures on those shows, he produced another mass-market book,

Sanity First: The Art of Sensible Living (1935). Jastrow's work, the *New York Times* reported, "aimed to give the layman a practical guide for a sane mental and spiritual life."[17]

Jastrow represented a Jewish version of the transition from a nine-teenth-century religious to a twentieth-century psychological culture. In the late 1920s one of his readers wrote, "I often wonder why you do not recommend spiritual help by means of minister, rabbi or priest." Jastrow agreed that religious faith helped people survive psychologically. "Without some conviction that despite the battle and the struggle, there is something worth living for as well as something to live by," he wrote, "a hopeless despair or feeble failure awaits the despondent under nervous stress." And yet, he continued: "The psychologist must recognize things as they are. . . . Fortunate are they who can use the path of prayer. There is little need to advise that path for those who tread it; for they do so of their own accord. But the psychologist, like all other men, knows many who find their codes and creeds in other directions; so he must speak to and for all."[18]

In speaking of "codes and creeds," Jastrow meant something more than met the eyes of his readers. "Creed" would have sufficed to describe faith-communities as Christians understood them. "Codes" was the name used by learned Jews to describe the corpus of rabbinic texts that informed men and women how to live. Jastrow's father was such a learned Jew. Though the popular psychologist described his father in *Keeping Mentally Fit* as a "philologist," Marcus Jastrow exceeded that label. He was a distinguished rabbi and scholar whose lexicon of the Talmud, completed in 1903, remains a standard tool for English-speaking students. Given his background, Jastrow's reflection on the good fortune of those who walked the "path of prayer" contained a poignant under-tone. That communion of people included most Jews prior to the assimi-lative encounter with European and American culture in the nineteenth and twentieth centuries. It continued to include a modern religious man like his father whose liturgy suggested someone other than the psycholo-gist as healer of the soul: *When they cry, the Lord listens, And delivers them from all their troubles; The Lord is near to the broken-hearted and saves those who are crushed in spirit.* The sense of transition from a religious to a secular world inhered in Jastrow's correspondence with readers, for that dialogi-cal format paralleled rabbinic responsa, the published answers of rabbis to questions about the many rituals and actions governing the daily life of Jews.[19]

Like Hugo Münsterberg, Joseph Jastrow gave little indication of his Jewish identity in his published writings. And yet, he was the son and son-in-law of eminent rabbis, a fond brother-in-law to Henrietta Szold, founder of the Zionist women's organization Hadassah, and husband of

Rachel Szold, an energetic organizer for both Jewish and women's causes and a leader of Madison's small Jewish community.

In a copious correspondence with her family, Rachel left a detailed record of the couple's life from marriage to retirement. Judaism and Jewish affairs were at the center of that life if only because of Rachel's frenetic activity and traditional streak. The couple had a large Jewish wedding in Baltimore the year Joseph secured his position at Wisconsin (1888) and maintained the custom of family gatherings on the High Holidays. Joseph and Rachel took quiet walks on Sabbath and festivals, though Joseph was not a synagogue goer. They debated Zionism, she coming to embrace the cause that made her sister famous and he, like many liberal Jewish intellectuals at the turn of the century, standing aloof from what he considered an elitist and impractical ideology. Joseph's command of Jewish history made him his wife's most valuable adviser when she prepared addresses on the subject for local women's clubs and associations. Frequently entertaining his colleagues at their home, Rachel liked to talk about Jewish literature and politics (Zangwill's *The Melting Pot* stimulated debates about intermarriage, which she opposed), and her husband undoubtedly took part in those conversations. Symbolic of the couple's involvement in local Jewish life, they adopted—fairly late in life—the infant son of a local Russian Jewish laborer whose wife died in the influenza epidemic of 1919. Joseph delighted in the child, whose father left a poignant statement concluding, "Some day he'll be a great man like Mr. Joseph Jastrow."[20]

An interesting sign of his Jewish background appeared in Jastrow's adaptation of the ideas of his first mentor, the philosopher Charles Sanders Peirce (1839–1914). Jastrow had the good fortune of being at Johns Hopkins during Peirce's five-year stay there and of collaborating with him on an experimental study of how people perceive small differences in sensation. Deeply impressed by Peirce's analysis of the role of logic and illogic in human thinking, Jastrow specialized in exposés of "fraudulent" thinking and established the psychology of delusion as a subdiscipline. In this respect, he sustained the legacy of Peirce while Peirce himself disappeared from the academic scene and waned in influence. When Jastrow adapted one of Peirce's most important essays, "The Fixation of Belief," he targeted Christianity, in a way Peirce did not, as the prime example of the forcible imposition of thought on a community of people. In his course at Wisconsin on the "Psychology of Belief" and in his popular writings, he spoke of the "sad page of history" that records the Church's techniques of censorship and suppression of thought. He also used the biblical and rabbinic phraseology of "the remnant" of Israel when he referred to the dissident few who fight in all times and places for freedom of thought: "There will always be a saving remnant," he wrote, "who enjoy a wide outlook and who are willing to give up dogma." Peirce envisioned a community of scientific (logical) thinkers who would provide an ethical foundation for modern society; that vision provided Jastrow with a nonreligious venue for expressing the rationalist Jewish morality in which he was raised.[21]

THE PSYCHIATRISTS: SIDIS AND MYERSON

Boris Sidis (1867–1923)

One of the most important psychopathologists in the United States at the turn of the century, Boris Sidis stood alongside William James, G. Stanley Hall, Hugo Münsterberg, Joseph Jastrow, and Morton Prince as an influential popularizer of psychology. More than the others, except for Prince, he established a reputation as a great psychotherapist, one whose abilities to help the afflicted led a former patient to give him an estate in Portsmouth, New Hampshire, where he set up the Sidis Psychotherapeutic Institute in 1909. Sidis invented a distinctive therapeutic method known as hypnoidization, a state of relaxation between hypnosis and normal mental activity. It was through that technique, we will recall, that he solved one of the most sensational psychiatric cases of the early 1900s, the total amnesia of Thomas Hanna. Sidis also created a special theory of reserve energy that coincided with that of William James. A vigorous and opinionated proponent of intensive parenting, Sidis turned the prodigious genius of his son William into a spectacular testimony of the kind of intelligence and creativity that he believed the right kind of home and school environment would yield. The full name of that child, William James Sidis, suggests a profitable way of describing the elder Sidis—as a Jewish epigone of William James.

   Boris Sidis grew up in the Ukraine and retained powerful memories of the first twenty years of his life as a Jew there. Born in Kiev to Moses and Fanny (Marmor) Sidis, Boris was well educated by private tutors until the age of seventeen, when he was sent to a government school in Kishinev. There Sidis got into serious trouble with the authorities as a result of some sort of political activity, which led to prison and several years of police surveillance after his release. Temperamentally unfit to live in tsarist Russia, Sidis emigrated to the United States in 1887 and settled in New York City. Virtually penniless on his arrival, he took on factory jobs and tutored other Jewish immigrants. Sidis moved to Boston in 1891 and, while continuing to tutor, he began taking classes at Harvard. There he moved ahead quickly, receiving a B.A. in 1894, an M.A. in 1895, and a Ph.D. in psychology under William James in 1897. James was so impressed with Sidis's dissertation, which appeared as *The Psychology of Sug-*

gestion in 1898, that he agreed to write the book's preface. A brilliant discourse on the dynamics of human suggestibility, the book catapulted Sidis to the top of his field.

If Sidis had an overriding intellectual concern, it was the role of fear, which led people to conform to bad values and stopped them from tapping their hidden reserves of mental energy. He interpreted this problem in terms of the Spinozan ideal of rationality: " 'A free man is he,' says Spinoza, 'who lives under the guidance of reason, who is not led by fear.' " In the Spinozan scheme, the nemesis of rationality was religious "enthusiasm," which Sidis decried in a way that swept away Jewish fanaticism and Christianity *in toto*. Observing that the "religious emotions" of Jews made them "highly susceptible to religious suggestions," he went on to argue that "the list of Jewish Messiahs is inordinately long" and that it "would take too much space to recount the names of all the 'saviours' who appeared among the Jews . . . down to our own times." Though he illustrated the point with a reference to the cult of Shabbetai Zvi, the implication for Christianity was grave. Shabbetai Zvi was a momentary, acute phenomenon among Jews, a deviation from the rationalist Judaism of Maimonides. The same could not be said, of course, for Christ, whose followers, according to Sidis's line of reasoning, were categorically guilty of irrationalism.[22]

In prophetic style, Sidis excoriated American parents for raising their sons and daughters to respect superficial values of appearance and strength rather than train them in the ways of intellectual and moral discipline. "Like the Israelites of old we worship golden calves and sacred bulls. Our daughters yearn after the barbaric shimmer and glitter of the bejewelled, bespangled, empty-minded, parasitic females of 'the smart set.' Our college boys admire the feats of the trained athlete and scorn the work of the 'grind.' If in the depths of space there is some solar system inhabited by really rational beings, and if one of such beings should by some miracle happen to visit our planet, he would no doubt turn away in horror." Sidis advised parents to raise their children according to the values of critical inquiry, not the autocratic dispensation of rules. "Everything should be open to the child's searching interest," he prescribed; "nothing should be suppressed and tabooed as too sacred for examination." Like patients who came to him for help with psychological problems, children "should learn to follow reason, rather than habit and routine."[23]

If only the right conditions existed, Sidis thought, children would naturally attain unimagined levels of genius. On this point, he both approximated and diverged from the theories of his mentor William James. Sidis dedicated two of his books to James, who, he wrote, "has inspired me with love for the study of the 'varieties' of human experiences, who has

given me his sympathy and hearty support in many an hour of trial."
With his teacher, Sidis developed a philosophy of life in which the individual might soar to great and unpredictable heights. He encouraged
James to read Freud's *Interpretation of Dreams* but could not stomach the
determinism in Freud's theory. It was as if one's future were foreordained
"in some sort of nautical almanac," he complained to James: "Where
would be our individuality, that chance element most dear to and valued
by us?" Teacher and student saw each other as creative individualists demanding a world of creative individualism. James said of Sidis's first book
that "the whole thing is bold, original and radical like yourself." Almost
simultaneously, each man had developed a theory about untapped reserves of energy that the most creative people, or people in crisis, managed to harness. In 1907, the year his address "The Energies of Men"
appeared in print, James told Sidis how much he liked Sidis's "theory of
reserve energy," and he observed that the "congruence of that theory
with the facts in my 'address' is striking, and makes for the truth of both."
James confessed that "just what we *mean* by energy in this connexion is
far from clear," and he sensed "that we are but stumbling at the threshold
of a big subject, which may open out amazingly in the near future, now
that ground is so emphatically broken."[24]

William James Sidis was supposed to prove what James and Sidis had
merely suggested about human potential, but he ended up proving
something else about the difference between the anxious Jewish immigrant who was his father and the more comfortably American man who
was his father's hero. To one who had been imprisoned as a college student in the Ukraine, the possibilities of education in America must have
seemed boundless. Sidis realized such rapid success, despite the difficulties facing the adult immigrant, that he must have fantasized what a
child born and raised in America might accomplish.

In 1894 Sidis married Sarah Mandelbaum, also an immigrant from
tsarist Russia (who worked her way to an M.D.), and the couple had two
children, William James (b. 1898) and Helen (b. 1910). Overlooking
their daughter, the Sidises schooled their son intensely; his natural gifts
were such that he entered Harvard at eleven, already fluent in several
languages and a master of mathematics and physics. (A few months after
enrolling he astonished the Harvard Mathematical Club with a lecture
on four-dimensional bodies that is still remembered as "the nonpareil of
achievements by a child prodigy.") James took an interest in the boy's
development but cautioned Boris about over-intellectualizing him. "I
congratulate you on W.J.S.—what you tell of him is wonderful," he wrote
Sidis when the youngster was still a toddler. Allowing that "his intellect
will take care of itself," James advised the overzealous father: "Exercise
his motor activities exclusively for many years now!" A prickly and rebel-

lious man, Sidis would not be deterred. Used to the intellectualism of eastern European Jewish life, he saw no reason for his son to depart from the path of the intellect. The boy, however, found that path hazardous (much more so than his childhood companion Norbert Wiener, another of Cambridge's Jewish prodigies). Spurned at Harvard and beyond as a misfit, he sank away from academia, worked as an adding-machine operator, produced a study of the Boston public transit system, nursed a powerful ambivalence toward his goal-directed immigrant father, and died a wreck of a man at forty-six.[25]

Abraham Myerson (1881–1948)

Reminiscent of the talmudic discussion about the relative merits of study and action, in which it is concluded that Torah study must lead to moral activity, Abraham Myerson recounted a dialogue he had with his father, a Lithuanian rabbi turned freethinking socialist: "My father and I finally agreed that the wise man has to know his fellow man and life far more than he needs to know books. Scholarship is only a means and not an end. The man who retreats to scholarship as an end retreats from wisdom and from life. The beginning and end of wisdom, therefore, is search and research into the nature and organization of man." Myerson not only echoed the Talmud but also transposed Psalm 111, which reads: "The beginning of wisdom is the fear of the Lord." By replacing "the fear of the Lord" with "research into the nature of man" Myerson crystallized the perspective of many secular Jewish thinkers who remained within the psychic structure of Judaism (otherwise, why paraphrase the Talmud and the Psalms?) while looking to science and the scientific ideal for a larger sense of purpose and meaning in the world.[26]

Born in Yanova, Lithuania, in 1881, Abraham Myerson was the fifth of eight children of Morris Joseph and Sophie (Segal) Myerson. Yanova lies about fifteen miles from Kovno, which was a center of secular literature in the dense yeshiva world of Lithuania. That proximity may have had something to do with the decision of Abraham's father to abandon a rabbinic career in favor of socialism. Morris Myerson was one of many young men in the 1880s "who would replace Jewish practices with a new faith" and who yearned to discover the "scientific causes" of the deterioration of Jewish life under the Tsars.[27]

In fear of being exiled for his radical views, Morris emigrated with his family to the United States in 1885, when Abraham was four. Growing up on the tough streets of the Boston waterfront, where his father made a living as a junk dealer, Abe Myerson worked his way from high school into Tufts Medical School, a journey that took seven years of saving money as a pipe cutter and streetcar conductor. He became a star pupil of psychiatrist Morton Prince and, to his great satisfaction, inherited Prince's chair in neurology at Tufts. Myerson completed his father's passage from religious to secular knowledge by imbuing his children with a passion for understanding the human mind—both his sons became psychiatrists and his daughter became a psychiatric social worker. Just as he attributed much of his success to his immigrant father's guidance, his own son Paul remembered being "protected through his growing affluence from the jarring decibels of Boston's slums." He fondly recalled "the special role [Abraham] played in his family constellation."[28]

In addition to attaining Prince's chair at Tufts, Myerson became a professor of clinical psychiatry at the Harvard Medical School, served for years as chief of neuropsychiatry at the Beth Israel Hospital, and was selected in 1913 as one of the first residents of Boston's innovative Psychopathic Hospital. He also became clinical director and pathologist at Taunton State Hospital and director of research at the Boston State Hospital in Matapan. The Myerson Building, built to house the laboratory of the Boston State Hospital, was named for him. He maintained a hectic private practice, in which he estimated seeing more than 25,000 patients between the 1910s and the early 1940s, and reached many readers through several books for the general public: *The Nervous Housewife* (1920), *The Foundations of Personality* (1921), *When Life Loses Its Zest* (1925), and *The Psychology of Mental Disorders* (1927).[29]

Myerson was a pioneer in the study of depression. Though he had abandoned the God of his ancestors, he retained a powerful concern about the purpose of life and the necessity of purposeful behavior. "If purpose means choosing means to an end—not a final end, but a goal— then every cell of the body and certainly every organism have purpose, unless there is no purpose anywhere," he wrote. A view of "a universe striving for some goal," he believed, "allows room for that comfort necessary to most people who reject orthodoxy." "For some," Myerson acknowledged, "this is 'base materialism,' " but for him it was "a working credo." Convinced of the purposefulness of existence even without any divine foundation, he immersed himself in the study of organic problems that stunted human development. Ironically, Myerson put the traditional religious problem of despair onto the psychiatric map when he introduced the concept of *anhedonia*, first in a professional journal and then in one of his most popular books, *When Life Loses Its Zest*. Anhedonia referred to that lack of desire which prevented people from living, as he liked to say, "with zest." A wiry, athletic man who craved physical activity, Myerson brooded about the problem of depression; when he found evidence that electric shock therapy could interrupt a long-standing depression, he became one of the first American doctors to advocate and train other doctors in its application. Once, on hearing a colleague claim that a combination of psychoanalysis and shock treatment cured a patient of depression, he said this reminded him of the fly, panting and exhausted because he and the bull had plowed a field together.[30]

Myerson agreed with Joseph Jastrow, who, paraphrasing Benjamin Disraeli, wrote, "All sensible men are of the same religion, but no sensible man ever tells." But he made an even more precise statement of the perspective of the Jewish psychological thinker. In a book Myerson wrote with Harvard literature professor Isaac Goldberg, the authors explained themselves: "The writers . . . are not in any dogmatic, religious sense, Jews, or anything else. They envisage the problems of the world as scientists, as citizens of that world, without abating by one jot their consciousness of Jewish origin or their interest in the history, the martyrdom, the psychology, the achievements, the faults, and the failures of their people." Wedded to a scientific ideal that linked them with other scientists seeking truth outside of traditional religion, yet carefully mindful of their background as Jews in an often hostile world, men like Abraham Myerson sallied forth into the arena of human nature, confident of the redemptive purpose of their inquiries and advice. "Above all," Myerson's daughter-in-law wrote, "he believed that in the future the organic sources of mental disturbances would be uncovered by science." That such a vision had its own messianic grandeur was made plain by the depth of Myerson's plaint: "I have seen people lose faith, hope, affection, interest, appetite for all of life and love, through illness. I have seen the hero become a coward, the philosopher a cringing fool, the scientist an ignoramus, the passionate lover with all his glow gone, and the wicked sinner apathetically good—while mentally sick."[31]

THE FREUDIANS: BRILL AND CORIAT

Abraham Arden Brill (1874–1948)

"I am Dr. A. A. Brill, who landed here alone in 1889 at the age of fourteen with a fortune of three cents," read an autobiographical statement submitted to the Office of War Information in 1943. "Through assiduous effort I have subsequently graduated from public school, college and university, and have prospered ever since as a psychiatrist. My successful career, for such as it is, I owe altogether to our great democratic country, which offers equal opportunities to all, regardless of race and religion." Despite the obvious protocol of this document, Abraham Brill meant every word of it (like most Jewish immigrants, he perceived America as a Promised Land without fully recognizing the realities of the nation's racial caste system). He looked back on his immigration to America as something foreordained. "I was brought up religiously and destined by my mother for the rabbinate," Brill reminisced at a celebration at the Waldorf-Astoria in honor of his seventieth birthday.

> Because I was born during the week that the Biblical story of Abraham was read in the synagogue, I was named after the patriarch Abraham, who was first named Abram. I was naturally impressed by his personality, by his trials and tribulations. Later on—much later—when I asked myself why I had been so obsessed to leave my home at so early an age and come to a strange country, where I knew no one, it occurred to me that the first verse of that weekly reading started as follows: "Now the Lord said unto Abram, 'Get thee out of thy country and from thy kindred, and from they father's house, unto the land that I will show thee.' "[32]

A *Galitzianer* (Galician Jew), Brill was probably near his adult height of 5'5" when he disembarked as a teenager in New York City at the end of the 1880s. His stocky frame contained enormous energies, which propelled him to become Sigmund Freud's first translator for the American market and the foremost of Freud's popularizers in the United States. "If psycho-analysis now plays a role in American intellectual life, or if it does so in the future," Freud wrote in the preface of the 1932 edition of *The Interpretation of Dreams*, "a large part of this result will have to be attributed to this and other activities of Dr. Brill's." Described by one colleague as "a transmission belt for revolutionary concepts of human behavior," Brill introduced into the American vocabulary such terms as *id, transference, displacement,* and the *unconscious.* Friends had to remind themselves that the "goateed, pot-bellied little man with twinkling eyes, robust humor, grace and tolerance" whom they knew in his later years "was the same man who, at the turn of the century, was the stormy petrel of American psychiatry." Although Brill's name is no longer well known, a sense of his reputation at mid-century can be gotten from a cartoon of 1955 in which a patient is asked, "And do you want it Freud, Jung or Brill?"[33]

Having to support himself at a series of jobs while pursuing his education—he carried garments, tended furnaces, gave lessons in violin and mandolin, taught other immigrants English—Brill graduated from grammar school in Manhattan's Thirteenth Ward when he was eighteen, attained U.S. citizenship at twenty, graduated from New York University at twenty-seven, and completed his medical degree at Columbia at twenty-nine in 1903. He met Freud during a visit to Europe in 1907 and returned a dedicated disciple. By 1911, the year he founded the New York Psychoanalytic Society, Brill was married to a "real American" (i.e., a native-born gentile), Kittie Rose Owen (who also became a doctor), and he held important posts at the Bronx Hospital and Columbia University. After the war, Brill developed a lucrative private practice, in one case

receiving as payment a collection of letters from D. H. Lawrence along
with the original manuscript of *Sons and Lovers*. (Freud once reprimanded Brill, "You have submitted far too much to the two big vices of
America: the greed for money and the respect of public opinion.") While
earning the affection and gratitude of many of his affluent patients, Brill
also did yeoman's work for the city's poorer and immigrant residents. He
helped establish the Vanderbilt Clinic, one of the city's first psychiatric
outpatient facilities, and served at the Bellevue, Manhattan, Beth Israel,
and Kingsbridge V.A. hospitals. Keenly aware of the challenges faced by
others like himself, Brill remained concerned about rising quotas against
Jews in medical schools after World War I. In the 1930s he helped produce a study of Jewish physicians in the United States that assessed the
problems faced by Jews wanting to become doctors.[34]

Brill sharply defined the contours of his Jewish identity even though
he comfortably married a (nonpracticing) Christian and the couple
agreed to raise their son and daughter without formal religion. "I was
the only Jew in the hospital among non-Jews who were more or less antisemitic," he related to his son. "I was broad-minded enough to understand their prejudices and not to react with hostility towards them," he
added, explaining why "they soon gave up their prejudices towards me
and accepted me as one of them." One of the earliest of his extant writings, a college essay on "Hiawatha" that dated probably to the very beginning of his studies at NYU (or possibly City College), shows the young
immigrant maintaining the tradition of avoiding the name of Jesus. "The
Jews had their Moses, the Christians their Saviour, the Arabs their Mo-
hammed, and the North American Indians their Hiawatha," he wrote.
Brill's teacher crossed out the word "Saviour" in red ink and replaced it
with "Christ," thereby preserving both the parallel structure of the sentence and the name of the Christian messiah. From his youth in Galicia
he retained a dislike for what he considered the fear-inducing authoritarianism of Catholicism, and a fondness for Hebrew scriptures, his favorite
passage being "the imagination of the human heart is evil from its youth."
Many decades after the religious studies of childhood, he still jotted
down an occasional Hebrew phrase in the drafts of his speeches.[35]

Time and again Brill cited Freud and Spinoza as intellectual fathers
in whom he perceived Jewish models of intellectual integrity. In a letter
to his son explaining why he and his wife decided not to raise the children in a formal religion, he wrote, "I have long before given up theism
and was guided by Spinoza whom I am still revering." Brill was conveying
the special symbolic importance that Spinoza held for Jewish intellectuals. Until the era of emancipation, Spinoza was *persona non grata* in the
Jewish world, a heretic pure and simple. In the middle of the nineteenth
century, however, a coterie of *maskilim* resurrected the sage of Amster-

dam and turned him into a culture hero who embodied the rationalist, scientific pursuit of knowledge in opposition to the forces of blind religious faith. For those intellectuals, Spinoza represented the pure spirit of Judaism stripped of dogma. Brill admired Spinoza in that way and perceived Freud as his fulfillment. "Freud was not a religious man in the dogmatic sense, but he was in my opinion a very religious person. I have compared him on many occasions to another Jew, who was rejected by the Jews because he could not accept their orthodox theology. That is Spinoza, who is called the 'God intoxicated man.' He certainly was very religious; yet, he was rejected and excommunicated because he could not follow dogmatic Judaism."[36]

Brill exemplified the immigrant psychological thinker whose successful assimilation increased his aura of mastery. "The story of Brill's life follows in the pattern of the Horatio Alger ideal of the American boy of fifty years ago: from poverty to prestige—an American saga," observed Clarence Oberndorf, an American psychoanalyst. "It is a narration of rise to greatness through pluck and perseverance, through work and wisdom, through fortitude and faith in self." Though a Jew, Brill found in America a "land which gave to him equal opportunity to develop his talents" and "which placed so few artificial barriers in his path." As a result, he was able both to realize his own potential and to help other Americans grapple with their problems. A "self-made" man like Brill boosted the image of psychoanalysis, which could suffer in America from connotations of European over-refinement and intellectualism. What made Brill's ascent so interesting was its dependence upon a Freudianism that questioned the conventional values associated with success.[37]

Isador Coriat (1875–1943)

Isador Coriat was one of the nation's foremost interpreters and popularizers of Freud. After the death of Harvard neurologist James Jackson Putnam in 1918, Coriat became the informal leader of Freudianism in the Boston area. Unlike Putnam, he did not belong to the upper echelon of New England society. Bypassing college, he, like Abraham Myerson, took the vocational road from high school to medical school.

The son of Clara Einstein and Harry (Hyram) Coriat, a Moroccan Jew who came to America in the 1860s, Isador Coriat was born in Philadelphia but raised primarily in Boston. The family belonged to Sephardic congregations in both cities. Coriat attended public school and entered Tufts Medical School, which did not require college courses as a prerequisite for admission and thus attracted young men from the region's poorer families. Married to a rabbi's daughter, Etta Dann, and a member of such organizations as the American Jewish Historical Society, Coriat did nothing to repudiate his Jewishness. Still, he probably experienced the insecurity of the second-generation Jewish professional who lived and worked in proximity to Boston brahmins who made no secret of their Mayflower lineage and proudly founded the Immigration Restriction League in the 1890s. Presumably out of a desire to upgrade his genealogy, Coriat identified his father as a "manufacturer" rather than a peddler, and he claimed descent from an "ancient Spanish family." His lineage allegedly included Thomas Coryat, who civilized the English by introducing them to forks in the early 1600s.[38]

To judge by one of the few extant photographs of Coriat, viewed in the light of his accomplishments, he was a man of puckish determination, which expressed itself in a willingness to risk the scorn of his anti-Freudian colleagues and in the expansiveness to publish the first American psychoanalyses of great literature (he began with *Macbeth*). A somewhat late convert to psychoanalysis, Coriat started out as a traditional neurologist, training with the most eminent psychiatrists in the country. He studied psychiatric diagnosis under Adolf Meyer at the Worcester State Hospital between 1900 and 1902 and then under Morton Prince at the Boston City Hospital, where he began working in the neurological department in 1905. Prince actively assisted Coriat's career at a critical stage, giving the younger man good referrals, appointing him as contributing editor to the *Journal of Abnormal Psychology*, and collaborating with him on an early article about psychotherapy. Coriat dedicated his first book on psychopathology, *Abnormal Psychology* (1910), to Prince. By 1914, five years after Freud's famous visit to Clark University, Coriat had become an adherent and a co-founder with Putnam of the Boston Psychoanalytic Society.[39]

We have little personal information about Coriat, but his writings and activities indicate an ongoing concern with Jewish matters. Coriat was instrumental in the early history of Boston's first Jewish hospital, Mount Sinai, for which he established a nerve clinic. When that hospital was succeeded by the Beth Israel Hospital, Coriat served as a consultant there from 1916 until 1930. Although he would become one of the nation's foremost proponents of Freudianism, and the leader of psychoanalysis in Boston after World War I, Coriat also conducted important research on amaurotic family idiocy (Tay-Sachs disease), a genetic affliction of eastern European Jews.[40]

Coriat openly discussed the anxiety experienced by Jews like himself who were assimilating into the nation's professional elite. Though lacking the finesse of Freud's dream interpretations, Coriat's simplified, accessible presentation of *The Interpretation of Dreams* reproduced the structure of that book, opening with an explanation of the theory of analysis followed by a specimen. Instead of Freud's specimen—the "Irma" dream

of July 24, 1895, which elicited the master's first successful interpretation—Coriat substituted an example from his own experience, an American Jewish example. The dream, which we encountered earlier, was that
of a medical "friend" of Coriat's who, as a Jew, worried that a colleague
and his wife who were his friends might reject him. Like Freud, Coriat
used an expository format resembling that of the Talmud and Midrash:
a piece of text is presented and then parsed word by word or phrase by
phrase. "Mrs. X remarked: 'That is a rabbi: we don't want any more rabbis in here.' "

> MRS. X REMARKED: "That is a rabbi: we don't want any more rabbis in
> here."
> RABBI. The subject had often thought that Mrs. X looked foreign and
> Jewish, but she was really not a Jewess. The subject
> himself was a Hebrew and had often felt, because of
> his religious belief, that perhaps he was only tolerated
> by the doctor and his wife. . . .

RABBIS also gave the free associations rabble or crowd, meaning that they
did not care for any more friends, but just a few intimate friends like the
dreamer, even though they were Jewish.[41]

Coriat perceived Freud as a Jewish hero, whose eightieth birthday he
helped commemorate at the Jewish Book Week celebration of the Boston Public Library in 1936. In reaction to critics who accused Freud of
soulless materialism, he reminded his audience of "one of Freud's most
monumental discoveries, what he terms the superego, which is synonymous with conscience." Coriat kept a copy of the commemorative article
published in *B'nai B'rith Magazine* in honor of Freud's first public lectures on psychoanalysis to his fellow members of the Jewish fraternal
society. The clipping contained the letter to B'nai B'rith in which Freud
observed the significance of Jewish ethics for his own development. Coriat shared Freud's view. "Our religious or political or moral views of
life," he wrote in *The Hysteria of Lady Macbeth*, "are in a large part determined by the educational complexes stored up during the earlier years
of our lives."[42]

THE ADLERIANS: WALTER BÉRAN WOLFE (1900–1935)
AND ALFRED ADLER IN AMERICA

The theories of Alfred Adler gained a powerful American foothold after
Adler moved to the United States and a young, Viennese-born Dartmouth man named Walter Béran Wolfe began translating and digesting

Adlerian psychology for a mass audience. Adler's first popular book in America, *Understanding Human Nature*, translated by Wolfe, appeared at the end of 1927. Less than six years later, Adlerian ideas were so well known that Sigmund Freud complained to his American readers of "Adler's Individual Psychology, which in America, for example, is looked upon as being equal in importance to our psycho-analysis . . . and is constantly mentioned in the same breath with it."

> I know you have heard a great deal about the sense of inferiority which is said to distinguish the neurotic subject. It crops up especially in the pages of works that have literary pretensions. A writer who brings in the expression "inferiority-complex" thinks he has satisfied all the demands of psychoanalysis and raised his work on to a higher psychological plane. . . . But, to the mass of mankind, a theory like this must be exceedingly welcome, which takes no complications into account, which introduces no new and difficult concepts, which knows nothing of the unconscious, which removes at a single blow the problem of sexuality, that weighs so heavily on everybody, and which confines itself to revealing the devices by means of which people try to make life comfortable.[43]

Though oversimplifying Adler, Freud was not exaggerating his impact in America. A 1934 textbook on mental hygiene for high school and college students, for example, described a college girl "who had a serious inferiority complex" because of her upbringing. In *New Techniques of Happiness*, Albert Edward Wiggam, a layman who wrote popular books on psychology and self-help, recommended Adler, "who seems to have had more common sense than any other of the famous Viennese psychologists." Dale Carnegie endorsed Adler in his inspirational best-sellers, *How to Win Friends and Influence People* (1936) and *How to Stop Worrying and Start Living* (1948). Though making scant and inaccurate reference to Freud, Carnegie extolled *What Life Should Mean to You*, which he called "Dr. Adler's splendid book." "I dislike repetition," Carnegie apologized as he reemphasized a point of Adler's that "is so important that I am going to repeat it in italics. *It is the individual who is not interested in his fellow man who has the greatest difficulties in life and provides the greatest injury to others. It is from among such individuals that all human failures spring.*" In suggesting ways of overcoming depression, Carnegie declared: "Here is the most astonishing statement I ever read from the pen of a great psychiatrist. This statement was made by Alfred Adler. He used to say to his melancholia patients: 'You can be cured in fourteen days if you follow this prescription. Try to think every day how you can please someone.' " "Dr. Adler urges us to do a good deed every day," Carnegie summarized after quoting two pages from *What Life Should Mean to You*.[44]

Adler first visited America in the winter of 1926–27 and was astounded by the warmth and scope of his reception. Lecturing to packed auditoriums in New York, Philadelphia, Boston, Chicago, Detroit, and smaller cities in the Northeast and Midwest, he exulted in letters to his family that the Americans were "spoiling" him by their lavish attention. After he returned to Vienna, he spent much of his time telling his colleagues how much more prepared for psychology the Americans were than the Europeans, and he emphasized that American parents paid more attention to their children and American educators inculcated mental hygiene in the schools more than their counterparts in Europe. Adler enjoyed speaking before all kinds of audiences, be they professors, administrators, doctors, teachers, parents, or anyone else with an interest in the development of healthy self-esteem in children, a topic that Americans valued. His message was simpler and more optimistic than Freud's; it also had more appeal for women (Adler emphasized the problem of masculine dominance and arbitrary gender roles) and less emphasis on childhood sexuality. All these characteristics made Adler's doctrine remarkably attractive to a middle-class public concerned about public schools and proper parenting and eager, in a society of individualist competition, to hear about how to reconcile the human urge to domination with the ethics of duty and social obligation. Adler visited again in 1928 and then moved to the United States the following year, establishing a residence on Gramercy Park North in midtown Manhattan. In 1933 he filed papers of intent to become an American citizen, and in 1935, when conditions for Jews deteriorated in Austria, he succeeded in bringing his estranged wife Raissa, a dedicated Communist and friend of Trotsky, and two of his four grown children, Alexandra and Kurt Adler, to join him in America.[45]

Unlike Freud, Adler did not like to write and did not write gracefully, which left a burden on his translators, especially Walter Béran Wolfe, his most valuable disciple. Because Wolfe died young (he was killed in an automobile accident in Switzerland when he was thirty-five), we have little biographical information about him. He was born in Vienna in 1900 to Maria (Béran) and Dr. Alexander Wolfe. The family immigrated to the United States when Walter was a boy. He grew up in St. Louis, graduated from Dartmouth College, and, returning to St. Louis, received his M.D. from the Washington University School of Medicine in 1924. After being commissioned a lieutenant in the U.S. Navy medical corps and serving as chief of the psychiatric ward at the naval hospital in San Diego, he took up postgraduate study in 1926 at the University of Vienna. In Vienna he got to know Adler and began assisting at his innovative child guidance clinics there, subsequently conducting child clinics in Paris and London as well. On returning to America, Wolfe maintained institutional connections with the Jewish world in New York, serving as psychiatrist for the Jewish Board of Guardians, as assistant psychiatrist at the mental hygiene clinic of Mt. Sinai Hospital, and director of the child guidance clinic of Beth Israel Hospital. A writer of poetry during his college days, Wolfe had just the right set of talents as a psychiatrist and author to provide a literary platform for Adler in America. One of Adler's close friends and first biographer, the English novelist Phyllis Bottome, lauded young Wolfe's translations for their "brilliant and living style and close approximation of Adler's own way of thinking." Wolfe managed to unravel Adler's dense German in such as way as to capture "the very essence and spirit of Adler himself." His death deprived Adlerian psychology of its most forceful American exponent.[46]

In addition to maintaining a thriving private practice at his upper East Side residence, Walter Béran Wolfe became a notable popularizer of psychology in his own right. In fairly rapid succession he produced *How to Be Happy Though Human* (1931), *Calm Your Nerves* (1933), *A Woman's Best Years: The Art of Staying Young* (1934), and the posthumously published *Successful Living* (1938), edited by his wife, Florence Topal Wolfe. Wolfe's experience of the powerful public response to Adler in the late 1920s convinced him that "the intelligent layman is interested . . . to know the whys and the wherefores of human behavior as never before in history." "It is to meet this need," he wrote in his first and most comprehensive book, "that the author has essayed the task of writing a Baedeker of the soul."[47]

Wolfe embellished Adler not only stylistically but also thematically. He liked to discuss personal development through the metaphor of self-sculpture: like the sculptor who studied all aspects of the craft in order to produce a thing of beauty, the individual needed to defeat ignorance and fear, the two most lethal enemies of mental health, in order to gain a rich knowledge of the world and its details. That pursuit of knowledge and experience required courage to break old patterns of behavior that locked one into stale convention. "You, as an individual citizen of this world, cannot be happy," he contended, "unless you are interested in the why and wherefore of the gang, of college suicides, prostitution, homosexuality, racketeering, war, prohibition, child labor, or religious persecution." The "first step in the fine art of being a complete human being," Wolfe claimed, was "the cultivation of awareness and interest in all that concerns humanity and the development of your sensitivity to new stimuli." The prerogative of maleness that the first generation of popular psychologists shared was expressed very clearly in Wolfe's treatise to his female clientele, *A Woman's Best Years*, a book that sold briskly, going through no fewer than eight printings in its first year. As a Jewish immigrant, Wolfe had good reason to emphasize that his advice about meaningful aging applied universally to "Rebecca Goldberg in the Bronx, Rosa Bernardino in Boston, Gretchen Jensen in Minneapolis, Mary O'Neill in Dallas, and Cora Dean in San Francisco," while as a male he tacitly assumed the right to define universals of behavior for women.[48]

PSYCHOLOGY AS A WEAPON AGAINST CHRISTIAN AUTHORITY

It will be fitting to recall here that popular psychology included many books by both psychologists and laypeople with explicit Christian preferences. In *Outwitting Our Nerves* (1922), for example, a best-seller that presented a version of Freudian psychology, psychiatrist Josephine Jackson argued that Christianity established "the highest ideal of character," which could help people in their effort to sublimate aggressive inner drives. Another popularization of Freud extolled "a certain Nazarene." In addition to making novel connections between Christianity and Freudianism, popular psychology sometimes urged readers to embrace Jesus as psychological healer or, on a darker note, assembled psychological data in an apocalyptic message about the decline of a godless America. Books of self-culture, which discussed self-improvement in nonpsychological language, also wandered into overt Christianity, sometimes affirming that "Christ unifies life for us."[49]

In this context, it was significant that Jewish authors not only abstained from Christian references but made Jewish ones. When Boris Sidis cited Maimonides, Ibn Gabirol, and Solomon Maimon as philosophical authorities in his *Foundations of Normal and Abnormal Psychology*, it was clear that a new element had entered the genre. Sensitive to customary Christian biases, these Jewish experts cited Hebrew scripture rather than the Gospels, and invoked the principle of Jewish moral "genius," sometimes with a slight polemical edge. The Golden Rule, Brill lectured, was "preached by Judaism long before Jesus uttered it in slightly changed phraseology in his Sermon on the Mount." Myerson made the same point by omission: "If the Greeks gave to the world beauty and attempted to give rationality and science, the Jews gave a penetrating insight into life, a code of morals, and the first passionate cries against human injustice and human misery."[50]

Jewish psychological thinkers entered an already existing battle between science and Christianity for the minds and souls of Americans. As early as 1890 Joseph Jastrow was asked to contribute to one of the first books in the United States to bring psychology and religion into the same arena: *Epitomes of Three Sciences: Comparative Philology, Psychology, and Old Testament History*. The volume's editor was Paul Carus (1852–1919), the scion of a distinguished family of German scholars and ministers, whose liberal views led him to resign a teaching post in Dresden and immigrate to the United States. Carus edited *The Open Court* and *The Monist,* two periodicals that propagated a "scientific conception of God as the impersonal world-order," and he also headed a Chicago publishing firm that produced classics in philosophy and science. His literary output was such that Carus "exercised a wide popular influence on behalf of a more rational attitude toward religion and ethics." With his 1890 anthology Carus enlisted the new psychology of Joseph Jastrow in his intellectual crusade: "Modern psychology will influence the religious development of humanity in no less a degree than modern astronomy has done. At first sight the new truths seem appalling. . . . However, a closer acquaintance with the modern solutions of the problems of soul-life shows, that, instead of destroying religion, they place it upon a firmer foundation than it ever before possessed."[51]

Jastrow's direct contribution, an overview of the development of modern psychology, was much less significant than his silent participation in a surprising theological debate that took place in the book's preface. Carl Heinrich Cornill, the illustrious German Protestant Bible critic who contributed the essay on Old Testament history, introduced his analysis with a gratuitous statement about the inferiority of the Hebrew scriptures to the Gospels. Cornill argued that the New Testament should be exempt from historical criticism, which would force it "down to the plane of the Old, whose inferior moral viewpoint is more congenial to the carnal side of human nature than the rigider, higher demands of Jesus." But Old Testament criticism was good because it liberated Christians: "It teaches us to understand and recognize as conditioned by time and historical circumstance that which otherwise is obscure and often actually repulsive, and it exonerates us from defending as Christian doctrine that in the Old Testament which is purely and specifically Jewish."[52]

In what amounted to a pre-emptive strike against the Protestant scholar, Carus prefaced Cornill's views with a claim of his own. "We look upon the New Testament in exactly the same light that Professor Cornill regards the Old Testament. . . . There are Jewish rabbis who, though they have no New Testament which they look upon as a fulfillment of the Old, accept the results of modern critical research as regards their own sacred scriptures; and yet their religion is not destroyed in this way." One of those rabbis was Marcus Jastrow, whose son Joseph may have advised Carus on this matter.[53]

When Carus passed from the scene after World War I, a Jewish publisher appeared with a similar sense of mission and an even greater appeal to an American audience that had tired of Christian pieties. Born Emanuel Julius into a Russian Jewish immigrant home in Philadelphia, Emanuel Haldeman-Julius (1889–1951) invented the Little Blue Books that saturated the American market in the 1920s and 1930s. A freethink-ing journalist who married a freethinking niece of Jane Addams, Marcet Haldeman, and agreed to hyphenate their new last name, Haldeman-Julius wrote for socialist newspapers in New York, Milwaukee, Chicago, and Los Angeles. True to his political commitments, he uprooted himself from city life and moved to Girard, Kansas, in 1915 in order to save the socialist paper *Appeal to Reason* from extinction. With money borrowed from his wife, who had inherited her family's bank in Girard, Haldeman-Julius bought the *Appeal to Reason* publishing plant and, in 1919, realized his dream of publishing inexpensive, 3 ½" × 5" numbered editions of literary classics for the intellectual satisfaction of the common man (booklet No. 1 was Oscar Wilde's *Ballad of Reading Gaol*). Seeing himself as a successor to Voltaire and Paine, Haldeman-Julius launched a thirty-year freethinking crusade against religious dogma in general and Chris-tianity in particular. Like Carus before him, Haldeman-Julius worshiped at the altar of science and defied the idols of irrationalism. His "Univer-sity in Print," the Little Blue Books, included more than two thousand titles and stacked up sales—amazingly—in the hundreds of millions.[54]

Haldeman-Julius belonged to an impressive group of Jewish entrepre-neurs who transformed the culture of print between the 1910s and 1940s. Their enterprises included the publishing houses of Alfred Knopf, Simon and Schuster, Viking, Random House, Boni and Liveright, Greenberg, Covici-Friede, Crown, Avon, Dial, Praeger, and Frederick Ungar, as well as the Book-of-the-Month Club and the Literary Guild. Some of those companies introduced a European and cosmopolitan quality into American publishing, while others became dynamos of the best-seller. Haldeman-Julius followed his own lights, aiming not to satisfy but to reshape mass tastes. He zeroed in like a zealot on "all forms of Christianity, be it Protestantism or Catholicism" for "the doses of poison" that the public "has been forced to swallow at the hands of religious mugwumps and charlatans." "The skeptic might be less inclined to scoff at the 'experience' of Christians," he wrote in regard to the Christian conversion experience, "if psychologists had not shown us the perversi-ties and peculiarities of the human mind, especially when under the sway of a highly emotional atmosphere of mysticism."

Completing the attack on Christian prerogative that opened in the Carus-Jastrow collaboration of 1890, the Little Blue Books subjected Jesus himself to psychiatric examination. When that exercise stimulated debate, Haldeman-Julius responded dryly: "The modern psychologist can only say that, if Jesus was the kind of man he is portrayed to have been, he was a crazy man." The Little Blue Books conveyed the same vehemence that the evangelicalism of the 1920s elicited from Sinclair Lewis and H. L. Mencken, but they also distilled an American Jewish propensity to identify the "true" values of America with those leaders who had ceased to be true Christians. Criticizing conventional associations of goodness with Christian piety, Haldeman-Julius wrote: "Speaking of Good men and patriots, what of Thomas Paine, Thomas Jefferson, Benjamin Franklin, George Washington? All of them . . . were un-Christian skeptics. . . . Lincoln was a good man, a man for whom I have again and again expressed my admiration—and Lincoln was not a Christian but a free thinker."[55]

From Joseph Jastrow to Emanuel Haldeman-Julius, Jews showed themselves eager to enter the marketplace of readers and, in that arena, to use psychology as a weapon against Christian domination of American culture. We should not be surprised, then, to find tensions and arguments between Jews and Christians surfacing in modern and apparently secular theories about the psyche and the social order.[56]

To the degree that their ideas of human nature and the psyche derived from their religious or moral heritage, the Jewish rationalist morality in which these men were raised began to surface in American popular thought. We have seen how some of those Jewish nuances appeared in secular form, but in the next two chapters we will gain a much fuller sense of the importance of ethnic and religious factors in American understandings of the psyche.

Hugo Münsterberg in 1901, probably the best-known psychologist in the United States before World War I. (Courtesy of the Harvard University Archives.)

Hugo Münsterberg with actress Anita Stewart on the movie set of the
Vitagraph Company in 1915. Münsterberg pioneered not only in the
psychological study of the industrial and legal system but also of the
movies, a medium that few scholars took seriously at the time. (Courtesy of
the Harvard University Archives.)

Joseph Jastrow, ca. 1900, the most prolific popularizer of psychology in the
United States between 1890 and 1940. (Courtesy of Duke University, Rare
Book, Manuscript, and Special Collections Library, Durham, North Carolina.)

Rachel Szold Jastrow, ca. 1895. Like her husband, Rachel Jastrow was from a learned, religious family, and she kept Joseph in contact with Jewish affairs. Her father was a prominent rabbi and her sister, Henrietta, founded the women's Zionist organization Hadassah. (Courtesy of Duke University, Rare Book, Manuscript, and Special Collections Library, Durham, North Carolina.)

Marcus Jastrow, ca. 1895. Joseph Jastrow's father, Marcus was an eminent rabbi and Talmudist. (Courtesy of Duke University, Rare Book, Manuscript, and Special Collections Library, Durham, North Carolina.)

Abraham Arden Brill. ca. 1905. Brill was Freud's first translator for the American market and the leading popularizer of Freudianism in the United States. (Courtesy of the Library of Congress.)

Abraham Brill's Orthodox father in Austro-Hungarian Galicia, perhaps
as he looked when his teenage son immigrated alone to America in 1889.
(Courtesy of the Library of Congress.)

Isador H. Coriat, ca. 1935. With A. A. Brill, Coriat was one of the most important disseminators of Freudiansim in America and author of the first popular book explaining Freud's theory of dreams to the lay reader. Photo by Fabian Bachrach (Reproduced by permission of the Boston Medical Library in the Francis A. Countway Library of Medicine.)

Kurt Lewin, ca. 1940. A refugee from Nazi Germany, Lewin produced highly influencial studies of authoritarian versus democratic styles of behavior and of the psychological dilemmas of ethnic minorities. (Courtesy of the Archives of the History of American Psychology—The University of Akron.)

Chapter 7

The Moronic Immigrant
and the Neurotic Jew:
Jews and American Perceptions
of Intelligence,
Personality, and Race

IN THE AUTUMN OF 1947 the ABC radio program *America's Town Meeting of the Air* conducted a forum called "What Can We Do to Improve Race and Religious Relationships in America?" One of the show's speakers, civic leader Charles Taft, son of a former U.S. president, announced, "I can help more tonight by talking, not about results of discrimination and prejudice, but about how and why people act that way." Prejudice, he continued, had not only economic and social but also psychological roots.

> Psychologists call it frustration. Watch the child that's punished by the bigger adult, his father or mother even, who then kicks the door or beats up the little neighbor who is unlucky enough to come along at just that moment. The "poor white" relieves his inferiority by looking down on the Negro; the German defeated in the first war by persecuting the Jews. Now unfortunately all of us individuals suffer in some degree from such states of mind and each one of us may unconsciously contribute thus to the volume of intolerance.

Taft's "interrogator" that evening, political commentator Max Lerner, agreed that psychology offered answers to the age-old problem but he made a more provocative analysis.

> What we're dealing with is not simply certain elements in human nature, Mr. Taft, I'm afraid. What we're dealing with is a specific neurosis, perhaps even a psychosis. . . . A neurosis, remember, which in Europe was capable of killing off six million Jews in cold blood, of burning them in the furnaces, of putting them into chambers that killed them—that kind of neurosis. I think it's true that we in America haven't begun to reach that extreme state of the neurosis, but I think also that we must examine our consciences and our hearts to find out why the germs of it are there.[1]

In the United States, World War II sparked strong public interest in the psychodynamics of prejudice and brutality, but Jewish thinkers had begun to use psychology to understand and combat prejudice decades earlier, largely because psychology itself was used as an instrument of prejudice. Jews were certainly not the only targets of discriminatory science, but they were the only ethnic minority (in Europe and the United States) for whom the practice of psychology became a critical means of protest against inimical views and policies.

The ethnic context of American psychological ideas is nowhere more evident than in the effort of experts to classify the intelligence and characteristics of different "racial" groups. Modern psychology raised momentous questions about whether ethnic groups inherited distinct intellectual abilities and personality traits, and leading psychological theorists often proved unable to separate personal biases from scientific conclusions.

Two allegations elicited a vocal response from a variety of Jewish thinkers who spearheaded a new American approach to the question of "racial" traits. One accusation held that immigrants and blacks were innately less intelligent than native-born white Americans, and the other claimed that Jews were innately neurotic. To refute those charges, Jewish intellectuals and psychological thinkers attacked the idea of genetically determined ethnic traits and insisted that social and cultural factors strongly affected a person's mental and emotional make-up. They found support in the American functionalist ideal, with its emphasis on the adaptable individual in an evolving society. The Jewish immigrant, they argued, exemplified the kind of adaptability that life in urban America demanded. As for Jewish neurosis, the popularizers of psychology developed a two-pronged argument—they denied that Jewish nervousness was an innate characteristic but also claimed that it included an admirable intellectuality and sensitivity, which Americans should emulate. In short, Jewish thinkers wanted to redefine American ideas of a healthy personality. That effort gained additional momentum during the interwar period when, in response to the rise of fascism and antisemitism, they used psychology to redefine bigotry as a psychopathic trait.

THE IRON CAGE OF INTELLIGENCE

The history of intelligence testing, one of psychology's most significant applications, is inseparable from the history of European and American racialism. The "father" of psychometric racism was Englishman Francis Galton (1822–1911), a gifted cousin of Charles Darwin who loved numbers and measurement as much as he loved his genealogy. In the 1880s Galton conducted a mammoth statistical study of Londoners, which he used to corroborate a theory he had laid out years earlier: intelligence was strictly hereditary and fixed according to race and social class. Galton disregarded the possibility that environmental influences such as wealth and social advantage might affect one's measurable intellectual achievements. His approach inspired a generation of American psychologists to do as he did and convert social prejudices into statistical measurements of mental aptitude.[2]

In the United States mental testing quickly became embroiled in the politics of immigration and race. The key figure in that story was Henry Goddard, one of the more prominent Ph.D.'s to come out of the prestigious psychology program at Clark University. Goddard worked at the Vineland Training School for the Feeble-Minded in southern New Jersey during the first years of the century. Adapting the innovative intelligence tests of French psychologist Alfred Binet, Goddard divided the Vineland students into three mental classes, which he designated as mental ages: idiots (mental age of 1–2), imbeciles (mental age of 3–7), and morons, a word he invented from the Greek term for "foolish" (mental age 8–12). Moron was the critical category, Goddard believed, because people so classified appeared to be normal, marrying inconspicuously and producing defective children who caused most of society's problems. In 1912 Goddard began administering mental tests to immigrants at Ellis Island and concluded that a high percentage of newcomers were morons. Although the total number of deportees from Ellis Island remained comparatively small—less than 3 percent—and most of those were not rejected for mental reasons, Goddard's testing program was a bad omen for immigrants.[3]

The men who followed Goddard's lead shared his hereditarian assumptions and stubborn refusal to consider an individual's background and circumstances. Stanford professor Lewis Terman, creator of the Stanford-Binet intelligence test and the leader of American intelligence testers, predicted in his influential 1916 book *The Measurement of Intelligence* that "there will be discovered enormously significant racial differences in general intelligence, differences which cannot be wiped out by any scheme of mental culture." A year later World War I gave American psychologists an unparalleled opportunity to demonstrate their importance as judges of intelligence. The U.S. Army commissioned Harvard psychologist Robert Yerkes, the president of the American Psychological Association, to operate a special testing unit that would classify soldiers according to their cognitive and perceptual abilities. Between the autumn of 1917 and the war's end the following fall, Yerkes and his corps of psychologists tested more than 1.7 million soldiers. Like Goddard and Terman, Yerkes thought that nationalities differed innately in intelligence, and he interpreted the Army test scores as proof that men of southern and eastern European descent (i.e., the "new" immigrants) were less intelligent than those of "Nordic" origin. Although the military debated the usefulness of intelligence tests for the placement of soldiers, the successful administration of so many tests in such a short time enhanced the prestige of psychology as an instrument for assessing individual aptitudes on a large scale. After the war, intelligence and personality testing enjoyed a boom; universities, public schools, and businesses used them to screen and place applicants. The sudden prestige of mental testing presented a serious problem for America's ethnic minorities.[4]

One member of Yerkes's team of Army testers, Princeton psychologist Carl Brigham, put those statistics to polemical use. At the peak of the immigration restriction movement, Brigham published *A Study of American Intelligence* (1923), which claimed that the Army tests proved native-born whites (Nordics) mentally superior to immigrants from eastern and southern Europe (Alpine and Mediterranean), who were in turn superior to blacks. He buttressed his argument with lengthy quotations from Madison Grant's *The Passing of the Great Race* (1916), the handbook of American racialism and nativism in the 1920s. In the tradition of Francis Galton, Brigham did not allow the hypothesis that anything other than genetics might account for differences in the way people responded to mental tests. Hence his gymnastic efforts to avoid the fact that immigrants who resided in the United States for sixteen to twenty years (i.e., those raised in America) scored the same as native-born whites, and his attempt to repudiate studies showing Jews equaling native-born whites in intelligence. Brigham dubiously concluded that Jews had a low average intelligence but a greater variability, which explained the examples of genius found by "investigators searching for talent in New York City and California schools."[5]

The force of psychological statistics overwhelmed the objections of America's deeper thinkers, who saw crude racial stereotyping beneath the stuffy charts of the country's mental technocrats. In 1908, before the mental testers had really gotten started, Harvard philosopher Josiah Royce came out with the eloquent *Race Questions, Provincialism and Other American Problems*, which exposed the dubious validity of racial theories of personality and ability. "The *Rassentheoretiker* [race theorist] frequently uses his science to support most of his personal prejudices," Royce observed, "and is praised by his sympathizers almost equally for his exact knowledge and for his vigorous display of temperament."

> I begin to wonder whether a science which mainly devotes itself to proving that we ourselves are the salt of the earth, is after all so exact as it aims to be. It is with some modern race-theories, as it is with some forms of international yacht racing. I know nothing about yachting; but whenever any form of the exalted sport of international yachting proves to be definable as a sort of contest in which the foreigner is invariably beaten, I for my part take no interest in learning more about the rules of that particular game.

"Our psychology is far too infantile a science," Royce continued, "to give us any precise information as to the way in which the inherited, the native, the constitutional aspects of the minds of men really vary with their complexions or with their hair." He insisted, however, that mental degeneracy was not a monopoly of any one race of people. When it appeared on a large scale it resulted from external conditions "of oppression and of other causes of degradation . . . continued through the generations."[6]

As Jews began to protest the racialist theories of prominent psychologists, they differed from Royce in two respects: they anchored their objections in the new theories of psychology and social science, and spoke from the vantage point of the outsider. While understanding the need of the immigrant to adapt to American society, they were more emotionally engaged than Royce with the predicament of the newcomer and they argued more vociferously, if not more elegantly, for a realignment of American values in order to accommodate the outsider.

Jews were remarkably prominent in the battle against racialist theories of intelligence. The two best-known opponents were journalist Walter Lippmann and anthropologist Franz Boas. In a series he wrote for the *New Republic* (of which he was a founder) in the fall of 1922, Lippmann decried the "gross perversion" of intelligence statistics by "muddle-headed and prejudiced men." He acknowledged that the Stanford-Binet tests might be useful for the placement of children in public schools but warned that "great mischief will follow if there is confusion about the spiritual meaning of this reform. If, for example, the impression takes root that these tests really measure intelligence, that they constitute a sort of last judgment on the child's capacity, that they reveal 'scientifically' his predestined ability, then it would be a thousand times better if all the intelligence testers and all their questionnaires were sunk without warning in the Sargasso Sea." With characteristic eloquence, Lippmann exposed the inability of the tests to measure intelligence, which had not been adequately defined to begin with, and to establish any claims about the hereditary nature of intelligence. He remarked on "how easily the intelligence test can be turned into an engine of cruelty . . . into a method of stamping a permanent sense of inferiority upon the soul of a child." Naming Stanford's Lewis Terman and Columbia's Edward Thorndike, Lippmann charged "the more prominent testers" with propagating a "dogma" that "could not but lead to an intellectual caste system in which the task of education had given way to the doctrine of predestination and infant damnation."[7]

Lippmann had a strong ally in the pioneering anthropologist Franz Boas (1858–1942). Because the Army intelligence tests gave such powerful, ostensibly scientific support to racism, Boas and his students made them a special target. A German Jew who had immigrated to the United States in the 1880s to escape the reactionary nationalism and antisemitism of Wilhelmine Germany, Boas boldly challenged the racialism that permeated European and American social science at the turn of the century. As early as 1904 he questioned America's cherished belief in the biological inferiority of African Americans, and in a powerful article on "The American People" (1909) he pierced the myth of a "pure" European or American race that would degenerate from intermixture with immigrants and blacks. Boas revolutionized American social thought by demonstrating in a variety of anthropometric and ethnographic studies that the environment in which people lived strongly affected both their physical and mental development. Culture, Boas argued, not race, explained the variety of human behavior.[8]

In 1908, starting with a sample of Jewish students in New York City, Boas initiated a massive, historic study of the physical proportions of the children of immigrants (the data encompassed nearly 18,000 people). To the astonishment of social scientists, Boas showed that the bodily form of the descendants of immigrants, including the shape of the head—which had been thought to be virtually unchanging within racial groups—changed noticeably as a result of the generational change from the Old World to the American environment. He noted also that the children of different nationalities tended to look more like each other, and like other Americans, than was true of their parents. Although Boas's new cultural anthropology did not stop the immigration restriction movement, by the late 1920s it had begun to affect other social scientists, including psychologists, who began to retreat from the old racialist interpretation of intelligence.[9]

One of Boas's students, psychologist Otto Klineberg (1899–1992), produced especially potent critiques of racialist assumptions about intelligence. A Canadian Jew with an M.D. from McGill University in Montreal, Klineberg earned a Ph.D. in psychology from Columbia in 1927. During his graduate studies, he attended anthropology classes given by Boas and was transformed by the experience. The Boas effect registered in Klineberg's dissertation, "An Experimental Study of Speed and Other Factors in 'Racial' Differences," which suggested that the very notion of speed in test-taking had to be scrutinized. Klineberg administered intelligence tests to three different groups of children—Yakima Indians, African Americans, and whites—and found that the white children consistently completed the task more quickly than the others. He observed, however, that the Yakima and the black children ignored the time element even when urged to perform as quickly as possible. When the time element was removed from the testing procedure, they did as well or better than their white peers. Tests that purported to measure intelligence, Klineberg argued, actually measured the social and cultural background of the test-taker. A misnomer often freighted with malice, "racial" really referred to cultural differences.

In his next project, *Negro Intelligence and Selective Migration* (1935), Klineberg tackled the popular argument of "selective migration," which psychologists used to explain the fact that African Americans in the northern states scored higher than their southern counterparts on intelligence tests. According to the racialist interpretation, that discrepancy meant that northern blacks were a special rather than a typical population: the most intelligent people had left the South for the opportunities of the North. Comparing the records of schoolchildren in both regions, Klineberg found no evidence that the smartest left the South. The superior environment of the North, not inborn racial traits, explained the superior scores of the northerners.[10]

In 1935 Klineberg produced a book, *Race Differences*, which dynamited the old racialist mythology. Opening with an overview of racial theories throughout history, Klineberg reminded Americans that virtually every civilization developed theories to explain its own superiority and the comparative inferiority of others. He undermined the pseudoscience of the two most influential race theorists, the Frenchman Arthur Joseph de Gobineau (1816–82) and the Germanophile Englishman Houston Stewart Chamberlain (1855–1927), by recalling such gems of analysis as Chamberlain's explanation that, even though Jews were not easy to distinguish from Germans, "when one of them enters a room, a German child, usually a girl, will unaccountably begin to cry." "The serious student demands objectivity," Klineberg insisted, "and will not content himself with value-judgments that cannot be verified." Openly criticizing policies such as immigration restriction and segregation that were based on racialist assumptions of human behavior, he tersely concluded, "there is no scientific proof of racial differences in mentality. . . . Our racial and national stereotypes—the 'pictures in our minds' of the Oriental, the Italian, the Jew, the Mexican—will be wrong much more often than right; they are based on current opinions which have never been verified, and they cannot be trusted in the treatment of human beings."[11]

Klineberg's writings had a powerful effect on scholars in the 1930s, well after the Johnson-Reed immigration restriction act of 1924, but Jewish popular psychologists had been publicly challenging race and intelligence testing since the 1910s. Isador Coriat referred to the tests as "practically worthless," and Boris Sidis called them "silly, pedantic, absurd, and grossly misleading." In a 1914 review for *Science* on "Heredity and Mental Traits," Jastrow cautioned psychologists that they had not created "a proper mode of recognition of the presence of the inherited traits," which, he emphasized, "are not as obvious as tallness or color in peas." In the 1920s, alongside Watson's behaviorism, which gave everything to environment and nothing to heredity, Alfred Adler's Individual Psychology acknowledged heredity without giving it determinative force on human development. "The thesis advanced by the group of psychological thinkers known as the Individual Psychologists," Adler declared in *Harper's Monthly Magazine,*

> —the thesis that talent is not inherited, and that the possibilities and potentialities of any individual for performance are not fixed—has been a bombshell in the camp of the old-line academic psychologists. . . . I have always found, particularly in Vienna, that the classes for talented children consisted mostly of relatively well-nourished individuals from the better classes, whereas in the untalented classes the poorly fed and poorly dressed children of the proletariat were to be found. . . . We can never tell what actions will characterize a man if we know only whence he comes. . . . The inherited instruments with which we fight the battle of life are very varied. *How we use these instruments,* however, is the important thing.[12]

In response to Brigham's provocative *Study of American Intelligence,* Abraham Myerson was singularly vocal. He challenged both the methodology of intelligence testing and Brigham's refusal to admit what the army tests clearly suggested: the "intelligence" of immigrants had to be environmentally sensitive because immigrants scored higher the longer they lived in the United States. Myerson cited the Jews as a prime example of such adaptation.

> We are very familiar with one large alien group, and we can state . . . that . . . if adaptation is the very hallmark of intelligence, then there has been a growth of innate intelligence in the space of one generation, which Dr. Brigham and the type of thinker he represents would be the first to deny as impossible. . . . One of the latest developments in psychology, the intelligence tests . . . *might be used—and in fact are being used, we believe by certain people—not to advance science or in the scientific spirit, but for race discrimination and in the spirit of propaganda.*[13]

Myerson was challenging psychological methodology on the grounds that it failed to understand subjects in their social context. He elaborated the point about Jewish adaptability in one of his books for the general public, *The Foundations of Personality* (1921), in which he insisted that "social heredity," rather than racial biology, explained human development: "Here is a race, the Jew, which in the Ghetto and under circumstances that built up a tremendously powerful set of traditions and customs developed a very distinctive type of human being. . . . With the old social heredity still at work, another set of customs, traditions and beliefs comes into open competition with it in the bosom of the American Jew. Nowhere is the struggle between the old and the new generations so intense as in the home of the Orthodox Jew." The second generation of Jewish men, Myerson explained, shaved their beards, abandoned or slackened their observance of the kosher dietary laws, and took up sports, while maintaining a love of scholarship. The Jews' "production of scholars and scientists" in the younger generation demonstrated their adaptability, but

> the remarkable rise of the Jewish prize fighter stands out as a divergence from tradition that mocks at theories of inborn racial characters. And a third generation differs in customs, manners, ideals, purposes and physique but little from the social class of Americans in which the individual members move.... A new social heredity has overcome—or at least in part supplanted—another social heredity and released and developed characters hitherto held in check. In every human being ... there are potential lines of development far outnumbering those that can be manifested, and each environment and tradition calls forth some and suppresses others.[14]

This was an important, perhaps unprecedented, invocation of cultural-historical factors as necessary for understanding personal development. Through their critique of the methodology of intelligence testing, Jews positioned themselves as leaders of a heterodox movement within American psychology, one that rejected the dominant approach of measuring intelligence and personality traits without factoring in the social background of the subject.[15]

Myerson's argument in defense of the Jewish immigrant exemplified the functionalist approach to human behavior that John Dewey championed. People in motion, not in castes, people adapting to a fluid social order, not petrifying into a rigid class system—this was the proper subject and the proper end of a practical, democratic psychology. Myerson's fellow Jews, in their heady and rapid adaptation to America, gave him the evidence he needed, and he gave them the theory on which their future depended.

Myerson injected the same polemical verve into the controversy over sterilization of the mentally deficient, long a pet project of the eugenicists. Between 1907 and 1935 roughly two dozen states passed laws allowing sterilization of the institutionalized feeble-minded, insane, epileptic, and, in a few cases, "moral degenerates and sexual perverts." Most institutional psychiatrists accepted the basic idea of eugenics—the creation of a smarter and nobler population through social engineering—and did not oppose proposals for sterilization of the mentally unfit. Myerson's influential study *The Inheritance of Mental Diseases* (1925) challenged hereditarian theories, opposed sterilization, and made him the most prominent opponent of such practices.

In the 1930s controversy erupted over a sterilization law proposed by members of the Galton Society, the home of those scientists who advocated "the right of every race to maintain its racial purity" through "migration control and selective breeding." The law in question would have authorized the state to sterilize any "socially inadequate person" who did not "maintain himself or herself as a useful member of the organized social life of the state." Myerson was quick to point out that "in Hitler's Germany, the Jew at one fell swoop is declared as of no value to the state," and that such a law would allow a majority in America "to decree by whatever means the nonpropagation of Italians, Jews and Negroes." "Any group that becomes dominant in the United States may declare all others alien to the fourth generation," Myerson railed, "and only the persons whose prolific ancestors came over in the remarkably small Mayflower can qualify as members of the American race." As the controversy raged, the American Neurological Association appointed Myerson chair of an investigative committee of three physicians and a geneticist, which published its findings in 1936. Myerson's committee solidly opposed involuntary sterilization and warned that existing scientific knowledge on the inheritance of mental disease was meager.[16]

Myerson's most ingenious contribution to American ideas about intelligence may have come in his study of the psychiatric histories of a number of America's leading families. Myerson discovered many cases of psychiatric hospitalization in those histories, especially manic-depressive disorders, and many recorded cases of aberrant behavior that would later have been classified as mental disorders. In a thinly veiled depiction of William James's family, for example, Myerson related the family history of "an immigrant . . . of great drive and intelligence" who produced an eminent son who suffered serious depressions and whose own children had their share of psychological afflictions including manic-depressive psychosis. In this clever reversal, he reminded his colleagues that immigrants—usually objectified by the eugenicists as a problematic population—fathered and mothered some of the nation's ideal figures. Shattering the eugenicist's premise of a naturally superior native elite, Myerson demonstrated that prestigious insiders as well as social outsiders contained genetic imperfections. "Had sterilization procedures of adequate type been carried out in the earlier part of the history of New England and of the United States," Myerson explained, "many highly important individuals and their family groups would not have appeared on the American scene, and consequently, it is very probable that . . . the development of the country would have been altered."[17]

THE MIXED BLESSING OF JEWISH NEUROSIS

The questions that Myerson raised in the intelligence and sterilization debates—about seeing individuals in their full social context, about the political uses of psychological data, and about the adaptability of Jewish immigrants—all surfaced even more conspicuously in another debate:

the problem of Jewish neurosis. In the 1880s, European psychiatry and anthropology began to identify Jews as prone to hysteria and neurasthenia and often explained the propensity genetically, as a condition produced by inbreeding. ("Neurasthenia" was a term coined by George Beard in 1869 to describe a state of nervous exhaustion; it fell into disuse in the early 1900s.) The notion of Jews as biologically and mentally impaired—oversexualized, ugly, and melancholic—had long been a staple of European thought. Although a panoply of antisemitic stereotypes crossed the Atlantic, Americans were less obsessed than Europeans with Jewish physicality and less vitriolic about Jews, who were only one of numerous stigmatized peoples. Nevertheless the stereotype of Jews as abnormally and problematically "nervous" gained a strong hold in the United States. As late as 1941 Otto Klineberg observed that "the racial literature is full of personality characterizations." Along with such notions as the "childlike cruelty of the Mediterraneans," the "irresponsibility of the Negro," and the "sense of honor of the Nordics," there persisted a belief in "the neuroticism of the Jew."[18]

To be more precise, a popular stereotype assigned Jews the twin traits of genius and neurosis (and this, despite the claims of intelligence testers that Jewish immigrants, like others, were mentally deficient). Historian Carl Wittke testified to that stereotype in his pioneering 1939 study of America's immigrants, *We Who Built America*, when he prefaced an account of the Jewish Lower East Side by commenting, "It is absurd, of course, to suppose that the ghetto swarms with nothing but geniuses." One of America's leading liberal ministers, John Haynes Holmes (who opened the doors of his Community Church in Manhattan to a clinic run by Walter Béran Wolfe), unassumingly entitled a chapter of *Through Gentile Eyes* (1938) "The Genius of the Jew." That chapter described the "primacy" of Jews "in worthy fields of human achievement" and "their possession of degrees of leadership out of all proportion to their actual numbers among mankind." A Jewish conceit helped sustain the notion of inherent collective genius, as Abraham Cahan illustrated through his protagonist David Levinsky, who expostulated on the mystique of talmudic reasoning:

> If it be true that our people represent an unusually high standard of mental aptitude, the distinction is probably due, to some extent at least, to the extremely important part which Talmud studies have played in the spiritual life of the race. . . . It is at once a fountain of moral and religious inspiration and a "brain-sharpener." "Can you fathom the sea? Neither can you fathom the depths of the Talmud," as we used to put it. We were sure that the highest mathematics taught in the Gentile universities was child's play compared to the Talmud.[19]

An instructive illustration of American images of the Jewish mind may be found in a book that scholars usually quote simply as evidence of nativism and antisemitism, Edward A. Ross's *The Old World in the New*. Tying intellectuality to a nervous temperament, Ross perceived Jews as "the polar opposite" of "the pioneer breed" of native Americans in respect to physique and temperament, because they were undersized, undermuscled, and "exceedingly sensitive to pain." Those features, though, did not sum up the Jews. "If the Hebrews are a race certainly one of their traits is *intellectuality*," wrote the Wisconsin sociologist, "the Russo-Jewish immigration is richer in gray matter than any other recent stream, and it may be richer than any large inflow since the colonial era." Mixed in with a hodgepodge of generalizations, some peculiar, some conventional, *adaptability* stands out as a paramount characteristic of Ross's Jew. Ross rooted Jewish adaptability in a particular kind of intelligence, one that grasped principles and universals. European racists had cultivated an image of Jews as natural abstract thinkers—gifted in mathematics, for example—but they associated that trait with inhuman coldness. Ross took a different, more positive view. As a strident reformer, he wrote appreciatively of the Jew that "he loves man rather than men, and from Isaiah to Karl Marx he holds the record in projects of social amelioration." "Flexible and rational," Ross continued, "the Jewish mind cannot be bound by conventions," and therein lay the Jew's "wonderful adaptability." The Jew shared with the native New Englander "his rationalism, his shrewdness, his inquisitiveness and acquisitiveness." Like the American founders, Jews possessed a tenacious intelligence that "masters circumstance instead of being dominated by it."[20]

In one of the first popular presentations of the work of Franz Boas, *McClure's* described Jewish mentality in a way that outdid Ross, who accepted the stereotype that Jewish intellectualism was accompanied by physical and emotional fragility. *McClure's* reported that from their oppression Jews had forged an especially efficient combination of mental and physical stamina. The stereotype of a Jewish physical "type," explained journalist Burton Hendrick, failed to withstand the evidence of the latest studies in physical anthropology, which showed that Jews displayed a full range of hair colors, facial shapes, and, most important, noses. "New York Jews Largely Blond, Blue-Eyed, and Straight-Nosed" was the subtitle that preceded Hendrick's observation that only a small percentage of Jews bore the "well-defined beaks that the comic papers attribute to the entire race," while "nearly sixty per cent of both Jews and Jewesses had that finely shaped straight nose that is commonly found in Greek sculpture." *McClure's* readers also learned that the smart Jew was not necessarily weak despite "the popular impression that the bright child is likely to be physically defective." According to "Professor Boas' investigations," Jews in America were physically stronger than their European parents and their mental achievement matched their physical prowess—"the child who is precocious mentally is also precocious physically." Even though Jews appeared more fragile than their gentile neighbors, they endured poor living conditions comparatively well. That physical endurance prompted "some scientists" to see "the great law of natural selection" in full operation—"in the face of ages of persecution and confinement within ghettos," Hendrick wrote, "the struggle for existence among the Jews has been so terrible that the weaker strains have been eliminated, leaving only the most efficient."[21]

Jews themselves parried the stereotype of Jewish nervousness in the same way, explaining its environmental causes and connecting it to the mythic notion of Jewish indomitability. As in the debate over intelligence, their defensive arguments had three focal points: the question of whether ethnic traits were inherited, the prospects for the assimilation of Jewish immigrants, and the historical-cultural context of Jewish neurosis.

Jewish psychological writers generally accepted the prevailing view that Jews, as a people, suffered from nervous disorders. "There need be no difference of opinion about the liability of the Jews to psychoneuroses," Myerson wrote. "Step into any clinic for nervous diseases in any large city in Europe or America and the Jew is unduly represented amongst the patients." Unlike their non-Jewish colleagues, however, Jewish doctors insisted that Americans properly contextualize the fact, which meant distinguishing between emotional disorders and other forms of mental illness, and understanding the environmental causes of maladies associated with Jews. In 1914 A. A. Brill published an impressive statistical comparison in response to the fact that "ever since modern psychiatry came into existence it has been understood that the Jews have contributed more to insanity than any other race." Based on statistics from New York City's institutionalized population, Brill established clearly that Jews had a substantially lower rate of insanity than the general population. "Alcoholic insanity," for example, proliferated among gentile patients but rarely appeared among Jews. While demolishing the insanity thesis, Brill acknowledged that Jews had a higher rate of manic depression and dementia praecox (schizophrenia). Those disorders, however, were classified as functional (amenable to psychotherapy) rather than organic.[22]

Arguments about Jewish neurosis highlighted the confusion surrounding the idea of race in the early twentieth century. From his investigations of cases of amaurotic family idiocy (Tay-Sachs disease) among immigrant Jews in Boston's Mt. Sinai Hospital, Isador Coriat commented, "Why amaurotic idiocy should be practically limited to Jewish families, is very difficult to understand unless we assume that the Jew possesses certain racial characteristics of organic inferiority through which he differs from the non-Jew." Later understood to be a genetic affliction of Ashkenazic Jews, the disease, marked by early blindness (hence "amaurotic"), mental deficiency, and death, prompted Coriat to consider the larger problem of endemic emotional problems in Jews. He recognized that the subject of "whether or not the Jew is a racial unity" was controversial and took no position on it. But he attributed the frequency of Tay-Sachs disease among Jews "to the fact that the Jew possesses a greater tendency to special types of organ inferiority in the central nervous system than the non-Jew." Having made that assumption, he relied on Adler's theory of organ inferiority to explain Jewish nervousness. "An organic or functional inferiority of the nervous system in certain individuals of Jewish birth or descent, probably explains the affective make-up of the Jew with his exaggerated emotional reactions. This elucidates his liability to . . . those disturbances of the sympathetic nervous system so often designated as Jewish neurasthenia or Hebraic debility."[23]

Though remaining cognizant of heredity as a possible factor, Jewish doctors emphasized the environmental causes of Jewish nervousness. If the primary explanation was in fact environmental, a more stable situation for Jews in America would diminish the number of neurotic personalities among them. Brill and Myerson explicitly addressed this question in the pages of *Mental Hygiene*, the organ of the influential National Committee for Mental Hygiene. Founded in 1917, the journal was aimed at virtually everyone concerned about the mental health of Americans: psychiatrists, psychologists, physicians, teachers, judges, and parents. Writing on "The Adjustment of the Jew to the American Environment," Brill's title brought to the forefront the question at the back of many people's minds: was Jewish neurosis an impediment to assimilation? Emphasizing that Jews were not particularly afflicted with *organic* (irremediable) mental problems, he explained that the *functional* nervous disorders comprised "those mental disturbances which are due mainly to mental conflicts."

> Individuals evincing this type of reaction are very sensitive mentally; they are unable to yield to strong but prohibited desires or to give vent to mental injuries through retaliation or other ways. They suffer in silence and then repress the desire or the mental injury into the unconscious part of the mind. Investigation shows that such repressions are not always successful, and that whenever they fail the result is either a mental or a nervous breakdown. It is from such forms of mental breakdown that the Jew suffers more than any other race.

"Jewish sensitiveness," concluded Brill, "is largely, if not wholly, the result of his past environment." Myerson concurred. Addressing the same audience two years later on "The 'Nervousness' of the Jew," he emphasized "how quickly racial characters can be changed under a fostering environment," as "exemplified by the development of the last generation in Jewish life in the free countries of Europe and America."[24]

Brill and Myerson followed the lead of Maurice Fishberg's influential anthropological study *The Jews: A Study of Race and Environment* (1911). Fishberg harnessed a battery of ethnographic and medical evidence to reject the theory that Jews constituted a separate race and to show how quickly they assimilated once they were allowed into modern society. He went so far as to suggest that Jews assimilated even more rapidly than "so called Aryan" immigrants—Germans and Austrians—who tended to preserve their native cultures. "Perhaps because the Jews have none of these national characteristics," he speculated, "they are more plastic and have a greater aptitude for adaptation to a new environment." Synthesizing and analyzing the psychiatric literature on Jewish neuroses, Fishberg noted that displays of hysterical emotion declined with assimilation, as Jews learned from "their Christian neighbours . . . that self-possession and calmness are usually of more benefit than alarm and excitement."[25]

Jewish psychological writers agreed that two forces had put the Jew under terrible mental pressure: Christianity and Judaism. They echoed an interesting apologia that dated back to eighteenth-century Germany, where Jewish physicians had begun to argue that Christian persecution and Jewish orthodoxy were responsible for mental disorders among Jews. Christian persecution, the argument went, forced the Jews into a fear-ridden, ghettoized way of life. Brill and Myerson candidly recounted the "oppressions and inhuman treatment from which the Jews have suffered for centuries." The result of this distressing history was a tendency among Jews toward apprehensiveness, melancholy, excessive familism, overdevelopment of urban habits and living by the wits, with a commensurate underdevelopment of the simplicity and physicality produced by rural life. A history of "fear emotions," Myerson suggested, "may, so far as we know, produce little by little permanent structural changes in the organism." Boris Sidis, who publicly recalled his memories of Russian pogroms, shared Myerson's concern in a popular book hypothesizing that all neurosis stems from the impulse of fear. And Isador Coriat linked Tay-Sachs disease to the mental strain endured by Russian Jews. He suspected that the parents of these unfortunate children "probably inherited a nervous disposition from their persecuted and maltreated ancestors."[26]

The other primary source of Jewish nervousness, according to these secular Jewish thinkers, was Orthodox Judaism. Like virtually all who had left the fold of rabbinic Judaism, the psychological writers believed that orthodox religion was fundamentally at odds with the modern societies in which emancipated Jews lived and worked. Unaware of the varieties of Orthodox Judaism, they interpreted "Jewish orthodoxy" to mean the cloistered religiosity of eastern Europe, steeped in suspicion of the out-side Christian world. Brill considered Jewish insularity the antithesis of mental health and highlighted the problem, ironically, with a quote from the rabbis: "The Talmudic saying, 'A pit cannot be filled from what has been taken from it,' is true psychologically." Most Western Jews no longer displayed the typology of the neurotic personality, Brill explained, but the Orthodox did. He likened the "voluntary clannish exclusiveness" of the Orthodox Jews to the mentality of the favorite child, who believes in his superiority to others. Both the favorite child and the Orthodox "are neurotic as a result of the conflicts between the taboos of the past and the demands of the present."[27]

The environmental causes of Jewish neurosis—Christian persecution and Jewish orthodoxy—had been identified, as had a solution: assimila-tion into modern society. But some of these thinkers went a step further, declaring that the American character would benefit from a touch of Jewish nervousness. Certain Jewish traits associated with the proverbial nervousness, they thought, were not all bad. The intense family life marked by extreme concern over the suffering of any member might stifle American individualism, but it had historically helped Jewish indi-viduals to survive. Walter Béran Wolfe criticized the "over-emphasis of the family" as a cause of neurosis, yet he extolled its historic value: "With-out the strong and beautiful family life in which individual Jews found the only available sphere of social significance, the Jews would have per-ished, and with them their valuable cultural contributions to our civiliza-tion." Wolfe gave psychological credentials to a widespread view of the Jewish family. As a Christian cleric declared at the 250th anniversary cele-bration of Jewish life in New York, "The integrity of the family for which the Jew has always stood, is a tradition which is of the deepest value in this day and nation."[28]

The same could be said of Jewish urbanism, another source of their nervousness. Though centuries of ghetto life may have accentuated that trait among Jews, Abraham Myerson reminded Americans that they themselves were rapidly urbanizing. They, too, were adapting habits that had enabled Jews to survive a more volatile environment. Sensitivity to one's fellows was essential to successful living in a crowded urban world, and Brill loved to talk about the gifts of the "neurotic" Jew in that regard. In a radio broadcast, "The Psychology of the Jew," Brill explained that, from living in a tense and sometimes hostile atmosphere, "the Jew learned to control his feelings and emotions better than the non-Jew." By that quality of self-control "the whole progress of civilization is mea-sured." Brill was fond of saying that his favorite people were neurotics, because he found them to be the most civilized. "Neurotics, or sensitive people (for that is the only difference between neurotics and ordinary individuals) vividly react to any manifestations of cruelty," he stressed in another radio broadcast. In Brill's cosmology, Jews and neurotics were gifted with the compassionate self-restraint on which modern urban civilization depended.[29]

Boris Sidis expressed a similar view in his theory of reserve energy, which focused on latent mental powers that people rarely tap. Sidis believed that the human brain was the same in primitive and sophisticated cultures: the "barbaric Teuton" and the modern German, for example, did not differ in their mental ability but in the degree to which they utilized stores of reserve energy. What determines whether a nation will tap its energy reserves? "Unusual combinations of circumstances, great radical changes of the environment," explained Sidis, because they "often loosen the inhibitions and . . . release some of the reserve energy." Crisis can bring out the best in people, powers they did not know they had. Whom did Sidis adduce as a prime example? The Jews. "The constant wars and national misfortunes of the Jews," he wrote, "released their reserve energy making of them a race of prophets, apostles and martyrs, deeply affecting the course of human civilization." Far from considering neurosis a simple misfortune, Sidis urged his readers to consider a more complicated reality, one that he encountered in his psychotherapeutic practice with immigrant Jews and Puritan descendants in the Boston area: "One may well ponder over the significant fact that it is *the neurasthenic, the 'psychasthenic' who is doing the world's work.*"[30]

In this spirit, Sidis and other Jewish popularizers of psychology encouraged Americans to place greater value on the scholarly, sensitive individual. They did so in a way that deviated from the American ideal of self-culture. Self-culture objected to superficiality and stressed thoughtfulness, but, compared to Jewish intellectualism, it allowed for a more easy-going, optimistic faith in the intuitive knowledge of the common man. It recommended "the wisdom of those who follow the plow." And self-culture coexisted with the beloved American ideal of the "gentleman-scholar," which emphasized social grace and popularity. That idea elicited a special derision from Jews for two reasons: it was used as a pretext for restricting Jewish admission to elite schools after World War I, and it conflicted with an intense, nearly absolute respect for the scholar in Jewish culture. "A passing mark is the gentleman's grade," Jastrow wrote disapprovingly in his advice column. "To show any genuine interest in studies is bad form and would defeat popularity." While assuring readers that he had "no intention to discourage fun and recreation and the lighter side of life or to ask people to be staid and sober," the psychologist nonetheless warned that "there should be a lighter side only as there is a more serious body of interests to support it." Walter Béran Wolfe derided the "cult of the hero and the beauty-prize winner." "A man with a sound mind and an unhealthy body can be a successful human being," he explained, "whereas a man with a sound body and an unhealthy mind surely becomes a failure in the terrific competition of modern times."[31]

To reckon with the myths and realities of Jewish neurosis, these popular psychologists emphasized the psychologically crippling effects of religious persecution and orthodox dogma, defended the neurotic as a creative force in society, and presented the once-ghettoized Jew as an exemplar of psychic survival in modern urban civilization.

THE PSYCHOLOGICAL CRITIQUE OF PREJUDICE AND FASCISM

It is commonly believed that racial and religious prejudice first came under psychological fire after World War II. No doubt the Holocaust shocked Americans into a more profound awareness of prejudice than they had had before. And it is true that systematic studies of the psychology of prejudice (sponsored by American Jewish organizations and conducted largely by Jewish scholars) appeared a few years after the war ended.[32]

But the psychological critique of prejudice had a longer history dating back to the 1910s and 1920s, when Jewish thinkers first used psychology to combat allegations that immigrants and blacks were inferior and that Jews were dysfunctionally neurotic. When Abraham Myerson charged that intelligence tests "*might be used—and in fact are being used . . . not to advance science or in the scientific spirit, but for race discrimination and in the spirit of propaganda*" (italics in original), he implicitly announced a Jewish countereffort against racialist theories of heredity and for an America that welcomed outsiders. A powerful device in that campaign was the inversion of stereotypes: the nervous Jew was an asset to American society, not a liability. Another inversion followed from the same line of reasoning: the prejudiced American was the real pathological personality and the real danger to American society.

During the interwar years, antisemitism in both America and Europe led Jewish thinkers to deploy psychology in an effort to expose and perhaps defuse the explosive motives behind bigotry. By 1941, when an eighty-three-year-old Franz Boas broadcast on NBC radio a call to his fellow scientists "to set free the minds of the youth of our generation, so that the young may learn to recognize bias and prejudice," Jewish psychological thinkers had already begun to define that task as their own.[33]

In the 1920s Abraham Myerson satirized Henry Ford's ignominious publication of antisemitic propaganda, and with the rise of Hitler in the early 1930s he depicted the "Jewish problem" as an explicit issue of so-

cial psychology. In a book written with Isaac Goldberg, a Harvard lecturer and advocate of psychoanalysis who had helped promote Isador
Coriat's writings in the Boston press, Myerson declared, "One of the
most fascinating chapters in social psychology has yet to be written: that
on the ambivalence of the Christian world towards the Jews." Having
established antisemitism on a psychological foundation, the authors psychoanalyzed "the paranoid, medieval Hitler" as harboring "an inferiority
complex with which he has succeeded in infecting a noble nation." Abraham Brill analyzed Nazism as "atavistic regression to primitive sadism,
which could only rise and flourish on German soil," for " 'schizoid Germany has repeatedly produced paranoid rulers" with "grandiose and
persecutory delusions."[34]

Hitler and Mussolini motivated another Jewish popularizer of psychology, Edmund Jacobson (1888–1983), to turn his pen from the therapeutics of relaxation to a psychological critique of fascism. Jacobson's case is
especially interesting because, until the late 1930s, he showed no particular interest in matters affecting Jews. The Chicago-born Jacobson held
both a Ph.D. in psychology from Harvard, where he studied with William
James, and an M.D. from the University of Chicago. He was best known
as the creator of progressive relaxation, a method of reducing tension by
methodically tensing and relaxing one's muscles, which has been called
"one of the most important developments in the history of psychiatry."
In 1929 he published *Progressive Relaxation*, a classic that remained in
print for more than fifty years. A few years later, he produced a popular
version of his innovative theory, *You Must Relax*, which was among the top
ten nonfiction best-sellers of 1934 and translated into more than a dozen
languages. Jacobson prided himself on having developed a democratic
method of relief from nervous tension, one with measurable physical
results and without the cost of expensive psychotherapies.[35]

As unrelated as muscle relaxation and democracy appeared, Jacobson
related the two when he explained why he wanted to reach a mass audience in an age of rising fascism. In *You Can Sleep Well: The A B C's of Restful
Sleep for the Average Person* (1938), he posed the rhetorical question: "Shall
we keep our facts to ourselves or, mindful of what has occurred in certain
foreign lands when science has fallen before political outbursts, do what
we can to share our secrets, so that a greater number will take interest
in them and . . . support and sustain our further scientific ventures?" In
the 1942 edition of *You Must Relax*, Jacobson added a chapter in which
he discussed the physiological and psychological conditions of Mussolini
and Hitler as well as Hitler's claim that he would wage "a war of nerves."
Hitler's plan would amount to nothing but his own destruction, Jacobson
predicted, because Mussolini had "declaimed that the democracies were
crumbling with age," yet his deteriorating physical condition proved that

"his very efforts to make his sayings come true added to the ruin of his body (as well as of his body politic)." In another book two years later, Jacobson catalogued the atrocities committed against Jews and others under Hitler and complained that people had underestimated the pathological cruelty of "the German people," not only their leaders. In the mind of a Jewish doctor such as Jacobson, the betterment of the nervous condition of a people and the free exchange of ideas between physicians and the public were features of an enlightened democracy. But under fascism both the people and their rulers were doomed to psychopathology.[36]

Jacobson's diagnosis was corroborated in the popular scientific press when the *Science News Letter* reported on the "Mass Neurosis Revealed in Nazi Scientific Journals," a summary of findings by psychologist Eugene Lerner of Sarah Lawrence College. After American entry into the war, the *Science News Letter* faithfully transcribed psychiatric literature pertaining to American soldiers, but in Lerner's case the subject of analysis was Nazi mental hygiene. Lerner sifted through German psychology journals to see what kinds of recommendations appeared there. "Dr. Lerner asks his readers what they would think of the state of public mental health in this country, if they read such statements as the following in our own scientific journals," the *News Letter* reported:

"Objective truth is less important than cultural stimulation."

"Propensity to specific crimes is inherited."

"Slums are caused by delinquent inhabitants, not vice versa."

"If the man in mental difficulties cannot find his way through his immediate relationship to God, the Party takes up the task, and here German psychotherapy can help."

Lerner's survey produced the following conclusions: (1) Germans displayed an "excessively dependent attitude"; (2) their "regressive, or infantile, traits" included a need for "obsessively rigid rules and regulations" and an "insistence on 'joy and ecstasy' and pathological hatred of anything rational or scientific"; and (3) they compensated for their inner dependence by "sadistic aggression" and "grandiose self-exaltation as a member of the elect 'Nordic' group" along with "psychopathic" hatred of "Jews, communists, democracies."[37]

In the thinking of Jewish psychological writers, racial or religious prejudice became a cardinal sign of psychopathology or maladjustment and, conversely, the well-adjusted person was free of such prejudices. Writing in the late 1920s, a little more than a decade after the lynching of Leo Frank and the resurrection of the Ku Klux Klan (both in 1915), and just a few years after the Scopes "monkey trial" in Tennessee, Joseph Jastrow explained in his syndicated column that a complex was a kind of fad for what people like and a prejudice or antipathy for what they dislike. A sports complex, like that of the golf fan, is acceptable "if not overdone," he advised. "But, to have a complex on the Negro question or on teaching evolution in the schools is not so harmless," he warned: "Because so highly charged with emotion, the complex . . . may overflow its proper bounds and cause disaster." Jastrow's selection of bigotry and religious fanaticism to exemplify a negative complex was not incidental. He understood racial and religious impulses as primitive maladaptive traits that interfered with social evolution. Similarly, Walter Béran Wolfe argued that the "individual who has reached social maturity . . . would never be guilty of condemning an entire race or nation with the cheap method of labeling it wicked or stupid or criminal." The stigma of neurotic maladjustment that had been cemented to the Jew was pried loose and affixed instead to the bigot.[38]

Of course, Jews were not the only Americans to rethink prejudice in psychological terms. Yet in the realm of popular thought it seems that they were more concerned than others about the problems of fascism and especially Nazism. If we compare Erich Fromm, for example, with the two other neo-Freudian writers of greatest influence in the interwar period, Karen Horney and Karl Menninger, we will notice the difference. Neither Horney's *The Neurotic Personality of Our Time* (1937) nor Menninger's *Man against Himself* (1938) showed an interest in a psychological critique of fascism or prejudice. This was so even though both books dealt extensively with the kinds of psychodynamics that would relate to that theme—Menninger analyzed the problem of human self-destructiveness and Horney the ways in which culture encourages certain types of anxieties and hostilities. But Erich Fromm's 1941 *Escape from Freedom* (which went through twenty-two printings in twenty years) delved deeply into the "Psychology of Nazism," to which he devoted an entire chapter. The book itself is an extended analysis of why people retreated from the freedoms of Weimar Germany into the oppressive and brutal behavior of the Third Reich.[39]

Jewish interest in psychological interpretations of fascism and prejudice took on great coherence in the thinking of Kurt Lewin (1890–1947). Lewin was associated with Gestalt psychology, a German school of thought created largely by Jewish thinkers who had studied in Berlin under the eminent philosopher-psychologist Carl Stumpf, a self-described "heretical Catholic." Lewin differed from his academic colleagues in one important respect: he wanted to apply theory to everyday life in order to humanize social relationships in the workplace, the school, and beyond. His socialist sympathies, developed during his student days, had something to do with this. A Prussian Jew and a Zionist who grew up strongly aware of the discriminatory effects of antisemitism,

Lewin applied his ethical idealism to the problem of minorities and prejudice. He immigrated to the United States after Hitler came to power in 1933. By then, Lewin had already developed pathbreaking insights into the effect of social context on a person's perceptions. In America he studied the self-perception of Jews and other stigmatized minorities and the effect of authoritarianism on individual behavior.[40]

In the "Psycho-Sociological Problems of a Minority Group," Lewin paved the way toward a new understanding of how prejudice affected the self-esteem of individuals in a stigmatized minority. Drawing on his own experience as a Jewish refugee from Nazism, Lewin compared the modern Jew and the ghetto Jew as models for understanding the psychology of minorities in general. Unlike Brill and the older generation of psychological thinkers, he cast the ghettoized Jewish male in a positive light, as a man who was sure of himself because he lived within the protective boundaries of his primary group. In contrast, the modern German Jew had a foot in two worlds and no secure grounding in either one. He was freed from the intramural tensions of ghetto life but was never fully accepted into gentile society. "This decrease of tension has brought no real relaxation to the life of the Jew," Lewin concluded, "but instead has meant perhaps even higher tension in some respects." At worst, the situation of the assimilated Jew devolved into a state of ethnic "self-hatred," a concept Lewin introduced into American thought in 1941.[41]

Having highlighted the fact of psychic disruption in stigmatized minorities, Lewin illustrated just as dramatically the psychic costs of authoritarianism. At the University of Iowa, where he worked from 1935 to 1944, Lewin supervised and publicized unusual experiments of authoritarian and democratic leadership styles. Those revealed that active, responsive children quickly became passive and depressed when their teachers switched from an open, flexible manner to one that was rigid and hierarchical. Co-operative "we" feelings occurred twice as often in the democratic setting than in the autocratic, which was dominated by hostile "I" feelings. At the same time, the flexibility of the democratic group allowed for greater individuality, whereas the children in the autocratic group "all had a low status without much individuality." To Lewin this experiment dramatized the precarious history of reason. It proved what "history shows . . . that the belief in reason as a social value is by no means universal, but is itself a result of a definite social atmosphere." To Americans "living in a thoroughly democratic tradition," it might seem natural that people would come to accept "the goddess of 'reason.' " But, he warned, "it is not an accident that the first act of modern Fascism in every country has been officially and vigorously to dethrone this goddess and instead to make emotions and obedience the all-ruling principles in education and life from kindergarten to death."[42]

Lewin gave new meaning to the American functionalist ideal, that belief in the ability of people to adapt to their social environment and in
psychology's responsibility to help them. His idealistic arguments about
reshaping personal behavior through democratic leadership in small
groups gained the attention of the American Jewish Congress, which
appointed him to create a research center on intergroup relations.
Under those auspices, Lewin developed "action research," a new approach in which "the need for action determines the content of the research." The action that Lewin envisioned was to change American customs and laws that separated people from each other, so as to reduce
prejudice against Jews and other stigmatized minorities. According to
Lewin, the social situation in which people found themselves determined
the kinds of attitudes they displayed. Without prejudicial social structures, prejudice would become pointless and disappear. If Americans
would only remove the artificial barriers that kept people apart, they
would wipe out the foundations of bigotry. Then, having been aided by
studies in the psychology of prejudice, they were sure to achieve the ideal
of democratic social evolution, a society of people freely adapting to each
other under conditions of freedom.[43]

The "outsider" perspective of Jewish thinkers, with their distinct sensi-
tivities, also shaped the way the concept of inferiority was applied to
American racial and religious minorities. Walter Béran Wolfe argued
that "the social, economic, religious or racial situations in which the
individual finds himself in a hated minority group" constituted a primary cause of an inferiority complex. "Members of any minority group,"
Wolfe claimed, "whether social, religious, or economic, suffer an accen-
tuation of their inferiority feeling because of the additional difficulties
of the world." In an instructive contrast to Jewish preoccupations with
victimization, Karen Horney (a German gentile émigré) offered an opposite psychological profile in *The Neurotic Personality of Our Time*, one
that emphasized the vindictive aggressiveness of the ethnic outsider. "In
persons in whom the craving for prestige is uppermost," Horney explained, "hostility usually takes the form of a desire to humiliate others.
This desire is paramount in those persons whose own self-esteem has
been wounded by humiliation and who have thus become vindictive.
Usually they have gone through a series of humiliating experiences in
childhood, experiences that may have had to do either with the social
situation in which they grew up—such as belonging to a minority group,
or being themselves poor but having wealthy relatives—or with their
own individual situation." Wolfe and Horney were looking at different
sides of the same coin; Wolfe profiled the wounded minority consciousness while Horney portrayed its wounding capacity. Most Jews in
America preferred Wolfe's analysis for public purposes and agreed with

Horney only in the private arena of Jewish humor, which acknowledged Jewish ambivalence and aggression.[44]

Growing throughout the 1930s, the Jewish psychological critique of prejudice and fascism culminated in a conference in San Francisco in 1944. Convened by Ernst Simmel, a prominent Berlin psychoanalyst who had become the most important Freudian in California (and an analyst to Hollywood celebrities), the meeting probed the psychological roots of antisemitism and yielded a book, *Anti-Semitism: A Social Disease*, which reinforced the new view of bigotry as pathological. Authored by Jewish social scientists who fled Europe in the 1930s, the book rested on the simple premise that "anti-Semitism requires investigation by the psychiatrist. . . . We considered it our duty to the immediate community—as well as to the larger community of the world—to submit the problem of anti-Semitism to the scrutiny of unbiased science." The science that Simmel and most of his conferees had in mind was psychoanalysis. Nothing less probing than Freud's dynamic psychology would reveal the "natural laws governing the *irrational* trends in men." According to contributor Otto Fenichel, another prominent student of Freud's, the Jew occupied a special place in the unconscious of the antisemite, representing both the authority that oppresses him and the primal instincts that he harbors within himself. Judaism, and the Jew's very existence, reminded the Christian of the most frightening elements of an authoritarian God. "He sees in the Jew everything which brings him misery." *Anti-Semitism: A Social Disease* answered the summons Abraham Myerson issued in 1933 for research into "one of the most fascinating chapters in social psychology . . . that on the ambivalence of the Christian world towards the Jews."[45]

To gauge the significance of the new, psychological critique of fascism and prejudice in the 1930s, we need only recall that it grounded two of the most important documents of the post–World War II era—George Kennan's "Long Telegram" of 1946 and the U.S. Supreme Court decision in the case of *Brown v. Board of Education* (1954). Kennan's famous message from Moscow set the foundations of the foreign policy of containment. In that document, Kennan stressed the psychological state of the Bolshevik regime, referring to "the Kremlin's neurotic view of world affairs" rooted in "the traditional and instinctive Russian sense of insecurity." He urged American officials to understand that the Bolsheviks harbored a profoundly prejudicial and paranoid view of the outside world, which he compared unfavorably to a democratic, scientific approach to human nature and society: "For it, the vast fund of objective fact about human society is not, as with us, the measure against which outlook is constantly being tested and reformed, but a grab bag from which individual items are selected arbitrarily and tendentiously to bolster an outlook already preconceived." In the *Brown* case, the Supreme Court made an extraordinary application of Adlerian and Lewinian psychology, noting of Negro schoolchildren that segregation produced "a feeling of inferiority as to their status in the community that may affect their hearts and minds in a way unlikely ever to be undone." "Whatever may have been the state of psychological knowledge at the time of *Plessy* v. *Ferguson*," the Court concluded, referring to the notorious 1896 decision authorizing segregation, "this finding is amply supported by modern authority."[46]

Jews participated energetically in public debate about the psyche as a racial repository of intelligence and personality because, in their view, as the psyche goes so goes the country. Theories that objectified and stigmatized ethnic minorities as mental and emotional defectives were fit for a fascist society, but not for the America that Jews colloquially understood as "a promised land." Turning conventional attitudes upside down, Jewish psychological thinkers showed that the neurotic moved civilization forward while the bigot, newly defined as a psychopath, threatened a return to barbarism. With similar motives, they added a distinct moral perspective to American inquiries into the nature of the unconscious. In that mysterious domain, they perceived yet another threat to the vision of a dynamic, tolerant, and democratic America.

Chapter 8

The Specter of the Mob:
Jews and the Battle for the
American Unconscious

BETWEEN THE 1890s AND 1940s Jewish interpreters of the psyche added a new dimension to public conversation about the mind and its unconscious or subconscious regions. They saw danger in the popular idea of a spiritualized psyche and campaigned against it, insisting instead that the mind contained no mystical or spiritual elements. Yet they also wanted to avoid the behaviorist pole of popular thought, which depicted the mind as a machine to be programmed. Both the transcendentalist and behaviorist views of the mind promised euphoric transformations of human nature that Jewish thinkers considered unrealistic and potentially chaotic. They wanted to guide the public toward a more restrained interpretation of the psyche, one that reflected the rationalist moralism in which they were raised and which resembled an older American tradition of disciplined self-control. Their "middle path" included a deep concern about a particular kind of evil, the destructive potential of the irrational mob. Into a generally cheerful American appraisal of human nature, which did not share darker European views of "the crowd," Jews introduced a more somber aspect. Only with an awareness of the danger of mass irrationalism, they believed, would Americans be properly equipped to produce an open and democratic society.

THE MYSTERY OF CONSCIOUSNESS

When John Locke denied the existence of innate ideas—denied, that is, that people are born with ideas implanted in their minds by God—he opened a path to a huge and vexing question: is there a spirit at work in the consciousness of human beings? Although we have no answer to that question, much of the excitement of modern intellectual life has come from a succession of thinkers who believed they had unlocked the mystery of consciousness.

In America, we have seen, popular discussions of consciousness veered toward transcendentalism on the one hand and behaviorism on the other. The transcendentalist camp included those who assumed that a soul animated the human being and that spiritual powers lay submerged in the depths of human consciousness. The behaviorist camp contained people of a very different disposition, those for whom "what you see is what you get." For them biology was everything; even the most intimate and deepest of thoughts could be explained in physical terms and could be altered by mechanical changes in the environment.

Although both perspectives kept a strong hold on the popular imagination, they fared very differently in the world of professional psychology. After the death of William James in 1910, the idea of a spiritualized psyche virtually disappeared among academic psychologists, though a rebellious minority sustained James's interest in the mysteries, or at least the profundities, of personal consciousness. The trend in academic psychology away from a spiritualized psyche reached a peak in Watson's behaviorism, which transformed the discipline in the 1920s. Although many professional psychologists were put off by Watson's utter rejection of *consciousness*—his belief that people operated like machines—they leaned in his direction, toward the laboratory rather than the séance chamber.[1]

Still, the transcendentalist view of the subconscious was to enjoy a long life in America. For a growing number of people who valued spirituality but gave up formal religion, the spiritualized subconscious turned out to be an extraordinarily effective way of merging body and soul. The mind-cure movement of the nineteenth century and the positive thinking movement of the twentieth century both clung to the splendid idea of a mind with infinite curative and regenerative powers. One of the most prolific inspirational writers of the twentieth century, Emmet Fox, illustrated the wonderful pliability of the concept in *Power though Constructive Thinking* (1932), a book that predated Norman Vincent Peale's blockbuster *The Power of Positive Thinking* by two decades: "The subconscious mind is active all the time and from the moment of incarnation it is busily building the new body, for it is the baby's own subconscious that builds its body in the uterus, and it builds it in its own image and likeness—that is why our bodies express the things that are in the soul. The mother supplies the material but the child's own soul builds its little body, and we learn in metaphysics that our environment is always but the outpicturing of our soul." Fox appealed to a multitude of Americans who resisted the efforts of scientists to eliminate spiritual factors from interpretations of the psyche. The idea of a subconscious or unconscious dimension of the mind proved too vital a tool for those who wanted to define their innermost sense of themselves in a way that combined the aura of science with the simplicity of faith.[2]

Jews were not impervious to this powerful strain of American thought, but unlike Christians nurtured in the idea of the Holy Ghost, their background did not prepare them to think in terms of actual infusions from an external source of spiritual power. Boris Sidis and William James each developed a theory of reserve energy, for example, but Sidis did not share James's interest in the metaphysics of mankind's latent powers. He simply recognized that people's potential accomplishments far exceeded what they actually achieved and that, in the right circumstances, they would instantiate creative power. In his psychological analysis of humor, for example, Sidis ascribed "true humor" to subconscious reserves of energy that emerged and put the individual "in touch with the infinite," but his infinite was not the Infinite of James or of the New Thought classic *In Tune with the Infinite*. Rather, it was "the infinite depth of the soul in the very failures, faults, defects, and imperfections" that gave rise to humor.[3]

Jewish columnist Herbert Kaufman also exhorted Americans to tap their reserves of power but, like Sidis, he did not wander into transcendentalism. Kaufman was one of the nation's most recognized newspapermen in the 1910s and 1920s. Born in Washington, D.C., in 1878, he graduated from Johns Hopkins, worked the journalism trade for a number of years, and went on to head up his own newspaper syndicate, the Herbert Kaufman Newspaper Syndicate (he also owned and edited *McClure's* after World War I). Kaufman's syndicated Sunday column, "Vim, Vigor, Victory," contained high-pitched self-help exhortations and aphorisms. Like *Poor Richard's Almanack* but more frenetically, Kaufman badgered his readers to waste no time and no opportunity to realize their potential for success and productivity. "*Certainly* there are forces *awaiting* management, with which *still* undetected realms will be *sensed* and *penetrated*. . . . We own hosts of *unrealized* assets, some of which offer *incredible* returns. . . . We appear to be *filled* with buttons for *Will* to touch. We must *hurry* and *locate* them. *Mythology* asserts that our *progenitors* were *Titans*. With due *help* from us, our *sons* can *eventually revert* to type. . . . We remain *dwarfs* only through *disregard* of our *potencies*."[4]

Like Kaufman, the Jewish popularizers of psychology were not averse to American pep, but they were remarkably uniform in rejecting the idea of a spiritualized psyche. One historian of the subject has correctly observed the extraordinary opposition of Joseph Jastrow, who carried on a "crusade to demystify the psychological term most subject to abuse by the general public—the subconscious." But Jastrow was not alone. Hugo Münsterberg played second fiddle to none on the matter of psychological metaphysics, which he summarily dismissed: "The story of the subconscious mind can be told in three words: there is none."[5]

In one of the first American symposia on the subconscious, published in 1910 as *Subconscious Phenomena*, six leading authorities—Jastrow, Münsterberg, Morton Prince, the French psychologists Pierre Janet and

Theodule Ribot, and British psychologist Bernard Hart—were asked to confront the conflict between the metaphysical and biological views of the subconscious. None of the six accepted a mystical or transcendentalist psyche, but a Jewish-Christian fissure divided the participants. The two Jewish contributors, Münsterberg and Jastrow, insisted more strenuously than the others on the purely physiological nature of subconscious activity. They agreed with the view that Boris Sidis had put forth in his influential *The Psychology of Suggestion: A Research into the Subconscious Nature of Man and Society* (1898), which denied metaphysical qualities to the subconscious. Ribot, however, objected to that interpretation; he thought Sidis extreme; he construed Sidis's theory as suggesting that the psyche was "stupid, uncritical, extremely credulous, without morality, and its principal mental mechanism is that of the brute—association by contiguity." Janet, Hart, and Prince shared at least some of Ribot's reservations, whereas Münsterberg and Jastrow were completely comfortable with an uncompromising physiological view of the mind. "Such physiological explanation," Münsterberg observed, "gives small foothold for that mystical expansion of the theory which seemed so easily reached from the subconscious mental life."[6]

The extremity, or vigor, of their position contrasted with that of Morton Prince, the renowned psychiatrist who convened the symposium. Though Prince denied to the subconscious those religious aspects that William James allowed, he nevertheless could not bring himself to view the mind in solely physical terms, as devoid of spirit. Prince described himself as a *panpsychist*, which meant that he considered all matter to be infused with spiritual force. Oddly akin to Christian Scientists, he thought matter was a fiction, though he reasoned from physics. Because the most basic units of physics were motion or energy rather than fixed substance, Prince surmised, the brain itself had to be a form of energy. "When the marshalling of the units of the immaterial, the spiritual energy of the universe, which is the body, reaches a certain complexity," he argued, "this immaterial body *is* the mind." Though he had abandoned Christianity, Prince still maintained a semblance of the American transcendentalist belief in the ubiquity of a universal spirit.[7]

A decade or so later, the younger Myerson joined the camp of Sidis, Münsterberg, and Jastrow in emphasizing the physical basis of existence. We may recall that Myerson was in the avant-garde of doctors who used electroshock and drugs to cure depression. Mind cure or mental healing remained foreign to him. At his most transcendental, Myerson invoked organic metaphors to account for the mysteriousness of the universe, likening individuals to "corpuscles in the blood stream of an organism too vast and complicated to be encompassed by one imagination." He discounted any notion of a submerged "self" with its own powers and personality. "There *is* a subconsciousness in that much of the nervous activity of the organism has but little or no relation to consciousness. . . . We are spurred on to sex life, to marriage, to the care of our children by instinct; but the instinct is not a personality any more than the automatic heartbeat is. . . . The uneasiness of a desire that arises from the activity of the sex organs is not a manifestation of a subconscious personality, unless we include in our personality our livers, spleen and internal organs of all kinds."[8]

Similarly, the Jewish followers of Freud and Adler guarded against spiritual incursions into their theory of the unconscious. Brill, Coriat, Adler, and Wolfe all deviated from Freud by accepting religion—rational religion—as a helpful resource for many people. That acceptance was probably mandatory in an American context, but it did not imply a greater fondness than Freud's for religious mysteries.

As we have seen, Freud and Adler differed from the third, gentile member of the psychoanalytic triumvirate, Carl Jung, on the question of spirituality. The two Jewish thinkers anchored themselves in a pure rationalism, while Jung took psychoanalysis in a vaguely Christian and metaphysical direction. When Brill wrote Freud about a visit to Oberammergau, the site of the annual passion play, in the summer of 1910, Freud replied, "I don't wonder that you found no pleasure in Oberammergau. . . . Nor would I, by the way, be able to handle the mystical pleasures of Christianity." In order to debunk mental telepathy and clairvoyance, Adler liked to tell the story of a seemingly oracular dream he had on April 14, 1912.

> I woke up at the exact time of the sinking of the *Titanic*, and so vivid had been my dream that I seemed to see a ship foundering in midocean, although I do not think that I invented the iceberg. It was a shock to discover next day that the ship had *really* sunk; but I was able to convince myself that it was not such a coincidence as it appeared, since I was in great anxiety at the time about the single copy of my book, *The Nervous Character*, which was on its way to America. In this case I had not taken a copy of it, which was my rule; and, had the ship sunk, I should have lost the work of years. The book, however, was not on the *Titanic*, and I soon received the news that it had arrived safely. You will find, if you carefully investigate all such cases of telepathy, that they usually have some such underlying anxiety in the background![9]

The distrust of mysticism in any form led Jewish followers of Freud to reject the attempt of some Americans to re-root psychoanalysis in American transcendentalist ideas of the Infinite. Harvard neurologist James Jackson Putnam, Freud's first prestigious American supporter, made that attempt. Sensing that Freud's hard-hitting materialism and rationalism needed readjusting for an American audience, Putnam tempered Freud with Emerson, emphasizing that "we live and breathe and have our being in an unpicturable world," a world of transcendent values. In contrast to Freud's grim view of psychic conflict, Putnam suggested that conflict can be resolved ultimately "as an evidence of perfect intelligence coalescing with perfectly disinterested love and perfect will." That platonic language belonged to Christian culture; it never appeared in Freud or his Jewish disciples, for whom "perfectly disinterested love" was a chimera, not a solution for psychic conflict. In proper transcendentalist fashion, Putnam recommended Emerson's path—spiritual pursuit of "the richer meanings which the universe offers to all who will seek for them"—and Emerson's assurance that "evil will bless."[10]

Another leading psychiatrist and popularizer of Freud who wanted to gloss psychoanalysis with transcendentalist optimism was William Alanson White. A tireless speaker and ardent penal reformer, White was chief administrator at St. Elizabeth's hospital in Washington, D.C., the federal hospital for the insane. As a result of White's reputation, Clarence Darrow selected him to be a primary expert witness in the Leopold and Loeb case of 1924. White, as one historian explains, "espoused a highly Romantic evolutionary faith cut from the same cloth as the liberal Protestantism of individuals such as Henry Ward Beecher," the charismatic and Romantic Brooklyn minister (and brother of Harriet Beecher Stowe), "whose sermons White had listened to in his youth." In a 1920s symposium on the unconscious, White showed the traces of Christianity that remained in the gut of the secular psychiatrist. "Life involves progress to higher levels of integration," he wrote. "This attainment of a new ideal, a mechanism to which the church gives the name conversion in certain instances, is the same mechanism that is involved whenever a new component is integrated, whenever a conflict is solved. . . . It is such considerations that go to make life the great adventure and salvation an ever present possibility for everyone."[11]

It was not uncommon for American interpreters to turn the Freudian unconscious, a zone of dire conflict, into a spiritual channel leading, as White put it, to salvation. In *The Freudian Wish and Its Place in Ethics* (1915), one of the most important of the early presentations of psychoanalytic theory, Harvard psychologist Edwin Bissell Holt avoided the religious idiom of salvation but, like White and Putnam, offered an extraordinarily optimistic vision of Freud in which all conflicts might be resolved through reasonable self-scrutiny. Tenacious conflicts in the unconscious that Freud found vexingly productive of evil seemed easily manageable to Holt. And in 1922, when Freudianism finally arrived on the national nonfiction best-seller list with psychiatrist Josephine Jackson's *Outwitting Our Nerves,* Freud would have been surprised to discover that "the Christian religion, which sets the highest ideal of character," made for a more graceful sublimation of conflicts in the unconscious.[12]

Jewish dissent from transcendentalist, not to mention explicitly Christian, versions of the unconscious marked Isador Coriat's ambivalent involvement with the popular Emmanuel movement. Based in the Emmanuel Episcopal Church of Boston, as we may recall, the Emmanuel movement ignited a "healing" craze from 1906 until 1912, after which time public interest in Freudianism overtook it. The brainchild of the church's rector, Elwood Worcester, the movement combined Protestantism and psychotherapy in an unusual way. Worcester believed that religion might once again be able to serve as a healing agent if it incorporated insights from psychiatry and psychology. Long lines of troubled souls entered the church's precincts, where they were first diagnosed for possible organic disorders, in which case they were referred to a physician, and then treated with a combination of positive mental suggestions, massaging of the head, and pastoral consolation. Worcester invited Isador Coriat to serve as the medical expert for the Emmanuel movement and to write several chapters of its guiding text, *Religion and Medicine: The Moral Control of Nervous Disorders* (1908). That book went through eight editions in seven months, doing as much as any single book to alert (and alarm) Americans about the dire necessity of treating their apparently mounting nervous disorders.[13]

Not yet a Freudian in 1908, Coriat was a Bostonian who matured professionally within that city's lush psychotherapeutic environment, and he appreciated the therapeutic creativity of Worcester's Emmanuel initiative. Nevertheless, he dissented from the transcendentalist conception of the subconscious espoused in *Religion and Medicine*. The chapters he authored differed in this respect from those written by Worcester and his Episcopal colleague Samuel McComb. Worcester's presentation of "The Subconscious Mind" took its inspiration from William James but went a bit farther in depicting the subconscious as a sacred region harboring "powers for good." Yet Worcester felt compelled to note that his coauthor Coriat did not accept the existence of such a spiritualized subconscious. Coriat's chapters maintained a scholarly, cautious tone, stressing the importance of "a thorough neurological, psychiatric, or general medical examination . . . before the institution of any form of psychic treatment." Coriat explained that he did not accept the transcendentalist idea of a *subliminal self* capable of establishing a spiritual connection to other people or to a universal spirit. On the contrary, he referred readers to the physiological interpretation of Jastrow's *The Subconscious* (1905).[14]

Coriat had warned about mystifications of the psyche a year earlier, in a 1907 article for *Good Housekeeping* addressed to women who might be affected by the vogue of mental healing. He stressed that the body was real and its afflictions not curable by wishful thinking. "The various meta-physical systems of mental healing completely ignore this interaction of body and mind," he explained; "one may as well try to defy the laws of gravitation as to cure an organic nervous affection by suggestion." The psychotherapist *must* implement a "rational practice" of explaining to the patient the nature of the disorder, he concluded, "and not dangle before his eyes the fetich [*sic*] of any mysterious magnetic force, or clothe any of our therapeutic procedures in a cloak of mystery."[15]

The differential between popular Jewish and Christian writers on the subconscious or unconscious helps us understand a key difference be-tween two of the most popular inspirational books of the twentieth cen-tury, Norman Vincent Peale's *The Power of Positive Thinking* (1952) and Joshua Loth Liebman's *Peace of Mind* (1946). Peale wedded liberal Prot-estantism to the psychological idea of great hidden powers within the subconscious mind, whereas Liebman took a completely different tack. Consistent with earlier Jewish psychological thinkers, *Peace of Mind* re-jected a spiritualized psyche. Liebman's unconscious was Freud's, a site of deep conflict. There were no hidden reserves of power for Liebman, no communion with a universal spirit. Peace of mind depended upon candid introspection and patient determination.[16]

SPIRITUALISM AND CHRISTIAN SCIENCE: THE MENACE OF THE SUPERNATURAL

Jewish rejections of a mystified subconscious reflected anxiety about mass enthusiasms, such as spiritualism and Christian Science, which pre-supposed a supernatural mental power. In the late nineteenth and early twentieth centuries, spiritualism and Christian Science powerfully at-tracted Christians who believed in a divine Unity but disliked Christian dogma and ritual.

The official history of American spiritualism began in 1847 when Mar-garet and Katherine Fox, two adolescent daughters of a Methodist farmer in Hydesville, New York, claimed to have received messages from a spirit who communicated through strange rappings in the old family farmhouse. After signing up with P. T. Barnum, the Fox sisters became nationwide celebrities, and their fame stimulated a rash of mediums and seances. Many socially prominent reformers and freethinkers flocked to spiritualism in the 1850s and 1860s, prompting Abraham Lincoln's wry observation, "Well, for those who like that sort of thing, I should think it is just about the sort of thing they would like." Spiritualism was a diverse rather than a centralized movement, and its advocates claimed eleven million adherents in the peak decade of the 1870s. In Boston the spiritualists established themselves as a stable religious denomination with an impressive house of worship, a prestigious Back Bay congregation, and a well-edited paper, the *Boston Banner of Light*. Spiritualism also correlated strongly with the advance of science; spiritualists despised the materialism of academic physiology and psychology but, as modern people, they insisted that "sightings" and "hearings" and "readings" constituted valid empirical data for the psychologist.[17]

Like Mormonism, Seventh-Day Adventism, Pentecostalism, and the Jehovah's Witnesses, Christian Science was an American creation. It originated in the mind-cure ideas of mesmerist Phineas Quimby, whose patients included a Maine woman named Mary Baker. After Quimby died in 1866, Baker relapsed into sickness after hurting her back from a fall on the ice. However, upon reading Matthew 9:2, in which Jesus heals a paralytic, she arose healed. Like Quimby, she considered herself a renewer of Christ's healing faith and, as Mary Baker Eddy (the name she acquired with marriage), she founded the first Church of Christ, Scientist (1879). By 1908, when Eddy founded the *Christian Science Monitor*, her *Science and Health: With Key to the Scriptures* (1875), the founding text of Christian Science, had sold approximately four hundred thousand copies. Eddy's key to understanding the universe was that *everything is spiritual*, nothing is material. Her doctrine held that "God is All, in all."

> What can be more than All? Nothing: and this is just what I call matter, *nothing*. . . . The Scriptures name God as good. . . . From this premise comes the logical conclusion that God is naturally and divinely infinite good. . . . Therefore the Science of good calls evil *nothing*. . . . Here is where Christian Science sticks to its text, and other systems of religion abandon their own logic. Here also is found the pith of the basal statement, the cardinal point in Christian Science, that matter and evil (including all inharmony, sin, disease, death) are *unreal*.[18]

Spiritualism and Christian Science had plenty of detractors, but it is a striking fact that the most publicly vociferous opponents of spiritualism in the early twentieth century—Jastrow, Münsterberg, and the magician Harry Houdini—were Jews. Houdini (1874–1926) debunked mediums because they undermined the whole premise of the modern magician, whose reputation depended on the ability to appear superhuman through the expert use of human skills. A man who put nearly as much effort into self-promotion as into magic, he was not about to let a quacksalving spiritualist do what no prestidigitating magician had done—exceed him as the world's most celebrated manipulator. The son of a Hungarian rabbi, Houdini (born Erich Weiss) also had aspirations toward scholarship and felt insecure about his lack of education. During the last decade of his life, he relentlessly exposed the tricks behind exhibitions of spiritualism and authored *Miracle Mongers and Their Methods* (1920) and *A Magician among the Spirits* (1924). Houdini achieved sufficient expertise to be asked to write the entry on conjuring for the thirteenth edition of the *Encyclopaedia Britannica* (1926).[19]

Hugo Münsterberg's angle of attack on spiritualism was even more devastating. His most famous case of medium exposure arose in 1909 when William James challenged him to investigate a performance by the notorious Italian medium Eusapia Palladino. An exotically charming middle-aged woman who caused tables to move and guitar strings to vibrate, Palladino tantalized audiences and professional investigators alike. James believed that she might prove to be "the crack in the levee" of scientific doubt through which "the whole Mississippi of supernaturalism may pour in," but the skeptic Münsterberg triumphed when, with the help of a man lying underneath Palladino's séance table, he caught her "levitating" the table with her foot. Münsterberg's evaluation was both kinder and crueler than a simple declaration of quackery. He excused Palladino of fraud and convicted her instead of mental illness, "a case of a complex hysteria in which a splitting of the personality has set in. . . . Such a split-off personality may enter into the most complex preparations of trickeries and frauds, may carry them through with a marvelous alertness, and yet as soon as the normal personality awakes, the whole hysteric action is forgotten. . . . It is a fraud for which no one is to be blamed as it belongs in the sphere of the hospital."[20]

For a full half-century between 1890 and 1940, Joseph Jastrow battled against all forms of irrational thinking based on the belief, no matter how vague, that supernatural forces were at work to grant individuals luck, health, or consolation. The entire enterprise of popular psychology, he believed, depended on persuading Americans to abandon myth and superstition. Jastrow lamented the fact that "reputable attempts to bring psychological doctrine to the masses" had to vie with "cure-alls for ills, formulae for character-reading, rules for prediction of fate, frothy inspirational appeals to master handicaps, to develop latent powers, and to ignore reality by a buoyant faith." All those techniques led "back to the jungles from which the folk-mind has never completely emerged." They prevented men and women from attaining "a wiser development of such powers as each possesses and a calm acceptance of their limitations." As late as 1940, well after the heyday of spiritualism, Jastrow was trying to rid the nation once and for all of the evils of phrenology, physiognomy, palmistry, graphology, fortune telling, divination, Malicious Animal Magnetism, and astrology.[21]

Jastrow felt that these popular indulgences were hijacking otherwise rational, progressive people from liberal religion and miring them in a diffusely Christian mysticism:

Surely it is not merely or mainly the evidences obtainable in the séance chamber, nor the irresistible accumulation of cures by argument and thought-healings, that account for the organized gatherings of Spiritualists and the costly temples and thriving congregations of Christ Scientist. It is the presentation of a practical doctrine of immortality and of the spiritual nature of disease in conjunction with an accepted religious system, that is responsible for these vast results. The "Key to the Scriptures" has immeasurably reinforced the "Science and Health," and brought believers to a new form of Christianity who never would have been converted to a new system of medicine presented on purely intellectual grounds.

Jastrow saw spiritualism and Christian Science as symbols of regress. Psychologists like himself who wrote for the general public were establishing a more rationalist view of human nature but, to his mind, Christianity, resurrected in new forms, had now returned to chip away at logic and science. Christian Science especially disturbed him because he recognized that it was gaining institutional respectability, something he did not have to fear from the eccentric and individualistic spiritualists. He perceived Mary Baker Eddy's church as the sun in a spiritualist solar system. "There can be no doubt," Jastrow wrote of the spiritualist associations in 1900, "that many of these systems have been stimulated into life or into renewed vigor by the success of 'Christian Science.' "[22]

Christians, of course, had their own problems with Christian Science. By the early 1890s there were enough Protestant pamphlets and books denouncing Christian Science to supply all the ministers who wanted to sermonize against it. Conservative Protestants usually indicted Christian Science for its heretical departures from Christian orthodoxies, whereas liberal Protestants tended to show a more indulgent attitude toward Mrs. Eddy's adherents. But both had to concede that underneath the peculiar doctrines of the sect, there existed a bonified Christian concern for healing. Even the irreverent Mark Twain, who classed Mary Baker Eddy among the world's third-rate minds, respected the commercial talent with which she "restored to the world neglected and abandoned features of the Christian religion." The growing popularity of the faith illustrated the fact that the healing message attracted Christians who felt its absence in the mainline churches.[23]

Unlike Christian critics, who derided Mrs. Eddy's religion for distorting the faith, Jews worried about the way it propagated Christian doctrines. Masses of Jews took an interest in Christian Science. By the 1920s there were estimates of 50,000 Jewish Christian Scientists in New York City alone. At its annual conference in 1912 the Reform movement's Central Conference of American Rabbis addressed the growing problem. Rabbi Maurice Lefkowitz delivered a report, "The Attitude of Judaism Toward Christian Science," which identified something Christian critics had missed: the inescapable Christianity within Christian Science. Lefkowitz insisted that Jews could not be both Christian Scientists and Jews. While recognizing that Mary Baker Eddy had denied Jesus his divinity, the rabbi pointed out that Christian Science nevertheless placed him on a pedestal of human spirituality. The Christian Scientist accepted the superhuman if not divine status of Jesus Christ.[24]

But the most vocal Jewish opponents of Christian Science were psychologists, not rabbis. None of the Jewish popularizers of psychology could find a kind word for Christian Science. In fact, the unanimity of their antagonism was noteworthy. Jastrow was the most tireless campaigner against Christian Science, but the others shared his viewpoint completely. Coriat made a midwestern speaking tour in 1909 during which, the press reported, he "leveled his lance at Christian Science and other like cults." Brill denied that anyone raised in Judaism could sincerely convert to Christianity, and he dismissed as "ludicrous" the attempt of Jews to reconcile the conflict between Old and New Worlds by joining Christian Science. Münsterberg tried to allay public anxieties about the powers of hypnotists by dismissing the "old mystical view of unscientific superstition ... that a man could exert secret influence from a distance ... could inflict pain and suffering on his enemy, and could misuse the innocent as instruments of his criminal schemes." He pointed out that Mary Baker Eddy encouraged precisely that superstition. A believer in Malicious Animal Magnetism, she prophesied that soon "the person or mind that hates his neighbor will have no need to traverse his fields to destroy his flocks and herds. . . . For the evil mind will do this through mesmerism." Walter Béran Wolfe deemed Christian Science one of numerous "modern equivalents of the savages' magic incantations and rites."[25]

THE JEW BEHIND JOHN WATSON

Opposed to a spiritualized subconscious, the Jewish popularizers of psychology also rejected the mechanistic mind of John Watson's behaviorism, a theory that some psychologists considered the most breathtaking reevaluation of human behavior since Darwin. The transcendentalist interpretation of the mind had grown out of one romantic strain of American Protestantism, and the behaviorist sprang from another: an optimistic environmentalism that defined human nature as completely open, vulnerable, and responsive to change. "It takes more time," Watson explained, but "we can change the personality as easily as we can change the shape of the nose."[26]

In a powerful new way, behaviorism questioned the idea of inherited traits, racial or otherwise, and promised a social revolution. "Pride of race has been strong, hence our Mayflower ancestry—our Daughters of the Revolution," Watson mocked. "We like to boast of our ancestry. It sets us apart. We like to think that it takes three generations to make a gentleman (sometimes a lot longer!) and that we have more than three behind us." In one rambunctious sweep, he cleared away all but the most serious genetic afflictions as obstacles to growth. The novelty and excite-ment of his project make it impossible not to quote once again the most-quoted passage of *Behaviorism* (1924). "Give me a dozen healthy infants, well-formed, and my own specified world to bring them up in and I'll guarantee to take any one at random and train him to become any type of specialist I might select—doctor, lawyer, artist, merchant-chief and, yes, even beggar-man and thief, regardless of his talents, penchants, ten-dencies, abilities, vocations, and race of his ancestors." "Please note," he stressed, "that when this experiment is made I am to be allowed to specify the way the children are to be brought up and the type of world they have to live in."[27]

In light of the resistance that Watson's perspective would encounter from the Jewish thinkers who shared his interest in popularizing psychol-ogy, it is perhaps ironic that behaviorism was inspired by a Jewish scientist. The ideal of social engineering by a corps of experts in human psychol-ogy—an ideal with chilling as well as liberating possibilities—originated with one of Watson's teachers, Jacques Loeb. When Watson depicted the human being as "nothing but an organic machine" whose behavior could be predicted and controlled by scientific experts, he echoed Loeb. In his single-minded materialism, his belief that physiology explained all of life's processes, he followed Loeb's philosophy of science.[28]

Jacques Loeb (1859–1924) came from the German Rhineland. Origi-nally named Isaak, he changed his name to Jacques as a young man, reflecting his father's Francophilia and his own desire to be a cosmopoli-tan who transcended the German nationalism of his day. Loeb grew up like many German Jews of his generation, in comfortable circumstances befitting his father's occupation as a wholesale merchant. After both his parents died from illness when he was a teenager, he turned away from the life that had been expected of him, which revolved around the fam-ily business. He enrolled in the Jewish *Askanische Gymnasium* in Berlin and took up the study of medicine at the University of Berlin, where he studied the physiology of the brain. His medical thesis, published in 1884, attacked the idea that there was a "metaphysiology" of the brain and insisted, instead, that every mental function could be explained in simple biological terms. Loeb's innovative research on the activity of dogs with brain lesions attracted the attention of William James, who recognized the uniqueness of his approach to the brain. In contrast to most German physiologists, who strove to isolate defects in order to produce better medical diagnoses, Loeb transcended medical concerns. He sought a general theory to explain the biological purposiveness of the animal mind.[29]

In 1890 Loeb met and married an American, Anne Leonard, a Smith College alumna and a German-trained Ph.D. Loeb's new wife was the daughter of a suspender manufacturer, Granville Hall Leonard, who happened to be the cousin of America's pioneering psychologist Granville Stanley Hall, the president of Clark University (and Freud's host in 1909). Hall provided Loeb with his first contacts in American academia and suggested that he get in touch with William Rainey Harper, president of the new University of Chicago. With few family ties in Germany and tenuous relations with German physiologists who did not appreciate the direction of his research, Loeb looked forward to a career and a life in America. He spent a frustrating year teaching psychology at Bryn Mawr College, where his Jewishness troubled some of his colleagues, and left for the University of Chicago in 1892, just a few months before Jastrow and Münsterberg came to town to exhibit psychology at the world's fair. At Chicago he taught physiology. His wife, Anne, served indispensably as his editor and translated his first two books, in addition to bearing four children in eight years (the first two—twin daughters—died). In 1900 John Watson entered the university as a graduate student. He studied biology and physiology under Loeb, who demonstrated to him "the fact that all research need not be uninteresting."[30]

Loeb had initially studied philosophy at the University of Berlin but quickly became disgusted at what he considered the inability of philosophers to penetrate to the fundamental problem of free will. Were people free to choose their actions? Mindful of that old philosophical concern, he turned to biology, believing that a close study of the mechanisms of animal behavior would yield answers that the "wordmongering" of philosophy would not. Biology, Loeb concluded, proves that free will is an illusion because human beings, like other animals, respond almost mechanically to a world of physical forces, of which their own reflexes constituted an important part. Loeb did not find this worldview depressing. On the contrary, he realized that the lawfulness of animal behavior made it possible to reshape the quality of human life. Once scientists discovered the relevant mechanisms, they could experiment with substitutes. When Loeb's study of sea urchins led him, in 1899, to invent a technique for inducing reproduction without sperm, he broke through the barriers that nature had seemingly imposed on animals. For Loeb the determinedness of life became a frontier of world-changing biological research. He forged the ideal of the scientist as an engineer rather than a mere observer of life processes. Fittingly, one of his students, Gregory Pincus, developed the birth control pill that freed women from one of biology's most stringent demands.[31]

The philosophy of science and life with which Loeb's name was most associated, the "mechanistic conception of life," was a direct response to theories of biological evolution that he considered dangerously metaphysical and potentially chauvinist. Loeb likened human reflexes and responses to the tropisms of plants. His theory that humans, like other animals and like plants, are designed to respond to stimuli in predetermined ways "puts an end to the metaphysical ideas that all matter, and hence the whole animal world, possesses consciousness." Loeb's mistrust of metaphysics was so deep that he could not tolerate the "clerical temperament" of those who tried to turn science into a cosmology. Once scientists and their sympathizers began to pontificate on the real nature of things and to advocate a scientific philosophy of life, they had succumbed to the clerical temptation of dogma.[32]

Loeb's worries were not abstract; he remained keenly aware of the efforts of Christian colleagues to reconcile science with Christianity. A British cleric and scientific popularizer who declared that the path of evolution led ever upward to Christianity gave the major academic lecture at the University of Chicago in 1893; Loeb could not believe that such a person was taken seriously. Even among those philosophers and scientists like John Dewey who had abandoned doctrinal Christianity, he perceived Christian metaphysics at work in the desire to find an ultimate pattern of meaning or truth in the "laws" of evolution. As a German Jew Loeb especially fretted about the way German thinkers assumed the evolutionary superiority of European civilization. The zoologist Ernst Haeckel, for example, was publishing widely popular books on evolution asserting that the "lower" races were "psychologically nearer to the mammals (apes and dogs) than to civilized Europeans," from which Haeckel concluded, "We must, therefore, assign a totally different value to their lives."[33]

True science, Loeb thought, would demolish such superstition and redeem civilization with values that were rational and just. As a pioneer of biological engineering, Loeb saw science not as an activity whereby people discovered fixed properties of evolution but, instead, as a means of altering evolution, of changing the conditions of life itself. His science steered entirely away from concerns about the "heritage" of human beings; those concerns, he knew, produced pernicious myths about race. The real excitement and the real challenge of biology, Loeb argued, lay in the possibility of restructuring life processes. That was the path to a rational and just world.[34]

As a Jewish atheist with socialist political views, Loeb retained an idealistic belief in principles of justice but did not believe that humans necessarily evolved toward a more humane social existence. "Economic, social, and political conditions or ignorance and superstition," he admonished, "may warp and inhibit the inherited instincts and thus create a civilization with a faulty or low development of ethics." Loeb spoke darkly of the ever-present possibility of ethical "mutants" who lacked an essential instinct much as an albino lacked pigment; "the offspring of such mutants may, if numerous enough, lower the ethical status of a community." Progress, then, was not inherent in human evolution. It was something that scientists might produce by bending the laws of human nature.[35]

NEITHER WATSON NOR JAMES: THE JEWISH MIDDLE WAY

The outlines of John Watson's behaviorism are visible in Jacques Loeb's "mechanistic conception of life," but Watson departed from Loeb in ways that made behaviorism unattractive to his Jewish colleagues in the enterprise of popular psychology. The utopianism of Watson's psychology, the powerful vision of a massive regeneration and purgation of American society, the sense of assurance that human nature might be radically transformed, all this was too much for Jews who shared his physiological view of consciousness but balked at his radical promises and his disregard for the ethic of self-examination. Whereas Watson's conduct suggested, in the words of his biographer, "that only the unexamined life was worth living," Jastrow, Brill, Münsterberg, and the others preached a *musar*-like message of self-discipline. As Münsterberg put it, there was "no conflict between the claim of science that we are mental mechanisms bound by law and the claim of our self-consciousness that we are free personalities." He understood modern psychology to mean that "we ought to look out for our inner world" because "we are that which we know ourselves to be in our practical life,—subjects which take free attitudes, and not simply objects."[36]

Jastrow likened behaviorism to "a blind man's version of the colorful world of mental behavior," and alluded to the all-important factor of cultural background that Watson's theory slighted. Though willing to give behaviorism credit when it illuminated the possibilities of "conditioned" human behavior, Jastrow urged that behaviorism deserved only "scant attention," except for the fact that John Watson had succeeded so well in popularizing it. He questioned Watson's idea "that it does not make much difference what we begin with or what kind of parents we have, since all that we shall ever become depends wholly on training from earliest infancy. . . . Whether we emerge from the process as doctor, lawyer, beggarman or thief (why not Indian chief?) is but the action of the environment and the conditions it offers." Jastrow's playful insertion of "Indian chief" into Watson's famous list of manufactured personalities was a clever allusion to the facts of ethnic and cultural background. He called into question any theory that failed to account for the effect of culture on individual destiny. Watson might produce a hypothetical doctor, but society, Jastrow knew, produced "doctors" and "Jewish doctors." That distinction was at its sharpest during behaviorism's ascent in the 1920s and 1930s, an era in which Jewish medical students faced new barriers to admission into American medical schools and Jewish doctorates in psychology were often denied positions for which they clearly qualified.[37]

Jewish popularizers of psychology did not see human beings as infinitely malleable, which meant potentially indistinguishable from one another. "To understand a human being you must understand his relative situation in the human group in which he moves," Walter Béran Wolfe commented. "He cannot be isolated in a laboratory and watched and observed as the behaviorists have attempted to do." It was difficult for Jewish thinkers to discount the complicated reality of ethnic traits that were virtually though not actually hereditary. "We may speak of one million men as if they were alike," Myerson explained in his 1934 textbook on social psychology, "but that does not alter the fact that Tom Jones is different from Max Cohen and Michael Flaherty."[38]

Comfortable with neither the mind-as-blank-slate of behaviorism nor the mind-as-divine-pathway of transcendentalism, Jews were conspicuous among popular writers on the mind for preaching a more conventional message of rational self-control. "I am arguing for a rational view of subconscious phenomena without making unwarranted assumptions or building up the subconscious into a miracle," Jastrow wrote. "Let us not raise vain hopes that we all have latent powers in some subcellar of the mind which we have only to tap by methods that advertisers boost and assert, but don't particularly make intelligible, and so introduce the millennium when we shall have perfect minds working in perfect order." To harness one's inner reserves of power in a real world of often depressing and exhausting obligations—that was the correct path for modern people, not a romantic flirtation with magical notions of rejuvenation or metamorphosis. "Living up to one's best is a lifetime discipline," Jastrow taught, "a lifetime ideal." While taking issue with Freudianism, he recommended the "heroic values of Freud's psychology" that "lie in the adequate recognition of the emotional life," because he, like Freud, emphasized the importance of exposing the opaqueness of emotions to the bright light of rational thought. To read Jastrow's admonitions about the power of emotions to upset reason, his exhortations about the dire necessity of using the mind to check emotional excesses, is to make contact with the classical, rationalist Judaism of his upbringing. "The primary use of intelligence should be to control emotions," Jastrow advised. "No one can go through life reasonably happy who cannot keep his emotions under adequate control."[39]

A Jewish Freudian like Isador Coriat also retained the rationalist moralism of Freud himself and followed a path between the transcendentalist and the behaviorist psyche. Coriat's *What Is Psychoanalysis?* (1917) did not cater to those who sought a philosophy of instinctual liberation in Freud's discovery of the repressed Id. Instead Coriat stressed the function of psychoanalysis as a liberator of reasonable ethics. His emphasis differed from that of the most influential Freudians of Christian background. William A. White's presentation of Freud, despite the title *Mechanisms of Character Formation* (1916), contained no explicit discussion of the ethical implications of psychoanalysis. Both White and James Jackson Putnam introduced their versions of Freud with quotations from Emerson, whereas Coriat chose a passage from Browning's *Rabbi Ben Ezra*, the dramatic monologue of an aged rabbi reviewing his life.

> So, still within this life,
> Though lifted o'er its strife,
> Let me discern, compare, pronounce at last,
> "This rage was right i' the main,
> "That acquiescence vain:
> "The Future I may face now I have proved the Past."

"Psychoanalysis," Coriat stressed in his book, "helps the patient to adequately meet the tasks of life and in a moral sense, it reeducates and reconstructs him."

To the rhetorical question he posed his readers, "What is the ethical value of psychoanalysis?" he gave an answer that recalled the *value* of repression. "Repression is the most important factor in our civilized life," he explained. "It keeps individuals from doing harm even if they have evil thoughts." Psychoanalysis allows those repressed feelings to be "utilized for a higher and more useful purpose" and in that way "encourages a more honest form of thinking, both in individuals and in social groups." In the end, Coriat's explanation of Freud hardly differed from the prescriptions of *musar.*

Q. What is the value of psychoanalysis in explaining character formation?

A. The unconscious is that region of the mind where the very springs of character take their source. . . . Psychoanalysis is able to penetrate to the origin of certain character traits and thus be helpful in eliminating characteristics which may be harmful to the individual.[40]

Walter Béran Wolfe echoed Coriat. "The individual who wishes social maturity," he urged, "must work at this task every day of his life." "The good life," he explained, "consists in utilizing the tremendous energy of the unconscious for the attainment of conscious, rational, and socially useful goals." Wolfe urged people to make a daily chart with checkmarks "for every good deed," which meant "every time you have identified yourself with someone and tried at least to make him a little happier." A crossmark would indicate "every unfriendly act and every omission or inhibition of human interest." He framed a "decalogue of all neurotic conduct" to help people on the road of self-examination and self-realization. Paralleling the traditional Jewish injunction to recite the *Shema* (the biblical declaration of God's oneness) twice a day, in the morning and the evening, he advised, "I want you to read it over every day, morning and night, until you can almost recite it. . . . What I want you to do is to cultivate an emancipated and enlightened egoism, not an immaculate saintliness. You need not go about in sandals and sackcloth to be a good social human being."[41]

"Judaism always preached the control of the emotions," Brill said in a lecture at New York University in the winter of 1937. "The old rabbis preached, 'He who conquers his primitive feelings is as strong as one who can conquer a city.' "

Brill and his Jewish comrades agreed on that moral perspective. They replaced the patient optimism of Judaism with a functionalist ideal in which humans painstakingly adjusted themselves to achieve greater internal harmony and social responsibility. Ill at ease with the euphoric transformations of human nature promised by transcendentalism and behaviorism, they followed a middle path, advocating a sober Jewish moralism that corresponded to an older, Franklinesque belief in a life of steady, perseverant self-improvement.[42]

That psychological moralism attracted Walter Lippmann, who incorporated it into *Drift and Mastery* (1914), a classic in the history of American social and political commentary. Lippmann (1889–1974) came from an affluent family of German Jewish New Yorkers. He was a prominent member of the illustrious Harvard class of 1909 that included T. S. Eliot. (At Harvard Lippmann studied psychology with Hugo Münsterberg, from whom he derived a personal interest in debunking spiritualism, a preoccupation that led to a friendship with Houdini in the 1920s.) The first influential layman in America to commend Freudianism, Lippmann discovered the Viennese doctor while vacationing in Maine with a patient of A. A. Brill. That patient, Alfred Kuttner, was a Jewish classmate of Lippmann at Harvard who suffered from serious bouts of depression and sought Brill's help. In the summer of 1912, the twenty-two-year-old Lippmann shared a cabin with Kuttner in the backwoods of Maine. Lippmann was there to write a book on politics (at the suggestion of a twenty-year-old friend from New York, Alfred Knopf) and Kuttner was busily working, as an assistant to Brill, on the first English translation of Freud's *The Interpretation of Dreams.* Once Kuttner began sharing the exciting new

ideas of Freud, Lippmann was hooked. He felt that Freud had given
him the explanation of human nature—specifically the relation between
rationality and irrationality—for which he had been searching. The inci-
sive sobriety of Freudianism liberated Lippmann, in the words of his
biographer, "from a Progressivism that saw man climbing ever upward
to perfection." "I feel about it as men might have felt about *The Origin of
Species!*" he wrote of Freud's work, which "for the first time in any psychology I know" provided "a picture of human nature in the act, so to speak,
of creating and expressing the character."[43]

The book that emerged from Lippmann's cabin in Maine was *A Preface
to Politics* (1913), but Freud served the brilliant young author even better
in *Drift and Mastery: An Attempt to Diagnose the Current Unrest*. Lippmann
called for a rationalist, scientific spirit as "the discipline of democracy,
the escape from drift, the outlook of a free man." Not unlike Jacques
Loeb's vision of society improved by biological engineers, Lippmann's
faith in progress revolved around a more candid psychological appraisal
of human emotionality and rationality. "Psychology," he wrote, "has
begun to penetrate emotional prejudice, to show why some men are so
deeply attached to authority." In wrestling with the problem of disorder
that came with the breakdown of traditional structures of authority—
church, family, community—the young idealist rejected both romantic
visions of the past and utopian visions of the future. He claimed that
"modern psychology, especially the school of Freud, has begun to work
out a technique for cutting under the surface of our thoughts," and with
that kind of scientific thinking about human nature Americans would
be more likely to "distinguish fact from fancy." Freudian morality helped
Lippmann imagine not a utopian society but one in which people pursued "a chastened and honest dream."[44]

THE EVIL OF THE MOB

Our Jewish thinkers believed that neither transcendentalist nor behaviorist approaches to the psyche allowed for a sharp enough appreciation
of evil, especially the evil of mass irrationalism. They introduced into
American popular thought a new concern about the destructiveness of
human nature that was expressed in mobs.

Seminal theories of the crowd developed in France at the end of the
nineteenth century, when strikes, socialist agitation, and scandals in high
places left the public uneasy about the future of the social order. Worried
about an uprising of the "republican" masses, a number of conservative
scholars and writers created the concept of the irrational mob. "To-day
the claims of the masses are becoming more and more sharply defined,"

wrote Gustave Le Bon, "and amount to nothing less than a determination to utterly destroy society as it now exists." A popular writer on psychology and sociology, Le Bon became the most famous of the European students of mass behavior with the publication of *The Psychology of Crowds* (1895), known in English as *The Crowd*. Padded with conservative stereotypes of races as having separate psychological constitutions and of crowd behavior as "female" by virtue of its irrational explosiveness, *The Crowd* distinguished itself by the simplicity of its thesis: "the unconscious action of crowds . . . is one of the principal characteristics of the present age." If leaders would learn about the psychology of crowds, argued Le Bon, they would then be able to mold unruly bodies of people into an orderly politics. "A knowledge of the psychology of crowds is to-day the last resource of the statesman," Le Bon declared. In the 1920s Benito Mussolini publicly praised Le Bon and acknowledged the lessons he had learned from *The Crowd*.[45]

Le Bon sold well in Europe, including England, but not in America. Americans of that era distrusted brooding portrayals of the crowd, which conflicted with a deeply held democratic optimism about the goodness of the common man.[46]

The one book about crowds that did enjoy remarkable success in the United States appeared, appropriately, in the same year that saw publication of Eleanor Porter's *Pollyanna*. Gerald Stanley Lee's *Crowds: A Moving Picture of Democracy* was the number-one nonfiction best-seller of 1913. (Mary Antin's *The Promised Land* took seventh place that year and Münsterberg's *Psychology and Industrial Efficiency* tenth). Lee (1862–1944) was an ordained Congregationalist minister whose Puritan ancestors settled in Connecticut in the 1640s. As a young man he had been deeply troubled by the loss of the solid church-oriented life of the old-stock New England towns and by the rise of cities populated by immigrants who were not Protestants. In middle age, having given up the pulpit for a career as a lecturer and writer, he perceived in the mysteries of crowd behavior a solution to the problems of urban America.[47]

Crowds begins by mimicking the standard diatribes of crowd literature, ridiculing socialism in the most juvenile fashion and despairing of the good old days when magazines contained large thoughts for small audiences. Then, in an abrupt about-face, the author praises the goodness of the "new kinds and new sizes of men" who make America's democracy a model of human collaboration for the greater good. In place of the Napoleonic figures who loom in French musings on the crowd, Lee cites the outstanding American businessman, like the president of a New England electric light company who "had besieged a city with the shrewdness of his faith, and conquered a hundred thousand men by believing in them more than they could." Inspired inventors and businessmen were millennial figures leading the masses toward Good through good works—they showed "what Christ meant . . . by saying He was the Way." With an irrepressible optimism that would have exasperated Le Bon, Lee held forth: "The men who are ahead make goodness start, but it is the crowds that make it irresistible. The final, slow, long, imperious lift on goodness is the one the crowd gives. . . . Crowds in the end will not accept less than the best."[48]

There was another reason American audiences avoided a darker crowd psychology. The most distinctive American form of crowd action in the early twentieth century was the southern lynch mob. Although not all Americans approved of that indigenous brand of mass behavior, which snuffed out the lives of more than one thousand African Americans between 1900 and 1920, neither did they want to point a spotlight at it that would renew the tension between North and South that had taken years to overcome. Though lynching became a regular theme in the pages of *The Crisis*, the official paper of the National Association for the Advancement of Colored People, edited by W.E.B. Du Bois, the majority of Americans overlooked the problem.[49]

Jews differed from that majority not because they suffered as blacks did from the American lynch mob, but because their sense of history and their reading of social behavior prevented them from sharing a conventional optimism. Unlike other popular writers on human nature, Jewish authors brooded about the dangers of mass irrationalism. In doing so they inverted the European theories of men like Le Bon who feared the force of democracy. While Le Bon claimed that knowledge of crowd psychology would enable the authorities to impose order on the people, Jewish psychological writers argued the opposite: the fulfillment of democracy depended upon the self-knowledge of the people. For them, democracy was not the problem; human suggestibility was. Once Americans learned to discard irrational and superstitious beliefs, they would rid American civilization of the excesses of the mob. Jewish psychological thinkers upheld American optimism but introduced an almost biblical note of warning. The Promised Land (true democracy) awaited Americans only if they proved themselves capable of psychological self-awareness, which meant rational self-restraint.

The first formal American study of the crowd was a doctoral thesis written in German by a brilliant young sociology student who had studied with John Dewey at the University of Chicago and then with Hugo Münsterberg and William James at Harvard. Robert Ezra Park became one of the greatest urban sociologists of the early twentieth century. At Harvard he had been impressed by one of William James's lectures, in which James praised Walt Whitman's glorious vision of the human crowd as the dynamo of democracy. That theme stimulated him to write a doctoral dissertation, *Masse und Publikum* (The Crowd and the Public), that he submitted to the faculty of the University of Heidelberg in 1904. (His study was not translated into English until the 1970s.) Park refused to accept the negative stereotypes that Le Bon and other European thinkers had heaped upon the crowd. Instead he stressed the ways in which crowd behavior divulged social conflicts and thereby enabled society to make changes that were vital to its survival. Park wrote in the American grain: America followed only one law, the law of progress based on confidence in the nation's foreordained ability to vanquish social problems on the road to pure democracy.[50]

Park was preceded, however, by a much more influential writer on mass behavior, Boris Sidis, who dwelled on the darker aspects of crowd psychology in his 1898 book, *The Psychology of Suggestion*. Sidis focused relentlessly on the dangerous propensities of human nature in its social context. He outlined a theory of behavior that rested, to a large extent, on the problem of human vulnerability to irrational appeals. "Not sociality, not rationality, but suggestibility," Sidis argued, "is what characterizes the average specimen of humanity, for *man is a suggestible animal.* . . . We do not in the least suspect that the awful, destructive, automatic spirit of the mob moves in the bosom of the peaceful crowd, reposes in the heart of the quiet assembly, and slumbers in the breast of the law-abiding citizen." Deriding Christian evangelism, Jewish messianism, political demagoguery, frontier vigilantism, and a host of other popular enthusiasms, Sidis concluded his lengthy study with the following italicized sentences: "*Society by its very nature tends to run riot in mobs and epidemics. For the gregarious, the subpersonal, uncritical social self, the mob self, and the suggestible subconscious self are identical.*"[51]

Several years prior to *The Psychology of Suggestion*, Sidis introduced American readers to the realities of the pogrom in an article for the *Atlantic Monthly*, "A Study of the Mob." He was the only prominent psychological thinker in America to have matured in tsarist Russia during the 1870s and 1880s, the dawn of a new era of antisemitic persecution. "A Study of the Mob" opened with two cases of mob action against Jews in the Ukraine, the region that was notorious for the Chmielnicki pogroms of 1648 and would become so again with the Kishinev massacre of 1903.

> In 1883, in the city of Ekaterinoslav, Russia, a Jewish merchant happened to quarrel with a peasant woman. "Murder! murder!" she screamed at the top of her voice. A crowd of idlers soon gathered about the two combatants. "Beat the Jews!" suggested someone in the crowd. A few stones flew in the direction of the Jew's store, more and more followed; then the mob made a rush for the building and destroyed it. . . . At about the same time, in one

of the suburbs of Nijni-Novgorod, the following incident occurred. A child
fell into a ditch; a Jewess pitied it, took it in her arms, and carried it into the
synagogue to warm it. A Christian woman witnessed the scene, and began to
cry out that a Christian child had been kidnapped for sacrificial purposes.
A crowd of about three thousand men gathered; a drunken fellow called
out, "Beat the Jews!" Thereupon an attack was made, and the mob, after
having demolished the Jewish synagogue, proceeded after the manner peculiar to all Russian anti-Jewish riots, breaking into Jewish houses, killing,
violating, and barbarously demolishing every person and thing they found
in them.[52]

Other Jews shared Sidis's wariness about the destructiveness of an irrational crowd. Most Americans discounted Freud's dark assessment of
human nature as mere German pessimism, even in the wake of World
War I, but Joseph Jastrow, though no Freudian, thought the war justified
the "baser side of living assumed in Freudian psychology." In Jastrow's
eyes, the war was a model of mass delusion. "In older days deluded patients heard divine voices in the air; now the inspired messages come
through an invisible telephone," he wrote. "The great German delusion,"
he presaged, "wears the garb of the twentieth century" because "liberty
is the political concept of the generation [and] the Germans maintained
the delusion that they were free." While paying lip service to "the values
regarded by the rest of mankind," they ruined them.[53]

The war merely sharpened an apprehensiveness about human behavior that Jastrow already shared with his Jewish colleagues, largely as a
result of their awareness of the history of antisemitic persecution in Christian cultures. "The hankering for magic is deeply rooted in the human
breast," Walter Béran Wolfe said of the human desire to find scapegoats.
"When Spain was going through its great depression in the fifteenth century, the Jews were the scapegoat, and their expulsion became an act of
highest piety." Writing in 1933 he perceived that "Hitlerite Germany, having learned nothing from history, follows the Spanish custom today."
Even Münsterberg remembered the Jewish timeline of persecution, despite his elevation of German over Jewish identity. To argue against the
practice of American policemen coercing confessions from potentially
innocent people, he cited the Inquisition, tsarist Russia, and the Dreyfus
case as stellar examples of such abuses. "When the conspiracy against
Dreyfuss sought to manufacture evidence against him," he admonished,
to illustrate how easily people incline toward emotional rather than objective conclusions, "they too made much of the fact that he trembled
and was thus hardly able to write when they dictated to him a letter in
which phrases of the discovered treasonable manuscript occurred."[54]

Münsterberg based his vocal opposition to the prohibition movement on similar anxieties about mass hysteria. "When a Chicago minister hangs the American flag over his pulpit, fastens a large patch of black color on it, declares that the patch stands for the liquor evil which smirches the country . . . and then madly tears the black cloth from the stars and stripes and grinds it under his heel," he wrote with some distress in 1908, "then thousands rush out as excited as if they had heard a convincing argument." Although he assured readers that he himself was a very light drinker and had no personal stake in the issue, Münsterberg objected to the way Prohibition took a matter of self-discipline and free will and turned the individual into a member of a mass. "The demand of true civilization is for temperance and not for abstinence," he argued, "but nothing is more characteristic of the hysterical caprice of the masses than the constant neglect of this distinction." Münsterberg died two years before Congress passed the Volstead Act (1918), enabling Prohibition on a national scale, but he was sure that "America under prohibition pushes the masses into gambling and reckless excitements and sexual disorder and money-crazes and criminal explosions of the mind."[55]

Münsterberg did not object to mass leisure; in fact, he was one of the first scholars to recognize the significance of movies as a new art form. But the spectacle of a large audience in a frenzied state led him to perceive latent fascism in ordinary customs of mass leisure (in this, he anticipated the critiques of mass culture made by German Jewish émigrés from Nazism in the 1940s). In the autumn of 1905 he remarked of the Harvard-Yale football game, which attracted thousands of fans, "Such frenzy, as I saw there, prepares the public systematically for hysteric emotions with all their consequences in social and political life."[56]

The boosterism and revivalism of the 1920s elicited criticism of mass behavior from intellectuals like Thorstein Veblen, who diagnosed an entire generation as suffering from dementia praecox, but Jews may have felt greater than average concern about the racial dimensions of popular irrationalism. Between 1915 and 1925, the Ku Klux Klan revived, businessman Leo Frank was lynched, a horrible series of "race" riots erupted, the most spectacular of which occurred in Chicago in 1919, and Henry Ford's *Dearborn Independent* published the *Protocols of the Elders of Zion* and other antisemitic screeds. In the eyes of many American Jews, the religious revivalism at issue in the Scopes trial of 1925 reinforced the mass irrationalism that fueled those notorious acts of racism. Hence Joseph Jastrow's warning that "to have a complex on the Negro question or on teaching evolution in the schools is not so harmless" because "when that kind of feeling rises it may break out in riots or mob rule."[57]

In such disquieting times it was the unique job of the psychologist, claimed Jastrow, to fathom "the persistence of the dominant human mo-

tives so deeply set in human nature" that they can be "kept under control
. . . only through constant discipline." The psychoanalysts Brill and Coriat agreed about the intractability of destructive instincts, which seemed
to verify the biblical statement that was Brill's favorite: "The imagination
of the human heart is evil from its youth." Coriat reminded readers that,
even though "the unconscious reveals very primitive and barbaric ways
of thinking," psychoanalysis can do "for the unconscious of the individual what education does for the race" by changing primal motives so
"that they become really civilized." Brill emphasized the importance of
sympathy, which he likened to a "heavy dam, which holds down and
controls our natural aggression" and which "like the dams of modesty,
disgust, or morality . . . must be carefully preserved." Adler and Wolfe
also placed a premium on sympathy, the quality that lay at the heart of
the Adlerian concept of communal feeling (*Gemeinschaftsgefühl*). They
interpreted evil as a product of human estrangement and, as an antidote,
they encouraged the development of a sincere appreciation for "the
stranger." "The secret of social success," Wolfe counseled, "lies in the
realization that every human being has a sense of strangeness in the
presence of another human being." The irrational violence of the mob
would be impossible if individuals would develop their capacity for mutual appreciation.[58]

Boris Sidis put the matter of evil bluntly. "Fathers and mothers," he
called out in a popular book on education, "*the true education of life is the
recognition of evil wherever it is met.*" Sidis warned that American optimism
was insufficient to prepare children for their civic responsibilities: "A
strong sense of recognition of evil should be the social sense of every
well-educated citizen as a safeguard of social and national life." The average citizen had to understand the vulnerability of people to the power
of irrational mass suggestion. "This knowledge," he insisted, "becomes
an imperative necessity to him who lives in a democracy."[59]

When Sidis and other Jewish thinkers publicized their warnings about
the potential of individuals to produce evil through superstitious mass
behavior, they were importing into American popular thought a paramount Jewish concern. Unlike the European theorists of the crowd who
wrote from an aristocratic fear of democratic excesses, Jews in America
wanted more democracy but feared that irrational mobs would under-
mine progress toward that goal. The numbing uniformity of their admonitions about self-discipline and rational control of the emotions, and
the distressed uniformity of their dislike for dramatic interpretations of
the mind—especially mystical interpretations—came, at least in part,
from a deeply historical sense of danger. They were optimists about
human potential but shared a sober wariness about those people whom
Jacques Loeb described as ethical "mutants."

These men were writing in an era of resurgent European antisemitism, with its mythical distinctions between a crude Jewish and a noble German (or Russian) soul. Such American mysticisms as mind cure and spiritualism had little to do with racial mythologies, but the bizarre history of antisemitic mythology left Jews deeply suspicious of any kind of romanticized irrational. Jewish thinkers did not necessarily believe that romantic views of the mind would yield racial bigotry, as happened in German culture, but they agreed with Münsterberg about the danger that "mental cures carry with them when they are based on any particular creed, and especially when they are tied up with a semi-religious arbitrary metaphysics. . . . What is gained if some nervous disorders are helped by belief, if the belief itself devastates our intellectual culture and brings the masses down again to a view of the world which has all the earmarks of barbarism?"[60]

Jews who wrote about psychology for the general public shared the goals of their colleagues from Protestant backgrounds. They hoped to alleviate mental suffering and produce a social order that would best protect the delicate mechanism of the human psyche. But they also created a separate stream of ideas that entered the mainstream of American thought about human nature. When they offered up a diagnosis of American society, they prescribed a place for the Jew, nerves and all, within it. Their preoccupation with the subjects of race, heredity, irrationalism, and evil reflected distinct Jewish fears about the collapse of rational civilized behavior, the only sanctuary for society's outcasts, dissenters, and scapegoats. Their profoundly rationalist moral perspective and deep discomfort with radical visions of psychic transformation added what they considered necessary ballast to public attitudes about the mind and soul.

The traumatic events of a second world war only reinforced the desire of Jewish thinkers to convince Americans of the dire necessity for continued examination of the psyche. There, in the innermost recesses of the mind, lay possibilities for redemption unknown to, or insufficiently explored by, traditional religion. That, at least, was the message a young rabbi brought to millions of Americans seeking peace of mind in a postwar world.

Part IV

Peace of Mind:
Judaism and the Therapeutic Polemics
of Postwar America

Chapter 9

Rabbi Liebman and the Psychic Pain of the World War II Generation

DURING THE FINAL WINTER of World War II *Science Digest* ran the story "Mental Crackups among Airmen." The magazine reported the findings of Lt. Col. Roy Grinker, a Freudian psychiatrist from Chicago serving in the Army Air Forces, on the problem of stress induced by air combat, which frequently led to nervous breakdowns. "No matter how carefully selected through psychiatric tests, almost every man will break down if the stress of air combat continues long enough," Grinker explained. After receiving appropriate psychotherapeutic treatment, however, a very high percentage of the soldiers returned to duty if not to combat. Most of the men, or, as the *Science Digest* phrased it, "the largest number of our mentally sickest returned soldiers," were people who longed to go home to wives or mothers "and be taken care of as though they were babies . . . reverting, or regressing as psychiatrists term it, to a babyish level." One of Sigmund Freud's last analysands, Grinker knew that Freud himself likened regression to an army detachment that retreated to earlier positions in order to avoid a powerful enemy (viz., psychic conflict). For Freud, regression was a deeply disturbing psychological function, involving a return to a childish lack of emotional and moral restraint, a weakened state that made individuals succumb to a primitive and dangerous "herd instinct." The success of psychiatrists like Grinker at restoring the psychological strength of American soldiers was therefore critical, not only to individuals but to the society into which they would return after the war.[1]

Several years before the war began, a rabbi came to Dr. Grinker to begin a regimen of psychoanalysis. The rabbi, Joshua Loth Liebman, was destined for extraordinary fame after the war as a result of a book called *Peace of Mind*, the most popular inspirational book to appear in America since 1900, and the first such best-seller to be written by a rabbi. Published in February 1946, *Peace of Mind* sold more than a million copies in its first three years, and was still among the top ten on the nonfiction best-seller list when Liebman died of heart failure in 1948 at age forty-one. By then, he was the most celebrated rabbi in America and the first to have an interfaith audience of national dimensions. Liebman's experience with psychoanalysis redefined his life and determined the central theme of *Peace of Mind*, which declared that men and women needed the insights of depth psychology if they hoped to gain inner peace. Religion alone, Liebman claimed, was insufficient, but psychology and religion working together "like twin angels" would "lift up ailing, bewildered man." More than any other American clergymen of his day, Joshua Liebman endorsed a Freudian approach to human nature and personified the postwar romance with psychology.[2]

Using Liebman's career as a prism, we will be able to see more clearly how three trends in American society intertwined with each other: the effect of World War II on American attitudes toward mental health; the remarkable ascendance of Freudian psychology to a dominant position in popular thought in the 1940s and 1950s; and the growing role of Jewish figures in America's "psychological" culture.

1946: *Peace of Mind* and *The Snake Pit*

"It may seem strange," Joshua Liebman averred in the opening sentence of his book, "for a man to write a book about peace of mind in this age of fierce turmoil and harrowing doubts."

> It may seem doubly strange for a rabbi, a representative of a people that has known so little peace, to engage in such an enterprise. However, I make no apologies for this attempt to find new answers to the basic problems of human nature. . . . I have written this book in the conviction that social peace can never be permanently achieved so long as individuals engage in civil war with themselves. I maintain that a co-operative world can never be fashioned by men and women who are corroded by the acids of inner hate.

Liebman possessed a keen sense for the shifting mood of the country after a decade and half of depression and war. He wanted to replace Marx—an exclusive focus on external conditions and political reform— with Freud. A committed liberal and civil rights advocate, Liebman conceded that "social circumstances do profoundly modify our human responses" and "unjust economic conditions do create neuroses and maladjustments." Nonetheless, he maintained, "whether under capitalism, socialism, or communism, men and women still face the purely personal and profoundly individual issues of life and death as well as the tangled interpersonal relations of parent and child, brother and sister, husband and wife." And with that shift of attention from outer to inner causes of human life, Rabbi Liebman ushered in the postwar preoccupation with individual happiness as a psychological imperative.[3]

"Questing Inward" was the name he chose for the first chapter, which opens with an autobiographical parable. When Liebman was a teenager, he composed a list of the world's goods, qualities such as health, love, beauty, talent, power, wealth, and fame that most people desire. But when he presented his list to "a wise elder who had been the mentor and spiritual model of my youth"—a rabbi (probably his grandfather)—the older man shook his head, crossed out the list with his pencil, and replaced it with three words: "peace of mind." That, the rabbi explained, was the "gift that God reserves for His special proteges." The passing years seemed only to confirm the lesson. "I have come to understand," Liebman told his readers, "that peace of mind is the characteristic mark of God Himself, and that it has always been the true goal of the considered life."[4]

Peace of mind did not refer to a monastic ideal ("it must not be identified with ivory-tower escapism"), nor could it be easily acquired ("it cannot be attained by taking a tablet before meals, or by enrolling for a 'course' three evenings a week"), nor did it reside in alcohol, drugs, or "sensual indulgence," diversions that seemed to be on the increase in America. Not even in "the sublime sharings of human love" would Americans find peace of mind. They would find it only by looking inward, a formidable task that required techniques beyond the traditional methods of religion. "There has been a new method of gaining insight into the deepest emotional and psychologic disturbances that threaten man's peace of mind," he explained, a method "pioneered by Sigmund Freud." Liebman wanted to correct the "erroneous impression" that psychoanalysis "reveals man solely as a creature of base passions and low desires," because "when we discover that it is the triumph of psychology to translate these energies into constructive, beautiful forms—then, and then only, shall we be in a position to speak honestly and act honestly."[5]

Peace of Mind was not the first attempt to reconcile religion and psychology, but it was the first to do so in a way that captivated millions of people. Liebman's clarion call was that "religion, which already has made its peace with Copernicus and with Darwin, will have to make peace with Freud." He did not mean Freud per se so much as "depth psychology" or "dynamic psychology," the analysis of inner drives and conflicts that distinguished the followers of Freud and Adler (he rarely mentioned Jung). By unearthing those inner conflicts that harked back to childhood and produced a lifetime of unproductive or destructive habits, people could find a new dynamism for change, a powerful motor for their spiritual lives. He explicitly addressed his message to "those disturbed and questing souls in this modern world who cannot 'go home again' to old theologies. . . . My words are not directed to those blessed souls that are quietly content in the arms of some traditional religion, nor are they intended for mystics who have found their own private way to serenity." The new path that Joshua Liebman hoped to open up to Americans was recognized by one of the nation's leading authorities on the psychology of personality, Harvard psychologist Gordon Allport, who testified that Liebman had shattered "the long-standing myth that religion and psychology are necessary antagonists" and demonstrated "that they converge upon a single goal—the enhancement of man's peace of mind."[6]

There were actually two best-sellers in 1946 that symbolized the immense postwar interest in mental health. *The Snake Pit*, an autobiographical novel by Mary Jane Ward, provided Americans with a potent new metaphor for understanding the plight of the insane. Aside from exposing the large gap between what the public thought asylums were like and the conditions that actually existed, *The Snake Pit* dramatized the vulnerability of a successful, intelligent, and well-educated person to mental breakdown. Stimulating mass anxiety about that possibility, the novel moves toward its conclusion with the wry comment of a nurse at the Juniper Hills Hospital, who says of the excess of incoming over outgoing patients, "I'll tell you where it's going to end. When there's more sick ones than well ones, by golly the sick ones will lock the well ones up."[7]

In November 1948 Twentieth Century Fox released a very successful movie version of *The Snake Pit*, which "adapted" Ward's story in order to propagandize virtues that did not appear in the original—the Freudian virtues that Liebman advocated in *Peace of Mind*. To this day there is a common misunderstanding that the movie version of *The Snake Pit* has the same theme as the novel on which it is based. After opening night at the Rivoli Theater in Manhattan, *New York Times* reviewer Bosley Crowther praised the film for following the book "with rare fidelity," and scholars have repeated his mistake ever since. The film's director and producer, Anatole Litvak, was a Ukrainian Jew who knew the political uses of film from his experience in the Soviet industry of the early 1920s and in the U.S. wartime industry of the 1940s, when he collaborated with Frank Capra on the War Department's "Why We Fight" series. Litvak radically altered Ward's story, turning it into a memorable Freudian melodrama. In the movie, a twenty-four-year-old woman suffers from an inability to love her husband. Through the patience and wisdom of a Freudian psychiatrist, she discovers a guilt complex based on primal love for her father, a revelation that liberates her to become a successful wife and mother. Around that plot, the film presents a sharp exposé of conditions in a mental asylum.

Ward's novel was indeed an exposure of the frightening conditions in mental asylums and a reminder of the thin line separating mental health and illness, but it was not a brief for Freud or psychoanalysis. Unlike the movie, the book does not focus on the protagonist's therapeutic dialogue with her psychiatrist, but on her interactions with nurses and patients. Unlike the movie, in which Olivia de Havilland portrays a sentimental and intellectually deferential young woman who secretly yearns to be a mother, the book depicts a witty, intellectually assertive, middle-aged writer who had once lived in a socialist co-operative in lower Manhattan and who would be happy to resume her career and her happily childless marriage. Near the end of the book the Freudianism of the protagonist's first doctor (a European) is damned with faint praise while the last word is given to another more traditional psychiatrist (an American), who admits that he lacks a satisfactory diagnosis but speculates that Virginia Cunningham suffered from a biochemical disturbance.[8]

Both Ward's novel and Litvak's film dramatized the grave regimentation of the mental asylum in a way that drew attention to something that caused great public anxiety and consternation in postwar America: the problem of mental disorders among the millions of returning citizen-soldiers. But it was Litvak's movie that capitalized on, and helped to sustain, the extraordinary role Freudianism played in the drama of wartime and postwar healing.

WAR AND THE FREUDIAN WAVE

Freudianism enjoyed its first American vogue after World War I, when shell shock dominated public attention. In 1918, for example, the *New York Tribune* headlined a story about shell shock, "Reassuring Information as to Its Nature and Treatment from Dr. I. H. Coriat, a Leading Psycho-Analyst." "By now the twitching figures, the quick starts, the periodic shudderings of the victims are fairly familiar as a reminder of our part in the war," the paper observed. The good news was that doctors like Coriat guaranteed that shell shock was a curable psychological disturbance, not unlike a breakdown suffered by a person from the stress and anxiety of daily life in a competitive world. "If the present conflict has one relieving feature," the newspaper reported, "it is that the very science which has expended itself on the aims of destruction has achieved still greater feats of skill in the study and the relief of its own destroying impulses." The hopefulness of that message goes a long way toward explaining the fact that, after the First World War, the center of psychoanalysis shifted from Vienna to Park Avenue, much as the center of international finance moved from London to Wall Street. As great as John Watson's influence was in the 1920s, writes a leading historian of that era, "it could not hold a candle to that of Sigmund Freud." And as much as Freudianism affected intellectuals and artists in the 1920s, it could not hold a candle to what it became after the Second World War.[9]

The most conspicuous differences between the two wars involved the length of time in battle and the numbers of soldiers, casualties, and psychiatric cases. In World War I, American troops served only a year and a half, from April 1917 to November 1918, compared to nearly four years (December 1941–September 1945) in World War II. Roughly 4.5 million Americans served in 1917–18, of whom more than 200,000 were wounded, 50,000 died in battle, and approximately 100,000 were admitted to hospitals for neuropsychiatric treatment. In the Second World War more than 10 million served in the armed forces, of whom nearly 600,000 were wounded, nearly 300,000 died, and approximately 850,000 were treated for neuropsychiatric problems. One of the statistics that most troubled people was the brute number of men declared psychologically unfit to serve in the military during World War II—more than 1.6 million were rejected at induction for psychiatric reasons. In addition, more than 160,000 men received an administrative discharge from the armed forces for one of the following reasons: psychopathic personality, mental deficiency, drug addiction, homosexuality, or alcoholism.[10]

The public did not have to wait for the end of the war to learn about the psychological problems it brought. From the beginning of American involvement the press kept up a fairly steady stream of reports about "war neuroses." The first successful campaign in the Pacific, the taking of Guadalcanal after months of combat, was accompanied by stories on the home front about "Guadalcanal Neurosis." The terrifying tactics of the Japanese, the physical results of which had appeared so shockingly in Bataan, were now examined in terms of psychic costs to American soldiers. "Never before in history," *Newsweek* reported about the victorious marines at Guadalcanal, "had such a picked group of toughened physical specimens been subjected to such prolonged and exquisite mental torture." This was the report of the chief psychiatrist at the Naval Hospital at Mare Island north of San Francisco, where many of the neuropsychiatric patients from the Pacific were recuperating. Lt. Commander Edwin Smith characterized the weakened state of these men as "a group neurosis that has not been seen before and may never be seen again." Smith discovered uniform symptoms of jumpiness at slight sounds, extreme sensitivity to mild reprimands, and acute fears of being considered cowardly. Reports on the psychological condition of soldiers (and their wives), on the high incidences of discharge for neuropsychiatric problems, and on the pressing need to help afflicted veterans readjust to noncombat duty and civilian life were routine in World War II.[11]

From the final autumn of the war through the first autumn of the peace, heart-wrenching personal stories saturated America's leading magazines. "Give Us a Break," pleaded an anonymous airman in the pages of the *Reader's Digest* in November 1944. "I was psychoneurotic," he began, as he related the horrors he witnessed in combat and the panic he experienced after being returned to the States in "Army pajamas and a robe" while his uniform was locked away. "We Psychos Are Not Crazy," was the headline of a confessional in the *Saturday Evening Post* that was written by a war correspondent, Henry Gorrell, who had suffered several bouts of nervous breakdown dating back to his being taken prisoner by Franco's forces during the Spanish Civil War. Gorrell complained, as did most writers on the subject, about the label "psychoneurosis"—which was often shortened to "psycho" when it wasn't disguised by "NP" (neuropsychiatric case). He explicitly advocated for the more respectful terminology— "combat fatigue" or "battle fatigue"—that eventually prevailed in the mass media. "Meet Ed Savickas," the *Ladies' Home Journal* urged in a story about a young husband and father of two from Elizabeth, New Jersey, who was "a victim of combat fatigue" but whose "chances of complete recovery give hope to thousands." Honorably discharged after frontline service in North Africa and Sicily, Savickas was working as an aircraft mechanic, seeing a psychiatrist once a month and slowly regaining his composure.

> When Eddie happened to mention he might like some Brussels sprouts, Stella knew they were out of season, but she tramped all over town till she found them—at seventy five cents a quart. That night she cooked them as tender and rich as she knew how, only to see him push his plate away and go into the living room unhappily supperless. . . . When they try a movie, Eddie is more than likely to get up in the middle and march out. Stella follows without question and makes no ill-timed remarks on the way home. Not that she is any 1945 version of Patient Griselda. . . . But she knows what the score is with Eddie. It was his thoughtfulness about little things that first attracted her to him, and the apparently regardless things he now does, she knows, aren't his fault. They're Hitler's fault, if anybody's.[12]

It was as if, following the war, mental imbalance had become a contagious disease. "Don't Let Them Tell You We're All Going Crazy!" *Better Homes and Gardens* admonished readers in 1947, lest they succumb to "the alarmists' charges that mental ills are increasing." The magazine hired an experienced medical writer to put the country's psychiatric dilemma in perspective. "We're all pretty glib in using words like psychoneurosis," he suggested. As if to forecast the release of *The Snake Pit* the following year, he added: "The next movie you attend may have as its hero a psychiatrist . . . who fishes a complex out of the patient's past to set the stage for a satisfactory clinch." Although this author's job was to reign in popular anxiety about the nation's mental health, he nonetheless subscribed to the new therapeutic ethos. "The ideal will not be reached," he knowingly observed, "until people are as casual about seeking psychiatric help as they are in getting a diagnosis of sinus trouble."[13]

The middle-class public took that advice seriously enough to justify Stephen Sondheim's lyrics in one of the great comic songs on Broadway in the 1950s, "Gee, Officer Krupke" from *West Side Story* (1955):

Officer Krupke, you're really a square;
This boy don't need a judge, he needs an analyst's care!
It's just his neurosis that oughta be curbed.
He's psychologic'ly disturbed!

The psychiatric expert that Americans were calling for and lyricists were parodying was a Freudian. It is hard to believe that a few hundred professionals could change the culture of a nation, but that is what happened in the United States after the Second World War. The *Manual of Military Neuropsychiatry*, edited by two Jewish psychiatrists, Harry Solomon and Paul Yakovlev, forecasted the postwar future in the words of one contributor: "Freud and his pupils, through psychoanalysis, have probably contributed more to the understanding of the complexities of the human personality than any other group of psychiatrists." Three years later a *Time* cover story on the psychology craze included a lexicon of "The Lingo," which contained only Freudian concepts (Oedipus complex, unconscious, subconscious, id, ego, superego, repression, sublimation, conversion) plus Adler's inferiority complex.[14]

The key to the popularity of the Freudians was the tempting prospect of "uncovering" repressed traumatic memories, which appeared to cause the neuroses and psychosomatic symptoms of soldiers. Roy Grinker, who came out of the war as a leading psychiatric authority, foreshadowed the postwar romance of uncovering the repressed in an interview with *Time* in the winter of 1944. Grinker explained that the Army used two psychotherapeutic methods, which *Time* dubbed the "Forget It" and the "Tell It" approaches. The first, used in the First World War, was better for returning soldiers to combat as quickly as possible. The patient was given rest, food, sedatives, and "psychiatric pep talks" to encourage him to return to the fray. The "Forget It" approach worked best for the soldier "whose ego is still pretty much in command of his cosmos." But Grinker considered this method unsatisfactory because he believed that the men who were "cured" by it would suffer from mental problems after the war. The soldier with more severe neurosis had to be treated by the "Tell It" method, which involved an abbreviated psychoanalysis. He was fed and rested and sometimes given sodium pentathol to "loosen his tongue." Then, seated in a darkened room with a psychiatrist, he was encouraged "to describe the horrors he has endured, relive the episodes that hurt his inner being. . . . When such a patient begins to depend on the psychiatrist, and accept him as a 'supporting presence,' he is likely to lose the outward signs of his neurosis—a stiff leg, deafness, forgetfulness, phobia. . . . Then begins a longer period, probably months, of making the patient independent of the psychiatrist." Only after the patient uncovered the traumatic episode that formed the nucleus of his affliction would he be freed "toward independence."[15]

The drama and catharsis of "uncovering," coupled with the idea of guilt as the source of mental affliction, captivated the mass media. Colonel Grinker told the *New York Times* about "the universality of guilt reactions" and the ways in which guilt—often over the death of comrades in battle—motivated many cases of war neurosis. Grinker, who was head of neuropsychiatry at Michael Reese Hospital in Chicago, and one of his residents, John Spiegel, wrote a small but important book, *War Neuroses* (1945), which distilled 1,200 cases of that affliction. With nearly fifty thousand copies distributed to military personnel, the book propagated the method of narcoanalysis that Grinker and Spiegel had developed, combining sodium pentathol with a brief, cathartic psychoanalysis. "It is the fusion of the technique of hypnotism with the ideas of psychoanalysis," wrote psychiatrists Bertram Wolfe and Raymond Rosenthal in a popular book on hypnotherapy, *Hypnosis Comes of Age*, "that represents the major innovation in hypnotic medicine to come out of the psychiatric emergency created by the Second World War."[16]

That approach became the focal point of a powerful documentary produced by the Army under the direction of Hollywood director John Huston (and narrated by his father, actor Walter Huston). *Let There Be Light* (1946) was not released for many years (perhaps the Army considered it too disturbing), but it testified to the magnetic power of psychoanalysis. Scripted by Charles Kaufman, who also wrote the screenplay for Huston's *Freud* (1962), *Let There Be Light* documented the treatment of soldiers hospitalized for war neuroses at the Mason General Hospital on Long Island. Case after case appeared before the camera—white and black men, southerners and northerners, native-born and immigrant—some stuttering, some overcome by vacillation, and a few suffering from paralysis or amnesia. One by one the patients were cured, however slowly, by talking out what had happened to them and bringing to the front of their minds those disturbing experiences and emotions that had lain buried in the psyche. Huston rendered their moments of catharsis so visible as to be poignant. To see a young man who had lost the use of his legs rise up from his bed and walk again after narcoanalysis was unforgettable, and to realize that unexpressed feelings of guilt might cause such an affliction was a revelation.

What the public missed from the suppression of *Let There Be Light* it absorbed through newspapers, magazines, and such movies as *The Snake Pit*, which made sure to focus the camera on a portrait of Sigmund Freud hanging in the office of the psychiatrist-hero, lest the audience forget who was "uncovering" the patient's hidden guilt. Psychiatrists propagandized the necessity of their trade by pointing out that the soldiers they had treated represented the fittest sector of the population: young healthy males who had been screened for service. And among psychiatrists in the postwar years, the Freudians were the ones with the greatest

sense of mission, the strongest *esprit de corps*, and the most tantalizing
tales of sickness and recovery. The paucity of hard evidence for the therapeutic effectiveness of psychoanalysis neither dampened their confidence nor curbed their enthusiasm. "Nothing could be farther from the
truth" than the idea that Freudianism was "a fanciful flight of the imagination," the partisans announced—"Freud elaborated his theories about
the unconscious mind on the basis of a close empirical study of the most
ordinary psychological events." And within that small but suddenly influential profession of psychiatry, Jewish doctors—especially Freudians—
were richly represented. A statistical breakdown of psychiatric residents
at the Menninger School of Psychiatry in 1958 found that about one-
third were Jewish (Jews comprised only 3 percent of the American population). Perhaps even more important, most of the celebrated émigré
psychoanalysts from Austria and Germany were Jewish.[17]

Joshua Liebman's Psycho-Spiritual Quest

Rabbi Joshua Liebman was probably the first American preacher of national standing to undergo psychoanalysis. That decision may have reflected the loneliness of a precocious child of divorced parents in an age
that did not smile on divorce. Born in 1907 to Simon and Sabina (Loth)
Liebman, Joshua grew up in Hamilton, Ohio, and later in Cincinnati.
His parents divorced when he was two, leaving him largely in the care of
his paternal grandparents. His grandfather, Lippman Liebman, was a
Reform rabbi and the person who first stimulated Joshua's interest in the
rabbinate. A short, stocky prodigy with a photographic memory, Joshua
entered the University of Cincinnati at fifteen and qualified for Phi Beta
Kappa in his junior year. To supplement his ordination, Liebman wrote
a dissertation on medieval Jewish philosophy, earning a doctorate in Hebrew letters from the Hebrew Union College in Cincinnati.

Somewhere around the age of thirty, by which time he had married his
cousin Fan Loth and was serving in his second pulpit at the distinguished
K.A.M. Temple in Chicago, he entered psychoanalysis with Roy Grinker.
He continued in therapy for about three years, during which time he
relocated to Boston to take the pulpit of Temple Israel. There he resumed analysis with Erich Lindemann, a psychiatrist at the Harvard Medical School whom Liebman considered, along with Grinker, a primary
inspiration to the writing of *Peace of Mind.* Like Grinker, Lindemann focused on the handling of stress and pioneered in the psychology of grief.
(Lindemann was known for his study of the victims of a tragic fire at
Boston's Coconut Grove nightclub in 1942, which claimed more than
four hundred young men and women.) Liebman's experience with psy-

choanalysis left him "enchanted with the world of the subconscious," his adopted daughter Leila recalled (sharing her father's interest, she became a child psychiatrist). The young rabbi soaked up the literature of depth psychology. By the time he sat down to write *Peace of Mind,* he had acquired an impressive if general understanding of the field.[18]

When Liebman succeeded Harry Levi as rabbi of Temple Israel in 1939, he inherited a pulpit that was ensconced in interfaith activity and modern broadcasting. Christians as well as Jews had attended Levi's Sunday services, which he began broadcasting throughout New England in 1924. Liebman extended Temple Israel's outreach even farther thanks to his oratorical gifts. By the mid-1940s he reached between one and two million listeners, of whom probably 70 to 80 percent were Christians. He received hundreds of letters after a regional show and thousands after each national broadcast. An outspoken Zionist and fighter for racial equality as well as an interfaith activist, Liebman devoted his inaugural radio sermon from Temple Israel, "Our Common Heritage," to an impassioned call for Christians and Jews to unite in the face of a common enemy: the abasement of human behavior not by science but by recent history. The first rabbi to lecture extensively at seminaries, colleges, and universities in New England, Liebman had an oratorical power that inspired vivid reminiscences. His fellow rabbi and colleague William Braude recalled an occasion in which Liebman entertained Braude's daughter at home. "I remember walking in one day as he was reciting Hamlet's 'To Be or Not To Be' to Dorothy and her friends, who were then nine or ten years old. They did not know what he was saying, but he held them spellbound. He could have done the same thing with the multiplication table. . . . Had he remained alive, he would have become a kind of Jewish and more intellectual Billy Graham."[19]

Liebman's relationship to his congregants was the crucible in which he forged his thinking about spiritual relief for the average American. From the very beginning of his career, Liebman relished his pastoral role. Though largely uninspired by his first pulpit in Lafayette, Indiana, the young rabbi confided to a close friend that, despite some disappointments he experienced as a teacher, "As pastor I have really made some lovely contacts and have perhaps brought a little courage and happiness into unhappy homes. Who can weigh or measure these intangibles?" Liebman searched the literature of philosophy and theology for insights into human nature and relationships, but the intellectual restlessness that generated *Peace of Mind* came from his frustrations as a pulpit rabbi. The banality of rabbinic sermons irritated him. Gloomily reflecting on the lack of originality both in his own sermons and in those of other rabbis, he confided to a friend that "the titles are all hackneyed and the content will be a re-statement of our old positions served 'with hash-brown potatoes or what have you.' In looking over some of the sermons of the rabbis of old . . . I am struck by the similarity of ideas and the sameness of approach in them all. . . . Are the basic points of view that can be expressed by us not extremely delimited and conducive to repetition?"[20]

Liebman also worried about impulses toward mystical and harmonial religion that had begun to penetrate the rationalist crust of American Jewish thought. Anticipating what would become a veritable mass movement of Jews into Eastern religion after the 1960s, a childhood friend of Liebman's took this path in the 1930s. The mystical-transcendentalist faith to which "Bill" turned appeared to give him an "assurance, a peace, a certitude as well as a cosmic support which we might well envy." Liebman was affected by this episode, in which he perceived something deeply unsettling. He wrote his most intimate correspondent, Rabbi Jacob Shankman: "Thank God that you have never changed and I hope shall never go saintly or mystical on me!"[21]

Liebman realized that if the pulpit remained empty of new ideas, more Jews might abandon Judaism as "Bill" had in search of a more "spiritual" faith. Or if they did not leave physically, they would impair Judaism by filling its pews with apathetic souls. The seeds of *Peace of Mind* appear in the first address Liebman delivered to the Brotherhood of Temple Israel in Boston soon after taking office there in 1939. He had begun to reassess the role of the synagogue as a spiritual institution: "The synagog [*sic*] serves its second great function when it helps you to gain a balanced emotional and philosophical attitude toward life, with its vicissitudes, its transitoriness, its defeats, and its possibilities. Without such a philosophy you cannot survive today with any measure of happiness or tranquility. . . . I certainly believe that philanthropy and charity are essential more perhaps than ever before. But they will not substitute for a rich philosophy of living for the individual."[22]

In ways that were remarkably prescient, Joshua Liebman argued in favor of a synagogue that met the deep inner needs of the person as effectively as it responded to the social needs of the Jewish community. These two sets of needs had been converging since the 1920s, as Jewish men and women began to demonstrate a keen interest in psychology.

THE JEWISH DRIFT TOWARD PSYCHOLOGY

In a sense American Jews had institutionalized a "talking cure" of their own as far back as the first decade of the century. A unique feature of the Yiddish press was the advice column that the *Forverts* (*Jewish Daily Forward*) installed in 1906 to help newcomers express their troubles and possibly find solutions. Editor Abraham Cahan wanted to create a space in his newspaper for the many "desolate souls who thirsted for a chance to unburden their hearts" and who sought "a meaning and some advice about the troubles that oppressed them." Keenly aware of the multitude of problems facing immigrants in New York City, especially such vexing personal problems as the separation of parents from children and husbands from wives, as well as interpersonal conflicts over assimilation, Cahan instituted a column known as the *Bintel Brief*, "bundle of letters." Readers submitted their problems, often with "a deep psychological description" of themselves and others, and the editors tried to solve them. The *Bintel Brief* was a huge success and an unprecedented venture in America's immigrant press, an example of the creativity that made Cahan's *Forverts* the most widely read of any foreign-language paper (in the 1920s it claimed a readership of 250,000).[23]

In the rush of confessionals, some writers brought up psychological problems and asked, as did the barber who had had a frightening dream about cutting the throat of a customer, "Is it madness?" The editor's reply was not theoretically sophisticated but, on the other hand, it showed a respect for psychic dilemmas and willingness to suggest psychiatric help that, in 1908, were unconventional even among native-born Americans. About the barber's disturbing urge to do what he had done in the dream, the *Forverts* commented: "Man's thoughts often weave automatically through 'idea-patterns,' as they are called in psychological science, and the muscles respond automatically to the ideas. . . . Every man can dream he commits a terrible crime, because in dreams the controllable will is slumbering. The writer of this letter must simply laugh off the dream and drive the whole matter out of his head. But if his nervous system is for some reason weakened and therefore his control over his will power likewise weak, he must consult a doctor."[24]

The sensitivity of the *Bintel Brief* corroborates evidence that Jews were more receptive than other immigrants to scientific information about nutrition, hygiene, health, and child development and less suspicious about the services provided by modern institutions. In 1914, for example, the Department of Health of New York City commended the Yiddish magazine *Unser Gesund* (Our Health) for its innovative effort to enlighten immigrants about the facts and myths of venereal disease. The department's medical adviser had been receiving inquiries from readers of the journal—"they were Hebrews, spoke English very indefinitely, had very up-to-date views on eugenics, asked about . . . many other questions which I could not hope to answer." The editor of *Unser Gesund*, Benzion Liber, authored *Sexual Life: A Popular Scientific Book* (1914), a Yiddish text dedicated as "a gift to the Jewish people" (*A matonoh dem yidishen folk*), in which he gladly reported that "people are becoming accustomed to the new role of the doctor, to his role as educator and enlightener."[25]

During the 1920s and 1930s the middle class of assimilated Jews who congregated in Reform temples proved a responsive audience for the ideas of Jewish psychological thinkers. Much as the Vienna lodge of B'nai B'rith gave Freud his first meaningful forum in the late 1890s, communal associations in American cities provided eager lay audiences for men whose rise as scientific experts signified the progress of American Jewry in general. Abraham Brill flourished on that circuit, which allowed him free expression of his strong ethnic sympathies, but the baptized Adler also spoke at Reform temples. By the late 1920s the interest of an educated Jewish laity in the world of psychology led the Reform rabbinate to extend its first invitation to a Freudian psychiatrist, Bernard Glueck, to speak at a meeting of the Central Conference of American Rabbis. A leader in the new field of forensic psychiatry and an expert witness for the defense in the trial of Leopold and Loeb, Glueck (1883–1972) was an immigrant from Poland who went on to become one of only two Jews to serve as president of the American Psycho-Pathological Association between 1910 and 1945 (the other was Abraham Myerson). "My practice, while not exclusively a Jewish practice," Glueck said, "gives me occasion to see many Jews in difficulties. I seldom see a patient coming to my office who has achieved that unity with himself and with his fellowmen and with the world about him, which somehow I conceive to be a characteristic of the religious state." Glueck encouraged the rabbinate to think of the great benefits Judaism might bring to its followers by incorporating a more therapeutic approach to human problems.[26]

The appeal of psychotherapeutics to Jews registered in the fact that hundreds of immigrants and children of immigrants studied to become psychiatrists, psychologists, neurologists, and social workers in the early 1900s. A highly selective census—the 1928 *Who's Who in American Jewry*—listed no fewer than 112 professionals in those fields, including a small but significant number of women such as Maida Solomon (1891–1988) who formed part of the first generation of psychiatric social workers.[27]

The study of psychology enticed an entire generation of Jews who came of age in America during the interwar years. A brief glimpse into the lives of four prominent psychologists raised in New York City suggests that, among other factors, the perception of having had an unhappy childhood pushed more than one intellectually inclined fledgling out of the parental nest and into the study of human nature. In contrast to Freud and Adler, who took the flaws of their nineteenth-century European parents in stride, Abraham Maslow (1908–70), Albert Ellis (1913–), Seymour Sarason (1919–), and Richard Lazarus (1922–) all left behind reminiscences that include acerbic commentary on the deficiencies of their parents and a sense that psychology gave them a tool for understanding themselves in spite of the disharmonies of childhood.[28]

Maslow, the son of a Brooklyn cooperage dealer who became one of the most influential American psychological thinkers of the postwar era, recalled his early life as "miserably unhappy." He felt extremely distant from both his parents and intensely disliked his mother, with whom he cut off all contact for a quarter of a century. Ellis, a best-selling author and creator of an influential therapeutic technique, Rational-Emotive-Behavioral Therapy (REBT), remembered a childhood in the Bronx marked by divorce and parental neglect. He described his father as a charming but domestically irresponsible salesman and "promoter" and his mother as a voluble woman with many friends and few maternal instincts. Lazarus, a psychologist of stress and coping who taught at Berkeley, recalled the tensions he felt with a father who showed "constant contempt and denigration of my competencies" and a depressed mother who turned for relief to Christian Science ("To preserve a hostile peace, my mother had to agree to raise her two boys as Jews"). Lazarus explicitly linked his "choice of vocation" to his "troubled childhood." Sarason, an educational psychologist who taught at Yale, also considered his childhood "a troubled one." Only in the home of his religious, Yiddish-speaking grandparents, which he remembered as "an oasis of conflict-free living," could he find the "warmth and stability" that he wanted from his parents. "My parents wanted to be Americans," he wrote, "and that meant that I was cut off from their near and historical pasts." Sarason believed that he was motivated toward psychology by a desire "to make sense of me and my past," especially the disjunction he felt between the Old World and American dimensions of his childhood.[29]

Though we must be cautious about generalizing from the testimony of a handful of men who made a life out of psychology, those reminiscences remind us of the unique advantages that the study of human nature held for many American Jews. It was probably not coincidental that none of the four sustained an interest in Judaism as a religious tradition even though they all grew up with at least a nominal Jewish education. Psychology gave them both a vocation and a cosmology. All four belonged to a generation of ambitious and energetic Jewish men and women who flooded America's colleges and universities in search not only of professions beyond the reach of their parents but also of secular knowledge to fill the religious void left by the immigrant generation. Theirs was the generation whose future was forecast by the momentous New York City communal survey of 1917, which discovered that only one-quarter of the city's Jewish children received a Jewish education. Fifty years later a different type of sociological survey found that nearly two-thirds of the people who came to psychoanalytic clinics in New York were Jews. Out of this generation came Henry Roth, who wrote *Call It Sleep* (1934), the first psychoanalytic novel about immigrant life and a beautifully wrought story about a young boy growing up on the Lower East Side. And the same generation included the Jewish women, Lucy Freeman and Joanne Greenberg, who authored the two most notable autobiographical accounts to popularize psychoanalysis in the years after World War II: *Fight against Fears* (1951) and *I Never Promised You a Rose Garden* (1964). In each story psychotherapy healed the breach that alienated the patient from her parents.[30]

In *Fight against Fears*, Lucy Freeman gave an eloquent account of the spiritual significance that some Jews perceived in psychoanalysis. A writer for the *New York Times* whose grandparents had emigrated from Germany and England, Freeman grew up in the 1920s and early 1930s amid the affluence of Westchester County and attended Bennington College in Vermont. Although she suffered from a chronic sinus condition, the dominant problem Freeman hoped to solve through analysis was spiritual. (The epigram of her book cleverly invoked Job: "Thou shalt lie down and none shall make thee afraid.") "Ostensibly I possessed all a girl needed for happiness. I worked on what I believed the world's finest newspaper, rubbed shoulders reporter-fashion with great and near-great. By society's standards I was successful—but I felt miserable. I had never known more people—nor been lonelier." As her psychotherapy progressed and she sorted out residual family conflicts, Freeman found herself gaining a depth, a capacity for more sincere engagement in the world, which had eluded her. "The idea that there is a conflict between psychoanalysis and religion (at least the psychoanalysis that I have known) is fantastic to me," she wrote. "Analysis gave me what feeling I possess for religion. . . . Now I find growing pride in being a Jew, a result of liking myself better as a whole. As long as I disliked almost everything else about myself, probably I also disliked being Jewish."[31]

PEACE OF MIND FOR AMERICAN WOMEN

Although we have no statistics to determine how many readers of *Peace of Mind* were women and how many were Jewish, there is reason to suspect that Liebman's message resonated with special force for both. Jews could delight in the fact that a rabbi had attained such celebrity and influence in American religious life. And women had all along been a driving force behind the therapeutic tendencies in American Protestantism that had also begun to surface in Judaism. *Peace of Mind* differed from the many books that emphasized material success and "personal power," the staples of the masculine self-help tradition. In fact Liebman's book began with the point that material successes are insufficient and often irrelevant to achieving a state of inner peacefulness. It spoke to a more "feminine" interest in the psyche for its own sake.[32]

To the degree that Liebman appealed to women, he offered an intellectual and spiritual alternative to the two Jewish "heroes" of postwar America, Hank Greenberg and Bess Myerson, whose reputations hinged on their bodies. The fame of the baseball star and the beauty queen converged in September 1945, when the Miss America pageant and the American League pennant race seized the nation's attention. Liebman appeared on the scene six months later. A Jewish student at Mount Holyoke College wrote her parents of Liebman's speaking engagement there a year after the appearance of *Peace of Mind*: "This week is some week! Rabbi Joshua Liebman is going to preach in *church*! A Christian girl's parents are coming up from New York especially to hear him!" A week later, she reported excitedly:

> Dear Folks, Rabbi Liebman was just wonderful! I have never been so moved in my entire life. If you've read "Peace of Mind," you know the general trend of his thought. However, to hear him speak was a thrill in itself. He had one of the best, if not *the* best speaking voices we've ever heard here. . . . But in the religious aspect, he was wonderful especially—he came right out and told how proud he was to belong to the Jewish faith. He even told some old rabbinical stories, from which one could get solace.[33]

This young woman's enthusiasm reflected both the importance of Liebman as a symbol of Judaism's ecumenical legitimacy and the appeal of his message to women.

Unlike most psychologists and psychiatrists who wrote advice for women in the 1940s, Liebman offered his readers a refreshingly unclichéd perspective. An issue of the *Ladies' Home Journal* that carried an extensive feature on Rabbi Liebman and his family also contained a regular column, "Making Marriage Work," by a Penn State psychologist. "If you're dissatisfied, restless, bored, don't waste time feeling sorry for yourself," the adviser wrote with gusto. "Join a club, cultivate new acquaintances, develop a hobby." The *Journal*'s readers learned also that "marriage offers the one best way of meeting most of your needs" and "to receive love and affection, you must give them without stint." The thoughtful insights in *Peace of Mind* about self-awareness and self-acceptance transcended such meat-and-potatoes psychological sermonizing. "In nearly 25 years of bookselling I have at last encountered an 'inspirational' book that I am able to read," wrote Elsie Stokes, the proprietor of a Nashville bookstore, to Liebman's publisher. "The flood of trash devoured under that name by the American public has always astounded and slightly disgusted me. . . . Now there is one, PEACE OF MIND, that I shall be proud to sell." Though Liebman was not preaching feminism, neither was he preaching against it; his overriding theme—personal liberation from the psychological shackles of religion and culture—appealed as strongly to women as to men.[34]

A more specific phenomenon of gender helped account for the timeliness of his book. Approximately 300,000 American soldiers died in World War II, leaving millions of wives, mothers, and sisters in grief and often without a major source of support. In *Peace of Mind* the theme of grief had special appeal, to judge by digests and references in popular magazines. In 1947, *Reader's Digest* underscored the therapeutics of grief by printing an abridged version of "Grief's Slow Wisdom," the chapter from *Peace of Mind* that dealt with death and mourning. Here Liebman counseled emotional honesty to a population inured by its culture to repress, conceal, or subdue feelings of sadness in the face of death: "*Express as much grief as you actually feel.* The pain that you feel now will be the tool and the instrument of your later healing." And his scenarios of grief often targeted women.

> A father dies, leaving a widow and a young child. At the time of the funeral the little boy is sent to some relative and the widowed mother and all the relatives conspire to conceal from the child the true situation. The father's name is not mentioned or, if mentioned, the conversation is quickly turned to some other channel. The theory behind all this conspiracy of silence about the death of the father is that the little boy should be shielded from grief and pain. This whole process of concealment, while motivated by the highest intentions, can prove to be terribly distorting to the child's emotional development.[35]

Joshua Liebman's message about grief resonated with special force in postwar America. To enhance its 1948 feature article on Liebman, *Look* selected excerpts from the chapter "Grief's Slow Wisdom" to accompany the article. In the layout for the Liebman story, the reader's attention is drawn as much to a large photograph of women weeping at a funeral as to the interview itself. The picture illustrated *Look*'s interpretation of Liebman's message: "These women are right in weeping unashamedly at the funeral of a loved one. By repressing this emotion, they might harm themselves psychologically." Following this piece of advice is *Look*'s list of "Don'ts" about grief: don't repress emotion, don't avoid talking about your feelings, don't avoid crying, don't avoid talking about the deceased, don't grieve excessively after a suitable mourning period, don't exclude children from the process, and don't find a substitute for the deceased too quickly because this might cause a "guilt complex."[36]

From *Peace of Mind*'s discourse on grief, Americans learned that Judaism had anticipated modern therapeutics of mourning. "Traditional Judaism," Liebman argued, "had the wisdom to devise almost all of the procedures for healthy-minded grief which the contemporary psychologist counsels." The rabbi went on to describe the rabbinic approach to mourning, which moved the mourner through several phases of graduated grief. "Where traditional Judaism was psychologically sound in its approach to death, much liberal religion has been unsound," Liebman charged. "Liberal rabbis and liberal ministers alike . . . arrange funerals in such a way as to make death itself almost an illusion." Linking Freud's insights about emotional repression with the rabbinic understanding of grief, he indicted "the whole superficiality of modern civilization."[37]

Peace of Mind followed "Grief's Slow Wisdom" with another chapter, "Intimations of Our Immortality," a chapter that nodded to Wordsworth and probably resonated with American women confronting the death of loved ones in the aftermath of war. Some evidence of this comes in the form of a little condolence book, *To Comfort You,* printed by Hallmark. The keepsake contained a poem by Liebman called "Our Memory Shall Be a Blessing," which echoed the theme of "Intimations of Our Immortality": we should take solace not from accolades of an afterlife but from the meaningful relationships we form during our lives. (This conventional Jewish focus on the here and now appeared earlier in Hugo Münsterberg's 1905 book *The Eternal Life* and in Harold Kushner's 1981 bestseller *When Bad Things Happen to Good People.*) In the condolence book, Liebman's meditation appeared alongside the poetry of well-known American authors, including Emily Dickinson.

The juxtaposition of Liebman and Dickinson tells its own story about women, publishing, and popular theology in the wartime and postwar years. Dickinson's poetry came into vogue many years after she lived and enjoyed a burst of attention between 1930 and 1960. In that period, three major editions of her poems, five editions of her letters, and three major biographies appeared. Like Liebman, Dickinson criticized the unfairness of Original Sin, and she once penned an insight into American popular theology that helps explain the impact of *Peace of Mind*: "When Jesus tells us about his Father, we distrust him. When he shows us his Home, we turn away, but when he confides to us that he is 'acquainted with Grief,' we listen, for that also is an Acquaintance of our own." Dickinson focused on death, dying, and immortality in a way that was not traditionally Christian. Her popularity in the middle decades of the century, especially among women, paralleled the success of Liebman's therapeutic message.[38]

JOSHUA LIEBMAN: THE FIRST ICONIC JEW OF POSTWAR AMERICA

Decades before Elie Wiesel and the mass-marketing of Holocaust awareness, the media transformed Joshua Liebman into the first "iconic Jew" of postwar America, the first celebrated Jewish figure identified with the

Jewish predicament and the human predicament after Hitler. *Ladies'
Home Journal* featured him in its series on American families, "How
America Lives." The layout for "Meet an American Rabbi and His Family"
contained two large-font inserts with Jewish quotations and commentary,
one of which evoked an interesting triple connection between Judaism,
healing or saving of life, and the Holocaust. " 'He who destroys one life,
it is as though he had destroyed the world. And he who saves one life, it
is as though he had saved the world.' This Talmudic precept has been
the guiding philosophy of this American rabbi who has brought a healing
message to a spiritually torn world. He exhorts his flock to live in the
image of the 'helping Jew' who has a moral offering to make to the
world." Beneath this passage, a smaller insert noted that "re-educating
their adopted daughter, Leila, to the 'blessings of immaturity' after the
horrors of a German concentration camp, has been the Liebmans' greatest joy." Highlighting the typicality of the Liebman's family life—including the Americanization of Leila, a Polish Jewish teenager only three
years out of Auschwitz—the *Journal* gave its readers a quick lesson in both
the problematic of Jewish history, symbolized by the Nazi horror, and the
solutions offered by Judaism, expressed by the talmudic injunction to
save life.[39]

The *Journal's* beautifully formatted, extensive feature story on Liebman and his family contained a large-font insert that read: "Mine has
been a rabbinate of trouble—of depression. Hitler's rise, world crisis,
global war, the attempted extermination of my people. My text has had
to be 'Comfort ye, Comfort ye, my people.' " *Newsweek* reprinted this
entire quotation in its story on Liebman, which, significantly, appeared
in an issue whose cover announced the theme of healing and renewal.
Showing a photograph of a paraplegic young man, presumably a veteran,
with a basketball on a basketball court, the cover read, "Paraplegics: The
Conquest of Unconquerable Odds." Among the intricate assemblages of
images and associations in mass magazines, that of "Rabbi Liebman,"
"consolation/healing," and the "ravages of war" marked a new and compelling combination in the late 1940s.[40]

The *Journal* emphasized and sharpened the symbolic association by
appending to its feature on Liebman his article, "Hope for Human
Brotherhood," which expounded on the problem of bigotry and prejudice in the postwar world. "We conveniently avoid recognition of the
guilt and hatred in our own souls, and we project these evils on to some
convenient bogeyman or scapegoat—the Jew, the Negro, the Catholic or
others," he explained, condensing Freud's theory of projection. "Today,
for the first time in history . . . we are just beginning to understand *why*
we hate and fear one another, and how such fear and hatred swell into
mass movements of bigotry and persecution. Our new knowledge of our-

selves offers boundless hope for human brotherhood. Insight brings healing." By virtue of both his Jewishness and his Freudianism, Liebman was taken as an authority on wartime suffering and prejudice.[41]

Joshua Liebman became a rabbi to the American public not simply because he was a brilliant orator but because he detected a massive public demand for a new kind of consolation and inspiration in the wake of war. In one unusual book, he responded to a religious restlessness and a curiosity about psychology that had been building for a generation. That a rabbi had emerged to accomplish that task was something new. Never before had a Jewish author speaking as a religious Jew attracted a national audience on the scale that Liebman achieved. Jews had written American best-sellers, as we have seen, but not inspirational best-sellers in which Judaism itself drove the plot. Now we must turn to the arguments and controversies that accompanied this first Jewish book into the American spiritual marketplace.

Rabbi Joshua Loth Liebman on the air, ca. 1946. Liebman was one of
America's most charismatic religious orators and the country's
most famous rabbi after the publication of *Peace of Mind*. He died two
years later at age forty-one. (From the Joshua Loth Liebman Collection,
Department of Special Collections, Boston University.)

Joshua Liebman with wife, Fan, and daughter, Leila. A survivor of the
Holocaust, Leila was adopted as a teenager by the Liebmans and,
inspired by her father's love of Freudian psychology, went on to become
a child psychiatrist. (From the Joshua Loth Liebman Collection,
Department of Special Collections, Boston University.)

Chapter 10

Peace of Mind:
A New Jewish Gospel of Love

A FULL-PAGE AD for *Peace of Mind* in *Life* magazine in 1946 pictured the book being handed down from above by a male hand. *Life* readers may have wondered if the hand was supposed to be the author's, the publisher's, or the Lord's, but in any case, it would have been Jewish insofar as the author was a rabbi, the publisher was Simon and Schuster, and the God in question was the God of Moses rather than Jesus.[1]

Joshua Liebman had written an emphatically *Jewish* book, the first of its kind to enter an inspirational mass market long monopolized by Protestants. By appealing to Americans on the basis of psychology rather than theology, Liebman could compete with his Christian peers. Theology favored believers over nonbelievers, whereas psychology placed everyone, Christian as well as Jew, on the same ground and recommended its prescriptions for maturity to one and all. In *Peace of Mind* Joshua Liebman said that spiritual growth depended on psychological maturity, but he also said something else that gave his book a polemical thrust. Judaism, Liebman preached, offered a unique healing message of self-acceptance, and self-acceptance formed the foundation for neighborly love. Behind the consolations that *Peace of Mind* offered its readers, the book transmitted a modern Jewish theology into American thought about human nature and the human condition.

WHY HISTORIANS FORGOT ABOUT *PEACE OF MIND*

Joshua Liebman was part of a postwar religious revival that also made celebrities of Norman Vincent Peale, Billy Graham, and Fulton Sheen. New churches and synagogues sprouted like mushrooms on the suburban landscape—by 1953 60 percent of Americans belonged to congregations, an all-time high. As for the other 40 percent (roughly 64 million people), a popular *Guide to the Religions of America* included them too on the simple grounds that "most of the millions who do not go to church *are* religious." Unfortunately, our understanding of the revival that Liebman, Peale, Sheen, and Graham represented has been badly damaged by a resilient stereotype, according to which postwar Americans sought a shallow, positive-thinking, feel-good religion to go along with the luxuries that inspired economist John Kenneth Galbraith to dub America "the affluent society." Critics claimed that the rejuvenation of religious life was more apparent than real, more a function of suburban social needs than of theological or spiritual demands. The motto of the era—one that has been parodied since the day it was uttered—was President Eisenhower's statement that American society had to be based on "a deeply felt religious faith—and I don't care what it is." Eisenhower alluded to a growing public feeling that Protestants, Catholics, and Jews shared a common sense of religious values transcending dogmatic differences. That was why it did not matter which faith Americans accepted, as long as they accepted one.[2]

The most influential critique of American religion to come out of that era, Will Herberg's *Protestant-Catholic-Jew* (1955), decried the "faith-for-the-sake-of-faith" attitude that seemed to prevail after the war. Herberg perceived the "cult of faith" as a sign of the "disintegration and enfeeblement of the historic religions"—"familiar words are retained, but the old meaning is voided." Phrases such as "have faith" and "don't lose faith" had once been "injunctions to preserve one's unwavering trust" in God, but in the postwar era they had degenerated into "an appeal to maintain a 'positive' attitude to life and not to lose confidence in oneself and one's activities. 'To believe in yourself and in everything you do': such, at bottom, is the meaning of the contemporary cult of faith, whether it is proclaimed by devout men from distinguished pulpits or offered as the 'secret of success' by self-styled psychologists."[3]

Protestant-Catholic-Jew portrayed the new consensus forming in America as Catholics and Jews entered what had once been a Protestant mainstream. The thick walls traditionally separating these three faiths had begun to thin. Americans began speaking of their society as a "Judeo-Christian" civilization. Considering that Jews constituted less than 4 percent of the U.S. population, the replacement of "Christian" by "Judeo-Christian" stood as a remarkable symbolic milestone. The very title of Herberg's book promoted his own people to a parity (an equal among three partners) that they would not have gained on the basis of ethnicity, where Jews coexisted with scores of other minorities. Norman Vincent Peale, Fulton Sheen, and Joshua Liebman personified the new religious pluralism, in which highly literate, nonparochial Protestant, Catholic, and Jewish preachers all addressed an ecumenical mass audience. But Herberg brooded over the theological cost of the new arrangement. He believed that the ecumenical melting pot destroyed the integrity of each religion. The triumph of Peale, Sheen, and Liebman meant the victory of blandness and conformity and the deterioration of an authentic Protestantism, Catholicism, and Judaism.[4]

Herberg's analysis was so trenchant and struck such a chord that it became the standard interpretation of postwar religion, and of *Peace of Mind*, for a full half-century. Herberg, however, grossly misrepresented *Peace of Mind* as a new kind of faith-healing, a doctrine of "if I believe, my troubles will disappear." He conveniently ignored Liebman's emphasis on the hard work and patience required to gain insight into one's own psyche. With the stroke of a gifted pen, Herberg established a caricature of Joshua Liebman that lasted fifty years. Histories of America in the 1940s, if they mention *Peace of Mind* at all, do so with condescension, noting that the book initiated "a spate of 'reassurance' tracts" and claiming that "the religious awakening of the 1940s had another, more rigorous side, rooted in theology." Even histories of American Jews in the postwar era saddle Liebman with this stereotype, linking his "pop religious psychology" with "simplistic guides to instant Judaism." A few discerning scholars of American religion have not fallen into Herberg's trap; they recognize that *Peace of Mind* was not a positive-thinking treatise. But their influence has been limited. As late as 1995 the prestigious Jewish journal *Commentary* published an article on the postwar religious revival that discussed Peale, Sheen, and Graham but made no mention of Liebman and hastily concluded that the revival was "Christian."[5]

Because of the general disregard of *Peace of Mind*, the Jewish features of the book have been largely overlooked and virtually no one has noticed the Jewish polemic lying between its covers. But once we look at Liebman's arguments, we are forced to reevaluate the entire world of postwar American religious thought, which contained more conflict and less conformity than we have been led to believe.

A NEW FREUDIAN *MUSAR*

Milton Steinberg (1903–50), a peer of Liebman who was one of the most gifted American rabbis of his generation, declared that *Peace of Mind* stood "as an indisputably Jewish contribution to the spiritual resources of the American community." Steinberg was in a position to know. He wrote his own minor classic, *Basic Judaism* (1947), a lucid exposition for the general reader that remained in print for the rest of the century, and a durable historical novel, *As a Driven Leaf* (1939), about a heretic of antiquity, Elisha ben Abuyah, who was torn—like most of Steinberg's twentieth-century readers—between Jewish and worldly values. The rabbi of the Park Avenue Synagogue in New York City, Steinberg belonged to the Conservative movement of American Judaism, which was much more tradition-minded than Liebman's Reform movement. He had little appetite for trendy mass-marketed books with sparse Jewish content.

In his review of *Peace of Mind*, Steinberg made a point of praising Liebman for refusing to water down his Jewish background and Jewish sources in order to appeal to a wider public. But what made Steinberg's assessment of *Peace of Mind* particularly astute was his ability to see that the book occupied a special place between two genres: American inspirational books and *musar*, Jewish ethical books. Though criticizing Liebman for putting religion into a psychological straitjacket, Steinberg recognized that *Peace of Mind* was much more sophisticated than the typical inspirational best-seller. He placed *Peace of Mind* into the tradition of Jewish ethical writing that included, at its best, such works as Luzzatto's *Path of the Upright*. Of course Steinberg realized that a *musar* book written for a large interfaith audience would look a lot different from those written over the centuries for strictly traditional Jews. But he saw one overriding criterion that qualified *Peace of Mind* as a classic of inspiration: the capacity to synthesize theology with the dominant intellectual trends of the age. "As in other ages," Steinberg wrote, "the core challenge to the human spirit . . . took the shape of the harmonization of religion and science, so today one of the most urgent ideological tasks is the establishment of a rapport between faith and its practical implications on the one hand, and psychiatric techniques and their presuppositions on the other. Rabbi Liebman, in other words, has undertaken an assignment at the very center of the thought life of our age."[6]

Among the connections Liebman made between tradition and modernity, he linked rabbinic and Freudian conceptions of human nature, becoming the first influential rabbi to do so. Liebman likened the Freudian idea of inescapable psychic conflict to the old *musar* idea of the *yetzer*. "Actually in Judaism there is a very realistic understanding of human nature as a battleground between 'the good impulse' and 'the evil impulse,' " he explained. And the Freudian process of *sublimating* unruly drives was comparable to the rabbinic idea of "sweetening" the evil impulse. "There is also a profound optimism that even the evil impulse can be made to serve a life-affirming purpose, for as the rabbis point out, without the driving energies of the emotions within man, 'no one would marry or beget a child or build a business.' All of the varying aspects of man, including his competitiveness and rivalry and passions, can be harnessed to the chariot of goodness. It is my faith that we can sublimate and master the evil within us in the service of righteousness and of life."[7] Liebman thrilled to the idea that Judaism's insights into human nature matched those of dynamic psychology. That idea fueled the Jewish polemic in *Peace of Mind*.

A voracious reader (he was known for reading even while he shaved), Joshua Liebman stayed abreast of the philosophical currents of the postwar world, and in *Peace of Mind* presented arguments about psychology and Judaism that had a clear philosophical goal. Liebman divided the religious philosophies of his day into two main groups: those that tried to incorporate the findings of science to produce a richer, humanistic religious life, and those that regarded science as peripheral or irrelevant to religious life. He, of course, identified with the first group: "It is basic to my own Jewish tradition that God reveals himself anew in every generation and some of the channels of this revelation in our day are in the healing principles and insights of psychology and psychiatry." The most prominent representatives of the second group, Liebman believed, were the European existentialists and neo-orthodox Protestants (he named Karl Barth and Emil Brunner) who had "completely lost faith not only in liberalism but in rationalism" and whose "attitude is one of basic gloom and pessimism." They conceived of the human being "as an unredeemed sinner, condemned by his very finiteness to anguish and anxiety." Liebman set himself against those religious thinkers:

> Temperamentally and theologically I am committed to seeing man, not as a hopeless sinner, but as a child of God created in His image. One of the fundamental issues that will be fought out in religious literature in these coming years lies just here—whether we shall view the human adventure with hope or despair; whether we shall look upon physical and social sciences and all other creations of human reason as indispensable allies in spiritual fulfillment, or whether broken-hearted and filled with guilt, we shall proclaim man's nothingness while waiting for the unmerited Grace of God.[8]

The science of psychology would also enrich religious life by giving people of different faiths a unique opportunity to transcend their dogmatic differences and recognize each other's common human nature. "There are no sectarian labels to our fears and aspirations," Liebman argued. "There is no essential difference between the anxieties, phobias, hopes and hungers of a Catholic, a Protestant or a Jew." In the kind of religion he promoted, one that harvested the insights into human behavior that social scientists provided, a new definition of spiritual maturity emerged. Maturity would no longer be defined in the old dogmatic terms, which assigned moral superiority to the believer who adhered most diligently to the tenets of Protestantism, Catholicism, or Judaism. (Other religions had not yet entered into the mainstream American vocabulary.) Instead, maturity belonged to those who learned to "understand themselves deeply, to master their undesirable traits and to fashion characters of strength and integrity." In other words, people who came to grips with their basic inner conflicts deserved to be called spiritually mature regardless of the religious doctrines they espoused.[9]

THE JEWISH POLEMIC IN *PEACE OF MIND*

And yet, despite his zeal for psychology, Liebman insisted on the ultimate value of religion and of Judaism in particular. In his call for "life-affirming" religious beliefs that gave people "a sense of relatedness to the Divine Power" without submerging them in a conviction of their sinfulness, Joshua Liebman saw Judaism as a model for all humanity. *Peace of Mind* asserted Judaism's place not simply as an equal partner with Christianity but as a religion of unequaled depth in its assessment of human nature. Liebman characterized Judaism as an affirmative, indomitable religion of love and criticized traditionalist Christianity for burdening the human psyche with excessive and improper guilt. In light of Christianity's traditional claim that it was the religion of love, superseding the "legalistic" faith of the Jews, Liebman's argument presented a sharp challenge to the status quo.[10]

Irrational guilt—and Christianity's alleged encouragement of it—was Liebman's primary target in *Peace of Mind*. He declared that Christianity, shaped by Christ's concept of the immorality of lustful thoughts and by Pauline, Augustinian, Lutheran, and Calvinist views of sin, promoted a "false conscience" based on the repression and condemnation of natural impulses. Because of its "doctrine that desire is equivalent to the commission of sin," Christianity "advises man to choke down every evil thought, lest he fall into the pit of eternal damnation." In short, Liebman was arguing that classical Christianity caused neurosis. After all, repression and misplaced guilt created many of the psychological and emotional problems that people face. But Judaism contained an antidote to the illness of self-condemnation. Instead of a morbid emphasis on original and intractable sin, Liebman urged, religion ought to give people "the faith first enunciated in Genesis, and continually stressed in classic Judaism, that man is truly created in God's own likeness."[11]

The critique of Christianity in *Peace of Mind* was measured and consistent with what many liberal Protestants believed, though it was uniquely provocative coming from a rabbi. Far from being antagonistic toward Christianity, Liebman dedicated himself to interfaith understanding through both his preaching and his many lectures at Protestant seminaries and colleges in New England. He praised Christianity for its contributions to civilization, and he cherished the sympathy and collaboration of American Christian leaders who protested the Jewish condition under Hitler and supported the Zionist ideal in Palestine. "American Christianity has given four and a half million Jews in this country, at least, renewed confidence in man, in human nature and in Godliness," he said in a wartime sermon called "A Jewish Tribute to American Christianity." And instead of the usual December harangues about the effects of Christmas on Jews, Liebman, in a sermon entitled "A Jew Looks at Christmas," said something very different: "It is Christianity alone which can convert the pagans and heathens of our day—Christianity which has the organization and the means and the proselytizing missionary spirit which may indeed create a world Christian community in which Judaism will have its place as creative partner, equal, and comrade."[12]

Though Liebman befriended Christianity, he felt that its conception of sin had left Westerners with a legacy of self-deprecation; conversely, he considered Jewish values essential to the new theology of *self-acceptance* he was promoting. "The man who has 'lived through' intense psychotherapeutic experience," he explained, based on his own venture into psychoanalysis, "has learned many lessons about his own inner nature but among the most valuable is this—*self-understanding rather than self-condemnation is the way to inner peace and mature conscience.*" Liebman recognized the truth in Christian and Jewish admonitions against self-centeredness, but he thought that most people had tendencies in the opposite direction, toward self-destructive emotions. "The attainment of proper self-love," he insisted, "must become the concern of every wise religion because as long as human beings are enslaved to wrong attitudes toward themselves they cannot help expressing wrong attitudes toward others." Alluding to Hillel's cryptic aphorism "If I am not for myself, who will be for me? And if I am for myself (only), what am I?" Liebman presented his readers the rhetorical question, "If the self is not loved, how can the neighbor be loved as oneself?" It was with these concerns in mind that Joshua Liebman called for a renewed awareness of the life-affirming ideas found in the book of Genesis and maintained in "classic Judaism."[13]

In sermons and speeches alike, Liebman harped on the idea of Judaism as a life-saving, because life-affirming, faith. He liked to contrast "the neo-Calvinist anthropology" of inveterate sin requiring total dependence on God's grace with "the Jewish anthropology" that placed "a saving faith in the possibility of man." He felt that people in Western culture were "under the spell . . . of a concept of human nature as hopeless, sinful, destined to perdition." With echoes of Boris Sidis's theory about the reserve energy of the Jewish people, Liebman claimed: "Judaism—which always emphasized the conviction that every human being is the child of God, thus bestowing upon man a sense of cosmic importance and status—created in our ancestors such a feeling of self-confidence despite hostility and persecution that they possessed an inner surplus with which they could bless society." The Jewish concept of providence, Liebman insisted, "is mainly man-conditioned or man-initiated and is not mere Divine grace." That faith in the human being distinguished Judaism's view of human nature. "Judaism has been able to avoid ultimate skepti-

cism and the denial of God because Judaism has always been truly realistic in its estimate of human nature. It has never glossed over the evils
that man can commit. On the other hand, it has maintained an unshakable faith that the good of human nature outweighs the evil."[14]

An admirer of William James, whom he considered one of his spiritual
"heroes," Liebman ingeniously adapted James's idea of religious
"healthy-mindedness" in a way that flattered Judaism. James had used
that term to describe "once-born," as opposed to "born-again" or "twice-
born" religious types. The "healthy-minded" religious person possesses
indomitable optimism, feels energetically engaged with the world, and
refuses to brood over the presence of sin and evil in society. James was
not thinking of Judaism when he formulated this concept—he referred
to the mind-cure and positive-thinking folks and, at the extreme end
of the spectrum, Christian Science, which denied evil altogether. But
Liebman played on the opposition between "healthy-minded" religion
and salvationist "born-again" Christianity, for he saw in it a means of
inserting Judaism into the American mainstream. "All men today," he
wrote, "need the healthy-mindedness of Judaism, the natural piety with
which the Jew declares, 'One world at a time is enough.' "[15]

Liebman offered up a fairly radical interpretation of the respective
roles of Judaism and Christianity in an era of unprecedented spiritual
upheaval. In a radio broadcast of 1940, "Where Jew and Christian Meet,"
he described Judaism as a healing faith for a war-torn world. "Judaism,"
he contended, "is a religion which can prove to be the antidote for the
pessimism of our age. . . . Judaism can teach humanity today the lesson
of optimism, of patience, of perspective, of faith in God, in life and in
man." Christianity also had a role to play: to "teach mankind humility
and repentance." Liebman's unusual comparison gave Judaism an upper
hand, based on his opinion that the Jewish soul had been seasoned for
love—the Jews suffered calamity without becoming either self-destructive
or hateful. "Israel that has suffered so much and yet has never grown
mad with the thirst for vengeance," he urged, "may be able to be an
example to our century that eventually will have to subdue all of the
hatreds that have been let loose by this war—if the earth is to become
good again."[16]

The "healthy-mindedness" of Liebman's Judaism centered on its capacity for instilling a spirit of human solidarity and neighborly love. In
one of his last articles, he told the readers of the *Ladies' Home Journal*,
"There is a real possibility that just as the Jewish people through the ages
achieved mutual solicitude under the threat of external danger, so now
the peoples of the world will yet achieve a new social solidarity and compassionate togetherness." "Love or Perish!" was the choice *Peace of Mind*
offered postwar America, as Liebman cited the "self-sacrificing devotion

to each other" of the Jews of the Warsaw Ghetto, and "the sense of mutual belongingness among the pioneering builders of contemporary Palestine." Those lessons illustrated "man's capacity to love his neighbor."[17]

Liebman's remedies for the spiritual and social problems of his age were both Freudian and Jewish. The insights of each dovetailed in his mind. Together, they offered Americans liberation from emotional repression and inappropriate guilt, on the one hand, and guidance to the Promised Land of human solidarity and renewal on the other.

A JEWISH BRIEF FOR "RELATEDNESS"

Because of Liebman's talent for synthesizing ideas, *Peace of Mind* was a landmark of popular theology, the first book to familiarize a mass audience with Jewish conceptions of God and humanity. Alongside the theme of self-acceptance, Liebman expounded the principle of human mutuality—loving the neighbor. Self-acceptance mattered, according to Liebman, because without it society was doomed to be little more than a collection of neurotically selfish and self-destructive individuals. On the other hand, men and women who were psychologically sound—who loved themselves properly—were able to love others. Only they could fully realize the biblical command to love the neighbor as oneself. Much of the excitement behind Rabbi Liebman's writing and speaking came from his exaggerated sense of what individual psychological insight would do for society at large. Having witnessed the inability of religion alone to create love of the neighbor and the stranger, he imagined that the reason was religion's inability to make people self-aware.

That was the specialty of dynamic psychology. Liebman felt sure that psychoanalysis had freed him from his own inner fears and insecurities and catapulted him to a much higher level of creativity and maturity. Once freed internally, he could reach out more effectively to help others. This was his revelation: the psychological health of the individual made it possible to fulfill the cherished Jewish principle of sustaining the community. For Judaism, which focused sharply on *this life* rather than the afterlife, the "unique human power for loving our fellow man" served as "the chief intimation of our immortality." What, exactly, was love? Liebman answered from the tradition of Jewish communalism: *love* meant "relatedness to some treasured person or group, the feeling of belongingness to a larger whole and of being of value to other men."[18]

"Relatedness," he often called it, or "right relatedness." Those terms were packed with meaning for Liebman—they signified the sum total of his education in ethics and psychology from both American and Jewish sources. When he spoke of human relatedness, he acknowledged his debts to the philosophers of the Chicago school of functionalist psychology, John Dewey and George Herbert Mead, and to Sigmund Freud "and his successors." Mead's writings, which were assembled for the first time and posthumously published in 1934 in the classic *Mind, Self, and Society,* appeared just as Liebman came of age in the rabbinate. Mead elaborated in sophisticated detail what he and Dewey and American social psychologists in general had been saying for some time, that the self cannot be understood apart from others and that self-realization happens always in a social context. Liebman likened that theory to the Freudian idea (or his interpretation of it) "that we are literally *made* by our contacts with others!" And Liebman also admired Alfred Adler, who constructed a universe around the idea of *communal feeling.* For Adler, it was impossible to speak of a psychologically healthy individual who did not fulfill his or her obligations to others. In addition to those great theorists, Liebman pointed to the entire world of contemporary science, from field theory in physics to Gestalt theory in psychology, all of which confirmed for him that "you can't understand an amoeba, a cell, a man or society in isolation."[19]

In the end, though, Liebman was a rabbi, and he grounded his idea of relatedness in Jewish sources. In his sermons he referred to the groundbreaking Jewish theologies of Franz Rosenzweig and Martin Buber well before either of these men were familiar names in the United States. Buber's *I-Thou* idea of human beings in vital relationship with each other and with God held special relevance for Liebman's philosophy of loving-the-self/loving-the-neighbor. As one reviewer observed of Liebman years after his death, "like Martin Buber, but in a more popular and engaging fashion, Liebman stressed that the essence of the good life is relationship and that the healing ingredient in that relationship is love." Liebman almost surely developed his ideas on that theme from other thinkers, but he recognized Buber's significance. In a 1940 broadcast Liebman emphasized the importance of brotherly love in Judaism by noting that "there is a Dialogue going on in the world between man and the Power that is greater than man, between what Martin Buber calls the 'I and the Thou.' "[20]

At bottom, Liebman's belief in human relatedness came from classical Judaism, "the intuitive wisdom of the prophets of Israel who sang the song of man's relatedness to man," as he put it in *Peace of Mind.* Only through a philosophy of love of one's fellows would modern men and women be able to stave off the plagues of isolation and despair. Liebman objected to existentialism because it isolated the individual, but so did much of Western thought. Philosophers "from Berkeley to Bertrand Russell," he claimed, "have needlessly tortured themselves with the idea that man is an isolated organism, excluded from real communication with his fellows." The redemptive force of dynamic psychology came from its focus on the individual's intimate relationships. Liebman thought that Freud had "revivified" classical Judaism's understanding of the individual as a socially obligated figure. "A lone human being is a destroyer of values," Liebman wrote; "a related human being is the builder of individual and social peace."[21]

No less a thinker than Reinhold Niebuhr, the greatest American theologian of the century, shared Liebman's idea that Jewish communalism offered a superior model of love. A decade after *Peace of Mind* appeared, Niebuhr compared Judaism and Christianity in an address before a joint meeting of the Jewish Theological Seminary and his own institution, the Union Theological Seminary, which stood across the street on Manhattan's Upper West Side. Given the celebrity of the Christian ideal of love, he noted the irony that a Jewish thinker, Martin Buber, had become the "most profound" exponent of "the biblical love doctrine." But he thought that even Buber did not convey the essence of the Jewish concept of love, which came out of the concrete mutual obligations of Jewish communal life. Echoing Liebman's theme in *Peace of Mind*, Niebuhr said that "the prophetic sense of justice . . . was more relevant to the problems of the community than the Christian ideal of love. . . . The superiority of the Jew's sense of justice may be derived from the fact that his norms were elaborated in a communal situation while the Christian norms transcend all communities."

Lest it be thought that he considered the Jewish communal ideal a relic of the past, Niebuhr shifted the scene to Detroit, where he had held a pulpit in the 1910s and 1920s. There, as chairman of a mayoral committee on race and civil rights, he first became acquainted with what he called the Jews' "undoubted capacity for civic virtue." His primary collaborator was a Jewish lawyer whose realism and civic commitment made a deep impression on Niebuhr. He also observed, "Jewish men of wealth were more emancipated from the prejudice of their class than Christian business men . . . and more generous in the support of communal projects which transcended the loyalties of a particular group." From his perspective as a left-leaning activist, Niebuhr perceived a "Jewish capacity for critical devotion to the community," which he equated with love in the larger collective sense.[22]

THE FUNCTIONAL JEWISH GOD OF MORDECAI KAPLAN

Not only did *Peace of Mind* provide a mass audience with its first taste of Jewish ideas of human mutuality, it also introduced the public to Mordecai Kaplan. Millions of people who had never heard the name before learned from Liebman that Kaplan was "a great Jewish theologian, who speaks of God in very profound terms." Kaplan left a strong imprint on *Peace of Mind.* He was one of the few people who read the manuscript, and Liebman saw fit to reproduce a thirty-eight-line meditation of Kaplan's, "God the Life of Nature," in the most theological chapter of *Peace of Mind,* "Thou Hast Enthralled Me, God."[23] Who was Mordecai Kaplan, and what did he think of God?

The most influential philosopher of American Judaism, Mordecai Menachem Kaplan (1881–1983) came of age just before the start of the twentieth century and lived nearly to its end. He entered America only three months after the Oklahoma Territory was opened for settlement and three years before Ellis Island was opened for immigration. Benjamin Harrison was president. When he died the Vietnam War had been over for nearly a decade, the Islamic revolution had already claimed Iran, and Ronald Reagan was president.

Kaplan was born into the deeply religious world of Lithuanian Jewry, the son of a Talmud scholar trained in the renowned Volozhin yeshiva. He and his family were among the 25,000 eastern European Jews who emigrated to the United States in 1889. Mordecai studied Talmud both under his father and at the Etz Chayim (Tree of Life) Yeshiva in his Lower East Side neighborhood, and he attended the Eldridge Street Synagogue, where his father not only prayed but also lectured. At twelve Kaplan began training for the rabbinate at the new Jewish Theological Seminary. He remained a student there for nine years while completing an undergraduate degree at City College (he and his schoolmates walked back and forth between the JTS on 57th Street and CCNY on 23rd Street). In 1900, two years before his ordination, he began graduate work at Columbia University. By that time, Kaplan had already been exposed to the radical idea of human authorship of the Bible; ironically he learned that from a biblical scholar whom his father had hired to be his tutor. And at Columbia he would be strongly affected by Felix Adler, founder of the Society for Ethical Culture and one of Columbia's few Jewish professors. The Jewish Theological Seminary itself encouraged his freethinking tendencies, for that institution—the center of the young Conservative movement—rejected Orthodox views about the divine origin of the Oral Law on which the entire system of commandments stood.[24]

The sociology and philosophy Kaplan learned at Columbia moved him completely out of the tradition, which he desperately wanted to "reconstruct." From a variety of teachers and sources, he became enthralled with a pragmatic approach to religion, one that replaced self-evident truths with observable effects. An admirer of William James and John Dewey, he wanted a Judaism that *worked,* an effective Judaism that maintained the powerful emotional life of the Jewish people but integrated the individual Jew into the world of modern America. From his teacher Felix Adler, whose Ethical Culture society promoted ethics without theology, Kaplan gained a deep sense of the importance of a universal ethics, a transcendent morality that was built into the universe and accessible to everyone. He also absorbed from Adler an important concept of God, which Adler borrowed from Matthew Arnold: God as "a power, not ourselves, which makes for righteousness." That formulation was Arnold's attempt to regain a truer sense of the Divinity at work in the Hebrew Bible, a God that he felt had been turned into an abstraction by centuries of theological speculation. The idea of God as a Power—an overriding force in the universe—rather than a Person appealed to the young scholar. A critical difference between Adler and Kaplan, however, involved the emotional and psychological content of religion. Kaplan felt his Jewishness strongly and therefore disliked Adler for abandoning Judaism in order to form the Ethical Culture movement. As much as he admired and shared Adler's belief in a transcendent moral order, Kaplan was primarily concerned about the future of the Jews as a faith community in America. Still, when he started his own school of thought, known as Reconstructionism, he called its organizational body the Society for the Advancement of Judaism, a name that was patterned on the Society for Ethical Culture.[25]

Like Adler's group, Reconstructionism remained a small movement, but Kaplan himself, as a teacher at the Jewish Theological Seminary for fifty-four years, shaped the thinking of generations of American rabbis. (It is telling that Kaplan's theology appeared in the writings of both Joshua Liebman and, a generation later, Harold Kushner, the best-selling rabbi of the 1980s.) When Kaplan momentarily resigned from the seminary in the 1920s, the outpouring of emotion from students and others sufficed to change his mind. Milton Steinberg, a student of Kaplan's at that time, presided over the student body and petitioned the JTS to regain the master teacher: "There is preeminently one man among our teachers who is responsible for what faith, and courage, and vision we may lay claim to. It is . . . he who has given the Judaism we are expected to teach the content and vitality we have elsewhere sought in vain. . . . His example has given us to understand that creative spiritual activity was still possible in Jewish life." Steinberg's passionate letter reflected the fact that Kaplan, in the words of his biographer, "had a mission to help save the Jews," a mission that "obsessed and motivated him throughout his life."[26]

Although Joshua Liebman, as a Reform rabbi, had never studied with Kaplan, he liked the way Kaplan combined an optimistic functionalist view of religion with a deep commitment to the inner life of the Jewish people. He praised Kaplan for recognizing "the importance of group

emotion and ritual and the indispensability of group discipline voluntarily chosen, not arbitrarily imposed—discipline in the form of religious
commandments and laws, rules of daily conduct, of ethical practice, of
ceremonial observance." Liebman knew that his own Reform movement
had lost sight of communal rituals. Kaplan discovered a way to maintain
old rites, such as Sabbath and festivals, by reinterpreting them in light
of the needs of modern people living by democratic values. Most of all,
Liebman appreciated the way Kaplan had reinterpreted the traditional
concept of salvation in the new language of psychological self-realization,
which Dewey had done so much to advertise. (For his publicity photo
Liebman chose to be pictured reading a book by Dewey.) Kaplan was one
of the first religious philosophers in America to adopt a psychologized
definition of salvation. In his 1937 classic, *The Meaning of God in Modern
Jewish Religion*, he defined personal salvation as "faith in the possibility of
achieving an integrated personality." And collective salvation he interpreted as the creation of the kind of society that "shall afford to each the
maximum opportunity for creative self-expression."[27]

Kaplan depicted a universe that Liebman understood. In that universe
God existed not as a Personality who enacted supernatural interventions
to "save" people, but as a force or Power that endowed people with the
ability to mature and follow the path of righteousness. In that universe,
men and women would find redemption as their psyches were freed from
age-old restraints. When Liebman wrote, "I believe that God is the Power
for salvation revealing Himself in nature and in human nature," he was
making a Kaplanian declaration of faith.[28]

In *Peace of Mind* Liebman offered up a "new God Idea for America."
His theological concoction was a potent blend of Kaplan's philosophy,
Freud's psychology, American democracy, and Liebman's favorite theme
from rabbinic Judaism, the idea of men and women being in partnership
with God. "The rabbis found God not as an aloof Principle far removed
from the habitations of men, but they found the evidences of God in His
relationship with men," he explained in a radio sermon on the Talmud.
"He is a working, creating God and he shows his power not through
miracle as some of the other religions believe but primarily through the
unrecognized miracle of daily living." According to that rabbinic view,
God *needed* people to bring about His plan for creation; the commandments had meaning only to the extent that men and women fulfilled
them. Yet fulfillment of the commandments depended on human freedom, and that is where psychology and democracy came into the picture.
The idea of people acting as God's partners in the divine plan "could
never be deeply felt so long as men lived in cultures that were not free
and equal." Centuries of European feudalism and authoritarianism,
Liebman believed, had engrained in people's minds an obsolete idea of

God as a despot ruling over powerless serfs. American self-reliance and democracy would not tolerate such a theology. Following Kaplan, who envisioned a democratic American Judaism, and Freud, who envisioned psychic liberation from paralyzing feelings of inferiority and anxiety, Liebman concluded:

> There is a chance here in America for the creation of a new idea of God; a God reflected in the brave creations of self-reliant social pioneers; a religion based not upon surrender or submission, but on a new birth of confidence in life and in the God of life. . . . God, according to Judaism, always wanted His children to become His creative partners, but it is only in this age, when democracy has at least a chance of triumphing around the globe, that we human beings can grow truly aware of His eternal yearning for our collaboration. . . . I am making the prophecy that it will be from the *democratic experience of our century that mankind will first learn its true dignity as independent and necessary partners of God.*[29]

THE CONTROVERSIAL THEOLOGY OF *PEACE OF MIND*

In its vigor and buoyancy, its messianic tone, its artful combination of democracy and psychology and theology, the "new God idea" of *Peace of Mind* must have been an epiphany for many readers, but it also fired controversy. Its optimistic faith in "man" nauseated a variety of opponents—both Christians and Jews—who insisted that any worthy religion had to stay focused on the omnipotence of God and the limitations of humans. Jewish intellectuals exceeded all others in the vitriol of their responses. Irving Kristol took offense at the message of *Peace of Mind* partly because it was popular and therefore tainted with the mark of mass culture. (He hinted that Liebman had "literary ties to the fraternity of vulgar journalism.") Panning the idea that psychoanalysis had something to offer religion, Kristol remarked acerbically, a year after Liebman's death, that *Peace of Mind* left thoughtful people with the impression that "today no one is so sick as our spiritual healers." Will Herberg derided Liebman's theology as euphoric. Against Liebman, he argued that equality and democracy have no meaning "except in terms of the common subjection of all men to the sovereignty of God."[30]

Will Herberg's voice was an influential one; he was the Paul Revere of postwar religion. Herberg (1901–77) was born in a *shtetl* near Minsk but came with his parents to America when he was three years old. His father fared poorly in America, as did his parent's marriage, which ended in divorce when Will was a teenager. Growing up in a poor section of Brooklyn, Herberg was restlessly intellectual and a diligent student at the Boys'

High School, but at City College he had problems and ended up being suspended. Almost immediately afterward, he joined the Young Workers League and became an avid polemicist for Communism. For two decades Herberg remained part of a dissident faction of American Communists and also served as educational director of a local branch of the International Ladies Garment Workers Union. But his politics changed radically in the spring of 1940, when he read Reinhold Niebuhr's *Moral Man and Immoral Society* (1932). That book challenged John Dewey and his many followers whose faith in rationalism and science failed "to recognise those elements in man's collective behavior which belong to the order of nature and can never be brought completely under the dominion of reason or conscience." Deeply impressed, Herberg immediately contacted Niebuhr at the Union Theological Seminary, where the two discussed the book and Niebuhr's critique of Marxism.[31]

The Protestant theologian's magnificent sense of power, justice, and the flawed quality of human nature gave Herberg a feeling of faith that had been totally absent from his secular upbringing. He contemplated converting to Christianity, but Niebuhr encouraged him to remain a Jew. He did so with a vengeance, quickly becoming one of the most compelling voices on the postwar scene. Herberg imported into Judaism the Protestant neo-orthodox emphasis on sin that he learned at the knee of Niebuhr. His enduring contribution to the history of Jewish theology, *Judaism and Modern Man* (1951), attempted to reconstruct Judaism in the image of Niebuhr's neo-orthodoxy, navigating a new course between the Scylla of fundamentalism and the Charybdis of religious liberalism.[32]

Even though Herberg skewered Liebman in *Protestant-Catholic-Jew*, both men had been struggling toward the same goal: to resuscitate a moribund Judaism. More eloquently than anyone else, Herberg sounded the alarm about the fate of American Judaism after the war. After surveying the intellectual climate in the nation's Reform, Conservative, and Orthodox Jewish congregations, he found that "nothing in the way of belief or practice—not even the belief in God or the practice of the most elementary *mitzvot*—may be taken for granted among synagogue members." What was more, he went on, "I was amazed at the indifference of many religious leaders in the face of this situation." That was in 1950, several years before he published the same criticism of American religion in general. Liebman, we recall, had been troubled by the banality of the synagogues in the 1930s; for him the answer was a whole new Freudian approach to human nature. But for Herberg, the revival of the synagogue demanded "a return to religious essentials."[33]

His return to those essentials took the form of *Judaism and Modern Man*, in which he made it plain that no secular system of thought, whether it was Marxism, psychoanalysis, or science in general, could satisfy "modern man in search of the absolute." An exercise in Jewish existentialism with debts not only to Niebuhr but also to Franz Rosenzweig and Martin Buber, the book urged people to develop a stronger sense of sinfulness over their egoistic separation from God. "The dereliction that overwhelms us," Herberg wrote in one of many vivid passages, "is at once the despair of being abandoned in the universe and the agonizing consciousness that we are ultimately responsible for our own condition." All people, he argued, felt guilt over the dereliction of their spiritual purpose. Unlike Liebman, who blamed religion for overburdening people with guilt, Herberg perceived guilt as "the mark of our human condition." "It is the consequence of our defying the essential law of our being. It is the consequence of sin." Herberg resented the way Liebman dazzled people with the grand promises of psychoanalysis, which prevented them from dealing with their existential guilt. "The popular psychologist is the priest and father-confessor of our time," Herberg chided, "who promises to give us 'peace of mind,' to relieve us of our anxieties, guilts and insecurities." Herberg respected "Freud and other explorers of the deepest recesses of the human psyche," but he described Liebman and his ilk as a "swarm of cult-priests and panacea-mongers spawned out of the troubles of our age. . . . Psychoanalysis—even the authentic kind, not to speak of the popular cult of 'peace of mind'—has no salvation to offer modern man. . . . It cannot really relieve him of his burden of anxiety . . . because, for all its insight, it operates on too superficial a level of human life."[34]

Had Liebman not died so young, we would probably now be speaking of the "Liebman-Herberg debates" that defined the postwar Jewish search for a new theology. And we would not be burdened, as we are now, by an oversimplified view of opposition between "liberal optimists" (the minimizers of sin) and "neo-orthodox realists" (the maximizers of sin). Liebman was a sharp debater for liberal religion, but he understood and appreciated the thinking of Herberg's mentor, Reinhold Niebuhr. Speaking before the National Conference of Jews and Christians in 1938, he praised two developments of contemporary Christianity: the Social Gospel of the Depression years, with its focus on social problems and injustice, and the "theological virility" personified by Niebuhr. "Judaism can take from Niebuhr the impetus to re-think and to re-discover the realism of Israel which also recognized the struggle between the good impulse and the evil impulse in all men and the always perishable victory [of] the good over evil." He applauded "the emphasis upon the tragic reality in life" as a valuable gift of "the new Christian theology to the religion of today and tomorrow. Too long have liberal Jews and Christians made of their religion and of their God a rose garden." And we will recall that Liebman condemned the liberal approach to death and mourning as a pathetic attempt "to make death itself almost an illusion," and recom-

mended a return to traditional Jewish practices that recognized the
depth of human grief.[35]

Christian reactions to *Peace of Mind* tended to follow the liberal-conser-
vative divide. Liebman's counterparts in liberal Protestantism were Harry
Emerson Fosdick (1878–1969) and Norman Vincent Peale (1898–
1993), both of whom wrote inspirational best-sellers with a psychological
slant. Like Liebman, Fosdick and Peale were powerful preachers driven
by deep pastoral instincts, instincts that led them to seek out innovative
ways of counseling their congregants. Within their respective branches
of the faith, both men pioneered in working with psychiatrists, Fosdick
in the 1920s and Peale in the 1930s. (Both were based in New York
City, Peale at the Marble Collegiate Church on Fifth Avenue and Twenty-
Ninth Street and Fosdick at the First Presbyterian Church on Fifth Avenue between Tenth and Eleventh Streets and later at the interdenominational Riverside Church on Morningside Heights.) Fosdick learned some
of the basics of psychotherapy in the early 1920s from a friend who happened to be one of the nation's leading psychiatrists, Thomas Salmon,
head of the National Committee for Mental Hygiene. He informally incorporated those techniques in his extensive pastoral work and became
a one-man band for religio-psychiatric counseling. As the leading liberal
Protestant in America and a professor at the Union Theological Seminary, Fosdick guided many ministers to make over their sermons in the
style of pastoral counseling. As for Peale, in the 1930s he found himself
with the same restless desire for more sophisticated methods, and collaborated with a Freudian analyst trained in Vienna, Smiley Blanton (a self-
described "Tennessee Methodist hillbilly"). In 1937 they set up a religio-
psychiatric clinic in the basement of Peale's church.[36]

Although Fosdick and Peale were forerunners of Liebman, they differed from him considerably in how they understood and spoke about
psychology. Neither ever really took to Freudianism. On the contrary,
they both harked back to the Emmanuel healing movement and to other
blends of Christian idiom and New Thought inspiration. Peale knew
more about Jung than Freud for the same reason that Christians with a
mystical or transcendentalist bent generally found Jung attractive; Jung's
idea of the inward quest leading to a cosmic consciousness harmonized
with Peale's idea about the divine contact made by positive thought. Nevertheless, all three preachers produced best-sellers in the 1940s. Fosdick's *On Being a Real Person* (1943) anticipated some of the points about
self-acceptance in *Peace of Mind*, and Peale's *A Guide to Confident Living*
(1948) reflected some of Liebman's light. Liebman and Fosdick ex-
changed compliments in private and public. "I have thought of you many
times as week after week I see your book *Peace of Mind* still leading the
non-fiction best seller list," Fosdick wrote Liebman. "It is very gratifying

and encouraging to know that a book like this is sustaining this preeminent position, and I congratulate you on behalf of the whole religious community for the splendid service which you have rendered in this book." And Liebman returned the kindness, observing in an article on postwar religious literature that "Dr. Fosdick . . . particularly in his 'On Being a Real Person,' has utilized the insights of modern psychology with rare artistry." Liebman died before Peale's ascent to celebrity, but in the early 1960s Peale persuaded *Reader's Digest* to rerun its original abridgment of *Peace of Mind.*[37]

Although liberal Protestants like Fosdick and Peale supported the theological optimism of *Peace of Mind*, they did not speak for all American Christians. Books by two rising stars of religious broadcasting, Monsignor Fulton Sheen and Billy Graham, carried titles—*Peace of Soul* (1949) and *Peace with God* (1953)—that implicitly challenged Liebman and in ways that suggested the old formula: Christianity = spiritual, Judaism = material. "Man needs peace," Graham wrote in his 1955 sequel, *The Secret of Happiness*, "not merely a nondescript, so-called peace of mind—but . . . . a peace of soul which permeates his entire being."[38]

Sheen refuted Liebman even more completely. Before *Peace of Mind* appeared, he was already on record as an eloquent challenger of "the superstition of scientism," the faith of Dewey that science would yield solid values. A highly educated, intellectually assertive, and prolific author, Sheen was not about to take Liebman's Freudianism lying down. In *Peace of Soul*, a book that has been called one of "the most powerful Catholic polemics of the postwar years," Sheen rejected the argument that psychoanalysis had come to replace the Catholic confessional, and reaffirmed the spiritual importance of guilt without psychological dispensations. Whereas Liebman accused traditional religion of overburdening modern men and women with guilt, Sheen argued the opposite: a sense of sin and acts of confession were the only source of salvation and inner peace. "It requires great moral effort to attain peace of soul, but even those who are indifferent to right and wrong sometimes achieve peace of mind," Sheen wrote, gravely misrepresenting what Liebman meant by his famous phrase. "Those who deny guilt and sin are like the Pharisees of old," the priest contended. On his popular Tuesday evening television show, "Life Is Worth Living," Sheen used the same kind of loaded language, which barely disguised the Jewish-Christian polemic he saw in the psychological evangelism of men like Liebman:

Paraphrasing the story of the Pharisee (who was a very nice man), we can imagine him praying in the front of the temple as follows: "I thank Thee, O Lord, that my Freudian adviser has told me that there is no such thing as guilt, that sin is a myth, and that Thou, O Father, art only a projection of my father complex. . . . I contribute 10 percent of my income to the Society for the Elimination of Religious Superstitions, and I diet for my figure three times a week. Oh, I thank Thee that I am not like the rest of men, those nasty people, such as the Christian there in the back of the temple who thinks that he is a sinner. . . . I may have an Oedipus complex but I have no sin."[39]

The reactions of Graham and Sheen to *Peace of Mind* were motivated not by antisemitism but by a revolutionary change that was happening before their eyes.[40] For the first time since the establishment of Christianity, a rabbi—a Jew speaking from a frankly and openly Jewish standpoint—was competing in a mass market of souls. Sheen himself represented the incursion of Catholicism into an inspirational arena run by Protestants. But Liebman personified a change of much greater significance. Sheen could speak ecumenically to all Christians about the saving grace of Jesus, but when Christians listened to and read Liebman, as they did in large numbers, they entered a new precinct of ideas. They heard Jesus and the leading lights of Christianity spoken of in relative terms. They heard Jewish sages cited as authorities to live by, and Jewish rituals hailed as superior mechanisms for human self-expression.

LEO BAECK: THE EMBODIMENT OF LIEBMAN'S GOSPEL OF LOVE

Those intellectuals and historians who have denied any theological significance to *Peace of Mind* and ignored its palpable Jewish content have also disregarded the relationship, both personal and intellectual, between Liebman and Leo Baeck (1873–1956), the spiritual leader of German Jewry who was liberated from the Theresienstadt concentration camp. It was Joshua Liebman who presented Baeck to a vast American audience in June 1948 in an article for the *Atlantic Monthly*, "A Living Saint: Rabbi Baeck," which *Reader's Digest* immediately abridged for its readers. "It was not until last winter that I heard from Baeck's gentle lips the soul-stirring epic of his survival," Liebman wrote. "None of the physical indignities devised by Nazi persecutors could touch Baeck's soul. At the camp he was made a 'horse' and harnessed to the garbage wagon. 'But,' he said to me with a smile, 'this was a quite happy period because the other "horse" harnessed to the cart was a distinguished philosopher. We had marvelous conversations on ethics and religion as we dragged the refuse through the mud.' " The preeminent leader of German Jewry (he was chief rabbi of Berlin, president of B'nai B'rith, and head of Germany's interdenominational rabbinical association), Baeck had been appointed to lead the nationwide Jewish communal organization established by the Nazis in 1933. Ten years later he was deported to Theresienstadt, where he became #187,894. Baeck ministered to the sick and dying in the camp and remained with the remnant of survivors for a full month after he had been authorized to depart for London. He became famous for the clandestine lectures on philosophy and Judaism he gave to hundreds of inmates under the cover of darkness. In May 1945, by which time the survivors had dwindled to a few hundred, Baeck was awakened from his sleep by a uniformed stranger (as told to Liebman, the stranger was Adolf Eichmann). As a result of confusion related to the listing of a deceased rabbi named Beck, the SS thought Leo Baeck had already been killed. The jackbooted official told the aged rabbi, "I see that we have made a mistake. Tomorrow morning I will remedy that mistake." That night the Russians liberated the camp.[41]

A doctor of philosophy, the Prussian-born Baeck was one of that elite of thinkers capable of synthesizing Jewish and secular knowledge into an innovative approach to Judaism. Liebman knew him first through the book that made his reputation, *The Essence of Judaism* (1905). That book was a powerful polemic that responded to *The Essence of Christianity* (1900), an influential work by the Protestant historian Adolf Harnack in which Harnack slighted the significance of Judaism. Against Harnack's dismissal of pharisaic Judaism, Baeck argued that the early rabbis, and Hillel in particular, had fashioned a vital faith that emphasized the principle of loving the neighbor.

When Baeck came to America in 1948, a few months before Liebman's sudden death, Liebman shared the platform with him at a number of events where the two became acquainted. "Only a few months ago I have met him for the first time," Baeck wrote to Liebman's widow in late June; "at once I became attached to him . . . captivated by the spell of his personality, by both the straightforwardness and the profoundness of his thinking, by the warmth and charm of his feelings." Just two months earlier, Baeck had been discussing his humanistic theology in a letter to Liebman. In *The Essence of Judaism*, he stressed an idea that Liebman also expressed in *Peace of Mind*, that the Jewish people had a unique spiritual possession: a hopeful, transcendent adaptability. And for Baeck's liberal theology, "man" was central because the ethically passionate person, exemplified by the Prophets, transformed the world. "The most real reality is man," he wrote to Liebman. "Everything gets its vitality and its actuality through man. . . . The strongest reality in man is his conscience: it is the firmest expression of his identity. . . . The proof of conscience is the deed, the duty by which man lays claim to himself and takes himself seriously so that he can trust himself and others may believe him.[42]

Because of the ordeal he endured at the hands of the Nazis, Baeck impressed Liebman as a modern saint whose story served as the ultimate parable of a life-affirming Judaism. The articles on Baeck in the *Atlantic Monthly* and *Reader's Digest* focused on the rabbi's extraordinary ability to transcend hatred and persecution. "He puts the meaning of life into a succinct aphorism," Liebman wrote, " 'The mark of a mature man is the ability to give love and to receive it—joyously and without guilt.' " Baeck epitomized the commandment to "love the neighbor as thyself" that Liebman considered a Jewish gift to the postwar world. Reciprocally, Leo Baeck encouraged the theology he saw taking shape in *Peace of Mind.* In Liebman's book he discerned "the distinct lineament, even the structure, of a real theology based on psychology—a commencement to be pursued." "We must be thankful to you for this," he wrote his younger colleague.[43]

As Baeck recognized, *Peace of Mind* had the merits and demerits of an inspirational best-seller. Written not for philosophers but for the multitude, the book sometimes got carried away with its missionary spirit, lapsing into purple prose and the kind of psychological reductionism that explained the atheist (and the Republican) as the product of an unresolved Oedipus complex. Nevertheless, Liebman masterfully combined insights from psychology, literature, and religion in a way that made many people want to be better, strive for wider horizons, overcome fears and insecurities, gain a productive self-awareness, and regain a spiritual life. He opened up a new line of thought about religion in the age of psychology and successfully conveyed the sense of hopefulness and human possibility that liberal theologians such as Kaplan and Baeck demanded. Remarkably, for a mass-marketed book, Liebman stuck to his guns about the unique spiritual role assigned to Judaism in the modern world. Whereas Baeck's *Essence of Judaism* was a polemical defense against the old charges of Jewish legalism, *Peace of Mind* was a polemical offensive promoting Judaism's distinct worth in a psychological age.

The therapeutic ideal that Joshua Liebman heralded contained as many problems as solutions for Americans in the late twentieth century. Liebman might well have been shocked at the narcissistic lengths to which the American people took his insistence on the need for self-acceptance. And, had he outlived the postwar psychology craze that captivated so many fine minds, he might have moderated his zeal about the redemptive powers of psychotherapy. But that is speculation.[44]

As a charismatic preacher, Liebman capitalized on the changes psychology had wrought in American religion. By placing all people on the same spectrum of normality and abnormality, and divorcing maturity from dogma, psychology created a spiritual democracy. As a result, for the first time in nearly two millennia, a rabbi had a solid platform from which to preach spiritual answers to an interfaith audience. A friend of Christianity, Liebman would not have preached the superiority of Judaism on the basis of faith alone. But, on the grounds of modern psychology, he could argue that Judaism offered special insight into the workings of the human mind and emotions.

The sudden appearance of a rabbi in a Christian inspirational realm was not a fluke. It was a sign of Jewish emergence from the margins to the middle of American religious debate. Under the noses of historians who have hastily dismissed the book as devoid of theology, *Peace of Mind* introduced, for the first time, a specific set of Jewish doctrines into the mass market of spiritual ideas.

Through *Peace of Mind*, a new Jewish gospel of love challenged an age-old status quo. After Liebman, it was harder to maintain that a Christianity of love had surpassed a Judaism of spiritless law. Jewish resistance to Christian models of spirituality caused consternation and debate, but so did the optimism of Joshua Liebman's theology, which infuriated those thinkers, both Jewish and Christian, who sought a graver, more ironic view of human nature. An emphatically Jewish book, *Peace of Mind* forces us to take a new look at the religious revival of the 1940s and 1950s. It is time to discard the stereotype of banal pulp preachers running a three-ring show of saccharine spirituality. Beneath the surface of the optimistic "cult of faith," a battle raged about the nature of God and humankind.

We will now turn to a more intimate side of the religious war: the story of a famous woman and a dispute between Catholics and Jews about the Freudian angel that glided through Joshua Liebman's America.

Clare Boothe Luce, 1955, eight years after her controversial confessional articles describing her conversion to Catholicism. She is pictured with Winston Churchill and, to the right rear, her husband, Henry Luce, during her tenure as U.S. Ambassador to Italy. (Courtesy of AP/Wide World Photos.)

Chapter 11

Clare Boothe Luce and the Catholic-Jewish Clash over Freud in America

"HE WHO BROUGHT YOU into the vineyard has not stopped leading you," Monsignor Fulton Sheen wrote to Clare Boothe Luce in the winter of 1946–47, a year after her celebrated conversion to Catholicism. "Out of all America, out of the world," Sheen continued, "He chose the darling of the worldlings to prove the power of His Grace." Sheen's choice of the word "worldling" coincided nicely with Brooks Atkinson's review of Luce's 1936 Broadway hit *The Women.* Atkinson liked the play's toothy portrayal of "unregenerate wordlings." Among Fulton Sheen's famous converts, Clare Luce was a star. Once an editor of *Vanity Fair,* she went on to become a well-known playwright and essayist as well as a member of Congress (1943–47). In the 1950s she served as U.S. Ambassador to Italy, and she was mentioned as a possible Republican candidate for the vice-presidency in 1956. Full of restless creative energy, gifted with words, bright and sharp-witted, Luce brought to American Catholicism an eloquence that exceeded what she had given Broadway. As she was preparing a massive religious confessional that would span three issues of *McCall's* in the spring of 1947, Sheen reminded her that her account would be "the greatest personal narrative of conversion ever done in this country." God, he said, "gave you everything . . . a brilliant intellect, an unusual charm and expansive personality . . . prestige and materialities . . . but He kept back one thing—His peace."[1]

Sheen (1895–1979), the charismatic radio and television priest, and Luce (1903–87), the beautiful writer, politician, and celebrity, were Catholicism's most vigorous, popular, and effective preachers in the 1940s and 1950s. As they guided Catholics into mainstream America after the war, they engaged in a culture clash with Jews like Joshua Liebman over Freudianism and the future of American religion. Sheen's *Peace of Soul* and Liebman's *Peace of Mind* symbolized the dissonance between Catholic and Jewish sensibilities, but Clare Luce's role in the conflict over Freud was dramatic enough to elicit a public accusation of antisemitism. By exploring the story behind that accusation, we will gain a sharper and more nuanced picture of the religious controversy surrounding the psychological revolution of the postwar years.[2]

SHEEN, LUCE, AND THE CATHOLIC POLEMIC AGAINST A JEWISH FREUD

The charge came in a 1948 issue of the *American Scholar.* In "Monsignor Sheen and Mrs. Luce," writer Fanny Sedgwick Colby complained that recent condemnations of psychoanalysis by the duo hurt rather than helped American Catholics. Colby was referring to a sermon Sheen gave on "Psychoanalysis and Confession" at St. Patrick's Cathedral in March 1947 and to a three-part series Luce wrote for *McCall's* (February-March-April 1947) describing her journey from hedonism to piety. She considered Sheen's and Luce's statements on modern psychology inaccurate and anti-intellectual, and perceived antisemitism in Luce's new cosmology. The *McCall's* articles, she observed, "leave with the careful reader an impression that responsibility for our present spiritual inadequacy rests not only on Freud, but as well on other outstanding thinkers of Jewish origin." "Indeed," she continued, "it would be possible for a careful reader to come to the reluctant conclusion that Mrs. Luce's thesis is this: We Christian innocents have been duped into our present godless condition by the unholy triumvirate of Communism, Psychoanalysis and Relativity. These three, symbolized by Marx, Freud and Einstein, are the result of the messianic impulse of the religiously frustrated Jewish ego."[3]

The *American Scholar* had its finger on the pulse of postwar America. Equations of Jewishness and cultural subversion were in the air. In his 1949 poem "A Case for Jefferson," Robert Frost wrote of his friend "Harrison" who "loves my country, too, but wants it all made over new." The poet describes the revolutionary as "Freudian Viennese by night" and "by day he's Marxian Muscovite," and then adds: "It isn't because he's Russian Jew," for Harrison is "Puritan Yankee through and through." This vague sense of Jews as subversive provided background to the battle over Freudianism that Joshua Liebman reignited in 1946.

Fifty years after the engagement of Sheen with Liebman, an internet site illustrated the degree to which concerns about Freudianism, and the identification of Jews with it, had penetrated the American Catholic imagination. In an electronic publication, the "Great Catholic Books Newsletter," the Catholic Resource Network posted an essay on Sheen and his importance to contemporary Catholics. Describing the bishop's lifelong struggle against atheism and Communism, the essay also devotes considerable space to Joshua Liebman and the challenge he posed to Catholicism. Misquoting and misconstruing Liebman in a way that reduced him to a caricature who "disposed of . . . the commandments of God" and "described religion as 'a fossil,' " the essay explains how "Sheen answered Liebman." *Peace of Soul*, it notes, met a warm acceptance in "the secular newspapers, whose editors recognized that true peace is possible only with a Christian solution of the problems that are torturing men's souls." Whereas Liebman spoke "for the Freudians," Sheen represented a "Christian psychology" that "to the credit of the American people . . . was so favorably received." The essay also cites Clare Boothe Luce's confessional series for *McCall's* to witness against "the godless and atavistic underbrush of Freudianism."[4]

What had Sheen and Luce said to spark such sharp and resilient controversy? Anticipating his thesis in *Peace of Soul*, Sheen derided Freudianism as a philosophy of life based on "materialism, hedonism, infantilism and eroticism." About transference—the transfer of libidinal emotions onto the psychoanalyst—he said that the process only worked when the patient was young and beautiful. Psychoanalysis was a rich person's sport that cared not for the poor. Sheen's characteristically colorful remarks started a small war between Catholic psychiatrists and the archdiocese of New York City. When church officials failed to comment upon, no less repudiate, Sheen's sermon, the chief psychiatrist of St. Vincent's hospital resigned both that post and his position as psychiatric consultant in the Chancery Office. Three of his Catholic colleagues joined him in a public denunciation of Sheen's statements, which they felt sure would discourage Catholic men and women from seeking psychiatric care now that it had been tainted as sinful. A. A. Brill stepped into the debate, suggesting to the *New York Times* that Sheen's sarcasm stemmed from jealousy over the success of Liebman's *Peace of Mind*.[5]

In his tirades against Freudianism, which continued through the 1950s, Sheen misrepresented the Jewish doctor in an invidious comparison with Jung. After World War II, such a comparison did not sit well with Jews, given Jung's infamous rapprochement with the Nazis. In 1934, as Freud's work was being banned in Germany, Jung wrote an article for "Aryan" psychotherapists in a Nazi-sponsored journal. That article, which parroted racist stereotypes of "the Aryan" and "the Jewish" psyche, argued that neither Freud nor Adler, as Jews, could be considered a "valid representative of European mankind." Twenty years later Sheen mimicked Jung in a popular book, *Life Is Worth Living* (1954). He praised Jung as "the greatest of all the psychiatrists" and quoted his opinion that "the kind of psychology Freud and Adler represent leaves out the spirit and is suited to people who believe they have no spiritual need and no spiritual aspiration." To repeat without qualification a characterization from the era of Nazism was disturbing enough, but Sheen outdid Jung by misquoting him in a way that exaggerated the alleged evils of Freud. He implied to his readers that the following was a verbatim quote from Jung's *Modern Man in Search of a Soul* (1933): "Freud himself, the founder of psychoanalysis, has thrown a glaring light upon the dirt, the darkness and the evil of the psychic hinterland and has presented these things as so much refuse and slag. It has awakened in many people an admiration for all this filth."

As a close reader would have noticed, something is wrong with the grammar of this passage—the "It" at the start of the second sentence has no antecedent. Sheen removed the text that came between those two sentences. Jung's actual words were: "Freud, himself, the founder of psychoanalysis, has thrown a glaring light upon the dirt, darkness and evil of the psychic hinterland, and has presented these things as so much refuse and slag; he has thus taken the utmost pains to discourage people from seeking anything behind them. He did not succeed, and his warning has even brought about the very thing he wished to prevent: it has awakened in many people an admiration for all this filth." Unlike Sheen, who glibly portrayed Freud as an almost diabolical materialist, Jung acknowledged Freud's contribution to civilization: "No wonder that to unearth buried fragments of psychic life we have first to drain a miasmal swamp. Only a great idealist like Freud could devote a lifetime to the unclean work. This is the beginning of our psychology. For us acquaintance with the realities of the psychic life could start only at this end, with all that repels us and that we do not wish to see."[6]

In the same book, Sheen not only reiterated his favorite image of the psychology-lover as a Pharisee but also conjured up an inventive new metaphor for the superiority of Christianity over Judaism. As he had been doing for years on radio and television, Sheen harped on the moral deficiencies of the "nice" people for whom "psychology . . . comes in handy to explain away their faults." He sardonically contrasted the duplicitous "nice" people with the honest "awful" people, those who admitted their failings and who "have never been introduced to their subconscious." "Nice people, if they are guilty of intemperance, will call themselves alcoholics. Awful people call themselves drunkards—sometimes just plain 'bums.' " As solutions to the moral and spiritual quandaries people faced, Sheen made another comparison in which he likened Judaism to radio and Christianity to television: "The Old Testament is something like radio: a speech without vision. But what discourse there is, for example, in those great commandments which were given to the Jews, and which have been the fabric of the world's civilization ever since." Yet for all its advantages, radio had one enormous limitation: "Love is not satisfied alone with hearing the speeches of the beloved; love also wants to see. . . . Vision must be added to revelation. This was done at the Incarnation of the Son of God in the Person of Jesus Christ." The force of Sheen's analogy came from its timing. He was speaking at the moment in the 1950s when television eclipsed radio; the visual dimension of television overawed audiences who, for a generation, had considered radio the superlative mass medium.[7]

The depth of Sheen's polemical challenge had a lot to do with television, which conferred on him a celebrity and authority far greater than he had attained through radio. Radio was the medium of the cloistered Catholic America that hung on into the 1930s, the Catholic America that listened to Father Charles Coughlin, Detroit's populist and antisemitic "radio priest." But television was the medium of the newly confident mainstream Catholicism, the Catholicism of the postwar years whose best incarnation was the suave, Louvain-educated Fulton Sheen. In 1940, to mark the tenth anniversary of Sheen's broadcasts for "The Catholic Hour," *Time* contrasted Coughlin and Sheen. "Take away Father Coughlin's microphone," the magazine editorialized, "and there would be little left but a parish priest." But Sheen was "a son of Mother Church in whom she can take greater pride" and "a persuasive, lucid speaker, with a well-cultivated voice who can make religion sensible and attractive to great masses of people."[8]

The book in which Sheen analogized Judaism and Christianity with radio and television, *Life Is Worth Living*, took its name from the priest's remarkable weekly television show. Produced by the archdiocese of New York, the show first aired on the Dumont network in February 1952 in the 8:00 P.M. Tuesday slot then dominated by "Mr. Television," Milton Berle. (The "standard Tuesday question" among Catholic priests, *Time* reported, was "Uncle Miltie or Uncle Fultie?") Sheen's set resembled a study; it contained only some books, a blackboard, and a statue of the Virgin Mary, which acquired the nickname "Our Lady of Television." Without the aid of cue cards or TelePrompTers, Sheen spoke extemporaneously for the full twenty-eight minutes of the broadcast, dressed in high-collared flowing robes, his piercing eyes bearing steadily on the camera. *Life Is Worth Living* outranked Dumont's erstwhile front-runner, *The Jackie Gleason Show*, and Sheen won an Emmy award after his first season on the air. In 1955 ABC bought the show, which had an estimated audience of thirty million viewers. Milton Berle told *Time*: "If I'm going to be eased off the top by anyone, it's better that I lose to the One for whom Bishop Sheen is speaking." It wasn't clear, though, that Berle and Sheen had the same One in mind.[9]

Although Sheen downplayed Catholic doctrine in order to hold an ecumenical audience, his themes remained clearly Christian, and the press highlighted his success at bringing nonbelievers, including Jews, into the Church. "In his words," *Time* reported, "range a message to all who call themselves Christians." The Antichrist, Sheen liked to say, "will come disguised as the Great Humanitarian. . . . He will write books on the new idea of God to suit the way people live. . . . Jews, Protestants and

Catholics should unite against a common foe. . . . If anti-Christ has his fellow-travelers, then why should not God and His Divine Son?" Announcing "Converter on Wax" in 1946, *Time* (whose owner was Henry Luce, Clare's husband) promoted a new record album containing eight of Sheen's speeches. The magazine noted Sheen's remarkable success at winning converts to Catholicism and quipped that the records "were issued by Sheen's longtime admirer, Edward Dukoff, who is press agent for Comedian Danny Kaye. Dukoff, a tall, nervous Jew, has so far not entered the Church." A few years later, in a story that was reprinted by *Reader's Digest, Time* said about the "Microphone Missionary" that he considered himself "a spiritual agriculturist [who] tills the soil" with the understanding that "all the tilling in the world would make no difference if the seed had not been dropped by God." To attest that "Sheen knows his agriculture," *Time* quoted one of his Jewish converts, "a middle-aged man in the textile business."

> I had been avoiding a decision for years. Sheen doesn't let you do that. He throws it right in your teeth. The one thing that was hard for me as a Jew to accept was the divinity of Christ. I kept putting if off. Then, when Sheen began to weed out those in the class that weren't really interested, he finished one lecture with: "What think ye of Christ?" I wandered around freezing in Central Park for hours that night, and the week that followed was the worst I ever spent. But I couldn't put off the decision any longer. Something about him wouldn't let me.[10]

Like Sheen, Clare Luce mixed a conviction of Christian superiority with her denunciation of Freudian psychology, and in her case that combination produced the accusation of antisemitism that appeared in the *American Scholar.* What did she actually say in the story of her spiritual journey to Catholicism?

Spread across the February, March, and April 1947 issues of *McCall's,* Luce's "The Real Reason" is a passionate description of a struggling soul's search for meaning in Marxism, Freudianism, Russian mysticism, and finally Catholicism. Despite her many successes by the early 1930s, Luce found herself unhappy and unable to explain why:

> Some vast uneasiness, restlessness, discontent, suffused the very interstices of my being. . . . I concluded, with considerable shame, that I must be a neurotic. Which I wasn't. I was just not at peace with my God. So how—in Heaven's name—could I long to be at peace with myself, or anyone? Now, in those days, the most fashionable ism for effecting a cure for any intense personal unhappiness whose immediate origin was difficult to define was Freudianism. Indeed, Freud was the patron saint of the liberal elite who believed that the individual could achieve health, wealth, wisdom and of

course popularity, by hauling away at his subconscious bootstraps. For the benefit of those who have written to me that "anyone who becomes a Catholic ought to be psychoanalyzed" I can reassure them: I was psychoanalyzed in the middle thirties. And it is quite clear to me now that this experience was also one of the real reasons I became a Catholic.[11]

Luce had begun psychoanalysis shortly after divorcing her first husband, socialite George Brokaw. She saw a prominent Viennese analyst, Dorian Feigenbaum ("one of the best in America, a pupil of a pupil of Freud's from Vienna"), who was on staff at Columbia University's Institute of Neurology. Like many men, Feigenbaum may have been sexually attracted to his witty and alluring patient; Luce's ironic description of the transference process implies as much. (Luce would again experience this problem a few years later, during a brief psychoanalysis prompted by frustration over Henry Luce's sexual apathy.) Despite any romantic feelings Feigenbaum may have stumbled over in trying to treat Luce, she took him seriously and gave up on psychoanalysis only after time allowed reasonable doubts to surface.

I think I first began to experience serious doubts about my analyst's dogmas as it became clear to me that Freudianism was a system of thought intended to explain everything about me, including my devotion to the "higher" things of life, in terms of disguised sexuality. . . . My world had seemed crass enough when I had come into his office. But I have believed passionately that there had been born, in the world, and were living in it now, men and women of high, pure and noble purpose . . . motivated, I felt sure, by a richer and sweeter, a more *ineffable* purpose than a sublimated infantile sexuality. The thought that they were not suddenly turned the world into a pageant of monstrous obscenity. During my analysis it began increasingly to seem that I was being "adjusted" to a world so shorn of beauty and goodness that a sane person might do better to leave it than try to live in it.[12]

Clare Luce's vivid reminiscence of a failed psychoanalysis did not mention Feigenbaum by name, but did refer at times to Jewish influences on psychoanalysis and other radical secular movements. After Bertrand Russell, she observed, "the Jewish pattern of history . . . is such as to make a powerful appeal to the oppressed and unfortunate at all times." As for her own flirtation with Marxism, she did not denounce that in conjunction with Judaism but wrote, "It was the emotional content, so subtly Christian and Jewish, that made Communism appealing to me for a long time." She incorrectly ascribed an "orthodox Jewish" background to both Freud and Marx, but only to suggest that their theories had a religious foundation.[13]

By ascribing a religious background to Freudianism, Luce, ironically, found a way to claim Freud for the Catholics. "The Catholic thinks that a child is born far on the leeward side of sainthood," she wrote: "Freud, whose own orthodox Jewish background profoundly influenced his thought, agrees."

> Indeed, Freud claims that a child is born with the mark of Cain not only upon his brow, but on every other part of his wee anatomy. The Freudian child springs from its mother's womb a brat, harboring aggressive and lustful intentions toward Pappa, Mamma, sister, nurse, and, as his little world expands, odd relations and playmates. If these intentions are clumsily or violently suppressed they boil and bubble and fester within him and become "complexes." If in maturity he fails to sublimate them successfully, they break out into anti-social actions which cause him and everybody else endless troubles and heartache. He then yearns "to return to the womb" which is fancy Freudian language meaning he wishes he had never been born. If this is not the doctrine of Original Sin, then I don't know a Catholic doctrine gone wrong, that is, turned into a heresy, when I see one.[14]

On the one hand, Luce seemed to be saying that traditional Judaism, like Catholicism, maintained a proper sense of human sinfulness, and that problems developed only when the religious sensibility was secularized, as in Freud's theory. Yet by defining Freud's assessment of human nature as essentially *Catholic*, a Catholic rather than a Jewish heresy, she both absolved Judaism and deprived it of ontological value. Her somewhat confused analysis expressed the ambiguous sympathy Luce felt for modern Jews. Of her analyst Feigenbaum she spoke finally with empathy, not hostility, "for he too was honestly trying to get along without God." "It was our joint misfortune that we happened for a number of months to get lost together," she recalled, "in the godless and atavistic underbrush of Freudianism." So, she implied, the "lost" secular soul, whether Jewish or Christian, entered out of desperation into the futile maze of psychoanalysis. But if Freudianism was a "Catholic doctrine gone wrong," then redemption for both the lapsed Christian and the secular Jew would have to come through the Church.[15]

LUCE AND THE CATHOLIC-JEWISH CULTURE CLASH

Luce's confessions conveyed no antisemitism, but they radiated a Christian self-assurance that must have seared Jewish readers. As a historian of converted Catholic intellectuals has observed, converts were more likely than born Catholics to address a wide audience; they "wanted to persuade other Protestants, Jews, atheists, and agnostics to follow their example." With a convert's passion, Luce asserted the primacy of Christianity; she believed that the true Catholic had to publicize the virtues of her faith. In several passages she referred to Jesus as "our Lord" and toward the end of her confessional she proclaimed the necessity of Christian belief. "It seems to me, today," she wrote, "that the differences between Christians of all denominations and unbelievers is wide and greater and more important to breach than the differences between let us say, Protestants and Catholics." Within that context, Luce's passages about the Jewishness of Marx and Freud might have excited her Catholic readers, who saw atheistic Communism as no better and perhaps worse than Nazism.[16]

Yet when she addressed Catholic audiences, Luce did not pander to that kind of emotionalism. In a 1947 speech on "Freedom and Catholicism" before Chicago's Archdiocese Council of Catholic Women, Luce opened with what was for the ladies in her audience the conventional wisdom on the subject: "Ever since Pius IX's time, Catholic statesmen and scholars have consistently and vociferously denounced and fought Communism." But she followed with a qualification: "But so have many Jews, Protestants and even Buddhists and Confucians." As if to reinforce the point that Communism and Judaism were not synonyms, as some of her listeners might have thought, she added the gratuitous information that "the great poet, Heinrich Heine, a German Jew, and a friend of Karl Marx, warned against his friend's philosophy."[17]

As a cosmopolitan convert, Luce distanced herself from both parochialism and pluralism; she objected to bigotry but without embracing the new "Judeo-Christian" rhetoric of the 1940s. In October 1947 she appeared with Max Lerner as a commentator on ABC's popular evening show "Town Meeting of the Air" to address the subject, "What Can We Do to Improve Race and Religious Relationships in America?" With the kind of historical and theological oversight that irritated Jews, Luce explained that the idea of interracial justice was "basically Christian doctrine, and it was put in the clearest, most simple fashion, in words that children could understand, 2,000 years ago in the Epistle of St. John. . . . 'And this commandment we have from God, that he who loveth God, loveth also his brother.' " A religious Jew would have cited prooftexts of much greater antiquity, the creation of all humanity "in the image of God," the commandments not to oppress the stranger and to love the neighbor as oneself. But Luce was simply voicing what she had learned in her Catholic instructions, that New Testament universalism superseded Old Testament particularism, and her motives were righteous: "That's good, plain, simple Christian talk and it's as plain as Peter's staff that anybody in this audience, or anybody who listens on the air, who hates any Jew or Catholic or Negro or Asiatic or man of any other racial or religious conviction than his own, simply because he holds that conviction, is not a Christian. He's just not a Christian."[18]

Luce's abstention from the "Judeo-Christian" crowd of religious liberals sometimes had a jarring quality. In one speech to the Women's Activities Committee of the National Conference of Christians and Jews, she exuded a Christian self-assurance that tested the limits of interfaith patience. The recently retired congresswoman discoursed upon the battle against atheism, secularism, and Communism, with many references to Christians, none to Jews, and quotations from Arnold Toynbee and T. S. Eliot, each of whom had spoken negatively about Judaism or Jews. When she referred to Our Lord, she meant Christ, for when she wanted to include her Jewish listeners she recognized "the God of Jewery" as a distinct entity. There was nothing inherently wrong with the distinction, but given the venue and her homage to Toynbee and Eliot, it is probably fair to say that Luce's characteristic feistiness crossed whatever line separated it from *chutzpah*.[19]

Unfortunately, not all of Luce's multitudinous fans were able or willing to distinguish between assertive Catholicism and antisemitism. Most of the letters Luce received contained no bigotry toward Jews, but a few did. An elderly correspondent from Brooklyn who sent some of his poetry took a *pro forma* compliment from the congresswoman as encouragement for an outpouring of both verse and prejudice. In one screed the gentleman linked Jews with atheistic Communism in a way that had become a minor convention among Catholics in the era of Father Coughlin:

> Many Jews have forsaken their torahs to become atheists and will argue with one openly on the streets that Russia is right. This fact has been shielded by the secular press and the truth is only obtained by reading the Catholic press, which dares to publish reality. There is no doubt at all in my mind that Russia, behind the scenes, has fostered the riots in the Holy Land. By throwing such a sop to the Jews they scratch the Jewish moneyed interests in the United States. The word "persecution" covers up many ills. . . . I daresay that the balance of reasoning power is in the Catholic Church today.

Another correspondent tersely expounded: "Zionism and Judaism and Bolshevism are about the same thing. All are enemies of Christianity, Christianity must defend itself against these evil forces."[20]

Luce did not dignify those letters with replies, but their existence reveals the continuing undercurrent of anti-Jewish sentiment beneath the Catholic-Jewish culture clash that first emerged in the 1920s. As paramount symbols of secular decadence for Catholics like Sheen and Luce in the 1940s, Freud and Marx merely succeeded to the role Hollywood played in the interwar era. The ubiquitous impact of Jewish moviemakers provoked the first Catholic reaction, as both Jews and Catholics struggled to make their mark on a post-Protestant American culture.

If movie censorship in America had an ethno-religious stamp, it was Catholic. In 1929 Martin Quigley, a devout Catholic who built a publishing empire out of the *Motion Picture Daily* and the *Motion Picture Herald*, began the campaign against cinematic indecency. Quigley collaborated with Father FitzGeorge Dinneen, a friend and a leader of the Chicago film board, and Father Daniel Lord, a Jesuit theologian and playwright, who wrote up an initial but ineffective production code. The second time around, Quigley teamed up with two men: John Cantwell, the bishop of Los Angeles, and Joe Breen, a "salty-tongued," "back-slapping Irish politician" reared in Philadelphia's Catholic school system who served as a public relations consultant to the Hays Office, as Hollywood's self-regulatory body, the Motion Picture Producers and Distributors of America, was commonly known. Cantwell and Breen were, in the words of historian Charles Morris, "more than a little anti-Semitic." The trio "orchestrated a public attack on the movie industry" in the course of which "Cantwell fulminated against the 'Jews' and 'pagans' who ran Hollywood."[21]

In the end, Jews and Catholics worked out a mutually satisfactory system under Breen's adept supervision, which guaranteed a kind of fantastic wholesomeness that was good for both profits and morals. Jewish writers and producers happily created iconic Catholics, especially the Irish American priest as virile moral crusader. Louis B. Mayer was philo-Catholic, and Columbia's Harry Cohn married Catholic women twice and raised his children as Catholics. Nevertheless, the censorship battle of the 1930s revealed that Catholics and Jews easily viewed each other as cultural antagonists, one standing for purity (repression) and the other for freedom (decadence).[22]

That potential for antagonism actually escalated in the 1930s and 1940s. The rise of fascism abroad alerted liberals to the vulnerability of democracy and unleashed a powerful suspicion about the incompatibility of Catholicism and American values. When the majority of American Catholics rallied behind the repressive regimes of Mussolini's Italy, Franco's Spain, and Vichy France, America's leading intellectuals, many of whom were liberals of Protestant and Jewish origin and Deweyite persuasion, focused on the Catholic Church as an enemy of freedom. In the late 1930s, before the full reality of Hitlerism and Stalinism had registered with Americans, the Spanish Civil War was the *cause célèbre* for the nation's liberals and leftists, who were shocked to find Catholic Americans coming out on the wrong side in an epic confrontation between democracy and authoritarianism.

Just a few years earlier, presidential candidate Al Smith had won the support of liberals by demonstrating that an American Catholic would follow the homogenizing, practical path of democracy rather than the divisive dogma of an orthodox faith. But by the 1940s liberal anxiety about Catholic endorsements of authoritarian parties abroad, the self-segregation of Catholic parochial education, the obedience of nuns, the hierarchicalism and supernaturalism of the Church, and the conspicuousness of Catholic antisemitism during the Depression had made Al Smith's Catholic Americanism seem like a relic. Suddenly the Church symbolized the rejection of those pluralistic, scientific values cherished by liberals as America's only hope in an age of religious bigotry and tribal retrenchment. So it was not a complete surprise when a liberal Protestant member of the Society for Ethical Culture, who swore no malice toward Catholic individuals, published an anti-Catholic book, *American Freedom and Catholic Power* (1949), which became a Book-of-the-Month club selection and elicited praise from John Dewey, Albert Einstein, and other prominent liberals of Protestant and Jewish background, the same types who had rallied behind Al Smith as a symbol of nonsectarian tolerance in 1928.[23]

The dispute between *Peace of Mind* and *Peace of Soul* over psychoanalysis and faith fit into that larger clash between Jews and Catholics (and Protestants and Catholics) over the direction America should take in the postwar world. When the *American Scholar* criticized Sheen and Luce for their statements against psychoanalysis and hinted that Luce had antisemitic motives, it sensed and entered into this ongoing ethno-religious conflict. Yet Clare Luce, unlike Father Cantwell of Los Angeles or Father Coughlin of Detroit, did not utter antisemitic statements. In fact she had a number of intense personal relationships with Jews and spoke out eloquently on the subject of postwar Jewish suffering. Let us now look further into the hidden personal story behind this key figure in the Catholic-Jewish conflict of the postwar years.

THE JEWISH MEN IN CLARE LUCE'S CLOSET

Luce had a series of fateful liaisons, connections, and collisions with Jews that mirrored her own sense of marginality. She was born out of wedlock and fated never to have a meaningful relationship with the man whose family name she carried, William Boothe. Her mother was an avaricious and unscrupulous social climber intent on one goal: to catapult Clare into the American upper class. As a result of those ambitions Ann Boothe refused to marry the Jewish businessman, Joel Jacobs, who supported her and her children lavishly for several years during Clare's adolescence and early adulthood. She continued to enjoy Jacobs's largesse even after she married another man.[24]

Although Clare picked up some of her mother's pretensions, she genuinely liked and cared about her generous Jewish guardian. Jacobs secured Clare's monetary needs when she went to the Castle School in Tarrytown-on-Hudson, paying for her train tickets, taxis, riding lessons, lunches, corsets, combs, tickets to plays, movies, musicals, operas, reviews, and vaudeville shows (she attended a show nearly every week). "Riggie," as Clare affectionately called Jacobs, thoughtfully sent her large baskets of fruit, flowers, and candy when she was away at school, bought her fine sets of books, and gave her shares of stock in his tire company. For her graduation he surprised her with a green Essex roadster. "Riggie is a wonderful man," an almost-sixteen-year-old Clare recorded in her diary, "and I just adore him. Jew? Yes. But any white Christian who was ½ as fine as he would be considered a miracle. Riggie thinks very wonderful things of me. . . . I shall do my best to make him really proud of me."[25]

Soon after high school Clare dated a middle-aged Jewish man but felt she had to keep a distance in deference to her mother's prejudices. "I like Mr. Strauss," she confided to her diary, "but, well, he *is* a Jew and folks around this hotel who amount to anything shun them. I don't care what people think, but mother seems to." Following her divorce from George Brokaw in 1929, she entered into relationships with two other Jewish men, both authority figures: her analyst Feigenbaum, and Bernard Baruch, with whom she carried on what may have been the most intense love affair of her life. The affair with Baruch, thirty-three years her senior, launched a new and vital phase of Clare's life, not only because of the passion she felt for the aristocratic statesman but because Baruch introduced her to important men and ruling ideas in American politics. (Her 1935 marriage to Henry Luce fit well into that line of interest.) In his autobiography Baruch referred to Clare as a "talented and charming" woman, a meager allusion to the once-passionate relationship that he apparently discarded with patrician detachment. Privately he described her as the brightest woman he knew and continued to hold her in high esteem. Luce could not have missed the parallel between Baruch and herself—they both were outsiders, he by religious and she by social background, who became consummate insiders through intellect and personality.[26]

With two Jewish men as her principal father figures, it was an ironic twist of fate that Luce's only child should be taken from her in an accident involving a Jewish man. While a freshman at Stanford in January 1944, Ann Clare Brokaw died in Palo Alto when the passenger door of the car in which she was riding flew open upon impact with an oncoming car. Ann was ejected and crushed between the car and a tree. Although the police report found no evidence of wrongdoing, Henry and Clare Luce may have suspected the other driver of negligence, for they made their own inquiry into the accident. They discovered that the driver was a German Jewish refugee named Kurt Bergel. He and his wife had escaped the Nazis and arrived penniless in the United States. Fluent in several languages, the Bergels had been language teachers in Germany and found the same work at a private school in Palo Alto. The investigator reported that Bergel was then teaching servicemen for the Army Specialists Training Unit at Stanford, that he and his wife earned a very modest income, and that Kurt was "reputed to be very serious and hard working, but gives the impression of never having been able to free himself from the recollection of the conditions in Germany from which he escaped." Bergel telegrammed the Luces to express how burdened he was with sadness over his part in the terrible accident. Writing on Clare's behalf, Henry Luce replied sympathetically to Bergel, and the Luces let the matter go.[27]

The unlikely collision of Clare Luce's life and that of an uprooted German Jew came during her first term as a congresswoman from Connecticut. Less than two years later, she delivered an electrifying speech on Capitol Hill about the fate of 100,000 homeless Jews in Europe. On December 19, 1945, the House of Representatives held its debate about a concurrent resolution urging the settlement of those displaced persons in Palestine. Jewish congressmen expressed the profound sentiments of American Jewry, while the Christian majority's views ranged from sincere expressions of religious obligation to pragmatic demurrals of American interventionism. To rebut the argument that humanitarian intervention might backfire and increase anti-Jewish sentiment, Luce offered a uniquely compelling combination of logic and moral commitment:

> Anti-Semitism will not be abated by the mere solution of the Palestine question, one way or another. Those who wish to think ill of the Jews will always be zealous in their search of reasons, and reasons will never be lacking. . . . The tragic result of such thinking is the disastrous belief that every man is his brother's enemy, no nation is a peaceful nation but a defeated or enthralled one, and in this instance that no Jew is a good Jew but a dead one. Some people who feel that way will express it in more diplomatic language. They will seize upon the opinion that to give the Jews in Europe sanctuary or a homeland in Palestine will fan the fires of anti-Semitism and, expressing a desire to save Jews, condemn great numbers of them to homelessness, persecution, and death. It is high time that we in America were brutally honest with ourselves about this Jewish question. . . . We talk hot for Palestine and blow cold the minute we are challenged to prove that we mean it. . . . Shall we make more promises to the ears of suffering Jewry with this

resolution, and break it to their hearts the minute it looks as though the promises we give are going to be the slightest bit troublesome? . . . I hope that this resolution will not be considered, as some seem to feel, a pious but meaningless gesture, which will soothe our consciences but commit us to nothing; a resolution which, in the words of many, "can do no harm and may catch or hold some Jewish votes." I hope it will pass and mean what it promises—a permanent homeland for suffering Jewry.[28]

Luce's subtle and somewhat tragic relations with Jewish men—the "stepfather" Jacobs, the suitor Strauss, the analyst Feigenbaum, the mentor-as-lover Baruch, the victim as inadvertent victimizer Bergel—played out also in her dreams. In June 1949 she informed her diary of a chaotic dream, in which people in a crowded theater surrounded her as she prepared to marry a young Jewish man named Kastner (she had once met a Jewish editor at *Life* with that name). But as she dressed for the wedding she cut her hand. Bleeding profusely, she realized that this accident may have saved her from a wedding she did not want. About this dream and another immediately preceding it, which also involved her bleeding but in an ambivalent Catholic context, she wrote that they evinced a feeling of "tremendous confusion." Whatever the confusion may have been in regard to symbols of her new Catholicism, the ambivalence surrounding her imagined wedding to a Jewish man reflected the intimacies and suffering of her actual experiences, and especially the confused affections and taboos attached to Jacobs and Baruch. For all that Luce rejected Freud, she shared his belief in the significance of dreams enough to record them with considerable precision.[29]

Near the end of her life Clare Luce revealed a final covert identification with Jews. She had taken a strong interest in the fate of Israel and published in the *National Review* an essay meant to counteract the wave of international antagonism building after 1973. In a letter to William F. Buckley accompanying her manuscript, she wrote, "I find that most of the people I talk to are very foggy about the Middle East situation, and either tend to blame it (and the energy crisis) on 'the New York Jews,' or on the greed of the oil cartel and our own oil companies. This is a simple, but I hope not too simple-minded attempt to put the Arab-Israeli conflict into some perspective for ordinary non-Jewish readers."[30]

A year and a half later, in a review of Golda Meir's autobiography for the *New Republic*, Luce spoke not from her political mind but from depths of private emotion. Confessing that her essay would not qualify as a review because she could find nothing critical to say about Meir's book, Luce defined her contemporary as a heroic figure. "I feel very deeply about the survival of Israel, which it does not seem to me can be taken for granted," she wrote as preface to her portrait of Meir's extraordinary

rise from humble origins in Russia and later Milwaukee. She pondered
that ascent as another ascendant woman of the same generation. Mindful
of how she had been transported from modest circumstances to an elite
boarding school with the help of Joel Jacobs, the man whom she swore
she would make proud one day, Luce wrote of the young Meir and her
husband: "No stroke of luck brought the young couple contacts with
well-to-do, no less rich or powerful friends who might have helped them
up the American ladder."[31]

CLARE LUCE AND THE JEWS: THE WOMAN AND THE SYMBOL

Clare Boothe Luce played a vocal part in the contest between a rising
American Catholic population that generally distrusted the vogue of psychology, and a rising American Jewish population that tended to accept
it. Of course, traditionalist Jews in the 1940s had little use for psychology,
and liberal Catholics had been dealing with Freud since the 1920s. By
the late 1950s Pope Pius XII called for a reconciliation of psychology
and Catholicism: "No one will deny that modern psychology, considered
as a whole, deserves approbation from the moral and religious point of
view." Pius did not really differ from Sheen, however, for he stressed the
limits of psychological authority and expressed an unmistakable reserve
about the spiritual and moral potential of psychotherapy. Reform and
Conservative Judaism allowed for a more affirmative take on psychology
and certainly on Freudian analysis, and even Joshua Liebman's stout
critic Will Herberg admired Freud. Perhaps the simplest measure of the
difference between Jewish and Catholic perceptions of psychotherapeutics was the fact that Jews constituted a large proportion of psychoanalysts
and Catholics did not, even though there were many more Catholics
than Jews in America.[32]

   In doing what she considered her calling, to promote Catholicism
in the American public square (as Liebman's *Peace of Mind* promoted
Judaism), Clare Luce made herself vulnerable to suspicions of antisemitism. Her vivid public refutation of Freud also gave her standing
within the hagiography of cultural conservatism, so much so that her
name may still be invoked today to witness against the "pharisees" of
psychoanalysis, as Sheen obsessively referred to them. If, however, we
distinguish between Clare Luce the woman and Clare Luce the symbol,
we will learn that her persona in the Catholic-Jewish culture clash of
postwar America was a complex one. She neither inherited nor sustained the parochial antisemitism of an interwar Catholic hero like
Charles Coughlin. On the contrary, her cosmopolitanism reflected both
the mainstreaming of American Catholicism after World War II and her

private experiences, which included intimate and psychologically potent relationships with Jews.

Clare Luce's intense involvement with a number of Jewish men gave her emotional life a complexity that her well-publicized Catholic ideology lacked. Even her intellectual effort to establish that Freudianism derived from Orthodox Judaism but resounded with Catholicism's Original Sin reflected a feeling, no matter how ill-defined, that both faiths somehow spoke a similar language. As a Catholic convert, however, she obviously could not pursue such implications. Those surfaced in dreams that involved Jewish and Catholic characters in convoluted relation to each other. Mindful of the social marginality she shared with Jews, and of her dependence on them at important stages in her life, Clare Luce never accepted completely the sharp dichotomy between Catholics and Jews that her new catechism prescribed.

Part V

Jews and the American Search
for Meaning, 1950–2000

Chapter 12

Jews and the Creation of American Humanism

IN SOME RESPECTS, the American psychological and spiritual scene of the last half of the twentieth century resembled that of the first. Traditional religion coexisted with positive-thinking and New Age spirituality, with the added attraction of Eastern spirituality. Spiritualism, not so much in the classical form of the séance as in ghost sightings, spirit channeling, and other paranormal activity, remained popular and found a new ally in beliefs about aliens from outer space. Popular psychology, with its distinctive mix of science and faith, not only endured but enlarged its place in American culture. And the evident desire of Jews to participate in public debate about human nature continued unabated. In conjunction with thinkers of Christian (usually Protestant) background, they pioneered the humanistic psychologies of personal growth and creativity that defined so much of American life and thought after the 1950s.

By far, the most important spiritual question of the era was this: How do we locate the authentic *person*, the genuine *self*, beneath the layers of conventional behavior that family and society imposed on the individual? This was an old question for Americans, one that stimulated Dickinson, Emerson, Thoreau, and other writers of the mid-nineteenth century. In the middle and late decades of the twentieth, Jews provided some of the essential answers. They did so in the arts—as writers of a new type of expressive, psychologically focused fiction and poetry—but also and with even greater consequence as psychologists and religious philosophers. Among the dozens of Jewish men and women who created innovative approaches and schools of human psychology in the postwar decades, Erik Erikson, Martin Buber, Erich Fromm, and Abraham Maslow stood out as guiding stars of the humanist enterprise. Their careers, and those of their most prominent Protestant counterparts, Paul Tillich, Rollo May, and Carl Rogers, are well known. Yet even as the Protestant roots of American humanism have not been fully remembered, the Jewish sources have never been coherently understood. In this chapter, we will explore these Jewish sources. We will see how some of the most important exponents of humanism spoke directly and sometimes defensively as Jews, sensitive to the destructiveness of fascism, aware of their outsider status, cognizant, as only immigrants could be, of the fluidity of personal identity, and deeply influenced by a Jewish concept of human relatedness.[1]

Humanism took root in the 1950s and early 1960s, years in which the Cold War and the civil rights movement dominated public attention. That period also saw the rise of psychiatrists to an almost hegemonic authority, which enabled them to define what was normal and abnormal. All too often, their definitions were arbitrary and supportive of a troubled status quo, one that kept many people confined to socially subordinate positions and labeled social misfits as deviants. R. D. Laing, a gifted and rebellious inquirer into mental illness, tersely summed up the problems that Cold War thinking, racial segregation, and psychiatric hubris had created: "A man who prefers to be dead rather than Red is normal. A man who says he has lost his soul is mad. . . . A man who says that Negroes are an inferior race may be widely respected. A man who says his whiteness is a form of cancer is certifiable."

By focusing on creativity, growth, and self-expression, those thinkers who considered themselves humanists led a countercultural crusade against all the institutions (the "military-industrial complex," segregation, the asylum, the authoritarian family) that diminished the individual and blocked what Abraham Maslow called "the highest reaches of human nature."[2]

JEWISH WRITERS AND THE SEARCH FOR HUMAN EMOTION

The new centrality of Jewish thinkers and themes in American conversation about human nature was anticipated by a book about Western literature that came from one of Hitler's Jewish refugees in Turkey. Writing in Istanbul during the 1940s, literary scholar Erich Auerbach (1892–1957) gave a powerful new reading of the Hebrew Bible in *Mimesis: The Representation of Reality in Western Literature*, one of the century's true masterpieces of scholarship. Before Hitler, the Berlin-born Auerbach had been a professor of philology at the University of Marburg. After the war he found his way to America, where he became a professor of literature at Yale. Translated from the German and published by Princeton University Press in 1953, *Mimesis* reversed an outworn interpretation of the Jewish Scriptures. Since the rise of Christianity, the Hebrew Bible had been interpreted as a secondary book to the Gospels, and one whose significance lay chiefly in its capacity to portend the coming of Jesus. With the rise of modern literary criticism in the nineteenth century, the Old Testament fared even worse. Literary scholars, most of them of Christian background, compared the Hebrew Bible to the Greek classics and found it wanting; its characters were demoted to the status of legendary composites, its laconic style dismissed as aesthetically unpleasant, and its fiery sense of righteousness deemed offensive. Auerbach put an end to that line of interpretation when he juxtaposed the Hebrew text with Homer and argued that "the two kinds of style they embody" formed the foundation on which Western literature built its depictions of reality.

With stunning eloquence, Auerbach discerned and explicated what Jewish readers had taken for granted for millennia: that the stories of the biblical characters were full of psychological nuance and human realism. The many descriptive gaps in the Bible invited interpretation about the motives and feelings of characters, whereas the complete descriptions in Homer left no mysterious hints for the reader to decipher. For all the aesthetic refinement of Greek literature, Homer's characters lacked the identifiable human substance of Abraham and Sarah, Isaac and Rebecca, Jacob and Rachel, of Joseph, Moses, Saul, David, and Absalom, all of whom "show a distinct stamp of individuality entirely foreign to the Homeric heroes." "And how much wider is the pendulum swing of their lives than that of the Homeric heroes!" Auerbach exclaimed.

> The poor beggar Odysseus is only masquerading, but Adam is really cast down, Jacob really a refugee, Joseph really in the pit and then a slave to be bought and sold.... So little are the Homeric heroes presented as developing or having developed, that most of them—Nestor, Agamemnon, Achilles—appear to be of an age fixed from the very first.... But what a road, what a fate, lie between the Jacob who cheated his father out of his blessing and the old man whose favorite son has been torn to pieces by a wild beast! ... The old man, of whom we know how he has become what he is, is more of an individual than the young man; for it is only during the course of an eventful life that men are differentiated into full individuality; and it is the history of a personality which the Old Testament presents to us as the formation undergone by those whom God has chosen to be examples.[3]

Auerbach's "rediscovery" of significance in a text associated with Jews was part of a new wave in postwar American letters, one that began to swell with Budd Schulberg's novel *What Makes Sammy Run?* (1941). That book signaled a new interest in Jewish characterizations of the human and the American predicament. Popular enough to reappear in *Reader's Digest*, the novel came on the heels of Sholem Asch's Jewish retelling of the life of Jesus, *The Nazarene*, which, translated from the Yiddish by Maurice Samuel, was a top-ten best-seller in both 1939 and 1940. (At the end of Asch's lavishly detailed story, Jesus's resurrection is left a matter of debate, and the Pharisees, portrayed as honorable men, have reached an agreement with Jesus about the commandments to love God and one's neighbor, though they differ "on the method by which to reach this goal.") Just as Asch redefined Jesus in Jewish terms, Schulberg redefined the American dream in both Jewish and psychological terms. Schulberg's novel is narrated by a Jewish newspaper columnist who becomes, in spite of himself, the best friend of Sammy Glick, a young man from a poor home on the Lower East Side whose ambition to become wealthy leads him to exploit everyone and everything on his way to the top of the motion picture industry. The narrator's refrain—*What makes Sammy run?*—is finally answered in psychological (Adlerian) terms: after being roughed up once too often, little Sammy Glickstein decides to become the dominator rather than the dominated. In Schulberg's story, the quintessential American competitor is an intensely neurotic overcompensator, a man incapable of forming sincere attachments to anyone. And yet, Sammy's personality is refreshingly open and unpretentious— his drives are the Ur-drives of American society.

"I wonder if the thing that makes Sammy so fascinating for us is that he is the *id* of our whole society," Sammy's only female friend tells the narrator.

> "What do you mean?"
>
> "Well, you know how the *id* is supposed to be the core of your basic appetites which the super-ego dresses in the clothes of respectability to present to the outside world? Somehow Sammy never had time to get dressed up in the way all those others have, Wilson and McCarter and Sir Anthony, all their sammyglickness covered up with Oxford manners or have-one-on-me sociability or Christian morals that they pay their respects to every Sunday morning when they don't have too big a hangover. I think that's what first hit me about Sammy. He wasn't something trying to be something else. He was the thing itself, the *id*, out in the open."[4]

Sammy Glick opened the doors to a genre of psychologically focused fiction that became the trademark of such innovative postwar Jewish writers as Saul Bellow, Philip Roth, and Allen Ginsberg. Theirs was a literature of voluble introspection; their heroes were neurotic existentialists given to rambling and acerbic reflections on their own inadequacies and on the stultifying conformity of the society they stubbornly refused to join. Psychiatrists typically figured into their dramas of the alienated individual. The purest, most outrageous examples were Roth's sexually manic analysand in *Portnoy's Complaint*, the anguished (and sexual) voice of Ginsberg in "Howl," and the articulate (and sexual) schlemiel that Woody Allen made a stock figure of American comedy. Less outrageous but equally pure was Bellow's Moses Herzog, a highly literate, narcissistic schlemiel of an English professor driven by a "steaming nervous vitality" to compose a furious series of angst-ridden, half-finished letters to everyone from Baruch Spinoza to Fulton Sheen. Bellow heralded the new style in his first novel, *Dangling Man* (1944), when the narrator, a Jewish inductee waiting interminably for his actual induction into the army, opens his reflections with a criticism of the "manly" emotional reticence associated with the era of Hemingway:

> There was a time when people were in the habit of addressing themselves frequently and felt no shame at making a record of their inward transactions. But to keep a journal nowadays is considered a kind of self-indulgence, a weakness, and in poor taste. . . . Today, the code of the athlete, of the tough boy—an American inheritance, I believe, from the English gentleman . . . is stronger than ever. Do you have feelings? There are correct and incorrect ways of indicating them. Do you have an inner life? It is nobody's business but your own. Do you have emotions? Strangle them.[5]

Bellow's character signaled a new creed of emotional expressiveness in 1940s America, one that had an unmistakable Jewish pedigree. In the words of one literary scholar:

> To a non-Jew, this is the most striking similarity among the Jewish-American writers, accounting for their warmth and perhaps even for their great appeal to the general American public. . . . Bellow's plea for energy and sensation in the face of correctness was a demand for an open society. It also involved a new model for the American . . . The Jews over the centuries had learned to live with chaos, and so could offer a more open kind of model, a type well-worn, harassed, and suffering, but large and dignified and persevering, finding his ideal in the human being itself.[6]

In other cultural venues, too, Jews called for a new openness to emotion, through the Method-acting that Lee Strasberg introduced into American drama, the renderings of masculine emotionality in Al Jolson's postwar movies, and the pathbreaking 1952 study by Mark Zborowski of comparative ethnic responses to pain. Shattering old derisive stereotypes of Jewish and Italian hospital patients as overly sensitive to pain, Zborowski established the new common sense: people from different cultural backgrounds had different ways of expressing pain and other emotions. Expressiveness was as normal as restraint.[7]

The expressive style of the postwar Jewish writers achieved its most enduring visual statement in Woody Allen's cinema and its most enduring aural monument in Allen Ginsberg's poetry. Take, for example, Allen's 1977 classic *Annie Hall* (a film that Allen originally named *Anhedonia*, the term Abraham Myerson introduced to the public in his 1925 book, *When Life Loses Its Zest*). In the film's introduction, we encounter a main character who discourses freely and rapidly on the anxiety of aging and isolation, making references to Freud's *Wit and Its Relation to the*

Unconscious as well as to Groucho Marx's quip about the Jew who
wouldn't want to belong to any club that would have someone like him
as a member. Allen's achievement was to take the heroic little man of
American comedy (Buster Keaton, Charlie Chaplin) and make him a
verbally heroic little man, unafraid of publicizing the angst within. Allen's innovative use of the Freudian confessional as a comedic device
epitomized the new sensibility.

Ginsberg did the same for Beat literature, to which he gave a verbal nuance and emotional candor that were lacking in his friend Jack Kerouac's
On the Road. William Carlos Williams acknowledged that accomplishment
in the introduction he wrote for Ginsberg's "Howl" (1956), a poem that
sold more than 100,000 copies in its first ten years. The act of trans-
forming the most painful emotions into a panoply of words, Williams
suggested, enabled Ginsberg to survive the harrowing experiences of
growing up with a paranoid schizophrenic mother and having an institutionalized lover, Carl Solomon, to whom "Howl" was dedicated. "In spite
of the most debasing experiences that life can offer a man," Ginsberg
proved that "the spirit of love survives to ennoble our lives if we have the
wit and the courage and the faith—and the art! to persist." In the final
section of "Howl," Ginsberg writes from San Francisco to Solomon, who
is confined in an asylum in New York:

> Carl Solomon! I'm with you in Rockland
>   where you're madder than I am
>   I'm with you in Rockland
>   where you must feel very strange
> I'm with you in Rockland
>   where you imitate the shade of my mother . . .
> I'm with you in Rockland
>   where you scream in a straightjacket that you're losing the
>   game of the actual pingpong of the abyss
> I'm with you in Rockland
>   where you bang on the catatonic piano the soul is innocent
>   and immortal it should never die ungodly in an armed
>   madhouse.[8]

Like most of the postwar Jewish writers of note, Ginsberg did not hide
the Jewish world out of which he came. The "Footnote to Howl," which
forms a second final section, adapts the mesmerizing cadence of the
Kedushah chant—"Holy, Holy, Holy, is the Lord of Hosts"—a fundamental part of the daily Hebrew liturgy; similarly, in "Kaddish," a heart-
wrenching lamentation that gives a harrowing picture of his mother's
disordered mind, Ginsberg builds on the plaintive Mourner's Kaddish:

Magnified Lauded Exalted the Name of the Holy One Blessed
is He!
    In the house in Newark Blessed is He! In the madhouse Blessed
is He! In the house of Death Blessed is He! . . .
Blessed be you Naomi in Hospitals! Blessed be you Naomi in
    solitude! Blest be your triumph! Blest be your bars!
    Blest be your last years' loneliness![9]

JEWISH NONCONFORMITY AND THE IDEA OF "INNER" IDENTITY

The explosive expressiveness of the new Jewish writers caught the public imagination because it gave a brilliant, almost baroque expression to the central image of the age, the image of the trapped individual seeking catharsis through emotional, sexual, and verbal liberation. There—in that theme—we find the grand junction where literature met psychology in the postwar decades.

One of the figures at the junction was Theodor Reik, a former student of Freud's who shared some of his teacher's ability to add a literary grace to the psychological "search within." In a number of books that read like novels, Reik reminded Americans of the Jewish origins of Freud and the Freudian movement.

Among popular writers of the postwar period, Reik was the one who first emphasized and explored Freud's Jewishness. He criticized Ernest Jones's otherwise excellent biography of Freud for not understanding "the Jewish element in Freud's personality," which escaped Jones because he "lived outside the culture pattern in which Freud was born and bred." Reik thought that Freud's love of Jewish humor expressed the ironic sense that lay at the core of his personality, and he liked to recite instances in which Freud referred or alluded to a Jewish joke as a way of making a larger point. In his early correspondence, for example, Freud expresses the hope that he will arrive at an understanding of the psychology of neurosis, "if my constitution can stand it." This, Reik explained, was an allusion to "the well-known anecdote" in which a destitute Jew sneaks onto a train headed for the spa at Karlsbad, is caught and brutally treated, sneaks back on, is again caught and roughed up, and so on. At one station an acquaintance sees him and asks where he is headed, to which the bedraggled fellow replies, "To Karlsbad, if my constitution can bear it." When Freud was recording his famous self-analysis, he sent part of it to a friend and, to underscore that the analysis was directed totally by his unconscious, he referred to the Jewish joke of the inexperienced horseman, Itzig, who is asked, "Where are you going?" and answers, "How should I know? Ask the horse!"[10]

Reik shared Freud's pride in Jewish heritage and did not hesitate to publish ethnocentric opinions that Freud expressed only among other Jews. In an account of biblical morality, for example, he wrote, "A special ethical sensitiveness and the highest appreciation of spiritual values formed a Jewish heritage still possessed by the latest descendants of the ancient Hebrew people." Reik wanted to emulate Freud by writing an epic psychoanalytic history based on biblical myths, specifically the myth of the Fall of Man. That took the form of *Myth and Guilt,* a grand "inquiry into the sense of guilt which haunts our civilization," the insight of which Reik attributed to his own intellectual openness. "I did not dwell in pre-fabricated thought houses," he observed, echoing Freud's autobiograph-ical reflections on his intellectual daring. Reik perceived his own origi-nality as part of a larger collective tendency of the Jews: "The Jews are among the nations decidedly not the collective counterpart of what is known as a 'good mixer,' but their function as ferment of civilization is still scarcely acknowledged."[11]

Reik relished and purveyed an image of Freud, and of the intellectu-ally defiant Jew, as an exemplary character type whose originality and creativity flew in the face of mass conformity. That theme reappeared, in less parochial form, in one of the most compelling concepts of the post-war era, Erik Erikson's concept of inner identity. Of all those who had studied under Freud, Erikson played perhaps the most important role for Americans. His ideas about identity crisis and the construction of a stable identity came out of his personal experience of immigration and adaptation to another culture.

Postwar America was ready for a new appreciation of the inner world of the immigrant, judging by the success of Oscar Handlin's Pulitzer Prize–winning book, *The Uprooted* (1951). In it the Harvard historian famously declared that his study of immigrants in American history had left him with the conviction that "immigrants *were* American history." Himself a child of Jewish immigrants, Handlin recast the immigrant as the archetype of the modern, mobile, anxiously striving American. "No one moves without sampling something of the immigrants' experience— mountaineers to Detroit, Okies to California, even men fixed in space but alienated from their culture by unpopular ideas or tastes. But the immigrants' alienation was more complete, more continuous, and more persistent. Understanding of their reactions in that exposed state may throw light on the problems of all those whom the modern world some-how uproots."[12]

Immigrants had unique opportunities to alter their entire way of life and their way of presenting themselves to others, and Jewish psychological thinkers, as immigrants or the children of immigrants, were uniquely situated to interpret that phenomenon. Abraham Maslow saved clippings over a seven-year period on the case of Stephen Weinberg, a Brooklyn boy who became the country's most notorious imposter between the 1920s and the early 1950s. The material was of use for Maslow's teaching on psychopathology, but he seems to have had additional interest in Weinberg's case. He kept these clippings next to the July 1941 *Reader's Digest* condensation of *What Makes Sammy Run?* Maslow evidently saw a connection between the two stories, the same motif that played on the mind of Erik Erikson. Erikson believed that Jewish adaptation to America produced two personality types, the orthodox dogmatist and the cultural relativist, for whom "geographic dispersion and cultural multiplicity have become 'second nature.' " In their most extreme forms, these two types were represented by "the bearded Jew in his kaftan, and Sammy Glick." Erikson came to the conclusion that the tension between these two extreme tendencies defined the psyche of the American Jew and especially of those creative thinkers for whom

> the Letter may have become political or scientific dogma (socialism, Zionism, psychoanalysis) quite removed from the dogma of the Talmud, yet quoted and argued in a way not unlike the disputation of passages from the Talmud in the tradition of their ancestors. . . . The psychoanalyst, however, knows that this same set of opposites, this conflict between the adherence to the Letter, and the surrender to the changing price of things pervades the unconscious conflicts of men and women of Jewish extraction who do not consider themselves, nor are considered by others, as "Jewish" in a denominational or racial sense. . . . Thus they have become . . . the mediators in culture change, the interpreters in the arts and sciences, the healers of disease and of inner conflict.[13]

The book in which that passage appeared, *Childhood and Society* (1950), culminated Erikson's journey from Vienna to America and generated an American interest in identity that endured into the next century. As Erikson's biographer has observed, the experience of changing his own identity as he settled in the United States stimulated this student of Freud to conceptualize the problem of an identity crisis. "Without a deep identity conflict," Erikson wrote, "I would not have done the work I did."[14]

That inner conflict reflected the facts of a complicated childhood. Erik was born in 1902 to Karla Abrahamsen, an educated, beautiful, and free-spirited child of an assimilated but religiously observant family of Danish Jews. The identity of his father remained a permanent secret of Karla's, but Erik's blond hair and blue eyes gave him the idea that his father was a gentile, perhaps—he fantasized—a gifted artist from Copenhagen's bohemian quarter, his mother's habitat in those years. When he was three, Karla married Theodor Homburger, a German Jewish doctor who adopted Erik and moved the new family to his home in Karlsruhe. There, Theodor and Karla became pillars of the Jewish community; they raised Erik and his two half-sisters in the practices of Orthodox Judaism, though Erik felt out of place in the synagogue, where his blond features apparently earned him the nickname "goy." As a teenager Erikson felt alienated from Judaism and attracted by Protestantism, which he encountered through both his mother's interest in Kierkegaard and his friendship with a boy whose father was a Lutheran minister. Without rejecting Judaism, Erikson believed he occupied a peculiar place between the Jewish and Protestant worlds; he had learned from his mother that he could be a good Jew while also imbibing the best of Christian thought. And his childhood, he later reflected, involved him in a necessary process of crossing borders of religion, nationality, and even descent (given his ambiguous relationship with his stepfather). Erikson understood Jewishness, at its best, as an ethical system that was "boundary obliterating," inclusive of all humanity. He found that quality exemplary: "the more worlds an individual unites in himself . . . the more inclusive he is, the truer he is."[15]

This idea, and Erikson's experience of America as a nation of immigrants, inspired his meditations on identity as something constructed rather than simply given. In 1927, as a young, idealistic, and artistically inclined man, Erikson went to Vienna and spent the next six years—a period he considered life-changing—working under Sigmund and Anna Freud. He shared with Anna a gift for understanding children and put his artistic ambitions to work in creative interactions with the youngsters he taught at the experimental Hietzing School that Anna established in an affluent district of Vienna. Like so many others after 1933, Erikson left Austria and immigrated to the United States. At that point he changed his name, reducing Homburger to a middle position and inventing for himself the family name Erikson, which met an unfulfilled longing to know his biological father and a more attainable desire to remake himself as an American. Erikson loved his adopted country. Greeted by a friendly immigration clerk in Boston, Erikson "was whistling 'Yankee Doodle' as he left the immigration office," and he maintained an unclouded optimism about America for the rest of his life. He considered the nation both a refuge from European fascism and a beacon that "stood for a humane attempt to reach a minimal level of economic, social, and psychological dignity for all." When he claimed that the working out of one's identity was the central psychological challenge of his age, he referred explicitly to the lessons of Americanization: "And so it comes about that we begin to conceptualize matters of identity at the very time in history when they become a problem. For we do so in a country which attempts to make a superidentity out of all the identities imported by its constituent immigrants."[16]

The idea of an inner identity first came to Erikson from Freud, and specifically from Freud's sense of having an "inner" Jewish identity that enabled him to maintain his intellectual and moral integrity. Erikson cited Freud's 1926 address to the Vienna branch of B'nai B'rith, which had given brother Sigmund a warm reception for ideas that were unwelcome in society at large. Freud wrote of the "inner identity" (*der inneren Identität*) that linked him to his fellow Jews; they shared "the same psychological make-up" (*der gleichen inneren Konstruktion*). This, Erikson observed, was "an untranslatable turn of phrase, which, I feel, contains what we try to formulate in the term 'identity.' " In Erikson's view, Freud had an unshakable originality and rationality, a solid core of personality that Freud himself linked to being a Jew. In the B'nai B'rith address, Erikson pointed out to his readers, Freud "mentioned two traits which he felt he owed [to] his Jewish ancestry: freedom from prejudices which narrow the use of the intellect, and the readiness to live in opposition." Those were the qualities, Erikson believed, that modern men and women needed to protect themselves from the seductive power of mass conformity, the herd mentality, and also from the peril of despair. Freud possessed "ego integrity," which was the highest stage of character development in Erikson's eight stages of personal growth.[17]

How to construct an authentic identity, a solid core of personality that would allow the individual to withstand pressures toward mindless conformity—that was the defining question of the postwar era. At its outer limits, the struggle for pure individuality took the form of outlandish demonstrations of sexual and social rebelliousness. It became possible, for a time, to idealize the psychopath or the schizophrenic, types that were thoroughly estranged from the social order. Norman Mailer, the writer who most flamboyantly embodied the countercultural spirit of the 1950s, not only celebrated "the White Negro" and "the hipster" as true individuals but tried even to smash the conventions of literature by producing, in lieu of the expected novel, a massive montage, *Advertisements for Myself* (1959), which was "a carnival of stories, broadsides, assaults, and self-promotions . . . a daring gambit, all-or-nothing, a challenge to conventional sensibility, an affront to taste, and a test of the limits of public utterance." Mailer built upon the message of the two most notable exponents of "anti-conformity" in the 1950s, psychiatrist Robert Lindner (author of *Rebel without a Cause* and *Must You Conform?*) and ex-Freudian Wilhelm Reich.[18]

Unlike Lindner, a family man who did not romanticize the outlaw, Reich outstripped even the most outlandish in the 1950s, when he entranced bohemian America with his remarkable call for orgasmic defiance of conformity. The most controversial of Freud's Jewish students in America, Reich (1897–1957) broke with Freud in the 1920s precisely over the question of the relation of the libido to society. Whereas Freud considered sexual repression an inevitable function of society—necessary to prevent a state of anarchic behavior—Reich argued the opposite. His was a gospel of healthy sexual release in which deadening social rules were broken by revolutionary (anti-authoritarian) sexual intercourse (the so-called "good" orgasm that prompted Woody Allen's quip that he had never known any other kind). Reich argued that society's repression of the individual did not stop at the mental level but intruded into the body itself. His notions of "muscular armor" and "character armor"—the physical and psychological incorporation of society's repressive rules—attracted cultural dissidents and radicals who sensed that the modern, bureaucratic state stifled the individual in the most intimate manner. Expelled in the early 1930s from both the German Communist Party and the International Psychoanalytic Association for his advocacy of sexual politics, he moved from Berlin to Denmark and then Norway, only to be driven out for the same reasons in 1939, when he emigrated to the United States. Quickly, he elicited similar hostility from the American government.

On the road to insanity (he eventually concluded that he came from outer space), Reich claimed to have discovered a cosmic life force, "orgone energy," that, when collected in boxes called "orgone accumulators," could be used to cure diseases. In the 1950s, when the Food and Drug Administration charged him with fraud, he refused to follow court orders banning both the orgone accelerator and all references to it in his writings. In an extraordinary act of repression, the federal government in 1956 outlawed and burned not only the boxes but also most of his books. Imprisoned for contempt of court, Reich died in a federal penitentiary the following year. The bizarre career of Wilhelm Reich illustrated as no other the drama of the individual struggling for freedom against forces of authority.[19]

Yet Reich was only the most extreme and tormented example of a widespread concern among émigré Jewish thinkers with the pernicious effects of mass society. In 1950s America they remained troubled, if not traumatized, by the German embrace of Nazism two decades earlier. Reich's *The Mass Psychology of Fascism* (1933) explored the same themes of mass reaction, irrationalism, and antisemitism that Erich Fromm investigated in *Escape from Freedom* (1941), that Theodor Adorno and the Frankfurt School took up in *The Authoritarian Personality* (1950), and that Hannah Arendt analyzed in *The Origins of Totalitarianism* (1951). And Fromm directly inspired an American Jewish sociologist, David Riesman, to theorize about the "other-directed personality" in *The Lonely*

Crowd (1950), one of the most influential critiques of American conformity ever published.[20]

For most Americans, the idiosyncratic rebellion of men like Reich and Mailer was not a useful answer to the problem of individuality versus conformity. Of the growing numbers of people who were moving away from traditional religion, most would find a model of authentic being in one of the most powerful waves of thought ever to hit the shores of American spiritual life: humanism.

THE PROTESTANT SOURCES OF HUMANISM

During the last half of the twentieth century, humanist psychology—the psychology of the human being as a creative, self-fulfilling creature—dominated American conversation about personhood. The primary formulators of that humanist philosophy of life were Protestant and Jewish thinkers who shared an interest in the psychodynamics of personal growth and interpersonal relationships. There were Catholics involved in the psychological enterprise of the age too, the most important being Harry Stack Sullivan, a lapsed Catholic whose theories of interpersonal behavior affected many thinkers long after his death in 1949. But Catholic thinkers did not rush as massively as their Jewish counterparts into psychology, partly, no doubt, because of the more tentative attitude of the Church toward that precocious social science. One way to understand the confluence of Protestant and Jewish innovators of the new humanism is to juxtapose two triumvirates: Rollo May–Carl Rogers–Paul Tillich and Erich Fromm–Abraham Maslow–Martin Buber. Although there were scores of people involved in the creation of postwar American humanism (known as the "third wave" succeeding the first two, Freudian and behaviorist psychology), this pair of "Big Three's" set much of the tone and content of public conversation about the spiritual situation of the individual. They converged at many points and yet retained distinct Protestant and Jewish qualities. In other words, ideas of individual fulfillment in postwar America were not simply "humanist" but also derived from specific Protestant and Jewish understandings of the human condition.

Together, Rollo May (1909–94), Carl Rogers (1902–87), and Paul Tillich (1886–1965) exerted an enormous force over Protestant views of human nature after the 1940s. May was a minister who had studied at the Union Theological Seminary, where he developed a strong bond to his teacher Paul Tillich. He also studied with Alfred Adler, who strongly impressed him. Though influenced by Freud and Adler, May believed that both men had erred in their "rationalistic faith in the idea that knowledge will lead to virtue." They omitted the element of religious tension, healthy guilt resulting from God's "impingement upon man's temporal life." May's first two books, *The Art of Counseling* (1939) and *The Springs of Creative Living* (1940), used the language of depth psychology to reclaim a Calvinist sense of sin. May explained how people eased their anxiety by grasping secular symbols of success rather than face their inner fears and trust in God. His 1950 classic, *The Meaning of Anxiety*, though written ecumenically for a mass audience, took up the problem of Christian existentialism, referring frequently both to the originator of that movement, Søren Kierkegaard, and to its contemporary leader, Tillich, who depicted the individual as existing in a state of tension between being and nonbeing.[21]

A refugee from Hitler, Tillich, who had studied psychology in Germany, inspired many Americans looking for a blend of humanism and religion and many Protestants disappointed by the sanguine character of liberal Christianity but uncomfortable with a return to orthodoxy. Like May, but from the side of religious philosophy, Tillich produced an intriguing combination of psychology and theology. May's message about learning to face one's existential anxiety creatively reflected the teachings of Tillich. In *The Courage to Be* (1952), one of his most popular books, Tillich argued that psychotherapy, in helping people fight the anxiety of guilt, had produced a modern equivalent of basic Protestant concepts of sin. In the Reformation, he wrote, the idea of "forgiveness of sins" and "justification through faith" dominated the thinking of Christians, whereas in his own time "the idea of acceptance" performed a similar role. "In the Lutheran formula that 'he who is unjust is just' (in the view of the divine forgiveness) or in the more modern phrasing that 'he who is unacceptable is accepted,' " Tillich observed, "the victory over the anxiety of guilt and condemnation is sharply expressed." Tillich understood the essential human challenge, the "courage to be," as "self-affirmation of being in spite of non-being." The modern language of self-acceptance represented a fulfillment of the "belief in forgiveness," and he argued that forgiveness was most deeply apprehended "in genuine Protestantism."[22]

Carl Rogers took that Protestant concern about acceptance to its furthest limit. Influential as the existentialist spirituality of May and Tillich was for the postwar generation, Rogers had an even greater impact both on pastors and on an educated public seeking a humanistic approach to human nature. Standing alongside Maslow as a "father" of humanistic psychology, Rogers insisted that the healthy, self-fulfilling individual be freed from all external constraints. His emphasis on the real person hidden beneath layers of social obligation resounded in an era that was so sharply focused on the problem of conformity. As a young man, Rogers pulled away from the conservative Protestantism of his parents, who wanted him to study at the Princeton Theological Seminary, and chose instead the more liberal Union Theological Seminary. Even a modernized theology was too much for him, however, and he switched paths from the ministry to psychotherapy though remaining "an old-time Protestant liberal" who was "too religious to be religious." Despite Rogers's desire for a purely scientific psychology, "an aura of liberal Protestant ethical idealism always lingered in the background whenever he spoke about acceptance."[23]

True to that liberalism, Rogers believed in the essential goodness of the human being who, "when functioning freely, is constructive and trustworthy." Like Tillich and May, he advocated a complete "openness to experience" and converted the functionalism of John Dewey into a full-blown humanism, speaking of the person as an "organism" that, when fully open to experience, would have no need of negative, defensive reactions to either external or internal stimuli. Self-accepting people, he wrote, "are able to trust their total organismic reaction to a new situation because they discover to an ever-increasing degree that if they are open to their experience, doing what 'feels right' proves to be a competent and trustworthy guide to behavior which is truly satisfying."[24]

Just as the humanist emphasis on *acceptance* of one's nature satisfied a deep Protestant preoccupation with the salvation of the individual's soul, Jews had an equally strong preoccupation with *relatedness*. Although May, Tillich, and Rogers were certainly concerned about the interpersonal dimension of maturity, and acknowledged that the individual was not a lone entity detached from others, the Jewish triumvirate of Fromm-Maslow-Buber placed much greater emphasis on the theme of relatedness.

THE JEWISH SOURCES OF HUMANISM: BUBER

"In the beginning is the relation," Martin Buber wrote in a paraphrase of his beloved Bible. Buber (1878–1965) never lived in America and visited only twice, in 1951 and 1957, but his idea of the I-Thou relationship appealed to Americans of all faiths. The attractiveness of Buber's thought came from the unique way in which he combined the background of an eastern European Jew with the concerns of a German philosopher. Though born in Vienna, he grew up with his grandparents in Lemberg (Lvov), where his grandfather Solomon Buber was a philanthropist and well-known scholar of rabbinic literature. Martin studied at the Universities of Berlin, Leipzig, Zurich, and Vienna, at the latter earning a doctorate in philosophy. Like many Germanic thinkers of his generation, he was profoundly troubled by the problem of human alienation in the modern world, the objectification of people as cogs in the machinery of mass society. And, again like his contemporaries, he drew upon the rich inheritance of German Romanticism in search of invisible sources of unification in the universe, bonds that restored some kind of organic wholeness to isolated human beings. His was a search for spiritual answers to the problems posed by man's ever-increasing technological prowess and self-awareness, which seemed to reduce the dignity of humanity while increasing its comforts and knowledge. The "history of the individual and that of the human race," Buber argued, "both signify a progressive increase of the It-world," which was his way of depicting the tendency to turn people, animals, and all of nature into things to be used, into an *it.* The only solution to that tendency was for people to regain the power of *encountering* each other with the directness that Buber associated with primitive humanity. He expressed the point in a haunting passage: "Even violence against a being one really confronts is better than ghostly solicitude for faceless digits! From the former a path leads to God, from the latter only to nothingness." Buber proposed that men and women should strive for "the life of dialogue," for an "I-Thou" or *dialogical* relationship with each other, with nature, and with God.[25]

Just as Tillich was the preeminent Protestant philosopher of the postwar years, Buber was the preeminent Jewish philosopher; as Tillich linked his idea of acceptance to Protestantism, Buber connected the I-Thou concept of relatedness to Judaism. "I am far from wishing to contend that the conception and experience of the dialogical situation are confined to Judaism," he wrote. "But I am certain that no other community of human beings has entered with such strength and fervor into this experience as have the Jews." He made that claim two years after Joshua Liebman made a case for Jewish relatedness in *Peace of Mind.* And, like Liebman, he affirmed the rabbinic idea of men and women in partnership with God. Addressing the problem of evil, Buber insisted that it began and ended with human beings. "The question is answered as far as Judaism is concerned," he explained, "by our being serious about the conception that man has been appointed to this world as an originator of events, as a real partner in the real dialogue with God." On this point, Buber differed from Tillich and Rogers, both of whom laid great stress on putting oneself at ease with (accepting) the flow of experience. In Buber's classically Jewish view, the ideal state of being was one of great initiative: the individual sanctified the mundane and attained a genuine relationship with the world not through acceptance but through activity. To be God's partner meant to exert oneself; refusal of that life of activity was a refusal of the partnership with God, which meant doing evil. That nuance between a Jewish and Protestant humanism paralleled the contrast between the struggling psyche of Joshua Liebman and the harmonized psyche of Norman Vincent Peale. It also reflected a more explicit concern with evil among liberal Jewish thinkers compared to liberal Protestants. But Buber rejected the Protestant neo-orthodox focus on evil, which echoed a belief in Original Sin that found no place in Jewish thought about human nature.[26]

The Jewish basis of Buber's philosophy became a polemical issue when Walter Kaufmann, a student of philosophy who fled Nazi Germany for a distinguished career at Princeton, produced a new translation of *I and Thou* in 1970. By that time Buber had a significant place in American Christian thought. He was commonly described as the personification of his philosophy, a man whose "teaching and writing career illustrates his personal application of the need for relatedness," as *Newsweek* commented in 1957, noting his ability "to combine what seems to be uncombinable things." What bothered Kaufmann was the tendency of Christians to appropriate Buber in a way that did a disservice to the Judaism from which his ideas sprang. Like Tillich and like all humanists of the period, Buber made a sharp distinction between formal religion and religiosity, the religious spirit that organized religion often suppressed or distorted. As a result of his poetic enthusiasm for the richness of the one-to-one relationship and his longtime involvement in interfaith dialogue, it was easy for Christian admirers to perceive his message as essentially Christian. "The book is steeped in Judaism," Kaufmann declared in the prologue to his new edition of *I and Thou.* "This is often overlooked and perhaps as often denied explicitly."[27]

Having converted from Protestantism to Judaism at twelve (a few months *after* Hitler came to power) only to discover later that all his grandparents were Jewish, Kaufmann emphasized the importance of the rabbinic concept of *teshuvah* (return, as in spiritual return, repentance) to Buber's philosophy. He remarked upon the failure of the original translator of *I and Thou* to render correctly the German *Umkehr* (turning back), which became, in the 1937 edition, "reversal" and in the revised 1958 edition "turning." The concept of *teshuvah* in Judaism, Kaufmann emphasized, means that "a man can at any time return and be accepted by God. That is all." He contrasted that simple doctrine with Christianity. "But the theology of Paul in the New Testament is founded on the implicit denial of this doctrine, and so are the Roman Catholic and the Greek Orthodox churches, Lutheranism and Calvinism. Paul's elaborate argument concerning the impossibility of salvation under the Torah ('the Law') and for the necessity of Christ's redemptive death presuppose that God cannot simply forgive anyone who returns." For the Jew, and for Buber, concluded Kaufmann, "man stands in a direct relationship to God and requires no mediator." In *I And Thou* Buber "deals with such immediate relationships, and in this as well as in his central emphasis on return he speaks out of the Jewish tradition."[28]

In the twenty-four years that separated Joshua Liebman's and Walter Kaufmann's polemic for the Jewish idea of relatedness, more than a few Christians had gotten the point. In Huston Smith's classic *The Religions of Man* (1958), Judaism appeared brilliantly as the faith that, more than any other, bequeathed to civilization a fundamental belief in the goodness of all Creation and in the morally redemptive bonds between human beings. In a more focused way, Protestant theologian John Hayward of the University of Chicago argued in *Existentialism and Religious Liberalism* (1962) that Judaism played a critical role for the religious humanist who wanted to believe in "man" but had to confront the existentialist allegation of humankind's pathetic condition. Like Huston Smith, Hayward contrasted the moral idealism of Judaism with the tragic rationalism of the Greeks and concluded that the "Jewish legacy more than anything else prevents the rationalism of liberals from reverting to a more melancholy, more nearly existentialist, point of view." Why? Because "the religious achievement of Judaism was to introduce an attitude of loving relationship between man and his environment and developing history."[29]

The Jewish Sources of Humanism: Fromm

Erich Fromm (1900–1980) was a seminal figure in the growth of American humanism, and he, too, upheld the Jewish ideal of relatedness. Like Buber, Fromm came out of an intellectual environment both deeply Jewish and deeply German. The adored only child of Orthodox Jewish parents with distinguished religious scholars on both sides (he was allegedly a descendant of Rashi, the supreme commentator on the Torah and Talmud), Erich Pinchas was himself an aspiring student of the Talmud, which he studied diligently into his mid-twenties. Fromm (whose surname means "pious") attributed his most basic values to the scholarly atmosphere in which he was reared. "My spiritual home was—one has to say—a medieval atmosphere, in which everything was directed to traditional learning, to the perfection of man, to spiritual values," he reminisced near the end of his life. Even as he entered into the routines of a bourgeois life befitting the son of a Frankfurt wine merchant, he always felt partially estranged from the activities of money-making and other secular preoccupations.[30]

In his late teens and early twenties Erich enjoyed a rare period of harmony between his religious and intellectual interests, studying with Rabbi Nehemiah Nobel of Frankfurt, a visionary Orthodox scholar, and associating with such great young thinkers as Franz Rosenzweig, Gershom Scholem, and his old schoolmate Leo Lowenthal, who became an important American sociologist. Fromm's doctoral dissertation in sociology at the University of Heidelberg, which he completed at age twenty-two, focused on the function of Jewish law as a basis for cohesion in several Diaspora communities. Soon after, he and another Orthodox Jew, Frieda Reichmann, a psychiatrist who exposed Fromm to Freudianism, started a therapeutic institute in Heidelberg for Jewish patients desiring psychoanalytic treatment. When he was twenty-seven, Fromm broke from Jewish practice and switched his allegiance to a Marxist brand of Freudianism; significantly, though, his first published article was an analysis of the biblical concept of the Sabbath. From then on, Erich channeled his respect for the Jewish prophetic tradition, which he considered the source of Western humanism, into pathbreaking studies of social psychology that had the critical edge of both Freud and Marx.[31]

In 1934 Fromm relocated to New York City along with the Institute for Social Research, that fruitful association of German critical thinkers now known as the Frankfurt School. He was but one of Freud's students and adaptors working in the United States in the 1930s, but he became the most important because of the depth of his scholarship and the range of his influence. (Fromm's verbal facility made several of his books best-sellers.) "Of all the neo-Freudians," an authority on American popular thought observed in the 1980s, "Erich Fromm has unquestionably been the most influential." Despite his abandonment of religion, Fromm's ideas penetrated deeply into America's Protestant seminaries (moreso even than Buber's), where a younger generation wanted to break away from their elders' emphasis on rational ideals and embrace a more critical, psychologically sophisticated view of social institutions, including organized religion. In *Escape from Freedom* (1941) and *Man for Himself* (1947) Fromm showed how human nature itself could be perverted by the isolation of the individual in a world of compelling authority figures and institutions (most notably, those of Nazism). He laid out a theory of the "character orientations" produced and encouraged by capitalist societies, in which the individual tailors his or her "personality" to meet the demands of the marketplace. His theory of the "marketing orientation" of modern people (akin to Buber's I-It relationship in which a person is perceived exclusively as an object) had an enduring effect on subsequent critiques of American society.[32]

Like all the American neo-Freudians, Fromm discarded the "darker" elements of Freud—especially his fatalistic view of people at the mercy of impulses—and focused on the social and cultural forces that conditioned human behavior. Those pressures, which derived from every layer of authority in society from the family to the factory, prevented the healthy, creative, authentic self from emerging. Fromm's conviction, that the core of the human being was a bundle of creative expression waiting

to be unwrapped, defined the underlying optimism of American humanists and distanced them from Freud, who saw people as engaged in the
thankless task of managing their nearly unmanageable lust and aggression. Fromm's particular departure from Freud had to do with the issue
of "relatedness." He focused on the "specific kind of relatedness of the
individual towards the world" rather than on the frustration or satisfaction of instinctual needs. The "main thesis of humanistic psychoanalysis,"
Fromm urged, was "that the basic passions of man are not rooted in his
instinctive needs, but . . . in the need to find a new relatedness to man
and nature." Appropriately, he introduced his powerful first book, *Escape
from Freedom*, with Hillel's aphorism about oneself and others, which in
1941 took on an existential urgency:

> If I am not for myself, who will be for me?
> If I am for myself only, what am I?
> If not now—when?[33]

The primary motif of Fromm's thought appeared in *Escape from Freedom*
and evolved in his subsequent books: the individual must, as Joshua Liebman put it, either love or perish. Like Buber, Fromm concentrated on
the problem of alienation that came with humanity's "emerging from
the original oneness with man and nature." The isolated individual of
modern times, he argued, would either "unite himself with the world in
the spontaneity of love and productive work" or "seek a kind of security"
that "destroys his freedom and the integrity of his individual self."[34]

Fromm wrote eloquently about the susceptibility of the lonely, insecure person to appeals of both authority and conformity, yet he also
exuded a tireless, sophisticated idealism about human potential. And as
a leavening for his mixture of pathos and hope, Fromm added the moral
perspective gained from Judaism. Declaring in an almost prophetic tone
that "*equality today means 'sameness,' rather than 'oneness,'* " he called for
the reclamation of what "equality had meant, in a religious context, that
we are all God's children . . . that while it is true that we are all one, it is
also true that each one of us is a unique entity, is a cosmos by itself. Such
conviction of the uniqueness of the individual is expressed for instance
in the talmudic statement: 'Whosoever saves a single life is as if he had
saved the whole world; whosoever destroys a single life is as if he had
destroyed the whole world.' "[35]

In Fromm's thought, the dignity of the individual could be redeemed
only through love, "the active and creative relatedness of man to his
fellow man." Love, he wrote, "permits the full unfolding of one's own
inner activity." When he spoke of creating a "sane society" he meant a
society in which relatedness prevailed; an "insane" way of life was one
defined by narcissism, the inability to perceive the uniqueness of other

people. Fromm's ideal of real individuality contrasted with that of Carl Jung, who also had an American following after the war. In the words of one scholar, Jung viewed "all forms of communion or community as flights from authentic individuality"—they were a necessary evil—whereas "Fromm saw individuation as a *prerequisite* to genuine relatedness, as did Martin Buber."[36]

In the work that most fully elaborates his humanism of relatedness, *The Art of Loving*, Fromm betrays how deeply the Judaism of his youth saturated the values of the atheist adult. Published in 1956, *The Art of Loving* went through twenty-nine printings and sold a million and a half copies in English by the end of the 1960s. (By 2000, the book had sold 25 million copies in fifty languages.) Such success was impressive for a Marxist critique of American emotional life that appeared at the height of the Cold War. "In a culture in which the marketing orientation prevails, and in which material success is the outstanding value," Fromm declared, "there is little reason to be surprised that human love relations follow the same pattern of exchange which governs the commodity and the labor market." The art to which he referred was seldom seen, and developed only by people who possessed what Fromm called a "productive orientation," a concept he first elaborated in *Man for Himself* (1947). In contrast to those personality types that fulfilled the most venal tendencies of a capitalist economy, the "productive" type sought "relatedness in all realms of human experience." The productive type, that is, the mature person, also had a healthy self-regard or self-love. Echoing Joshua Liebman's motif in *Peace of Mind*, Fromm objected to Christian indictments of self-love and argued that "the idea expressed in the Biblical 'Love thy neighbor as thyself!' implies that respect for one's own integrity and uniqueness, love for and understanding of one's own self, cannot be separated from respect and love and understanding for another individual."[37]

As he moved through his argument about the nature of mature love and its evolution in Western history, Fromm drew on his Jewish education and placed himself in a line of radical Jewish thinkers whom he deemed the true inheritors of the Jewish spirit. He married Maimonides to Freud in order to criticize the infantile conception of God to which, in his view, most people adhered. In the *Guide for the Perplexed*, Maimonides discoursed on the problems of anthropomorphizing God and insisted that God could not be identified by adjectives (e.g., wise, just) that applied to people. Freud, for his part, thought that God was a projection of neurotic needs for a father figure. Fromm also objected to such diminished conceptions of God, but he parted from Freud by favoring the attitude of "the truly religious person" who "follows the essence of the monotheistic idea . . . knowing that he knows nothing about God." Hav-

ing established the unknowability of God, Fromm went on to argue: "The
love of God is neither the knowledge of God in thought, nor the thought
of one's love of God, but the act of experiencing the oneness with
God. . . . This leads to the emphasis on the right way of living." He then
claimed that Eastern religions (Taoism, Buddhism, Hinduism) and also
Judaism exemplified that approach, whereas Christianity (except for
Meister Eckhart, his favorite mystic) did not, because it elevated thought
over action and belief over deed. "The emphasis of the Jewish religion
was . . . on the right way of living, the Halacha," Fromm explained. "In
modern history, the same principle is expressed in the thought of Spinoza, Marx and Freud." In Western culture, then, the truest source of a
mature rather than infantile love of God, and a mature practice of love
as human relatedness, was Judaism and those visionary Jews to whom
Fromm looked for inspiration.[38]

    That Fromm's humanism had deep Jewish roots became startlingly
clear in *You Shall Be as Gods* (1966), which was subtitled *A Radical Interpretation of the Old Testament and Its Tradition*. Although the book elaborated
an argument already present in *The Art of Loving*, here Fromm finally
brought the old apparatus of rabbinic exegesis out of the closet into
which he had put it at age twenty-seven, dusted it off, and produced a
thoroughly original piece of writing: a brief for humanism composed for
the general reader and based on a sophisticated Jewish analysis of the
Bible with many detailed references to talmudic and rabbinic commentaries. He argued that the Hebrew Bible and rabbinic Judaism contained
the seeds of a grand and radical humanist tradition in Western thought.
The Bible showed a "remarkable evolution from primitive authoritarianism and clannishness to the idea of the radical freedom of man and the
brotherhood of all men." Moreover, the entire Jewish tradition from the
Pharisees through the Hasids promoted a belief in the human being as
an unfolding personality commanded to "be holy" as God is holy. As
Joshua Liebman had stressed the Jewish concept of people being in partnership with God, Fromm affirmed the same idea but with a rich array
of midrashic prooftexts illustrating the remarkable boldness that the
God of the rabbis seemed to accept from mere humans. ("Man is not
God, but if he acquires God's qualities, he is not beneath God, but walks
with him.") Most important, Fromm contended, the Hebrew Bible established unequivocally that people, in serving the one God, should never
reduce themselves to serving men. By liberating human beings from "in-
cestuous" ties to land and blood, obedience to God placed them on a
path of "imitating" the divine attributes of mercy and justice. "Man, the
prisoner of nature, becomes free by becoming fully human. In the biblical and later Jewish view, freedom and independence are the goals of

human development, and the aim of human action is the constant process of liberating oneself from the shackles that bind man to the past, to nature, to the clan, to idols."[39]

You Shall Be as Gods was intended both as an apologetic text for the tradition that Fromm loved and as a kind of guide for the perplexed humanist, both the religious humanist and the "non-theistic humanist" (as he called himself) who needed "the experiential reality" behind the idea of God if not God per se. He opened with the old Jewish complaint about Christian misrepresentations of the Torah as a nationalistic book focused on an angry and vengeful God. "Among most Christians the Old Testament is little read in comparison with the New Testament," he observed. "Furthermore, much of what is read is often distorted by prejudice." Fromm then gave his readers a short grand tour through the postbiblical Jewish tradition, including an autobiographical account of his own rich education in the sources of Judaism. Paying homage to the three great rabbis who instructed him, he explained, "Not being a practicing or a 'believing' Jew, I am, of course, in a very different position from theirs. . . . Yet my views have grown out of their teaching, and it is my conviction that at no point has the continuity between their teaching and my own views been interrupted."[40]

In part, Fromm wanted to reconnect secular Jewish idealists with the "revolutionary" principles of their ancestors. He believed that "the universalism and humanism of the prophets blossomed in the figures of thousands of Jewish philosophers, socialists, and internationalists, many of whom had no personal connection with Judaism." And, having reached his sixties, he was prepared to reflect on the possibility that the *halakhah*, and the observance of the Sabbath in particular, might contain valuable lessons and methods for the struggle to affirm life in a society that turned people "into appendices of machines." The sanctification of all activity on the Sabbath was an antidote for the poisons of modern society; it was an incarnation of the humanist ethic. "I do believe that the principle of the Sabbath rest might be adopted by a much larger number of people—Christians, Jews, and people outside of any religion. The Sabbath day, for them, would be a day of contemplation, reading, meaningful conversation, a day of rest and joy, completely free from all practical and mundane concerns."[41]

For both Buber and Fromm (not to mention Liebman), relatedness was an overriding ideal because it expressed the essence of Jewish life, that dense system of mutual obligations to which Jews themselves, and nearly everyone else, attributed their remarkable survival in the West. (*Life Is With People* was an apt title for the study of the *shtetl* that anthropologists Mark Zborowski and Elizabeth Herzog published in the wake of its annihilation.) Buber and Fromm grew up immersed in a European Jewish world that gave them an immediate and direct understanding of Jewish spiritual life. Out of that experience, they forged their distinctive brands of humanism.

THE JEWISH SOURCES OF HUMANISM: MASLOW

The third partner of the Jewish humanist triad, Abraham Maslow (1908– 70), grew up in an entirely different and essentially secular environment. Nevertheless, his hugely influential concept of self-actualization, which became an American mantra after the 1960s, also reflected Maslow's experience as a Jew and also looked toward an ideal of relatedness.

"He wrote with none of the dark grandeur of a Freud or the learned grace of an Erik Erikson," *Esquire* magazine observed in 1983, more than a decade after a fatal heart attack claimed Maslow at age sixty-two. "And yet, Abraham Maslow had done more to change our view of human nature and human possibilities than has any other American psychologist of the past fifty years." The *Los Angeles Times* predicted that Maslow "will rank as one of the key figures of 20th-century psychology—perhaps second in importance only to Freud." Joyce Carol Oates agreed. The novelist eulogized "Maslow's amazingly fertile mind; his combining of teacher, seer, reporter, physician, visionary, social planner, critic . . . his unstoppable optimism. Maslow's lifelong emphasis on the importance of man's subjective life lead us again to the realization (so clear in imaginative literature, so muddled elsewhere) that it is here, in the soul, inside the fantastically complex phenomenon of man, that the salvation of the entire world will take place."[42]

By his early twenties, Maslow had already decided not to hide or compromise his identity but, like Freud, to maintain a proud sense of himself as a man whose Jewishness encouraged intellectual independence and even rebelliousness. "Testicles seem to be a missing blessing on this campus," Maslow wrote in his diary in the early 1930s, when he was a graduate student in psychology at the University of Wisconsin.

> I can't imagine any one in this goddamned department standing up to a dean and spitting in his eye. They are all so cautionary. No one of them minds me because I am a Jew. At the same time if any of them had the hiring of me they would none of them take me on so sensitive are they to the folkways round here, to just the general feeling in the air about Jews. . . . This Jewish problem! I had about made up my mind to dodge it. To change my name. . . . But then I read Ludwig Lewisohn's 'Island Within,' & he

changed my mind for me. I wouldn't dream of it now. If I'm a Jew, I am a
Jew & I'll stuff it down your throats if you don't like it.

Maslow remained conscious of the joys and advantages of being among
other inquisitive Jews in an environment where one felt mentally free:
"Sometimes I think how fine it would be for Jews to segregate voluntarily,
particularly in the matter of education. Jewish Universities & colleges as
places where Jewish native talent could develop without too harsh a contact with raw anti-Semitism." As it happened, Maslow spent his teaching
career at two schools, Brooklyn College and Brandeis University, in
which Jewish students predominated. That circumstance would affect his
creation of a unique theory of personal creativity and attainment.[43]

Unlike Erich Fromm, Maslow grew up in a family with no distinguished
ancestors and a fairly weak religious life, but as the first child of immigrant Jewish parents in Brooklyn, he was encouraged to succeed educa-
tionally. At the City College of New York, Maslow was awakened by
Charles Sumner's *Folkways* (1906), which excited his desire to one day
write a comprehensive theory of society, and then by the expansiveness
of John Watson's behaviorism, which left him determined to make that
intellectual contribution through the field of psychology. For him,
though, a science that denied spiritual realities was no better than a religion that cultivated irrational beliefs. Neither Freudianism nor Watson's
behaviorism, he thought, was capable of dealing with the spiritual, or
"higher" realities of human life. A proper science of human nature would
merge the necessary rationalism of science with the necessary idealism
of religion. Whereas a humanist like Viktor Frankl explicitly rejected the
idea of making psychology into a substitute for religion, Maslow vowed
to do just that. Having utterly rejected Judaism and all religion, which he
associated with the superstitiousness of his mother, whom he despised,
Maslow hoped to build a humanist psychology that would develop into
"the life-philosophy, the religion-surrogate, the value-system, the life-pro-
gram" that idealistic people found in neither religion nor science. Maslow's *Toward a Psychology of Being* (1962) was the manifesto of that total
psychology.[44]

The key concept of Maslow's humanism was self-actualization, which
referred to the drive that Maslow believed inhered in human life, a drive
toward the fulfillment of one's native abilities and talents, including,
most of all, the ability to love and to experience that state of harmony
with the world that is usually associated with mystics. That quasi-mystical
state, in which one's perceptions are heightened, the ordinary acquires
the aura of the sublime, and everything coheres in a wondrous unity,
Maslow called a peak-experience. He liked to speak of self-actualizers,

"S.A.'s," who often enjoyed peak-experiences. Such people possessed Fromm's "productive orientation" and Buber's "I-Thou" disposition; they saw the world and other people as wholes and not as parts. They were able to do so because they had met their "deficiency needs," the basic need of humans for physical and emotional security, and were therefore able to move on to a higher level of existence in which they satisfied their "growth needs." Those who had not satisfied their deficiency needs, however, used other people as instruments for achieving a feeling of security. Maslow's theory of self-actualization built upon the work of a number of eminent psychological thinkers, especially Kurt Goldstein and Gordon Allport, who rejected a standard view of the human being as an organism driven by a need for equilibrium, rest, and quiescence. From years of contemplating the restless men and women who were high achievers, Maslow knew that the old theory could not explain the world of human potential. For people "who are predominantly growth motivated," he noticed, "gratification breeds increased rather than decreased motivation, heightened rather than lessened excitement."[45]

Maslow's contact with ambitious and intellectually restless Jewish students at Brooklyn College laid the foundation for his theory of self-actualization. In the 1930s the average Brooklyn College student was typically a child of Jewish immigrants, scored high on college entrance tests, and often skipped grades before arriving at college. Like Maslow himself, many of those students were intellectually confident and ambitious. Soon after he began teaching there in 1937, Maslow found himself serving informally as a psychotherapist to students who sought him out. A turning point came in 1938, when Maslow was approached by a brilliant female student of psychology who complained of insomnia, lack of appetite, disturbed menstruation, and chronic boredom. Her symptoms reminded Maslow of those described by Abraham Myerson in *When Life Loses Its Zest,* a book he admired. The young woman had graduated from Brooklyn College the previous year and was supporting her entire family with a dull but well-paying job as a supervisor at a chewing gum factory. In her talks with Maslow, she confessed that she was frustrated by the emptiness of her life and by a feeling that she would be forever trapped in the same kind of job. Maslow told her that the problem might be the lack of a meaningful outlet for her intelligence. After following his suggestion that she continue her studies at the graduate level at night, she began to regain a sense of vitality and her symptoms disappeared. By his own account, Maslow's theory of self-actualization came out of this and other such cases. When he moved to Brandeis in 1950, Maslow once again drew much of his data from questionnaires and assignments he gave to his mostly Jewish students.[46]

Maslow saw himself as an intellectually sensitive Jew in opposition to the gentile world, a world that seemed brutal during his childhood and conformist during his early years as a scholar.

> I was on the outside looking in, especially since I never lived in fully Jewish neighborhoods. In one I remember there was a little enclave of Jewish families, surrounded by Italians and Irish, so that going out of that area, going to the library for instance, meant going through the Irish neighborhood. And there was guerrilla warfare, you had to sneak and hide and run and so on. Going in the other direction was Italian territory. I got ganged often enough, and grew up thinking of Irish and Italians, Christians in general, Churches, religions, as a child, as cruel and nasty.[47]

Maslow's idea of himself as a boy whose intellectual aspirations brought him into conflict with gentile brutishness remained with him but took on a more subtle form when he became an adult. As we have seen, Maslow was highly critical of his gentile peers in the graduate program in psychology at Wisconsin, where he felt isolated as a Jew. He saw himself as a humanist misfit among academic drones. He sought a more holistic and philosophical approach to psychology, while they ridiculed his wider interests and concentrated on "getting ahead," which was "synonymous with doing one piffling experiment after another and publishing as a result one piffling paper after another." Maslow's defensively Jewish identity, his sense of being on the outside, a nonconforming cosmopolitan among academic provincials, extended so far as to include his feelings of masculine pride. "It is fashionable now to despise Gestalt psychology. Accordingly, they all despise it. If it were the folkway to admire it, they would admire it. . . . They seem to be a bunch of intellectual castrates, timid and womanish. But God damn it, I'll keep my own intellectual virility if it kills me."[48]

After he returned to New York to begin teaching at Brooklyn College in 1937, Maslow followed the teachings of the émigré psychoanalysts who lived and taught in the city and developed a circle of (eminent) Jewish friends whom he met at the New York Psychoanalytic Institute: Abraham Kardiner, David Levy, Bela Mittelmann, and David Rapaport. Since most academic psychologists kept their distance from the psychoanalysts, Maslow remembered as a point of pride that he was virtually the only American psychologist who faithfully attended the weekly lectures of Alfred Adler at the Gramercy Park Hotel and of Erich Fromm at the Institute for Social Research at Columbia University. As he began to contemplate the "ideal personality" that became the "self-actualizing" personality of his theory, his reference points were the inquisitiveness and originality in this milieu of cosmopolitan Jewish scholars and those selected non-Jews whom he considered exceptional.[49]

Maslow conceived of self-actualization not as a purely individual matter but as a means of creating healthy relationships between people. Like many Jewish socialists concerned with the creation of just social relations, he interpreted his own idealism as a secular expression of Judaism's prophetic call for justice. A more concretely Jewish perspective, however, is visible in Maslow's emphasis on engagement in the world rather than withdrawal from it. He criticized Zen monks and Buddhists as well as followers of a Christian monastic ideal because, as he wrote in his notebooks, "to integrate and become serene at cost of giving up world, escaping and avoiding it, is a sort of phoniness. One condition of comprehensive inner peace is the peace of other people. . . . Much harder job but very necessary."[50]

Wrestling with the problem of self-fulfillment versus selfishness, Maslow turned to two other Jewish socialists, Erich Fromm and Alfred Adler. He admired Fromm's interpretation of "Selfishness, Self-Love, and Self-Interest" in *Man for Himself,* where Fromm distinguished between healthy self-interest and selfishness and favorably compared Spinoza's ideal of enlightened self-interest to the Christian ideal of self-subordination espoused by Calvin and Luther. Maslow turned even more often to Adler, who is cited in many of his notes and lectures. As much as he appreciated Freud's genius, Maslow preferred Adler's psychology and subscribed to his argument that self-affirmation was valuable only when it enhanced the good of the community.[51]

In the early 1950s Maslow began to envision a utopia, which he dubbed Eupsychia, a place of the psychologically "good"—men and women who were both highly individualistic and highly engaged with others. "Intrinsic human nature," Maslow wrote in his notes on Eupsychia, "says that fullest individualism can be built only on basis of sociability, and that fullest sociality can be built only on basis of fullest individuals." Such an ideal rested on Maslow's devout belief in the reality of universal values that transcended any and all cultures. Without transcendent values, Maslow worried, "we would simply have no criterion for criticizing, let us say, the well-adjusted Nazi in Nazi Germany." The personality ideal that Maslow attacked ferociously—the ideal of the "adjusted" personality—reminded him not only of those colleagues in graduate school who (in his opinion) did whatever was necessary to "get ahead" but also of the worst-case scenario, the ordinary Nazi, which he often cited as a negative model. "Sickness might consist of not having symptoms when you should," he wrote in *Toward a Psychology of Being*: "Which of the Nazis at Auschwitz or Dachau were healthy? Those with stricken conscience or those with a nice, clear, happy conscience?" The kind of person whom Maslow considered "profoundly human" was someone like Abraham Lincoln or William James, who was "saddened by stupidity, viciousness, phoniness, etc."[52]

Since the interpersonal dimension of human life stood at the heart of Maslow's humanism, the problem of evil was never far from his mind. In an interview for *Psychology Today* two years before his unexpected death, Maslow said, "The next thing I want to do with my life is to study evil and understand it." "Evil people are rare," he observed, "but you find evil behavior in the majority of people." Stopping short of Rogers's belief in the essential goodness of human nature, Maslow thought people were not inherently bad but he remained unsure of whether human nature was basically good or neutral. "Both the all-good theory of self and the all-bad theory of self are inadequate," he reflected in the notes for a book on the subject, because "even perfectly reasonable and natural human wishes, can generate real trouble, hatred, and fear and hopelessness that can stultify the individual profoundly and help to make a poor human being." By the end of the 1960s, he was deeply disturbed by what he considered the misguided idealism of the youth rebellion (which he compared to the spurious idealism of the Hitler youth who overthrew Weimar culture). Dismayed by the cult of instant nirvana and spontaneity-for-spontaneity's-sake that had become a vogue, partly as a result of the misuse of his own theories, Maslow prefaced the second edition of *Toward a Psychology of Being* with the rueful observation that there were actually very few self-actualized people, compared to how many there might be. He attributed that shortage to "fear of human goodness and greatness." Therefore, he explained, a good world would have to wait for a humanistic account of evil, "one written out of compassion and love for human nature rather than out of disgust with it or out of hopelessness."[53]

Sounding like Boris Sidis in *Philistine and Genius*, Maslow declared the good citizen, the mature person, to be a warrior against evil. "A healthy person, a fully rational person, a fully human person," he wrote, "is a firm fighter against evil." Despite his deeply American optimism, Maslow shared with Buber and Fromm a wariness about human nature unbound. The great *I* of humanism must, in the end, remain faithful to the *You*. The ties of human obligation had to grow along with the self-obligated individual, or the individual would destroy humanity.

An eccentric yet very possibly correct observation about Maslow's humanism came from a Catholic psychologist, William Coulson, a student and colleague of Carl Rogers who became disgusted with the obstreperous individualism of the new humanism and turned back to traditional Catholicism:

> We had trained people who didn't have Rogers' innate discipline from his own fundamentalist Protestant background, people who thought that being

themselves meant unleashing libido. Maslow did warn us about this. Maslow believed in evil, and we didn't. He said our problem was our total confusion about evil. . . . Their religion was sort of Tillichian: the courage to *be*, the importance of taking risks, the importance of inventiveness. I think the fact that Maslow was a Jew enabled him to see some of the harm, because he had a sense of tribe. He had a people whom he knew were being hurt by this, and as an elder of the tribe he had an obligation not to allow it to continue.[54]

It has long been known that American Jews participated vigorously in postwar critiques of conformity and in the humanist enterprise generally. The names in this chapter, from Ginsberg to Maslow, are not obscure. But until now we have understood neither the degree to which Jewish themes and values entered into public conversation about human nature nor the coherence of that Jewish engagement. That oversight is part of a larger failure to comprehend the importance of both the Protestant and Jewish backgrounds of the founders of humanism. Mixed into the universalist message of human potential were questions and concerns that engaged those thinkers not only as individuals but as Protestants and Jews. Even the most influential jeremiads against the self-centeredness of American humanism—Philip Rieff's *The Triumph of the Therapeutic* (1966), Daniel Bell's *The Cultural Contradictions of Capitalism* (1976), and Christopher Lasch's *The Culture of Narcissism* (1978)—had strong Jewish and Protestant overtones.[55]

An important corollary of the humanist ideal was the desire of women for fuller realization of their potential not only as wives and mothers but also as persons. Jewish women were in the avant-garde of that movement. Next, we shall try to determine why.

Erik Homburger Erikson. Erikson's famous concept of identity reflected some of the complexities of his life as a Jew and an immigrant. (Courtesy of the Archives of the History of American Psychology–The University of Akron.)

Erich Pinchas Fromm, ca. 1940. An Orthodox Jew and adept student of the Talmud into his twenties, Fromm became a key figure in the growth of American humanism, into which he conveyed the ethical values of his religious background. (Courtesy of the Erich Fromm Archiv, Tübingen, with special thanks to Dr. Rainer Funk, literary executor of Erich Fromm.)

Abraham Maslow. Along with Carl Rogers, Maslow was known as the founding father of humanist psychology, and his concept of self-actualization deeply affected American culture. The ideas of Rogers and Maslow reflected important parts of their Protestant and Jewish backgrounds. (Courtesy of the Archives of the History of American Psychology—The University of Akron.)

Joyce Brothers, 1957, two years after winning the top prize on *The $64,000 Question* on national television, the first woman to do so. Part of a postwar wave of Jewish women who became important public moralists in America, Brothers was the country's most widely known psychologist between the 1950s and 1990s and a guide for millions of women trying to achieve a "liberated" marriage without abandoning traditional roles as wives and mothers. (Courtesy of the Library of Congress.)

Chapter 13

Joyce Brothers:
The Jewish Woman as Psychologist
of Suburban America

IF ONE PERSON REPRESENTED psychology to the average American after
the 1950s, she was Joyce Brothers. Brothers was the first public psychologist whose career began not on radio or in the newspapers—although
she would enjoy many years of syndication in both those media—but on
television. In 1958 she debuted on NBC as the star of "The Joyce Brothers Show." It was the heyday of the great suburban migration, and women
wrote in to Dr. Brothers wanting advice about everything from buying a
home to disciplining children.

The show's format was simple (and in black and white): a male side-
kick read letters from viewers to Dr. Brothers, who sat at a desk and
answered them. Brothers carefully combined feminine delicacy (a soft
voice, slow, graceful body movements) with an attitude of serious scientific authority, which she conveyed through her tone and her unflinching
gaze at the camera. In one episode, for example, a young newlywed in
the Bronx wrote in asking about the psychology of buying a new home.
The woman referred to a statistic that Dr. Brothers had given in a previous show, that three-fourths of very young brides lived with their families
for a year or so after marriage, and she added that she and her husband
were in that situation. The young woman wanted to know what "psychological factors" of home buying might lead her and her husband to make
a wrong decision. Dr. Brothers explained that realtors typically advertise
one feature of a house to the man and another to the woman. Sales
pressure, she pointed out, worked well on both husbands and wives. The
woman sees a house as a projection of her personality, so the realtor is
likely to say, "This house seems just right for you." Brothers warned her
female viewers to beware of such a sales technique, not to get carried
away with the "personality" aspect of home buying, and to be mindful of
practical needs for space. She buttressed her opinions with an array of
statistics and references to psychological studies about homebuyers.[1]

Here was a novel scenario. A lone female authority figure on the powerful new medium of television, assisted by a subordinate male her
own age, used the data of psychology to arm women against the psychological techniques of salesmen—while at the same time her authority

helped to generate sales for her sponsors, Supp-hose stockings and
Bamberger's, a New Jersey department store chain. Less surprising was
the fact that Joyce Brothers was Jewish. If a woman was going to end up
as a psychological adviser to Americans, the odds were very good that
she would be Jewish.

In the 1950s six Jewish women were on their way to achieving positions
of authority over public attitudes about how to live in the suburban age:
Ayn Rand, whose philosophical novels *The Fountainhead* and *Atlas
Shrugged* attained a cultic status among younger Americans; Esther Pauline and Pauline Esther Friedman who, as Ann Landers and Abigail Van
Buren, commanded the advice column for decades; Betty Friedan, whose
1963 feminist classic, *The Feminine Mystique,* developed out of a survey
she conducted among her fellow Smith College alumnae in 1957; Gertrude Berg, who moved her show *The Goldbergs* from radio to television
and, in 1955, from the Bronx to the suburbs; and Joyce Brothers, who
started her television career by winning the top prize on *The $64,000
Question* on CBS in 1955, the first woman to do so.

Brothers's career is of special interest for several reasons. Like Ann
Landers and Abigail Van Buren, she held a vast audience for many years,
yet, unlike them, she departed from the traditionally female role of the
folksy advice columnist and succeeded in the male-dominated discipline
of psychology. Though not as innovative as Betty Friedan and Ayn Rand,
Brothers spoke much more effectively to the average person, and her
writings more faithfully represented the lifespan of a generation of
American women who married, raised families, and matured between
the 1940s and the 1980s. Strangely, historians have completely disregarded her.

Joyce Brothers did more than anyone else to advance a practical feminism for the average American, but she also went awry by idolizing the
"modern marriage," which became her Golden Calf. With the best of
intentions for the personal fulfillment of American women, Brothers revealed the moral drift of unbounded psychology. The pragmatism that
made her such a success at translating psychological ideas for the multitude also left her unable to keep in touch with transcendent Jewish values. Her case is especially compelling because, unlike a charlatan such
as Bruno Bettelheim, who fabricated credentials and browbeat down-
hearted women with puffed-up theories, Joyce Brothers kept her nose
close to the ground of daily life and expected no more of her readers
than she did of herself. Before examining her career, we will glance at
the larger story of Jewish women in America striving for expression and
authority as public moralists.[2]

JEWISH WOMEN AS PUBLIC MORALISTS

The only woman whom history records as a presence at Sigmund Freud's sole visit to America in 1909 was Emma Goldman (1869–1940). "Among the array of professors, looking stiff and important in their university caps and gowns," Goldman recalled of that day at Clark University, "Sigmund Freud, in ordinary attire, unassuming, almost shrinking, stood out like a giant among pygmies. He had aged somewhat since I had heard him in Vienna in 1896. He had been reviled then as a Jew and irresponsible innovator; now he was a world figure; but neither obloquy nor fame had influenced the great man." The free-spirited Goldman lived in America from 1886 to 1919, the year she was deported to the Soviet Union along with many other radicals. The sexual freedom of women had long been a primary concern of hers. She maintained numerous lovers without a thought of wedlock—marriage, she argued, reduced a woman to chattel—and was frequently arrested for disseminating birth control information. In Freud, Goldman saw a genius who had finally shown that society, by repressing female sexuality, created mental disturbances in women, rendering them inferior to men. She considered psychoanalysis and feminism partners in the liberation of female potential. As an anarchist, she was a staunch atheist but, like her comrades on the Lower East Side who instituted an annual Yom Kippur ball, Goldman kept her Jewish affinities. Her primary lovers, for example, were Jewish men, and she criticized radical Jews who hid their identity "in chameleon-like acceptance of every Gentile habit." Her depiction of Freud as a reviled Jew registered pride in the idea of the Jewish outsider as an intellectual rebel.[3]

Nine decades later, a woman who was Goldman's diametrical opposite illustrated the continuing visibility of Jewish women in public debate about psychological questions. In the late 1990s family therapist Laura Schlessinger became by far the most listened-to radio "psychologist" in the United States. At her peak, "Dr. Laura" (her Ph.D. from Columbia University was in physiology) claimed 20 million listeners, second only to conservative talk-show host Rush Limbaugh, and she wrote several best-selling books. Born in Brooklyn in 1946 to a Catholic mother and a Jewish father, Schlessinger "identified Jewishly" but had little religious knowledge and, as a young woman in the 1960s, lived a somewhat free-spirited life. In her forties, she formally converted to Judaism and followed an Orthodox path. That change paved the way to her career as a public moralist—she became "much more interested in advocating moral and ethical behavior in spite of whatever psychological turmoil is present." Schlessinger hammered on the theme of personal moral accountability and scorned psychologized justifications for destructive behavior. Yet her sense of "mission" and accusatory style were not characteristic of Modern Orthodox Jews, with whom she identified until her sudden break with Judaism in August 2003. She spoke of homosexuality, in particular, with a strident tone that most Modern Orthodox rabbis would have found objectionable. Her pronouncements against abortion also obscured the complexity of traditional Jewish thought on the issue. Because she tied her views so clearly to Judaism, Schlessinger became an anomalous figure: the only Orthodox Jew ever to gain such an immense audience, yet one whose success in the "shock jock" style of 1990s radio distanced her from rabbinic standards of propriety.[4]

Of much greater influence than Schlessinger, whose impact was spectacular but brief, dozens of Jewish women entered the more serious domain of professional psychology and psychiatry. A partial list of those who were already working in America before 1945 would include the well-known émigré psychologists Else Frenkel-Brunswik (1908–58) and Charlotte (Malachowski) Bühler (1893–1974); émigré psychoanalysts Frieda Fromm-Reichmann (1889–1957), Margaret (Schoenberger) Mahler (1897–1985), Helene Deutsch (1884–1982), Therese Benedek (1892–1977), Bertha Bornstein (1900–1971), and Marianne Kris (1900–1980); Gestalt psychologists Eugenia Hanfmann (1905–83), Tamara Dembo (1902–93), and Mary Henle (1913–); Stella Chess (1914–), a pediatric psychiatrist at Bellevue Hospital in New York City; Phyllis Greenacre (1894–1989), psychiatric consultant at the Westchester County (N.Y.) Department of Child Welfare and professor of psychiatry at the Cornell University Medical College; Marguerite Hertz (1899–1992), professor of psychology at Western Reserve University and a founder of the Rorschach Institute; Adele Jaffa (1870–1953), one of California's first child psychologists; Maida Solomon (1891–1988), one of the nation's first psychiatric social workers; and Bernice Neugarten (1916–2003), a psychologist who helped shape the field of adult development and aging.[5]

A number of those women, along with others who appeared on the American scene after the war, contributed to public conversation about human nature, especially in regard to the psychology of women and children. And so did two Jews living in England, Anna Freud and Melanie Klein. Let us also recall that Jewish women authored two of the most popular books on Freudian psychology in the postwar years, *Fight Against Fears* (1951) by Lucy Freeman, and the best-selling *I Never Promised You a Rose Garden* (1964) by Joanne Greenberg (under the pseudonym Hannah Green). The latter fictionalized the author's own recovery from schizophrenia under the care of Frieda Fromm-Reichmann at Chestnut

Lodge, an exclusive psychiatric hospital near Washington, D.C. A gifted Jewish child who was an outcast among her upper-class Protestant schoolmates, the protagonist of that story inhabited an illusory world "in which the Jews, or Deborah, always lost." The psychoanalyst behind *Spellbound* (1945), the first Hollywood blockbuster to place a woman (portrayed by Ingrid Bergman) in the role of Freudian detective, was May Ginsburg Romm, a Russian Jew who came to America at age twelve, made her way through medical school, and established herself in Los Angeles with the help of A. A. Brill. Eventually she became renowned as analyst to a host of celebrities, including producer David O. Selznick, who, to the dismay of director Alfred Hitchcock, gave Romm complete supervisory control over the script of *Spellbound*.[6]

Joanne Greenberg's novel and May Romm's scripting were part of a tradition of intellectual and literary restlessness among Jewish women in America, a tradition that sometimes expressed itself in the idiom of psychology. Women began knocking at the doors of institutional Judaism in the 1800s, calling for the right to participate as equals and even to become rabbis. In 1889 Mary Cohen, superintendent of Philadelphia's Hebrew Sunday School, the first institution in which women could publicly teach Judaism, raised the question of women's ordination in a story in the *Jewish Exponent*. Cohen represented a rising middle class of women who wanted to relocate themselves from the periphery to the center of public life. Traditionally, a Jewish woman might be educated, but she could not channel her knowledge into significant discussions of Jewish life and law—talmudic debate was the absolute prerogative of men. So intellectually ambitious women gravitated toward the world of secular knowledge, where they stood a greater chance of being heard.[7]

The eastern European Jews who poured into America at the turn of the twentieth century formed a massive foundation of female intellect on which several generations of readers and writers would stand. Although it is tempting to exaggerate the rapidity of Jewish advances from the immigrant ghetto to the educated middle class, by the 1920s the legendary rise of the American Jew, male and female, had some truth to it. Boys were still favored over girls when it came to higher education, but the girls persevered, often working to help support their families while they attended local colleges. Even during the Depression, sending daughters to college remained an important goal of many Jewish families. In 1934, when Jews constituted roughly one-quarter of New York City's population, more than 50 percent of the city's female college students were Jewish. And historians have found evidence that, among the city's high school students in the 1930s and 1940s, Jewish women showed a disproportionate interest in literary activities. By that time a number of writers, some of immigrant background and others American-born, had demonstrated the possibilities of literary careers for talented women: Emma Lazarus, Mary Antin, Anzia Yezierska, Fannie Hurst, Edna Ferber, Gertrude Stein, and Dorothy Parker (whose father was Jewish). To women, America meant, among other things, a dynamic new outlet for consumers and producers of literature.[8]

The striving of Jewish women for education and higher literacy was not simply a result of Jews moving as a group into the middle class; other groups did that without conspicuous public accomplishments by women. Rather, there was a strong cultural basis for female achievement. Since the early 1900s Jewish women had been making themselves known as political and labor leaders (e.g., Emma Goldman, Zionists Henrietta Szold and Golda Meir, trade unionist Rose Pesotta), entertainers (Fanny Brice, Sophie Tucker, Theda Bara, Gertrude Berg), and practitioners in the law, teaching, and social work. They shared a Jewish background "that was not burdened with crippling notions of femininity," as one scholar has put it. That helps to account for the disproportionate presence of Jewish women as leaders in the feminist movement of the 1960s.[9]

Ayn Rand (born Alissa Rosenbaum, 1905–82) was one of those bright, educated, and determined women who made herself into a public philosopher with a devoted coterie of followers (including Alan Greenspan, chairman of the Federal Reserve Board in the 1990s and early 2000s) and a readership of millions. Rand was born in St. Petersburg to a middle-class couple, Zinovy Rosenbaum, the owner of a pharmacy, and his wife, Anna, a teacher of languages. Sent to an excellent college preparatory school, she completed an undergraduate degree at the University of Leningrad in the years following the Bolshevik revolution. Rand saw her family ruined by the nationalization of her father's business, and barely escaped the purges of the universities in the 1920s, a procedure that elevated the children of manual workers and expelled those, like her, who came from "bourgeois" households. Those experiences molded the philosophy of life she developed after her escape to the United States in 1926. With remarkable swiftness, Alissa Rosenbaum, who took the name Ayn Rand after emigrating, learned English and began writing scripts in Hollywood. Her ultimate aim, though, was to produce philosophical fiction. When she did, her philosophy was a direct rejection of the Russian ideal of *sobornost*, which had roots in orthodox Christianity and translates roughly as "commonality." *Sobornost* called for the absorption of the individual into the larger body of society; in Bolshevism it found a secular form. For Rand, nothing was more dreadful than the submergence of individual identity in a social mass. In a dystopian novel, she created a hero, Equality 7–2521, who triumphantly rediscovers the word "I."[10]

Through a series of novels, *We the Living* (1936), *The Fountainhead* (1943), *Anthem* (1946), and *Atlas Shrugged* (1957), known for their iconic, two-dimensional characters, Rand outlined a "new, nonreligious morality" of rational self-interest that elevated the human spirit above the animalistic without bending it toward a deity. She believed that both the state and religion warred against the dignity of the individual. Her ideal system, an economy of unfettered capitalism, nurtured creative individuals who refused to compromise the aesthetic purity of their ideas to satisfy the crass interests of philistines. Rand antagonized the Right with her atheism, the Left with her capitalism, and the critics with her prose, but many readers thrilled to her bold characterizations of the defiant individualist. Through her one-time disciple and lover, Nathaniel Branden (a Canadian Jew, born Nathan Blumenthal), Rand's conception of the self-sufficient individual became the basis of a "psychology of self-esteem," which Branden espoused in a series of popular inspirational books.[11]

The year Rand culminated her literary career with *Atlas Shrugged*, Betty Friedan (born Bettye Naomi Goldstein in 1921) began the research for a revolutionary book that examined self-esteem from a different angle. Friedan exemplified the Jewish woman who turned to psychology for answers about such troubling questions as antisemitism, fascism, and the subordination of women. Born and raised in Peoria, Friedan was the daughter of Harry Goldstein, an immigrant from Kiev who owned a successful jewelry store, and Miriam Horwitz, a second-generation Jew of Hungarian descent and a college graduate who had written a local newspaper column before becoming a homemaker. Harry was a religious skeptic who admired Robert Ingersoll, the great agnostic orator who lived in Peoria in the 1800s. Betty followed the same path, doubting the existence of God from an early age. But the social prejudice she experienced during adolescence made her status as a Jew painfully real. Ostracism, she later recalled, inspired her "passion against injustice." A lonely, intellectual girl, she went on to a rich education at Smith College, a school that was unusual in the late 1930s for its hiring of Jewish professors and European émigrés, including the great German Jewish Gestalt psychologist Kurt Koffka. At Smith, Friedan took up writing and radical politics, and majored in psychology in an effort to understand the personal, psychological underpinnings of oppressive social structures. She graduated summa cum laude, one of the best students in the school's history. "Through her education in psychology," her biographer observes, Friedan "acquired a way of looking at the world."[12]

After a year as a graduate student in psychology at Berkeley, where she studied with Erik Erikson and began contemplating the formation of female identity, Friedan decided against an academic career. America had entered the war and, as a dedicated Marxist yearning to fight fascism and antisemitism, she chose to become a progressive journalist. But Betty also wished to combine a career with an "egalitarian" marriage. After the war she married Carl Friedan and by 1952 was the mother of two children in a New York suburb. Frustrated with the life of a homemaker even as she began a successful career writing for women's magazines, Friedan entered psychotherapy, an experience she described as a "rebirth." She concluded that she had "lost her sense of self" by accepting the "false dichotomy of being a woman or exercising her mind." That train of thought led to the argument of *The Feminine Mystique*: society did not consider the frustration of female potential to be a problem because "woman is seen only in terms of her sexual role." It led also to the famous phrase "The Problem That Has No Name," which meant that suburban women suffered from an undefined identity crisis. Friedan resented the way male editors revised her magazine articles to remove any feminist suggestions that might disturb the "mystique" of "the happy home-maker." She retaliated in *The Feminine Mystique*. In that book Friedan wanted "to get her readers to feel what she had experienced—self-realization and discovery through therapy" so that other women would put a premium on "self-esteem, ideas, and education."[13]

The popularity of *The Feminine Mystique* had something to do with its dramatic exaggerations. Nearly always busy as a writer or a community organizer, Friedan never had been the passive "mystified" housewife that the suburbs supposedly spawned. Her book derived from a survey she conducted of her Smith classmates fifteen years after graduation, yet her depictions of suburban malaise did not accurately reflect what those women said about their lives. Her thesis, that a virtual conspiracy of mass media had created the feminine mystique, echoed her Marxism but slighted the complexity of the subject. Nevertheless, Friedan's analysis of the psychodynamics of suburban womanhood struck a powerful chord.[14]

If Betty Friedan was the emblematic public moralist for American feminists, two other Jewish women, Ann Landers and Abigail Van Buren, fulfilled that role for a much larger and more diverse audience. The newspaper advice column was one of the most resilient and attractive institutions in the world of mass media. Originating in London in the 1690s, the custom evolved in America from the Silence Dogood column that Benjamin Franklin wrote for the *New England Courant* in the 1700s to the "modern" columns of Beatrice Fairfax (Marie Manning) and Dorothy Dix (Elizabeth Gilmer), which began in the 1890s and ran for many decades. After World War II, when Landers and Van Buren became the new avatars of the advice column, the multitude of people who solicited their help were from the lower and middle classes, many of them teenagers struggling with sex, and many of them adults (especially southerners who had recently migrated to the North and West) who distrusted or feared official agencies such as psychiatric clinics and marriage counsel-ing services. A far cry from the cynical Miss Lonelyhearts of Nathaniel West's novel, the women who wrote the majority of columns took their readers very seriously and offered them "contact with a wider world in which there are other anxious persons and in which there is a friendly authority."[15]

Ann Landers and Abigail Van Buren were the pen names of twin sisters Esther Pauline Lederer (1918–2002) and Pauline Esther Phillips (1918–). Esther and Pauline were two of four daughters born to Rebecca and Abraham Friedman, Russian Jewish immigrants who settled in Sioux City, Iowa, in 1910. Abraham started as a pushcart peddler and ended up owning several vaudeville and movie theaters. Both girls graduated high school in Sioux City and enrolled in nearby Morningside College, where they started a gossip column for the college weekly, but did not graduate, leaving school to marry (in a double wedding) just before turning twenty-one, and to raise families. Roughly a decade and a half later, in October 1955, restless to resume the role of newspaper columnist, Esther talked her way into taking over the "Ann Landers" column at the *Chicago Sun-Times*. Three months later Pauline followed suit at the *San Francisco Chronicle* under the new pseudonym Abigail Van Buren. The twins added a sharp edge of humor that had not been typical of advice columns, and that quality, along with a terse common sense, accounted for their meteoric rise. They quickly went into syndication and within a few years far outpaced their competitors. By 1976 Ann Landers, the most widely read of all, had more than 50 million readers in 750 daily newspapers; by 1996, she had 90 million readers in more than 1,200 daily newspapers.[16]

Landers and Van Buren accurately represented the values of the aver-age American Jew of the 1950s, 1960s, and early 1970s. They believed in God and Country, espoused liberal Judaism and liberal politics, frowned on public expressions of religious and racial intolerance but disliked traditionalist forms of Christianity, accepted sexual drives as good (i.e., not sinful), tolerated abortion, and, though not endorsing homosexuality, attacked homophobic intolerance. After the sexual revo-lution of the 1960s and 1970s, the opinions that once defined Landers and Van Buren as liberals began to sound conservative in the nation's most cosmopolitan areas. Nevertheless, compared to the famous advice columnists who preceded them, they were less likely to blame women for problems of love, sex, and marriage and more likely to recommend men-tal health services. A statistical study of their newspaper columns, along with those of Joyce Brothers, concluded that these three leaders of popu-lar advice had the overall effect of debunking myths and correcting mis-leading information about mental health and marriage. Landers and Van Buren reflected an American Jewish inclination to accept scientific expertise, and at the same time maintained the image of the Jewish mother as a down-to-earth, humorous authority on affairs of the heart and the family. (That stereotype became so much a part of the popular culture that it underwrote a marketing bonanza of inspirational books: *Chicken Soup for the Soul* [1993] and its bevy of descendants, which went on to include *Chicken Soup for the Teenager's, Mother's, Sister's, Woman's, Pet Lover's, Nurse's, Teacher's, Survivor's,* and *Writer's Soul.*)[17]

GERTRUDE BERG: THE JEWISH MOTHER AS SITCOM PSYCHOLOGIST

The prototype for the Jewish mother in the mass media was Gertrude Berg. Though now largely forgotten, Berg was for many years the best-known Jewish woman in America. She created and starred in the radio series *The Goldbergs,* which, along with *Amos 'n' Andy,* established the new genre of the sitcom in the late 1920s. Throughout the golden age of radio, Berg, as Jewish mother Molly Goldberg, "filled the air ... with heavy accents and Yiddish phrases." In 1949 she adapted the show for television, keeping her fictive Jewish family in the American living room for another six years. Unlike *Amos 'n' Andy,* which came out of the black-face tradition and perpetuated demeaning stereotypes, *The Goldbergs* was "owned and operated" by Jews and became the first ethnic comedy in the history of broadcasting that was both successful *and* socially unobjectionable. Berg's audience was enormous and the longest-lasting of any show to come out of radio (in contrast, protest over racial stereotyping shut down *Amos 'n' Andy* soon after it migrated to television).[18]

Gertrude (Edelstein) Berg (1899–1966), unlike the immigrant Molly Goldberg, was born in New York City. An artistically ambitious young woman, she studied playwriting for a time at Columbia University, began writing radio scripts, and broke through with *The Rise of the Goldbergs,* which she pitched to NBC in 1929. Surrounded by husband Jake, daughter Rosalie, son Sammy, and uncle David, Molly Goldberg became the mythic Jewish mother for two generations of Americans. She combined Old World charm and moral compass with a passion for democratic values and secular progress. Radio, and early television, obeyed a very strict code of moral imagery that exalted the individual's ties to family, community, and country and condemned avarice and bigotry as "un-American." (The networks prohibited racial epithets and hateful language, for example, though comic stereotypes abounded and the social order was never challenged.) Molly Goldberg worked perfectly within that system of values. The rough edges of inner-city life, immigrant malaise, and disordered Jewish families were either nonexistent or muted in her world, and Berg's writing and acting were skillful enough to make her *the* image of the sensible, warm-hearted Jewish American mother.[19]

Berg's Molly was also a moral guide. Espousing the precept that "you must love and obey God but you have to love and obey Him by loving your neighbor," she helped those around her. Molly's didactic style expressed Gertrude Berg's own wish to be a public moralist. In the mid-1930s, several years after her breakthrough in radio, Berg wrote a syndicated advice column for the Jewish press. Her attitudes were those of an educated, politically liberal woman who thought that American mothers should produce independent, self-respecting children. Modern psychology, she believed, would help women understand the changing dynamics of family life. As Molly, Berg imbued these attitudes with a strong Jewish flavor.[20]

Like other television comedies of the 1950s, *The Goldbergs* worked psychology for jokes about the superiority of common sense over academic knowledge and the inability of most people to comprehend the psychoanalytic terms that had passed into everyday speech. That type of humor became especially useful when the Goldberg family left the Bronx for a new home in the suburban town of Haverville in 1955, because Berg found in psychology a convenient symbol for the larger world into which the immigrant family had moved. In Haverville (a name that plays on both the obvious—a place where people *have* more material things—and on the Yiddish word for "friend"—a place of new and not exclusively Jewish friends), the suburban children go to college and major in psychology. A 1955 episode on dream interpretation, for example, focused on a (gentile) woman who became obsessed with the psychoanalytic terms she learned from her collegiate daughter, a psychology major. "That Mrs. Van Nest is making the whole neighborhood unconscious," Uncle David complains to Molly in his thick Yiddish accent. But Berg distilled humor from psychological terminology even at the start of her television series in 1949, when the Goldberg family was set in the Bronx. In one early episode, Molly instructed her husband, "It all comes from the subconscious that goes into the conscious," a line that captures the intelligence of Berg's comedy. The humor comes from the sound of Molly's dialect but not from a burlesque of Molly, who has pithily expressed an abstract concept.[21]

If we compare *The Goldbergs* to other television comedies, we will appreciate Berg's ability to dignify psychology even as she spoofed it. A month after Berg's dream-interpretation episode, another popular sitcom, *The Bob Cummings Show,* sported with psychology in a more frivolous way. Produced and written by Paul Henning, one of the best comedy writers of early television, *The Bob Cummings Show* was not mere slapstick. In its final episode of the 1955 season, Cumming's nephew Chuck, a main character played by Dwayne Hickman, wants to borrow his bachelor uncle's fancy car. To achieve his end, he tries to use psychology to convince his mother to persuade Uncle Bob to lend the car. With mock innocence, he tells her that teenagers, according to the psychology he learned in school, must be treated with a lot of love or their libidos will suffer. Chuck further complains to his uncle that he has an "injured id"— "Mom keeps frustrating me, Uncle Bob, filling me with repressions and inhibitions." Bob, who is impatient to get ready for a date, makes light of the comment, but Chuck, proud of his scheme, brags to a friend that he's got his mother "buffaloed with all this psychology jazz." After Chuck's hijinks turn Uncle Bob's date into a fiasco, Bob recoups by persuading his voluptuous young companion that the evening's upsets have hurt his libido, which can be repaired only with her romantic attention. In this comedy, psychology is a sales device, a new lingo for an old game in which the crafty male tries to fool the unsuspecting female.[22]

Molly Goldberg's encounters with psychology are more complex. Though Berg was not above spoofing the profession, she also dignified psychology in a way that was uncommon in prime-time entertainment. On the one hand, traditional common sense usually prevails over psychological theory when it comes to solving problems within the family. But sometimes psychology is needed. When teenaged Rosalie wants plastic surgery to straighten her nose, Molly insists, "Our behavior to Rosie must be pure psychology." Molly's son, Sammy, has been studying psychology at college, and she respects his diagnosis of his sister's problem: Rosie has an "inferiority complex. . . . She thinks she's an ugly duckling."

> Jake: "So college professor, what's your suggestion?"
> Sammy: "Well, you've got to try and build up her ego. . . ."
> Molly: "Oy, Samele, your words are pearls. Pearls!"

Recognizing that Rosalie is more likely to forego the surgery if she is encouraged to make an independent decision, Molly eschews an authoritarian response in favor of a more sophisticated approach.

> Molly: "Jake, let Rosie think that her nose is her own and she can do with
> it what she pleases. That's psychology, Jake."

When Jake sardonically replies, "Well, Madame Freud," Molly answers: "Jake, I'd rather she had a scar on her nose than a scar on her subconscious!" Molly's "psychology" is a subtle blend of native wisdom (the proverbial "reverse psychology" of the desperate parent) and a real acknowledgment of the "pearls" of psychological insight. Rosalie, as it turns out, decides to keep her nose as it is. In postwar suburban America, the lesson appears to be that a Jewish girl will be accepted if she accepts herself.[23]

One of the final episodes of *Molly*, the show's title in its last season, used psychology in a way that foreshadowed the feminist revolution about to unfold with *The Feminine Mystique*. In the episode "Dreams," the comic story of Mrs. Van Nest, the neighbor who had become obsessed with tidbits of psychoanalysis, opened a tinderbox of unfulfilled female dreams on the suburban frontier. After Mrs. Van Nest pays Molly a visit, Molly and Jake talk.

> Jake: "Are you happy?"
> Molly: "Very, but maybe I'd be happier if I knew a little about psychology, for instance."
> Jake: "Maybe you'd be happier, but I wouldn't."

The episode revolves around the interpretation of Molly's dreams, which seem to suggest that she feels stunted in her life as a homemaker. "The dustcloth and the mop are the symbols of your imprisonment," Mrs. Van Nest, the Joseph of Haverville, tells Molly.

> Mrs. Van Nest: "You are sublimating your own personality. Oh, you're too intelligent to waste yourself, Mrs. Goldberg. Oh, get out into the world. You weren't meant to be a hausfrau!"
> Molly: "But I love it."
> Mrs. Van Nest: "Oh, you think you love it, but you're just wasting your life."

The armchair psychoanalysis throws Molly into a pensive state. She considers ways of dealing with the revelation that "I'm a potential. And I should be expressed. Because of mine emotions." In the end, nothing comes of Molly's suspicion that "a new world is opening up to me!" The skepticism of husband Jake, and the silliness of Mrs. Van Nast, resolve in a finale that finds Molly falling back on the customs of family life with only the promise of new consumer goods before her. But the "Dreams" episode expressed an undercurrent of genuine discontent and an unspoiled faith in the explanatory potential of psychology. After all, it was the field that young Sammy, the next generation of Goldbergs, was studying in college with Molly's blessing.[24]

In her ambivalent retreat from the feminist implications of her "psychoanalysis," Molly Goldberg reacted to strong crosscurrents of 1950s America. Her creator was unusual but not freakish in being both a mother and a professional. Admittedly, many authorities warned about the dangers of mothers abdicating their duties in the home and of women "masculinizing" themselves (and feminizing their husbands) through independent careers. Yet mothers like Molly Goldberg whose children were old enough for school were taking on jobs outside the home—39 percent of them did so by 1960. Most worked in order to increase the family's purchasing power, and the minority who sought rewarding careers faced considerable resistance. Employers usually took women less seriously than men, assuming that their ultimate goal was marriage and children rather than career. And many husbands believed that a working wife was a sign of their own failure to provide adequately for their families. At the same time, images of successful careerwomen, some married and with children, abounded in the years after the war. Rather than Rosie the Riveter, the wartime ideal of female labor, the model working woman of the 1950s was a sleek, well-groomed business-woman, journalist, or civic leader. Popular magazines ran many stories of successful professional women, highlighted the difficulties of domes-ticity as well as its rewards, and rarely preached a gospel of female passiv-ity. Though most women in the 1950s were wives and mothers and home-making remained a supreme value, there was another message that mirrored Molly Goldberg's: the mother and wife was also "a potential."[25]

Jewish Values and the Rise of Dr. Joyce Brothers

At nearly the exact moment of Gertrude Berg's farewell to television, another Jewish woman appeared who would enjoy an even longer and more influential career as a public moralist, a woman who spoke with the full authority of a professional psychologist and who also happened to be a wife and mother. Nineteen fifty-five was not only the year the Goldbergs moved to the suburbs; it was also the year in which Joyce Brothers became the first woman to win *The $64,000 Question.*

A freshly minted Ph.D. in psychology, wife of a young M.D., and mother of a two-year-old girl, Brothers made up her mind to become a contestant on the popular quiz show in order to boost the young family's meager income. Showing the pluck that would distinguish her as a celeb-rity psychologist for more than four decades, Brothers realized that she had to develop a novel expertise, something to attract the network's at-tention. She decided on boxing, knowing that a woman who could an-swer questions on that subject would titillate the public. After months of round-the-clock research into the rules and history of the game, she be-came an authority, and her hunch paid off. The petite, pretty blond psy-chologist surprised even the show's producers with the extent of her knowledge of boxing. Not only did Brothers win the grand prize but she also doubled her money two years later on *The $64,000* Challenge, single-handedly defeating a team of seven famous boxers. Her celebrity led to guest appearances on other television shows and in 1958 to an offer from NBC to host her own afternoon show counseling women on love, marriage, sex, and children. Within two months of her debut Brothers was receiving nearly 2,000 letters a week. "A smooth blend of Dorothy

Dix and Sigmund Freud," *Newsweek* called her, whose "heart-to-heart talks frequently cover topics formerly considered taboo for television . . . female frigidity, the menopause (in men and women), sexual satisfaction, and toilet training."[26]

The assertive intellectuality of Joyce Brothers cannot be called a "Jewish" trait, of course, but it certainly conformed to the values with which she was raised. Brothers's parents emphasized the education of their daughters in a way that was not unusual for Jewish families but was for other Americans. Joyce Diane Bauer was born in New York City in 1929 to second-generation Jews, Estelle (Rappaport) and Morris Bauer. Estelle's mother had immigrated from the Ukraine and worked alongside her husband in their dry-goods store. She passed on a love of work to Estelle, who followed a similar path in New York, becoming a lawyer and forming a partnership with her husband. Joyce and her sister grew up in a household where it was normal for a wife and mother to have a satisfying and prestigious career. They, too, were expected to be literate and verbal. "There was nothing our daughters couldn't discuss with us," Estelle reminisced. "The supper table was always lively with conversation." Joyce's own memories agreed with Estelle's: "Mother went off to work with Dad every morning. That was the way things were at our house. And when our parents were at home, their lives revolved around us. We had a wonderful childhood."[27]

Brothers attributed her determination to succeed to her parent's conviction that girls were intellectually as valuable as boys. The turning point for her came in an encounter with a professor of psychology at Columbia who tried to discourage her from pursuing a doctorate. He granted that she had the highest qualifying marks of those who were admitted to the Ph.D. program in 1949, but speculated that, as a woman, she would likely defer a career to raise a family, thus taking up a place that would be better occupied by a male. "If I had not been brought up to think that I had as much right as anyone else, male or female, to learn and to work," Brothers explained to her readers, "Professor Q's awe-inspiring position and his fatherly disapproval might have made me back down." She persevered, earning a Ph.D. in psychology at Columbia in 1953.[28]

Though her family lived in a largely Christian community on Long Island, Brothers grew up with a clear sense of their difference as Jews. A precocious child (she graduated from Cornell when she was eighteen), Joyce learned early on from her mother that such family customs as the celebration of Hanukkah set them apart from their neighbors. This feeling of being on the social periphery may have been the reason she highlighted social prejudice as "one of the most common manifestations" of difficult people in her first inspirational book, *Woman* (1961): "They don't like the members of another race or of a different religion, or they

don't like men who are fat or women who are thin. The list is endless."
She married medical student Milton Brothers on July 4, 1949, when she
was nineteen, and for four decades the couple maintained a home not
unlike that of her parents, with two busy professionals (now doctors instead of lawyers) wrapped in a secular Jewish sensibility. Milton, for example, had a policy never to charge rabbis or rabbinical students for medical
treatment (he also did not charge relatives or other doctors, their wives
or children).[29]

The ideal of female success and fulfillment that Brothers preached
throughout her long career reflected her understanding of how a Jewish
woman should behave. She contrasted herself with other well-educated
women in America whose desire for autonomy conflicted with their husbands' desire for a warmly attentive wife. Soon after she inaugurated her
column, "On Being a Woman," for *Good Housekeeping*, Brothers compared two wives she knew, one of whom was the "sort of woman many
other women envy" because of her sophistication, charm, and efficiency,
while the other, an Italian American, was less chic and sometimes over-
emotional. Asking herself which wife would make a better marriage,
Brothers recommended the latter because she knew how to pamper her
husband. "In America today, there is little doubt that Italian (and Jewish)
wives are most freely showered with gifts and appreciation," she wrote.
"I believe this is linked to the way women raised in these two cultural
traditions are likely to pamper their husbands." (By pampering, Brothers
meant attending to the husband's desire for physical and emotional comfort: "Lasagna—or chicken soup with homemade noodles—served up
with a large dose of motherly sympathy.") At the same time, Brothers's
prescriptions for the good wife included the kind of praise for the career
woman that contrasted with the mores of Italian Catholics as much as
it agreed with the sensibility of American Jews. "My mother had always
practiced law . . . and raised a family, too," she told her readers. "I had
always assumed that any woman could combine a career with marriage
and a family if she wanted to."[30]

The rise of Joyce Brothers was unique and unprecedented. Radio had
its psychology experts, but never before had a psychologist created such a
powerful niche in broadcasting as Brothers did on television. And never
before had a psychological authority entered so fully into popular culture. A reviewer for the *New York Times* did not exaggerate when she said,
in the early 1980s, that Brothers "*is* psychology to millions of Americans."
Aside from her series of television shows, Brothers conducted her business on the radio and through popular magazines, particularly *Good
Housekeeping*, for which she served as a regular columnist during the
1960s and 1970s. Brothers was the proverbial good sport—she appeared
in cameo roles in dozens of movies and television shows, often spoofing

herself. Her appearances achieved an almost cultic stature in the annals of American comedy. Among her more memorable performances were her parody of the psychological adviser to confused suburban women on *Mary Hartman, Mary Hartman* (1977); her psychoanalytic dialogue with "Johnny," the streetwise shoeshine-man/informer on *Police Squad!* (1982); and her leap from the Brooklyn Bridge, along with scores of other loners, at the finale of *The Lonely Guy* (1984). Though she continued to dispense advice and appear in television skits into the twenty-first century, Brothers exerted her greatest effect in the 1960s, 1970s, and 1980s. By using her own life cycle as a focal point of her books—from being a young mother in the 1950s to becoming a widow in the 1990s—she mapped the rites-of-passage of an entire generation of American women.[31]

THE SUBURBAN FEMINISM OF DR. BROTHERS

Although her audience included women in cities and small towns, Brothers's career coincided with the rise of the suburb. Suburban women formed the nucleus of her audience, which meant that she was often responding to those people who left the older ethnic neighborhoods and parishes of cities like New York, where her first show was broadcast on WNBC-TV, to settle in places like Molly Goldberg's Haverville. Her suburban fans, like Molly, had moved away from relatives and centered themselves more completely on their nuclear families in detached, single-family homes. The prototype for those homes, Levittown, was built by Levitt and Sons in 1947, not far from where Brothers grew up on Long Island. By the early 1960s, when she was a fixture on television, New Jersey and Pennsylvania each had a Levittown, and numerous other Levitt developments bearing British pastoral names like Strathmore popped up in semi-rural townships within commuting distance of Manhattan. Other builders followed the Levitt innovation of affordable mass-produced housing, and the West Coast had its own innovators. Of the thirteen million housing units built in nonfarm areas between 1946 and 1958, 85 percent were suburban. That trend continued as nearly every major city lost population in the postwar years. In 1950 37 million Americans lived in suburbs; by 1970 70 million did. Television kept the same pace. In 1946 several thousand TV sets existed for a population of 140 million; by 1957 there were 40 million sets. By 1970 virtually every American household had at least one.[32]

Although critics who lived in cities and college towns loved to decry the idiocy of suburban life, the main quality that differentiated the new suburbanites was a desire for greater privacy than they had before as urbanites. That fact helps to explain the initial popularity of Joyce Brothers's televised advice. The visual dimension of television, and Brothers's ability to relate to the camera, generated a greater feeling of personal connection than radio could give. There, present in the living room of a wife who was the only adult at home in the afternoon, was a real psychologist, not simply a voice that one assumed to be a psychologist.[33]

Brothers developed a unique style of addressing her listeners, a mixture of scientific authority and demure femininity that made her more reputable than the chat-show host, yet much more sympathetic and less condescending than male authority figures of her day. She studiously avoided the pronoun "I" if she could say instead, "studies show" or "psychologists have found." Fond of statistics, which she mixed thoroughly into her advice, Brothers combined a high native intelligence with an indomitable work ethic (she virtually eliminated her social life to prepare her shows and articles). Critic Marya Mannes, who had little in common with the housewives whom Brothers primarily addressed, nonetheless said what many women were thinking when they watched Brothers win *The $64,000 Question*:

> Here was this demure little blonde in her twenties who had total recall in a man's world and was a psychologist (registered) too. . . . Dr. Brothers works very hard, is patently sincere, and says nothing that is not eminently reasonable. . . . Part of Dr. Brothers's success (she is syndicated all over the country) lies in her ability to answer complex problems in simple language: she eschews the jargon of psychologists, psychiatrists, and educators. . . . She can discuss sexual maladjustment as an electrician might discuss a faulty connection, and dispose of male appetite as a form of athlete's foot. That she achieves this with an air of dedicated and genuine sympathy is a small miracle.[34]

Despite the intrinsic limitations of over-the-air advice, Brothers managed to shore up the esteem of housewives without ridiculing their husbands. In an effort to reinforce marriage amid the physical and social instability of suburbanization, she preached the value of "pampering" a husband while also encouraging women to balance their marital obligations in a way that allowed room for their personal needs. Both were tactics in the struggle to make marriage and womanhood a richer experience. She introduced millions of homemakers to the new feminism of the 1960s by steering clear of ideology and staying focused on the practical matters of family life. By 1969, in her fifth year as *Good Housekeeping*'s resident psychologist, she was writing "In Defense of Selfishness," a homemaker's version of Adam Smith's philosophy of economics—"by 'selfishly' taking care of yourself, you'll find you can take a lot better care of your family."[35]

Her ideas about women's place in marriage and society developed over a thirty-year period and can be charted through the titles of some of her books: *Woman* (1961), *The Brothers System for Liberated Love and Marriage* (1972), *How to Get Whatever You Want Out of Life* (1978), *What Every Woman Should Know about Men* (1981), *The Successful Woman* (1988), and *Widowed* (1990). Only the first of these, *Woman*, did not sell to a large audience. In that book, Brothers emphasized the importance of character over the more superficial aspects of a woman's identity. "When a life is built exclusively on face and figure," she advised, "the possessor is driven to preserve these foundations. . . . The truth is that no woman, whether she is a beauty or just an average girl, can ever be secure unless she develops an inner quality, an assurance that is independent of her outer appearance. . . . And when a woman has this quality, physical beauty becomes secondary and strangely unimportant." Brothers also pleaded with housewives not to turn their homes into the be-all and end-all of existence. "Millions of people are ill fed and ill housed" and "others are persecuted because of the color of their skin or because of their religion," she cried out in anticipation of the civil rights and war-on-poverty initiatives of the Kennedy-Johnson years, "and you have been working yourself into a rage because a bureau drawer refuses to budge."[36]

In 1961, when *Woman* appeared, housewives had not yet become, either for Brothers or for most other Americans, an identifiable social group with its own historical burden, but that same year John F. Kennedy established the President's Commission on the Status of Women, the first official federal recognition that "prejudice and outmoded customs act as barriers to the full realization of women's basic rights." A decade later, the world of American women was a different place. *The Feminine Mystique* appeared in 1963. Two years later, the Supreme Court ruled in *Griswold v. Connecticut* (1965) that there was a constitutional "right to privacy" in regard to reproductive matters, a precedent for *Roe v. Wade* (1973). The National Organization for Women formed in 1966, protestors staged a major demonstration at the Miss America pageant in Atlantic City in 1968, and by 1970 Betty Friedan had begun to seem like a matron lagging behind the fast-paced movement for women's liberation. "Not since Emma Goldman," an historian of feminism observes, "had feminists called for such far-reaching change."[37]

Brothers's first popular book for women, *The Brothers System for Liberated Love and Marriage* (1972), domesticated some of those changes, applying them to the vast majority of home-centered women whom the most vocal feminist leaders bypassed and sometimes discounted. "Today's feminists are quite right in urging more responsibilities, more freedoms, more equality for women," she declared, "but responsibility, freedom, and equality can be achieved within the framework of marriage—and that's what most women want." Describing "Sophie," a homemaker who typi-fied the "enormous cross section of young married women" who wrote to her, Brothers explained, "Sophie is one of those women that the ex-tremists in the contemporary feminist movement forget about." Sophie did not agree with those who believed, or whose speeches implied, that "marriage is passe, homemaking a drudgery and children a drag." Still, Brothers approved of *Ms.*, "one of the new magazines for the new woman," and especially recommended an article in which a busy woman wrote "with pungent and pointed details of why she wants A Wife."[38]

The Brothers "system" of liberated love and marriage started from a simple premise: "The cards in modern marriage are stacked against women. They are expected to give without ever thinking of getting." True to form, Brothers rallied the statistics for her case, citing surveys between 1960 and 1970 that "shocked" professionals with the finding that mar-ried women were one of the unhappiest groups in American society. That finding, she noted, crossed the boundaries of race and social class. Wives across the spectrum felt discouraged. "Every human being has a need and the right to develop and function to top potential. That need, that right, has been denied to many married women, not consciously, but as a natural consequence of that clinging cultural stereotype that all it takes to fulfill a 'normal' woman is a husband and children." Brothers went on to tell her readers about another psychological study suggesting that women had a greater potential for happiness than men because they were more flexible, more realistic about what to expect from life, and "more able to express their emotions." And yet, according to the statis-tics, "married *men* are the happiest people around." "Why," Brothers asked her readers, "is your husband happier than you? In a country dedi-cated to the pursuit of happiness, this is not an unreasonable question. And yet it is an unusual one; a question rarely posed."[39]

Brothers considered her own life a model for the American woman's pursuit of happiness. Her husband was not happier than she, and she, as her readers well knew, managed to live out the dream of female success in America, enjoying both a career and a family. She told the story that became a fixture of her inspirational writing, the true story of her deter-mination to obtain a Ph.D. in psychology despite the effort of Columbia's "Professor Q" to discourage her. That victorious struggle taught her "how vital it is to put yourself first." It "was really my first step in working out the Brothers System." She had also worked out the other basic principle of the "liberated marriage," an egalitarian cooperation rather than a "master-slave" relationship. Drawing on the pioneering ideas of Kurt Lewin about the moral superiority of a democratic over an authoritarian style of interaction, Brothers claimed that the wife in an authoritarian marriage became incapacitated in times of crisis because of her habitual passivity, whereas the wife in a "flexible power structure" responded effectively with self-confidence. Just as Joshua Liebman had rejected the master-slave model of religion in the hope of attaining a "mature" spiritual life in line with American democracy, Joyce Brothers rejected the same model for the same reason, so that marriage would be "no longer a refuge for the immature." The Brothers System, she promised, would bring Americans "closer than we have ever been to attaining the romantic ideal of marriage that is so uniquely American."[40]

BROTHERS AND THE AMBIGUOUS VALUES OF PSYCHOLOGY

Brothers shared two secrets of her success, which conformed nicely to American and Jewish traditions of conduct. Like Benjamin Franklin, she made lists of goals. "Part of my system is that before I go to bed every night, I spend a few minutes thinking about what I have to do the next day. It's almost always more than I'll be able to do—I've learned that from experience. So once I've thought through what I *should* do, I make another mental list of the three most important things: things that I absolutely *must* do." Her system also called for contracts between spouses. "The idea of contracts has always appealed to me," she explained, "possibly because my father always used to make contracts with me when I was little." Brothers's recommendation of informal spousal contracts recalled the Jewish tradition of the marriage contract between husband and wife, the *ketubah*, which becomes the wife's property to protect her interests throughout the marriage and in the event of divorce. (In the standard *ketubah*, the groom pledges to maintain the bride in "the custom of Jewish husbands, who work for their wives, honoring and supporting them, and maintaining them in truth.")[41]

The statistical and tactical thinking behind the Brothers system of love and marriage, however, began spiraling out of control in the course of the 1970s. Within six years of *The Brothers System for Liberated Love and Marriage*, Brothers was cluing her readers in on psychological techniques of manipulation so that they might learn *How to Get Whatever You Want Out of Life* (1978). "Most people consider the idea of manipulating others, getting them to do what you want them to, rather distasteful," Brothers observed, but only to affirm "the fact" that "we all manipulate people at one time or another without even being conscious of it. Wealth Seekers tend to manipulate intuitively and are quite adept at the art, but there are ways and means of manipulation that you may not have discovered or that do not come naturally to you. They can be learned. See Chapter Seventeen." Chapter 17, "The Manipulative Handbook," elaborated the main point of Chapter 16, "How to Make People Do What You Want."

In some respects, this was the heart of a book that paused only occasionally to remind readers that "money isn't everything" and that helping your opponent save face was often the best way to succeed. Flattery, rewards, guilt, and fear were the four essential "psychological tools" for getting people to do what you want. Since "everyone has an inferiority complex," everyone was susceptible to flattery. "Rewards are the pleasantest of psychological tools, but the manipulator should use them sparingly," Dr. Brothers admonished, otherwise the "operant conditioning" of the rewarded subject would be lessened by his or her expectation to be rewarded for every display of the desired behavior.[42]

It is difficult to understand how the idealism of *The Brothers System for Liberated Love and Marriage* degenerated in only six years to the Machiavellian psychotechnics of *How to Get Whatever You Want Out of Life*, but the signs of a loosening moral compass appeared in another book sandwiched between those two. *Better Than Ever* (1975) was written for women entering middle age and exhorted "the woman who wants her second-chance years to be the best of all" not to give in to the demons of fat, lethargy, and self-pity. Characteristically, Brothers used her own life story as a model of female indomitability. She reported that, despite the fears that came with her forties, she lost weight, got into great physical shape by swimming, improved her sex life with her husband, Milt (well known to readers since her previous book), from a "4" to a "10," and "started over" when she and Milt bought an old Connecticut farmhouse that they enjoyed renovating together on weekends away from Manhattan. Her ambitions for personal change and rejuvenation culminated with the announcement that "soon I am going to try to carve out a second career for myself—in politics this time." Although nothing came of her desire to become a U.S. Senator, Brothers knew that her readers appreciated the spunk of someone who preferred "to pin my hopes to a star rather than to the lowest branch of the smallest tree." *Better Than Ever* offered many useful tips and much encouragement to middle-age women but, tucked into the middle of the book, a disturbing new suggestion peered out at the reader.[43]

"I have to admit that I have completely reversed my attitude toward extramarital affairs," Brothers declared. Only three years earlier, in *The Brothers System for Liberated Love and Marriage*, she opposed the idea that "marriage should be so liberated as to embrace extramarital affairs." By 1975, however, she recommended that possibility, not for "the promiscuous wife" but only for "the mature woman who is in full control of herself." For such a woman, a fling might invigorate marriage. Brothers insisted that her change of mind had an empirical basis.

At least that is what increasing numbers of women all over the country are telling me. They are telling me about brief romantic flings with the veterinarian (more women seem to have affairs with vets than with men in other occupations, I don't know why), with old beaux whom they ran into many years later, with the handsome young man who delivered the dry cleaning— and even with the Boy Scout leader. . . . Men have been having affairs for centuries without endangering their marriages; it seems that now women are availing themselves of the same privilege.

The key, she warned, was the ability to keep the affair a secret. Whatever benefits the dalliance might have for one's marriage would be nullified if the truth got out. Brothers's new advice might have been good news for veterinarians, delivery boys, and wives who didn't mind living double lives and lying to their husbands, but it raised obvious ethical questions. In her desire to strengthen the place of women within marriage, to show how the married woman might realize the ideal of being the happiest of people, Brothers had made that goal the ultimate criterion of value, for which even honesty and trust might be sacrificed.[44]

Her first book of the 1980s, *What Every Woman Should Know about Men* (1981), combined the same amoral utilitarianism with a streak of female chauvinism. Brothers presented new information about the biological differences between men and women and emphasized the superiority of females in terms of both biology and mentality. Women, her evidence suggested, were better able than men to withstand various afflictions, like strokes, and their brains functioned in a way that made them "more perceptive about people." Because the "key to survival in the nuclear age is going to be perception," the more that women enter into statecraft the better will be the diplomatic results. With those considerations in mind, Brothers urged women to consider the deliberate selection of female children. Couples using amniocentesis seemed to prefer males, but "there are cosmic consequences to such sex control," she warned, "and women who want sons should take time to think about them." A surplus of males would lead to more crime, wars, male homosexuality, prostitution, polygamy, and the loss of women's freedom, "since females will be a rare commodity." Then, after presenting data about the allegedly superior traits of the first-born child, she recommended, "when the day comes that sex-selection techniques are available . . . this would be an overpowering argument for choosing first a girl."[45]

In *Widowed* (1990), published a year after Milt's death, Brothers brought to the surface a tension between Judaism and psychologism that had been latent during her triumphant years as a celebrity. The book contained her reflections on the late years in the lifespan of an American woman, "the last stage in the role of wife," and her recommendations about handling the perplexities of bereavement and the frustrations of widowhood. White women of her generation were outliving their husbands by at least seven years. Though she was just over sixty, Brothers had the company of many widows. Less triumphal a tale than her earlier books, *Widowed* candidly exposed the inevitable compromises that Brothers, her husband, and her daughter had to make for her success. Readers who remembered her triumph on *The $64,000 Question*, for example, learned that she had her mother take care of her two-year-old daughter while she "got up at six in the morning and studied until one the next morning." ("But I had an important goal," she added, "so it was easy to do.") They also discovered that Brothers and her husband fought on their honeymoon and "all through our marriage." Sex, too, had not been all it appeared. Although in the 1975 book *Better Than Ever* Brothers had boasted that her sex life with her husband was a "10," fifteen years later, despite the nostalgia that attends a recently deceased spouse, she looked back and concluded that sex, after years of marriage, "tends to be a familiar pleasure that you take for granted."[46]

Underneath the inspirational story of a woman's triumph over adversity, *Widowed* revealed a troubled outlook in which social science replaced religion. With her husband gone, Brothers felt that life itself had lost meaning and she sank into a nearly suicidal despair. Judaism proved of little use to Brothers in her time of grief. "I regretted I was not sitting *shiva*," she remarked, referring to the seven-day period of mourning among family and friends prescribed by Judaism, because that ritual "would have provided a transition between the old and the new." She abstained because "Milt had made me promise not to. . . . I am not sure he was right, but it was important to me to do as Milt had wanted." Yet the custom of sitting *shiva* focuses on the welfare of the survivor, not on honoring the wishes of the deceased. The decision to forgo the consolations of Judaism was hers alone, and it was consistent with the logic of a secular Jew for whom marriage had become the highest ideal and final source of meaning.[47]

The path of consolation she ended up choosing was work, specifically the work of a celebrity. The day after Milton's funeral, Brothers received a call from television variety-show host Pat Sajak, who, not knowing of her husband's death, asked her to do a comedy skit for his show. She agreed. Although she admitted afterward that she felt "as if I were being mugged" during the skit, she noted that the *National Enquirer* praised her courage in concealing her pain "in the best tradition of 'the show must go on.'" But Joyce Brothers was a psychologist, not an entertainer, and her audience, unlike that of a comedian, would not have expected her to perform a few days after her husband's funeral. What was the psychological lesson of her decision?[48]

In the end, Brothers turned to science and statistics to comprehend her own grief, giving only a nod to Judaism. "Tears of sadness or anger contain leucine-enkephalin, one of the brain's natural pain relievers," she explained to her readers. "Crying does not just feel good," she quoted from a recent study, "it appears to be an evolutionary device for adapting to emotional stress." Having established the scientific credibility of crying, Brothers shared a Jewish interpretation of it. "According to the Talmud, when God banished Adam and Eve from the Garden of Eden, Adam protested that the punishment was too severe. They would not be able to cope with the world outside the Garden of Eden. God considered Adam's plea and found it valid, so he gave Adam and Eve two gifts to help them cope with the hardships of the world. The first was the Sabbath for rest and contemplation; the second was the tear." A Jewish interpretation of human life and human travail, however, was peripheral to her outlook, which focused on the physiology of tears and the sociology of the widowed. Discussing the difficulties that older widows faced in remarrying, she listed the gloomy statistics and concluded, "When I look at the facts of second marriages in this way, I understand that my chances of remarrying are slim." While her readers must have found such a prediction odd—given Brothers's wealth, celebrity, and age—it illustrates how deeply statistical thinking had pervaded her outlook. Brothers offered real insight into the loss of status suffered by the widowed woman, who "in the human ranking order . . . becomes a second-class citizen unless she fights against it" and risks a "feeling of inferiority" that "will only deepen her loneliness." And yet, behind her assessment was the assumption that there was no larger, transcendent ground of being, nothing to dignify the individual life and allow it to retain meaning despite the loss of a spouse. Judaism had given way to social science.[49]

If spiritual and moral confusions entered into the advice that Joyce Brothers dispensed over the years, they were confusions of her time. Women of her generation were born into a very different world of marital and sexual values than the world into which they moved after 1960. They had all learned to prize marriage and family, but as they moved away from their religious traditions they could not always be sure how to fit the ideal of marriage and family into a larger moral framework. Their confusions were those of men and women who had placed too much faith in psychology and the human sciences, which, after all, were better at producing data than values. Having left behind the coherent values of a fully articulated religion, Joyce Brothers, like many other Americans, was unable to construct an alternative moral framework of equal coherence. Her excesses were, in part, materialist excesses, and she had no monopoly on those in the "affluent society" that America became after World War II.

They were also excesses of a pragmatism that had been at the heart of much American thinking about human nature since Dewey and James, according to which what *works* defines what is *true*, and what we should do. There had always been a lingering question, *works to what end?* Brothers may have taken her readers to the outer limits of pragmatism as a tool for determining the values of married life. She did have an end, though—the ideal "liberated" marriage in which women realized their human potential as women and homemakers. Her ideal reflected a new regard for female individualism in America and also something in the American Jewish culture of her upbringing, a respect for the intelligence and secular potential of girls. But the ideal of liberated marriage was not in itself sufficient to generate moral and spiritual values. And, as the extraordinary career of Joyce Brothers illustrates, psychology could not do that either.

Chapter 14

Holocaust, Hasidism,
Suffering, Redemption

"WE NEED HIM NOW," read a *Publishers Weekly* headline a few weeks after the terrorist attacks of September 11, 2001. "At a time when many author tours and media appearances have been canceled or rescheduled," the journal noted, "one author seems to be in greater demand than ever." The author was Rabbi Harold Kushner, who, in 1981, had written *When Bad Things Happen to Good People*, an inspirational book on the old problem of theodicy—how can a benevolent and omnipotent God allow the innocent to suffer? By the time a twentieth anniversary edition appeared, Kushner's slim volume had sold four million copies. Of America's clergy, he was the one most often identified as an authority on coping with inexplicable suffering and loss. The morning of the ghastly airplane hijackings, Kushner himself was about to board a flight at Boston's Logan Airport, and the next day he appeared on a number of network television shows and gave interviews to newspapers across the country. He had just published his sixth best-seller, *Living a Life That Matters: Resolving the Conflict between Conscience and Success*, but in the aftermath of national tragedy the little classic from the 1980s, which *Publishers Weekly* called "the perennial book of comfort," took on extra meaning.[1]

This final chapter of our story considers the ways in which Jews and Judaism figured into American meditations on evil, suffering, and redemption in the final decades of the twentieth century. To fully understand Kushner's important place in popular thought, we must examine the larger impact of both the Holocaust and Hasidism in America after the 1950s.

Neither the Holocaust nor Hasidism was an American phenomenon but, as the "lessons" of each were distilled by a variety of American interpreters, they formed a unique pair of lenses through which to view suffering and redemption. A public fascinated by therapeutic spirituality found in Auschwitz a model of ultimate suffering and in the Hasid a model of the God-intoxicated man whose passion for living triumphed over the worst kind of evil. Viktor Frankl's psychological commentary on the meaning of existence after Auschwitz found a ready audience in America, and Elie Wiesel ascended to an almost saintly status through his unique way of writing and speaking about that symbol of Hell on earth. Wiesel's Hasidic background loomed large in the saga he detailed, and his depictions of Hasidic "souls on fire" offered a prospect of religious redemption from the spiritual chaos of the Holocaust.

In one form or another, Hasidism also entered the mass market of inspirational literature written by rabbis. One of the most prolific rabbinic authors of inspirational books for the general public was Abraham Twerski, a Hasidic rabbi and psychiatrist specializing in recovery from addiction, who combined traditional Jewish morality with the post-Christian Twelve Step philosophy of Alcoholics Anonymous, producing a thoroughly American brand of *musar*. Hasidism also filtered into Harold Kushner's interpretation of suffering via the "theology of pathos" of Abraham Joshua Heschel, the most charismatic Jewish religious philosopher of postwar America. Kushner tapped a deep American receptivity to both the Holocaust and certain Hasidic motifs, and galvanized controversy with his idea of a limited and essentially empathetic God. This was his offering to a post-Holocaust world and an American public that had largely accepted Joshua Liebman's summons, years earlier, for a more therapeutic spiritual life.

THE HOLOCAUST AND
THE SPIRITUAL EXPERTISE OF THE UPROOTED JEW

The Holocaust was an event in the history of Europe, not the United States, yet Americans have been surprisingly interested in its commemoration and interpretation. This has partly to do with the determination of American Jews to commemorate it. But, as with everything else in the public marketplace, there is a demand as well as a supply side to what the public wants to recall. The steady public demand for books about the Holocaust, for example, cannot be explained simply by the desire of Jews to incorporate the event into American culture.[2]

For liberal Christians, the Holocaust has served as a uniquely poignant venue for expressing a variety of religious feelings about the tortured historical relationship of Jews and Christianity. Some have interpreted it as an invitation to vicarious guilt—"if I had been there, wouldn't I too have sinned against the Jews?"—and the theme of innocent suffering, epitomized by Jews who were killed not as dissenters or combatants but simply for who they were, resonated with Christian imagery of the Crucifixion. On the other, evangelical side of the Christian spectrum, the spectacular sales of *The Late Great Planet Earth* (1970), Hal Lindsey's lurid doomsday prophesy, shows that a sizable number of evangelical Protestants have interpreted the establishment of Israel in 1948 as the pivotal event leading to Armageddon and the Second Coming. Within that cosmology Hitler's genocidal campaign may be viewed as a culmination of the age-old persecution of the Jews that, according to God's mysterious but certain plan, precedes the Jewish return to the Holy Land (and, ultimately, their "return" to Christ). According to evangelical theologian Carl F. H. Henry, writing in the early 1980s, "Hitler's demonic assault on Jewry became the human occasion of Jewish clamor for an erstwhile neglected possibility of a national homeland," an epic "regathering of world Jewry" that fulfills "ancient prophetic promises of messianic end-time."[3]

In the mainstream of postwar American society, where many people preferred psychological and therapeutic forms of spirituality, the Holocaust provided a spectacular model of psychic tribulation and recovery; an eloquent Jewish interpreter of that psychic saga could attain an almost cultic status.

To some extent, Jews acquired a mystique after World War II; their experience of dislocation and persecution seemed to confer upon them a special sagacity about the human condition. An older myth of Jewish "genius" gave way to the new concept of the Jew as the prototypical "marginal man" who achieved insight into the social order from standing outside it. Although sociologist Robert Park originated the term in the 1920s, "the marginal man" entered the American vocabulary primarily through one of his students, Everett Stonequist, whose book by that name appeared in the late 1930s. In his introduction to *The Marginal Man*, Park explained that this distinct "personality type" was someone who had to live in two worlds at the same time, a fate that conferred upon him "the role of a cosmopolitan and a stranger . . . the individual with the wider horizon, the keener intelligence, the more detached and rational viewpoint. He occupies the position which has been, historically, that of the Jew in the Diaspora. The Jew, particularly the Jew who has emerged from the provincialism of the ghetto, has everywhere and always been the most civilized of human creatures." Stonequist reinforced that image of the Jew, whose "special position and mentality" made for a unique perspicacity and intellectual creativity.[4]

If, as the myth proposed, living on the margin endowed the Jew with exceptional insight, then the articulate Holocaust survivor, a Jew who was forced to the outer limits of the social universe, would have to be a superlative commentator on the human condition. The first of this new type of marginal man on the American scene was Bruno Bettelheim, who, in 1943, published a report based on his relatively brief time in Buchenwald in the late 1930s, "Individual and Mass Behavior in Extreme Situations." (He claimed that inmates rapidly reverted to infantile and passive behavior, and he reprimanded Jews, including Anne Frank's father, Otto, for submitting to the Nazis rather than dying in combat against them.) Although Bettelheim was ultimately exposed as an unreliable authority who lied about various aspects of his life, his essay was the first and for many years the most impressive eyewitness account of what happened to the psyche in the concentration camps. In the long run, though, the Viennese pioneer of "existential analysis," Viktor Frankl (1905–97), had a more enduring effect on American thinking about the human condition as revealed in the miseries of Auschwitz.[5]

Frankl's story has become famous. He grew up in the Jewish middle class of Vienna and became enthralled, in his early days, with Freud and Adler. After graduating from the University of Vienna Medical School in 1930, he became chief of a Viennese neurology and psychiatry clinic. Along with his wife and parents (none of whom survived the concentration camps), Frankl was deported in 1942, spending three years in four camps, including Auschwitz-Birkenau. He arrived in the camps with a manuscript—sewn into the lining of his coat—containing a new theory of human nature and psychotherapy that focused on a special kind of problem, the loss of meaning. The theory, logotherapy (literally, "meaning therapy"), became the "third school of Viennese psychiatry," after Freudian and Adlerian psychology. Frankl liked to say that Freud focused on the will-to-pleasure, Adler on the will-to-power, and he on the will-to-meaning, since logotherapy asserted that humans, unlike animals, seek meaning in their lives and, lacking it, fall into a state of despair.

Inevitably, his manuscript was confiscated and destroyed, so Frankl began to reconstruct it while still in the concentration camps by jotting notes on tiny pieces of paper stolen for him by a fellow inmate. A year after the war ended, he published a manuscript that not only reconstructed his earlier, lost work but also revised it to include insights about human nature he gained during his years as a prisoner. *Man's Search for Meaning* (1962), an adaptation of that original book, became one of the most influential commentaries on the human condition in America and sold more than two million copies in English by the time Frankl penned a preface for the revised 1984 edition.[6]

Frankl's personal ordeal seemed to legitimize his theory of human nature. Even though he developed logotherapy before the war, few realized this, because the preface of *Man's Search for Meaning*, written by the venerable Harvard psychologist Gordon Allport, states that Frankl's experience as a prisoner in the camps "led to his discovery of logotherapy." Therefore, nearly everyone interpreted his insights on the "search for meaning" as a kind of revelation issuing from the tribulations of the Holocaust. "A psychiatrist who personally has faced such extremity," wrote Allport in his preface, "is a psychiatrist worth listening to." The passage of years did not diminish the belief in a vital and perhaps mysterious connection between the extreme suffering of the Holocaust survivor and a "singular lucidity" about human nature: "He who suffers," wrote one of Frankl's interpreters in 1999, "is in a privileged position to describe the true meaning of his life."[7]

Historians have raised serious questions about the moral compromises Frankl may have made as a doctor under National Socialism prior to his deportation to the camps, but most readers of *Man's Search for Meaning*, unaware of that debate, have undoubtedly been affected by the sobering candor with which Frankl opened his account. He explained that most people survived the camps through a desperate fight for existence in a horrid zero-sum game where one's neighbor or oneself would be next aboard the final transport to the crematorium. The heroes often sacrificed their lives in revolt or for the sake of others. "The best of us," he confessed, "did not return." But in the degradation of the concentration camps, Frankl discovered the error of Freud's belief that, when reduced to the basest level of existence, people would seem more and more alike as creatures of brute instinct. On the contrary, he noted, the differences between people emerged more clearly under those conditions. Inmates who had some larger goal or purpose to fulfill were much more likely to hold on and, if they were lucky, to survive and live productively again after the war. Those who stopped believing that their lives had a transcendent meaning were more likely to give up and perish under the rigors of the camps. Frankl felt certain that his own overriding purpose, to rewrite and publish his manuscript, contributed to his survival.[8]

Even before the war, Frankl had unequivocally rejected deterministic theories of human nature (such as Freud's) and insisted that people retained the freedom to choose how they would respond to their circumstances. He believed in God, or a "Supermeaning" (he would not be pinned down on this point), and emphasized the transcendent, spiritual element of human nature. The horrors of the war only confirmed Frankl's hostility toward reductionist or mechanistic theories of human nature.

> If we present a man with a concept of man which is not true, we may well corrupt him. . . . I became acquainted with the last stage of that corruption in my second concentration camp, Auschwitz. The gas chambers of Auschwitz were the ultimate consequence of the theory that man is nothing but the product of heredity and environment—or, as the Nazi liked to say, of "Blood and Soil." I am absolutely convinced that the gas chambers of Auschwitz, Treblinka, and Maidenek were ultimately prepared not in some Ministry or other in Berlin, but rather at the desks and in the lecture halls of nihilistic scientists and philosophers.[9]

Frankl's belief that nihilism produced the Holocaust and that "man's search for meaning" offered a possible escape from it (he never lost sight of the role of luck) gave his personal story a powerful religious aura: it was a story of radical suffering and redemption through faith, not necessarily faith in God but, at the very least, faith in something greater than and outside of oneself. Such a story appealed to traditionally religious people and to those, like Frankl, who no longer practiced a specific religion but believed in a spiritual reality beyond the merely human. Christians were especially moved by Frankl's refusal to assign collective guilt to the Christian world for the destruction of European Jewry, an equanimity that struck some Jews, especially survivors, as inappropriate to the times. (His infrequent reference to the specifically Jewish element of the Nazi slaughter, along with his marriage to a Christian and a comfortable return to Vienna after the war, no doubt exacerbated the irritation of those who felt he had failed to own up to the catastrophic fate of his people.) Yet he had many Jewish as well as Christian advocates. Christian theologians could claim that "logotherapy offers a philosophy of life and a method of counseling which is more consistent with a basically Christian view of life than any other existing system in the current therapeutic world," while Leo Baeck considered Frankl's philosophy of meaning essentially Jewish, and a much younger contemporary, the Canadian Orthodox rabbi and self-help author Reuven Bulka, established a Jewish logotherapy based on the "kinship" between Judaism and Frankl's thought.[10]

By the end of the twentieth century, when the problem of despair among America's burgeoning population of aged people suddenly became a visible social problem, a whole new audience emerged for Frankl's belief that people could always find meaning in their lives. The nascent field of religious gerontology—pastoral therapy for the aged— drew considerable inspiration from logotherapy, which, "by emphasizing that a human being is not simply a psychosomatic organism . . . introduces an understanding of personhood which affirms one's capacity to find meaning in life in every stage of life, indeed, even in the midst of suffering and dying." Fifty years after Frankl's liberation from the concentration camps, when *Man's Search for Meaning* had sold ten million copies worldwide, his assessment of coping with moral evil translated easily to a problem of natural evil: the bodily degeneration of old age and the psychic malaise that often accompanies it.[11]

Yet the person who most embodied the Jewishness of the Holocaust was not Frankl, and not Anne Frank, but Elie Wiesel, whose memoir *Night* stood with *The Diary of Anne Frank* and *Man's Search for Meaning* as one of the most widely read of Holocaust narratives. Neither Frank—if only because of the tender age at which she was cut down—nor Frankl personified the specifically Jewish drama of the Holocaust as Wiesel did in a long career of poetic meditations heavily laced with motifs from his Hasidic background. A man whose face seemed to carry the full weight of sadness engendered by Auschwitz ("a face that has seen the worst that men can do to one another and . . . seems to be looking at you from a long way off, from 'the kingdom of night' "), and whose gestures and voice conveyed the sensibility of Lamentations, Wiesel served as a living touchstone of suffering and redemption, a "modern Job," as many perceived him, but a Job whose faith in God did not fully survive his ordeal. "His books speak for our suffering," the Jesuit magazine *America* observed; "though their message is sober, their very existence is a sign of hope." For many Americans, Wiesel represented the modern soul wrestling with God. "Strangely enough," he wrote for the *Christian Century* in 1981, "the child knew what the adult would not."

> Yes, in my small town somewhere in the Carpathian Mountains, I knew where I was. I knew why I existed. I existed to glorify God and to sanctify his word. I existed to link my destiny to that of my people, and the destiny of my people to that of humanity. . . . I knew that God was at the same time near and far, magnanimous and severe, rigorous and merciful. . . . I knew that I was in exile and that the exile was total, universal, even cosmic. I knew as well that the exile would not last, that it would end in redemption. . . . Now I no longer know anything.[12]

Wiesel's story, known to his many readers, is that of a devout young Jew born in 1928 in the Transylvanian town of Sighet, raised by intellectual parents who bought him books by Freud and Goethe, and enchanted by a Hasidic grandfather who told him tales of the great Hasidic rebbes. Deported with his family during Passover 1944, Wiesel emerged alone from the death camps a year later, lived in France and then Israel, where he worked as a journalist, and a decade after his liberation wrote a Yiddish manuscript about his ordeal. After extensive editing, that story, *Night*, appeared in French in 1958. Neither French nor American publishers in the late 1950s were enthusiastic about a memoir as harrowing as Wiesel's, but his agent in the United States, where Wiesel had taken up permanent residence, finally found a willing young publisher, Arthur Wang of Hill and Wang. The book appeared in 1960 and sold very slowly—slightly more than a thousand copies in its first year and a half. That soon changed. By 1997, when Bantam Books renewed its license for the book (paying Wiesel an advance in seven figures), *Night* was still selling 300,000 copies annually. Among Wiesel's many honors, he received the Congressional Gold Medal of Achievement in 1985 and the Nobel Peace Prize in 1986 for his eloquent concern about human rights across the world. His exquisite connection to the Holocaust made Wiesel an iconic figure. To American Christians he evoked images of Crucified Modern Man; to American Jews he became, in the words of theologian Eugene Borowitz, "the closest thing we have . . . to a superstar."[13]

Unlike Anne Frank, who wrote in her diary that "in spite of everything, I still believe that people are truly good at heart," and unlike Frankl, who insisted that one could choose life no matter how closely death loomed, Wiesel, in *Night*, gave his readers no reassurances about human nature or the possibility of spiritual transcendence—in fact, he forced them into a vicarious experience of his own suffering and despair. In 1974 scholar Lawrence Cunningham beautifully expressed the book's impact on contemporary thought. Observing that *Night* enacted a reversal of the book of Exodus, depicting a journey into bondage and despair rather than out of it, Cunningham suggested that Wiesel forced people "to see the grim visage of postmodern man: the possible death of history; the dying of persons, peoples and comfortable divinities. *Night* insists that the old order has been overturned and the form of the question has been radically changed. God may still live, but if He does, He has much to answer for."[14]

Wiesel's capacity to evoke the spiritual and theological crisis of the Holocaust had something to do with the translation of his story from an angrier Yiddish to a more sympathetic English version. In Yiddish Wiesel emphasized the destructive activities of outsiders: the murderousness of the Germans and their collaborators and the indifference of the rest of the gentile world. His title was *And the World Was Silent*, and his dedication was "to the eternal memory of my mother Sarah, my father Shlomo, and my dear little sister Tzipora, who were killed by the German murderers." In *Night*, however, that dedication became briefer and more detached: "In memory of my parents and my little sister, Tzipora." The Yiddish narrator said of one important character, "The murderers had left him for dead," whereas in English he switched to the passive voice—"he was taken for dead." The Yiddish version recalled the first invasion of Jewish homes in Wiesel's hometown: "We were lucky; in our house they only screamed and threatened, but in the homes of our neighbors they beat and tortured." But that detail is deleted from *Night*, in which the narrative focuses more exclusively on the thoughts and feelings of the victims. In Yiddish, when Wiesel spoke of his first night in Auschwitz, he declared that he would never forget the cremation of his mother and little sister, but in English the personal reference disappears and Wiesel laments more generally "the little faces of the children, whose bodies I saw turned into wreaths of smoke."[15]

Through such subtle changes, Wiesel distanced himself from the situation he describes, becoming more of an observer of humanity in general; he moved his readers away from his anger and toward his crisis of faith, away from the social causes of evil and toward the effects of evil on the individual psyche. The change in the book's title placed his personal crisis at the center of the narrative, because in the passage that introduces the metaphor of a spiritual "night" Wiesel also declares: "Never shall I forget that nocturnal silence which deprived me, for all eternity, of the desire to live. Never shall I forget those moments which murdered my God and my soul and turned my dreams to dust. Never shall I forget these things, even if I am condemned to live as long as God Himself."

By focusing not on the outer world of perpetrators but on the inner world of victims, on the trauma sustained by the human psyche under the worst conditions imaginable, *Night* established a new and mesmerizing model of psychic pain and survival. Wiesel brandished the image of the God-forsaken, damaged soul and at the same time suggested that, through the telling of his story, he would regain his soul, his sense of life-affirming meaning in a death-ridden universe. Through his storytelling, which included a continuing series of novels, memoirs, and essays, he thought he might restore some of the dignity to those Jewish victims whom God had apparently failed to protect.[16]

More than any other individual in the United States, Wiesel stimulated an outpouring of literature about the theological implications of the Holocaust, yet he knew himself to be a storyteller, not a philosopher or theologian, and he was generally perceived as the consummate narrator of the death and resurrection of the Jewish people. A 1978 volume devoted to Wiesel's impact on American understandings of the Holocaust noted that he, "more than any other single writer of the postwar years, educated this generation to the absolute need not only to remember but continually to confront the anguish and mystery of the Holocaust." Wiesel accomplished that feat by creating his own genre of midrash, stories that infiltrate his experience of the Holocaust with allusions to biblical, rabbinic, and kabbalistic motifs, often invoking the venerable Jewish concept of "quarreling" with God. An honorary doctorate bestowed on Wiesel by Manhattanville College in 1972 included the citation: "You celebrate the truth and magic of man's imagination, of his awesome power to tell stories." To his largely Catholic commencement audience that day, he emphasized the redemptive value of his stories. "My idea in my storytelling," he said, "is to make Jews better Jews, and Christians better Christians, and in general, if possible at all, make man a little warmer, so he will not feel crushed by his own solitude." That seemed to be the message that others received from Wiesel. "Wiesel's stories bring us to the heart of darkness, but they do not leave us in despair," wrote a reviewer for the evangelical magazine *Christianity Today.* "Wiesel is a contemporary Job, demanding a hearing, a contemporary Jacob, wrestling with God to understand, in the face of monstrous evil, the meaning of God's apparent silence. The outcome of Wiesel's struggle ought to concern every Christian."[17]

Wiesel's ability to turn storytelling into a method of spiritual healing or reconciliation hinged on his Hasidic background, from which he drew a deep love of imaginative and fantastic inspirational stories. "I would give much to be able to relive a Sabbath in my small town, somewhere in the Carpathian Mountains," Wiesel recalled in an effort to explain what could never be communicated about the Holocaust and what he must communicate. "The whiteness of the tablecloths, the blinking candle flames, the beaming faces around me, the melodious voice of my grandfather, the *Hasid* of Vizhnitz, inviting the angels of the Sabbath to accompany him to our home." Having unburdened himself of the pain of *Night*, Wiesel began to explore biblical, talmudic, and Hasidic stories as a way "to avoid painful subjects." "I recount the adventures of the Besht," he said, referring to Hasidism's founder, Israel Baal Shem Tov, "so as not to dwell on the end of his descendants." Wiesel told all sorts of Jewish stories in his many books, but his Hasidic renderings were particularly evocative to audiences seeking, after the 1960s, more emotionally driven types of religious devotion. They appealed "to young Jews looking for authenticity," but also to Christians. It was by writing "out of the particularity of his own Jewishness," Protestant theologian Robert McAfee Brown observed of Wiesel, that "he touches universal chords." That particularity centered on the Hasidism he imbibed from his grandfather. "Christians must approach, with profound gratitude," Brown wrote, the "strangely hopeful song that Eli Wiesel has recovered from his Hasidic childhood."[18]

After *Night*, Wiesel's most popular and enduring book was *Souls on Fire* (1972), a journey through the forest of legends and stories surrounding some of the greatest figures of Hasidism. *Souls on Fire* was the most accessible, appealing, and artfully crafted presentation of Hasidic lore to appear in the American market, a distinction that the book may still hold today. Where *Night* was a labor of necessity, in which Wiesel the storyteller had to use his literary skill to document human atrocities, *Souls on Fire* was a labor of love. In it, Wiesel could situate himself as a great Jewish storyteller among the greatest of Jewish storytellers, the Hasidim. Weaving a few childhood memories and brief meditations on the Holocaust into his literary portrait of the Hasidic masters, Wiesel offered his readers a vision of a vanished world that somehow remained alive, promising human redemption through the power of imagination rather than reason. "I can still hear my grandfather telling me," he wrote, " 'In the Besht's universe, no one felt left out.' . . . I can still hear my grandfather's voice: 'There will, of course, always be someone to tell you that a certain tale cannot, could not, be objectively true. That is of no importance; an objective Hasid is not a Hasid.' "[19]

In the concluding chapter of *Souls on Fire*, Wiesel tells of Rabbi Mena-chem Mendl of Kotzk, one of the most enigmatic and tormented of the Hasidic leaders and the one whom Wiesel sees as a link between a pre-Holocaust past and post-Holocaust future, a harbinger of hope for gener-ations born long after he has passed away. "A stranger in his own genera-tion," Wiesel relates, "Mendl of Kotzk seems to belong to ours; he could be our contemporary. His anger is our anger, our revolt reflects his." We meet Mendl, who left behind no possessions and no writings, through one of the strangest stories about him: A wintry Sabbath eve in the 1830s; a group of passionate disciples sit around the Sabbath table waiting for the Rebbe to begin the blessings over wine and bread; the Rebbe's mind seems far removed from the scene; his breath becomes short and halting, like that of a sick man; his eyes gaze into the Sabbath candles; time passes, he says nothing, his students become uneasy and then frightened; they wonder where their master is traveling in his mind; the waiting and the silence continue until, suddenly, Rabbi Menachem Mendl, his face filled with fury, throws his head back and . . . This is the end of the story; no one knows what happened next, except that, after he said whatever he said, he fainted, was carried to his quarters and fell into a bizarre depres-sion for the remaining twenty years of his life. Among the stories that exist about the secret happening of that Sabbath eve, one holds that, in reaction to a wave of pogroms, the Rebbe flew into a rage and roared, "I demand that justice be done, I demand that the Supreme Legislator obey his own Laws!"

Wondering about the trauma and withdrawal of Menachem Mendl of Kotzk, Wiesel asks: "Could he have foreseen that one hundred years after his retreat another fire would set the continent ablaze, and that its first victims would be Jewish men and women abandoned by God and by all mankind? Could it be that from that moment on he planned to fight fire with fire—attempting to prepare us, demanding that we be strong, intransigent, capable of resisting evil no matter what form it takes, the comfort of faith included; capable of resisting even God and the hope in God?" For Wiesel, the story of Menachem Mendl is a story of "throwing off despair through despair." Thanks to that anguished saint, Wiesel con-cludes, "we hear a voice and we know . . . that history is not deserted; somebody is there and he is calling us."[20]

In this and the other stories of *Souls on Fire*, Wiesel anchors reality in the psychic world of the Hasid, the God-intoxicated Jew who, according to some accounts, was capable of dancing and singing even at the thresh-old of the Nazi death camp or who, like Mendl of Kotzk, expressed a soul-encompassing defiance of evil in a less visible way. As Wiesel personi-fied the ultimate victim, his Hasidic ancestors represented the ultimate spiritual survivor because they possessed an unbreakable bond to God and life. As a reviewer for the Catholic magazine *Commonweal* expressed it, "*Souls on Fire* is a toweringly inspiring document of faith in man's inexplicable, yet unwavering capacity to begin again."[21]

In Wiesel and his tacit principle of therapeutic storytelling, we see how the Holocaust fit into the powerful psychotherapeutic sensibility of postwar America, a sensibility centered on the theme of psychic damage and restoration. This is not to say that Wiesel was not primarily addressing the problem of morality in his numerous books about the Holocaust—he was—and it is not to slight his moral activism as a spokesman for oppressed people worldwide, for which he received the Nobel Peace Prize. But the image of inextinguishable suffering he projected, and the longevity of *Night* and *Souls on Fire* over his other books, outweighed, in the end, the various moral questions raised in his many novels and his many speeches for human rights. That image led many to suppose "the Holocaust has left a scar that will remain imprinted on [the Jews] and their descendants until the end of time." He was, *TV Guide* reported in 1988, "a symbol of life and of hope," not of moral reckoning, an icon of damage whose suffering entitled him to a special hearing and whose Hasidic heritage seemed the only possible source of repair for evils inflicted by a heartless gentile world.[22]

To Americans reading *Night* in the 1960s, the motif of the long-suffering yet still hopeful victim had peculiar relevance because of the drama of the civil rights movement. *Night* awoke from its initial retail slumber between 1962 and 1964, the movement's peak years. By then, images of peaceful African American protestors being brutalized by mobs and policemen had entered the country's visual vocabulary. Those images, however, were soon accompanied by outbursts of long-repressed anger, the kind of anger over injustice that Wiesel had toned down as he edited his memories of Auschwitz for a non-Jewish audience in Europe and America. *The Autobiography of Malcolm X*, which appeared in 1965, forced its readers to answer difficult questions about their own past and present. Wiesel's questions, however, were sufficiently removed from the daily reality of Americans and sufficiently framed as universal questions about the human condition as to create a zone of comfort for the earnest reader. And, by the early 1970s, when revolts at home and war in Vietnam had stretched the American social fabric to a breaking point, *Souls on Fire* offered a romantic alternative vision out of the Hasidic past:

> *They knew how to worship. And trust. They had mastered the art of giving and receiving. Of sharing and taking part. In their communities, no beggar ever went hungry on Shabbat. In spite of their poverty, their misery, they asked nothing of others. And were endlessly surprised by and grateful for the smallest expression of warmth, of generosity. Therefore, they could not survive in a society ruled by cold cruelty, a cruelty both impersonal and absurd.*[23]

The Emergence of Hasidism in American Life

Souls on Fire reflected an American curiosity about Hasidism that waxed with the romanticism and humanism of the 1960s but first appeared a generation earlier, when Martin Buber's classic Hasidic tales were translated into English. The "Hebrew Humanism" of Buber and Fromm was rooted in a reverence for the Jewish alternative that these inquisitive and rebellious young thinkers saw in Hasidism. Rejecting the supreme rationalism of the older generation of modern, "enlightened" Jews, who regarded Jewish mysticism and Hasidism as aberrations, a younger generation followed the path indicated by Buber in his German presentations of the spirit of Hasidism: *The Stories of Rabbi Nachman* (1906), *The Legends of the Baal Shem* (1922), and *The Great Maggid and His Successors* (1922). Those works helped shape the conclusions of Fromm's 1922 doctoral dissertation on the sociology of Jewish law, which depicted Reform Judaism as a lifeless ideological substitute for baptism and exalted Hasidism as an authentic movement that radiated the social energy of the Jewish community, avoided dogmatism, and retained the legitimacy of Jewish law. In 1947 Schocken, the transplanted German Jewish publishing house, presented an American audience with its first taste of Buber's delightful *Tales of the Hasidim.* Buber's reading of Hasidism was highly personal. By highlighting the vivid, enigmatic, and wondrous legends of the Hasids (and separating them from the stringent orthodoxy of Hasidic life), he offered a modern public an indigenous Jewish antidote to the alienation of "modern man."[24]

The first mass exposure of Americans to Hasidism as a living force in their own society came with the publication of Chaim Potok's 1967 bestseller *The Chosen.* Like *Night*, Potok's novel was a coming-of-age story with a deeply Jewish content, and like Wiesel, Potok grew up in a Hasidic environment. The memorable character of Reb Saunders, the father of one of the two teenage boys at the heart of the story (presented to millions by the superb actor Rod Steiger in a 1982 movie adaptation), resembled the stormy and inspired figures that inhabited Buber's *Tales of the Hasidim* and Wiesel's *Souls on Fire.* Reb Saunders's son Daniel is a prodigy destined to succeed his father as the religious leader of their Brooklyn community, but Daniel, like Potok, had more worldly aspirations. Potok left the Hasidic fold of his immigrant parents to become a Conservative rabbi (a negligible position in the eyes of Hasidim) and to pursue his real goal of writing novels; Danny Saunders wants to become a psychologist and sneaks away whenever possible to the public library to bury himself in the writings of Freud. In the end, the conflict between father and son and between Hasidic and modern American ways resolves when Reb Saunders agrees to Danny's decision to attend Columbia University and acknowledges that his son can be a modern psychologist and an observant Jew at the same time.[25]

Potok's novel illustrated the effect that the postwar romance with psychology could have even on the most traditional sectors of the Jewish world, and it mirrored the actual story of a Hasidic rabbi from Milwaukee, Abraham Twerski, who became a psychiatrist and a significant writer of inspirational books for the general public. Twerski was part of a generation of rabbis who followed Joshua Liebman's lead into the mass market.

At first, in the 1950s and 1960s, rabbinic authors of mass-market inspirational books were, like Liebman, preachers of liberal Judaism. In *Man's Best Hope* (1961), Roland Gittelsohn, Liebman's successor at Temple Israel, echoed the rationalist message that religion had to "re-think" itself in terms of the scientific discoveries of Darwin, Einstein, and Freud, and castigated people who had "blind faith" in a religious doctrine. In a similar vein, Israel Chodos of Temple Sinai in Los Angeles urged Americans to *Count Your Blessings* (1955), a book that echoed Liebman's plea to Americans not to submit to philosophies of cynicism and despair and exhorted them to keep the spirit of rationalist idealism, fighting such social evils as prejudice and poverty. Like Rabbi Robert Kahn of Temple Emanu-El in Houston, who explained that his *Lessons for Life* (1963) derived from traditional Jewish texts, these authors distinguished themselves in the market by referring to the rabbinic tradition as a moral guidepost for modern people.[26]

By the 1990s, publishers had added Orthodox writers—including two towering figures in the Orthodox world, Rabbi Joseph Soloveitchik and the Lubavitcher Rebbe, Menachem Mendel Schneerson—to the field of rabbinic authors addressing a general American audience. And, despite the skepticism of those Jewish critics of Joshua Liebman who had claimed that traditional Judaism had nothing to learn from psychology, several important Orthodox authors of contemporary *musar* systematically incorporated insights from modern psychology into their thought. Abraham Twerski, the first and most prolific Orthodox rabbi to enter the American mass market, was one of them.[27]

Twerski's success as an inspirational writer reflected his ability to blend the folksy, homiletic style of Hasidism with the simple down-to-earth message of Alcoholics Anonymous. His adaptation of the Twelve Step self-improvement plan resembled the very first instance of the "Americanization" of *musar*, the use of Benjamin Franklin's chart of thirteen virtues in Menachem Mendel Lefin's *Accounting of the Soul.*

Abraham Twerski was born in 1930, one of five sons of Jacob Israel Twerski and Leah Halberstam, both of whom came from distinguished Hasidic families in Russia. Immigrating to the United States in 1927, the Twerskis settled in Milwaukee. Jacob served as rabbi of a local congregation there until 1939, when he established a new congregation, Beth Yehudah, in the family's home. Abraham was entranced by the procession of people who came to his father for advice and consolation, and he decided he wanted this kind of relationship with people himself. He recognized, however, that in America clergymen were no longer the sole dispensers of spiritual comfort. Dreading the prospect of being an overseer of ceremonial functions with little pastoral engagement, the younger Twerski resolved upon a different path. "If I had to become a psychiatrist to do what I had to do as a rabbi," he recalled, "then that's what I was going to do."[28]

Twerski's medical path led him into the "recovery" movement, which became, in the 1970s and 1980s, one of the most powerful self-improvement philosophies the country had ever seen. In 1959, after assisting his father for seven years and graduating from Marquette University Medical School, he left the pulpit to enter the University of Pittsburgh Western Psychiatric Institute, where he completed his psychiatric training in 1963. In 1972 Twerski founded the Gateway Rehabilitation Center in western Pennsylvania, a leading center for the treatment of drug and alcohol abuse. When his father died the following year and one of his brothers took the family pulpit, absolving Abraham of that responsibility, he expanded his psychiatric ministry. Twerski began writing self-help books in 1978 and ultimately produced more than twenty in this genre, some for a general audience, including several best-sellers, and some specifically for Jews. His adaptation of the Twelve Step formula for Orthodox (and other) Jews appeared in such books as *Living Each Day* (1988) and *Self-Improvement?—I'm Jewish!* (1995). His books for the mass market include *Like Yourself* (*and others will too)* (1978), *Self Discovery in Recovery* (1984), *Who Says You're Neurotic?* (1984), *When Do the Good Things Start?* (1988), *Waking Up Just in Time* (1990), *I'd Like to Call for Help, but I Don't Know the Number* (1991), *I Didn't Ask to Be in This Family* (1992), *Life's Too Short* (1995), *Addictive Thinking* (1997), and *That's Not a Fault: It's a Character Trait* (1999).[29]

In Twerski's books, alcoholism is often the backdrop for *musar*'s drama of good and evil impulses at war, of muddled self-justification defying clear-sighted self-awareness. Two acclaimed films of 1962, *Days of Wine and Roses* and *Long Day's Journey into Night*, riveted public attention on the fierceness and intractability of addiction. Twerski began practicing psychiatry the following year and quickly encountered the human wreckage of an alcohol- and drug-oriented culture. One of his earliest books, *Caution: 'Kindness' Can Be Dangerous to the Alcoholic* begins with a moving dedication to "Isabel," a woman whose story made a deep impression on Twerski: "As a first-year psychiatric resident, I was assigned to the walk-in clinic. One day a woman came in asking for help. The woman gave the high points of her history. When she was twenty-four, married, and with a baby, she was drinking so heavily that her husband asked for a divorce. Recognizing that she was not fulfilling her functions as a wife and mother, she gave her husband the divorce and custody of the child. Free of all restraints, she now indulged in alcohol even more heavily." Accustomed to the fiercely family-oriented world of Hasidism, the young Twerski must have been impressed by this woman's decision to abandon her child and husband in order to pursue the decadent pleasure of drinking. Making her story even more compelling, Isabel's degradation was a descent from the top of the social ladder.

> Even at sixty-one, when I first met her, Isabel was an attractive woman. She must have been stunning in her younger years, when she was much sought after as a companion, being wined and dined by the social elite. As the years went on and alcohol took its toll, Isabel's social life deteriorated drastically. Between the ages of thirty and fifty-seven, she had more than 65 hospitalizations for 'drying out.' her behavior had become so intolerable that her family eventually detached themselves completely from her, even refusing to respond to calls from the hospital. She made several token visits to Alcoholics Anonymous (AA), but she never took the program seriously. Eventually she ended up in the skid-row flophouses.

The tenacity of Isabel's bout with alcohol made her recovery mysterious and profoundly challenging to Twerski's sense of human existence. "At the time she consulted me, Isabel had been sober for four years. . . . Isabel's motivation for sobriety continued to elude me, and although I continued to see her until her death at seventy-four, I never did discover any specific reason for her turning her life around. All I can conclude is that within every person there is a nucleus of self-respect and dignity which, no matter how deeply concealed, exists obstinately."[30]

Perhaps evocative of the dramatic redemptionist mood of Hasidism, the story of Isabel drew Twerski into a world that redefined his understanding of human nature. Having stepped outside his father's Hasidic cloister, the younger Twerski brought his pastoral skills into the netherworld of alcohol and drugs. As he himself understood, he was confronting a situation of malaise amid affluence that increasingly defined American life in the postwar era. The descent of Isabel from wealth and prestige was a parable of American spirituality, which required individuals so often to handle not dire want but bewildering excess.

Twerski's encounters with alcoholics changed his understanding of human behavior. He was exposed to psychoanalysis in medical school but rejected it as a therapeutic method, preserving instead a fairly traditional conviction that immediate action had redemptive potential even without a sophisticated understanding of one's psychological problems. "Sometimes the best psychotherapy is when we are told to make some changes in our behavior," he advised, "instead of looking for deep-rooted sources for our problems." Yet Twerski decisively broke with an old-fashioned moralism that emphasized the stubborn will as the chief stumbling block to self-improvement. Not only did he grasp the biochemical nature of some behavior, but over time he realized that a logical critique was often useless in helping patients overcome self-defeating behavior rooted in self-deprecation. He ended up accepting the premise that psychological blocks were essentially involuntary and therefore tantamount to physical disabilities, though subject to remedy.[31]

Alcoholics Anonymous gave Twerski a vital framework in which to combine his psychiatric training and Hasidic background. AA was founded in 1935 by two alcoholics, both originally from Vermont, one a failed New York stockbroker and the other a doctor in Akron, Ohio. "Bill W.," the broker, was an ambitious man driven to prove his worth in the business world. He made a lot of money on Wall Street in the 1920s and lost it after the stock market crashed. His personal trajectory from stolid Yankee origins and a good marriage to a life of fast money, failed business, and drunken binges gave AA a foundational story that exposed the tragic consequences of the American dream for individuals without a spiritual grounding. At the moment when Bill W. bottomed out, he experienced a spiritual illumination that was reinforced by an intense reading of William James's observations on spiritual malaise and awakening in *The Varieties of Religious Experience.* Fortified philosophically by James and practically by a small network of recovering drinkers he met in Akron, Bill W. turned his conversion experience into weekly meetings with a group of fellow alcoholics in the parlor of his Brooklyn home. Four years after he and "Dr. Bob" founded Alcoholics Anonymous, the group published a book by that name which outlined the Twelve Steps for personal recovery.[32]

After vehement religious debates within the fledgling organization, in which conservatives demanded and liberals refused an explicitly Christian statement of belief, the Twelve Steps were formulated as a nonsectarian monotheistic creed. Focusing on man's ultimate and utter dependence on divine help, the first of the Twelve Steps recognizes the gravity of the alcoholic's problem, and the remainder delineate a careful agenda of moral and spiritual reformation.[33]

Derived from mainstream Christianity but tempered by a pragmatic, grass-roots ecumenicism, the Twelve Step program was the first spiritually focused organization to which Jews could belong without compromising their Judaism. The significance of the religious dynamic in Alcoholics Anonymous was captured in Abraham Twerski's comment that he discovered in AA meetings the kind of sincere and even selfless fellow-feeling that was often absent from synagogues. He was moved by the example of men and women who would willingly be awakened in the middle of the night to go out and help a fellow alcoholic. Recovering alcoholics, Twerski observed, "will often exhibit a sense of responsibility far superior to that of the non-alcoholic in relationship to their families, friends, and God." In the almost heart-rending existentialism of AA, Twerski saw a primordial religious experience, a dead reckoning with the helplessness and interdependence that define human life.[34]

He was attracted as well by the pragmatism of the Twelve Steps. With roots running back to the American Puritan tradition of rigorous self-examination and public spiritual testimony, the AA system offered a practical, nonanalytic therapy that resonated with traditional Judaism much more than conventional psychoanalysis did. With *musar*'s evil impulse, the *yetzer*, in mind, Twerski emphasized the

> important similarity between the Torah approach to behavior and the Twelve Step program approach. One does not enter into a discussion or argument with the *yetzer hara*. Whatever reasons you can propose for one position, the *yetzer hara* will give several logical reasons to the contrary. . . . When the Israelites received the Torah, they accepted it with the declaration of 'We will do and we will listen (understand).' The principle is stated here: First do as you are instructed, whether or not you understand why. After you have done what you are told, you may try to fathom why.[35]

Twerski's psychological orientation gives his thought an empathic quality and optimism typical of American inspirational writing in the postwar era, though foreign to classical *musar*. He focuses on the same theme that motivated Joshua Loth Liebman: the importance of self-acceptance. To grow and mature, he writes, "it is first necessary to realize that groundless assumptions of inadequacy are at the root of many of our problems. If we can only discover that we are really much better than we think we are, we may be able to enjoy a happier and more productive life." This insight was a foundation stone for Twerski, one he laid early in his career as an inspirational writer. His first book, *Like Yourself* (*and others will, too)*, contends that many psychological problems, aside from those with a biochemical cause, come from one major personality trait: negative self-image.[36]

Using the confessional format as a way of establishing emotional rapport with his readers, Twerski openly describes his own confrontation with unpleasant inner impulses and his all-too-human deduction that he must be an unworthy person to harbor such feelings. Beset by a crisis of self-esteem, Twerski explains to his American readers, he finally found an answer in the Talmud, which explained that people were given the commandments precisely because they were endowed with animal impulses. "The discovery of animalistic traits within myself," he explains to his readers, "was no reason for me to consider myself to be a 'bad' person."

> Many people are indeed incapable of tolerating themselves, because they harbor self-directed feelings of negativity. Their discomfort with themselves may be so great that they employ a variety of tactics, some of them quite drastic, to escape or to deny their identity as they perceive it. . . . These people are in actuality fine, competent, and likeable people. . . . Instead of seeing themselves as they really are, they somehow develop a distorted image of themselves, and it is this distorted image, *which they assume to be the real image*, that becomes intolerable.

Betty Ford acknowledged the accessible, nurturing tone of Twerski's writing. "Abe Twerski provides us with an understanding of our spiritual side," she wrote in praise of *I'd Like to Call for Help, but I Don't Know the Number.* "It's like a conversation with a warm and trusted friend."[37]

The challenges of adapting *musar* to the American mass market also stimulated Twerski to introduce a novel pictorial dimension into some of his most popular books: Charlie Brown and the other characters of Charles M. Schulz's *Peanuts* comic strip. Twerski became convinced of the therapeutic value of cartoon humor when he once tried in vain to convince a patient that he had a drinking problem. Finally, Twerski showed the man a few *Peanuts* comic strips with Charlie Brown missing the football time and time again but rationalizing that things were going to be different *this year,* rather than learning from his mistakes and trying to change. The patient was able to recognize his own weaknesses in the comic strip. "Charlie Brown had been able to reach this patient in a way that I could not," Twerski observed. "As a psychiatrist I appeared formidable and threatening. . . . However, Charlie Brown was innocent and harmless. . . . Insights that come from the patient rather than from the therapist are always more effective."[38]

Twerski viewed Charles Schulz as a sort of untutored genius whose insights into human nature wanted an explicitly psychotherapeutic expression. He recalled having said half-jokingly to Schulz, "I'm your Americus." The choice of words was fascinating, suggesting the image of the Hasidic Jew Americanizing an American cultural icon. Just as Vespucci perceived that America was not Asia, so Twerski, by recognizing the psychological value of Schulz's work, aimed to give it a new and redeeming significance. Of course, in the same moment that he recontextualized Schulz's humor, Schulz reshaped *musar,* crowning an adaptation to American mores that had begun nearly two centuries earlier in Lefin's *Accounting of the Soul.*[39]

The Holocaust and Hasidism in
Harold Kushner's Theology of Suffering

Although Twerski became an important figure in the world of recovery from addiction and his writings reached a sizable audience, including many Orthodox Jews, neither he nor any other rabbi gained an audience approaching that of Conservative rabbi Harold Kushner. After the success of *When Bad Things Happen to Good People,* Kushner had the midas touch, producing an unbroken series of best-sellers: *When All You Ever Wanted Isn't Enough* (1986), *Who Needs God?* (1989), *To Life!* (1993), *How Good Do We Have to Be?* (1996), and *Living a Life That Matters* (2001). Kushner was the Jewish inspirational writer par excellence, combining rabbinic knowledge and pastoral experience with a snappy intelligence, a provocative style, and the ability to distill theological ideas for the lay reader. Those qualities made him a real force in public conversation about the nature of humanity and divinity.[40]

Until 1981, Harold Kushner was a suburban rabbi little known outside his local community. The outline of his biography resembled that of many of his colleagues. He was born in 1935 in Brooklyn into a synagogue-going, middle-class family. His father, Julius, was a businessman, and his mother, Sarah (Hartman), was a teacher. Kushner earned a B.A. and M.A. from Columbia University and then enrolled in the Jewish Theological Seminary. Ordained in 1960, which was also the year he married Suzette Estrada, he spent two years as an army chaplain at Fort Sill, Oklahoma, before becoming a pulpit rabbi, first in Great Neck, New York, and then in Natick, Massachusetts, a suburb of Boston.

In 1963 the Kushners had their first child, Aaron, whose fate prepared the way for his father's. Aaron was diagnosed with progeria, a rare genetic disease that produces premature aging. He died when he was fourteen. As a pastor, Kushner had already grown uncomfortable with the platitudes that so often passed for wisdom to bereaved people. Assurances that "God wanted it this way" left him cold, and he found that his parishioners often blamed themselves for misfortunes that struck their loved ones. After Aaron's death, he resolved to do something for himself—to relieve his own suffering—and for others by writing a book to offer what he considered a much better and more compassionate explanation of tragic loss. "In addition to his full-time duties as rabbi in a suburban New England town," *Time* reported not long after the publication of *When Bad Things Happen to Good People,* "Harold Kushner has become rabbi to a nationwide congregation."[41]

A generation of Americans raised in the Bible would have been stirred by the quotation from the Book of Samuel that Kushner selected to accompany the dedication of *When Bad Things Happen to Good People.* "And David said: While the child was yet alive, I fasted and wept, for I said, Who knows whether the Lord will be gracious to me and the child will live. But now that he is dead, why should I fast? Can I bring him back again? I shall go to him, but he will not return to me." Kushner began with a sharply democratic, almost populist tone, as if to soothe the masses who had been let down by the theological dogma of their religious leaders: "This is not an abstract book about God and theology. It does not try to use big words or clever ways of rephrasing questions in an effort to convince us that our problems are not really problems, but that we only think they are. This is a very personal book, written by someone who believes in God . . . and was compelled by a personal tragedy to rethink everything he had been taught about God and God's ways." And thus, despite the familiarity of the biblical passage about David, Rabbi Kushner prepared his readers for a different and very unbiblical interpretation of God, a radical departure that he thought would disqualify the book from gaining the kind of success it quickly achieved.[42]

The overwhelming enthusiasm for his book shocked Kushner. *Redbook* published an excerpt in the fall of 1981 just before the Jewish New Year. When Kushner and his family returned home from High Holiday services, their phone was ringing continuously with calls from people who did not realize it was Rosh Hoshanah. "These were phone calls," Kushner recalled, "from people with problems," often suffering from tragedies of their own and questioning "long-held religious beliefs about the goodness or even the existence of God." A woman from Chicago whose son died of cancer wrote Kushner, "I hated and blamed God. But your book was the real turnaround in my mourning. You let me love the Lord again." A mother from Nevada who gave birth to a baby with Down syndrome wrote him, "You were the first person to express to me that I have a right to feel anger. Maybe now I can believe in a more realistic God." The *Redbook* article condensed some of the most riveting and poignant passages of Kushner's book:

> We all have read stories of little children who were left unwatched for just a moment and fell from a window or into a swimming pool and died. Why does God permit such a thing to happen to an innocent child? It can't be to teach a child a lesson about exploring new areas—by the time the lesson is over, the child is dead. Is it to teach the parents and baby sitters to be more careful? That is too trivial a lesson to be purchased at the price of a child's life. Is it to make the parents more sensitive, more compassionate people, more appreciative of life and health because of their experience? Is it to move them to work for better safety standards and in that way save 100 lives in the future? The price is still too high and the reasoning shows

too little regard for the value of an individual life. I am offended by those who suggest that God creates retarded children so that those around them will learn compassion and gratitude. Why should God distort someone else's life to such a degree to enhance my spiritual sensitivity?[43]

When Bad Things Happen to Good People was perhaps the most provocative work of theodicy ever written for a popular audience in America. Kushner took the traditional and vexing question—would a God who is both omnipotent and good allow the innocent to suffer?—and answered with a resounding "No." Outraged at the idea of a God who specifically determined all the fortunes and misfortunes of people, Kushner proposed instead a limited God who did not cause suffering but empathized with those who suffered. His was a God who set the world in motion according to natural laws and human freedom and had no power to alter those laws and that freedom. The water that nourishes us may also drown us; our freedom to do good assumes the possibility we will do bad. Those guidelines of the universe, not God's will, determine who lives and dies, who suffers and who escapes suffering. Therefore, Kushner argues, the question "Why did God do this to me?" is the wrong question, and to become angry with God for one's unmerited suffering makes no sense. Neither, he stressed, does it make sense for people to blame themselves for misfortunes beyond their control, to assume that those misfortunes are God's punishment, a retribution for something they did wrong or a chastisement to make them better people. They may choose to interpret their suffering as an opportunity to change something about themselves, but that is their choice rather than God's will. "It is so easy to make us feel that we are bad people," Kushner explains, "that it is unworthy of religion to manipulate us in that way."[44]

In his argument for a limited God, Kushner was actually reaffirming what Joshua Liebman and other liberal rabbis had been saying for years. In *Peace of Mind*, Liebman addressed the problem of evil and suffering and observed that his reading of the Prophets led him "to make [a] radical revision of my idea of God. At first it seems daring, if not heretical, for us to say that God is not omnipotent—that He, too, is limited. . . . If I did not believe that God is *limited* by the very nature of the world He created, then I would have to surrender my faith." Boston rabbi Roland Gittelsohn, in *Man's Best Hope* (1961), recommended Liebman's interpretation and agreed, "If God could change the past or abrogate the law of gravity . . . I could no longer believe in God. . . . I believe in a God of order, not one of caprice or whim." Liebman, Gittelsohn, and Kushner all considered it "childish" to think of God as a dispenser of personal favors or "an Oriental monarch," as Liebman put it, "to be bribed into overlooking violations of the principles upon which the earth and human society must rest." Liebman and Kushner were both influenced in this way by Mordecai Kaplan, who was Kushner's teacher at the Jewish Theological Seminary; Kaplan's God was even more impersonal than theirs.[45]

Though Kushner's limited God was not new, Kushner was the first rabbi to devote an entire book to that concept, making it a nearly un-avoidable part of all subsequent American discussions of the theology of evil and suffering. Like *Peace of Mind* years earlier, *When Bad Things Happen to Good People* generated a host of responses. The universality of the book impressed *Publishers Weekly*: "Kushner's book should be read by all people in trouble, no matter what their religious faith is or whether they have any faith in a deity at all." Kushner himself attributed some of the book's success to the support of liberal Protestant theologians and minis-ters who discussed it in their sermons, distributed it to their parishioners, and recommended it to funeral homes, which, as one Catholic priest observed, were "ordering the book by the gross." *The National Catholic Reporter* called the book a must for "every pastor's bookshelf and at every patient's bedside." "Not everyone will agree with all Kushner says," the paper observed, referring to Kushner's theology of a limited God, "but no one will be left unmoved by his compassion."[46]

That was probably a predominant view among Christian readers seek-ing the practical consolation and advice Kushner offered, but there were others less accommodating. The Jesuit magazine *America* rejected Kush-ner's humanism, his belief that everything that matters "begins and ends with this world" and depends on the ability of men and women to "give meaning" to events, rather than "find" the ultimate meaning inherent in a God-created universe. Writing for the *National Review* on "When Bad Things Happen to Good Religion," religious thinker Richard John Neuhaus also derided Kushner's "feel good" theology as "radically an-thropocentric," and, referring to Martin Buber, suggested that for Kush-ner "it seems very doubtful that there is any Thou there." Neuhaus echoed the Orthodox Jewish journal *Tradition*, which dismissed "Kush-nerism" as blind to Jewish doctrine, a mere "therapy . . . to make its clients feel good." Even some of Kushner's colleagues in Conservative Judaism stigmatized his limited God as an alien notion without basis in Jewish tradition.[47]

Despite the attempts of some critics to relegate Kushner to the back-lists of "pop" religious psychology, his analysis was thoughtful and urgent enough to become a reference point for American theologians dealing with theodicy, whether or not they accepted his argument. He forced a confrontation between a fundamental notion of traditional Judaism and Christianity—the presence of an omnipotent God—and the very real problems that notion presented to people in distress. After Kushner, who had done so much to democratize theodicy, giving the average person a way of thinking about God and evil, it was difficult for a spiritual leader to simply reiterate the old assurances about God's will for suffering humanity. Serious readers of Kushner recognized that he certainly was not promoting easy answers to make people feel better but, rather, that his writing conveyed a brooding existential concern about the ever-present possibility of despair in the face of a seemingly chaotic universe. Though he was not an original theorist, and did not pretend to be one, Kushner offered a credible refutation of the traditionalist idea of a "self-restricting" God, according to which an omnipotent Deity, capable of intervening at any time in human affairs, decides not to invade the realm of free moral choice. Precisely because Kushner is so intensely concerned about the nature of God, and intent on preventing people from falling into religious despair, he wants to consider what kind of God would have the power to stop the suffering of a child and not utilize it. Of course, there is more than one way of answering that question, but Kushner's is a credible option. As a pastor rather than a theologian, he learned from experience that many people were spiritually liberated once they realized they did not have to ask, "Why did God do this to me?"[48]

Although his young son's affliction inspired *When Bad Things Happen to Good People*, the Holocaust stood in the background of Kushner's theology of suffering. This was partly because the Holocaust had become a benchmark of theodicy by the 1980s. Previously, theologians dealing with the question of evil referred to the Lisbon earthquake of 1755 as the quintessential disaster wreaking havoc on innocent people (followed by fires and a flood of the Tagus River, the quake destroyed the city, killing tens of thousands of people). But "the paradigm evil event to which virtually all theodicists now refer," observed Christian philosopher Stephen Davis in 1981, "is the Holocaust, i.e., the murder of six million Jews and millions of others by the Nazis during World War II." Unlike the Lisbon earthquake, which signified natural evil, the Holocaust represents moral evil, a shift of considerable importance. "We twentieth-century people—with the advances in technology we have seen, with the rise of mass organization and totalitarian political ideologies–are acutely conscious of the tremendous power human beings have to inflict suffering on each other," writes Davis. The peculiar nature of the Nazi slaughter of innocents has created the epochal question: "Are there any theodicies . . . which are credible when they try to account for the Holocaust?"[49]

Since Harold Kushner's limited God is powerless to prevent people from doing harm to one another—to prevent that would be to eliminate moral freedom—the world bears the risk of murder on the scale of the Holocaust. "When people ask, 'Where was God in Auschwitz?' " Kushner writes, "my response is that it was not God who caused it. It was caused by human beings choosing to be cruel to their fellow men." For Kushner the Holocaust is the historical litmus test of God's nature: "I cannot make sense of the Holocaust by taking it to be God's will. Even if I could accept the death of an innocent individual now and then without having to rethink all of my beliefs, the Holocaust represents too many deaths, too much evidence against the view that 'God is in charge and He has His reasons.' I have to believe that the Holocaust was at least as much of an offense to God's moral order as it is to mine, or how can I respect God as a source of moral guidance?" If Kushner's God cannot prevent evil from occurring, then what can his God do? If his God is a "source of moral guidance," how so? The God that Rabbi Kushner does feel comfortable worshiping, the God he *can* recommend to other suffering people, is a God who places within people the capacity to feel compassion. Taking note of Christianity's conception of a God who suffers, and of the rabbinic idea of God suffering in exile with the people of Israel, Kushner acknowledges, "I don't know what it means for God to suffer. . . . But I would like to think that the anguish I feel when I read of the sufferings of innocent people reflects God's anguish and God's compassion. . . . I would like to think that He is the source of my being able to feel sympathy and outrage." On the most general level, Kushner expresses a conventional idea that people, in trying to "imitate" God's ways, would try to imitate the quality of mercy and lovingkindness that the Bible ascribes to God. But the idea of God as a source of empathy reflects a more specific neo-Hasidic trend in American Jewish thought.[50]

That trend is most closely associated with Abraham Joshua Heschel (1907–72), the most influential philosopher of Judaism after World War II and a formative figure in the Conservative movement to which Harold Kushner belonged. Outside Jewish and intellectual circles, Heschel was perhaps best known for his activism in the civil rights, antiwar, and interfaith movements of the 1960s. *Time* eulogized him as having "fused the Judaic strands of Abraham's mysticism and Joshua's militant vigor." But Heschel's literary talents also commended him to many, especially Jews seeking an inspired alternative to the perfunctory Judaism that Will Herberg exposed in the 1950s. His paean to the lost world of Jewish eastern Europe, *The Earth Is the Lord's* (1950), which shared the romantic tone of Buber's *Tales of the Hasidim* and Wiesel's *Souls on Fire,* and his extraordinary meditation on *The Sabbath* (1951) and its "architecture of time," revealed a writer whose poetic instincts flowed as well in English as in Yiddish, Hebrew, and German. The "genuinely precious is encountered in the realm of Time, rather than in Space," he wrote in his elegy to the vanished Jews of eastern Europe, whose "mixture of intellectualism and mysticism . . . is often bewildering to analytical observers." In *Man Is Not Alone* (1951) and *God in Search of Man* (1955), Heschel de-

scribed the experience of religious awareness with great aesthetic precision, accomplishing with language what he lacked in the way of systematic theology.[51]

Of exalted Hasidic lineage (his namesake, Abraham Joshua Heschel
of Apt, the Apter Rebbe, was one of the figures in Buber's *Tales of the
Hasidim*), Heschel, like Buber and Fromm, combined a German university education with deep learning in Jewish texts. Out of a yearning for
a spiritually passionate Judaism capable of meeting the demands of the
modern world, he created his own brand of neo-Hasidism. As a boy he
was exposed to and mesmerized by the legends and teachings of Menachem Mendl of Kotzk, the Hasidic master with whom Elie Wiesel identified in *Souls on Fire*. Heschel appreciated the Kotzker Rebbe's struggle
with depression and his radically individualist search for God beyond
the dictates of the commandments. Like Buber and Wiesel, Heschel left
Hasidism in order to extol its virtues. After his escape to America in 1940,
he affiliated not with Orthodoxy but with Conservative Judaism, which
allowed a more flexible interpretation of how to apply the traditional
commandments to modern conditions. The core of Heschel's neo-Hasidism was the mystical-ethical principle: "Not only is God necessary for us,
but we are for God. God acts through us."[52]

Heschel developed a "theology of pathos" in which God expresses concern for people's moral and spiritual welfare empathetically. In *Man Is
Not Alone* Heschel interpreted the sensibility of the Prophets (the subject
of his doctoral dissertation at the University of Berlin) as "the proclamation of the divine *pathos*."

> The Bible tells us nothing about God in Himself; all its sayings refer to
> His relations to man. . . . Zeus is passionately interested in pretty female
> deities. . . . The God of Israel is passionately interested in widows and or-
> phans. Divine concern means His taking interest in the fate of man; it means
> that the moral and spiritual state of man engages His attention. It is true
> that His concern is, to most of us, one of the most baffling mysteries, but it
> is just as true that to those whose life is open to God His care and love are
> a constant experience.

Heschel considered "man's relationship to God" not as a "passive reli-
ance upon His Omnipotence" but an "active assistance," and he talked
about prayer not as an activity in which God granted something but
rather as one in which the person praying gained the satisfaction of
"knowing that God shares our prayer."[53]

Those are the dominant themes in Harold Kushner's theology of consolation. Along with Mordecai Kaplan, Heschel was the dominant intellectual force at the Jewish Theological Seminary when Kushner studied
there in the late 1950s. The view of God and the Holocaust that eventu-

ally appeared in *When Bad Things Happen to Good People* was anticipated in *Man Is Not Alone*, where Heschel declared the responsibility of people, not God, for what happened at Auschwitz: "Does not history look like a stage for the dance of might and evil . . . and God either directing the play or indifferent to it? The major folly of this view seems to lie in its shifting the responsibility for man's plight from man to God." Kushner also echoed Heschel's theology of pathos, of God expressing divine capacity through emotions of compassion. Hence Kushner's statement that his own anguish over the suffering of innocents "reflects God's anguish and God's compassion," and his conviction that God supplies the moral instinct of men and women by being "the source of my being able to feel sympathy and outrage." When Kushner recommended the power of prayer, it was not to petition God to cure the sick but to grant the sufferer the consoling "knowledge that we are not alone, that God is on our side." And when he told his readers that one of their greatest sources of comfort in times of distress and sadness would be the sharing of their experience with others, he was conveying the essence of Heschel's neo-Hasidic principle: "Not only is God necessary for us, but we are for God. God acts through us." As Kushner himself expressed it: "God, who neither causes nor prevents tragedies, helps by inspiring people to help. As a nineteenth-century Hasidic rabbi once put it, 'human beings are God's language.' God shows His opposition to cancer and birth defects, not by eliminating them or making them happen only to bad people (He can't do that), but by summoning forth friends and neighbors to ease the burden and to fill the emptiness."[54]

In American popular culture, the Holocaust and Hasidism became symbols of suffering and redemption and, as such, provided a powerful backdrop for Harold Kushner's American theodicy. Kushner's controversial interpretation of evil brought together several different trends of American and Jewish thought: (1) the deeply rationalist perspective that had been a trademark of modernized Jews in Europe and America since the nineteenth century; (2) the charismatic neo-Hasidism associated with Martin Buber, Elie Wiesel, and Abraham Joshua Heschel; (3) a view of the Holocaust as the quintessence of evil, the litmus test for modern theodicies; and (4) American receptivity to psychologically focused, therapeutic forms of spiritual experience.

When Bad Things Happen to Good People also fit into a larger trend among Jewish interpreters of human nature that dated back nearly a century to Boris Sidis's warnings about the evil of irrational mob violence. Sidis hoped to defy evil by exposing its psychological roots, whereas Kushner, like Viktor Frankl and Elie Wiesel (and Abraham Twerski), wanted to defy it by inspiring people with a countervailing will-to-life. Sidis worried about pogroms under the Tsar; Kushner meditated upon the significance of Hitler's ultimate pogrom. Both the psychologist and the rabbi, and the array of Jewish thinkers and writers who came between them, hoped that, by affecting American beliefs about the mysterious workings of the mind and soul, they might make Americans more resistant to that evil urge, the *yetzer,* which stood poised at every moment to unleash the chaos of human destructiveness.

Conclusion

MODERN AMERICAN IDEAS of human nature, as we have seen in the preceding pages, developed out of complicated interactions among a wide array of men and women, some secular, others religious, some of Jewish origin, many of Protestant background, and others raised Catholic. By focusing on Jewish figures here, we have glimpsed an important and neglected part of that story but certainly not the whole story.

We are like the viewer of that curious drawing used to illustrate the quirks of human perception (a reversible figure-ground drawing), in which a white vase appears against a black background or two black profiles face each other against a white background.[1] While fixing on one image we cannot fully access the other. In order to focus on the Jewish presence in this history of American thought and culture, we have had to place some Christian presences in the background even as we emphasized others. In reality, neither Jewish nor Christian perspectives have existed in isolation, and "the Christian presence" itself contains many internal variations, not least of which is the historic tension between Protestants and Catholics, which did not really subside in the United States until the 1960s. A book of a thousand pages would not do justice to the complex intellectual and cultural engagements behind modern American understandings of the human condition.

Hopefully we will soon have more histories of ideas about the mind and soul that are able to reflect the country's ever-growing ethnic and religious diversity and to clarify the subtle ways in which ideas move into the mainstream from more remote or exclusive sources. It has gone without saying in this account that "thinkers" comprise not only those geniuses who are capable of producing bold new concepts of human existence but also, and perhaps even more important, men and women whose careers take them into the popular arena, the mass market of ideas. Unless we want to confine ourselves to the history of scholars and intellectuals, we cannot afford to overlook figures such as Joshua Liebman and Joyce Brothers who, though often ignored or disdained by scholars and intellectuals because of their popularity, served a vital function as distillers of psychological and theological ideas for the man and woman on the street. If we learn anything from the story told here, it is that the history of American ideas about human nature is not a rarefied history confined to the dense bookshelves of the most extraordinary thinkers. It is a story of constant flow between academic knowledge and the mass media, and of ethnic and religious tensions that expand, contract, and fluctuate with the crises of each generation.

More specifically—and we cannot emphasize this point enough—we have seen that the emergence of America's powerful psychological or "therapeutic" culture was not simply a secularization of a once-Protestant society or a shift away from the Protestant work ethic toward a "culture of narcissism." Beneath the great shift in American culture toward psychological evaluations of human conduct was a dynamic interaction between Jews and Christians and a dynamic tension between Jewish and Christian values.

Sometimes that tension turned on alliances between secular or liberal thinkers of Jewish and Protestant background—a William James and a Boris Sidis, a Carl Rogers and an Abraham Maslow—rebelling against religious dogmas and prejudices to create a more cosmopolitan and humanist America. But even within those liberal alliances, important differences between Jewish and Christian values appeared, as they did between Joshua Liebman and Norman Vincent Peale, those great liberal preachers of the postwar years. (And, we must remember that Jews debated among themselves—as in the Herberg-Liebman and Harold Kushner controversies—as to what represented Jewish values.) Sometimes Jewish-Christian tension appeared in a classic confrontation of popular theologies, like that between a Jewish *Peace of Mind* and a Catholic *Peace of Soul*, and sometimes it registered in the very different paths chosen by a Clare Luce and a Joyce Brothers. Often, apprehension about ethnic stereotypes (the "moronic" immigrant and the "neurotic" Jew) and irrational mob violence shaped Jewish contributions to popular psychology, much as Jewish doctrines of human partnership with God and human "relatedness" to one another reshaped what had once been a thoroughly Christian and Protestant conversation about the human condition.

It should give us pause to realize that *Peace of Mind*, which heralded the postwar fascination with "self-acceptance" (that great bull's-eye for critics of American narcissism), also introduced elements of the venerable *musar* tradition of self-discipline and vaunted the precept of "loving one's neighbor as oneself." Old simplifications about a massive twentieth-century "decline" from solid Protestant values of hard work and self-denial to flimsy values of selfishness must be measured against a much more historically sophisticated view, one that registers the religious and ethnic complexities behind changes in American values and can accommodate the fact of conflicting "love of self" and "love of neighbor" impulses in postwar culture.

The continuing activity of Jews as public moralists, whether they speak as rabbis, psychologists, philosophers, journalists, or creative writers, represents an important story line in the history of the modern psyche, and one that has not diminished after several generations of assimilation in America. A case in point: journalist Wendy Kaminer, one of the most visible critics of American popular psychology and religion at the end of the twentieth century. A third- or fourth-generation secular American Jew who came of age in the late 1960s, Kaminer has produced social criticism with an unmistakable Jewish edge. In *I'm Dysfunctional, You're Dysfunctional* (1992), she ridiculed the excesses of self-help psychology and theology, including such Jewish practitioners as EST founder Werner Erhard (Jack Rosenberg), but she did so with a vigilant eye for Christian valences in pop psychology. She found those antisemitic at worst and morally escapist at best.

Though generally dismayed by authors of inspirational books, Kaminer approved of Rabbi Harold Kushner, and echoed both his and Joshua Liebman's complaint about traditional Christian messages of personal submission: "I still can't help worrying about the public impact of a mandate to submit, which appears in its simplest, most vulgarized form in much popular religious literature." She liked the way Kushner, like Liebman before him, "qualifies the ideal of self-surrender with self-reliance—with the image of Moses walking up Mount Sinai." In a subsequent book, *Sleeping with Extra-Terrestrials* (1999), Kaminer proved herself a successor to Joseph Jastrow, writing as an agnostic Jew on a crusade to debunk irrationalism and mysticism, with a special lance leveled at Christian sources of those twin evils. In the garb of the 1990s Kaminer espoused the Jewish rationalist moralism that had been the trademark of Jastrow and his comrades at the century's beginning (she even shared their fondness for the values of John Dewey, who had become obsolete to most people of her generation).[2]

But by Kaminer's time, the spectrum of spiritual tastes among American Jews was much wider than it had ever been before. Varieties of Hasidism and neo-Hasidism, as we have seen, achieved a surprising prominence in America. Jewish mysticism did a booming business in the 1990s, when Kabbala became a choice item in America's transcendental grabbag. The charm of Eastern spirituality, especially Buddhism, worked powerfully on American Jews—"BuJews"—who were overrepresented as both practitioners and abbots in the United States. Healing rituals of all kinds, including good old-fashioned magic, swept up Jews along with everyone else in a fin-de-siècle explosion of therapeutic religious ceremonies. And the Jewish Renewal movement, which mixed neo-Hasidism with the sensibility of the sixties' counterculture, built the psychotherapeutic ideal of spiritual "healing" into its very structure. By the 1990s so many American rabbis and laypeople were writing inspirational books about Judaism and spirituality that a separate publishing house, Jewish Lights, emerged to specialize in the genre. To catalogue the varieties of American Jewish religious experience at the turn of the twenty-first century would require a book in itself.

Jewish inspirationalists, Orthodox and otherwise, remain as popular as ever—witness the success of journalist Mitch Albom's *Tuesdays with Morrie* (1997) and Hasidic rabbi Shmuley Boteach's *Kosher Sex* (1999), among other titles. "Dr. Ruth" Westheimer has enjoyed a long career as a high-profile sex therapist, and Dr. Joyce Brothers has continued to receive calls for interviews on everything from the tragedy of September 11 to the press's treatment of singer Michael Jackson. In the popular apocalyptic movie *Independence Day* (1996), a Jewish character not only provides the genius necessary to save the world from destruction but, when the end seems near, his father dons a yarmulke and offers consolation to a properly ecumenical group of Americans by reading from a Jewish prayer book.

We conclude, then, with an awareness that the story of American ideas about the mind and soul is one in which Jews have been central actors rather than exotic, peripheral characters. To interpret the modern history of American thought, faith, and culture as an exchange between Jewish and Christian values, rather than a linear development out of a Protestant heritage, is to add a vital and energizing complexity to our national self-understanding. A civilization so rich in ethnic and religious nuances demands no less.

Notes

INTRODUCTION. JEWS AND THE AMERICAN SOUL

1. We are fortunate to have an extremely rich historical literature on the Protestant context of modern American ideas about human nature. See, for example, Donald Meyer, *The Positive Thinkers: A Study of the American Quest for Health, Wealth and Personal Power from Mary Baker Eddy to Norman Vincent Peale* (New York, 1965); Richard Weiss, *The American Myth of Success: From Horatio Alger to Norman Vincent Peale* (Urbana, 1969); John Owen King III, *The Iron of Melancholy: Structures of Spiritual Conversion in America from the Puritan Conscience to Victorian Neurosis* (Middletown, Conn., 1983); E. Brooks Holifield, *A History of Pastoral Care in America: From Salvation to Self-Realization* (Nashville, 1983); Robert C. Fuller, *Americans and the Unconscious* (New York, 1986); John C. Burnham, *How Superstition Won and Science Lost: Popularizing Science and Health in the United States* (New Brunswick, 1987); James Hoopes, *Consciousness in New England: From Puritanism and Ideas to Psychoanalysis and Semiotic* (Baltimore, 1989); and Ann Taves, *Fits, Trances, & Visions: Experiencing Religion and Explaining Experience from Wesley to James* (Princeton, 1999). See Chapter 5 for additional references to historical literature citing the Protestant background of secular psychological theories.

2. I have addressed aspects of this subject in several articles: Andrew R. Heinze, "Jews and American Popular Psychology: Reconsidering the Protestant Paradigm of Popular Thought," *Journal of American History* 88 (December 2001), 950–78; "*Peace of Mind* (1946): Judaism and the Therapeutic Polemics of Postwar America," *Religion and American Culture* 12 (Winter 2002), 31–58; "*Schizophrenia Americana*: Aliens, Alienists and the 'Personality Shift' of Twentieth-Century Culture," *American Quarterly* 55 (June 2003), 227–56; "Clare Boothe Luce and the Jews: A Chapter from the Catholic-Jewish Disputation of Postwar America," *American Jewish History* 88 (September 2000), 361–76; and "The Americanization of *Mussar*: Abraham Twerski's Twelve Steps," *Judaism* 48 (Fall 1999), 450–69.

3. Thematically, this book stands in the middle of a large intersection. It focuses on subjects at the heart of intellectual and religious history—the dialectic between theological and psychological, and Jewish and Christian, perspectives on self and society; cultural history—the development of a mass market of inspirational and self-help literature; immigration and ethnic history—the dynamics of assimilation and acculturation, and public definitions of race; and Jewish history—the problem of interpreting secular Jewish intellectuals and defining Jewish theological adaptation in modern societies.

4. In a few cases I was unable to determine whether a historical figure was Jewish. I suspected, but was unable to prove, that two psychologists who wrote

for the general public, David Harold Fink and Abraham Sperling, were Jews. Fink wrote a pair of best-sellers, *Release From Nervous Tension* (1943) and *People Under Pressure* (1956), and Sperling wrote *Psychology for the Millions* (1946) and *Psychology Made Simple* (1957). With the help of Ms. Cheri Gay of the Detroit Public Library, I was able to determine that Fink grew up in or near a Jewish area of Detroit. And Fink married a woman whose last name, Zimmerman, is often Jewish, but those facts were insufficient to establish a Jewish identity. Sperling grew up in New York City and taught at City College, but City College archival material did not reveal much else about his background. For her assistance, thanks to Ms. Sydney Van Nort, archivist at the Morris Raphael Cohen Library of City College. On Fink (b. 1894), who died with his fifty-five-year-old wife, Ruth, in an apparent double-suicide in their home in Carmel, California, see the obituaries in the *Monterey Herald*, July 22, 1968; and *Carmel Pine Cone*, August 1, 1968. See also *San Francisco Chronicle*, March 11, 1956, p. 24.

5. Albert Einstein, *Out of My Later Years* (New York, 1950), 249.

6. In the 1980s historian David Hollinger boldly addressed the problem of how to analyze the thought of America's secular Jewish intellectuals. Hollinger pointed out that "a persistent inhibition," based on a legitimate desire to avoid ethnic stereotyping, had kept scholars from investigating the ways in which Jewishness may have figured into what those intellectuals chose to write and talk about. See David A. Hollinger, *In the American Province: Studies in the History and Historiography of Ideas* (1985; Baltimore, 1989), 56, 58–73. Those pages reproduce Hollinger's innovative 1975 article on the subject: David A. Hollinger, "Ethnic Diversity, Cosmopolitanism, and the Emergence of the American Liberal Intelligentsia," *American Quarterly* 27 (May 1975), 133–51. See also David A. Hollinger, "Jewish Intellectuals and the De-Christianization of American Public Culture in the Twentieth Century," and "The 'Tough-Minded' Justice Holmes, Jewish Intellectuals, and the Making of an American Icon," in David A. Hollinger, *Science, Jews, and Secular Culture: Studies in Mid-Twentieth-Century American Intellectual History* (Princeton, 1996), 17–59.

CHAPTER 1. JEWS AND THE PSYCHODYNAMICS OF AMERICAN LIFE

1. Edwin Tenney Brewster, "Dreams and Forgetting: New Discoveries in Dream Psychology," *McClure's* 39 (October 1912), 714–19; *Philadelphia Inquirer*, May 15, 1910. See also *Chicago Evening Post*, March 3, 1911; *Providence Journal*, August 14, 1910; *Boston Transcript*, April 30, 1910; *Louisville Courier*, May 14, 1910; *Baltimore Sun*, June 1, 1910; *San Francisco Call*, July 3, 1910; *Pittsburgh Gazette-Times*, October 26, 1910; *Springfield Republican*, February 13, 1911; and *New Orleans Picayune*, March 19, 1911.

2. Robert L. Gale, "Samuel Sidney McClure," in *American National Biography*, 24 vols. (New York, 1999), 14:887–89.

3. Herbert Nichols, "The Psychological Laboratory at Harvard," *McClure's* 1 (October 1893), 409; "Professor Münsterberg is a wizard" comes from the editor's note attached to Hugo Münsterberg, "Why We Go to the Movies," *The Cosmopolitan* 60 (December 1915), 22.

4. I. Zangwill, " 'Incurable.' A Ghetto Tragedy," *McClure's* 1 (November 1893), 478.

5. *Encyclopaedia Britannica; or a Dictionary of Arts and Sciences, Compiled upon a New Plan*, 3 vols. (Edinburgh, 1771), v. 3, p. 618; and *Webster's Third New International Dictionary of the English Language Unabridged* (Springfield, Mass., 1993), 1832.

6. Eliza Chester, "Training the Will," in *Ideal Home Life*, ed. Hamilton Wright Mabie (Philadelphia, 1909), 85–86.

7. James Allen, *As a Man Thinketh* (New York, n.d.), 30, 90–91. This booklet was published by the Little Leather Library Corporation, probably between 1900 and 1910. Allen wrote a number of books in the genre of New Thought, which will be discussed later in this book.

8. Robert Baird, *Religion in America; or, an Account of the Origin, Relation to the State, and Present Condition of the Evangelical Churches in the United States with Notices of the Unevangelical Denominations* (New York, 1856), 568; and John Frost, *The Pictorial Family Encyclopedia of History, Biography and Travels* (New York, 1856), 329–35.

9. Isaac Leeser, "The Jews and their Religion," in *An Original History of the Religious Denominations at present existing in the United States, Containing authentic Accounts of their Rise, Progress, Statistics and Doctrines written expressly for the work by eminent Theological Professors, Ministers, and Lay-Members, of the respective Denominations*, ed. I. Daniel Rupp (Philadelphia, 1844), 351.

10. John Watson, "The Life of the Master," *McClure's* 15 (May 1900), 11, 14.

11. Lester F. Ward, *The Psychic Factors of Civilization* (Boston, 1893), 105; and R. Travers Herford, *Pharisaism: Its Aim and Its Method* (New York, 1912), v–vi, 59, 333.

12. The stories of Mrs. L., who is so named, and Mr. M., whom I named for convenience, are found in H. Addington Bruce, "The Marvels of Dream Analysis," *McClure's* 40 (November 1912), 113–19, with quotations from pp. 115, 116, 119. The full account of Mrs. L. may be found in A. A. Brill, *Psychanalysis: Its Theories and Practical Application* (Philadelphia, 1913), 85–95; the quotation is from p. 93.

13. H. Addington Bruce, "Stammering and Its Cure," *McClure's* 40 (February 1913), 96; H. Addington Bruce, "Lightening Calculators: A Study in the Psychology of Harnessing the Subconscious," 39 (September 1912), 586–96; and Brewster, "Dreams and Forgetting," 715.

14. Burton J. Hendrick, "The Jewish Invasion of America," *McClure's* 40 (March 1913), 125–65, with quotations from pp. 125, 163, 165. A comment should be made here about this writer for *McClure's*. Burton J. Hendrick, who twice won the Pulitzer Prize for biography in the 1920s, was an important though sometimes troubling writer on Jews in America. Often dismissed as antisemitic, his writings were more complicated than that stigma suggests. His 1923 brief for immigration restriction, *The Jews in America*, contains some standard stereotypes about "the Jewish race" and is clearly biased against eastern European Jews (though not against Sephardic and German Jews, whom he praises). On the other hand, one of the book's explicit purposes is to rebut the antisemitism that had cropped up after World War I and which he characterizes as a blight on American civilization. Hendrick squarely denounces the propaganda of "Jewish

domination" spread by Henry Ford and others, and documents the falsehood of charges about Jewish control of business and finance. See Burton J. Hendrick, *The Jews in America* (New York, 1923).

15. For the beginning of Cahan's serialization, corresponding roughly to the first four chapters of the complete novel, but with textual differences, see Abraham Cahan, "The Autobiography of an American Jew: The Rise of David Levinsky," *McClure's* 40 (April 1913), 92–106. Subsequent installments appeared in the May, June, and July issues.

16. Ray Stannard Baker, *The Spiritual Unrest* (New York, 1910), 119; and Ray Stannard Baker, *New Ideals in Healing* (New York, 1908), v–vi.

17. Baker, *New Ideals in Healing*, 27.

18. Ibid., 62, 64, 68–69. On Cabot, see Sanford Gifford, "Medical Psychotherapy and the Emmanuel Movement in Boston, 1904–1912," in *Psychoanalysis, Psychotherapy and the New England Medical Scene, 1894–1944*, ed. George E. Gifford, Jr. (New York, 1978), 106–8.

19. Cabot is quoted in Barbara Miller Solomon, *Ancestors and Immigrants: A Changing New England Tradition* (1956; Chicago, 1972), 145. The myths and realities of Jewish nervous disorders are discussed above in Chapter 7, "The Moronic Immigrant and the Neurotic Jew." Abraham Brill noted that many foreigners were institutionalized in the early 1900s simply because the psychiatric personnel could not understand them. See his lecture to the staff of the New Jersey State Hospitals of Marlboro, Trenton, and Skillman: A. A. Brill, "The Broader Aspects of Psychiatry," lecture, Marlboro, New Jersey, October 15, 1946, folder "Lectures, 1946," box 11, Abraham A. Brill Papers, Manuscript Division, Library of Congress.

20. Elwood Worcester, Samuel McComb, and Isador H. Coriat, *Religion and Medicine: The Moral Control of Nervous Disorders* (New York, 1908), 154–55.

21. Baker, *New Ideals in Healing*, 75–77.

22. William James, *The Principles of Psychology*, 2 vols. (New York, n.d.), 1:379. This edition is the Dover unabridged and unaltered republication of the original 1890 text published by Henry Holt and Company. For background on the emergence of dual personality ideas in European and American psychology around the turn of the century, see Adam Crabtree, *From Mesmer to Freud: Magnetic Sleep and the Roots of Psychological Healing* (New Haven, 1993), 283–306; and Alan Gauld, *A History of Hypnotism* (Cambridge, 1992), 363–418. For the motif of the "double" and split personality in European and American literature during this period, see Karl Miller, *Doubles: Studies in Literary History* (Oxford, 1985); and John Herdman, *The Double in Nineteenth-Century Fiction: The Shadow Life* (New York, 1991).

23. Boris Sidis, *The Psychology of Suggestion: A Research into the Subconscious Nature of Man and Society* (1898; New York, 1916), 224. For a detailed account of the Hanna case, see Boris Sidis and Simon P. Goodhart, *Multiple Personality: An Experimental Investigation into the Nature of Human Individuality* (New York, 1905), 83–226. For the Beauchamp case, see Morton Prince, *The Dissociation of a Personality* (New York, 1905); and Nathan G. Hale, Jr., *Freud and the Americans: The Beginnings of Psychoanalysis in the United States, 1876–1917* (New York, 1971), 117–21.

24. *Boston Sunday Herald*, August 26, 1906. The story of Susan Norris first appeared in the *Boston Herald*, August 2, 1906, under the striking headline: "Woman Exhibits Three Identities." Isador Coriat researched the Norris case as a contribution to the pathology of memory; see Isador H. Coriat, "The Lowell Case of Amnesia," *Journal of Abnormal Psychology* 2 (August-September, 1907), 93–111.

25. John Higham, *Send These to Me: Immigrants in Urban America* (Baltimore, 1984), 175, 197. Higham lays out this line of argument in the essay "Integrating America: The Problem of Assimilation," 175–97.

26. Theodore Roosevelt to Hugo Münsterberg, January 19, 1916, Hugo Münsterberg Papers, Rare Books and Manuscripts, Boston Public Library. (Roosevelt and Münsterberg began corresponding in 1901.) On the hyphenated Americanism phenomenon, see John Higham, *Strangers in the Land: Patterns of American Nativism, 1860–1925* (1955; New York, 1974), 198–200, 234–63.

27. For the quote from the congressional report, see Elizabeth Lunbeck, *The Psychiatric Persuasion: Knowledge, Gender, and Power in Modern America* (Princeton, 1994), 123. The original source is Harry H. Laughlin, "Analysis of the Metal and the Dross in America's Modern Melting Pot," in U.S. Congress, House Committee on Immigration and Naturalization, *Hearings*, 67th Cong., 3rd sess., November 1922.

28. Thomas W. Salmon, "Immigration and the Mixture of Races in Relation to the Mental Health of the Nation," in William A. White and Smith Ely Jelliffe, *The Modern Treatment of Nervous and Mental Diseases*, 2 vols. (Philadelphia, 1913), 1:258, 275.

29. Edward Alsworth Ross, *The Old World in the New* (New York, 1914), 285–87, 299. Ross was not unerringly pejorative. A few years later, as the nativist movement was reaching a peak, he took a much milder tone toward immigrants in *What Is America?* That book noted the good and bad effects of the new immigration but primarily pointed out the problem that comes from the isolation of ethnic enclaves and the importance of the new Americanization movement for encouraging immigrants to participate more fully in American institutions. See Edward Alsworth Ross, *What is America?* (New York, 1919). For an interpretation of Ross as a key figure in the development of liberal but racialist social science, see Dorothy Ross, *The Origins of American Social Science* (Cambridge, 1991), 229–40.

30. On adjustment psychology, see Donald S. Napoli, *Architects of Adjustment: The History of the Psychological Profession in the United States* (Port Washington, N.Y., 1981).

31. William I. Thomas and Florian Znaniecki, *The Polish Peasant in Europe and America*, 2 vols. (1918–21; New York, 1958), 2:1469, 1476.

32. Psychological concepts attain different degrees of credibility and popularity in different societies. Philosopher Ian Hacking has charted the rise and fall of such classifications as multiple personality, suggesting why a given classification flourishes in certain times and places and not in others, and how that classification might affect the ways in which individuals and groups interpret themselves and others. See Ian Hacking, *Rewriting the Soul: Multiple Personality and the Sciences of Memory* (Princeton, 1995); *Mad Travelers: Reflections on the Reality of Transient*

Mental Illnesses (Charlottesville, 1998); and *The Social Construction of What?* (Cambridge, Mass., 1999).

33. W.E.B. Du Bois, *The Souls of Black Folk* (1903; New York, 1989), 3; and Dickson D. Bruce, Jr., "W.E.B. Du Bois and the Idea of Double Consciousness," *American Literature* 64 (June 1992), 299–309. Du Bois first wrote about Negro double consciousness in a magazine article in 1897. On the theme of dual identity in African American literature, see Eric J. Sundquist, *To Wake the Nations: Race in the Making of American Literature* (Cambridge, Mass., 1993), 564–77. For an analysis of "doubleness" in American ethnic literature and of Du Bois, Horace Kallen, and Randolph Bourne as theorists of a new kind of integrated American identity, see Werner Sollors, *Beyond Ethnicity: Consent and Descent in American Culture* (New York, 1986), 249–54, 174–207.

34. Abraham Cahan, "The Autobiography of an American Jew: The Rise of David Levinsky," *McClure's* 40 (April 1913), 92–93; and Abraham Cahan, *The Rise of David Levinsky* (1917; New York, 1960), 3.

35. Mary Antin, *The Promised Land* (1912; New York, 1997), 1–3. In his introduction to this edition, Werner Sollors calls Antin's portrait "remarkable . . . in the detailed psychological observations that she makes about her own development."

36. Horace M. Kallen, "Democracy Versus the Melting-Pot: A Study of American Nationality," *The Nation* (February 18, 1915), 193–94. For a concise background on Kallen's pluralism, see Higham, *Send These to Me*, 205–15; and Susanne Klingenstein, *Jews in the American Academy, 1900–1940: The Dynamics of Intellectual Assimilation* (1991; Syracuse, 1998), 34–50.

37. Boris Sidis, *The Psychology of Suggestion: A Research into the Subconscious Nature of Man and Society* (1898; New York, 1916), 258–59.

38. Boris Sidis, "The Psychotherapeutic Value of the Hypnoidal State," in *Psychotherapeutics: A Symposium*, ed. Morton Prince et al. (Boston, 1910), 121–44. In a case that he reported for a popular audience, Sidis described a young man suffering from nervous spasms whose psychotherapy depended on the analyst's ability to understand Yiddish, the language to which the patient spontaneously reverted under hypnosis. See Sidis, *Nervous Ills: Their Cause and Cure* (Boston, 1922), 220–29.

39. Joseph Jastrow, *Piloting Your Life: The Psychologist as Helmsman* (New York, 1930), 356–57.

40. Morton Prince, *The Unconscious: The Fundamentals of Human Personality Normal and Abnormal* (New York, 1914), 217–19.

41. For these and other Jewish references, see Abraham A. Brill, *Psychanalysis: Its Theories and Practical Application* (Philadelphia, 1913), 31, 71–72, 85–95, 96–112, 120–44, 230–31, 263–64, 315.A comparison of Jewish and non-Jewish Freudians yields the same result: Jews appear in the writings of Brill and Coriat but not in such comparable authors as James Jackson Putnam, William A. White, and E. B. Holt. See James Jackson Putnam, *Human Motives* (Boston, 1915); Edwin B. Holt, *The Freudian Wish and Its Place in Ethics* (New York, 1915); and William A. White, *Mechanisms of Character Formation: An Introduction to Psychoanalysis* (New York, 1920). For additional examples of the introduction of Jewish refer-

ences, see Louis Waldstein, *The Subconscious Self (and Its Relation to Education and Health)* (New York, 1909), 134–35; and Abram Lipsky, *Man the Puppet: The Art of Controlling Minds* (New York, 1925), 180.

42. See "An Example of Dream Analysis," in Isador H. Coriat, *The Meaning of Dreams* (1915; Boston, 1920), 13–42. On dissociation as understood by Freud and Freudian analysis, see Jerome L. Singer, ed., *Repression and Dissociation: Implications for Personality Theory, Psychopathology, and Health* (Chicago, 1990).

43. Brill, *Psychanalysis*, 96–112.

Chapter 2. Benjamin Franklin in Hebrew: The *Musar* Sage of Philadelphia

1. *The Autobiography of Benjamin Franklin*, ed. Leonard W. Labaree, Ralph L. Ketcham, Helen C. Boatfield, and Helene H. Fineman (New Haven, 1974), 146–47. For the depiction of Franklin as "friend of the human race," see Carl L. Becker, *The Heavenly City of the Eighteenth-Century Philosophers* (New Haven, 1932), 34. For concise treatments of Franklin's thought, see Paul K. Conkin, *Puritans and Pragmatists: Eight Eminent American Thinkers* (New York, 1968), 73–108; and Daniel Walker Howe, *Making the American Self: Jonathan Edwards to Abraham Lincoln* (Cambridge, Mass., 1997), 21–47.

2. *Autobiography of Benjamin Franklin*, 148–56.

3. Ibid., 157.

4. On Lefin, see Hillel Levine, "Menahem Mendel Lefin: A Case Study of Judaism and Modernization" (Ph.D. diss., Harvard University, 1974); and Nancy Beth Sinkoff, "Tradition and Transition: Mendel Lefin of Satanow and the Beginnings of the Jewish Enlightenment in Eastern Europe, 1749–1826" (Ph.D. diss., Columbia University, 1996).

5. Nissim ben Jacob ibn Shahin, *An Elegant Composition Concerning Relief After Adversity*, ed. William M. Brinner (1977; Northvale, N.J., 1996), 132.

6. For an introduction to *musar* literature, see Joseph Dan, "Ethical Literature," in *Encyclopaedia Judaica*, 16 vols. (Jerusalem, 1971), 6:922–32; and the appropriate sections of Israel Zinberg, *A History of Jewish Literature*, 12 vols. (Cincinnati, 1975–78), which is a translation of Israel Zinberg, *Di Geschichte fun der Literatur bay Yidn*, 10 vols. (New York, 1943). In Hebrew, see Dov Katz, *Tenu'at ha-Musar* (Tel Aviv, 1952); and Joseph Dan, *Sifrut ha-Musar v'ha Derush* (Jerusalem, 1975).

7. Menachem Mendel Lefin, *Accounting of the Soul* (New York, 1995), section 1; and Richard F. Teichgraeber III, *Sublime Thoughts/Penny Wisdom: Situating Emerson and Thoreau in the American Market* (Baltimore, 1995), 268, 271–72. In quoting from *Ḥeshbon ha-Nefesh*, I rely primarily on the translation of Shraga Silverstein (New York, 1995); it should be noted, however, that this bilingual edition omits several concluding passages from the original, which are included in a current Hebrew edition: *Sefer Ḥeshbon ha-Nefesh* (Jerusalem: Merkaz ha-Sefer, 1988).

8. *Autobiography of Benjamin Franklin*, 18; Cotton Mather, *Bonifacius: An Essay upon the Good*, ed. David Levin (Cambridge, Mass. 1966), 102–3; and "Tzahalon," *Encyclopaedia Judaica*, 16:919.

9. Shlomo Fox Ashrei, ed., *Orchos Chaim of the Rosh* (New York, 1992), 8; and Moshe Chaim Luzzatto, *The Path of the Upright*, ed. Mordecai M. Kaplan (1936; Northvale, N.J., 1995). Luzzatto's list in Hebrew reads: *zehirut, zerizut, nikiyut, perishut, taharah, ḥasidut, anavah*, and *kedushah*.

10. *Autobiography of Benjamin Franklin*, 1; and Moses Maimonides, *Shemonah Perakim* [Hebrew] (Jerusalem, 1997), 35. See also Aristotle's *Nicomachean Ethics* (Mineola, N.Y., 1998), 26–33: this is the unabridged Dover republication of *The Ethics of Aristotle*, trans. D. P. Chase (London, 1911). On Greek wisdom and Franklin's idea of virtue, see Mitchell Robert Breitwieser, *Cotton Mather and Benjamin Franklin: The Price of Representative Personality* (Cambridge, 1984), 192–201.

11. Mather, *Bonifacius*, 27.

12. Breitwieser, *Cotton Mather and Benjamin Franklin*, 178.

13. John Locke, *An Essay Concerning Human Understanding* (Chicago, 1956), 154, 359–68; and Henry F. May, *The Enlightenment in America* (New York, 1976), 7–10, 38. For the significance of Locke's writings on religious toleration for Jews in the British Commonwealth, see Jacob Katz, *Out of the Ghetto: The Social Background of Jewish Emancipation, 1770–1870* (New York, 1978), 38–40. On the implications of Lockean thought for Jewish thinkers in the eighteenth century, see David B. Ruderman, *Jewish Enlightenment in an English Key: Anglo-Jewry's Construction of Modern Jewish Thought* (Princeton, 2000), 9, 22, 114–15, 281–84.

14. Hillel Levine, "Between Hasidism and Haskalah: On a Disguised Anti-Hasidic Polemic" [Hebrew], in *Perakim be-Toldot ha-Ḥevrah ha-Yehudit be-yimei ha-Beinayim uve-Et ha-Ḥadashah*, ed. I. Etkes and J. Salmon (Jerusalem, 1980), 182–91, esp. 187–90; Levine, "Menahem Mendel Lefin," 179–97; Sinkoff, "Tradition and Transition," 117–50; and Nancy Sinkoff, "Benjamin Franklin in Jewish Eastern Europe: Cultural Appropriation in the Age of the Enlightenment," *Journal of the History of Ideas* 61 (January 2000), 133–52.

15. *Autobiography of Benjamin Franklin*, 157–58; and Lefin, *Accounting of the Soul*, sections 18–20.

16. A. R. Malachi, "Benjamin Franklin and Hebrew Literature" [Hebrew], *Ha-Doar*, January 27, 1956, pp. 328–29; and *Kerem Ḥemed* (Vienna, 1833), republication of a letter from Yaakov Shmuel Bick to Tuvia Feder, Tevet 19, 5575 (1815), pp. 96–98. Franklin's *Way to Wealth* appeared in Hebrew in the 1860s, and in 1901 a Warsaw publisher brought out the *Lebens beshraybung fun Binyamin Franklin*, his life story in Yiddish. For finding the citation of the Yiddish translation of a Franklin biography, I thank Roy E. Goodman, Curator of Printed Materials of the American Philosophical Society Library, and Seth Jerchower, Public Services Librarian, Center for Judaic Studies Library of the University of Pennsylvania.

17. Zinberg, *Geschichte fun der Literatur bay Yidn*, 5:198; see esp. 184–224, 320–39 (in the English translation, *A History of Jewish Literature*, 6:155–90, 271–86).

18. Lefin, *Accounting of the Soul*, section 27.

19. Ibid., section 110.

20. *Autobiography of Benjamin Franklin*, 158; Roger Smith, *The Norton History of the Human Sciences* (New York, 1997), 250–54; Robert Boakes, *From Darwin to*

Behaviourism: Psychology and the Minds of Animals (Cambridge, 1984), 92–95; and Edward S. Reed, *From Soul to Mind: The Emergence of Psychology from Erasmus Darwin to William James* (New Haven, 1997), 93.

21. Lefin, *Accounting of the Soul,* sections 52, 67.

22. Ibid., sections 41, 43.

CHAPTER 3. JEWS AND THE CRISIS OF THE PSYCHE

1. Roger Smith, *The Norton History of the Human Sciences* (New York, 1997), 145, 143–53; Harold Bloom, *The Western Canon* (New York, 1995), 46; and Charles Taylor, *Sources of the Self: The Making of the Modern Identity* (Cambridge, Mass., 1989), 185.

2. Smith, *History of the Human Sciences,* 118–43; Taylor, *Sources of the Self,* 143–91; and Roy Porter, *The Creation of the Modern World: The Untold Story of the British Enlightenment* (New York, 2001), 106–7, 205–23. On the persistence of magical thinking in colonial America, see Jon Butler, *Awash in a Sea of Faith: Christianizing the American People* (Cambridge, Mass., 1990).

3. Porter, *Creation of the Modern World,* 291–94; Smith, *History of the Human Sciences,* 220–21, 368; and H. Stuart Hughes, *Consciousness and Society: The Reorientation of European Social Thought, 1890–1930* (1958; New York, 1977), 66.

4. Porter, *Creation of the Modern World,* 436–45; and Edward S. Reed, *From Soul to Mind: The Emergence of Psychology from Erasmus Darwin to William James* (New Haven, 1997), 14–15, 83.

5. Reed, *From Soul to Mind,* 7, 159; and Dorothy Ross, *G. Stanley Hall: The Psychologist as Prophet* (Chicago, 1972), 138–43. In France, where Catholicism rather than Protestantism prevailed as the religion of the state, the same essential battle was waged by psychological authorities in the universities against a secular approach that threatened to destabilize the unity and purity of the *moi* ("I"), the God-given rational personality. See Jan Goldstein, "The Advent of Psychological Modernism in France," in *Modernist Impulses in the Human Sciences, 1870–1930,* ed. Dorothy Ross (Baltimore, 1994), 190–209.

6. Henri F. Ellenberger, *The Discovery of the Unconscious: The History and Evolution of Dynamic Psychiatry* (New York, 1970), 57–101. In 1784 a commission of inquiry that included Benjamin Franklin determined that there was no evidence for Mesmer's magnetic fluid and ascribed his therapeutic success to the influence of imagination.

7. Robert C. Fuller, *Americans and the Unconscious* (New York, 1986), 179–80; R. Laurence Moore, *In Search of White Crows: Spiritualism, Parapsychology, and American Culture* (New York, 1977), 4, 9–10ff.; and Ellenberger, *Discovery of the Unconscious,* 83–85.

8. Bernice Glatzer Rosenthal, "Introduction" and "Political Implications of the Early Twentieth-Century Occult Revival," in *The Occult in Russian and Soviet Culture,* ed. Bernice Glatzer Rosenthal (Ithaca, 1997), 5, 9–10, 394–97; in the same volume, Maria Carlson, "Fashionable Occultism: Spiritualism, Theosophy, Freemasonry, and Hermeticism in Fin-de-Siècle Russia," 140.

9. Rosenthal, "Introduction," *Occult in Russian and Soviet Culture*, 6, 10; in the same volume, Judith Deutsch Kornblatt, "Russian Religious Thought and the Jewish Kabbala," 90–91.

10. Quoted from Roger Scruton, *A Short History of Modern Philosophy: From Descartes to Wittgenstein* (1981; London, 1999), 178; Christopher Janaway, "Schopenhauer," in *German Philosophers: Kant, Hegel, Schopenhauer, and Nietzsche*, ed. Roger Scruton et al. (Oxford, 2001), 270–76; Smith, *History of the Human Sciences*, 208; and William J. McGrath, *Freud's Discovery of Psychoanalysis: The Politics of Hysteria* (Ithaca, 1986), 141–51. On German philosophies of self, see Karl Ameriks and Dieter Sturma, eds., *The Modern Subject: Conceptions of the Self in Classical German Philosophy* (Albany, 1995).

11. Johann Wolfgang von Goethe, *The Sorrows of Young Werther*, trans. Harry Steinhauer (New York, 1970), 56. On Schleiermacher's theology, see Friedrich Schleiermacher, *On Religion: Speeches to its Cultured Despisers*, ed. Richard Crouter (Cambridge, England, 1996); for example: "What is revelation? Every original and new intuition of the universe is one, and yet all individuals must know best what is original and new for them" (49). On Schleiermacher's references to Judaism, see Michael A. Meyer, *The Origins of the Modern Jew: Jewish Identity and European Culture in German, 1749–1824* (1967; Detroit, 1984), 104–5.

12. Meyer, *Origins of the Modern Jew*, 101–14.

13. Michael A. Meyer, *Response to Modernity: A History of the Reform Movement in Judaism* (New York, 1988), 91, 94–97.

14. Ibid., 98–99.

15. On Adler, see Benny Kraut, *From Reform Judaism to Ethical Culture: The Religious Evolution of Felix Adler* (Cincinnati, 1979).

16. Felix Adler, *The Reconstruction of the Spiritual Ideal* (New York, 1924), 17, 36; and Felix Adler, *The Moral Instruction of Children* (New York, 1909), 130. The latter book presents a series of lectures Adler delivered in 1891.

17. Noah H. Rosenbloom, *Tradition in an Age of Reform: The Religious Philosophy of Samson Raphael Hirsch* (Philadelphia, 1976), 205.

18. Samson Raphael Hirsch, *The Pentateuch* (Gateshead, 1989), commentary on Leviticus 19:18.

19. Ibid., Leviticus 26:16.

20. On Salanter and the *Musar* movement, see Immanuel Etkes, *Rabbi Israel Salanter and the Mussar Movement: Seeking the Truth of Torah* (Philadelphia, 1993); and Hillel Goldberg, *Israel Salanter: Text, Structure, Idea—The Ethics and Theology of an Early Psychologist of the Unconscious* (New York, 1982).

21. Israel Salanter, *Iggeret ha-Musar*, in *Sefer Or Yisrael*, ed. I. Blazer (n.p., 1997), 151; Zalman F. Ury, "Salanter's Musar Movement," in *Studies in Judaica*, ed. Leon D. Stitskin (New York, 1972), 239–42; and Etkes, *Rabbi Israel Salanter*, 101.

22. Etkes, *Rabbi Israel Salanter*, 322.

23. Gershom Scholem, *Major Trends in Jewish Mysticism* (1946; New York, 1995), 341.

24. Ibid., 340–43.

25. Roman A. Foxbrunner, Ḥabad: The Hasidism of R. Shneur Zalman of Lyady (Northvale, N.J., 1993), 119, 125–26.

26. Ibid., 117, 120–21.

CHAPTER 4. FREUD AND ADLER:
THE RISE OF JEWISH PSYCHOANALYTIC MORALISM

1. Friedrich Nietzsche, "Letter to Overbeck," February 23, 1887, in *The Portable Nietzsche*, ed. Walter Kaufmann (New York, 1976), 455.

2. Sigmund Freud, *Wit and Its Relation to the Unconscious* (New York, 1993), 112. This edition is a reprint of the 1916 authorized edition, translated by A. A. Brill from the original 1905 *Der Witz und seine Beziehung zum Unbewussten*.

3. Ibid., 167.

4. Ibid., 167–69.

5. See Kaufmann, *Portable Nietzsche*, 450; and Friedrich Nietzsche, *The Birth of Tragedy* and *The Genealogy of Morals*, trans. Francis Golffing (New York, 1956), 188.

6. Jacques Barzun, *From Dawn to Decadence: 500 Years of Western Cultural Life, 1500 to the Present* (New York, 2000), 662; Nathan G. Hale, Jr., *Freud and the Americans: The Beginnings of Psychoanalysis in the United States, 1876–1917* (New York, 1971); Nathan G. Hale, Jr., *Freud and the Americans: The Rise and Crisis of Psychoanalysis in the United States, 1917–1985* (New York, 1995). For comparative treatment of Freud and Adler in Jewish history, see two fine books on Viennese Jewry: Robert S. Wistrich, *The Jews of Vienna in the Age of Franz Joseph* (Oxford, 1990), which has a forty-five-page chapter on Freud, but two pages on Adler, and Steven Beller, *Vienna and the Jews, 1867–1938: A Cultural History* (Cambridge, England, 1989), which has thirty-four pages on Freud, and three on Adler.

7. Edward Hoffman, *The Drive for Self: Alfred Adler and the Founding of Individual Psychology* (Reading, Mass., 1994), 76–77; and Peter Gay, *Freud: A Life for Our Time* (New York, 1998), 221–24. See also Bernhard Handlbauer, *The Freud-Adler Controversy* (Oxford, 1998).

8. Alfred Adler, notebook, folder "Miscellany, Notes and Memoranda," box 3, Alfred Adler Papers, Manuscript Division, Library of Congress, Washington, D.C.

9. Sigmund Freud, *Introductory Lectures on Psychoanalysis*, trans. James Strachey (New York, 1977), 282 (this volume appeared in 1917 as *Vorlesungen zur Einführung in die Psychoanalyse*).

10. See for example, Alfred Adler, *The Neurotic Constitution: Outlines of a Comparative Individualistic Psychology and Psychotherapy*, trans. Bernard Glueck and John E. Lind (1912; New York, 1917), 36–37.

11. William M. Johnston, *The Austrian Mind: An Intellectual and Social History, 1848–1938* (Berkeley, 1972), 3; and Yosef Hayim Yerushalmi, *Freud's Moses: Judaism Terminable and Interminable* (New Haven, 1991), 9–10. See also Dennis B. Klein, *Jewish Origins of the Psychoanalytic Movement* (New York, 1981).

12. Johnston, *Austrian Mind*, 23. For a detailed study of the demography and social structure of Jews in Vienna, see Marsha L. Rozenblit, *The Jews of Vienna*,

1867–1914: Assimilation and Identity (Albany, 1983). On the cultural impact of Vienna's Jews, see Wistrich, *Jews of Vienna*; Beller, *Vienna and the Jews*; and Carl E. Schorske, *Fin-de-Siècle Vienna: Politics and Culture* (New York, 1981), esp. 181–207.

13. Thorstein Veblen, "The Intellectual Pre-Eminence of Jews in Modern Europe," in *The Viking Portable Veblen*, ed. Max Lerner (New York, 1948), 467–79; and Adam Gopnik, "What Steinberg Saw," *New Yorker*, November 13, 2000, p. 142.

14. For an interesting short discussion of the possible reasons for the creativity of Vienna's Jews, which includes the quoted phrase, they "lost touch with mysticism and the soil," see Johnston, *Austrian Mind*, 23–29. For a complete analysis, see Beller, *Vienna and the Jews*.

15. Ernest Jones, *The Life and Work of Sigmund Freud*, 2 vols. (New York, 1953–57) 1:1–13; Gay, *Freud*, 4–9; Hoffman, *Drive for Self*, 4–18; and Phyllis Bottome, *Alfred Adler: A Biography* (New York, 1939), 11.

16. William J. McGrath, *Freud's Discovery of Psychoanalysis: The Politics of Hysteria* (Ithaca, 1986), 317; and Bottome, *Alfred Adler*, 11.

17. McGrath, *Freud's Discovery of Psychoanalysis*, 53–55.

18. Peter Gay, *A Godless Jew: Freud, Atheism, and the Making of Psychoanalysis* (New Haven, 1987), 124, 148.

19. Gay, *Freud*, 7; Hoffman, *Drive for Self*, 7.

20. The reminiscence of Walter Rathenau is quoted from Alan Levenson, "Radical Assimilation and Radical Assimilationists in Imperial Germany," in *What Is Modern about the Modern Jewish Experience?*, ed. Marc Lee Raphael (Williamsburg, Va. 1997), 41. On Wagner's and Liszt's assessment of Felix Mendelssohn, see Ezra Mendelsohn, "Should We Take Notice of Berthe Weill?: Reflections on the Domain of Jewish History," *Jewish Social Studies* (n.s.) 1 (Fall 1994), 25.

21. Wistrich, *Jews of Vienna*, 205–37.

22. Fritz Stern, *The Politics of Cultural Despair: A Study in the Rise of the Germanic Ideology* (Garden City, N.Y., 1965), 10, and Fritz Stern, *Einstein's German World* (Princeton, 1999), 32.

23. Stefan Zweig, *The World of Yesterday* (New York, 1943), 12.

24. Beller, *Vienna and the Jews*, 211.

25. Sigmund Freud, *An Autobiographical Study* (1935; New York, 1963), 14–15; Hilda C. Abraham and Ernst L. Freud, eds., *A Psycho-Analytic Dialogue: The Letters of Sigmund Freud and Karl Abraham, 1907–1926* (New York, 1965), 46; and Sander L. Gilman, *The Case of Sigmund Freud: Medicine and Identity at the Fin de Siècle* (Baltimore, 1993), 218.

26. Bottome, *Alfred Adler*, ix, 40; and Alexandra Adler, "Human Values in Psychotherapy," in *Aldred Adler: His Influence on Psychology Today*, ed. Harold H. Mosak (Park Ridge, N.J., 1973), 142–43.

27. Ernst L. Freud, ed., *The Letters of Sigmund Freud and Arnold Zweig* (New York, 1970), 44; and Albert Einstein, *Ideas and Opinions* (New York, 1954), 185–86. The quotation from Einstein is from a 1934 essay, "Is There a Jewish Point of View?"

28. Yerushalmi, *Freud's Moses*, 51–52; Hoffman, *Drive for Self*, 110; and Adler, *Understanding Human Nature*, 225.

29. Alexander King, *Peter Altenberg's Evocations of Love* (New York, 1960), 58. On the German Jewish subculture of Enlightenment values, see Jehuda Reinharz and Walter Schatzberg, eds., *Jewish Response to German Culture: From the Enlighten-*

ment to the Second World War (Hanover, N.H., 1985) and David Sorkin, *The Transformation of German Jewry, 1780–1840* (New York, 1987).

30. Gerhard Wehr, "C. G. Jung in the Context of Christian Esotericism and Cultural History," in *Modern Esoteric Spirituality*, ed. Antoine Faivre and Jacob Needleman (New York, 1995), 389.

31. For the quotations see McGrath, *Freud's Discovery of Psychoanalysis*, 118; and Ernest Jones, *The Life and Work of Sigmund Freud*, 2 vols. (New York, 1953–57), 2:153.

32. Bottome, *Alfred Adler*, 39; and Adler, *Understanding Human Nature*, 215.

33. On post-biblical Jewish family life, see "Family," in *Encyclopaedia Judaica*, 16 vols. (Jerusalem, 1971), 6:1169–72; and Steven M. Cohen and Paula E. Hyman, *The Jewish Family: Myths and Reality* (New York, 1986). Also illustrative is Shonie B. Levi and Sylvia R. Kaplan, *Across the Threshold: A Guide for the Jewish Homemaker* (New York, 1959). For an example of Midrash, which was the most popular kind of scriptural commentary, see *The Weekly Midrash: Tz'enah Ur'enah— The Classic Anthology of Torah Lore and Midrashic Commentary*, trans. Miriam Stark Zakon, 2 vols. (Brooklyn, 1994).

34. Freud, *Autobiographical Study*, 13–14; and Alfred Adler, "The Science of the Individual Personality," lecture, Conway Hall, London, May 11, 1936, folder "Lectures, 1935–1936," box 2, Adler Papers, Manuscript Division, Library of Congress, Washington, D.C.

35. Freud, *Introductory Lectures on Psychoanalysis*, 333–35; Alfred Adler, *Understanding Human Nature*, trans. Walter Béran Wolfe (Garden City, N.Y., 1927), 149–57; McGrath, *Freud's Discovery of Psychoanalysis*, 27; and Alexandra Adler, "Human Values in Psychotherapy," 142–43. In a brief historical overview of psychological theories, psychologist Ross Stagner comments on the relationship between Jewish exegesis and psychoanalysis: "Most of the psychological material in the Old Testament relates to emotions such as shame and guilt. It is no surprise that Sigmund Freud, whose psychoanalytic theory focused on these emotions, was steeped in the Judaic literature and showed a concern about dynamics, as opposed to reason, as the keystone of human psychology." See Ross Stagner, *A History of Psychological Theories* (New York, 1988), 33.

36. Philip Rieff, *Freud: The Mind of the Moralist* (New York, 1959), 12–13, 18; Adler, *Neurotic Constitution*, 127–207, 281–333, 361–435.

37. Sigmund Freud, *The Ego and the Id*, trans. James Strachey (1923; London, 1961), 18; and Adler, *Understanding Human Nature*, 286. See also McGrath, *Freud's Discovery of Psychoanalysis*, 321.

CHAPTER 5. POPULAR PSYCHOLOGY:
THE GREAT AMERICAN SYNTHESIS OF RELIGION AND SCIENCE

1. Ernst L. Freud, ed., *The Letters of Sigmund Freud and Arnold Zweig* (New York, 1970), 136.

2. David D. Hall, "The World of Print and Collective Mentality," in *New Directions in American Intellectual History*, ed. John Higham and Paul K. Conkin (Baltimore, 1979), 173; David D. Hall, *Worlds of Wonder, Days of Judgment: Popular Reli-*

gious Belief in Early New England (New York, 1989), 26; and Jon Butler, *Becoming America: The Revolution Before 1776* (Cambridge, Mass., 2000), 111. See also David D. Hall, *Cultures of Print: Essays in the History of the Book* (Amherst, 1996), 36–78; and E. Jennifer Monaghan, "Literacy Instruction and Gender in Colonial New England," in *Reading in America: Literature and Social History*, ed. Cathy N. Davidson (Baltimore, 1989), 53–80; Janet Duitsman Cornelius, *'When I Can Read My Title Clear': Literacy, Slavery, and Religion in the Antebellum South* (Colombia, S.C., 1991), 3–4, 125–50. The figures on African American literacy in 1913 come from C. Vann Woodward, *Origins of the New South, 1877–1913* (1951; Baton Rouge, 1974), 368.

3. Jefferson's statement is from the Virginia Statute of Religious Freedom, written in 1779 and enacted into law in 1786. On Jefferson and the ideal of self-construction, see Daniel Walker Howe, *Making the American Self: Jonathan Edwards to Abraham Lincoln* (Cambridge, Mass., 1997), 261–63.

4. The final edition of *Poor Richard's Almanack* (1758) reproduced the maxims from the preceding editions and was later republished many times as *The Way to Wealth* and *Franklin's Way to Wealth*. For a facsimile, see *Poor Richard's Almanack; being the almanacks of 1733, 1749, 1756, 1757, 1758, first written under the name of Richard Saunders, by Benjamin Franklin* (Garden City, N.Y., 1928). On Franklin's desire to establish a world of print "liberated from the pulpit," see Hall, *Cultures of Print*, 157.

5. Horatio Alger, Jr., *Bound to Rise* (1873; New York, 1910); for the chapter "In Franklin's Footsteps" see pp. 32–37.

6. William Dean Howells, *The Rise of Silas Lapham* (1885; New York, 1965), 5. On the genre of success writing, see Richard Weiss, *The American Myth of Success: From Horatio Alger to Norman Vincent Peale* (1969; Urbana, 1988).

7. Joan Shelley Rubin, *The Making of Middlebrow Culture* (Chapel Hill, 1992), 1–33; and Richard F. Teichgraeber III, *Sublime Thoughts/Penny Wisdom: Situating Emerson and Thoreau in the American Market* (Baltimore, 1995).

8. Edward Everett Hale, *How to Do It* (1874; Boston, 1900), 263–65.

9. Dorothea Brande, *Wake Up and Live!* (New York, 1936), 187.

10. George M. Beard, *American Nervousness: Its Causes and Consequences* (1881; New York, 1972), 7, 101–13; and Donald Meyer, *The Positive Thinkers: A Study of the American Quest for Health, Wealth and Personal Power from Mary Baker Eddy to Norman Vincent Peale* (New York, 1965), 22–26.

11. Leo Marx, *The Machine in the Garden: Technology and the Pastoral Ideal in America* (1964; New York, 2000), 122, 247; Roderick Nash, *Wilderness and the American Mind* (New Haven, 1967), 143; and Edward Alsworth Ross, *Social Control: A Survey of the Foundations of Order* (New York, 1901), 1.

12. Edward Alsworth Ross, *Civic Sociology: A Textbook in Social and Civic Problems for Young Americans* (Yonkers-on-Hudson, 1926), 42–43, 138, 141.

13. Duane Schultz, *A History of Modern Psychology* (New York, 1975), 150; Frederick Lewis Allen, *Only Yesterday: An Informal History of the Nineteen-Twenties* (1931; New York, 1964), 164–65; and Hugo Münsterberg, *Psychotherapy* (New York, 1909), 77.

14. See the chapter on Leopold and Loeb in Paula S. Fass, *Kidnapped: Child Abduction in America* (New York, 1997), 57–93. The quoted passages are from pages 83 and 92. See also Catherine Lucille Covert, "Freud on the Front Page: Transmission of Freudian Ideas in the American Newspaper of the 1920s" (Ph.D. diss., Syracuse University, 1975), 1–73; see p. 8 for the comment of the psychiatric witness for the defense. Had that macabre case occurred in Germany, Austria, or France, the Jewish identity of the criminals would undoubtedly have provided the most desirable explanation for decadence (as it did in the Dreyfus case of the 1890s), because continental psychologists tended to contrast the Aryan and the Jewish psyche. It was significant that in the United States, despite the rising antisemitism of the early and mid-1920s, the Jewishness of Leopold and Loeb was not newsworthy; on the contrary, the press sympathetically emphasized the essential similarity of the Leopold and Loeb families to those of other Americans (see Fass, *Kidnapped,* 84).

15. Alice Payne Hackett, *70 Years of Best Sellers: 1895–1965* (New York, 1967), 108–73; Ellen Herman, *The Romance of American Psychology: Political Culture in the Age of Experts* (Berkeley, 1995), 1; Philip Rieff, *Freud: The Mind of the Moralist* (New York, 1959), 355; and Philip Rieff, *The Triumph of the Therapeutic: Uses of Faith after Freud* (New York, 1966).

16. Joseph Jastrow, *Piloting Your Life: The Psychologist as Helmsman* (New York, 1930), xiv; Joseph Jastrow, *Keeping Mentally Fit* (Garden City, N.Y., 1928), vii.

17. Robert C. Fuller, *Americans and the Unconscious* (New York, 1986), 198.

18. The shift from a public to an academic philosophy is a primary theme of Bruce Kuklick, *The Rise of American Philosophy: Cambridge, Massachusetts, 1860–1930* (New Haven, 1977). On complaints about the "effeminacy" of Protestantism after 1900, see E. Brooks Holifield, *A History of Pastoral Care in America: From Salvation to Self-Realization* (Nashville, 1983), 218.

19. *St. Louis Post Dispatch,* August 1, 1915. On the transition from old to new therapies, see Nathan G. Hale, Jr., *Freud and the Americans: The Beginnings of Psychoanalysis in the United States, 1876–1917* (New York, 1971), 47–68; and John Chynoweth Burnham, "Psychiatry, Psychology and the Progressive Movement," *American Quarterly* 12 (Winter 1960), 459–60.

20. *New York Times,* August 1, 1915; *Boston Advertiser,* September 1, 1915; and *Boston Globe,* July 25, 1915.

21. The quote is from Dewey's *Human Nature and Conduct* (1922)—see Larry A. Hickman and Thomas M. Alexander, eds., *The Essential Dewey: Volume 2—Ethics, Logic, Psychology* (Bloomington, 1998), 25. See also Robert B. Westbrook, *John Dewey and American Democracy* (Ithaca, 1991), 286–93; John M. O'Donnell, *The Origins of Behaviorism: American Psychology, 1870–1920* (New York, 1985), 170–75; Merle Curti, *Human Nature in American Thought: A History* (Madison, 1980), 187–215; and Duane Schultz, *A History of Modern Psychology* (New York, 1975), 107. For the larger Euro-American philosophical context, which gave rise to a new conception of experience as the center of human consciousness, see James T. Kloppenberg, *Uncertain Victory: Social Democracy and Progressivism in European and American Thought, 1870–1920* (New York, 1986), 81–93.

22. Bruce Kuklick, *Churchmen and Philosophers: From Jonathan Edwards to John Dewey* (New Haven, 1985), 232. For other scholarly assessments of the continuity between Dewey's Protestant heritage and his philosophy, see Westbrook, *John Dewey and American Democracy*, 36; Kloppenberg, *Uncertain Victory*, 44; and Paul K. Conkin, *Puritans and Pragmatists: Eight Eminent American Thinkers* (New York, 1968), 345.

23. Carl L. Becker, *The Heavenly City of the Eighteenth-Century Philosophers* (New Haven, 1932), 47; Kuklick, *Churchmen and Philosophers*, 238–53; and Darnell Rucker, *The Chicago Pragmatists* (Minneapolis, 1969), 57–67. See Dewey's seminal essay, "The Reflex Arc Concept in Psychology," in Hickman and Thomas, *The Essential Dewey*, 2:3–10. The article appeared in *Psychological Review* 3 (July 1896), 357–70. Compare Dewey's scientific idealism, with its psychological and sociological focus, with that of his contemporary Charles Sanders Peirce, which focused on language. For both, the self was something brokered rather than independent; Dewey's self appeared at moments when the human organism was out of adjustment, while Peirce's self appeared through the words that interpreted the world. See John Patrick Diggins, *The Promise of Pragmatism: Modernism and the Crisis of Knowledge and Authority* (Chicago, 1994), 163, 183–84.

24. Karl E. Scheibe, "Metamorphoses in the Psychologist's Advantage," in *The Rise of Experimentation in American Psychology*, ed. Jill G. Morawski (New Haven, 1988), 59–60. Dorothy Ross, *The Origins of American Social Science* (Cambridge, 1991), explains the close connection between American exceptionalism and social science and discusses the darker functionalism of nativists like Edward A. Ross as well as the cosmopolitan Deweyan model.

25. Barbara Sicherman, *The Quest for Mental Health in America, 1880–1917* (New York, 1980), 278–79, 333, 335, and the chapter "Psychological Medicine Comes of Age," pp. 228–80; David J. Rothman, *Conscience and Convenience: The Asylum and Its Alternatives in Progressive America* (Boston, 1980), 293–323; and Gerald N. Grob, *Mental Illness and American Society, 1875–1940* (Princeton, 1983), 46–71. On Clifford Beers and the mental hygiene movement, see Sicherman, *Quest for Mental Health*, 281–327; and Grob, *Mental Illness and American Society*, 147–78.

26. Burnham, *How Superstition Won and Science Lost*, 23; and G. Stanley Hall, *Adolescence: Its Psychology and Its Relations to Physiology, Anthropology, Sociology, Sex, Crime, Religion and Education*, 2 vols. (New York, 1905), 2:304, 357.

For some additional linkages between America's psychological theorists and the Puritan or Protestant heritage, see Lucille C. Birnbaum, "Behaviorism in the 1920's," *American Quarterly* 7 (Spring 1955), 20, 30; Burnham, "Psychiatry, Psychology, and the Progressive Movement," 458, 463; Dorothy Ross, *G. Stanley Hall: The Psychologist as Prophet* (Chicago, 1972), 138–45; Leila Zenderland, *Measuring Minds: Henry Herbert Goddard and the Origins of American Intelligence Testing* (Cambridge, 1998), 30–43; Katherine Pandora, *Rebels within the Ranks: Psychologists' Critique of Scientific Authority and Democratic Realities in New Deal America* (Cambridge, 1997), 25–34; Robert Boakes, *From Darwin to Behaviourism: Psychology and the Minds of Animals* (Cambridge, 1984), 68; Agnes N. O'Connell and Nancy Felipe Russo, eds., *Models of Achievement: Reflections of Eminent Women in Psychology*, 2 vols. (Hillsdale, N.J., 1988), 2:46; and J[ill] G. Morawski, "Not Quite New

Worlds: Psychologists' Conceptions of the Ideal Family in the Twenties," in *In the Shadow of the Past: Psychology Portrays the Sexes*, ed. Miriam Lewin (New York, 1984), 97–125.

27. On the development of an American literature of melancholy and "psychomachia" rooted in Puritan narratives, see John Owen King III, *The Iron of Melancholy: Structures of Spiritual Conversion in America from the Puritan Conscience to Victorian Neurosis* (Middletown, 1983). On the evolution of American ideas about consciousness from the Puritans to the founders of American psychology, see James Hoopes, *Consciousness in New England: From Puritanism and Ideas to Psychoanalysis and Semiotic* (Baltimore, 1989).

28. William James, *On Vital Reserves: The Energies of Men; The Gospel of Relaxation* (New York, 1911), 5, 70–71. This book contains two addresses by James, one to the American Philosophical Association in 1906, which was slightly altered for publication in the *American Magazine* (1907), and one to a gathering of teachers published as a pamphlet, *Talks to Teachers on Psychology: and to Students on Some of Life's Ideals* (New York, 1899). See also Meyer, *Positive Thinkers*, 30.

29. William James, *The Varieties of Religious Experience: A Study in Human Nature* (New York, 1961), 396, 398–99. See also Weiss, *American Myth of Success*, 207–14; Fuller, *Americans and the Unconscious*, 95; and Barbara Ross, "William James: A Prime Mover of the Psychoanalytic Movement in America," in *Psychoanalysis, Psychotherapy and the New England Medical Scene, 1894–1944*, ed. George E. Gifford, Jr. (New York, 1978), 17–19.

30. Meyer, *Positive Thinkers*, 30–31; and James, *On Vital Reserves*, 34–35.

31. On the mind-cure movement, see Gail Thain Parker, *Mind Cure in New England: From the Civil War to World War I* (Hanover, N.H., 1973). For the relationship of William James to mind cure, see pp. 151–68, and for the adaptation of Freud by Horatio Dresser, see pp. 146–49. For a study of New Thought focused on concepts of gender (though tending to reinforce an exaggerated claim that "New Thought and psychology were one and the same," p. 243), see Beryl Satter, *Each Mind a Kingdom: American Women, Sexual Purity, and the New Thought Movement, 1875–1920* (Berkeley, 1999). On mind cure as a preparation for Freud in America, see Hale, *Beginnings of Psychoanalysis*, 225–49; and Joseph Adelson, "Freud in America: Some Observations," *American Psychologist*, 11 (September 1956), 468–69.

32. John B. Watson, "The Heart or the Intellect?" *Harper's Monthly* 156 (February 1928), 346–47.

33. Horace Bushnell, "Christian Nurture," in *The American Intellectual Tradition: A Sourcebook, Volume 1: 1630–1865*, ed. David A. Hollinger and Charles Capper (New York, 2001), 425. The original source is Horace Bushnell, *Views of Christian Nurture, and of Subjects Adjacent Thereto* (Hartford, 1847).

34. Watson, "Heart or the Intellect," 351–52. On behaviorism, see O'Donnell, *The Origins of Behaviorism*; Curti, *Human Nature in American Thought*, 372–406; C. James Goodwin, *A History of Modern Psychology* (New York, 1999), 302–18; and Lucille C. Birnbaum, "Behaviorism in the 1920's," *American Quarterly* 7 (Spring 1955), 17–20, 30. On Watson, see Kerry Buckley, *Mechanical Man: John Broadus Watson and the Beginnings of Behaviorism* (New York, 1989).

CHAPTER 6. JEWISH PSYCHOLOGICAL EVANGELISM:
A COLLECTIVE BIOGRAPHY OF THE FIRST GENERATION

1. Joseph Jastrow to Hugo Münsterberg, November 13, 1892, Hugo Münsterberg Papers, Boston Public Library (hereafter Münsterberg Papers). See also Joseph Jastrow to Henrietta Szold, April 24, 1893, Letters, 1890–1894, Joseph Jastrow Papers, Duke University, Rare Book, Manuscript and Special Collections Library (hereafter Jastrow Papers). A. A. Roback, *History of American Psychology* (New York, 1952), 133–34; Kurt Danziger and Paul Ballantyne, "Psychological Experiments," in *A Pictorial History of Psychology*, ed. Wolfgang G. Bringmann et. al. (Chicago, 1997), 233–34; and exhibition pamphlet "An Exhibit in Honor of the 75th Anniversary" of the American Psychological Association, prepared by the Archives of the History of American Psychology (Akron, 1967), with thanks to Dr. David Baker, Director of the Archives of the History of American Psychology.

2. Hugo Münsterberg to Joseph Jastrow, June 22, 1914, Münsterberg Papers.

3. One of the most important characteristics they had in common was gender. See Elizabeth Lunbeck, *The Psychiatric Persuasion: Knowledge, Gender, and Power in Modern America* (Princeton, 1994), and Mari Jo Buhle, *Feminism and Its Discontents: A Century of Struggle with Psychoanalysis* (Cambridge, Mass., 1998).

4. The French Jewish philosopher Henri Bergson's *Creative Evolution* (1912) was a best-selling book that ignited a Bergson vogue in America, but it is virtually impossible to discern any specifically Jewish significance in the book, which made no references to history or contemporary society that bore on Jewish concerns and said nothing about theology or religion that reflected a Jewish education or inclination. It is of incidental interest that two influential Jewish thinkers, Walter Lippmann and Horace Kallen, wholeheartedly propagated Bergson's philosophy of flux, which they evidently perceived as an antidote to conservative views that might block Progressive change. Nevertheless, both Bergsonism and Progressivism would have gone on without their efforts.

On the periphery of the story told here is Abraham Aaron Roback (1890–1965), a Russian-born Canadian Jew who became a psychologist in the United States. Roback wrote for the Jewish press in addition to publishing pamphlets and books on popular psychology, though not with major publishers. I thank Nicole Barenbaum of the University of the South for sharing her manuscript essays on Roback: "Jewish 'Chuzpah'? A. A. Roback's Correspondence with Sigmund Freud" (2002), and "The Outskirts of Psychology: Roback on Coué, Freud, and Popular Psychology in the 1920s" (2002).

5. *Boston Traveller*, December 16, 1916; *Boston Globe*, December 17, 1916; *Passaic News*, December 16, 1916; *Chicago Post*, December 16, 1916; "Munsterberg's Last Message," *Utica Press*, December 18, 1916; *Syracuse Post Standard*, December 18, 1916; *Springfield* (Mass.) *Republican*, December 18, 1916; and *Chicago Staats-Zeitung*, December 19, 1916. Numerous obituaries are collected in the Hugo Münsterberg scrapbook, MS Acc. 2499b (774), Münsterberg Papers.

6. George C. Cohen, letter to *Louisville Courier-Journal*, December 21, 1916; and "Ex-Pupil Tells How Muensterberg's Mind Dominated Class," *New York Morning Telegraph*, December 24, 1916; and Gustave A. Feingold, "Hugo Muensterberg, An Appreciation by One of his Students," *Hartford Times*, February 6, 1917.

7. "Muensterberg Heard From: Brookline Woman Says Famous Harvard Psychologist Sent Her Spirit Message," *Boston Evening Transcript,* December 27, 1916; " 'I Still Live,' Munsterberg's 'Spirit' Message," *New York Tribune,* December 28, 1916; and "Two Psychologists," *Des Moines Register,* January 5, 1917.

8. Phyllis Keller, *States of Belonging: German-American Intellectuals and the First World War* (Cambridge, Mass., 1979), 7–8. Keller devotes pp. 6–118 to a biographical portrait of Münsterberg. Although overly psychologized, Keller's interpretation of Münsterberg's personality is keenly perceptive. For an excellent biography that contextualizes Münsterberg within the history of psychology, see Matthew Hale, Jr., *Human Science and Social Order: Hugo Munsterberg and the Origins of Applied Psychology* (Philadelphia, 1980). There is also a very good chapter on Münsterberg in Bruce Kuklick, *The Rise of American Philosophy: Cambridge, Massachusetts, 1860–1930* (New Haven, 1977), 196–214.

9. Keller, *States of Belonging,* 9–12, 64–65.

10. Ibid., 16, 46.

11. See the Münsterberg-James correspondence in the William James Papers, Houghton Library, Harvard University [bMS Am 1092.9 (357–92) and (3263–3305)]. In a letter of March 17, 1909, Münsterberg reminisced to James: "It is a fact that my whole conflict with Wundt which went on for years originated, as he has delightfully described it himself, with my putting you publicly at the head of the profession."

The quote from James on the acceptance of Jews in universities comes from a letter to Pauline Goldmark regarding the appointment of Goldmark's brother-in-law, Felix Adler, by Columbia University in 1902. See William James to Pauline Goldmark, August 1, 1902, William James Papers, Houghton Library, Harvard University [bMS Am 1092.1]. James wrote, "I cannot tell you how glad I was to hear of Adler's appointment to Columbia, not only for his personal sake, but for progress in general." In his fifties and early sixties James had a crush on Pauline Goldmark, a young woman from an extraordinary Jewish family. See Linda Simon, *Genuine Reality: A Life of William James* (New York, 1998), 260–61, 282, 359–60.

12. See also the correspondence between James and Julius Goldstein, the German Jewish philosopher who translated *A Pluralistic Universe* into German, in the William James Papers, Houghton Library, Harvard University [bMS Am 1092.1]. In a letter of June 15, 1910, James congratulated Goldstein on "your splendid address on race-theories. What mockery is carried on to-day under the name of Science!"

On Münsterberg, James, and their relationship to the changing character of Harvard after 1900, see Simon, *Genuine Reality,* 325–29.

For Münsterberg's belief that antisemitism stunted his career in Germany, see Hale, *Human Science and Social Order,* 53. Keller writes, "It is questionable whether his credentials as a German national would have been as fully accepted in Germany as they were in America." See Keller, *States of Belonging,* 114, 55.

13. For a description of the poem, see Hale, *Human Science and Social Order,* 135. Münsterberg's wife, Selma Oppler, was the daughter of Moritz Münsterberg's first cousin, a military surgeon who had converted to Protestantism

and thereafter won appointment to the post of chief physician in the Prussian army. See Keller, *States of Belonging*, 23.

14. Hale, *Human Science and Social Order*, 194; *Brooklyn Eagle*, January 5, 1917; and *The Churchman*, December 30, 1916.

15. *Peoria Star*, December 22, 1916.

16. The index card was attached to the following letter to his sister-in-law: Joseph Jastrow to Bertha Szold Levin, June 29, 1915, "Letters 1909–1945," Jastrow Papers.

17. *New York Times*, January 9, 1944; V.A.C. Henmon, "Joseph Jastrow," *Science* 99 (March 10, 1944), 193; Arthur L. Blumenthal, "The Intrepid Joseph Jastrow," in *Portraits of Pioneers in Psychology*, ed. Gregory A. Kimble et al. (Washington, D.C., 1991), 75–87; Thomas C. Cadwallader, "Origins and Accomplishments of Joseph Jastrow's 1888-Founded Chair of Comparative Psychology at the University of Wisconsin," *Journal of Comparative Psychology* 101 (September 1987), 235; and Edward G. Boring, *A History of Experimental Psychology* (1929; New York, 1950), 541. Because Jastrow was a founding figure of American psychology and its most prolific popularizer, historians usually mention him but without any sense of his distinguished rabbinic ancestry or any implication that his Jewish identity affected his thought. The one exception is Blumenthal, cited above, who suggested that "the rabbi's wayward son finally found himself in a pulpit, as a sermonizing crusader, as his father had been, yet with a congregation likely much larger than any his father ever dreamed of." See Blumenthal, "Intrepid Joseph Jastrow," 86. One of Jastrow's radio lectures, "The Devil Take the Hindmost," May 30, 1938, NBC (Blue), is available at the Motion Picture, Broadcasting and Recorded Sound Collections, Library of Congress, Washington, D.C.

18. Joseph Jastrow, *Piloting Your Life: The Psychologist as Helmsman* (New York, 1930), 360–61.

19. The liturgical passage is from Psalm 34, recited in the Sabbath morning service.

20. Rachel Szold Jastrow's illustrative letters are an essential part of the Joseph Jastrow Papers at Duke University. See for example Rachel's correspondence to her family dated March 29, 1888, undated 1891, May 15, 1893, May 23, 1893, December [?] 1894, undated [1894?], May 9, 1895, October 12, 1897, October 20, 1897, December 1, 1905, February 12, 1907, May 23, 1907, June 11, 1907, January 28, 1908, November 20, 1908, and March 23, 1919. At the end of his life, Jastrow finally turned to a subject of direct interest to Jews—a psychological profile of Hitler and Nazism—but he died before finishing these manuscripts. See also Alexandra Lee Levin, "The Jastrows in Madison: A Chronicle of University Life, 1888–1900," *Wisconsin Magazine of History* 46 (Summer 1963), 243–56. The story of the adoption of the infant by the Jastrows is recorded in a four-page statement of Harry Bold, the child's father, a native of Kiev who worked for a furniture company in Madison. Distraught by his wife's death, he departed Madison with his three older children. See the folder "Pictures, Writings, and Miscellany," Jastrow Papers.

As a young man Joseph wrote to Rabbi and Mrs. Szold about the Jewish New Year, "I do not know whether it is so for you, but for me the year really does begin at this season, when I come again in your midst." Joseph Jastrow to Dr. and Mrs. Szold, September 8, [1884?], Letters, 1875–1889, Jastrow Papers.

21. Typescript Course Lecture "Psychology of Belief," "Volumes," Jastrow Papers. For an explicit adaptation of Peirce, see Joseph Jastrow, "Belief and Credulity," *Educational Review* 23 (January 1902), 22–49 (for quotations, p. 25 and p. 27). Thomas Cadwallader highlights the influence of Peirce on Jastrow in Cadwallader, "Origins and Accomplishments," 232. The Jewish concept of a saving "remnant of Israel" is based on a number of passages in Prophets and is included in the daily prayer service. In *Romans*, Paul adapts the idea, but it is safe to say that Jastrow acquired the concept from his Jewish education and it is sure that he did not suggest the Christian meaning.

In "The Fixation of Belief," Peirce did not take any specific religious system to task, and he wrote from a tacitly Protestant perspective, as suggested by the two examples he chose to illustrate the inertia of human belief: what shall we say, he asked, "to a reformed Mussulman who should hesitate to give up his old notions in regard to the relations of the sexes; or to a reformed Catholic who should still shrink from reading the Bible." See Charles S. Peirce, "The Fixation of Belief," in *Charles S. Peirce: The Essential Writings*, ed. Edward C. Moore (Amherst, N.Y., 1998), 136. The essay originally appeared in *Popular Science Monthly* in 1877.

22. Boris Sidis, *Nervous Ills: Their Cause and Cure* (Boston, 1922), 361; and Boris Sidis, *The Psychology of Suggestion: A Research into the Subconscious Nature of Man and Society* (1898; New York, 1916), 327.

23. Boris Sidis, *Philistine and Genius* (New York, 1911), 28; and Sidis, *Nervous Ills*, 360.

24. For the book dedication see Boris Sidis and Simon P. Goodhart, *Multiple Personality: An Experimental Investigation into the Nature of Human Individuality* (New York, 1905). For the correspondence see the following letters in the William James Papers: Sidis to James, October 9, 1905 [bMS Am1092.9 (3768–3777)]; James to Sidis, October 28, 1897 [bMS Am1092.9(619)]; and James to Sidis, June 20, 1907 [bMS Am1092.9(619)].

25. William James to Boris Sidis, September 4, 1901, and September 11, 1902, William James Papers [bMS Am1092.9(619)]. On the death of William James Sidis, Ernest Jones wrote to Abraham Brill, "P.S. I suppose you saw about the end of a child prodigy? Boris Sidis died in time." EJ to AB, July 22 [1944], box 9 "Jones-Brill Correspondence," Brill Papers. For an analysis of William James Sidis, see Kathleen Montour, "William James Sidis, The Broken Twig," *American Psychologist* 32 (April 1977), 265–79; for the quote "nonpareil of achievements" see p. 269. See also Norbert Wiener, *Ex-Prodigy: My Childhood and Youth* (1953; Cambridge, Mass., 1972), 131–38; and Amy Wallace, *The Prodigy* (New York, 1986).

26. Abraham Myerson, *Speaking of Man* (New York, 1950), 10. This posthumously published book was edited by Myerson's daughter-in-law, Mildred Ann Myerson.

27. Moses Rischin, *The Promised City: New York's Jews, 1870–1914* (1962; New York, 1977), 41, and the entire chapter "Torah, Haskala, and Protest," 34–47, on the ideological shifts in the world of the eastern European Jewish immigrants to America. On the tension between secular and Orthodox ideas in Lithuania,

see Marc B. Shapiro, *Between the Yeshiva World and Modern Orthodoxy: The Life and Works of Rabbi Jehiel Jacob Weinberg, 1884–1966* (London, 1999), 1–17.

28. Paul G. Myerson, "Abraham Myerson," in *Psychoanalysis, Psychotherapy and the New England Medical Scene, 1894–1944*, ed. George E. Gifford, Jr. (New York, 1978), 243. See also *Dictionary of American Biography* (supp. 4), 617–18; *New York Times*, September 3, 1948; and *Who's Who in American Jewry 1928*, 506.

29. Myerson, *Speaking of Man*, 253–70. Myerson's other books were *The Inheritance of Mental Diseases* (Baltimore, 1925), *Social Psychology* (New York, 1934), and *Eugenical Sterilization* (New York, 1936). He coauthored *Preventive Medicine and Hygiene* (New York, 1927) and *The German Jew: His Share in Modern Culture* (New York, 1933).

30. Myerson, *Speaking of Man*, 34, 40–41, 263–68. The poignancy of Myerson's concern about people falling into a state of anhedonia comes through even in his clinical studies. See Abraham Myerson, "Neuroses and Neuropsychoses," *American Journal of Psychiatry* 94 (January 1938), 962–63. For his introduction of the term, see Abraham Myerson, "Anhedonia," *American Journal of Psychiatry* 2 (July 1922), 87–103.

31. Joseph Jastrow, "Manners and Morals: An Unconventional Dialogue," *Unpopular Review* 8 (October 1917), 330; Abraham Myerson and Isaac Goldberg, *The German Jew: His Share in Modern Culture* (New York, 1933), ix; and Myerson, *Speaking of Man*, 38, 270.

32. Statement to Office of War Information, April 17, 1943, folder "Autobiographical Statement," box 12, Abraham A. Brill Papers, Manuscript Division, Library of Congress (hereafter Brill Papers). A. A. Brill, keynote address, 70th birthday celebration, Waldorf Astoria Hotel, New York City, October 12, 1944, folder "Lectures, 1944," box 11, Brill Papers.

33. Sigmund Freud, *The Interpretation of Dreams* (New York, 1998), xxxii. This edition is a reprint of the *Standard Edition* (London, 1953) translated by James Strachey. Albert Deutsch, "About Dr. Brill, the Jovial Crusader Who Overcame Freud's Detractors," *PM*, March 4, 1948; cartoon, June 15, 1955, from unidentified magazine, folder "Miscellany, Clippings," box 13, Brill Papers.

In 1923 Freud wrote Brill, "When I saw you last I recognized what the peculiar nature of our relation is and I think I have not been mistaken. There is something unalterable in it, and intimacy of the kind present in blood-relationship." See Freud to Brill, April 25, 1923, "Freud-Brill Correspondence," box 9, Brill Papers.

34. Folder "Miscellany, Passports & Identification Forms," box 12; and "Reflections and Reminiscences," January 9, 1947, folder "Lectures, 1947," box 11, Brill Papers; *Bulletin of the American Psychoanalytic Association* 4 (May 1948), 1–3; *New York State Journal of Medicine* (April 15, 1948), 939; C[larence]. P. Oberndorf, "A. A. Brill," *Psychoanalytic Quarterly* 17 (April 1948), 149–54; *American Journal of Psychiatry* 104 (March 1948), 581; and Jacob A. Goldberg, "Jews in the Medical Profession—A National Survey," *Jewish Social Studies* 1 (July 1939), 327–36. On the receipt of D. H. Lawrence memorabilia, see Yale University Library *Gazette*, 37 (January 1963), 102, a clipping of which is contained in "Family Papers, Memorials," box 1, Brill Papers. For Freud's reprimand, see Freud to Brill, January 7, 1923, "Freud-Brill Correspondence," box 9, Brill Papers.

When his will was probated in 1948, Brill's total estate was valued at $451,381.95. Between the mid-1930s and mid-1940s Brill gave cash gifts to his son, Edmund, totaling about $50,000, to his wife, Rose, about $25,000, and to his daughter, Gioia, about $25,000. See "Family Papers, Estate Tax Returns," box 1, Brill Papers. On the financial rewards of Brill's practice, see also "Lewisohn-Brill Correspondence," box 9, Brill Papers.

35. A. A. Brill to Edmund Brill, undated [1939], folder "Letter to Edmund R. Brill," box 9; "Writings, College Essays," box 5; "Thoughts of Life and Death," speech before the Vidonian Club, New York City, December 7, 1946, folder "Miscellany, Vidonian Club," box 12; and "Determinism in Psychiatry," lecture before the Jewish Academy of Arts and Sciences, January 23, 1938, folder "Lectures, 1938," box 11, Brill Papers. Brill's favorite biblical quotation comes from Genesis 8:21: "For the imagination (impulse) of the heart of man is evil from his youth." See also Nathan G. Hale, Jr., *Freud and the Americans: The Beginnings of Psychoanalysis in the United States, 1876–1917* (New York, 1971), 389–96.

36. A. A. Brill to Edmund Brill [notation by Edmund (?) "Early 1939 or 1940"], "Letter to Edmund R. Brill," box 9; and "Moses and Monotheism," lecture before congregation Rodeph Sholom, November 5, 1939, folder "Lectures, 1939," box 11, Brill Papers. For the Spinoza cult of nineteenth-century European Jewry, see Shmuel Feiner, *Haskalah and History: The Emergence of a Modern Jewish Historical Consciousness* (Oxford, 2002), 146–49.

37. Oberndorf, "A. A. Brill," 153.

38. Barbara Sicherman, "Isador H. Coriat: The Making of an American Psychoanalyst," in *Psychoanalysis, Psychotherapy and the New England Medical Scene*, 164, 168–69; C. P. Oberndorf, "Isador Henry Coriat," *The International Journal of Psycho-Analysis* 24 (1943), 93–94; Arthur J. Linenthal, *First a Dream: The History of Boston's Jewish Hospitals, 1896–1928* (Boston, 1990), 536; and *Who's Who in American Jewry 1928* (New York, 1928), 125.

39. Sicherman, "Isador H. Coriat," 163–77; MDFLHale, *Beginnings of Psychoanalysis*, 377–79. See also Isaac Goldberg, "The Hysteria of Lady Macbeth: A Novel Use of Famous Imaginary People as Subjects for Psychological Study, First Undertaken by a Boston Scientist, Dr. Coriat," *Boston Evening Transcript*, June 13, 1917; and "Freud, Fry and Phantasy," *Boston Transcript*, April 4, 1925.

40. Linenthal, *First a Dream*, 62–64; Isador H. Coriat, "Amaurotic Family Idiocy," *Archives of Pediatrics* 30 (June 1913), 404–15; and Isador H. Coriat, "Some Familial and Hereditary Features of Amaurotic Idiocy," *American Journal of Insanity* 75 (July 1918), 121–31. Amaurosis is a type of idiocy marked by blindness; amaurotic family idiocy was coined as a term by Dr. Bernard Sachs in a 1896 article "A Family Form of Idiocy, Generally Fatal, Associated with Early Blindness," *Journal of Nervous and Mental Disorders* 23 (1896), 475–79. Coriat's articles on this subject provided important corroboration of the disease that would be named after Sachs and English ophthamologist Warren Tay.

41. Isador H. Coriat, *The Meaning of Dreams* (1915; Boston, 1920), 14, 32, 34.

42. Isador H. Coriat, "The Eightieth Birthday of Sigmund Freud," remarks made at a meeting of Jewish Book Week at the Boston Public Library, May 17, 1936, p. 9, Isador Henry Coriat Papers, The Francis A. Countway Library of Medicine, Boston (hereafter Coriat Papers); and Isador H. Coriat, *The Hysteria of Lady*

Macbeth (New York, 1912), 10. For the B'nai B'rith clipping, see Scrapbook #2 of the Coriat Papers.

43. Sigmund Freud, *New Introductory Lectures on Psycho-Analysis* (New York, 1933), 93, 192, 194. Even Freud's disciple Coriat invoked the inferiority complex in an analysis of a dream, and several years before Adler's name was known to the public; see Isador H. Coriat, *Repressed Emotions* (New York, 1920), 205–13. Coriat believed that Adler's organic approach was "of great value for the future development of psychoanalysis," as he correctly perceived that it would appeal to those "who are either inclined to functional or to physical interpretations of the development of the neurosis" (177).

44. Edwin A. Kirkpatrick, *Mental Hygiene for Effective Living* (New York, 1934), 2–3; Albert Edward Wiggam, *New Techniques of Happiness* (New York, 1948), 67–68; Dale Carnegie, *How to Win Friends and Influence People* (New York, 1937), 85; and Dale Carnegie, *How to Stop Worrying and Start Living* (New York, 1948), 137–39.

45. Edward Hoffman, *The Drive for Self: Alfred Adler and the Founding of Individual Psychology* (Reading, Mass., 1994), 173–247, 296–302.

46. *Who's Who in American Jewry, 1928,* 760; Phyllis Bottome, *Alfred Adler: A Biography* (New York, 1939), 100; and Hoffman, *Drive for Self,* 197, 301.

47. W[alter] Béran Wolfe, *How to Be Happy though Human* (New York, 1931), viii.

48. Ibid., 9–10; and W[alter] Béran Wolfe, *A Woman's Best Years: The Art of Staying Young* (New York, 1935), 241.

49. Josephine A. Jackson and Helen M. Salisbury, *Outwitting Our Nerves* (1921; Garden City, N.Y., 1944), 75; Frederick Pierce, *Our Unconscious Mind: And How to Use It* (New York, 1922), 230–31; Alexander B. MacLeod, *Mental Hygiene as Taught by Jesus* (New York, 1925); William L. Stidger, *Finding God in Books* (New York, 1925), 162–71, and Hugh Black, *The Practice of Self-Culture* (New York, 1904), 210. On the difficulties of American success literature in confronting both industrialism and the new immigration of the late 1800s, see Richard Weiss, *The American Myth of Success: From Horatio Alger to Norman Vincent Peale* (1969; Urbana, 1988), 64–96.

50. Boris Sidis, *The Foundations of Normal and Abnormal Psychology* (Boston, 1914), 187, 196; A. A. Brill, "The Psychopathology of the Cripple," lecture delivered to the Society for the Aid of the Crippled in Palestine at the Jewish Club, New York City, January 25, 1937, folder "Lectures, 1937," box 11, Brill Papers; and Myerson and Goldberg, *German Jew,* 18.

51. [Paul Carus, ed.,] *Epitomes of Three Sciences: Comparative Philology, Psychology, and Old Testament History* (Chicago, 1890), 8; Allen Johnson and Dumas Malone, eds., *Dictionary of American Biography* (New York, 1958), vol. 2, part 1, p. 548. One of the first editors to introduce Buddhism and eastern religion to an American audience, Carus once wrote, "I have said repeatedly that I am a Buddhist, but you must not forget that I am at the same time a Christian in so far as I accept certain teachings of Christ. I am even a Taoist, in so far as I accept certain doctrines of Lautsze. I am an Israelite, in so far as I sympathize with the aspirations of the Israelitic prophets." See Harold Henderson, *Catalyst for Controversy: Paul Carus of Open Court* (Carbondale, Ill., 1993), 116.

52. *Epitomes of Three Sciences,* 104–5.

53. Ibid., 7. In a good comparative example from the British academic world, anthropologist Harvey Goldberg finds hints of ideological struggle between the mid-twentieth-century English anthropologists Meyer Fortes and his friend Edward Evans-Pritchard. "With elegant British ambiguity," Evans-Pritchard "generously likened the Old Testament to Nuer Religion," whereas Fortes made biblical references equally to Judaism and Christianity. In Fortes's writings, "Jewish and Christian examples often appear in close proximity, almost as if to hint, contra *Nuer Religion,* that neither religion is more primitive than the other." See Harvey E. Goldberg, "The Voice of Jacob: Jewish Perspectives on Anthropology and the Study of the Bible," *Jewish Social Studies* [n.s.] 2 (Fall 1995), 50.

54. Dale M. Herder, "Haldeman-Julius, the Little Blue Books, and the Theory of Popular Culture," *Journal of Popular Culture* 4 (Spring 1971), 881–91.

55. E. Haldeman-Julius, *An Agnostic Looks at Life: Challenges of a Militant Pen* (Girard, Kans., 1926), 14, 16, 78. This volume is Big Blue Book No. B-25. For the original psychological critique of Jesus, see E. Haldeman-Julius, *Studies in Rationalism* (Girard, Kans., 1925), Big Blue Book No. 7. For a crisp overview of the Jewish publishing companies, see Howard Sachar, *A History of the Jews in America* (New York, 1992), 768–72. See also "Publishing," in *Encyclopaedia Judaica,* 16 vols. (Jerusalem, 1971), 13:1371–72.

Although Janice Radway exaggerates in arguing that Jewish publishing entrepreneurs viewed culture not as "something offered for contemplation and study, a thing to be valued in its own right" but rather as "a sign of achievement and a mark of social position," she, like Joan Shelley Rubin before her, presents an interesting interpretation of the cultural conflicts that the Book-of-the-Month Club men stimulated; see Janice Radway, "The Scandal of the Middlebrow: The Book-of-the-Month Club, Class Fracture, and Cultural Authority," *South Atlantic Quarterly* 89 (Fall 1990), 703–36; and Joan Shelley Rubin, "Self, Culture, and Self-Culture in Modern America: The Early History of the Book-of-the-Month Club," *Journal of American History* 71 (March 1985), 782–806.

56. It is interesting to note that two non-Jewish scholars made important inroads into the problem of interpreting the distinctive significance of secular Jewish thinkers. In 1974 sociologist John Murray Cuddihy published *The Ordeal of Civility: Freud, Marx, Lévi-Strauss, and the Jewish Struggle with Modernity.* In a brilliantly rambunctious style, Cuddihy claimed that the psychological and social dynamics of Jewish assimilation underlay the seminal theories of Karl Marx, Sigmund Freud, and Claude Lévi-Strauss and of secular Jewish thinkers in general. He argued that a " 'secret,' intraethnic war has been encoded in various ways in the literary and ideological product of the Jewish social critics of the Diaspora" (p. 225).

Historian David Hollinger carved out another path for understanding the activities of Jewish intellectuals, one that was less flamboyant but more empirically viable than Cuddihy's. In an effort to trace the "de-Christianization" of American academic and public thought in the twentieth century, Hollinger found that "an informal alliance" of liberal or secular Protestants and Jews had taken shape in the interwar and postwar years. Their objective: to replace "the old Protestant cultural hegemony" with an elite of intellectuals from various faiths and no faiths at all. See David A. Hollinger, *Science, Jews, and Secular Culture* (Princeton, 1996), 17, 28–29. Hollinger first suggested this line of argument in a fine intellectual biography of the philosopher Morris Raphael Cohen; see David A. Hollinger, *Morris R. Cohen and the Scientific Ideal* (Cambridge, Mass., 1975), 59–60, 249.

By the 1980s a full-blown academic field of Jewish Studies had emerged in the United States, within which scholars examined the nuances of Jewish assimilation in Western society. They discovered that, beneath the secular surface of many Jewish thinkers, there existed a layer of ethnic motives, often apologetic but usually reflecting Jewish ambivalence about the sacrifices that came with the desire to assimilate into the gentile world.

CHAPTER 7. THE MORONIC IMMIGRANT AND THE NEUROTIC JEW:
JEWS AND AMERICAN PERCEPTIONS OF INTELLIGENCE, PERSONALITY, AND RACE

1. "What Can We Do To Improve Race and Religious Relationships in America?" *Town Meeting* (Bulletin of America's Town Meeting of the Air, ABC, October 7, 1947), vol. 13, no. 24, pp. 7–8, 10.

2. Robert Boakes, *From Darwin to Behaviourism: Psychology and the Minds of Animals* (Cambridge, 1984), 44–48; and for a history of the eugenics movement in the United States, see Mark H. Haller, *Eugenics: Hereditarian Attitudes in American Thought* (New Brunswick, N.J., 1963). In one instance Jews entered into Galton's compass, marking an early example of polemical battle between philosemitic and antisemitic interpretations of psychological data. In 1883 an Anglo-Jewish statistician, Joseph Jacobs, asked Galton to do a photographic study of East End Jews using a method he, Galton, had developed to establish the characteristic "type" of a group from a composite of pictures. Both Galton and Jacobs operated on the assumption that "races" had enduring collective personalities that were detectable in pictures, and both agreed that this pictorial study showed a distinct Jewish typology. But Galton argued that the faces revealed a capacity for cold economic appraisal whereas Jacobs saw evidence of idealistic intellectuality. See Mitchell B. Hart, *Social Science and the Politics of Modern Jewish Identity* (Stanford, 2000), 178.

3. On Goddard, see Leila Zenderland, *Measuring Minds: Henry Herbert Goddard and the Origins of American Intelligence Testing* (Cambridge, 1998). See also Michael M. Sokal, ed., *Psychological Testing and American Society, 1890–1930* (New Brunswick, N.J., 1987); C. James Goodwin, *A History of Modern Psychology* (New York, 1999), 219–42; and Alan M. Kraut, *Silent Travelers: Germs, Genes, and the "Immigrant Menace"* (New York, 1994), 57–68.

4. Lewis M. Terman, *The Measurement of Intelligence* (Boston, 1916), 91–92; JoAnne Brown, "Mental Measurements and the Rhetorical Force of Numbers," in *The Estate of Social Knowledge,* ed. JoAnne Brown and David K. van Keuren (Baltimore, 1991), 134–52; and Goodwin, *History of Modern Psychology,* 234–41.

5. Carl C. Brigham, *A Study of American Intelligence* (Princeton, 1923), 187–90. The popularity of racialist science among some intellectuals is well illustrated by the fact that the textbook at issue in the Scopes "monkey trial," George Hunter's

Civic Biology, emancipated American high schoolers from fundamentalist views of creation while indoctrinating them in the latest pseudo-science about racial genetics. See Paul A. Carter, *The Twenties in America* (Arlington Heights, Ill., 1975), 95.

6. Josiah Royce, *Race Questions, Provincialism and Other American Problems* (New York, 1908), 8–9, 33, 46–48.

7. Walter Lippmann, "The Mental Age of Americans," *New Republic,* October 25, 1992; "The Abuse of the Tests," *New Republic,* November 15, 1922; and "A Future for the Tests," *New Republic,* November 29, 1922. Despite his opposition to nativist hereditarianism, Lippmann favored immigration restriction. See Ronald Steel, *Walter Lippmann and the American Century* (New York, 1980), 247–48. About half a year after Lippmann's series, Harvard psychologist E. G. Boring weighed in with a more muted but important criticism of the hereditarian case—see Edwin G. Boring, "Facts and Fancies of Immigration," *New Republic,* April 25, 1923; and "Intelligence as the Tests Test It," *New Republic,* June 6, 1923. For a few other critiques not cited here, see Brown, "Mental Measurements," 144–46.

8. George W. Stocking, Jr., *Race, Culture, and Evolution: Essays in the History of Anthropology* (New York, 1968), 163–94, 300–301; Carl N. Degler, *In Search of Human Nature: The Decline and Revival of Darwinism in American Social Thought* (New York, 1991), 84–104, 167–86; Graham Richards, *'Race,' Racism and Psychology: Towards a Reflexive History* (London, 1997), 122–59; Franz Samelson, "From 'Race Psychology' to 'Studies in Prejudice': Some Observations on the Thematic Reversal in Social Psychology," *Journal of the History of the Behavioral Sciences* 14 (1978), 265–78; and Julia E. Liss, "Franz Boas," in *A Companion to American Thought,* ed. Richard Wightman Fox and James T. Kloppenberg (Oxford, 1998), 81–83. For Boas's early writings on the American Negro and the article "The American People," see the posthumously published collection, Franz Boas, *Race and Democratic Society* (New York, 1945), esp. 54–95.

9. Stocking, *Race, Culture, and Evolution,* 175–80. Carl Brigham himself retracted his earlier argument, but after *A Study of American Intelligence* had done its damage. See Carl C. Brigham, "Intelligence Tests of Immigrant Groups," *Psychological Review* 37 (March 1930), 158–65.

10. John P. Jackson, Jr., *Social Scientists for Social Justice: Making the Case against Segregation* (New York, 2001), 20–23; and Otto Klineberg, *Negro Intelligence and Selective Migration* (New York, 1935). Another of Boas's Jewish students, anthropologist Melville Herskovits, simultaneously attacked other aspects of the same problem. See Melville Herskovits, *The American Negro: A Study in Racial Crossing* (New York, 1928); and Melville Herskovits, *The Anthropometry of the American Negro* (New York, 1930).

11. Otto Klineberg, *Race Differences* (New York, 1935), 1–5, 12, 345–46.

12. "Talks on Mental Hygiene Are Heard by Jewish Women," undated clipping from an unidentified Providence newspaper, scrapbook #1, Isador Henry Coriat Papers, Francis A. Countway Library of Medicine, Boston; Boris Sidis, *The Foundations of Normal and Abnormal Psychology* (Boston, 1914), v; Joseph Jastrow, "Heredity and Mental Traits," *Science,* October 16, 1914, p. 556; and Alfred Adler, "Character and Talent," *Harper's Monthly* 155 (June 1927), 64, 66, 71.

13. Maurice B. Hexter and Abraham Myerson, "13.77 versus 12.05; A Study in Probable Error: A Critical Discussion of Brigham's 'American Intelligence,' " *Mental Hygiene* 8 (January 1924), 82.

14. Abraham Myerson, *The Foundations of Personality* (Boston, 1921), 31–32. See also Abraham Myerson, *Social Psychology* (New York, 1934), 379–80. The concept of "social heredity" already existed in American psychology, but Myerson gave it historical and cultural specificity.

15. A Jewish psychologist, Saul Rosenzweig, was the first to raise the issue of the background (gender, ethnic, racial, social) of the subject in psychological experiments. See Saul Rosenzweig, "The Experimental Situation as a Psychological Problem," *Psychological Review* 40 (July 1933), 337–54. See also Jill G. Morawski, "Impossible Experiments and Practical Constructions," in *The Rise of Experimentation in American Psychology*, ed. Jill G. Morawski (New Haven, 1988), 72–93.

16. Abraham Myerson, "A Critique of Proposed 'Ideal' Sterilization Legislation," *Archives of Neurology and Psychiatry* 33 (March 1935), 454–55, 462–63; Haller, *Eugenics*, 130–41; and Gerald N. Grob, *Mental Illness and American Society, 1875–1940* (Princeton, 1983), 175–77. The important 1936 study cautioned: "We do not believe that society needs to hurry into a program based on fear and propaganda"—see Abraham Myerson et al., *Eugenical Sterilization: A Reorientation of the Problem* (New York, 1936), 183. William Alanson White was also an important spokesman against sterilization but, in contrast to Myerson, did not emphasize the ethnic dimension of the subject.

17. Abraham Myerson and Rosalie D. Boyle, "The Incidence of Manic-Depressive Psychosis in Certain Socially Prominent Families," *American Journal of Psychiatry* 98 (July 1941), 11–21.

18. Otto Klineberg, "Mental Testing of Racial and National Groups," in H. S. Jennings et al., *Scientific Aspects of the Race Problem* (Washington, D.C., 1941), 254; Sander L. Gilman, *Jewish Self-Hatred: Anti-Semitism and the Hidden Language of the Jews* (Baltimore, 1986), 288–89; and Sander L. Gilman, *The Case of Sigmund Freud: Medicine and Identity at the Fin de Siècle* (Baltimore, 1993), 20–21. On the rise of Jewish race science as a reaction to antisemitism, see John M. Efron, *Defenders of the Race: Jewish Doctors and Race Science in Fin-de-Siècle Europe* (New Haven, 1994). For an extensive comparison of European and American views of Jews, see Frederic Cople Jaher, *A Scapegoat in the New Wilderness: The Origins and Rise of Anti-Semitism in America* (Cambridge, Mass., 1994). On racialist antisemitism at the turn of the century, see Robert Singerman, "The Jew as Racial Alien: The Genetic Component of American Anti-Semitism," *Anti-Semitism in American History*, ed. David A. Gerber (Urbana, 1986), 103–28. On stereotypes of Jews as tubercular and weak, see Kraut, *Silent Travelers*, 145–46, 155–56.

19. Carl Wittke, *We Who Built America: The Saga of the Immigrant* (n.p., 1939), v; John Haynes Holmes, *Through Gentile Eyes* (New York, 1938), 12; and Abraham Cahan, "The Autobiography of an American Jew: The Rise of David Levinsky," *McClure's* 40 (April 1913), 96. The myth of Jewish genius that circulated in America differed dramatically from a popular European stereotype that depicted the Jewish mind as "imitative" at best and incapable of creative genius. On Germanic attitudes about Jewish mentality, see Steven Beller, *Vienna and the Jews,*

1867–1938: A Cultural History (Cambridge, 1989), 77–82; and Sander Gilman, *The Jew's Body* (New York, 1991), 128–49.

20. Edward Alsworth Ross, *The Old World in the New: The Significance of Past and Present Immigration to the American People* (New York, 1914), 157–64. The view that Jews and Anglo-Saxons were equally indomitable was not peculiar to Ross. George Beard said the same; see George M. Beard, *American Nervousness: Its Causes and Consequences* (1881; New York, 1972), 172.

21. Burton J. Hendrick, "The Skulls of Our Immigrants," *McClure's* 35 (May 1910), 42, 44. For a sample of views about Jewish genetic tenacity, see Arnold White, *The Modern Jew* (New York, 1899), 56; and John Foster Fraser, *The Conquering Jew* (New York, 1916), 1, 51, 295.

22. A. Myerson, "The 'Nervousness' of the Jew," *Mental Hygiene*, 4 (January 1920), 65, 71; and A. A. Brill and Morris J. Karpas, "Insanity Among Jews," *Medical Record* 86 (October 1914), 576–79. In an article for *Good Housekeeping*, Coriat emphasized the difference between functional (emotional) disorders like neurasthenia that were curable through "mental therapeutics" and organic disorders that were not; see Isador H. Coriat, "Suggestion in the Treatment of Nervous Disease," *Good Housekeeping* 44 (May 1907), 558–60. A recent study roughly corroborated Brill, finding that Jewish males were more inclined than other men to suffer major depressions and less inclined to have alcohol-related problems; see Itzhak Levav, Robert Kohn, Jacqueline M. Golding, and Myrna Weissman, "Vulnerability of Jews to Affective Disorders," *American Journal of Psychiatry* 154 (July 1997), 941–47.

23. Isador H. Coriat, "Some Familial and Hereditary Features of Amaurotic Idiocy," *American Journal of Insanity* 75 (July 1918), 127–28, 130.

24. A. A. Brill, "The Adjustment of the Jew to the American Environment," *Mental Hygiene* 2 (April 1918), 220; and Myerson, " 'Nervousness' of the Jew," 71. On the Mental Hygiene movement see Grob, *Mental Illness and American Society*, 144–78.

25. Maurice Fishberg, *The Jews: A Study of Race and Environment* (New York, 1911), 531, 555.

26. Brill, "Adjustment of the Jew," 220; Gilman, *Case of Sigmund Freud*, 20–21; Myerson, " 'Nervousness' of the Jew," 70; Sidis, *Nervous Ills*; and Isador H. Coriat, "Amaurotic Family Idiocy," *Archives of Pediatrics* 30 (June 1913), 413–14. William Alanson White, a leading American psychoanalyst, seconded the idea that emotional repression borne of persecution caused physiological problems in Jews. Noting that diabetes had "long been believed" to be "of nervous origin," White attributed the prevalence of that disease among Jews to a brutal history. "Here certainly no argument is needed to demonstrate the larger factor that repression may well play in a race which, in Europe particularly, has continuously been the object of prejudice and so suppressed in all manner of ways for centuries." See William A. White, *Mechanisms of Character Formation* (1916; New York, 1920), 256–58.

On the persistence of Lamarckian assumptions (that environmental stimuli can produce genetic traits) in American thought see Stocking, *Race, Culture, and Evolution*, 234–69; Ronald L. Numbers, *Darwin Comes to America* (Cambridge, Mass., 1998), 33–43; and Merle Curti, *Human Nature in American Thought* (Madison, 1980), 274–90.

27. Brill, "Adjustment of the Jew," 223–25. Brill's talmudic quotation comes from Tractate Berakhot 3b. I thank Serguei Dolgopolski for help in locating that passage.

28. Wolfe, *How to Be Happy though Human*, 240; and *The Two Hundred and Fiftieth Anniversary of the Settlement of the Jews in the United States, 1655–1905* (New York, 1906), 86. A positive view of the Jewish family appeared even in the raucously nativist writings of Edward A. Ross: "The Jewish immigrants cherish a pure, close-knit family life and the position of the woman in the home is one of dignity. More than any other immigrants they are ready to assume the support of distant needy relatives." See Ross, *Old World in the New*, 149.

29. Myerson, " 'Nervousness' of the Jew," 69, 72; A. A. Brill, "The Psychology of the Jew," for broadcast on WMCA (New York), December 11, 1932, folder "Radio Scripts, 1932," box 12, Brill Papers; A. A. Brill, "Sigmund Freud, The Man and His Work," lecture given before the Group [?], New York City, October 24, 1939, folder "Lectures, 1939," box 11, Brill Papers; and A. A. Brill, "Should Voluntary Mercy Death (Euthanasia) Be Legalized?" for broadcast on WMCA (New York), February 16, 1943, folder "Radio Scripts, 1943," box 12, Brill Papers.

30. Sidis, *Foundations of Normal and Abnormal Psychology*, 223, 225–26. Italics are Sidis's.

31. John Cowper Powys, *The Art of Forgetting the Unpleasant* (Girard, Kans., 1928), 24; Joseph Jastrow, *Piloting Your Life: The Psychologist as Helmsman* (New York, 1930), 316, 318; W[alter] Béran Wolfe, *Calm Your Nerves: The Prevention and Cure of Nervous Breakdown* (New York, 1933), 62–64; and Wolfe, *How to Be Happy though Human*, 241–43. See also Boris Sidis, *Philistine and Genius* (New York, 1911). For another example of the contrast with American self-culture, see Hugh Black, *The Practice of Self-Culture* (New York, 1904), 125. On the stereotypical over-intellectuality of Jews as a pretext for collegiate discrimination, see, for example, Thomas Bender, *New York Intellect* (Baltimore, 1987), 288–92.

32. In his study of Jewish organizational efforts to combat prejudice, Stuart Svonkin discusses the influential Studies in Prejudice series that appeared in 1949–50 but overlooks the Jewish psychologists who began this line of inquiry before World War II. See Stuart Svonkin, *Jews Against Prejudice: American Jews and the Fight for Civil Liberties* (New York, 1997), 37. On the Frankfurt School of largely German Jewish scholars who produced the Studies in Prejudice series, see Martin Jay, *The Dialectical Imagination: A History of the Frankfurt School and the Institute of Social Research, 1923–1950* (Boston, 1973), esp. 219–52. As Jay notes, the Institute for Social Research was originally supposed to investigate the sources of antisemitism in Germany, but its personnel, as committed Marxists who deemphasized ethno-religious questions, tended to avoid the subject as long as possible. Furthermore, the Institute's first publications on authority and Nazism appeared only in German, even though the Institute had already relocated to New York City. Until the war began the Frankfurt scholars "remained impervious to the entreaties of their new colleagues at Columbia to integrate their work into the American social-scientific mainstream" (114).

33. Boas, *Race and Democratic Society*, 2. On American antisemitism after World War I, see Leonard Dinnerstein, *Anti-Semitism in America* (New York, 1994), 78–127.

34. Abraham Myerson, *The Terrible Jews, by One of Them* (Boston, 1922), 42–43; Abraham Myerson and Isaac Goldberg, *The German Jew: His Share in Modern Culture* (New York, 1933), 11, 160; and A. A. Brill, "The Family Faces the Future," address before the Conference on Maternal Health and Child Welfare, New York City, February 19, 1943, folder "Lectures, 1943," box 11, Brill Papers. See also Myerson, *Social Psychology,* 585.

35. F. J. McGuigan, "Edmund Jacobson (1888–1983)," *American Psychologist* 41 (March 1986), 315; *New York Times,* January 14, 1983; "Edmund Jacobson," *Contemporary Authors* (Detroit, 1974), First Revision, vols. 9–12, p. 427; Edmund Jacobson, *Progressive Relaxation: A Physiological and Clinical Investigation of Muscular States and Their Significance in Psychology and Medical Practice* (Chicago, 1929), 377; and Edmund Jacobson, *You Must Relax: A Practical Method for Reducing the Strains of Modern Living* (1934; New York, 1942), 24, 26. Concerned about the inability of psychiatry to determine therapeutic success with scientific precision, Jacobson became the "father of electromyography," inventing apparatus that recorded levels of muscular tension in microvolts. See McGuigan, "Edmund Jacobson," 315.

36. Edmund Jacobson, *You Can Sleep Well: The A B C's of Restful Sleep for the Average Person* (New York, 1938), ix–x; Jacobson, *You Must Relax,* 14–15; and Edmund Jacobson, *The Peace We Americans Need: A Plea for Clearer Thinking about Our Allies, Our Foes, Ourselves and Our Future* (Chicago, 1944), 70–71.

37. *Science News Letter,* May 9, 1942.

38. Jastrow, *Keeping Mentally Fit,* 178–79; and W[alter] Béran Wolfe, *Successful Living* (New York, 1938), 19–20.

39. Karen Horney, *The Neurotic Personality of Our Time* (New York, 1937); Karl Menninger, *Man Against Himself* (New York, 1938); and Erich Fromm, *Escape from Freedom* (1941; New York, 1961). On the sensitivity of German-speaking émigrés, most of them Jewish, to the problem of fascism, see Anthony Heilbut, *Exiled in Paradise: German Refugee Artists and Intellectuals in America from the 1930s to the Present* (Boston, 1983).

40. Mitchell G. Ash, *Gestalt Psychology in German Culture, 1890–1967: Holism and the Quest for Objectivity* (Cambridge, England, 1995), 263–75. On the migration of Gestalt psychology to America, see Michael M. Sokal, "The Gestalt Psychologists in Behaviorist America," *American Historical Review* 89 (December 1984), 1240–63; and Mitchell G. Ash, "Émigré Psychologists after 1933: The Cultural Coding of Scientific and Professional Practices," in *Forced Migration and Scientific Change: Émigré German-Speaking Scientists and Scholars after 1933,* ed. Mitchell G. Ash and Alfons Söllner (Washington, D.C., 1996), 117–38. The importance of Lewin to American psychological thought began to appear in the late 1920s; see Kurt Koffka, "On the Structure of the Unconscious," in *The Unconscious: A Symposium,* ed. C. M. Child et al. (1928; Freeport, N.Y., 1966), 59–63.

41. Kurt Lewin, *Resolving Social Conflicts: Selected Papers on Group Dynamics,* ed. Gertrud Weiss Lewin (New York, 1948), 153, 156–58, 186–200. This posthumously published volume includes "Psycho-Sociological Problems of a Minority Group" (1935). In "Self-Hatred among Jews" (1941), Lewin contended that "Jewish self-hatred is a phenomenon which has its parallel in many underprivileged groups," and he claimed that "one of the better known and most extreme cases of self-hatred can be found among American Negroes" (189). African American

psychologist Kenneth Clark, whose evidence about Negro self-esteem affected the Supreme Court decision in *Brown v. Board of Education* (1954), drew upon Lewin's concept of self-hatred—see Jackson, *Social Scientists for Social Justice*, 57, 122. On the relation of Jewishness to Lewin's psychological theories, see Mitchell G. Ash, "Cultural Contexts and Scientific Change in Psychology: Kurt Lewin in Iowa," *American Psychologist* 47 (February 1992), 204; and Miriam Lewin, "The Impact of Kurt Lewin's Life on the Place of Social Issues in His Work," *Journal of Social Issues* 48 (Summer 1992), 15–29.

42. Lewin, *Resolving Social Conflicts*, 77, 79, 83. The paper that is cited here, "Experiments in Social Space," appeared in the *Harvard Educational Review* in 1939. The experiments were first reported in Kurt Lewin, Ronald Lippitt, and Ralph K. White, "Patterns of Aggressive Behavior in Experimentally Created 'Social Climates,' " *Journal of Social Psychology* 10 (May 1939), 271–99.

43. Lewin's project preceded and inspired reformers who used social scientific data to attack segregation after World War II. See Jackson, *Social Scientists for Social Justice*, 66–74, 109. See also pp. 103–6 for the crisis that came out of the effort to merge the "objectivity" of social science with the political agenda of the American Jewish Congress. On the relationship between Lewin's psychological theories of prejudice and ethnic marginality and those of the Chicago school of functionalist sociology, see Daryl Michael Scott, *Contempt and Pity: Social Policy and the Image of the Damaged Black Psyche, 1880–1996* (Chapel Hill, 1997), 22–26.

44. Wolfe, *Calm Your Nerves*, 13; W[alter] Béran Wolfe, "Adler and Our Neurotic World," introduction to Alfred Adler, *The Pattern of Life* (New York, 1930), 14; and Horney, *Neurotic Personality*, 178.

45. Ernst Simmel, ed., *Anti-Semitism: A Social Disease* (New York, 1946), xix, 29. On Simmel and Fenichel, see Nathan G. Hale, Jr., *Freud and the Americans: The Rise and Crisis of Psychoanalysis, 1917–1985* (New York, 1995), 50–51, 149–52.

46. Kennan's "Long Telegram" is reprinted in Thomas G. Patterson and Dennis Merrill, eds., *Major Problems in American Foreign Relations: Volume II, Since 1914*, 4th ed. (Lexington, Mass., 1995), 244–47; and the *Brown* decision is excerpted in Marvin Meyers, John G. Cawelti, and Alexander Kern, eds., *Sources of the American Republic: A Documentary History of Politics, Society, and Thought*, rev. ed., 2 vols. (Glenview, Ill., 1969), 2:489–90. Daryl Scott observes that the "damage imagery" of the *Brown* decision "provided a ring of moral righteousness in a society devoted to therapeutic concerns." See Scott, *Contempt and Pity*, 136. On psychology and *Brown*, see also Jackson, *Social Scientists for Social Justice*, 109–96; and Ellen Herman, *The Romance of American Psychology: Political Culture in the Age of Experts* (Berkeley, 1995), 193–99.

CHAPTER 8. THE SPECTER OF THE MOB:
JEWS AND THE BATTLE FOR THE AMERICAN UNCONSCIOUS

1. On the trend of psychology away from metaphysical notions of the psyche, see John C. Burnham, *How Superstition Won and Science Lost: Popularizing Science and Health in the United States* (New Brunswick, 1987), 9–15, 90–91. Those academic psychologists like Columbia's Gardner Murphy who sustained the spirit

of Jamesian transcendentalism after 1920 focused less on the metaphysics of the subconscious than on the depths of human personality. See Katherine Pandora, *Rebels within the Ranks: Psychologists' Critique of Scientific Authority and Democratic Realities in New Deal America* (Cambridge, 1997), 20–25, 51–52, 124–30. On the variety of popular psychologies in the 1920s, see John C. Burnham, *Paths into American Culture: Psychology, Medicine, and Morals* (Philadelphia, 1988), 70–81.

2. Emmet Fox, *Power Through Constructive Thinking* (1932; New York, 1940), 148; and Robert C. Fuller, *Americans and the Unconscious* (New York, 1986), 175.

3. Boris Sidis, *The Psychology of Laughter* (New York, 1913), 67–73, 293.

4. *Boston Sunday Herald*, January 28, 1917. For biographical details on Kaufman, see *Who's Who in American Jewry, 1928* (New York, 1928), 352.

5. Fuller, *Americans and the Unconscious*, 129; and Hugo Münsterberg, *Psychotherapy* (New York, 1909), 125.

6. Hugo Münsterberg et al. (Theodore Ribot, Pierre Janet, Joseph Jastrow, Bernard Hart, and Morton Prince), *Subconscious Phenomena* (Boston, 1910), 35, 16–32, 40–52; Boris Sidis, *The Psychology of Suggestion: A Research into the Subconscious Nature of Man and Society* (1898; New York, 1916), 3, 201–15; and Hugo Münsterberg, "A Symposium on the Subconscious," *Journal of Abnormal Psychology* 2 (April–May, 1907), 32–33. See also Münsterberg, *Psychotherapy*, 82; Joseph Jastrow, *The Subconscious* (Boston, 1905); Joseph Jastrow, *Character and Temperament* (1915; New York, 1921), 139–40; and R. W. Rieber and Kurt Salzinger, eds., *Psychology: Theoretical-Historical Perspectives* (New York, 1980), 277.

7. Morton Prince, *Clinical and Experimental Studies in Personality*, ed. A. A. Roback (1929; Cambridge, Mass., 1939), 507, 591; and Münsterberg et al, *Subconscious Phenomena*, 98–101.

8. Abraham Myerson, *The Foundations of Personality* (Boston, 1921), 28, 95, 97.

9. Sigmund Freud to A. A. Brill, July 24, 1910, "Freud-Brill Correspondence," box 9, Brill Papers. (In German the passage reads: "Wundere mich nicht dass Sie kein Vergnügen in Oberammergau gefunden haben. . . . Auch ich wurde mich übrigens in die mystischen Genüsse der Christenheit schwer hineinfinden.") The quotation from Adler appears in Phyllis Bottome, *Alfred Adler: A Biography* (New York, 1939), 39–40. On Jewish versus Christian inflections of psychoanalysis, see Chapter 4 above, "Jewish Rationalist Moralism and the Drama of Family Life."

10. James Jackson Putnam, *Human Motives* (Boston, 1915), 52, 65, 170–71; F. H. Matthews, "The Americanization of Sigmund Freud: Adaptations of Psychoanalysis Before 1917," *Journal of American Studies* 1 (April 1967), 47; and Nathan G. Hale, Jr., "James Jackson Putnam and Boston Neurology: 1877–1918," *Psychoanalysis, Psychotherapy and the New England Medical Scene, 1894–1944*, ed. George E. Gifford, Jr. (New York, 1978), 153–54.

11. William A. White, "Higher Levels of Mental Integration," in *The Unconscious: A Symposium*, ed. C. M. Child et al. (1928; Freeport, New York, 1966), 248–50. The quotation about White comes from Fuller, *Americans and the Unconscious*, 115.

12. Edwin B. Holt, *The Freudian Wish and Its Place in Ethics* (New York, 1915); Josephine A. Jackson and Helen M. Salisbury, *Outwitting Our Nerves* (1921; Garden City, 1944), 75; Nathan G. Hale, Jr., *Freud and the Americans: The Beginnings of Psychoanalysis in the United States, 1876–1917* (New York, 1971), 377, 380–82, 394, 426–29; and Fuller, *Americans and the Unconscious*, 113–20.

13. Sanford Gifford, "Medical Psychotherapy and the Emmanuel Movement in Boston, 1904–1912," *Psychoanalysis, Psychotherapy and the New England Medical Scene*, 106–18; Hale, *Beginnings of Psychoanalysis*, 232–41; and Ann Taves, *Fits, Trances, & Visions: Experiencing Religion and Explaining Experience from Wesley to James* (Princeton, 1999), 319–25.

14. Elwood Worcester, Samuel McComb, and Isador H. Coriat, *Religion and Medicine: The Moral Control of Nervous Disorders* (New York, 1908), 14–15, 37–38, 261. Coriat authored chapters 8–13, pp. 179–265. See especially his chapter, "Diseases of the Subconscious," 199–217.

15. Isador H. Coriat, "Suggestion in the Treatment of Nervous Disease," *Good Housekeeping* 44 (May 1907), 559.

16. Donald Meyer noticed this distinction between the two in his classic analysis of the mental healing tradition in America. See Donald Meyer, *The Positive Thinkers: A Study of the American Quest for Health, Wealth and Personal Power from Mary Baker Eddy to Norman Vincent Peale* (New York, 1965), 266, 269, 328.

17. Sydney E. Ahlstrom, *A Religious History of the American People* (New Haven, 1972), 488–90. See also R. Laurence Moore, *In Search of White Crows: Spiritualism, Parapsychology, and American Culture* (New York, 1977); and Ann Braude, *Radical Spirits: Spiritualism and Women's Rights in Nineteenth-Century America* (Boston, 1989).

18. Mary Baker Eddy, *Miscellaneous Writings, 1883–1896* (1896; Boston, 1924), 26–27; Ahlstrom, *Religious History of the American People*, 1020–26; and Stephen Gottschalk, *The Emergence of Christian Science in American Religious Life* (Berkeley, 1973).

19. Houdini's battles against spiritualism occupy a large part of the biography by Kenneth Silverman, *Houdini!!! The Career of Ehrich Weiss* (New York, 1996).

20. Hugo Münsterberg, *American Problems: From the Point of View of a Psychologist* (New York, 1910), 144–45; and Linda Simon, *Genuine Reality: A Life of William James* (New York, 1998), 366–68.

21. Carl Murchison, ed., *A History of Psychology in Autobiography*, 4 vols. (1930; New York, 1961), 1:160; and Joseph Jastrow, "This Superstitious World," *Science Digest* (September 1940), 56, 58. For Jastrow's formidable output on the dangers of spiritualism and other irrationalist fashions and folklore, see *Fact and Fable in Psychology* (Boston, 1900), an anthology of eleven articles published between 1888 and 1900; "Modern Spiritualism," *The Dial* 34 (February 1, 1903), 79–82; "Fact and Fable in Animal Psychology," *Popular Science Monthly* 69 (August 1906), 138–46; "The Unmasking of Paladino," *Collier's* 45 (May 14, 1910), 21–22; "The Case of Paladino," *American Review of Reviews* 42 (July 1910), 74–84; "Malicious Animal Magnetism," *Hampton's* 25 (October 1910), 447–58 (see also the reply to Jastrow by a Christian Scientist, *Hampton's* 26 [February 1911], 266–68); "The Will to Believe in the Supernatural," *Nineteenth Century* 69 (March 1911), 471–86; "The Psychology of Conviction," *Scientific Monthly* 5 (December 1917), 523–44; "Do the Dead Come Back? A Psychological Interpretation of Human Gullibility," *Forum* 63 (February 1920), 145–63; "The Case of Sir Oliver Lodge," *The Review* 2 (March 6, 1920), 225–27; "Spiritualism and Science," *American Review of Reviews* 61 (May 1920), 504–11; "Professor Jastrow Replies," *The Review* 3 (No-

vember 24, 1920), 498–99; "Conan Doyle, Spiritualist, on Tour," *The Independent and the Weekly Review* 102 (April 29, 1922), 416–18; and "Metaphysics," *Literary Review* 4 (September 8, 1923), 17–18.

22. Joseph Jastrow, "The Modern Occult," *Popular Science Monthly* 57 (September 1900), 461, 462, 466, 469, 471. See also Jastrow, "Psychology of Conviction," 542–43. On James and spiritualism, see Simon, *Genuine Reality,* 189–211, 287–89, 305–8, 320–21, 342–43. For Jastrow's judgment on James's flirtations with spiritualism, see "Spiritualism and Science," 511.

23. Gottschalk, *Emergence of Christian Science,* 203–13; and Mark Twain, *Christian Science* (1907; New York, 1996), 292–93.

24. Gottschalk, *Emergence of Christian Science,* 84, 204–5; and Michael A. Meyer, *Response to Modernity: A History of the Reform Movement in Judaism* (New York, 1988), 314.

25. *St. Paul Pioneer Press,* February 8, 1909; A. A. Brill, "The Adjustment of the Jew to the American Environment," *Mental Hygiene* 2 (April 1918), 227, 229; Hugo Münsterberg, "Hypnotism and Crime," *McClure's* 30 (January 1908), 319; W[alter] Béran Wolfe, *Calm Your Nerves: The Prevention and Cure of Nervous Breakdown* (New York, 1933), 178. See also Münsterberg, *Psychotherapy,* 381; Abraham Myerson, *The Psychology of Mental Disorders* (New York, 1927), vii; and Edmund Jacobson, *You Must Relax: A Practical Method for Reducing the Strains of Modern Living* (1934; New York, 1942), 26. See also Scrapbook #3 of the Isador H. Coriat Papers, Francis A. Countway Library of Medicine, Boston, which contains many newspaper clippings documenting Coriat's effort to debunk mental telepathy, spiritualism, and mind cure as well as other superstitions about psychology, such as the belief that anyone can be hypnotized at the will of a criminal to commit a crime.

26. John B. Watson, *Behaviorism* (New York, 1925), 3, 247.

27. Ibid., 82–83.

28. Kerry Buckley, *Mechanical Man: John Broadus Watson and the Beginnings of Behaviorism* (New York, 1989), 40–41, 137.

29. Philip J. Pauly, *Controlling Life: Jacques Loeb and the Engineering Ideal in Biology* (New York, 1987), 9–27.

30. Ibid., 28–29, 62–65. For the quotation from Watson, see p. 172.

31. Jacques Loeb, *The Mechanistic Conception of Life,* ed. Donald Fleming (1912; Cambridge, Mass., 1964), xi–xiii; and Pauly, *Controlling Life,* 93–99, 189–93. Near the end of his life, in the 1920s, Americans spoke of Loeb in the same breath with Einstein; the biologist-as-hero in Sinclair Lewis's 1925 novel *Arrowsmith* was largely inspired by him. See Charles E. Rosenberg, "Martin Arrowsmith: The Scientist as Hero," in *Twentieth Century Interpretations of Arrowsmith,* ed. Robert J. Griffin (Englewood Cliffs, N.J., 1968), 47–56.

32. Jacques Loeb, *The Mechanistic Conception of Life: Biological Essays* (Chicago, 1912), 72–74; and Pauly, *Controlling Life,* 73–74.

33. Ernst Haeckel, *The Wonders of Life: A Popular Study of Biological Philosophy* (New York, 1905), 316, 335, 393–400; and Pauly, *Controlling Life,* 139–40, 144–45. Similarly, David Hollinger has observed of philosopher Morris Raphael Cohen, the first Jew to enter the field of American philosophy, that "Cohen was more offended by idealism's lingering Christian theism than were many of his

otherwise more 'insurgent' contemporaries. . . . Cohen was impatient with 'moderns' who smuggled their own ancestral theology into their philosophy." See David A. Hollinger, *Morris R. Cohen and the Scientific Ideal* (Cambridge, Mass., 1975), 55.

34. Pauly, *Controlling Life*, 86. See also Fleming's introduction to the 1964 edition of *The Mechanistic Conception of Life*, xiv–xv.

35. Loeb, *Mechanistic Conception of Life*, 31.

36. Buckley, *Mechanical Man*, 179; Münsterberg, *Psychology and Life*, 32–33; and Hugo Münsterberg, *The Eternal Life* (Boston, 1905), 14–15. On the utopian dimensions of behaviorism, see J[ill] G. Morawski, "Not Quite New Worlds: Psychologists' Conceptions of the Ideal Family in the Twenties," in *In the Shadow of the Past: Psychology Portrays the Sexes*, ed. Miriam Lewin (New York, 1984), 97–125.

37. Joseph Jastrow, *Piloting Your Life: The Psychologist as Helmsman* (New York, 1930), 241, 244. See also Joseph Jastrow, "Has Psychology Failed?" *American Scholar* 4 (Winter 1935), 264. On antisemitism in American academic psychology, see Andrew S. Winston, " 'The Defects of His Race': E. G. Boring and Anti-Semitism in American Psychology, 1923–1953," *History of Psychology* 1 (February 1998), 27–51.

38. Alfred Adler, *The Pattern of Life*, ed. W. Béran Wolfe (New York, 1930), 9–10; Abraham Myerson, *Social Psychology* (New York, 1934), 396; A. Myerson, "The 'Nervousness' of the Jew," *Mental Hygiene* 4 (January 1920), 66; Jastrow, *Piloting Your Life*, 76; and Boris Sidis, *The Foundations of Normal and Abnormal Psychology* (Boston, 1914), 396.

39. Joseph Jastrow, *Sanity First: The Art of Sensible Living* (New York, 1935), 92–93; Jastrow, *Piloting Your Life*, 45; Joseph Jastrow, "Has Psychology Failed?" *American Scholar* 4 (Winter 1935), 266; Joseph Jastrow, *The House That Freud Built* (New York, 1932), 291; and Henry Elkind, ed., *The Healthy Mind: Mental Hygiene for Adults* (New York, 1929), 242, 245, 248. Also, Joseph Jastrow, *The Subconscious* (Boston, 1905), 543; and Joseph Jastrow, "On the Trail of the Subconscious: The Byways of the Mind," *Scientific American, Supplement* (June 22, 1912), 395.

40. Isador H. Coriat, *What Is Psychoanalysis?* (New York, 1917), 85–86, 108, 117–18. For comparison to White, see William A. White, *Mechanisms of Character Formation: An Introduction to Psychoanalysis* (1916; New York, 1920). The epigram to Coriat's book is the final line of the quoted stanza: " 'The Future I may face now I have proved the Past.' " Browning knew Hebrew, studied some rabbinic texts, and wrote several sympathetic poems about Jewish figures.

41. W[alter] Béran Wolfe, *Successful Living* (New York, 1938), 27; and Wolfe, *Calm Your Nerves*, 40–41, 176–82, 204, 212.

42. A. A. Brill, "Immunity to Immorality," lecture before the School of Education, NYU, March 4, 1937, folder "Lectures, 1937," box 11, Brill Papers.

43. Ronald Steel, *Walter Lippmann and the American Century* (New York, 1980), 44–46.

44. Walter Lippmann, *Drift and Mastery: An Attempt to Diagnose the Current Unrest* (1914; Englewood Cliffs, N.J., 1961), 150–51.

45. Gustave Le Bon, *The Crowd: A Study of the Popular Mind* (1895; London, 1930), 5, 16, 21. On the social and intellectual context of French theories of the crowd, including a chapter on Le Bon, see Susanna Barrows, *Distorting Mirrors:*

Visions of the Crowd in Late Nineteenth-Century France (New Haven, 1981); and Robert Allen Nye, *The Origins of Crowd Psychology: Gustave Le Bon and the Crisis of Mass Democracy in the Third Republic* (London, 1975). Freud's theory of group psychology drew on Le Bon's *The Crowd*, which Freud called "deservedly famous." See Sigmund Freud, *Beyond the Pleasure Principle, Group Psychology and Other Works*, ed. James Strachey (1955; London, 1973), 72ff. *Group Psychology and the Analysis of the Ego* appeared in 1921.

46. Henry Steele Commager, *The American Mind: An Interpretation of American Thought and Character since the 1880s* (New Haven, 1950), 333–35. An interesting exception is Everett Dean Martin, *The Behavior of Crowds: A Psychological Study* (New York, 1920), which explicitly takes up Le Bon's subject but disagrees with his critique. Martin relies on Freud and Adler to explain human motivation, and he concludes with a call for educational reform along the lines of pragmatic humanism set out by William James and John Dewey. In the end, Martin follows a very different path from Le Bon; his book fits into the American tradition of self-culture, which decries commercialism and conformity and calls for the invigoration of individualism. A few scholars have cited psychologist William McDougall's *Group Mind* (New York, 1920) as an example of a darker crowd psychology in America, but McDougall explicitly distances his more optimistic interpretation from Le Bon's, and his book focuses not really on crowd psychology but on the formation of nations and national characteristics. An Englishman with frank Anglo-American biases who immigrated to the United States in middle age after the poor reception of *The Group Mind* in England, McDougall is very different from the Jewish writers treated here in that he upheld racialist ideas that were on the way to being discredited by most American social scientists. He warned about the dangers of racial intermixture and advocated the complete separation of blacks out of American society (by relocation to their own territory). See McDougall, *Group Mind*, 176 and William McDougall, *The American Nation: Its Problems and Psychology* (London, 1925), 153–65.

47. On Lee, see Gregory W. Bush, *Lord of Attention: Gerald Stanley Lee & the Crowd Metaphor in Industrializing America* (Amherst, Mass., 1991). Bush observes that Lee appropriated "the veneer of crowd psychology alongside a mystical identification with machines and electricity" (65).

48. Gerald Stanley Lee, *Crowds: A Moving-Picture of Democracy* (Garden City, N.Y., 1913), 89–90, 184–85, 189.

49. On Du Bois's exposes of lynching in *The Crisis*, see David Levering Lewis, *W.E.B. Du Bois: Biography of a Race, 1869–1919* (New York, 1993), 411–12, 426–27, 514–15, 539–40.

50. Robert E. Park, *The Crowd and the Public, and Other Essays*, ed. Henry Elsner, Jr. (Chicago, 1972), xxxi; Bush, *Lord of Attention*, 24, 72; and Simon, *Genuine Reality*, 267.

51. Sidis, *Psychology of Suggestion*, 17, 364. Sidis has been largely overlooked as a forerunner of American meditations on the crowd, even though Robert Park himself acknowledged Sidis very clearly in *The Crowd and the Public*. Sidis does not appear, for example, in the historical overview of American theories of crowd psychology in Clark McPhail, *The Myth of the Madding Crowd* (New York, 1991); his name appears once but without any substantive comment on his writings or

his significance in Bush, *Lord of Attention*, 27. Sidis is recognized by Eugene Leach, " 'Mental Epidemics': Crowd Psychology and American Culture, 1890–1940," *American Studies* 33 (Spring 1992), 14–16.

52. Boris Sidis, "A Study of the Mob," *Atlantic Monthly* 75 (February 1895), 188–97.

53. Hale, *Beginnings of Psychoanalysis*, 430; and Joseph Jastrow, "Delusion, Mass Suggestion, and the War: A Dream and the Awakening," *Scientific Monthly* 8 (May 1919), 430. See also Joseph Jastrow, "Mania Teutonica: A Psychological Study of the War," *Outlook* (January 9, 1918), 58–60; and Joseph Jastrow, "A Pacifist Defense of America's War," *North American Review* 206 (August 1917), 199–208.

54. Wolfe, *Calm Your Nerves*, 139–40; and Hugo Münsterberg, *On the Witness Stand: Essays on Psychology and Crime* (Garden City, N.Y., 1912), 73–74, 115. See also Hugo Münsterberg, *Tomorrow: Letters to a Friend in Germany* (New York, 1916), 73, 81–82; and John Cowper Powys, *The War and Culture: A Reply to Professor Münsterberg* (New York, 1914), 79.

55. Hugo Münsterberg, "Prohibition and Social Psychology," *McClure's* 31 (August 1908), 441–42; and Hugo Münsterberg, *American Problems: From the Point of View of a Psychologist* (New York, 1910), 21.

56. Hugo Münsterberg to Nicholas Murray Butler, November 29, 1905, Hugo Münsterberg Papers, Rare Books, Manuscript and Special Collections, Boston Public Library, Boston. For Münsterberg's prescient appreciation of moving pictures, see Hugo Münsterberg, *The Photoplay: A Psychological Study* (New York, 1916).

57. Jastrow, *Keeping Mentally Fit*, 42, 178–79. See also E. Haldeman-Julius, *The Big American Parade* (Boston, 1929), 141–43, 145, 150, 152. Veblen's 1922 essay, "Dementia Praecox," is republished in Loren Baritz, ed., *The Culture of the Twenties* (Indianapolis, 1981), 29–40.

58. Jastrow, *Piloting Your Life*, 38; A. A. Brill, "Should Voluntary Mercy Death (Euthanasia) Be Legalized?," radio address, WMCA (New York City), February 16, 1943, folder "Radio Scripts, 1943," box 12, Brill Papers; Isador H. Coriat, *Repressed Emotions* (New York, 1920), 143–44, 146; Wolfe, *Calm Your Nerves*, 207; and Bottome, *Alfred Adler*, 114. Consternation about the behavior of fascist crowds in Germany and Austria prompted Freud's daughter, Anna, and his last student, Heinz Hartmann, a Jewish refugee who came to the United States in 1941, to develop an ego psychology that emphasized the supreme importance of controlling the instinct toward aggression. See Nathan G. Hale, Jr., *Freud and the Americans: The Rise and Crisis of Psychoanalysis, 1917–1985* (New York, 1995), 233.

59. Sidis, *Philistine and Genius*, 38, 40; and Sidis, *Psychology of Suggestion*, 3–4.

60. Münsterberg, *Psychotherapy*, 381, 384.

CHAPTER 9. RABBI LIEBMAN AND THE PSYCHIC PAIN OF THE WORLD WAR II GENERATION

1. *Science Digest* 17 (January 1945), 51; Sigmund Freud, *Introductory Lectures on Psychoanalysis*, ed. James Strachey (1916–17; New York, 1977), 341; and Sigmund Freud, *Beyond the Pleasure Principle, Group Psychology and Other Works*, ed. James Strachey (1955; London, 1973), 117, 122; *Group Psychology and the Analysis of the*

Ego, the volume that contains the reference to regression and the herd instinct, was first published in 1921. See also "Regression," in *Encyclopedia of Psychoanalysis*, ed. Ludwig Eidelberg (New York, 1968), 371–72. For reminiscences about Grinker's analysis with Sigmund Freud, see Roy Grinker, Sr., *Fifty Years in Psychiatry: A Living History* (Springfield, Ill., 1979), 6–15; and Roy R. Grinker, Jr., "My Father's Analysis with Sigmund Freud," in *Sigmund Freud and His Impact on the Modern World*, ed. Jerome A. Winer and James William Anderson (Hillsdale, N.J., 2001), 35–47.

2. The information about Liebman's psychoanalysis with Roy Grinker came from Liebman's daughter, Leila Liebman, in a telephone conversation, February 24, 1993. For the quotation, see Joshua Loth Liebman, *Peace of Mind* (New York, 1948), 177.

A valuable study for gauging the relative significance of *Peace of Mind* and inspirational books in general is Louis Schneider and Sanford M. Dornbusch, *Popular Religion: Inspirational Books in America* (Chicago, 1958). Page 162 presents a list of sales figures for sixteen inspirational best-sellers, which places *Peace of Mind* ahead of every book published between 1900 and 1955 except *The Power of Positive Thinking* and Catherine Marshall's biography of her husband, *A Man Called Peter*. The figure given for *Peace of Mind*, however, seems lower than that suggested by other sources in the publishing trade. Nevertheless, the comparisons reveal that Liebman's book far outsold those of America's most famous inspirational writers, such as Emmet Fox, Bruce Barton, Harry Emerson Fosdick, Fulton Sheen, and, if we except *The Power of Positive Thinking* from his corpus, even Norman Vincent Peale. Of the thirty authors covered by Schneider and Dornbusch, representing the best-selling inspirational writers in the United States between 1875 and 1955, Liebman is the only Jewish author.

3. Liebman, *Peace of Mind*, xi–xii.

4. Ibid., 3–4.

5. Ibid., 6–10.

6. Ibid., 20. The quotation from Allport appears in the advertisement of *Peace of Mind* in *Life*, September 30, 1946, p. 17.

7. Mary Jane Ward, *The Snake Pit* (New York, 1946), 277–78.

8. Bosley Crowther, "The Screen in Review," *New York Times*, November 5, 1948; and Ward, *Snake Pit*, 274. Even Gerald Grob's authoritative history of mental illness in America makes the mistake of identifying the theme of the movie and the original book as the same. See Gerald N. Grob, *The Mad among Us: A History of the Care of America's Mentally Ill* (New York, 1994), 206.

9. "Shell Shock: Its Cause, Character and Cure," *New York Tribune*, December 29, 1918; and William E. Leuchtenberg, *The Perils of Prosperity, 1914–32* (Chicago, 1958), 163.

10. William Menninger, *Psychiatry in a Troubled World* (New York, 1948), 338–47.

11. "Guadalcanal Neurosis," *Time*, May 24, 1943; "Isle of Nightmare," *Newsweek*, May 24, 1943; "What's New in Medicine," *Science Digest* 11 (April 1942), 48–49; George W. Gray, "Nerves in the War," *Harper's* 184 (May 1942), 630–38; Walter Freeman, "Wartime Neuroses," *Hygeia* 20 (July 1942), 492–93, 530–32; "War Nerves," *Newsweek*, January 4, 1943; Louis P. Thorpe, "Diagnosing War Neuroses," *Education* 63 (May 1943), 549–54; "Neuroses Caused by Petty Troubles," *Science*

Digest 14 (August 1943), 49; "Spit It Out, Soldier," *Time*, September 13, 1943;
Will O'Neil, "750,000 Unwanted Men," *Hygeia* 21 (September 1943), 650–52,
692–95; Frederick C. Painton, "There is No Such Thing as Shell Shock," *Reader's
Digest* 43 (October 1943), 59–63; "The Heavy-Laden," *Time*, February 7, 1944;
"Neurotics are not Insane," *Science News Letter*, March 4, 1944; "Soldiers Wounded
in Mind," *Science News Letter*, April 22, 1944; Marjorie Van de Water, "Mental Combat Casualties," *Science News Letter*, June 17, 1944; John Eisele Davis, "War Neuroses," *Hygeia* 22 (July 1944), 496–97, 554–55; "Dog's Neurosis," *Newsweek*, August
21, 1944; John A. P. Millett, "Honorable Discharge," *American Scholar* 13 (October
1944), 429–36; "M. J. Farrell, "Plain Truths about the 'N.P.s,' " *The Rotarian* 65
(October 1944), 19, 55; "Heartsickness," *Time*, January 29, 1945; "Mental Crackups among Airmen," *Science Digest* 17 (January 1945), 51; Leslie B. Hohman,
"Combat Fatigue," *Ladies' Home Journal* 62 (February 1945), 146–47; "John Eisele
Davis, "Psychiatry and the Veteran," *American Scholar* 14 (April 1945), 249–51;
William C. Menninger, "The Mentally or Emotionally Handicapped Veteran," *Annals of the American Academy of Political and Social Science* 239 (May 1945), 20–28;
"Twilight Healing," *Reader's Digest* 47 (July 1945), 89–92; S. W. Morris, "Sports
Heal War Neuroses," *Recreation* 39 (October 1945), 343–44, 390; "Neurotic He-
roes," *Time*, January 14, 1946; Greer Williams, "How Far Can We Safely Invade
the Mind?" *Saturday Evening Post*, May 25, 1946; "Mama's Boys," *Time*, November
25, 1946; and "War and Jap Nerves," *Newsweek*, December 16, 1946.

    12. "Give Us a Break," *Reader's Digest* 45 (November 1944), 8–10; Henry T.
Gorrell, "We Psychos are Not Crazy," *Saturday Evening Post*, May 19, 1945; and
J. C. Furnan, "Meet Ed Savickas," *Ladies' Home Journal* 62 (February 1945), 141–
44.

    13. Donald G. Cooley, "Don't Let Them Tell You We're All Going Crazy!" *Better
Homes and Gardens* 25 (July 1947), 33–34, 126.

    14. Harry C. Solomon and Paul I. Yakovlev, eds., *Manual of Military Neuropsychi-
atry* (Philadelphia, 1945), 244; and "Are You Always Worrying?" *Time*, October
25, 1948, 64–72.

    15. "The Heavy-Laden," *Time*, February 7, 1944.

    16. *New York Times*, May 17, 1944; Bernard Wolfe and Raymond Rosenthal,
Hypnotism Comes of Age (Garden City, N.Y., 1948), 45; Roy R. Grinker and John P.
Spiegel, *War Neuroses* (Philadelphia, 1945); Roy R. Grinker and John P. Spiegel,
Men Under Stress (Philadelphia, 1945); Nathan G. Hale, Jr., *Freud and the Ameri-
cans: The Rise and Crisis of Psychoanalysis, 1917–1985* (New York, 1995), 191.

    17. Hale, *Rise and Crisis of Psychoanalysis*, 205–8; 223. The quotation comes
from Wolfe and Rosenthal, *Hypnotism Comes of Age*, 50. For a chronicle of Freudianism and the complex relationships between Jewish analysts, writers, and producers in show business during the 1940s and 1950s, see Stephen Farber and
Marc Green, *Hollywood on the Couch: A Candid Look at the Overheated Love Affair
between Psychiatrists and Moviemakers* (New York, 1993), 19–82.

    18. Author's telephone interview with Dr. Leila Liebman, February 23, 1993.

    19. Arthur Mann, ed., *Growth and Achievement: Temple Israel, 1854–1954* (Cam-
bridge, Mass., 1954), 45–116; Joshua Loth Liebman, "Our Common Heritage,"
typescript for broadcast on WBZ, WBZA (Boston), November 19, 1939, box 52,
Joshua Loth Liebman Papers, Department of Special Collections, Mugar Memo-

rial Library, Boston University (hereafter LP/BU); Harold B. Clemenko, "The Man Behind 'Peace of Mind,' " *Look*, January 6, 1948, pp. 16–17; and William G. Braude, "Recollections of a Septuagenarian," reprinted from *Rhode Island Jewish Historical Notes* 8 (November 1981) for the multi-media exhibit "Remembering Joshua Loth Liebman" at Temple Israel, Boston, Joshua Loth Liebman Papers, American Jewish Archives, Cincinnati (hereafter LP/AJA). On the innovation of Sunday services in a few Reform congregations, see Michael A. Meyer, *Response to Modernity: A History of the Reform Movement in Judaism* (New York, 1988), 290–91.

20. Joshua Liebman to Jacob K. Shankman, undated, but written in several installments after Yom Kippur 1931 or 1932 from the Fowler Hotel in Lafayette, Indiana; and Joshua Liebman to Jacob K. Shankman, undated, probably 1932 or 1933, written from the Fowler Hotel in Lafayette, Indiana, LP/AJA.

21. Joshua Liebman to Jacob K. Shankman, undated, probably 1934, on K[ehillat].A[nshe].M[aarab]. letterhead, Chicago, LP/AJA. As we have already seen, Jews who wanted a more harmonial religious faith had been moving toward Christian Science, a trend that culminated in the creation of Jewish Science in the 1920s. The key text of Jewish Science was a book called *Peace of Mind*, written by Rabbi Morris Lichtenstein. An intriguing hybrid of American transcendentalism and talmudic morality, Lichtenstein's *Peace of Mind* agreed with Christian Science about the way in which negative thoughts obstruct the basic joyousness of life but called it a "manifest absurdity . . . to contend, as do the followers of some religious sects, that man is wholly spirit, that matter is only a figment of the imagination, and an error of mortal mind." See Morris Lichtenstein, *Peace of Mind* (New York, 1927), 22, 32, 321–26, 357. On Jewish Science, see Rebecca Trachtenberg Alpert, "From Jewish Science to Rabbinical Counseling: The Evaluation of the Relationship between Religion and Health by the American Reform Rabbinate, 1916–1954" (Ph.D. diss., Temple University, 1978), 61–64, 72–85.

22. Joshua Loth Liebman, "First Address to Brotherhood of Temple Israel," October 18, 1939, box 46, LP/BU.

23. Abraham Cahan, *Bleter fun Meyn Leben*, 5 vols. (New York, 1926–31), 4:477–78.

24. Isaac Metzker, ed., *A Bintel Brief* (New York, 1971), 72–73.

25. B[enzion] Liber, *Das Geschlechts Leben: A Popular-Wissenschaftlich Buch* (1914; New York, 1918), 8–9, 15. See also Andrew R. Heinze, *Adapting to Abundance: Jewish Immigrants, Mass Consumption and the Search for American Identity* (New York, 1990), 170–71; Jenna Weissman Joselit, *The Wonders of America: Reinventing Jewish Culture, 1880–1950* (New York, 1994), 64–66; and Andrew R. Heinze, "Mass Consumption, Schmass Consumption: On Jewish Things and American Popular Culture," *Reviews in American History* 24 (March 1996), 75.

26. Bernard Glueck, "The Clinical Significance of Religion," *Central Conference of American Rabbis Yearbook* (Cincinnati, 1927), 344, 346. On Glueck, see *Who's Who in American Jewry, 1928*, 228; *New York Times*, October 9, 1972. For examples of the Temple lecture circuit, see A. A. Brill, "Women, Their Status in Modern Life," lecture to the Sisterhood of Congregation B'nai Jeshurun (NYC), February 26, 1934, folder "Lectures, 1934," box 11; "Psychoanalysis and Morals," lecture to Congregation Rodeph Shalom (NYC), April 28, 1933, folder "Lectures, 1933," box 11; "Mass Psychoses of Our Age: How Can We Cure Them?," outline of lec-

ture to Congregation Rodeph Shalom, February 18, 1934, Folder "Lectures, 1934," box 11, Brill Papers; and Alfred Adler, folder "Lectures, 1935–1936," box 2, Alfred Adler Papers, Manuscript Division, Library of Congress, Washington, D.C. On the development of Jewish marriage counseling in the 1930s, see Alpert, "From Jewish Science to Rabbinical Counseling," 115–16.

27. *Who's Who in American Jewry, 1928* (New York, 1928). On Maida Solomon, see Paula E. Hyman and Deborah Dash Moore, eds., *Jewish Women in America: An Historical Encyclopedia*, 2 vols. (New York, 1997), 2:1286–87.

28. See also Irving D. Yalom, *Momma and the Meaning of Life: Tales of Psychotherapy* (New York, 1999), 4; and for a different, Latin American Jewish perspective, Salvador Minuchin, *Family Healing: Tales of Hope and Renewal from Family Therapy* (New York, 1993), 6, 17, 25.

29. Undated journal entry, ca. 1932, folder #7, "Journal Entries by Maslow," M1910/421, Abraham Maslow Papers, Archives of the History of American Psychology, University of Akron; author's interview with Albert Ellis, August 9, 2000 (transcript available); Seymour B. Sarason, *The Making of an American Psychologist: An Autobiography* (San Francisco, 1988), 25–34; and Richard S. Lazarus, *The Life and Work of an Eminent Psychologist: Autobiography of Richard S. Lazarus* (New York, 1998), 1–6, 18. As the title of the Lazarus autobiography reminds us, psychologists are not exempt from narcissism, so the dramatic portrayals of lone individuals enduring contemptuous or neglectful parents must be taken as evidence of the authors' perceptions, which may or may not do justice to what happened in their families. As the contrast with Freud and Adler suggests, the cultural and the generational environment of these American psychologists influenced those perceptions—or at least the recording of those perceptions.

30. Hale, *Rise and Crisis of Psychoanalysis*, 223, 292–95; and Henry Roth, *Call It Sleep* (1934; New York, 1964). *Call It Sleep* had lain dormant and unrecognized for two decades when, in 1956, Alfred Kazin and Leslie Fiedler brought the book to public attention. It went on to become a best-seller and is now considered a classic. Fiedler treats it at length in his own great work of Freudian literary criticism, *Love and Death in the American Novel* (New York, 1960).

31. Lucy Freeman, *Fight against Fears* (New York, 1951), 18, 252–54.

32. On the masculinity of the self-help tradition, see Richard Weiss, *The American Myth of Success: From Horatio Alger to Norman Vincent Peale* (1969; Urbana, 1988). Weiss writes, "As men became cogs in complex organizational structures, their sense of personal significance diminished. The increasing concern for individual power reflected anxiety over the loss of it" (230).

33. Letters from Eleanor Neiditz to parents, April 14 and 21, 1947, in author's possession, with thanks to Eleanor Caplan (née Neiditz). On Hank Greenberg and Bess Myerson as heroes, see Edward S. Shapiro, *A Time for Healing: American Jewry since World War II* (Baltimore, 1992), 15.

34. Clifford R. Adams, "Making Marriage Work," *Ladies' Home Journal* 65 (January 1948), 26; and Elsie Stokes to Simon and Schuster, February 15, 1946, box 5x, LP/BU.

35. *Reader's Digest* 51 (October 1947), 88, 89. In her study of late-twentieth-century readers, Wendy Simonds gives a good sense of how women may respond to literature of consolation. One respondent said: "The grief books . . . most of

them say the same things, but I get a lot of *comfort* from seeing it in print. . . . [It is] more comforting than having other people tell it to me verbally. It seems more real." See Wendy Simonds, *Women and Self-Help Culture: Reading Between the Lines* (New Brunswick, N.J., 1992), 27.

36. Clemenko, "The Man Behind 'Peace of Mind,' " 15–18.

37. Liebman, *Peace of Mind*, 116–18.

38. Quoted in John B. Pickard, *Emily Dickinson: An Introduction and Interpretation* (New York, 1967), 36; see pp. 127–28 for a selected list of Dickinson volumes appearing between 1930 and 1960.

39. David Davidson and Hilde Abel, "How America Lives: Meet an American Rabbi and his Family," *Ladies' Home Journal* 65 (January 1948), 123–31. The talmudic passage about saving a life has a complex history because of an ambiguity about whether it originally referred to Jews in particular or embraced all people. One version reads *nefesh aḥat me-b'nei adam* ("a single soul from the children of man") while the other reads *nefesh aḥat me-b'nei yisrael* ("a single soul from the children of Israel"). The American version routinely conveys the universal message, which accords so well with the nation's democratic values. Compare Mishnah Sanhedrin 4:5 in Philip Blackman, ed., *Mishnayoth, Volume IV, Order Nezikin* (1963; New York, 1990), 254, with I. Epstein, ed., *Hebrew-English Edition of the Babylonian Talmud: Seder Nezikin, Sanhedrin* (London, 1994), 37a.

40. Davidson and Abel, "How America Lives," 126; and "No Peace for Liebman," *Newsweek* March 22, 1948, p. 84.

41. Joshua Loth Liebman, "Hope for Human Brotherhood," *Ladies' Home Journal* 65 (January 1948), 132. In a 1944 sermon delivered on WBZ radio, Liebman said, "The people who are hated whether they be Catholics or Jews or Negroes do not experience the two prerequisites for growth: namely, approval and affection. Their personalities tend to shrink and to contract rather than to expand and the whole progress of a country is impeded when any fragment of a population loses confidence and courage. . . . The panic of the persecuted and the phobia of the persecutor together are the architects of chaos." See the manuscript sermon "Brotherhood or Chaos," in commemoration of the Eleventh Annual Brotherhood Week, February 20, 1944, box 5x, LP/BU.

CHAPTER 10. *PEACE OF MIND*: A NEW JEWISH GOSPEL OF LOVE

1. *Life*, September 30, 1946.

2. Leo Rosten, ed., *A Guide to the Religions of America* (New York, 1955). The Rosten volume is based on an extensive series of articles about America's diverse religious groups that *Look* published between 1952 and 1955. The book contains detailed statistics on church membership. For Eisenhower's comment, which was not at all ridiculous in its original context, see *New York Times*, December 23, 1952.

3. Will Herberg, *Protestant-Catholic-Jew: An Essay in American Religious Sociology* (New York, 1955), 97–98, 103–4.

4. On the rise of the Judeo-Christian idea, see Deborah Dash Moore, "Jewish GIs and the Creation of the Judeo-Christian Tradition," *Religion and American*

Culture 8 (Winter 1998), 31–53; and Mark Silk, "Notes on the Judeo-Christian Tradition in America," *American Quarterly* 36 (Spring 1984), 65–85. For earlier antecedents, see Benny Kraut, "A Wary Collaboration: Jews, Catholics, and the Protestant Goodwill Movement," in *Between the Times: The Travail of the Protestant Establishment in America, 1900–1960,* ed. William R. Hutchison (Cambridge, 1989), 193–230.

5. Herberg, *Protestant-Catholic-Jew,* 103, 111; William Graebner, *The Age of Doubt: American Thought and Culture in the 1940s* (Boston, 1991), 61; Edward S. Shapiro, *A Time for Healing: American Jewry since World War II* (Baltimore, 1992), 163; and Paul Johnson, "God and the Americans," *Commentary* 99 (January 1995), 39.
Surprisingly, a leading historian of American religion, George Marsden, also notes Peale and Sheen while omitting Liebman, and echoes the Herberg thesis; see George M. Marsden, *Religion and American Culture* (San Diego, 1990), 214–15, 225. Similarly, a 1982 scholarly survey of American inspirational literature focuses entirely on Christian authorship, with only a brief and misdated mention of *Peace of Mind;* see Roy M. Anker, "Religion and Self-Help" in *Concise Histories of American Popular Culture,* ed. M. Thomas Inge (Westport, Conn., 1982), 328–45. Nor does Liebman appear in Robert G. Goldy, *The Emergence of Jewish Theology in America* (Bloomington, 1990). Herberg's equation of *Peace of Mind* with Peale's positive thinking is echoed in Rebecca T. Alpert, "Joshua Loth Liebman: The Peace of Mind Rabbi," in *Faith and Freedom: A Tribute to Franklin H. Littell,* ed. Richard Libowitz (Oxford, 1987), 190.
For more accurate assessments of Liebman see Donald Meyer, *The Positive Thinkers: A Study of the American Quest for Health, Wealth and Personal Power from Mary Baker Eddy to Norman Vincent Peale* (New York: Doubleday, 1965), 325–30; Sydney E. Ahlstrom, *A Religious History of the American People* (New Haven: Yale University Press, 1972), 955; Edwin S. Gaustad, ed., *A Documentary History of Religion in America since 1865* (Grand Rapids: Eerdmans, 1990), 516; and Arthur Mann, "Joshua Loth Liebman: Religio-Psychiatric Thinker," in *Growth and Achievement: Temple Israel, 1854–1954,* ed. Arthur Mann (Cambridge, 1954), 100–116. I first discussed this interpretive problem in Andrew R. Heinze, "The First Mass Market Rabbi," *Midstream: A Monthly Jewish Review* 42 (June/July 1996), 14–17; and more fully in Andrew R. Heinze, "Peace of Mind (1946): Judaism and the Therapeutic Polemics of Postwar America," *Religion and American Culture* (Winter 2002), 33–34. The same stereotype plagued the historical memory of Fulton Sheen; see Thomas C. Reeves, *America's Bishop: The Life and Times of Fulton J. Sheen* (San Francisco, 2001), 368–69.

6. Steinberg's review appeared in *The Reconstructionist,* June 28, 1946, pp. 28–30.

7. Joshua Loth Liebman, ed. *Psychiatry and Religion* (Boston, 1948), 36–37.

8. Joshua Loth Liebman, "Thoughts on Religious Literature in Our Time," *Publishers' Weekly,* February 14, 1948, p. 960; and Liebman, *Psychiatry and Religion,* 33.

9. Liebman, "Thoughts on Religious Literature," 961.

10. On the ultimate value of religion and the special qualities of Judaism, see especially the final chapter "Where Religion and Psychology Part—And Meet," in Joshua Loth Liebman, *Peace of Mind* (New York, 1968), 163–86. All subsequent

citations of *Peace of Mind* are from the 1968 Simon and Schuster printing (the forty-third).

11. Ibid., 33, 171.

12. Joshua Loth Liebman, "A Jewish Tribute to American Christianity," sermon typescript, undated, circa 1943, box 5x; and Joshua Loth Liebman, "A Jew Looks at Christmas," sermon typescript, December 27, 1940, box 44, LP/BU.

13. Liebman, *Peace of Mind*, 58.

14. "The American Jewish Adventure," address to the National Jewish Welfare Board (Chicago), May 9, 1948, LP/AJA; and Joshua Loth Liebman, "God and the World Crisis—Can We Still Believe in Providence?" *CCAR Yearbook* (Cincinnati, 1941), 261–62, 268–69.

15. See the chapter "The Religion of Healthy-Mindedness," in William James, *The Varieties of Religious Experience* (1902; New York, 1961), 79–113; and Liebman, *Peace of Mind*, 134. In *The Varieties of Religious Experience* James makes scant reference to Judaism; he focuses on Christian experience but refers fairly often to eastern religion, especially Buddhism, and occasionally to Islam. For Liebman's reference to James as a spiritual hero, see Joshua Loth Liebman, "How to Remain Normal in Abnormal Times," address at Ford Hall (Boston), March 22, 1942, box 46, LP/BU.

16. Joshua Loth Liebman, "Where Jew and Christian Meet," broadcast typescript, "Message of Israel," November 16, 1940, LP/AJA; Joshua Loth Liebman, untitled speech delivered to Boston Chamber of Commerce, March 27, 1940, box 46, LP/BU; and Joshua Loth Liebman, "The Mystery of the Lost Hatred," broadcast typescript, "Message of Israel," October 30, 1943, box 1, LP/BU.

17. Joshua Loth Liebman, "Hope for Human Brotherhood," *Ladies' Home Journal* 65 (January 1948), 134; and Liebman, *Peace of Mind*, 68–69.

18. Liebman, *Peace of Mind*, 61–62.

19. Ibid., 62–65.

20. David Polish, review of Liebman's posthumously published *Hope for Man* (1966), *Chicago Tribune*, August 7, 1966; Joshua Loth Liebman, "Why Wars Come," broadcast typescript, "Message of Israel," November 9, 1940, LP/AJA; and Joshua Loth Liebman, "The Meaning of Life," 7, address given at the Hebrew Union College Institute of Religion and Psychiatry, March 1948, LP/AJA.

21. Liebman, *Peace of Mind*, 62, 64–65.

22. Reinhold Niebuhr, *Pious and Secular America* (New York, 1958), 91–93; and Richard Wightman Fox, *Reinhold Niebuhr: A Biography* (New York, 1985), 92–93.

23. Liebman, *Peace of Mind*, 157, 156–59. See the acknowledgements of *Peace of Mind*; see also Alpert, "Joshua Loth Liebman," 177–92, who notes the influence of Kaplan on Liebman's deemphasis of the revelation at Sinai, his reference to God as "the Power for salvation revealing himself in nature," and his stress on the need for a new concept of God appropriate for a democracy like America (190).

24. Mel Scult, *Judaism Faces the Twentieth Century: A Biography of Mordecai M. Kaplan* (Detroit, 1993), 19–51.

25. Ibid., 79–87; Michael A. Meyer, "Beyond Particularism: On Ethical Culture and the Reconstructionists," *Commentary* 51 (March 1971), 71–76; Charles S. Liebman, "Reconstructionism in American Jewish Life," *American Jewish Year Book*

1970 (New York, 1970), 3–99; Richard Libowitz, *Mordecai M. Kaplan and the Development of Reconstructionism* (New York, 1983), 1–42; and Matthew Arnold, *Literature and Dogma* (1873; New York, 1970), 46. In the first chapter of this classic, "Religion Given," Arnold gives his dramatic rereading of the Hebrew Bible, to which he ascribed enormous importance. Kaplan (and Liebman) must have been moved by Arnold's steady focus on the real-life meaning of religion for people, rather than theological expositions of dogma.

26. Scult, *Judaism Faces the Twentieth Century*, 76. The quotation from Steinberg appears on p. 274.

27. Joshua Loth Liebman, address in honor of Mordecai Kaplan before the Reconstructionist Foundation (New York City), October 14, 1945, box 1, LP/BU; and Mordecai M. Kaplan, *The Meaning of God in Modern Jewish Religion* (1937; New York, 1962), 53–54. See also Andrew R. Heinze, "Judaism and the Therapeutic," *The Reconstructionist* 61 (Spring 1996), 27–35; and Harold M. Schulweis, "A Critical Assessment of Kaplan's Ideas of Salvation," in *The American Judaism of Mordecai Kaplan*, ed. Emanuel S. Goldsmith, Mel Scult, and Robert M. Seltzer (New York, 1990), 260–61.

28. Liebman, *Peace of Mind*, 159. See Kaplan, *Meaning of God in Modern Jewish Religion*, 40ff.

29. Liebman, *Peace of Mind*, 159–62; and Joshua Loth Liebman, "How to Find God—The Talmud: Its Help for Modern Living," broadcast typescript, WBZ, WBZA, March 18, 1945, box 9, LP/BU.

30. Irving Kristol, "God and the Psychoanalysts," *Commentary* 8 (November 1949), 434; and Will Herberg, *Judaism and Modern Man* (New York, 1951), 66. Here, Herberg creates a false dichotomy. Judaism accommodates and promotes both the theme of human dependence and that of human partnership with God. In the words of one of the greatest American rabbinic thinkers, "We meet God in the covenantal community as a comrade and fellow member. Of course, even within the framework of this community, God appears as the leader, teacher, and shepherd"; see Joseph B. Soloveitchik, *The Lonely Man of Faith* (New York, 1992), 45.

31. Harry J. Ausmus, *Will Herberg: From Right to Right* (Chapel Hill, 1987), 1–29, 65–66; and Reinhold Niebuhr, *Moral Man and Immoral Society: A Study in Ethics and Politics* (1932; New York, 1960), xii.

32. Ausmus, *Will Herberg*, 91–107.

33. Will Herberg, "The Postwar Revival of the Synagogue," *Commentary* 9 (April 1950), 323, 325.

34. Herberg, *Judaism and Modern Man*, 29–30, 118. For Herberg's appreciation of Freud, see Will Herberg, "Freud, Religion and Social Reality," *Commentary* 23 (March 1957), 277–84.

35. Joshua Loth Liebman, "A Jewish Evaluation of Christianity," address to the National Conference of Jews and Christians, November 30, 1938, box 13, LP/BU; and Liebman, *Peace of Mind*, 116–18. The problem with the tendency of scholars to dichotomize postwar thought as liberalism versus neo-orthodoxy is not that they are wrong but that they make no allowance for the more subtle reality of intersections between the two. See for example Goldy, *Emergence of Jewish Theology*, 4–5. A case in point: in the acknowledgments of *Judaism and Modern Man*, Herberg be-

stows high praise on his friend Milton Steinberg, who was a close friend of Liebman's and who gave *Peace of Mind* its most astute and powerful review.

36. E. Brooks Holifield, *A History of Pastoral Care in America: From Salvation to
Self-Realization* (Nashville, 1983), 219–21, Meyer, *Positive Thinkers*, 211–19, 259–
89; Carol V. R. George, *God's Salesman: Norman Vincent Peale and the Power of Positive
Thinking* (New York, 1993), 89–91; and Robert Moats Miller, *Harry Emerson Fosdick: Preacher, Pastor, Prophet* (New York, 1985), 251–84.

37. Harry Emerson Fosdick to Joshua Loth Liebman, April 9, 1947, box 3,
LP/BU; Liebman, "Thoughts on Religious Literature in Our Time," February
14, 1948, p. 960; and *Reader's Digest* 81 (November 1962), 107–10. See also
George, *God's Salesman*, 91; and Holifield, *History of Pastoral Care*, 220.

38. Billy Graham, *The Secret of Happiness: Jesus' Teaching on Happiness as Expressed
in the Beatitudes* (Garden City, N.Y., 1955), 3; and Billy Graham, *Peace with God*
(Garden City, N.Y., 1953).

39. Fulton Sheen, *Peace of Soul* (New York, 1949), 84, 87; and "Microphone
Missionary," *Time*, April 14, 1952, p. 73. The same "parable" as that told on television is recorded in *Peace of Soul* (p. 53) and is echoed in many passages throughout the book. For Sheen's refutation of scientism, see Fulton J. Sheen, *Philosophies
at War* (New York, 1943), 50–58. For the quotation about *Peace of Soul* as a Catholic polemic, see Reeves, *America's Bishop*, 202.

40. This is not to say that Graham and Sheen, as traditional Christians, were
immune to stereotypes of Jews as usurpers of Christian civilization; however, without evidence we cannot make assumptions about that. In 2002, a tidbit from
the taped conversations of Richard Nixon revealed Graham agreeing with the
president that Jews had a pernicious effect on American society through their
involvement in the media. (Graham made a public apology for his remark and
claimed that it did not represent his thinking on Jews; Graham had been a vocal
opponent of antisemitism over the years.) As for Sheen, who also spoke out
against antisemitism, the destruction of nearly all his enormous private correspondence makes it impossible to characterize his attitudes toward Jews with any
precision. Tensions between Catholic and Jewish thinkers, including Sheen, over
such subjects as psychoanalysis are described in the next chapter.

41. Joshua Loth Liebman, "A Living Saint: Rabbi Baeck," *Atlantic Monthly* 181
(June 1948), 40–43; and Joshua Loth Liebman, "The Most Unforgettable Character I've Met," *Reader's Digest* 53 (July 1948), 12–16.

42. Leo Baeck to Fan Liebman, June 25, 1948, box 3; Leo Baeck to Joshua
Loth Liebman, April [?] 1948, box 3, LP/BU. On *The Essence of Judaism* and
Baeck's response to Harnack, see Albert H. Friedlander, *Leo Baeck: Teacher of There-
sienstadt* (New York, 1968), 51–102; and William E. Kaufman, *Contemporary Jewish
Philosophies* (1976; Detroit, 1992), 125–41.

43. Liebman, "The Most Unforgettable Man," 15; Liebman, "A Living Saint,"
43; and Leo Baeck to Joshua Loth Liebman, April 22, 1948, box 3, LP/BU.

44. A fascinating example of the psychology craze's impact on the finest of
scholars is David M. Potter, *People of Plenty: Economic Abundance and the American
Character* (Chicago, 1954). See especially the discussion of the psychology of
American child-rearing, a subject far from Potter's field of pre–Civil War American history, pp. 194–99.

CHAPTER 11. CLARE BOOTHE LUCE AND THE
CATHOLIC-JEWISH CLASH OVER FREUD IN AMERICA

1. Fulton J. Sheen to Clare Luce, [1946? 1947?], folder 15, container x31; Fulton J. Sheen to Clare Luce, November 23, 1946, folder 1, container x31; and Fulton J. Sheen to Clare Luce, [1946?], folder 1, container x31, Clare Boothe Luce Papers, Library of Congress, mm 82030759 (hereafter Luce Papers). For the Brooks Atkinson quote, see Sylvia Jukes Morris, *Rage for Fame: The Ascent of Clare Boothe Luce* (New York, 1997), 13.

2. For the same reasons (noted in Chapter 10) that historians ignored Joshua Liebman, they overlooked the significance of Sheen and Luce in the postwar years and of the Catholic-Jewish conflict that is the focus of this chapter. I have commented on this oversight in Andrew R. Heinze, "Clare Boothe Luce and the Jews: A Chapter from the Catholic-Jewish Disputation of Postwar America," *American Jewish History* 88 (September 2000), 361–76.

Scholars have only recently begun to treat Sheen; see Thomas C. Reeves, *America's Bishop: The Life and Times of Fulton J. Sheen* (San Francisco, 2001); Mark S. Massa, *Catholics and American Culture: Fulton Sheen, Dorothy Day, and the Notre Dame Football Team* (New York, 1999); and Christopher Lynch, *Selling Catholicism: Bishop Sheen and the Power of Television* (Louisville, 1998). Published scholarship on Luce is virtually nonexistent; she appears briefly in Patrick Allitt, *Catholic Converts: British and American Intellectuals Turn to Rome* (Ithaca, 1997), 130, but aside from Morris's account of her early years (cited above), we have only older, more personal biographies: Alden Hatch, *Clare Boothe Luce: Ambassador Extraordinary* (London, 1956), Stephen Shadegg, *Clare Boothe Luce: A Biography* (New York, 1970), and Wilfred Sheed's colorful reminiscence-cum-biography *Clare Boothe Luce* (New York, 1982).

3. Fanny Sedgwick Colby, *The American Scholar* 17 (January 1948), 38–39.

4. "Archbishop Fulton J. Sheen—Author, Orator and Missionary," *Great Catholic Books Newsletter* 2:2, pp. 2–5 (http://www.ewtn.com/library/christ/sheen.txt). Copyright held by Trinity Communications, 1994. I first checked this website in 2000; the article cited was still posted when this book went into production in 2003.

5. Reeves, *America's Bishop*, 198–99; "Are You Always Worrying," *Time*, October 25, 1948, p. 70; and *New York Times*, July 6, 1947.

6. Fulton J. Sheen, *Life Is Worth Living* (Second Series) (New York, 1954), 55, 131–32; and C. G. Jung, *Modern Man in Search of a Soul* (1933; New York, n.d.), 208–9, 214, 224. On Jung's 1934 article for the *Zentralblatt für Psychotherapie*, see Frederic V. Grunfeld, *Prophets without Honor: A Background to Freud, Kafka, Einstein and Their World* (New York, 1979), 58–59.

7. Sheen, *Life Is Worth Living*, 7, 112.

8. "Monsignor's Tenth," *Time*, March 11, 1940.

9. "Microphone Missionary," *Time*, April 14, 1952; Massa, *Catholics and American Culture*, 82–83, 93–94; and Charles R. Morris, *American Catholic: The Saints and Sinners Who Built America's Most Powerful Church* (New York, 1997), 225–26.

10. "Signs of the Times," *Time*, February 3, 1947; "Converter on Wax," *Time*, May 6, 1946; "Microphone Missionary," *Time*, April 14, 1952; and *Reader's Digest*

61 (July 1952), 57–62. See also Fulton Oursler, "A Bargain in Brimstone," *Reader's Digest* 50 (June 1947), 8–10; Fulton Sheen, "The Life of Christ," *Collier's*, January 8, 1954, pp. 20–25; Howard Cohn, "Bishop Sheen Answers His Fan Mail," *Collier's*, January 24, 1953, pp. 22–24; and "Psychiatry & Faith," *Time*, April 18, 1949.

11. Clare Boothe Luce, "The 'Real' Reason," *McCall's* (February 1947), 135. The complete citation for this series is as follows: (February 1947), pp. 16, 117–18, 120–35; (March 1947), pp. 16, 153–54, 156, 160–61, 167–68, 171–73, 175–76; (April 1947), pp. 26–27, 76, 78, 80, 85, 88, 90.

12. Luce, "Real Reason," *McCall's* (March 1947), 153; and Morris, *Rage for Fame*, 160, 358.

13. Luce, "Real Reason," *McCall's* (March 1947), 167.

14. Ibid., 156, 160.

15. Ibid., 16.

16. Allitt, *Catholic Converts*, ix; and Luce, "Real Reason," *McCall's* (April 1947), 88.

17. Clare Boothe Luce, typescript of speech "Freedom and Catholicism" or "Christianity and the Red Religion," delivered before the Archdiocese Council of Catholic Women, Chicago, November 20, 1947, p. 21, folder 1, container 682, Luce Papers.

18. "What Can We Do to Improve Race and Religious Relationships in America?," *Town Meeting* (Bulletin of America's Town Meeting of the Air, ABC, October 7, 1947), vol. 13, no. 24, pp. 13–14. This item may be found in folder 32, container 681, Luce Papers.

19. Clare Boothe Luce, typescript of speech, "Brotherhood Is Freedom," to the Women's Activities Committee of the National Conference of Christians and Jews, Washington, D.C., February 23, 1949, folder 11, container 683, Luce Papers.

20. Clarence Edward Heller to Clare Boothe Luce, June 23, 1946, folder 7, container 120; and undated typescript, "The Evil Protocols of the (Jewish) Zionists. (Politically)," Congressional File, Subject File (1943–46)—Anti-Semitism, folder 6, container 594, Luce Papers. On Catholic, especially Irish Catholic, anti-semitism in New York City, see Ronald H. Bayor, *Neighbors in Conflict: The Irish, Germans, Jews, and Italians of New York City, 1929–1941* (Baltimore, 1978), 87–108, 150–63. On the antisemitic excesses of the Catholic counterculture, see James Terence Fisher, *The Catholic Counterculture in America, 1933–1962* (Chapel Hill, 1989), 83–88.

21. Morris, *American Catholics*, 200–204; quotes from p. 203.

22. Ibid., 208.

23. The author of *American Freedom and Catholic Power* was Paul Blanshard. See John T. McGreevy, "Thinking on One's Own: Catholicism in the American Intellectual Imagination, 1928–1960," *Journal of American History* 84 (June 1997), 97–131; and John T. McGreevy, *Catholicism and American Freedom: A History* (New York, 2003), 166–88. See also James Gilbert, *Redeeming Culture: American Religion in an Age of Science* (Chicago, 1997), 84–89. For insight into some of the Jewish liberal intellectuals who opposed certain elements of Catholicism, see David A. Hollinger, "Jewish Intellectuals and the De-Christianization of American Public Culture in the Twentieth Century," and "The 'Tough-Minded' Justice Holmes,

Jewish Intellectuals, and the Making of an American Icon," in David A. Hollinger, *Science, Jews, and Secular Culture: Studies in Mid-Twentieth-Century American Intellectual History* (Princeton, 1996), 17–59.

24. Morris, *Rage for Fame,* 54.

25. Clare Boothe Luce Diary, March 11, 1919, folder 1, container x21, Luce Papers. See also Morris, *Rage for Fame,* 64.

26. Clare Boothe Luce Diary, November 26, 1919, folder 1, container x21, Luce Papers; Bernard M. Baruch, *Baruch: The Public Years* (New York, 1960), 240; and Morris, *Rage for Fame,* 5, 207.

27. The Luce-Bergel correspondence and the investigator's report, as well as news clippings are in folder 18, container x3, Luce Papers.

28. U.S. Congress, *Congressional Record,* Proceedings and Debates of the 79th Congress, First Session (Washington, D.C., 1945), 12391–92.

29. Clare Boothe Luce Diary, June 4, 1949, container 56, folder 9, Luce Papers.

30. Clare Boothe Luce to William F. Buckley, November 27, 1974, folder 17, container 311, Luce Papers. The article, "Ultimatum to the UN: Israel and the Arab Godfather," appeared in the *National Review,* January 31, 1975.

31. Clare Boothe Luce, review of Golda Meir, *My Life, New Republic,* April 17, 1976, pp. 25–27.

32. "Applied Psychology: An Address of Pope Pius XII to a Congress of the International Association of Applied Psychology," *The Pope Speaks* 5 (Summer 1958), 11–20; and Nathan G. Hale, Jr., *Freud and the Americans: The Rise and Crisis of Psychoanalysis, 1917–1985* (New York, 1995), 223. For an early Catholic response to Freud, which depicts Jesus as "the Great Psychiatrist," see John Rathbone Oliver, *Psychiatry and Mental Health* (New York, 1932), 287. See also J. Godfrey Raupert, *Human Destiny and the New Psychology* (Philadelphia, 1921); and E[dward John] Boyd Barrett, S.J., *Psycho-Analysis and Christian Morality* (London, 1924).

CHAPTER 12. JEWS AND THE CREATION OF AMERICAN HUMANISM

1. Jews were at the forefront of a number of psychotherapeutic "schools" including Gestalt therapy (Frederick and Laura Perls and Paul Goodman), Transactional Analysis (Eric Berne), Cognitive Therapy (Aaron Beck), Rational Emotive Behavior Therapy (Albert Ellis), Reality Therapy and Choice Theory (William Glasser), and Positive Psychology (Martin Seligman), and Nathan Ackerman and Salvador Minuchin were important figures in the development of Family Therapy. Viktor Frankl's logotherapy loomed large among humanist psychologies and is discussed in Chapter 14 in the context of approaches to evil and suffering.

2. Laing's passage was written in 1964 as part of the preface to the Pelican edition of R. D. Laing, *The Divided Self: An Existential Study in Sanity and Madness* (1959; n.p., 1982), 11–12; and Abraham H. Maslow, *Toward a Psychology of Being* (1962; New York, 1968), 72. See also Phyllis Chesler, *Women and Madness* (Garden City, N.Y., 1972).

3. Erich Auerbach, *Mimesis: The Representation of Reality in Western Literature* (1953; Princeton, 1974), 7–23. For the quoted passages see pp. 17–18. For a retrospective on *Mimesis*, see Seth Lerer, ed., *Literary History and the Challenge of Philology: The Legacy of Erich Auerbach* (Stanford, 1996).

4. Sholem Asch, *The Nazarene* (New York, 1939), 697; and Budd Schulberg, *What Makes Sammy Run?* (New York, 1941), 212. Schulberg's novel also appeared in abridged form in *Reader's Digest* 39 (July 1941), 128–84.

5. Saul Bellow, *Dangling Man* (1944; New York, 1975), 7; and Saul Bellow, *Herzog* (1961; New York, 1964), 218.

6. Keith Opdahl, "The 'Mental Comedies' of Saul Bellow," in *From Hester Street to Hollywood: The Jewish-American Stage and Screen*, ed. Sarah Blacher Cohen (Bloomington, 1983), 187.

7. William Graebner, *The Age of Doubt: American Thought and Culture in the 1940s* (Boston, 1991), 127–29; and Mark Zborowski, "Cultural Components in Response to Pain," *Journal of Social Issues* 8 (1952), 16–30. To fully appreciate Zborowski's reinterpretation, compare it to Lorraine Maynard and Laurence Miscall, *Bellevue* (New York, 1940), 5, 57. Zborowski's 1952 study formed the basis of a book that became a classic in its field; see Mark Zborowski, *People in Pain* (San Francisco, 1969).

8. Allen Ginsberg, *Howl and Other Poems* (1956; San Francisco, 1966), 7–8, 19–20.

9. Allen Ginsberg, *Kaddish and Other Poems, 1958–1960* (San Francisco, 1961), 32.

10. Theodor Reik, *The Search Within: The Inner Experiences of a Psychoanalyst* (1956; New York, 1969), 32–34.

11. Theodor Reik, *Myth and Guilt: The Crime and Punishment of Mankind* (New York, 1957), 387, 396, 431–32.

12. Oscar Handlin, *The Uprooted: The Epic Story of the Great Migrations That Made the American People* (Boston, 1951), 6.

13. The Weinberg clippings may be found in the folder "Psychopathic Personality," M449/331–32, Abraham Maslow Papers, Archives of the History of American Psychology, University of Akron (hereafter Maslow Papers); and Erik H. Erikson, *Childhood and Society* (1950; New York, 1963), 355.

14. Lawrence J. Friedman, *Identity's Architect: A Biography of Erik H. Erikson* (New York, 1999), 433.

15. Ibid., 32–42, 54.

16. Erikson, *Childhood and Society*, 282; and Friedman, *Identity's Architect*, 20.

17. Erikson, *Childhood and Society*, 281, and see also pp. 268–69.

18. Mark Schechner, *After the Revolution: Studies in the Contemporary Jewish American Imagination* (Bloomington, 1987), 172, and see also pp. 173–79 for the linkages between Mailer, Lindner, and Reich. On Lindner, see Fred Waage, "Traumatic Conformity: Robert Lindner's Narratives of Rebellion," *Journal of American Culture* 22 (Summer 1999), 25–32. For background on the response of American intellectuals to the problem of conformity, see Richard H. Pells, *The Liberal Mind in a Conservative Age: American Intellectuals in the 1940s and 1950s* (New York, 1985), 183–261.

19. See "Wilhelm Reich," in *Twentieth-Century Literary Criticism* (Detroit, 1992), 57:337–92; and the chapter "From Socialism to Therapy, II: Wilhelm Reich," in Shechner, *After the Revolution*, 91–101.

20. For Riesman's debt to Fromm, see David Riesman (with Nathan Glazer and Reuel Denney), *The Lonely Crowd: A Study of the Changing American Character* (1950; New Haven, 1970), 22. The "other directed personality" derived from Fromm's theory of character orientations, of which the one most typical of the modern age was the "marketing orientation," in which superficial traits of personality define one's fate in the market economy. See Erich Fromm, *Man for Himself* (1947; New York, 1966), 67–82. Riesman was an analysand of Fromm in the late 1940s; I received this information from Dr. Rainer Funk, Fromm's literary executor, in a personal communication on April 8, 2003, at the Erich Fromm-Archiv in Tübingen. According to Funk, reference to Riesman's therapy with Fromm appears in the Erich Fromm Papers at the New York Public Library but is not accessible, as of this writing, due to restrictions on that collection.

21. E. Brooks Holifield, *A History of Pastoral Care in America: From Salvation to Self-Realization* (Nashville, 1983), 251–57; Rollo May, *The Art of Counseling* (New York, 1939), 69; and Rollo May, *The Meaning of Anxiety* (1950; New York, 1977), 381–82. For the impact of Tillich on May, see Rollo May, *Paulus: Reminiscences of a Friendship* (New York, 1973).

22. Paul Tillich, *The Courage to Be* (New Haven, 1952), 164.

23. Holifield, *History of Pastoral Care*, 295–96, 299.

24. Carl R. Rogers, *On Becoming a Person: A Therapist's View of Psychotherapy* (Boston, 1961), 189, 194.

25. Martin Buber, *I and Thou*, ed. Walter Kaufmann (New York, 1970), 69, 75, 87. The phrase "I-Thou" came from the first English translation of Buber's *Ich und Du*, by Ronald Gregor Smith (1937). But, as Walter Kaufmann points out in his more fluid translation of Buber's opaque original, the German *du* does not translate naturally into the archaic and stylized *Thou* of modern English. See Kaufmann's evaluation of Buber's book in the prologue, pp. 14–48. On the background of Buber's thought, see Laurence J. Silberstein, *Martin Buber's Social and Religious Thought: Alienation and the Quest for Meaning* (New York, 1989), 18–42; and Maurice Friedman, *Martin Buber's Life and Work: The Early Years, 1878–1923* (Detroit, 1988).

26. The quotes from Buber, which originally appeared in a 1948 book, *Israel and the World*, are taken from Adrienne Koch, *Philosophy for a Time of Crisis: An Interpretation with Key Writings by Fifteen Great Modern Thinkers* (New York, 1959), 186–87. Vis-à-vis the idea of experience in Tillich and Rogers, see Buber's statement in *I and Thou*: "Those who experience do not participate in the world. For the experience is 'in them' and not between them and the world. The world does not participate in experience. It allows itself to be experienced, but it is not concerned, for it contributes nothing, and nothing happens to it" (Kaufmann edition, p. 56).

Buber emphasizes the *limits* against which people must struggle to achieve a true mutuality, and, against Rogers, he rejects the idea that in dialogue one encounters an intrinsic goodness, preferring to describe human nature as thoroughly at odds with itself and having the potential to move in a positive, rather than a negative, direction. See the exchange between Buber and Rogers in Judith Buber Agassi, ed., *Martin Buber on Psychology and Psychotherapy* (Syracuse, 1999), 246–70.

Like the Russian Jewish psychologist Lev Vygotsky, Buber believed that all of modern psychology was in a state of crisis, that no single "school" could even approach the total understanding of human existence to which all of them aspired, and that the solution lay in a transcendent, unifying concept of human relatedness. Compare the emphasis on human activity in the realization of the I-Thou relationship to Vygotsky's unifying principle of *Tatigkeit*, socially meaningful activity. See Lev Vygotsky, *Thought and Language*, ed. Alex Kozulin (Cambridge, Mass., 1997), xix–xxiv.

27. "Of Man Unto Man," *Newsweek*, April 1, 1957, p. 82; Buber, *I and Thou*, 32; and Sydney E. Ahlstrom, *A Religious History of the American People* (New Haven, 1972), 982–83. See also "Jewish Religiosity" in Martin Buber, *On Judaism* (New York, 1995), 79–94.

28. Buber, *I and Thou*, 36–37.

29. Huston Smith, *The Religions of Man* (New York, 1958), 254–300; and John F. Hayward, *Existentialism and Religious Liberalism* (Boston, 1962), 64–65.

30. The quotation from Fromm comes from Rainer Funk, *Erich Fromm: His Life and Ideas* (New York, 2000), 6.

31. For biographical detail on Fromm's childhood and early adulthood, see Funk, *Erich Fromm*, 6–77, and Don Hausdorff, *Erich Fromm* (New York, 1972), 11–20. For a thorough bibliography of Fromm's writings, see Rainer Funk, ed., *Erich Fromm: Gesamtausgabe*, 12 vols. (Stuttgart, 1999), 10:373–500.

32. The quotation on Fromm's importance comes from Robert C. Fuller, *Americans and the Unconscious* (New York, 1986), 126. For Fromm's impact on Protestantism, see Holifield, *History of Pastoral Care*, 276–87, 290–91. Seward Hiltner, a leader of Protestant pastoral psychology, wrote his dissertation on Fromm, and the journal *Pastoral Psychology* devoted an issue to him (September 1955). Karen Horney credited Fromm as "the first in German psychoanalytic literature" who "recognized the importance of cultural factors as a determining influence in psychological conditions," and "who, through his profound knowledge of both sociology and psychoanalysis, made me more aware of the significance of social factors." See Karen Horney, *The Neurotic Personality of Our Time* (New York, 1937), 20; and Karen Horney, *Our Inner Conflicts: A Constructive Theory of Neurosis* (1945; New York, 1972), 12.

33. Erich Fromm, *Escape from Freedom* (New York, 1941), 12; Erich Fromm, *The Sane Society* (1955; New York, 1988), v; and Daniel Burston, *The Legacy of Erich Fromm* (Cambridge, Mass., 1991), 56–71.

34. Fromm, *Escape from Freedom*, 22–23.

35. Erich Fromm, *The Art of Loving* (1956; New York, 1970), 12.

36. Fromm, *Sane Society*, 35–41; and Burston, *Legacy of Erich Fromm*, 72.

37. Fromm, *Art of Loving*, 3, 49; and *Man for Himself*, 84. For the sales figure in 2000, see Funk, *Erich Fromm*, 139.

38. Fromm, *Art of Loving*, 66.

39. Erich Fromm, *You Shall Be as Gods: A Radical Interpretation of the Old Testament and Its Tradition* (Greenwich, 1966), 54, 57.

40. Ibid., 8, 14.

41. Ibid., 69, 157, 180.

42. George Leonard, "Abraham Maslow and the New Self," *Esquire* 100 (December 1983), 326; "Abraham Maslow: Father of Humanistic Psychology," *Los Angeles Times*, April 6, 1975; and Joyce Carol Oates, "The Potential of Normality," *Saturday Review*, August 26, 1972, p. 55.

43. Abraham Maslow, undated journal entry (Fall 1931?), "Journal Entries by Maslow," folder #7, M1910/421, Maslow Papers. Maslow's fears about finding a job were neither irrational nor exaggerated—see Andrew S. Winston, " 'The Defects of His Race': E. G. Boring and Anti-Semitism in American Psychology, 1923–1953," *History of Psychology* 1 (February 1998), 27–51.

44. Edward Hoffman, *The Right to Be Human: A Biography of Abraham Maslow* (Los Angeles, 1988), 31–33; and Abraham H. Maslow, *Toward a Psychology of Being* (1962; New York, 1968), iii–iv. See also Abraham H. Maslow, *Religions, Values, and Peak-Experiences* (1964; New York, 1970), 11–18, 36–47. For Frankl's separation of psychotherapy from religion, see Viktor E. Frankl, *The Doctor and the Soul: From Psychotherapy to Logotherapy* (1955; New York, 1983), xxi.

45. Maslow, *Toward a Psychology of Being*, 29–30. For a good example of the public reception of the idea of the peak-experience, see Ardis Whitman, "Overtaken by Joy," *The Reader's Digest* 86 (April 1965), 105–9. The ebullient response to Maslow is illustrated by the collection of letters from his readers in the Maslow Papers. Gorden Allport noticed the resemblance between Maslow's investigations of subjective experience and those of William James in *The Varieties of Religious Experience*. See Gordon W. Allport to Abraham Maslow, April 11, 1957, Folder "Peaks," M447/325–26, Maslow Papers.

46. Hoffman, *Right to be Human*, 130–45; for the data from Brandeis student assignments, see for example folder "Peak Research," M447/325–26, Maslow Papers.

47. "Abraham H. Maslow: The Mystery of Health," self-study typescript from taped conversations (marked confidential), written in late 1963 or 1964, Maslow Papers.

48. Journal entry, January 5, 1932, folder #7, "Journal Entries by Maslow," M1910/421, Maslow Papers.

49. Abraham Maslow to Jean Mandler, November 2, 1967, depot box 12, Maslow Papers. See also Erich Fromm to Abraham Maslow, June 22, 1937, and June 2, 1939, in Erich Fromm Papers, Erich Fromm-Archiv, Ursrainer Ring 24, Tübingen, Germany.

50. Hoffman, *Right to Be Human*, 16; "SA" undated typescript, folder #5, "Notes on Self Actualization," M1910/421, Maslow Papers.

51. Fromm, *Man for Himself*, 118, 134–35; "Selfishness and Unselfishness," typescript of lecture notes dated March 22, 1943, folder "Selfish," M449.1/334; notes on Madelaine Ganz, *The Psychology of Alfred Adler and the Development of the Child* (1953), folder "Selfish," M449.1/334; and "Self-Esteem," typescript of taped lecture, folder "Self-Esteem," M449.10, Maslow Papers. Fromm's discussion of selfishness first appeared in Erich Fromm, "Selfishness and Self-Love," *Psychiatry* 2 (November 1939), 507–23.

52. "SA and Identification," typescript document with subtitle "Chat with Haigh 4/16/51," folder #5, "Notes on Self Actualization," M1910/421, Maslow Papers; Hoffman, *Right to Be Human*, 258; Maslow, *Toward a Psychology of Being*, 7; and "Notes from A. H. Maslow," dated June 5, 1967, folder #5, "Notes on Self Actualization," M1910/421, Maslow Papers.

53. The *Psychology Today* interview from 1968 (when Maslow was sixty) is reprinted in *Psychology Today* 25 (January/February 1992), 69–73, 89; the quotation appears on p. 69. "Notes from A. H. Maslow," dated June 5, 1967, folder #5, "Notes on Self Actualization," M1910/421; "Evil" typescript, folder "Abe on Evil," M436/297, Maslow Papers; and Maslow, *Toward a Psychology of Being*, iv. See also the revised edition of Abraham H. Maslow, *Motivation and Personality* (New York, 1970), xix.

54. Typescript, "Evil," originally "Notes for Motivation and Personality Revision Preface," dated November 9, 1969, folder "Abe on Evil," M436/297, Maslow Papers; and William Marra, "An Interview with Dr. William Coulson," *The Latin Mass: Chronicle of Catholic Reform* 3 (January-February 1994), 14, 17. In light of Coulson's reflection, we might note that Catholics also preferred Buber to Protestant humanists on this very issue of evil, emphasizing Buber's insistence on personal responsibility and noting that "for Buber's thought evil presents itself . . . as the aimless whirl of undirected human potential." See Sister Helen James John, "Eichmann and Buber: A Message of Responsibility," *Commonweal*, July 6, 1962, pp. 374, 376.

55. See the discussion of Rieff, Bell (both Jewish), and Lasch in Peter Clecak, *America's Quest for the Ideal Self: Dissent and Fulfillment in the 60s and 70s* (New York, 1983), 229–76. We should note that the influential critique by economist John Kenneth Galbraith, *The Affluent Society* (1958), also invoked Protestant moral values.

CHAPTER 13. JOYCE BROTHERS:
THE JEWISH WOMAN AS PSYCHOLOGIST
OF SUBURBAN AMERICA

1. "Dr. Joyce Brothers," September 26, 1961, NBC (TV), B:02289 [131212], Museum of Television and Radio, Los Angeles. Brothers had three television shows, "The Joyce Brothers Show" (NBC, 1958–63), "Consult Dr. Brothers" (ABC, 1961–66), and "Tell Me, Dr. Brothers" (syndicated, 1964–70). Virtually all those shows appear to have been lost or destroyed. With the exception of the episode cited here, which is a six-minute fragment, the nation's primary archives for television have nothing other than Brothers's guest appearances on other shows. In a telephone conversation with the author, Dr. Brothers said that she possesses no recordings of her television shows. The Joyce Brothers Papers at Cornell University contain 789 videotapes, but the collection is not yet catalogued and remains closed until 2022.

2. On Bettelheim, see Richard Pollak, *The Creation of Dr. B: A Biography of Bruno Bettelheim* (New York, 1997).

3. Emma Goldman, *Living My Life* (1931; New York, 1977), 172–73, 455–56; Nathan G. Hale, Jr., *Freud and the Americans: The Beginnings of Psychoanalysis in the United States, 1876–1917* (New York, 1971), 269–70; and Mari Jo Buhle, *Feminism and Its Discontents: A Century of Struggle with Psychoanalysis* (Cambridge, Mass., 1998), 1–3.

4. "Dr. Laura Wants You to Stop Whining," *Psychology Today* 31 (February 1998), 28; M. Sue Bergin, "Who You Gonna Call? Dr. Laura," *San Francisco Chronicle*, January 26, 1997, pp. 30–31; and *Forward*, August 15, 2003, pp. 1, 6. See, for example, her *New York Times* best-seller, *How Could You Do That? The Abdication of Character, Courage, and Conscience* (New York, 1996). Orthodox Judaism does not consider homosexual conduct as more or less a transgression than driving on the Sabbath or eating nonkosher food; hence it would be highly unusual for an Orthodox rabbi to single out homosexuality for condemnation. Orthodox rabbinic opinion on abortion ranges from strict to lenient, depending on the circumstances.

5. For a starting point on this subject, see Rhoda K. Unger, "Psychology," in *Jewish Women in America: An Historical Encyclopedia*, 2 vols., ed. Paula E. Hyman and Deborah Dash Moore (New York, 1997), 2:1104–13; and Mitchell G. Ash, "Women Émigré Psychologists and Psychoanalysts in the United States," in *Between Strength and Sorrow: Women Refugees of the Nazi Period*, ed. Sibylle Quack (Washington, D.C., 1995), 239–64. There is no comprehensive history of women as psychological thinkers, but in respect to psychoanalysis, see Buhle, *Feminism and Its Discontents*. See also Agnes N. O'Connell and Nancy Felipe Russo, eds., *Models of Achievement: Reflections of Eminent Women in Psychology*, 2 vols. (Hillsdale, N.J., 1988).

6. Hannah Green, *I Never Promised You a Rose Garden* (New York, 1964), 57; and Stephen Farber and Marc Green, *Hollywood on the Couch: A Candid Look at the Overheated Love Affair between Psychiatrists and Moviemakers* (New York, 1993), 35–54. We should also note psychologist Phyllis Chesler, whose *Women and Madness* (New York, 1972) became a feminist classic and sold two million copies in a quarter-century.

7. Pamela Nadell, *Women Who Would Be Rabbis: A History of Women's Ordination, 1889–1985* (Boston, 1998), 1–23; Alvin H. Rosenfeld, "Inventing the Jew: Notes on Jewish Autobiography," *Midstream* 21 (April 1975), 57, 66–67; and Joyce Antler, *The Journey Home: Jewish Women and the American Century* (New York, 1997), 17–39, 150–75.

8. Deborah Dash Moore, *At Home in America: Second Generation New York Jews* (New York, 1981), 103; Beth S. Wenger, *New York Jews and the Great Depression: Uncertain Promise* (Syracuse, 1999), 63; Diana B. Turk, "College Students," in *Jewish Women in America*, 1:258, 261; and Paula S. Fass, *Outside In: Minorities and the Transformation of American Education* (New York, 1989), 82–83.

9. The quotation is from historian Deborah Dash Moore, with her permission, from a private correspondence, January 26, 2003. For a brief explanation of the comparative empowerment of women in eastern European Jewish culture, see Andrew R. Heinze, *Adapting to Abundance: Jewish Immigrants, Mass Consumption, and the Search for American Identity* (New York, 1990), 106–9. For a quick and

comprehensive illustration of the extraordinary attainments of Jewish women in America, see Hyman and Moore, *Jewish Women in America.*

10. Chris Matthew Sciabarra, *Ayn Rand: The Russian Radical* (1995; University Park, Pa., 1999), 24, 66–95, 110–11, 389.

11. Ibid., 96–122. For a selection of essays on Rand, see "Ayn Rand," in *Contemporary Literary Criticism* (Detroit, 1994), 79:356–97. On Branden, see *Contemporary Authors* (Detroit, 1989), 27:62–66.

12. Daniel Horowitz, *Betty Friedan and the Making of The Feminine Mystique* (Amherst, Mass., 1998), 86; on Friedan's childhood and education, see pp. 16–87.

13. Ibid., 101, 161, 219; and Betty Friedan, *The Feminine Mystique* (New York, 1963), 61.

14. Horowitz, *Betty Friedan,* 193–94, 197–223. See especially the chapters "The Problem That Has No Name," "The Happy Housewife Heroine," "The Crisis in Woman's Identity," "The Sexual Sell," and "The Forfeited Self," in Friedan, *Feminine Mystique,* 15–79, 206–32, 310–37.

15. Walter Gieber, "The 'Lovelorn' Columnist and Her Social Role," *Journalism Quarterly* 37 (Fall 1960), 499–514 (the quotation is from p. 514). See also Susan Schmidt Dibner, "Newspaper Advice Columns as a Mental Health Resource," *Community Mental Health Journal* 10 (Summer 1974), 147–55; and W. Clark Hendley, "Dear Abby, Miss Lonelyhearts, and the Eighteenth Century: The Origins of the Newspaper Advice Column," *Journal of Popular Culture* 11 (Fall 1977), 345–52.

16. Christopher Buckley, "You Got a Problem?" *New Yorker,* December 4, 1995, pp. 80–85; Abigail Van Buren, *The Best of Dear Abby* (Kansas City, 1981), 9–19; Timothy J. Gilfoyle, "Chicago's Emissaries of Culture: Interviews with Eppie Lederer and Lois Weisberg," *Chicago History* 29 (Spring 2001), 52–65; "Database: A Century of Advice," *U.S. News & World Report,* July 8, 1996; and Malcolm E. Lumby, "Ann Landers' Advice Column: 1958 and 1971," *Journalism Quarterly* 53 (Spring 1976), 129–32.

17. David I. Grossvogel, *Dear Ann Landers: Our Intimate and Changing Dialogue with America's Best-Loved Confidante* (Chicago, 1987), 12–18; James W. Tankard, Jr., and Rachel Adelson, "Mental Health and Marital Information in Three Newspaper Advice Columns," *Journalism Quarterly* 59 (Winter 1982), 592–97, 609; and Joseph J. Moran, "Newspaper Psychology: Advice and Therapy," *Journal of Popular Culture* 22 (Spring 1989), 119–27. For the views of Landers and Van Buren on homosexuality, see Ann Landers, *Ann Landers Talks to Teen-Agers About Sex* (Englewood Cliffs, 1963), 80–92; and Van Buren, *Best of Dear Abby,* 61–76.

18. J. Fred MacDonald, *Don't Touch That Dial! Radio Programming in American Life, 1920–1960* (1979; Chicago, 1991), 98. For the comparison with *Amos 'n' Andy,* see Melvin Patrick Ely, *The Adventures of Amos 'n' Andy: A Social History of an American Phenomenon* (New York, 1991). Berg's show started in 1929 as *The Rise of the Goldbergs* before NBC shortened the title to *The Goldbergs.* The radio show aired in the years 1929–34, 1938–45, and 1949–51, and the television show from 1949 to 1955, switching in its last year to the title *Molly.*

19. Jeffrey Shandler, "Gertrude Berg," in *Jewish Women in America,* 1:139–41; Michele Hilmes, *Radio Voices: American Broadcasting, 1922–1952* (Minneapolis, 1997), 1–6, 288–90; Donald Weber, "The Jewish-American World of Gertrude

Berg: The Goldbergs on Radio and Television, 1930–1950," in *Talking Back: Images of Jewish Women in American Popular Culture*, ed. Joyce Antler (Hanover, N.H., 1998), 85–99; and Joyce Antler, " 'Yesterday's Woman,' Today's Moral Guide: Molly Goldberg as Jewish Mother," in *Key Texts in American Jewish Culture*, ed. Jack Kugelmass (New Brunswick, N.J., 2003), 129–46. On radio morality, see MacDonald, *Don't Touch That Dial*, 44–47.

20. Antler, " 'Yesterday's Woman,' " 134; and Riv-Ellen Prell, *Fighting to Become Americans: Jews, Gender, and the Anxiety of Assimilation* (Boston, 1999), 170–72.

21. *The Goldbergs*, October 10, 1949, "Rosalie's Essay"; *Molly*, November 10, 1955, "Dreams." UCLA Film and Television Archive, Los Angeles.

22. *The Bob Cummings Show*, December 31, 1955. UCLA Film and Television Archive, Los Angeles.

23. *The Goldbergs*, October 10, 1949, "Rosalie's Essay"; *Molly*, October 27, 1955, "Rosie's Nose." UCLA Film and Television Archive, Los Angeles.

24. *Molly*, November 10, 1955, "Dreams." UCLA Film and Television Archive, Los Angeles. By the time she moved the Goldbergs to Haverville (1955), Berg's insights may have been more significant for what they forecast than for how many they affected. Her audience was presumably dwindling; the Yiddish-dialect mother was out of place in the suburbs, which downplayed overt ethnic traits in the interest of social homogeneity.

25. Joanne Meyerowitz, "Beyond the Feminine Mystique: A Reassessment of Postwar Mass Culture, 1946–1958," in *Not June Cleaver: Women and Gender in Postwar America, 1945–1960*, ed. Joanne Meyerowitz (Philadelphia, 1994), 229–62. See also, in the same volume, Susan M. Hartmann, "Women's Employment and the Domestic Ideal in the Early Cold War Years," 84–100; and Rosalind Rosenberg, *Divided Lives: American Women in the Twentieth Century* (New York, 1992), 160–62.

26. "Sex Is on the Air," *Newsweek*, September 29, 1958, p. 65; John Lardner, "The Air: Science in the World of Soap," *New Yorker*, September 13, 1958, pp. 131–35; and John Lardner, "The Book-Swallower," *Newsweek*, November 16, 1959, p. 104. See also "Winner Takes All," *Newsweek*, December 19, 1955, p. 44; and "$150,000 etc. Question—The Quiz Mind," *New York Times Magazine*, February 17, 1957, pp. 25ff.

27. Ruth Winter, "The Hanukkah Memory That Live On," *Good Housekeeping* 191 (December 1980), 72; and Joyce Brothers, *The Successful Woman: How You Can Have a Career, a Husband and a Family—and Not Feel Guilty about It* (New York, 1988), 192–93. See also Sydney Stahl Weinberg, "Joyce Brothers," in *Jewish Women in America*, 1:191.

28. Joyce Brothers, *The Brothers System for Liberated Love and Marriage* (New York, 1972), 58.

29. Joyce Brothers, *Woman* (Kingswood, U.K., 1962), 230; and Joyce Brothers, *Widowed* (New York, 1990), 41.

30. Joyce Brothers, "On Being a Woman," *Good Housekeeping* 165 (September 1964), 32; and Brothers, *The Brothers System*, 52–53. Brothers's long-running column for *Good Housekeeping* began in February 1964.

31. *New York Times*, January 12, 1982. Joyce Brothers's appearances on *Mary Hartman, Mary Hartman* (1977), *Police Squad* (1982), *Moonlighting* (1987), *Late*

Night with Conan O'Brien (1993, 1994), and *Grace Under Fire* (1995) may be viewed at the Museum of Television and Radio in Los Angeles or New York City.

32. Dewey W. Grantham, *Recent America: The United States since 1945* (Arlington Heights, Ill., 1987), 160, 196; and William E. Leuchtenberg, *A Troubled Feast: American Society since 1945* (Boston, 1983), 65–67, 75–76. On the interrelationship of television, women, and suburbia in the postwar years, see Lynn Spigel, *Make Room for TV: Television and the Family Ideal in Postwar America* (Chicago, 1992).

33. On the motives of suburbanites and their high-culture critics, see the classic sociological study by Herbert Gans, *The Levittowners: Ways of Life and Politics in a New Suburban Community* (1967; New York, 1982).

34. Marya Mannes, "Little Brothers Is Watching You," *The Reporter,* February 15, 1962, 43–44. See also "Scattering Confetti," *Newsweek,* June 12, 1961, p. 63.

35. Joyce Brothers, "In Defense of Selfishness," *Good Housekeeping* (January 1969), 48–52. And compare "Why Not Pamper Your Husband?," *Good Housekeeping* 165 (September 1964), 30–32, and "It's Time to Give Yourself a Break," *Good Housekeeping* 165 (October 1964), 62–68. See also Brothers's advice to men on the meaning of masculinity, "How to Appeal to Women," *Mechanix Illustrated* 66 (August 1970), 35–37, 118–20.

36. Brothers, *Woman,* 132, 225.

37. Rosenberg, *Divided Lives,* 202.

38. Brothers, *The Brothers System,* 157–58, 210.

39. Ibid., 40–42, 47–50.

40. Ibid., 58, 107–9.

41. Ibid., 214, 285. See also Joyce Brothers, "Make Your Marriage a Love Affair," *Reader's Digest* 102 (March 1973), 79–82. For a concise description of the *ketubah,* see Philip Birnbaum, *Encyclopedia of Jewish Concepts* (New York, 1993), 298–99.

42. Joyce Brothers, *How to Get Whatever You Want Out of Life* (New York, 1978), 158.

43. Joyce Brothers, *Better Than Ever* (New York, 1975), 179.

44. Ibid., 152–56. See also the reviews of *Better Than Ever* in *Library Journal,* December 15, 1975, p. 2330; and *Publishers Weekly,* October 13, 1975, p. 96. Compare Brothers's position on extramarital sex to that of Albert Ellis, who does not see such liaisons as inherently immoral provided that the spouses are honest with each other, in *The Art and Science of Love* (New York, 1960), 55–56.

45. Joyce Brothers, *What Every Woman Should Know about Men* (New York, 1981), 21, 40, 45, 47.

46. Brothers, *Widowed,* 32, 48–49, 51, 142.

47. Ibid., 9, 17–18, 77.

48. Ibid., 78–79.

49. Ibid., 85–86, 103, 175.

CHAPTER 14. HOLOCAUST, HASIDISM, SUFFERING, REDEMPTION

1. Daisy Maryles, "We Need Him Now," *Publishers Weekly,* October 1, 2001, p. 16; and Robert Dahlin, "America Confronts Grief," *Publishers Weekly,* December 17, 2001, pp. 38–39. See also Deirdre Donahue, "Kushner's 'Bad Things Hap-

pen' Reassures," *USA Today*, September 13, 2001; and Marc Silver, "Why Bad Things Can Inspire a Good Life," *U.S. News & World Report*, October 8, 2001, p. 10.

2. For a probing though not completely satisfactory explanation of this phenomenon, see Peter Novick, *The Holocaust in American Life* (Boston, 1999), especially pp. 207–63, where Novick raises a host of important questions about the "meaning" of the Holocaust to Americans. On representations of the Holocaust in American popular culture, see Jeffrey Shandler, *While America Watches: Televising the Holocaust* (New York, 1999).

3. Novick, *Holocaust in American Life*, 236–37; "Why Christians Can't Forget the Holocaust," *U.S. Catholic* 55 (July 1990), 6–13; John M. Mulder, "The Terminal Generation," *Theology Today* 33 (January 1977), 443; and Carl F. H. Henry, *God, Revelation and Authority, Volume VI: God Who Stands and Stays, Part Two* (1983; Wheaton, Ill., 1999), 488. For a good illustration of some of the differences between liberal and evangelical Protestants, and between evangelicals themselves, in regard to the significance of the Holocaust for Christian approaches to Jews, see Stephen T. Davis, "Evangelical Christians and Holocaust Theology," *American Journal of Theology and Philosophy* 2 (September 1981), 121–29; David P. Gushee, "The Good News after Auschwitz: A Biblical Reflection," in *"Good News" after Auschwitz? Christian Faith within a Post-Holocaust World*, eds. Carol Rittner and John K. Roth (Macon, Ga., 2001), 157–72; Kenneth A. Myers, "Adjusting Theology in the Shadow of Auschwitz," *Christianity Today*, October 8, 1990, pp. 41–43; Richard J. Mouw, "The Chosen People Puzzle," *Christianity Today*, March 5, 2001, pp. 70–78; and Yaacov Ariel, "Jewish Suffering and Christian Salvation: The Evangelical-Fundamentalist Holocaust Memoirs," *Holocaust and Genocide Studies* 6 (Spring 1991), 63–78. I thank Doug Milford of Wheaton College for directing me to pertinent sources on evangelical Christian thought about the Holocaust.

4. Everett V. Stonequist, *The Marginal Man: A Study in Personality and Culture Conflict* (1937; New York, 1961), 76, 81.

5. Richard Pollak, *The Creation of Dr. B: A Biography of Bruno Bettelheim* (New York, 1997), 358–83.

6. For a biography of Frankl, see Haddon Klingberg, Jr., *When Life Calls Out to Us: The Love and Lifework of Viktor and Elly Frankl* (New York, 2001). An obituary appeared in the *New York Times*, September 4, 1997. See also Viktor E. Frankl, *Man's Search for Meaning: An Introduction to Logotherapy* (1962; New York, 1984). The book first appeared in English in 1959 under the title *From Death-Camp to Existentialism: A Psychiatrist's Path to a New Therapy* and in German in 1947 as *Ein Psycholog erlebt das Konzentrationslager* (*A Psychologist Experiences the Concentration Camp*). Frankl submitted a preview of his story to American readers in Viktor E. Frankl, "The Search for Meaning," *Saturday Review*, September 13, 1958, p. 20.

7. Frankl, *Man's Search for Meaning*, 7; and Wenceslao Vial Mena, *La Antropología de Viktor Frankl: El Dolor, Una Puerta Abierta* (Santiago, Chile, 1999), 302, and for the quote "singular lucidity" (*singular lucidez*) see the abstract on the book's back cover. See also Timothy Pytell, "The Missing Pieces of the Puzzle: A Reflection on the Odd Career of Viktor Frankl," *Journal of Contemporary History* 35 (April 2000), 300–301.

8. Pytell, "Missing Pieces of the Puzzle," 285–95; and Frankl, *Man's Search for Meaning*, 17–100.

9. Viktor E. Frankl, *The Doctor and the Soul: From Psychotherapy to Logotherapy* (1955; New York, 1986), xxvii. Though Frankl admired Freud, he sharply criticized the determinism of psychoanalysis; see Viktor E. Frankl, *The Unconscious God: Psychotherapy and Theology* (1948; New York, 1975), 20–28.

10. Robert C. Leslie, *Jesus and Logotherapy: The Ministry of Jesus as Interpreted Through the Psychotherapy of Viktor Frankl* (New York, 1965), 9; "Reuven P. Bulka: Work, Love, Suffering, and Death," *Jewish Book News*, March 12, 1998, pp. 39–43; and Reuven P. Bulka, *The Quest for Ultimate Meaning: Principles and Applications of Logotherapy* (New York, 1979), vii, 9–10. In 1976 Bulka founded the *Journal of Psychology and Judaism*, based on his synthesis of Judaism and logotherapy. For an extensive deliberation on the religious dimensions of Frankl's thought and its relation to Christianity, see Mena, *La Antropología*. For an overview of controversies surrounding Frankl, see Klingberg, *When Life Calls Out to Us*, 221–42; Pytell, "Missing Pieces of the Puzzle," 281–306; and Karlheinz Biller, Jay I. Levinson, and Timothy Pytell, "Viktor Frankl—Opposing Views," *Journal of Contemporary History* 37 (January 2002), 105–13.

11. Melvin A. Kimble, ed. *Viktor Frankl's Contribution to Spirituality and Aging* (New York, 2000), 21.

12. John B. Breslin, "Elie Wiesel, Survivor and Witness," *America*, June 19, 1976, pp. 537, 539; Elie Wiesel, "Recalling Swallowed-Up Worlds," *Christian Century*, May 27, 1981, p. 609; Mark Chmiel, *Elie Wiesel and the Politics of Moral Leadership* (Philadelphia, 2001), xi; and Maurice Friedman, "Elie Wiesel—The Modern Job," *Commonweal*, October 14, 1966, p. 48. See also Robert McAfee Brown, "Wiesel's Case Against God," *Christian Century*, January 30, 1980, pp. 109–12. Along with Robert McAfee Brown and Harry James Cargas (author of *Reflections of a Post-Auschwitz Christian*, 1989), Carol Rittner and John K. Roth have devoted themselves to incorporating Wiesel into Christian thought; they introduce a recent volume with two quotations, one from Luke and one from Wiesel; see Rittner and Roth, eds., *"Good News" after Auschwitz?*

13. For a good overview, see Samuel G. Freedman, "Bearing Witness: The Life and Work of Elie Wiesel," *New York Times Magazine*, October 23, 1983, pp. 32–36, 40, 65–69. See also Paul Nathan, "Another Hard Sell," *Publishers Weekly*, August 25, 1997, p. 27; Elizabeth Devereaux, "Elie Wiesel," *Publishers Weekly*, April 6, 1992, pp. 39–40; *Time*, October 27, 1986, p. 66; and *U.S. News & World Report*, October 27, 1986, pp. 67–68. For a sense of the adulation Wiesel has enjoyed among Christians, especially American Christians, see Robert McAfee Brown, *Elie Wiesel: Messenger to All Humanity* (Notre Dame, 1983); and Carol Rittner, ed., *Elie Wiesel: Between Memory and Hope* (New York, 1990). Like *Night*, Wiesel's subsequent books were translated into English from French, the language in which he preferred to write.

14. Lawrence S. Cunningham, "Elie Wiesel's Anti-Exodus," *America*, April 27, 1974, p. 327.

15. Eliezer Wiesel, *Un Di Velt Hot Geshvign* (Buenos Aires, 1956), 10, 18, 70; and Elie Wiesel, *Night* (1960; New York, 1971), 15, 20, 44. For a comparison of the Yiddish and French versions of *Night* (the English edition was based on the

French), see Naomi Seidman, "Elie Wiesel and the Scandal of Jewish Rage," *Jewish Social Studies* (New Series) 3 (Fall 1996), 1–19; and Ruth R. Wisse, *The Modern Jewish Canon: A Journey Through Language and Culture* (New York, 2000), 212–16. Wiesel himself noted the difference between the original Yiddish memoir and the French in Elie Wiesel, *All Rivers Run to the Sea: Memoirs* (New York, 1995), 320.

16. Wiesel, *Night*, 44; and Elie Wiesel, "Why I Write," in *Confronting the Holocaust: The Impact of Elie Wiesel*, ed. Alvin H. Rosenfeld and Irving Greenberg (Bloomington, 1978), 201–6.

17. Alvin H. Rosenfeld, "Introduction," and Byron L. Sherwin, "Wiesel's Midrash: The Writings of Elie Wiesel and Their Relationship to Jewish Tradition," both in *Confronting the Holocaust: The Impact of Elie Wiesel*, xii, 117–32; "The Real State of the World," *Nation*, June 12, 1972, p. 741; and L. Eugene Startzman, "Elie Wiesel Poses Hard Questions from the Holocaust," *Christianity Today*, October 7, 1983, p. 99.

18. Wiesel, "Recalling Swallowed-Up Worlds," 611–12; Robert McAfee Brown, "The Power of the Tale," *Christian Century*, June 3–10, 1981, p. 650; Freedman, "Bearing Witness: The Life and Work of Elie Wiesel," p. 40; and Robert McAfee Brown, "Eli [*sic*] Wiesel's Song: Lost & Found Again," *Commonweal*, July 12, 1974, p. 384.

19. Elie Wiesel, *Souls on Fire: Portraits and Legends of Hasidic Masters* (New York, 1972), 7, 19.

20. Ibid., 228–31, 252–54.

21. Michael J. Bandler, "A Nostalgic Glimpse at Hasidism: Souls on Fire," *Commonweal*, April 28, 1972, p. 196.

22. *Christian Century*, May 15, 1985, p. 497; and John Weisman, "If Only We'd Had TV during Hitler's Time," *TV Guide*, December 31, 1988, p. 6. On the longevity of *Night* and *Souls on Fire*, see for example, "Now Is a Good Time to Sample Writings of Jewish-Americans," *Los Angeles Times*, November 28, 1991.

23. Wiesel, *Souls on Fire*, 256 (emphasis in original).

24. Erich Fromm, *Das jüdische Gesetz: Zur Soziologie des Diaspora-Judentums* (1922; München, 1996), 190. Fromm's dissertation was prepared for publication by Rainer Funk, the director of the Erich Fromm Archiv in Tübingen, and Bernd Sahler; it has not been translated into English. For a famous critique of Buber's version of Hasidism, see Gershom Scholem, "Martin Buber's Hasidism," *Commentary* 32 (October 1961), 305–16. For an anticipation of American interest in Hasidism prior to Buber's translation, see Jacob S. Minkin, *The Romance of Hassidism* (New York, 1935).

The rise of Hasidism to prominence in American thought is perfectly illustrated by the eminent philosopher Robert Nozick, a devout rationalist, who included "the tales of the Baal Shem Tov" in a short list of great spiritual narratives, the others being Plato's dialogues, the Gospels, and the Pali canon. See Robert Nozick, *The Examined Life: Philosophical Meditations* (New York, 1989), 253.

25. Chaim Potok, *The Chosen* (New York, 1967). On Potok, see Edward A. Abramson, *Chaim Potok* (Boston, 1986).

26. Roland B. Gittelsohn, *Man's Best Hope* (New York, 1961), 12, 16–17; Israel Chodos, *Count Your Blessings* (New York, 1955); and Robert I. Kahn, *Lessons for Life* (Garden City, N.Y., 1963), 14. See also Sidney Greenberg, *Say Yes to Life: A*

Book of Thoughts for Better Living (New York, 1982), and three works by Louis Binstock: *The Power of Faith* (New York, 1952), *The Road to Successful Living* (New York, 1958), and *The Power of Maturity* (New York, 1969).

27. In addition to Twerski, Reuven Bulka, who is cited above, has combined psychology and *musar*, as has Zelig Pliskin, a Jerusalem-based rabbi from Baltimore who is perhaps the most eminent specialist in *musar* today. Pliskin self-publishes most of his books in Hebrew and English. See, for example, Zelig Pliskin, *Begin Again Now: A Concise Encyclopedia of Strategies for Living* (Brooklyn, 1993). During a personal meeting in 1995, Rabbi Pliskin spoke to me with great enthusiasm about such psychotherapeutic techniques as "mirroring" and mentioned that he enjoyed attending psychology conferences in Israel. His stated aim—"to help every individual maximize his or her potential"—illustrates the interweaving of traditional Judaism and humanist psychology.

For the posthumously published inspirational thoughts of the Lubavitcher Rebbe, transcribed from sermons by one of his disciples, see Menachem Mendel Schneerson, *Toward a Meaningful Life: The Wisdom of the Rebbe* (New York, 1995). In preparing the Rebbe's teaching for a general audience, Simon Jacobson, the editor of this volume, opens the book with a carefully worded explanation: "Although he was a Jewish leader, the Rebbe taught—and embodied—a distinctly universal message, calling upon all humankind to lead productive and virtuous lives, and calling for unity between all people" (p. ix). The mass market was not well suited to the crystalline intensity of a theologian like Joseph Soloveitchik. His classic work *The Lonely Man of Faith*, published in an Orthodox journal in 1965 and then in book form by Doubleday in 1992, appealed primarily to learned readers with strong interests in religious philosophy. Perhaps in an effort to extend the book's appeal beyond Jews, Orthodox or otherwise, the publisher placed on the cover a photo of an anonymous, clean-shaven man, presumably considered a better representative of universal angst than the full-bearded, decidedly rabbinic-looking Soloveitchik. For an example of a book by a Modern Orthodox rabbi that stayed within the parameters of American inspirational writing, see Maurice Lamm, *The Power of Hope: The One Essential of Life and Love* (New York, 1995).

28. Author's interview with Abraham J. Twerski, January 21, 1998; and *Encyclopaedia Judaica*, vol. 17 (Supplement), 587.

29. For a fuller discussion of Twerski, including his efforts to inform Orthodox Jews about psychotherapy, addiction, and spouse abuse, see Andrew R. Heinze, "The Americanization of Mussar: Abraham Twerski's Twelve Steps," *Judaism* 48 (Fall 1999), 450–69. For a critique of the excesses of the recovery movement, focusing on its Christian antecedents, see Wendy Kaminer, *I'm Dysfunctional, You're Dysfunctional: The Recovery Movement and Other Self-Help Fashions* (New York 1993), 9–28.

30. Abraham J. Twerski, *Caution: 'Kindness' Can Be Dangerous to the Alcoholic* (New York, 1981), xv–xvii.

31. Abraham J. Twerski, *When Do the Good Things Start?* (New York, 1988), 16, 52; Abraham J. Twerski, *Like Yourself* (*and others will too)* (Englewood Cliffs, N.J., 1978), 25–26; Abraham J. Twerski, *Who Says You're Neurotic? How to Avoid Mistaken*

Diagnoses When the Problem May Be a Physical Condition (Englewood Cliffs, N.J., 1984), 52; and Twerski interview.

32. *Alcoholics Anonymous Comes of Age: A Brief History of AA* (1957; New York, 1975), 52–77, 160–67.

33. Ibid., 160–67. The Twelve Steps are: "(1) We admitted we were powerless over alcohol—that our lives had become unmanageable. (2) We came to believe that a Power greater than ourselves could restore us to sanity. (3) We made a decision to turn our will and our lives over to the care of God *as we understood Him.* (4) We made a searching and fearless moral inventory of ourselves. (5) We admitted to God, to ourselves, and to another human being the exact nature of our wrongs. (6) We were entirely ready to have God remove all these defects of character. (7) We humbly asked him to remove our shortcomings. (8) We made a list of all persons we had harmed, and became willing to make amends to them all. (9) We made direct amends to such people whenever possible, except when to do so would injure them or others. (10) We continued to take personal inventory and when we were wrong promptly admitted it. (11) We sought through prayer and meditation to improve our conscious contact with God *as we understood Him,* praying only for knowledge of His will for us and the power to carry that out. (12) Having had a spiritual awakening as the result of these steps, we tried to carry this message to alcoholics, and to practice these principles in all our affairs." See *Twelve Steps and Twelve Traditions* (New York, 1952).

34. Abraham J. Twerski, *Self-Discovery in Recovery* (n.p., 1984), 118. (This book was published under the auspices of the Hazelden Foundation, an important provider of services related to chemical dependency.) Freemasonry has historically been attractive to Jews and also requires monotheistic belief, but it is primarily a social rather than a spiritual organization.

35. Ibid., 94–96.

36. Abraham J. Twerski, *I Didn't Ask to Be in This Family* (New York, 1992), 111; and Twerski, *Like Yourself,* 6.

37. Abraham J. Twerski, *I'd Like to Call for Help, But I Don't Know the Number: The Search for Spirituality in Everyday Life* (New York, 1991), 24–25. For the comment by Betty Ford, see the back cover of the original 1991 edition of the book.

38. Twerski, *I Didn't Ask,* 113; and Twerski, *When Do the Good Things Start?,* 7, 9–10.

39. Twerski interview.

40. Kushner's first three best-sellers—*When Bad Things Happen to Good People, When All You Ever Wanted Isn't Enough,* and *Who Needs God?*—creatively adapt the distinctive themes of three scriptural books (Job, Ecclesiastes, and Psalms, respectively).

41. *Time,* July 19, 1982, p. 80; Elizabeth A. Schick, ed., *Current Biography Yearbook, 1997* (New York, 1997), 288–90; and *Contemporary Authors,* New Revision Series, vol. 84, (Farmington Hills, Mich., 2000), 268–74. See also *People,* October 19, 1981, pp. 97–98.

42. Harold S. Kushner, *When Bad Things Happen to Good People* (1981; New York, 1983), 1.

43. *Time,* July 19, 1982, p. 80; and *Redbook* 157 (October 1981), 60.

44. Kushner, *When Bad Things Happen,* 6–30, 97.

45. Joshua Loth Liebman, *Peace of Mind* (New York, 1948), 160–61; and Gittelsohn, *Man's Best Hope*, 114–15.

46. *Publishers Weekly*, August 7, 1981, p. 74; and *National Catholic Reporter*, January 28, 1983, p. 10. See also *Christian Century*, April 21, 1982, pp. 488–89, and May 26, 1982, p. 632; *U.S. Catholic* 47 (July 1982), 48–49; *American Legion* 111 (November 1981), 25; *Glamour* 81 (February 1983), 168; *New York Times*, January 3, 1983; and *Cosmopolitan* 194 (February 1983), 34.

47. *America*, March 26, 1983, p. 246–47; Richard John Neuhaus, "When Bad Things Happen to Good Religion," *National Review*, November 10, 1989, pp. 53–54; Mordechai Winiarz, "Is Religion for the Happy Minded? A Response to Harold Kushner," *Tradition: A Journal of Orthodox Thought* 22 (Fall 1986), 62; and *Time*, July 19, 1982, p. 80. See also *Commonweal*, January 28, 1983, pp. 54–57.

48. See Burton Cooper, "When Modern Consciousness Happens to Good People: Revisiting Harold Kushner," *Theology Today* 48 (October 1991), 290–300. Cooper, a professor of theology at the Louisville Presbyterian Theological Seminary, makes a case that Kushner's popularity and significance come from his ability to address people with a "modern consciousness," a perspective framed by science, and speak to their need for religious faith. The "mainline Protestant denominations," Cooper argues, "so concerned with the vitality of fundamentalist and conservative churches, on the one hand, and their own apparent malaise, on the other, can vitalize themselves by taking the clue to their method and mission from Kushner" (p. 291). Cooper's commentary on the "existentialism" of Kushner's writing is especially interesting. For other indications of Kushner's relevance to American theodicies, see for example Patrick D. Miller, "Hallelujah! The Lord God Omnipotent Reigns," *Theology Today* 53 (April 1996), 1; Mary Caygill, "When Faith is Tested," *Anglican Theological Review* 81 (Winter 1999), 184–86; and Edesio Sanchez, "God on Trial: The Book of Job and Human Suffering," *Interpretation* 53 (July 1999), 305–6.

49. Stephen T. Davis, ed., *Encountering Evil: Live Options in Theodicy* (Atlanta, 1981), 6. The same passage about the Holocaust, slightly reworded, appears in the 2001 edition of the book. The elevation of the Holocaust to prime position in contemporary theodicy is a cultural phenomenon rather than a logical necessity. As Christian theologian John Hicks observed years ago, "If, for example, divine providence had eliminated Hitler in his infancy we might now point instead to Mussolini as an example of a human monster whom God ought secretly to have excised from the human race; and if there were no Mussolini we should point to someone else. . . . Or, again, if He had secretly prevented the Second World War, then what about the First World War, or the American Civil War, or the Napoleonic wars. . . . There would be nowhere to stop, short of a divinely arranged paradise in which human freedom would be narrowly circumscribed." See John Hicks, *Evil and the Love of God* (1966; San Francisco, 1977), 327.

50. Kushner, *When Bad Things Happen*, 81–82, 85.

51. *Time*, January 8, 1973, p. 43; and Abraham Joshua Heschel, *The Earth Is the Lord's: The Inner World of the Jew in East Europe* (New York, 1950), 3, 15. For an idea of Heschel's impact, especially on Jewish-Christian relations, see the March 10, 1973, issue of *America*, which is devoted to Heschel; and *Time*, March 19, 1956, p. 64; Abraham Joshua Heschel, "Sacred Images of Man," *Christian Century*,

December 11, 1957, pp. 1473–75; *Time,* January 25, 1963, p. 66; Abraham Joshua Heschel, "Protestant Renewal: A Jewish View," *Christian Century,* December 4, 1963, pp. 1501–4; *Time,* March 14, 1969, p. 63; *Newsweek,* January 8, 1973, p. 50; Peter Steinfels, "Beliefs," *New York Times,* January 10, 1998; and Michael A. Chester, "Heschel and the Christians," *Journal of Ecumenical Studies* 38 (Spring-Summer 2001), 246–70. See also Susannah Heschel, "Introduction," in *Moral Grandeur and Spiritual Audacity: Essays, Abraham Joshua Heschel,* ed. Susannah Heschel (New York, 1996), vii–xxx.

52. Quoted in Edward K. Kaplan and Samuel H. Dresner, *Abraham Joshua Heschel: Prophetic Witness* (New Haven, 1998), 132. On the influence of the Kotzker Rebbe, see pp. 36–40, 69–71.

53. Abraham Joshua Heschel, *Man Is Not Alone: A Philosophy of Religion* (Philadelphia, 1951), 143–44, 242–45. See also Rivka Horwitz, "Abraham Joshua Heschel on Prayer and his Hasidic Sources," *Modern Judaism* 19 (October 1999), 293–310.

54. Ibid., 151; and Kushner, *When Bad Things Happen,* 85, 129, 140.

Conclusion

1. That drawing was the creation of Danish psychologist Edgar Rubin, who discovered this perceptual phenomenon in 1915.

2. Wendy Kaminer, *I'm Dysfunctional, You're Dysfunctional: The Recovery Movement and Other Self-Help Fashions* (New York, 1993), 19–20, 128, 138, 147–49; and Wendy Kaminer, *Sleeping With Extra-Terrestrials: The Rise of Irrationalism and Perils of Piety* (New York, 1999) (see the repeated references to Dewey in the latter work).

Index

Abnormal Psychology (Coriat), 11, 122
abortion: Landers and Van Buren on, 303; Schlessinger on, 298; and Orthodox Judaism, 408n. 4
Abraham, Karl, 75
acceptance, and Protestant humanism, 274–75
Accounting of the Soul (Lefin), 40–49, 61, 339
Ackerman, Nathan, 402n. 1
action research, Lewin's concept of, 162
adaptability, as Jewish trait, 151–52, 154
Addams, Jane, 129
addiction: and the Twelve Step program, 335–38; Twerski on, 335–39. *See also* alcoholism; drug addiction
adjustment, concept of, 29
adjustment psychology, criticized by Maslow, 288
Adler, Alfred, 64–86: accepts value of religion, 168; his affinity for Torah, 76; his concept of duty, 69, 125; on heredity and intelligence, 146–47; his love of Bible stories, 79; and Maslow, 287–88; and Rollo May, 273; rationalism of, 77–78, 169; as socialist, 66, 68, 76; as speaker on Jewish circuit, 208; on spiritualism, 78; his split with Freud, 67; in United States, 125; universalism of, 75–76; upbringing of, 71–73
Adler, Felix, 58, 80, 228
Adler, Viktor, 69
Adlerian psychology: appeal of to women, 125; contrasted to psychiatry and psychology, 79–80; description of, 68; on evil, 190; as Jewish development, 80–81; and Jewish neurosis, 153; as moral regimen, 79–80, 190; optimism of, 125; and self-realization, 226; in United States, 123–27
Adlerian terms, in American parlance, 2, 124, 162, 163–64, 202, 306, 316, 376n. 43
Adolescence (Hall), 98
Advertisements for Myself (Mailer), 271

advertising, and TV psychology, 295–96
advice: literature of, 88–89; male bias of psychological, 126–27, 211; on marriage, 211, 312–20; newspaper columns, 33, 110–11, 167, 206–7, 302–3; rise of psychological, 91–93
African Americans: deemed mentally inferior, 142–43; defended by Boas, 144; defended by Klineberg, 144–45; and ethnically split personality, 30; and Lewin's theory of self-hatred, 383n. 41; and literacy, 88; and lynching, 186
aging, and logotherapy, 326
alcoholic insanity, 152
Alcoholics Anonymous, 337–38
alcoholism: mentioned in *Peace of Mind*, 197; and military discharges, 200; public attention to, 335; and the Twelve Steps, 335–38; Twerski on, 335–39
Alger, Horatio, Jr., 89
alienation, as problem for humanism, 275, 280
alienists, versus "new psychiatrist," 97–98
Allen, Frederick Lewis, 92
Allen, Woody (Allen Stewart Konigsberg), 264, 265–66, 272
Allport, Gordon: and Frankl, 324; and Maslow, 286, 406n. 45; and *Peace of Mind*, 198
Altenberg, Peter, 77
amaurotic family idiocy. *See* Tay-Sachs disease
America, as Promised Land, 118, 164, 186
American Nervousness (Beard), 91
American Neurological Association, 149
American Psychological Association, 142
American Psycho-Pathological Association, 208
American Scholar, 242, 252
Americanism, "100 percent" versus "hyphenated," 27
Americans: as audience for psychology, 90–93; as readers, 88–89
amnesia, 25–26, 113
Amos 'n' Andy (radio show), 304

281, 301, 313, 321, 324, 327, 333, 340, 391n. 2, 408n. 6; gender as factor of inspirational, 210–13, 312–15, 370n. 3, 394n. 35; Little Blue Books, 128–29; self-help and inspirational, 87–90, 93, 195, 301, 304, 312–15, 334–39, 391n. 2. *See also specific titles*
Bornstein, Bertha, 298
Boston: psychiatric care in, 104, 117, 121, 171, 204; spiritualism in, 172–73
Boston Psychoanalytic Society, 122
Boston Psychopathic Hospital, 117
Bottome, Phyllis, 75, 126
Bound to Rise (Alger), 89
bourgeoisie, German Jewish, 56, 71
brain. *See* mind
Brande, Dorothea, 90
Brandeis University, and Maslow's ideas, 285–86
Branden, Nathaniel (Nathan Blumenthal), 301
Braude, Rabbi William, 205
Breen, Joe, 251
Brentano, Franz, 70, 77
Brice, Fanny, 300
Brigham, Carl, 143, 146, 379n. 9
Brill, Abraham, 17–18, 20, 33–36, 183; accepts value of religion, 168; background of, 118–21; on behaviorism, 180; on Christian Science, 176; criticizes Fulton Sheen, 243; financial success of, 375n. 34; and Freud, 119, 120, 374n. 33; on Jewish neurosis, 152–56; on rational self-control, 183, 190; and Romm, 299; as speaker on Jewish circuit, 208; on sympathy, 190
Brill, Kittie Rose (Owen), 119
Brooklyn College, and Maslow's ideas, 285–86
Brothers, Joyce, 295–96, 303, 308–20; on adultery, 316–17; broadcasting style of, 312; on ethnic differences, 310; on female indomitability, 316, 317; and ideal of liberated marriage, 312–20; Jewish self-awareness of, 309–10; as model of female success, 314–16; in popular culture, 310–11; as a pragmatic feminist, 313–15, 320; on prejudice, 309–10, 313; upbringing of, 309
Brothers System for Liberated Love and Marriage, The, 313–14, 316
Brown, Rev. Robert McAfee, 330

Brown v. Board of Education (1954), 163
Browning, Robert, 182, 388n. 40
Bryn Mawr College, 178
Buber, Martin; and American humanism, 261, 275–77; Christian appropriation of, 277; contrasted to Tillich and Rogers, 404n. 26; and German critique of mass society, 275–76; and Herberg's Judaism, 232; and idea of relatedness, 276; on Jews as model community, 276; and Liebman's Judaism, 226; and neo-Hasidic revival, 333
Buckley, William F., Jr., 255
Bühler, Charlotte, 298
Bulka, Rabbi Reuven, 326, 415n. 27
Bushnell, Rev. Horace, 101

Cabot, Richard, 22–23
Cahan, Abraham, 20–21, 30–31, 150, 206–7
Call It Sleep (Henry Roth), 209
Calm Your Nerves (Wolfe), 126
Calvinism, 96, 99–100, 101–2, 274
Cantwell, John (bishop of Los Angeles), 251
capitalism: and personality types, 272, 279, 404 n. 20; in thought of Ayn Rand, 301
Capra, Frank, 198
Carnegie, Dale, 124
Carus, Paul, 127–28, 376n. 51
"Catholic Hour, The" (radio program), 245
Catholicism: in Austria-Hungary, 120; and Buber, 407n. 54; and controversy over Freud, 241–57; converts to, 241, 245–46, 248; enters cultural mainstream, 217, 218, 236, 241–42; and fascism in Europe, 251–52; and psychoanalysis, 235, 256; reconciled with psychology, 53
Catholics: antisemitism among, 250, 251; Liebman as negative symbol for, 242; psychiatrists among, oppose Sheen, 243; and psychology, 256, 289; Sheen and Luce as heroes for, 241–42
censorship, motion picture, 251
Central Conference of American Rabbis, 175, 208
Chamberlain, Houston Stewart, 146
Chaplin, Charlie, 265
character armor (Reichian), 272
Chesler, Phyllis, 408n. 6
Chess, Stella, 298